GILL SHAKESPEARE FOCUS

KING L[obscured]R

Leaving Certificate English

Text, analysis, commentary notes and sample essays

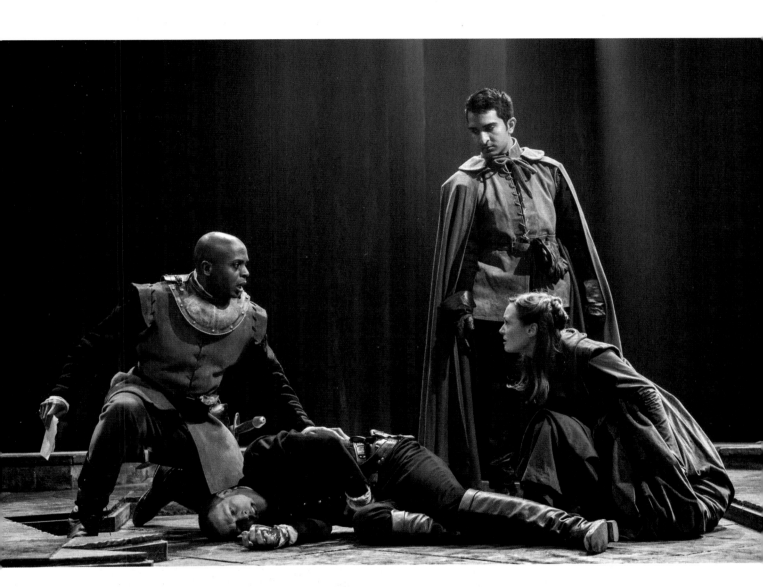

MARTIN KIERAN AND FRANCES ROCKS

Gill Education
Hume Avenue
Park West
Dublin 12
www.gilleducation.ie

MIX
Paper from responsible sources
FSC® C167221

Gill Education is an imprint of M.H. Gill & Co.

ISBN: 978 07171 98986

Cover design: O'Brien Creative

Print origination: Carole Lynch

For permission to reproduce photographs, the authors and publisher gratefully acknowledge the following: © Adobe Stock: iii, iv, vT, 17, 28, 31, 48, 53, 62, 76, 94, 100, 106, 109, 122, 125, 142, 160, 164, 168, 183, 192, 199, 226, 258, 260, 264B, 269; © Alamy: vii, viiiT, ixT, vB, 118, 259, 264T; © Anthony Woods: 26, 47, 77, 134, 222, 233, 279; © ArenaPAL/Billie Rafaeli: 200; © ArenaPAL/Elliot Franks: xiT, 119; © ArenaPAL/Johan Persson: i, 14, 29, 32, 64, 96, 101, 123, 126, 144, 157, 190, 220, 239, 249, 252, 267, 284; © ArenaPAL/Marilyn Kingwill: xT, 250, 266; © ArenaPAL/Nigel Norrington: 91, 236, 246; © ArenaPAL/Pete Jones: xiC; © Arnau Bosc: 271; © British Library: ixB; David Iliff, via Wikimedia Commons (CC BY-SA 3.0): vi; © FreeImages: 161; © Getty Images: 181, 289; © Isidro Ferrer, CDN (Centro Dramatico Nacional de España): 273; © iStock/Getty Premium: viiiB, 63, 73, 99, 133, 149, 156, 202, 248, 254, 261, 263, 265; © Marie Lazar: 275; © Photostage/Donald Cooper: xC, xB, xiB, 13, 25, 52, 90, 132, 141; Photo by Manuel Harlan © RSC: ii, xii, 1, 15, 18, 49, 55, 74, 107, 110, 120, 150, 162, 165, 169, 184, 194, 203, 223, 241, 247, 295; Photo by Donald Cooper © RSC: 243; Photo by Ellie Kurttz © RSC: 245; © Shutterstock: 256; © Solent News/Shutterstock: 268; © Stratford Festival, *King Lear*, 2014 – Stephen Ouimette as the Fool, Colm Feore as King Lear and Jonathan Goad as Kent, photographer David Hou, director Antoni Cimolino, designer Eo Sharp, lighting designer Michael Walton: 105, 229.

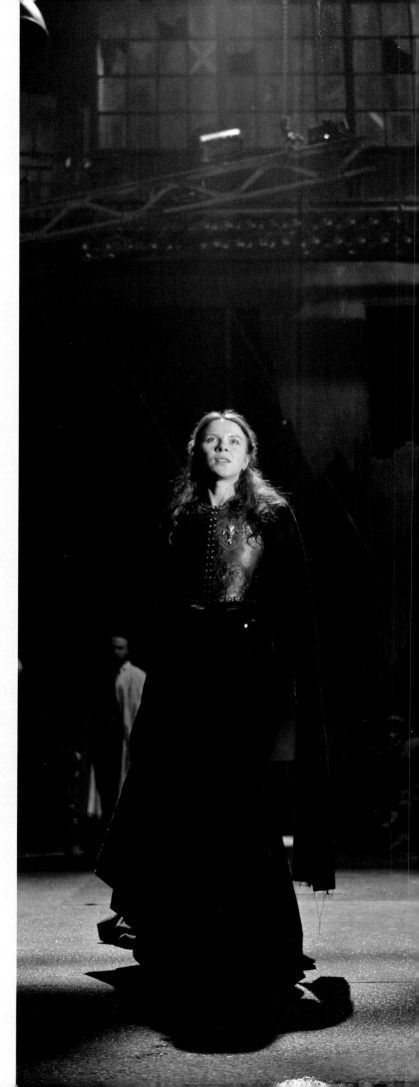

The authors and publisher have made every effort to trace all copyright holders, but if any has been inadvertently overlooked we would be pleased to make the necessary arrangement at the first opportunity.

Contents

**These key scenes require close, detailed study.*

ACT 4

ACT 5

**These key scenes require close, detailed study.*

CHARACTER STUDIES

KEY THEMES IN *KING LEAR*

DRAMATIC TECHNIQUES IN *KING LEAR*

EXAM FOCUS

SAMPLE ESSAYS ON *KING LEAR*

USING *KING LEAR* AS A COMPARATIVE TEXT

Introduction

- The epic tragedy *King Lear* is widely regarded as one of Shakespeare's most intense and powerful tragedies. Written in 1605, it tells the story of the elderly ruler of ancient Britain who attempts to divide his kingdom between his three daughters: Goneril, Regan and Cordelia.
- Before giving up his power, Lear challenges his daughters to prove which one of them loves him best. Although Cordelia loves her father, she refuses to exaggerate her feelings as her sisters do. Lear becomes enraged and banishes her for ever.
- In a similar misunderstanding, the Earl of Gloucester is misled by his scheming son, Edmund, into believing that his legitimate son, Edgar, wishes to murder him.
- The play raises many questions about power, deception, cruelty, love and justice.

Leaving Certificate exam questions relate mainly to characters, relationships, themes and dramatic techniques – all of which are closely interlinked.

Shakespeare's Life

Since William Shakespeare lived more than 400 years ago, the little we know about his life comes mainly from public records. For example, we are sure that he was baptised in Stratford-upon-Avon, 100 miles north-west of London, on 26 April 1564.

We also know that Shakespeare's life revolved around two locations: Stratford and London. He grew up, had a family and bought property in Stratford, but he worked in London, the centre of English theatre. As an actor, a playwright and a partner in a leading acting company, he soon became prosperous and well-known.

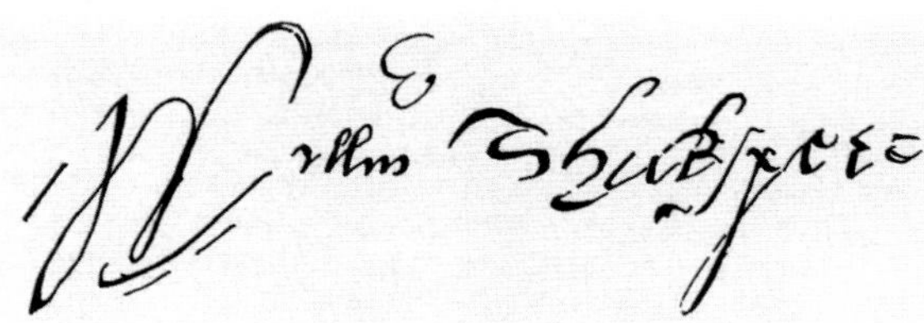

1564	Born in Stratford-upon-Avon
1582	Marries Anne Hathaway
1583	His daughter Susannah is born
1584	Birth of twins, Judith and Hamnet
1585	Moves to London
1590	Writes his first play
1595	Makes his name as a London playwright with *Romeo and Juliet*
1596	Death of his son Hamnet
1599	Invests in the Globe Theatre
1605	Writes *King Lear*
1606	First record of a stage performance of *King Lear* in Whitehall, London
1608	First printed copies of *King Lear*
1609	Becomes part-owner of the new Blackfriars Theatre
1612	Retires and returns to Stratford-upon-Avon
1616	Dies aged 52

(Dates of plays are approximate.)

Shakespeare's birthplace, Stratford-upon-Avon

Shakespeare's Theatre

Throughout Shakespeare's lifetime, professional theatre was a highly successful business that provided popular entertainment for people of all backgrounds. Shakespeare wrote for a specific acting company, known first as the Lord Chamberlain's Men and later as the King's Men.

Plays were performed in the royal courts, as well as in town squares, churches and guildhalls around the country. In London, the largest theatres were open-air arenas with room for several thousand people. These buildings were made mainly of wood. Indoor playhouses accommodated up to 500 people, all of whom were given seats. Lighting was provided by candles, making indoor theatres suitable for winter and evening productions.

William Shakespeare (1564–1616)

The Swan

Built in 1595–6, the Swan Theatre was located in the Southwark district of London, close to the River Thames. It had a capacity of 3,000 spectators and was described by Johannes de Witt, a Dutchman visiting the English capital, as 'the finest and biggest of the London theatres'. De Witt also drew a sketch of the building and a copy of this famous drawing is probably the single most reliable source of information about the interior layout of Elizabethan London theatres.

The Globe

From 1599, London's most important outdoor theatre was the Globe, also in Southwark, where Shakespeare's best-known dramas were first produced. The building was about 36 feet high and had a diameter of 84 feet. The inside of the structure contained three tiers of galleries that surrounded an uncovered yard roughly 56 feet in diameter.

The grounds surrounding the theatre would have been bustling with playgoers and local people. Stallholders sold merchandise and refreshments, creating a lively market-day atmosphere. The Globe would have particularly attracted young people and there were many complaints of apprentices avoiding work in order to go to the theatre.

Staging

The bare stages of Shakespeare's day had very little scenery and few props except for objects required by the plot. Setting and mood were suggested by the power of the play's language.

There was a roof over the stage, but no curtain. Rhyming couplets signalled the end of a scene. Colourful costumes were common, often denoting a character's social status or nationality. Exits and entrances were in plain view of the audience, but actors could also descend from the 'heavens' above the stage or enter and exit via the 'hell' below through a trapdoor.

The Actors

Women never performed in stage dramas (acting was seen as a disreputable profession), and young boys usually played female characters. During Elizabethan times, there was a fast turnover of plays – and little or no time for rehearsal – so actors needed to have excellent recall. Indeed, they sometimes received scripts just hours before the play started and relied on prompters who sat behind the scenes and whispered the lines.

Actors performed on a stage space that thrust into the yard area and had three sides where audience members could watch the action. Acoustics were poor and actors were often forced to shout their lines and use exaggerated theatrical gestures. Speech patterns were heightened for dramatic effect.

A 1596 sketch of a performance on the thrust stage (extending into the auditorium) of the Swan Theatre by Johannes de Witt

Audiences

Shakespeare's theatre was full of life.
Poorer people ('groundlings') would pay a few pennies to stand in front of the stage while the better-off paid more for places in the sheltered side galleries. A trumpeter, perched on the roof, would hurry latecomers into the theatre when a performance was due to begin.

Plays were staged in the afternoon and the audience would talk, wander around and eat and drink during performances, so authors had to come up with ways of holding their attention. Since there were no backdrops or artificial lighting, audiences had to use their imagination.

The New Globe Theatre

The continuing popularity of Shakespeare's plays means that the Globe Theatre lives on in a modern reconstruction close to the original site in Southwark. Completed in 1997, the theatre serves not only as a museum, but also as a working playhouse.

The new Globe Theatre

King Lear Fact File

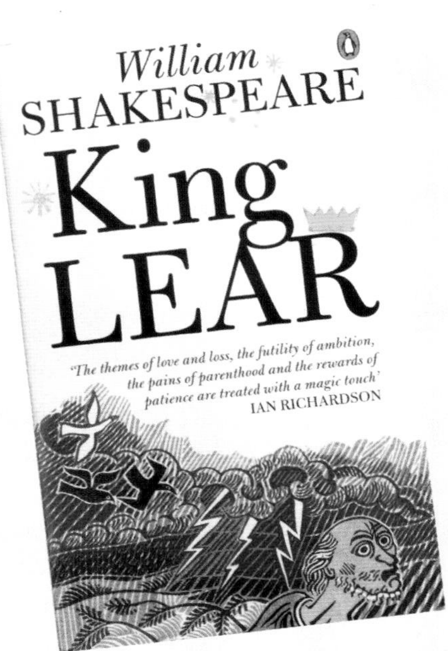

- The legend of the old king and his three daughters was well known in England for centuries before Shakespeare wrote his play.
- One early account of Lear can be found in *The History of the Kings of Britain*, written by Geoffrey of Monmouth in 1135. This account inspired several 16th-century versions.
- Irish writer Nahum Tate re-wrote the play in 1681 – with a happy ending in which Lear and Cordelia survive, and Cordelia marries Edgar. It remained popular with London audiences until the early 1800s.
- *King Lear* is filled with more references to animals and nature than any of Shakespeare's other plays. The word 'nature' (or variations of it) occurs more than 40 times in the text.
- The playwright George Bernard Shaw loved *King Lear*, saying, 'No man will ever write a better tragedy'. However, Russian writer Leo Tolstoy described an 'exaggerated' plot with 'pompous, characterless language'.
- Shakespeare's *King Lear* contains the earliest-known reference to the phrase 'football player'. In Act 1 Scene 4, Kent insults Oswald, calling him a 'base football player'.
- These days, anyone going to a performance of *King Lear* usually says, 'I'm going to see a play'. However, back in Shakespeare's lifetime, people talked about 'going to hear a play'.

Shakespeare's Text and Line Numbers

Over the years, Shakespeare's plays have been printed in various formats. Most popular versions of *King Lear* have some modernised spelling and punctuation. Line numbers may also differ slightly, depending on the particular edition.

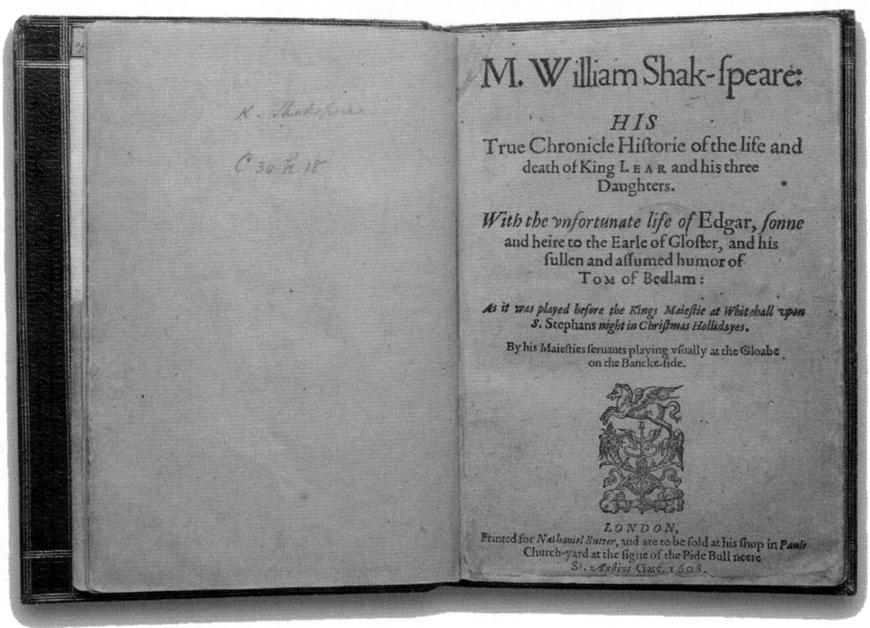

M. William Shak-ſpeare:

HIS

True Chronicle Hiſtorie of the life and death of King LEAR and his three Daughters.

With the vnfortunate life of Edgar, *ſonne* and heire to the Earle of Gloſter, and his ſullen and aſſumed humor of TOM of Bedlam:

As it was played before the Kings Maieſtie at Whitehall vpon S. Stephans *night in Chriſtmas Hollidayes.*

By his Maieſties ſeruants playing vſually at the Gloabe on the Bancke-ſide.

LONDON,

Printed for *Nathaniel Butter*, and are to be ſold at his ſhop in *Pauls* Church-yard at the ſigne of the Pide Bull neere St. *Auſtins* Gate. 1608.

Key Scenes in *King Lear*

In preparing for the Single Text *King Lear* question, it is important to become familiar with the entire play. Your written work should show engagement and creative thought, supporting the points you make with close reference to key scenes. Some moments in the play (including the six scenes listed below) are particularly revealing and worth studying in detail.

• Act 1 Scene 1
King Lear's palace

Lear announces plans to retire and calls on his daughters to express their love for him. Acting on impulse, he disinherits Cordelia and hands over power to Goneril and Regan. These decisions will determine the play's tragic outcome.

• Act 1 Scene 2
Gloucester's castle

The Earl of Gloucester's family is also divided. His younger son, Edmund, believes he should have the same rights as his legitimate brother, Edgar, and he convinces his father that Edgar is plotting against him.

• Act 2 Scene 4
Gloucester's castle

Lear's anguish reaches its height when Regan and Goneril disrespect him. He begins to lose his mind. Lear meets the Earl of Gloucester, an old friend, who is concerned for the king's well-being.

Act 3 Scene 4
Outside a hovel on the heath

Lear, Kent and the Fool find Edgar disguised as the deranged beggar Poor Tom. This marks a turning point for Lear, who begins to sympathise with deprived and vulnerable human beings.

Act 4 Scene 7
The French camp near Dover

The exhausted king wakes from sleep and recovers his senses. He is reunited with Cordelia, who has returned with an army from France. Father and daughter ask each other for forgiveness.

Act 5 Scene 3
The British camp near Dover

Cordelia is imprisoned and executed. Lear is unable to accept that she is dead and he himself soon dies of overwhelming grief. Gloucester's son, Edgar, is left to rule Britain and restore order.

- **Remember that commentaries and study guides are there to be challenged.**
- **Be confident when expressing and developing your own ideas.**
- **Identify the main elements of the question so that your answer is relevant.**
- **When responding to exam questions, avoid unfocused narrative.**

Characters

The Royal House of Britain

LEAR – King of Britain

GONERIL – his eldest daughter

REGAN – his second daughter

CORDELIA – his youngest daughter

DUKE OF ALBANY – Goneril's husband

DUKE OF CORNWALL – Regan's husband

The Gloucester Family

EARL OF GLOUCESTER – Lear's loyal friend

EDGAR/POOR TOM – Gloucester's older son

EDMUND – Gloucester's younger, illegitimate son

Other characters

The Fool – Lear's loyal court jester

Earl of Kent/Caius – Lear's devoted supporter

Oswald – Goneril's steward

King of France – he marries Cordelia and is willing to support her efforts to rescue Lear

Duke of Burgundy – another suitor for Cordelia. He rejects her when he learns that she has no dowry

Curan – Gloucester's servant

Old Man – tenant of Gloucester

Doctor – attendant to Cordelia

Knights of Lear's entourage, gentlemen, soldiers, attendants, messengers, servants

The action of the play takes place in various parts of the kingdom of Britain.

Act 1
Scene 1*

INTRODUCTION

- Lear announces that he will step down from his role as king.
- His plan is to divide his kingdom between his three daughters.
- He asks each of them to publicly declare their love for him.
- Gloucester's sons, Edmund and Edgar, are introduced.

*** This key scene requires close, detailed study.**

King Lear's palace

Enter Kent, Gloucester and Edmund

Kent

I thought the king had more affected the Duke of Albany than Cornwall.

Gloucester

It did always seem so to us: but now, in the division of the kingdom, it appears not which of the Dukes he values most; for qualities are so weighed that curiosity in neither can make choice of either's moiety.

Kent

Is not this your son, my lord?

Gloucester

His breeding, sir, hath been at my charge: I have so often blushed to acknowledge him, that now I am brazed to it.

Kent

I cannot conceive you.

Gloucester

Sir, this young fellow's mother could: whereupon she grew round-wombed, and had, indeed, sir, a son for her cradle ere she had a husband for her bed. Do you smell a fault?

Kent

I cannot wish the fault undone, the issue of it being so proper.

Gloucester

But I have, sir, a son by order of law, some year elder than this, who yet is no dearer in my account; though this knave came something saucily into the world before he was sent for, yet was his mother fair; there was good sport at his making, and the whoreson must be acknowledged. Do you know this noble gentleman, Edmund?

Edmund

No, my lord.

Gloucester

My lord of Kent. Remember him hereafter as my honourable friend.

Edmund

My services to your lordship.

1 affected: *favoured*

5 qualities...moiety: *merits so similar, it is impossible to say what share either might inherit*

9 brazed to it: *used to it*

10 I cannot conceive you: *I do not understand you*

14 issue: *consequence*

16 by order of law: *within marriage*

17 knave: *rogue, scamp*

20 whoreson: *bastard*

Kent

I must love you and sue to know you better.

Edmund

Sir, I shall study deserving.

Gloucester

He hath been out nine years, and away he shall again.
The king is coming.

Trumpet fanfare. Enter Lear, Cornwall, Albany, Goneril, Regan, Cordelia and Attendants.

Lear

Attend the lords of France and Burgundy, Gloucester.

Gloucester

I shall, my liege.

Exeunt Gloucester and Edmund

Lear

Meantime we shall express our darker purpose.
Give me the map there. Know that we have divided
In three our kingdom; and it is our fast intent
To shake all cares and business from our age,
Conferring them on younger strengths, while we
Unburthened crawl toward death. Our son of Cornwall,
And you, our no less loving son of Albany,
We have this hour a constant will to publish
Our daughters' several dowers, that future strife
May be prevented now. The princes, France and Burgundy,
Great rivals in our youngest daughter's love,
Long in our court have made their amorous sojourn,
And here are to be answered. Tell me, my daughters,
Since now we will divest us both of rule,
Interest of territory, cares of state,
Which of you shall we say doth love us most?
That we our largest bounty may extend
Where nature doth with merit challenge. Goneril,
Our eldest-born, speak first.

Goneril

Sir, I love you more than words can wield the matter,
Dearer than eye-sight, space, and liberty,
Beyond what can be valued rich or rare,
No less than life, with grace, health, beauty, honour,

26 sue: *try*

31 liege: *lord*

32 darker purpose: *secret intention*

39 constant will: *resolute plan*

40 several dowers: *separate marriage settlements*

43 amorous sojourn: *courting visit*

45 divest us both of: *rid us of*

48 bounty: *reward*

49 nature...challenge: *tenderness and virtues are combined*

51 wield: *handle*

As much as child ever loved or father found;
A love that makes breath poor and speech unable,
Beyond all manner of 'so much' I love you.

Cordelia

Aside

What shall Cordelia do?
Love, and be silent.

Lear

Of all these bounds, even from this line to this,
With shadowy forests and with champains riched,
With plenteous rivers and wide-skirted meads,
We make thee lady. To thine and Albany's issue
Be this perpetual. What says our second daughter,
Our dearest Regan, wife of Cornwall? Speak.

61 champains riched: *fertile plains*
62 wide-skirted meads: *broad meadows*

Regan

Sir, I am made of that self mettle as my sister,
And prize me at her worth. In my true heart
I find she names my very deed of love;
Only she comes too short: that I profess
Myself an enemy to all other joys,
Which the most precious square of sense possesses
And find I am alone felicitate
In your dear highness' love.

66 self mettle: *same spirit*
71 the most precious square of sense possesses: *is perfectly obvious*
72 felicitate: *happy*

Cordelia

Aside

Then poor Cordelia!
And yet not so, since, I am sure, my love's
More ponderous than my tongue.

75 ponderous: *weighty*

Lear

[*to Regan*] To thee and thine hereditary ever,
Remain this ample third of our fair kingdom;
No less in space, validity, and pleasure,
Than that conferred on Goneril. Now, our joy,
Although the last, not least; to whose young love
The vines of France and milk of Burgundy
Strive to be interessed; what can you say to draw
A third more opulent than your sisters? Speak.

78 validity: *value*
82 Strive to be interessed: *are hoping to marry*
83 opulent: *wealthy*

Cordelia

Nothing, my lord.

Lear

Nothing!

Cordelia

Nothing.

Lear

Nothing will come of nothing: speak again.

Cordelia

Unhappy that I am, I cannot heave
My heart into my mouth: I love your majesty
According to my bond; no more nor less.

Lear

How, how, Cordelia! mend your speech a little,
Lest it may mar your fortunes.

Cordelia

Good my lord,
You have begot me, bred me, loved me; I
Return those duties back as are right fit,
Obey you, love you, and most honour you.
Why have my sisters husbands, if they say
They love you all? Haply, when I shall wed,
That lord whose hand must take my plight shall carry
Half my love with him, half my care and duty.
Sure, I shall never marry like my sisters
To love my father all.

Lear

But goes thy heart with this?

Cordelia

Ay, good my lord.

Lear

So young, and so untender?

Cordelia

So young, my lord, and true.

Lear

Let it be so; thy truth, then, be thy dower:
For, by the sacred radiance of the sun,
The mysteries of Hecate, and the night;
By all the operation of the orbs
From whom we do exist, and cease to be;

88 heave: *drag with great effort*

90 bond: *duty as a daughter*

92 mar: *spoil*

93 begot: *fathered*
bred: *reared*

98 take my plight: *accept me in marriage*

103 untender: *unkind, insensitive*

107 Hecate: *goddess of witchcraft*

108 operation of the orbs: *working of the stars*

111 Propinquity and property of blood: *family links*

113 Scythian: *brute, savage*

114 makes his generation messes: *devours his own children*

119 dragon and his wrath: *Lear compares himself to a fierce creature*

120 set my rest: *rely on*

121 kind nursery: *loving care*

126 plainness, marry her: *honest speech will be her only dowry*

128 Pre-eminence: *high status*

134 sway: *power*

136 coronet: *crown*

140 make from the shaft: *avoid the arrow (of my anger)*

141 fork invade: *arrow penetrate*

Here I disclaim all my paternal care,
Propinquity and property of blood,
And as a stranger to my heart and me
Hold thee, from this, for ever. The barbarous Scythian,
Or he that makes his generation messes
To gorge his appetite, shall to my bosom
Be as well neighboured, pitied, and relieved,
As thou my sometime daughter.

Kent

Good my liege –

Lear

Peace, Kent!
Come not between the dragon and his wrath.
I loved her most, and thought to set my rest
On her kind nursery. Hence, and avoid my sight!
So be my grave my peace, as here I give
Her father's heart from her! Call France. Who stirs?
Call Burgundy. Cornwall and Albany,
With my two daughters' dowers digest this third.
Let pride, which she calls plainness, marry her.
I do invest you jointly with my power,
Pre-eminence, and all the large effects
That troop with majesty. Ourself, by monthly course,
With reservation of an hundred knights,
By you to be sustained, shall our abode
Make with you by due turns. Only we still retain
The name, and all the additions to a king;
The sway, revenue, execution of the rest,
Beloved sons, be yours: which to confirm,
This coronet part betwixt you.

Kent

Royal Lear,
Whom I have ever honoured as my king,
Loved as my father, as my master followed,
As my great patron thought on in my prayers –

Lear

The bow is bent and drawn, make from the shaft.

Kent

Let it fall rather, though the fork invade
The region of my heart: be Kent unmannerly,
When Lear is mad. What wilt thou do, old man?

Thinkest thou that duty shall have dread to speak,
When power to flattery bows? To plainness honour's bound,
When majesty stoops to folly. Reserve thy state,
And, in thy best consideration, check
This hideous rashness. Answer my life my judgement,
Thy youngest daughter does not love thee least;
Nor are those empty-hearted whose low sound
Reverbs no hollowness.

Lear

Kent, on thy life, no more.

Kent

My life I never held but as a pawn
To wage against thy enemies; nor fear to lose it,
Thy safety being the motive.

Lear

Out of my sight!

Kent

See better, Lear; and let me still remain
The true blank of thine eye.

Lear

Now, by Apollo –

Kent

Now, by Apollo, king,
Thou swearest thy gods in vain.

Lear

O, vassal! miscreant!

Laying his hand on his sword

Albany and Cornwall

Dear sir, forbear.

Kent

To Lear

Do. Kill thy physician, and the fee bestow
Upon thy foul disease. Revoke thy gift;
Or, whilst I can vent clamour from my throat,
I'll tell thee thou dost evil.

Lear

Hear me, recreant!

146 Reserve thy state: *keep your royal power*

148 Answer my life my judgement: *I am willing to risk my life on my opinion*

151 Reverbs no hollowness: *does not sound insincere*

152 pawn: *someone to be used by others for their own purposes*

156 blank: *target*

157 Apollo: *Sun god*

158 vassal: *miscreant, worthless slave*

160 physician: *doctor*

161 Revoke thy gift: *cancel giving Cordelia's share of the kingdom to her sisters*

162 vent clamour: *shout cries of protest*

163 recreant: *traitor*

On thine allegiance, hear me!
Since thou hast sought to make us break our vow,
Which we durst never yet, and with strained pride
To come between our sentence and our power,
Which nor our nature nor our place can bear,
Our potency made good, take thy reward.
Five days we do allot thee, for provision
To shield thee from diseases of the world;
And on the sixth to turn thy hated back
Upon our kingdom: if, on the tenth day following,
Thy banished trunk be found in our dominions,
The moment is thy death. Away! by Jupiter,
This shall not be revoked.

174 trunk: *body*

175 Jupiter: *ruler of the gods in Roman mythology*

Kent

Fare thee well, king, since thus thou wilt appear,
Freedom lives hence, and banishment is here.

To Cordelia

The gods to their dear shelter take thee, maid,
That justly thinkest, and hast most rightly said!

To Regan and Goneril

And your large speeches may your deeds approve,
That good effects may spring from words of love.
Thus Kent, O princes, bids you all adieu;
He'll shape his old course in a country new.

181 large speeches may your deeds approve: *may your grand words be backed up by actions*

Exit

Flourish. Re-enter Gloucester, with France, Burgundy, and Attendants

Gloucester

Here's France and Burgundy, my noble lord.

Lear

My lord of Burgundy.
We first address towards you, who with this king
Hath rivalled for our daughter. What, in the least,
Will you require in present dower with her,
Or cease your quest of love?

188 rivalled: *competed*

189 present dower: *marriage gift brought by a bride to her husband*

Burgundy

Most royal majesty,
I crave no more than what your highness offered,
Nor will you tender less.

192 tender: *formally offer*

Lear

Right noble Burgundy,
When she was dear to us, we did hold her so,
But now her price is fallen. Sir, there she stands.
If aught within that little seeming substance,
Or all of it, with our displeasure pieced,
And nothing more, may fitly like your grace,
She's there, and she is yours.

Burgundy

I know no answer.

Lear

Will you, with those infirmities she owes,
Unfriended, new-adopted to our hate,
Dowered with our curse, and strangered with our oath,
Take her, or leave her?

Burgundy

Pardon me, royal sir;
Election makes not up on such conditions.

Lear

Then leave her, sir; for, by the power that made me,
I tell you all her wealth.
To France
For you, great king,
I would not from your love make such a stray,
To match you where I hate; therefore beseech you
To avert your liking a more worthier way
Than on a wretch whom nature is ashamed
Almost to acknowledge hers.
I tell you all her wealth.

France

This is most strange,
That she, that even but now was your best object,
The argument of your praise, balm of your age,
Most best, most dearest, should in this trice of time
Commit a thing so monstrous, to dismantle
So many folds of favour. Sure, her offence
Must be of such unnatural degree,
That monsters it, or your fore-vouched affection
Fall into taint; which to believe of her,
Must be a faith that reason without miracle
Could never plant in me.

195 aught: *anything at all*
little seeming substance: *small deceitful object*
196 pieced: *assembled*
197 fitly like: *suitably please*
199 infirmities she owes: *weaknesses she possesses*
203 Election: *choice*
209 avert: *turn away*
214 argument: *the main subject*
balm: *healing substance*
216 dismantle: *take to pieces*
219 fore-vouched: *previously confirmed*
220 Fall into taint: *become spoiled*
221 reason...in me: *it would take something extraordinary to convince me*

223 that glib and oily art: *plausible and false words*

230 still-soliciting: *always begging*

234 tardiness in nature: *natural reticence, shyness*

235 history: *private thoughts*

238 regards: *other considerations*

247 respects of fortune: *consideration of status and wealth*

Cordelia

I yet beseech your Majesty,
If for I want that glib and oily art,
To speak and purpose not, since what I well intend,
I'll do it before I speak, that you make known
It is no vicious blot, murder, or foulness,
No unchaste action, or dishonoured step,
That hath deprived me of your grace and favour;
But even for want of that for which I am richer,
A still-soliciting eye, and such a tongue
That I am glad I have not, though not to have it
Hath lost me in your liking.

Lear

Better thou
Hadst not been born than not to have pleased me better.

France

Is it but this, a tardiness in nature
Which often leaves the history unspoke
That it intends to do? My lord of Burgundy,
What say you to the lady? Love's not love
When it is mingled with regards that stand
Aloof from the entire point. Will you have her?
She is herself a dowry.

Burgundy

Royal Lear,
Give but that portion which yourself proposed,
And here I take Cordelia by the hand,
Duchess of Burgundy.

Lear

Nothing: I have sworn; I am firm.

Burgundy

I am sorry, then, you have so lost a father
That you must lose a husband.

Cordelia

Peace be with Burgundy!
Since that respects of fortune are his love,
I shall not be his wife.

France

Fairest Cordelia, that art most rich, being poor;
Most choice, forsaken; and most loved, despised!

Thee and thy virtues here I seize upon:
Be it lawful I take up what's cast away.
Gods, gods! 'tis strange that from their coldest neglect
My love should kindle to inflamed respect.
Thy dowerless daughter, king, thrown to my chance,
Is queen of us, of ours, and our fair France:
Not all the dukes of waterish Burgundy
Can buy this unprized precious maid of me.
Bid them farewell, Cordelia, though unkind:
Thou losest here, a better where to find.

Lear

Thou hast her, France. Let her be thine, for we
Have no such daughter, nor shall ever see
That face of hers again. Therefore be gone
Without our grace, our love, our benison.
Come, noble Burgundy.

Flourish. Exeunt all but France, Goneril, Regan, and Cordelia

France

Bid farewell to your sisters.

Cordelia

The jewels of our father, with washed eyes
Cordelia leaves you. I know you what you are
And like a sister am most loath to call
Your faults as they are named. Use well our father:
To your professed bosoms I commit him
But yet, alas, stood I within his grace,
I would prefer him to a better place.
So, farewell to you both.

Regan

Prescribe not us our duties.

Goneril

Let your study
Be to content your lord, who hath received you
At fortune's alms. You have obedience scanted,
And well are worth the want that you have wanted.

Cordelia

Time shall unfold what plighted cunning hides;
Who cover faults, at last shame them derides.
Well may you prosper!

254 kindle to inflamed respect: *arouse to burning love*

257 waterish: *feeble*

258 unprized: *unvalued*

264 benison: *blessing*

271 professed bosoms: *publicly declared love*

277 fortune's alms: *a charitable gift*

278 well are...wanted: *deserve to be regarded as worthless*

279 plighted: *concealed*

280 derides: *mocks*

France

Come, my fair Cordelia.

Exeunt France and Cordelia

Goneril

Sister, it is not a little I have to say of what most nearly appertains to us both. I think our father will hence to-night.

283 appertains: *concerns*

Regan

That's most certain, and with you; next month with us.

Goneril

You see how full of changes his age is; the observation we have made of it hath not been little; he always loved our sister most; and with what poor judgement he hath now cast her off appears too grossly.

289 too grossly: *so obviously*

Regan

It is the infirmity of his age: yet he hath ever but slenderly known himself.

290 infirmity: *weakness*

Goneril

The best and soundest of his time hath been but rash; then must we look from his age to receive, not alone the imperfections of long-engraffed condition, but there withal the unruly waywardness that infirm and choleric years bring with them.

294 long-engraffed: *firmly established*

295 choleric: *angry, rash*

Regan

Such unconstant starts are we like to have from him as this of Kent's banishment.

297 unconstant starts: *impulsive actions*

Goneril

There is further compliment of leave-taking between France and him. Pray you, let's hit together: if our father carry authority with such dispositions as he bears, this last surrender of his will but offend us.

300 let's hit together: *let's join forces*

Regan

We shall further think on it.

Goneril

We must do something, and in the heat.

304 in the heat: *at once*

Exeunt

Key Scene Analysis

Court gossip (lines 1–31)

The scene opens in the royal palace. Two of Lear's closest advisers, the earls of Gloucester and Kent, discuss the king's decision to divide his kingdom between his three daughters: Goneril, Regan and Cordelia. The audience also learns that Gloucester has two sons. The older, Edgar, is his legitimate heir. Gloucester makes a joke about his younger son, Edmund: 'this knave came something saucily into the world'. His embarrassment about Edmund's illegitimacy raises immediate questions about his character. What kind of father is he? Is he a responsible man?

The 'love test' (lines 32–184)

Shakespeare introduces the play's protagonist (central character) scanning the map of Britain before handing over his kingdom. Lear says that he wishes to prevent 'future strife' between his sons-in-law and he thinks that 'younger strengths' will govern better than he can, now that he has grown old.

The vain king seems to be playing to the court audience by demanding that his daughters put on a public show of affection for him. Yet he persists in the 'love test' as a way of rewarding the daughter who says she loves him best. Goneril, the eldest, tells her egotistical father exactly what he wants to hear: 'I love you more than words can wield the matter'. She clearly knows how to play the hypocritical game of flattering Lear.

Which of you shall we say doth love us most?
Lear
Act 1 Scene 1, l.47

Cordelia lets the audience know that she does not wish to participate in this false show, so she decides to 'Love, and be silent'. Regan rivals Goneril in exaggerating her feelings for Lear: 'I find she names my very deed of love;/ Only she comes too short'. In contrast, Cordelia is sure that her genuine feelings are of more worth than her sisters' public displays: 'my love's/ More ponderous than my tongue'. She is not prepared to humour her father's vanity and tells him that she loves him 'According to my bond; no more nor less'.

Cordelia then tries – without success – to explain her attitude by saying that if she loved her father to the same extent as her sisters, she would never marry: 'Why have my sisters husbands, if they say/ They love you all?' But Lear finds her honesty cold and 'untender'. For someone who is so concerned with appearances, he now finds himself being publicly humiliated.

Lear cautions Cordelia to 'mend your speech a little'. He invites her to flatter him: 'what can you say to draw/ A third more opulent than your sisters?' Her response comes as a shock: 'Nothing, my lord'. Ironically, all the play's suffering and tragedy will flow from this word 'Nothing'.

The elderly king becomes enraged, saying that he will deprive his youngest daughter of her inheritance, 'thy truth, then, be thy dower'. In a state of arrogant fury, he discards all of his 'paternal care', announcing that he will not spend his retirement with Cordelia as he had planned, but will divide his time between his other two daughters' palaces. He will, however, continue to have his personal army of 'an hundred knights'.

Audiences will be instantly aware of the king's poor political judgement. Dividing the kingdom between two new rulers is not a good idea. Lear is also unable to see that he cannot retain the official title and symbols of kingship if he is to truly give up his power. It is evident that he has little understanding of his own family and that he cannot distinguish between flattery and sincere expressions of affection. We can only wonder about the consequences of his weaknesses both as a king and as a father.

Honest Kent (lines 118–184)

Kent is an experienced courtier who courageously challenges the king's 'hideous rashness' and speaks up for Cordelia. He is concerned for Lear because he knows that Goneril and Regan are self-interested opportunists. But Kent is also completely honest and he plainly tells Lear, 'thou dost evil'.

The audience will sympathise with Kent's honourable behaviour. Unfortunately, his reward is on-the-spot banishment from the royal court on pain of death. Before leaving, he assures Cordelia that she has been truthful, and he warns her sisters that their future actions should live up to their promises. His farewell speech has a formal tone foreshadowing the tragedy to come, now that the self-centred king is left without the one daughter who loves him most and the one courtier he can trust.

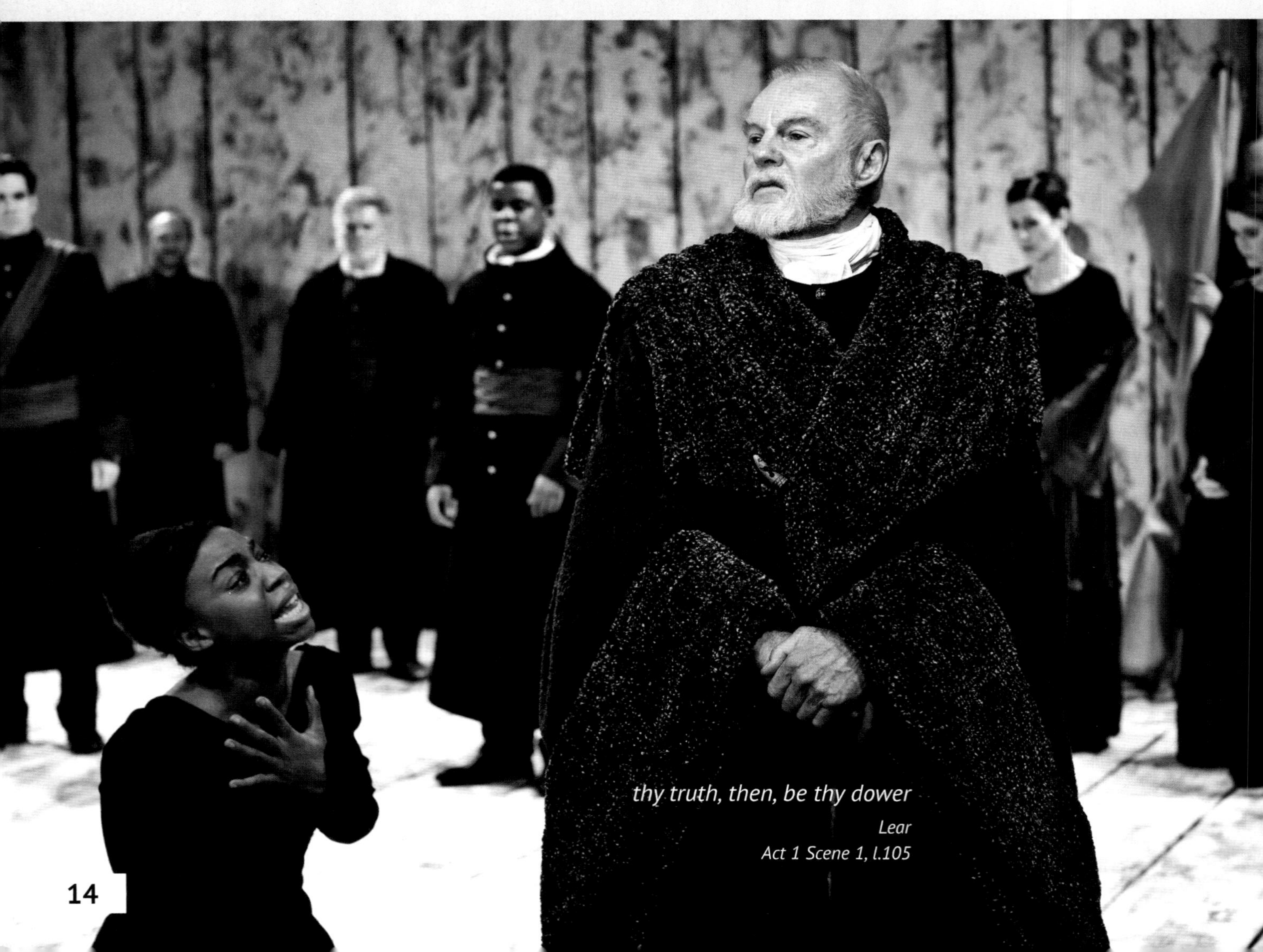

thy truth, then, be thy dower
Lear
Act 1 Scene 1, l.105

A rejected daughter (lines 186–264)

The princes of France and Burgundy, two suitors interested in marrying Cordelia, arrive to hear her father's decision. But once again, Lear humiliates his daughter publicly ('her price is fallen'), explaining that she no longer has either land or money. Burgundy soon cancels his offer of marriage, but France believes that Cordelia 'is herself a dowry' and will be very happy if she will accept him as her husband.

Plain speaking versus hypocrisy (lines 266–304)

Cordelia makes it clear to her sisters that she is aware of their real nature. She warns them to look after Lear, but also wishes that he was well away from them. In response, Goneril and Regan also speak plainly, telling her that she has got what she deserved – nothing. As she leaves, Cordelia warns them that their hypocrisy will eventually be revealed: 'Time shall unfold what plighted cunning hides'.

In their closing conversation, Goneril and Regan prove Cordelia's words true. Coldly, they discuss their father's true personality: 'he hath ever but slenderly known himself'. The audience sees what they really think about the old king as they describe his many failings – particularly his unpredictable behaviour ('unconstant starts'). The two sisters agree to 'hit together' because they fear their father's reckless judgement. They also know that they must act quickly ('in the heat'). Shakespeare closes the scene on a tense note, leaving the audience fearful for Lear's uncertain future.

Both Lear and Cordelia have much in common. She was abrupt and dismissive, making no allowance for his old age or vanity. He then retaliated rashly by abandoning her. Which character is likely to gain the audience's sympathy?

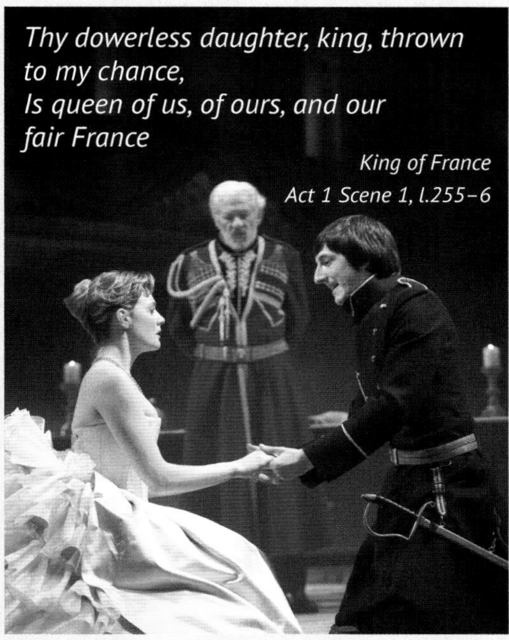
Thy dowerless daughter, king, thrown to my chance,
Is queen of us, of ours, and our fair France

King of France
Act 1 Scene 1, l.255–6

Shakespeare's Dramatic Style

Shakespeare creates a growing sense of unease throughout this dramatic opening scene which focuses on Lear's divided family and the **tension** within the royal court. The playwright lets the characters set the uneasy mood and introduces key themes including deception, power, justice and injustice.

The playwright uses **memorable images** which enrich and illustrate the story of Lear and his disordered world. Neither Lear nor Gloucester 'see' their own children for what they really are. This shared character flaw will crucially affect the outcome of the play. Shakespeare foreshadows this with several references to sight: 'Dearer than eye-sight', 'avoid my sight', 'See better, Lear'. The misguided king fails to see through the hypocrisy of Goneril and Regan, or to recognise the honesty of Cordelia and Kent. There is obvious irony in Lear's trust and regard for the daughters who love him least.

The **violent atmosphere** of Lear's court is emphasised through the powerful use of animal imagery: 'Come not between the dragon and his wrath', 'a thing so monstrous'. This highlights the vile cruelty of human nature at its worst. Kent uses the imagery of illness when he attempts to steer Lear towards sound judgement, remarking, 'Kill thy physician and the fee bestow/ Upon thy foul disease'.

There is an ominous sense of impending tragedy all through Act 1 Scene 1, **foreshadowing** many of the play's future events. Lear and Gloucester are blind to the consequences of their actions, leading the audience to imagine that both characters will continue to suffer.

Critical Analysis

Do you have any sympathy for Lear in Act 1 Scene 1?

Write a paragraph (about 150 words), giving reasons for your response and developing your answer with reference to the text.

Sample Paragraph 1

Lear is a really old man who doesn't want to be king but he still wants all the benefits of being king still. He wants everyone to big him up day and night. He can't believe when his younger daughter Cordelia – a daughter on who he totally doted won't say out loud that she really loves him. He really loses it then and bans her from the palace and gives her share to her two big sisters. Her boyfriends are told she won't have any wedding money and the earl of burgundy just takes off. But the king of france has sympathy for her and she will marry him. Meantime Lear banishes Kent who really tried to talk some sense into him. The big sisters decide to 'hit together in the heat' as they really don't know what this old man will do next. *(145 words)*

Examiner's Comment

- Limited response – more of a summary of the scene than an analysis of Lear's character.
- The question of sympathy needs to be addressed directly.
- Some repetitive expression and grammatical errors.
- Needs more focus and suitable references to support points.

Sample Paragraph 2

Lear abdicates his 'cares and business' to the next generation of 'younger strengths'. But this decision is affected by serious misjudgement. He believes he can get rid of the responsibilities of being king while retaining its privileges, 'the additions to a king'. But his most serious mistake is the foolish 'love test'. His vanity is breath-taking, and he enjoys lavish displays of affection from Goneril and Regan. At first, I sympathised with the old man at Cordelia's refusal to flatter him: 'So young, and so untender?' But I was repulsed by his irrational anger when he banishes her, 'as a stranger to my heart'. Kent is the next victim – simply because he dared to speak the truth about the king's 'hideous rashness'. I was sickened by his humiliation of Cordelia before the men who wanted to marry her, 'now her price is fallen'. Overall, my initial impression of Lear is almost completely unsympathetic. *(155 words)*

Examiner's Comment

- A much more focused answer which addresses the question directly.
- Uses apt reference to illustrate a changing response to Lear's character.
- Genuine engagement with the text evident ('His vanity is breath-taking').
- Varied expression adds to the top-grade quality of this confident answer.

Class/Homework Exercise

Based on your study of Act 1 Scene 1, what is your opinion of Lear both as a king and as a father?

Write a paragraph (about 150 words), developing your response with reference to the text.

Exam Focus

Act 1 Scene 1 can be used successfully in response to a range of examination questions about the play's central themes, characters, relationships and the playwright's dramatic style.

This **key scene** has important dramatic functions:

- Establishes the unpredictable court setting at a time of great change.
- Presents first impressions of Lear and his three daughters.
- Offers initial views of Kent and Gloucester.
- Introduces key themes – power, deception, justice, and family conflict.
- Involves the audience in the tense atmosphere of instability and intrigue.
- Foreshadows disaster and tragedy ahead.

Key Quotes

Quote	Comment
this knave came something saucily into the world before he was sent for *(Gloucester to Kent, l.17–19)*	The moral bankruptcy of Lear's court is shown by the bragging Gloucester openly boasting about his son Edmund's conception outside marriage – and within his son's hearing. The term 'knave' clearly suggests that he regards Edmund as socially inferior.
To shake all cares and business from our age *(Lear to his daughters and court) l.35*	Lear makes the fatal decision to abdicate his power. But does he really hope that he can still hold on to the rights, but not the responsibilities, of kingship?
I cannot heave/ My heart into my mouth *(Cordelia to Lear) l.88–9*	Cordelia refuses to take part in Lear's 'love test' which demands public declarations of affection for her aged father in order to gain land and power. Her honesty will also lead to disaster.
let me still remain/ The true blank of thine eye *(Kent to Lear) l.155–6*	Having offended Lear by supporting Cordelia and behaving honorably, the loyal courtier Kent asks to remain as Lear's honest adviser.
a tardiness in nature/ Which often leaves the history unspoke/ That it intends to do *(France to Lear) l.234–6*	France also defends Cordelia, pointing out that she is a naturally reserved type of person who keeps her qualities and good intentions to herself.
The best and soundest of his time hath been but rash *(Goneril to Regan) l.292*	In their private conversation, Lear's two daughters accurately sum up the king's flawed character. He acts without due thought and his judgement is faulty.

Act 1
Scene 2*

INTRODUCTION

- Edmund resents being treated as inferior because he is illegitimate.
- His legitimate brother, Edgar, will inherit Gloucester's estate.
- Edmund ruthlessly plots against his family to pursue his own interests.
- From Edmund's viewpoint, there is no justice under the law.

* This key scene requires close, detailed study.

The Earl of Gloucester's castle

Enter Edmund, with a letter

Edmund

Thou, nature, art my goddess; to thy law
My services are bound. Wherefore should I
Stand in the plague of custom, and permit
The curiosity of nations to deprive me,
For that I am some twelve or fourteen moonshines
Lag of a brother? Why bastard? wherefore base?
When my dimensions are as well compact,
My mind as generous, and my shape as true,
As honest madam's issue? Why brand they us
With base? with baseness? bastardy? base, base?
Who, in the lusty stealth of nature, take
More composition and fierce quality
Than doth, within a dull, stale, tired bed,
Go to the creating a whole tribe of fops,
Got between asleep and wake? Well, then,
Legitimate Edgar, I must have your land:
Our father's love is to the bastard Edmund
As to the legitimate: fine word, legitimate!
Well, my legitimate, if this letter speed,
And my invention thrive, Edmund the base
Shall top the legitimate. I grow; I prosper:
Now, gods, stand up for bastards!

Enter Gloucester

Gloucester

Kent banished thus! and France in choler parted!
And the king gone to-night! Prescribed his power!
Confined to exhibition! All this done
Upon the gad! Edmund, how now! what news?

Edmund

So please your lordship, none.

Putting the letter in his pocket

Gloucester

Why so earnestly seek you to put up that letter?

Edmund

I know no news, my lord.

Gloucester

What paper were you reading?

3 in the plague of custom: *denounced by the conventions of society*
4 curiosity of nations: *intrusive laws*
6 Lag of: *younger than*
bastard: *child of unmarried persons*
base: *low social status*
7 dimensions...compact: *well-designed and proportioned*
9 issue: *child*
14 fops: *fools*
21 top: *rise above*
23 choler: *anger*
24 Prescribed: *reduced*
25 Confined to exhibition: *restricted to a limited allowance*
26 Upon the gad: *in a rush*

Edmund

Nothing, my lord.

Gloucester

32 terrible dispatch: *hastily consigning*

No? What needed, then, that terrible dispatch of it into your pocket? The quality of nothing hath not such need to hide itself. Let's see. Come, if it be nothing, I shall not need spectacles.

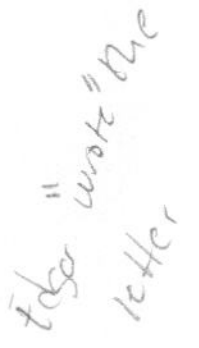

Edmund

38 perused: *scanned*
for your over-looking: *for you to see*

I beseech you, sir, pardon me. It is a letter from my brother, that I have not all over-read; and for so much as I have perused, I find it not fit for your over-looking.

Gloucester

Give me the letter, sir.

Edmund

I shall offend, either to detain or give it. The contents, as in part I understand them, are to blame.

Gloucester

Let's see, let's see.

Edmund

44 an essay...of my virtue: *a way of testing my integrity*

I hope, for my brother's justification, he wrote this but as an essay or taste of my virtue.

Gloucester

47–48 idle and fond bondage: *redundant and stupid enslavement*

49 sways...suffered: *governs because it is endured*

[Reads]

'This policy and reverence of age makes the world bitter to the best of our times; keeps our fortunes from us till our oldness cannot relish them. I begin to find an idle and fond bondage in the oppression of aged tyranny; who sways, not as it hath power, but as it is suffered. Come to me, that of this I may speak more. If our father would sleep till I waked him, you should enjoy half his revenue for ever, and live the beloved of your brother, Edgar.' Hum! Conspiracy! 'Sleep till I waked him, you should enjoy half his revenue.' My son Edgar! Had he a hand to write this? a heart and brain to breed it in? When came this to you? Who brought it?

Edmund

58 casement: *window*
closet: *private room*

It was not brought me, my lord; there's the cunning of it. I found it thrown in at the casement of my closet.

Gloucester

You know the character to be your brother's?

Edmund

If the matter were good, my lord, I durst swear it were his; but, in respect of that, I would fain think it were not.

Gloucester

It is his.

Edmund

It is his hand, my lord, but I hope his heart is not in the contents.

Gloucester

Hath he never before sounded you in this business?

Edmund

Never, my lord. But I have heard him oft maintain it to be fit, that, sons at perfect age, and fathers declined, the father should be as ward to the son, and the son manage his revenue.

Gloucester

O villain, villain! His very opinion in the letter! Abhorred villain! Unnatural, detested, brutish villain! Worse than brutish! Go, sirrah, seek him; I'll apprehend him. Abominable villain! Where is he?

Edmund

I do not well know, my lord. If it shall please you to suspend your indignation against my brother till you can derive from him better testimony of his intent, you should run a certain course; where, if you violently proceed against him, mistaking his purpose, it would make a great gap in your own honour, and shake in pieces the heart of his obedience. I dare pawn down my life for him, that he hath writ this to feel my affection to your honour, and to no other pretence of danger.

Gloucester

Think you so?

Edmund

If your honour judge it meet, I will place you where you shall hear us confer of this, and by an auricular assurance have your satisfaction, and that without any further delay than this very evening.

59 character: *handwriting*

60 durst: *dare*

61 would fain think it were not: *would like to think it was not his*

65 sounded you: *tried to discover your opinions*

67 sons at perfect age: *mature grown-up sons*

68 ward: *someone under control of a guardian*

72 sirrah: *young sir*

75–76 derive...intent: *find out what he intends to do*

76–77 should...course: *will not go wrong*

80 pawn down: *gamble*

84 meet: *suitable*

85 auricular assurance: *proof by hearing*

Gloucester

He cannot be such a monster –

Edmund

Nor is not, sure.

Gloucester

To his father, that so tenderly and entirely loves him. Heaven and earth! Edmund, seek him out: wind me into him, I pray you. Frame the business after your own wisdom. I would unstate myself, to be in a due resolution.

91–92 wind me into him: *discover what he is thinking*
93 unstate… resolution: *give up all I possess to be sure*

Edmund

I will seek him, sir, presently, convey the business as I shall find means, and acquaint you withal.

95 acquaint you withal: *let you know how I get on*

Gloucester

These late eclipses in the sun and moon portend no good to us. Though the wisdom of nature can reason it thus and thus, yet nature finds itself scourged by the sequent effects. Love cools, friendship falls off, brothers divide. In cities, mutinies; in countries, discord; in palaces, treason; and the bond cracked 'twixt son and father. This villain of mine comes under the prediction; there's son against father. The king falls from bias of nature, there's father against child. We have seen the best of our time. Machinations, hollowness, treachery, and all ruinous disorders, follow us disquietly to our graves. Find out this villain, Edmund, it shall lose thee nothing. Do it carefully. And the noble and true-hearted Kent banished! His offence, honesty! 'Tis strange.

Exit

96 eclipses: *blotting out of light by the position of a planet*
portend: *foretell*
98 sequent: *succeeding*
103 bias of nature: *his natural course*
104 Machinations: *scheming plots*

Edmund

This is the excellent foppery of the world, that when we are sick in fortune, often the surfeits of our own behaviour, we make guilty of our disasters the sun, the moon, and stars, as if we were villains on necessity, fools by heavenly compulsion, knaves, thieves and treachers, by spherical predominance, drunkards, liars and adulterers, by an enforced obedience of planetary influence; and all that we are evil in, by a divine thrusting on. An admirable evasion of whoremaster man, to lay his goatish disposition to the charge of a star! My father compounded with my

110 foppery: *foolishness, stupidity*
111 surfeits: *over-indulgences*
114 treachers: *traitors*

118 goatish disposition: *lechery*
119 compounded: *conceived*

mother under the dragon's tail, and my nativity was under Ursa Major, so that it follows I am rough and lecherous. I should have been that I am had the maidenliest star in the firmament twinkled on my bastardizing.

Enter Edgar

Pat he comes like the catastrophe of the old comedy. My cue is villainous melancholy, with a sigh like Tom o' Bedlam. O, these eclipses do portend these divisions! fa, sol, la, mi.

Edgar

How now, brother Edmund! What serious contemplation are you in?

Edmund

I am thinking, brother, of a prediction I read this other day, what should follow these eclipses.

Edgar

Do you busy yourself about that?

Edmund

I promise you, the effects he writes of succeed unhappily as of unnaturalness between the child and the parent; death, dearth, dissolutions of ancient amities; divisions in state, menaces and maledictions against king and nobles; needless diffidences, banishment of friends, dissipation of cohorts, nuptial breaches, and I know not what.

Edgar

Do you busy yourself with that?

Edmund

When saw you my father last?

Edgar

The night gone by.

Edmund

Spake you with him?

Edgar

Ay, two hours together.

Edmund

Parted you in good terms? Found you no displeasure in him by word or countenance?

121 Ursa Major: *Great Bear constellation*

124 Pat: *right on time*

125–26 Tom o' Bedlam: *a madman*

128 contemplation: *thoughts*

135 dearth: *scarcity*
dissolutions of ancient amities: *breaking up of old friendships*

137 needless diffidences: *avoidable loss of trust*

137–38 dissipation of cohorts: *dispersal of soldiers*

138 nuptial breaches: *marriage breakdown*

Edgar

None at all.

Edmund

Bethink yourself wherein you may have offended him, and at my entreaty forbear his presence until some little time hath qualified the heat of his displeasure; which at this instant so rageth in him, that with the mischief of your person it would scarcely allay.

Edgar

Some villain hath done me wrong.

153 have a continent forbearance: *keep a low profile*

155 fitly: *at a suitable time*

Edmund

That's my fear. I pray you, have a continent forbearance till the speed of his rage goes slower; and, as I say, retire with me to my lodging, from whence I will fitly bring you to hear my lord speak. Pray ye, go; there's my key. If you do stir abroad, go armed.

Edgar

Armed, brother?

Edmund

Brother, I advise you to the best. I am no honest man if there be any good meaning towards you. I have told you what I have seen and heard but faintly, nothing like the image and horror of it. Pray you, away.

163 anon: *soon*

Edgar

Shall I hear from you anon?

165 credulous: *easily taken in*
noble: *honourable*

168 practices: *trickery*

169 wit: *intelligence*

170 meet: *correct*
fashion fit: *shape to suit my purposes*

Edmund

I do serve you in this business.

Exit Edgar

A credulous father and a brother noble,
Whose nature is so far from doing harms,
That he suspects none: on whose foolish honesty
My practices ride easy. I see the business.
Let me, if not by birth, have lands by wit:
All with me's meet that I can fashion fit.

Exit

Key Scene Analysis

Edmund's soliloquy (lines 1–22)

The opening monologue shows the true feelings and evil intentions of Gloucester's younger son. Edmund is angry at the preferential treatment shown to people regarded as illegitimate, simply because they are born outside marriage. He chooses to make nature his 'goddess' and plans to displace his legitimate brother Edgar and claim his inheritance: 'I must have your land'. To achieve this, he will use a forged letter to trick his father and gain what he believes is his entitlement: 'Edmund the base/ Shall top the legitimate'.

The letter (lines 28–61)

Edmund exaggerates his attempts to hide a letter so that Gloucester will demand to know more about it. Keen to give the impression that he means no harm, Edmund pretends that he is reluctant to hand it over. However, Gloucester insists on reading what is written and is horrified to discover that Edgar is suggesting that the two brothers should unite to murder their father and divide his wealth between them: 'you should enjoy half his revenue for ever'. Horrified at his ungrateful son, the old earl demands that Edgar be apprehended at once.

The sub-plot closely reflects the main storyline as both fathers are shocked by the unexpected behaviour of children who have always appeared to love them. Gloucester seems completely out of touch with his two sons and deeply disappointed that children can be so disrespectful to their elderly parents, 'the oppression of aged tyranny'.

A rash father and a devious son (lines 63–95)

Gloucester immediately jumps to the conclusion Edmund has planned, furiously condemning the absent Edgar as an 'Unnatural, detested, brutish villain!' Acting as a peacemaker, Edmund advises his father to keep calm and 'suspend your indignation against my brother'. But Gloucester is desperate to know the truth about Edgar's intentions: 'wind me into him'. Audiences are likely to wonder why he does not check the truth of Edmund's invented story by directly confronting his older son. His sudden suspicions indicate a severe lack of communication between himself and his children.

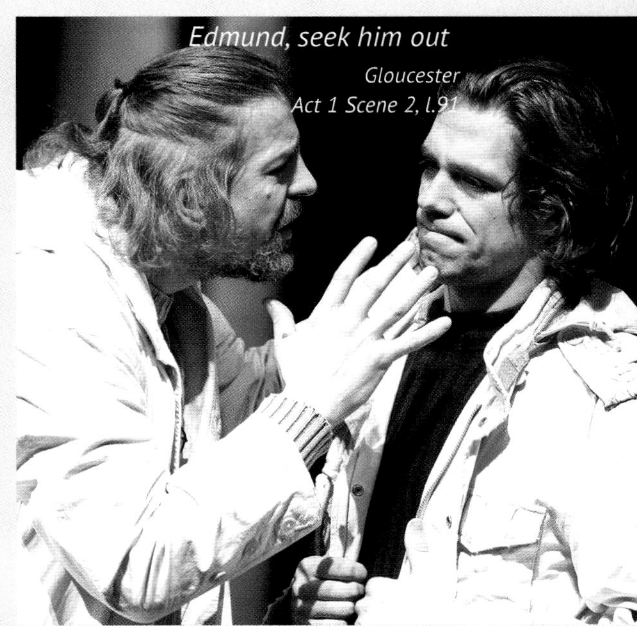
Edmund, seek him out

Gloucester
Act 1 Scene 2, l.91

Gloucester agrees with Edmund's suggestion to spy on Edgar so that he can end this uncertainty 'by an auricular assurance'. Edmund is delighted at this and pretends to comfort his father by saying that he will organise everything and 'acquaint you withal'. Throughout this frantic encounter, Gloucester appears as a naive, irrational character who is still stunned by what happened earlier in Lear's court. Like the elderly king, of course, he is influenced by individuals who are not what they seem.

The Gloucester family sub-plot has obvious parallels with the main plot. Just as Lear has children who are scheming against him, Gloucester has a deceitful son. Like the king, he mistakenly condemns the wrong person.

Superstitious Gloucester (lines 96–109)

Gloucester reflects on how things change, blaming this on the stars, 'late eclipses in the sun and moon portend no good'. He is a superstitious man who lives through his senses. Lear has also shown a similar trait in his personality, 'By all the operation of the orbs/ From whom we do exist, and cease to be'. The illusions of both characters emphasise the pagan background of the story, which is set in pre-Christian times.

Edmund's realism (lines 110–127)

Edmund mocks his father's beliefs that the stars are to blame for man's actions: 'This is the excellent foppery of the world'. He feels that people often delude themselves with this superstitious explanation, 'An admirable evasion'. It is ironic that one of the play's greatest villains holds such a rational view. Edmund asserts that he himself would have been exactly as he is regardless of what star shone on his conception. He sneers at the sight of Edgar as he approaches and delights in mocking Gloucester's previous speech: 'O, these eclipses do portend these divisions!'

Treachery (lines 128–164)

The unsuspecting older brother is easily taken in by Edmund's treachery. Although he rightly deduces that 'Some villain hath done me wrong', Edgar never suspects his own brother. Like Gloucester, he places himself under Edmund's control, timidly inquiring, 'Shall I hear from you anon?' He has much in common with his gullible father and accepts everything his persuasive brother says as the truth. Edgar is clearly honest and trusting, but is far from being sharp and worldly-wise.

This revealing scene is dominated by Edmund. He is an astute judge of character and correctly identifies his father as 'credulous' and his brother as being too 'noble' for his own good. This allows him to deceive both of them effortlessly. Edmund is a realist and a schemer who is determined to rise in the world. Always the opportunist, he can now see his plans taking shape and he swears to get what he deserves: 'if not by birth, have lands by wit'.

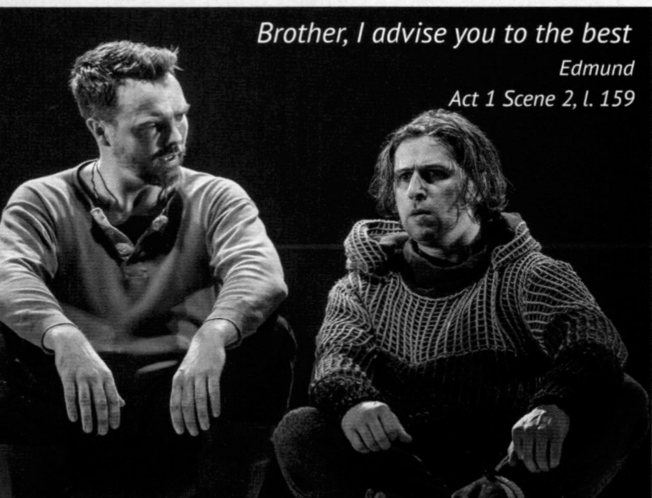

Brother, I advise you to the best
Edmund
Act 1 Scene 2, l. 159

Edmund sees 'nature' as a malicious force which can overturn civilisation and order. He is clever and persuasive, easily manipulating his father and brother. Somewhat surprisingly, he can charm audiences, who sympathise with him despite his cold-hearted scheming.

Shakespeare's Dramatic Style

Shakespeare has set the scene for the developing drama and the audience has much more knowledge of what is going on than some of the main characters. The playwright makes **effective use of dramatic irony to increase the tension** in the play. We learn that Edmund is filled with hidden bitterness and has a grudge against his own family. Now that he has taken justice into his own hands, anything could happen.

It's clear that Edmund will let nothing stand in the way of his lust for power. He **reveals his true character in compelling soliloquies**. The audience knows about his evil plans in advance. He deceives the unsuspecting Gloucester by pretending to support Edgar, claiming that he accidently found the incriminating letter 'thrown in at the casement'. Lying comes easy to Edmund: 'I hope his heart is not in the contents', and he even swears that he would die for Edgar: 'I dare pawn down my life for him'.

Critical Analysis

Based on your reading of Act 1 Scene 2 of *King Lear*, discuss the dramatic significance of the Gloucester family sub-plot.

Write a paragraph (about 150 words), developing your response with reference to the text.

Sample Paragraph 1

The sub plot is very like the main story of King Lear losing out, there are many things in common. Both fathers are very old men and have children who don't really get on with them. Edmund hates Gloucester. Edmund is very clever and comes up with a secret plan to inherit land 'Edgar I will soon have your land'. he does not like his father because the old man is always showing off about how Edmund was illigitimate. I think Gloucester is as bad a father as Lear and the sub plot is very intresting because we like Edmund even though he is an evil son who has some right to be annoyed. Edgar is innocent too. he just believes Edmund as does Gloucester. I think this subplot is very dramatic in the play. *(135 words)*

Examiner's Comment

- Unfocused paragraph that includes some observations regarding Gloucester's family.
- Needs more engagement with the playwright's use of the sub-plot and its impact.
- Note-like expression and some mechanical flaws. Basic-grade standard.

Sample Paragraph 2

In Act 1 Scene 2, the Gloucester sub-plot reinforces the main plot's message – which is about moral blindness. Both Lear and Gloucester are gullible and rash. These faults lead them into making serious misjudgements about their children, Cordelia and Edgar, who are then banished. Lear roars 'avoid my sight'. Both fathers are fooled by outward appearances. The Gloucester sub-plot highlights how older people are vulnerable to the evil schemes of their ungrateful children. Goneril and Regan used the 'glib and oily art' of flattery and lies to deceive Lear. Edmund uses the forged letter to trick Gloucester, 'I hope for my brother's justification, he wrote this but as an essay or taste of my virtue'. By matching the plot and sub-plot so closely, Shakespeare succeeds in making the tragic story more believable. This gets the audience engaging more in the important theme of moral blindness. *(145 words)*

Examiner's Comment

- Top-grade response shows a good understanding of the sub-plot's importance.
- Focused throughout – with strong supportive reference and quotation.
- Some insightful discussion points are well developed.
- Impressive expression (e.g. 'corresponding sub-plot highlights the vulnerability of the old').

Class/Homework Exercise

Based on the evidence of Act 1 Scene 2, describe the relationship between Gloucester and his two sons.

Write a paragraph (about 150 words), developing your response with reference to the text.

Exam Focus

Act 1 Scene 2 can be used successfully in response to a range of examination questions about the play's central themes, characters, relationships and the playwright's dramatic style.

This **key scene** has important dramatic functions:

- The Gloucester sub-plot mirrors the conflict within Lear's family.
- Establishes Edmund's complex character.
- Reveals more about Edgar and Gloucester's gullibility.
- Develops themes of deception, envy, vengeance, justice and injustice.
- Increases dramatic tension through irony and foreshadowing.

Key Quotes

Quote	Comment
Thou, nature, art my goddess; to thy law/ My services are bound *(Edmund) l.1–2*	In this revealing soliloquy, Gloucester's younger son, Edmund, vows to follow the laws of nature where only the strongest survive and the weak become victims. He is extremely hurt and resentful that he is regarded as inferior because of his illegitimacy.
What needed, then, that terrible dispatch of it into your pocket? *(Gloucester to Edmund) l.32*	Gloucester's curiosity is immediately aroused when Edmund pretends to hide a letter from Edgar. Its contents will suggest that Edgar is plotting against their father.
These late eclipses in the sun and moon portend no good to us *(Gloucester to Edmund) l.96–7*	The old earl is highly superstitious and believes that man's actions and circumstances are governed by heavenly influences.
in palaces treason;/ and the bond cracked 'twixt son and father *(Gloucester to Edmund) l.100–1*	Gloucester is shocked at the recent events in court when Lear was deceived by his two elder daughters and banished Cordelia. Ironically, Gloucester makes exactly the same mistake, believing the hypocritical Edmund while proceeding to exile his loyal son, Edgar.
Some villain hath done me wrong *(Edgar to Edmund) l.152*	Edgar is speaking the truth, but does not realise that the villain is his brother Edmund.
Let me, if not by birth, have lands by wit:/ All with me's meet that I can fashion fit *(Edmund) l.169–70*	Edmund decides that he will seize power through the strength of his intellect and he intends to use everyone and everything to his advantage. For him, the end justifies the means. He is the ultimate exploiter.

Act 1
Scene 3

INTRODUCTION

- Goneril complains about the disorderly behaviour of Lear's knights.
- She is intent on challenging her father.
- Oswald is loyal to Goneril and agrees to disrespect the former king.

The Duke of Albany's palace

Enter Goneril and her steward, Oswald

Goneril

Did my father strike my gentleman for chiding of his Fool?

Oswald

Yes, madam.

Goneril

By day and night he wrongs me; every hour
He flashes into one gross crime or other,
That sets us all at odds. I'll not endure it.
His knights grow riotous, and himself upbraids us
On every trifle. When he returns from hunting,
I will not speak with him. Say I am sick.
If you come slack of former services,
You shall do well; the fault of it I'll answer.

Oswald

He's coming, madam, I hear him.

Horns within

Goneril

Put on what weary negligence you please,
You and your fellows; I'd have it come to question.
If he distaste it, let him to our sister,
Whose mind and mine, I know, in that are one,
Not to be over-ruled. Idle old man,
That still would manage those authorities
That he hath given away! Now, by my life,
Old fools are babes again; and must be used
With cheques as flatteries, when they are seen abused.
Remember what I have said.

Oswald

Well, madam.

Goneril

And let his knights have colder looks among you;
What grows of it, no matter; advise your fellows so:
I would breed from hence occasions, and I shall,
That I may speak: I'll write straight to my sister,
To hold my very course. Prepare for dinner.

Exeunt

1 chiding: *scolding*

4 flashes...or other: *suddenly does something offensive*

6 upbraids: *finds fault with*

7 trifle: *unimportant matter*

9 come slack of former services: *are not as attentive as before*

Horns within: *the sound of hunting horns*

12 weary negligence: *jaded indifference*

13 come to question: *made an issue of*

14 distaste: *dislike*

20 cheques as flatteries: *sharp reprimands in addition to praise*
seen abused: *seem deluded*

24 I would breed from hence: *I would like to use this*

Analysis

Goneril's changing character (lines 1–26)

Lear's oldest daughter openly shows her lack of feelings for her father by complaining about him to her servant, Oswald. She calls him an 'Idle old man' and is irritated that Lear is behaving as if he were still in power. Goneril is frustrated that he 'still would manage those authorities/ That he hath given away'. She is also angry that the old king has her household in uproar, 'His knights grow riotous', and that he continuously finds fault, 'himself upbraids us/ On every trifle'. Shakespeare leaves his audience to decide whether her criticisms are genuine or not.

She tells Oswald that if Lear asks to speak to her when he returns from hunting, he is to make up an excuse for her absence: 'Say I am sick'. She also instructs Oswald to be openly disrespectful to Lear, 'come slack of former services' and even to adopt an attitude of 'weary negligence'. Goneril's earlier declarations of love ring hollow now when she declares that 'Old fools are babes again'. Will the audience feel sympathy for Lear who is, after all, Goneril's father, a guest in her home, and the former king?

Goneril appears to be the stronger of the two sisters and she will urge Regan to follow her lead in the treatment of their father: 'I'll write straight to my sister, / To hold my very course'. At this stage, neither sister intends to physically harm Lear, but they are keen to free themselves from the current arrangement by which they are expected to look after the elderly king and his hundred knights.

This short scene also introduces Oswald, a loyal servant who does whatever Goneril tells him, regardless of the morality or consequences. Interestingly, Oswald will serve as a contrast to Kent, whose loyalty is based on honour and decency.

Key Quotes

Quote	Comment
His knights grow riotous, and himself upbraids us/ On every trifle *(Goneril to Oswald) l.6–7*	Goneril's fury at Lear and his knights' behaviour is conveyed to her trusted servant, Oswald. Has she a genuine grievance or is she just making an excuse for her callous treatment of her father?
Say I am sick *(Goneril to Oswald) l.8*	Lear's daughter now decides that she will not greet her father on his return from his hunting trip and she instructs Oswald to make up an excuse.
Put on what weary negligence you please *(Goneril to Oswald) l.12*	She further orders Oswald and the other servants to treat the old king with cynical indifference to provoke Lear.
Old fools are babes again *(Goneril to Oswald) l.19*	Lear is contemptuously dismissed as having reverted to the behaviour of a naughty child who must be reprimanded.

Act 1
Scene 4

INTRODUCTION

- A disguised Kent returns to Lear's service.
- The old king struggles to cope with his changed circumstances.
- Lear has his first angry confrontation with Goneril.
- The Fool, Lear's court jester, is introduced.

A hall in the Duke of Albany's palace

Enter Kent, disguised

Kent

If but as well I other accents borrow,
That can my speech defuse, my good intent
May carry through itself to that full issue
For which I razed my likeness. Now, banished Kent,
If thou canst serve where thou dost stand condemned,
So may it come, thy master, whom thou lovest,
Shall find thee full of labours.

2 defuse: *disguise*
intent: *purpose*
3 issue: *end*
4 razed my likeness: *changed my appearance*
7 full of labours: *a diligent worker*

Horns within. Enter King Lear, Knights, and Attendants

Lear

Let me not stay a jot for dinner. Go get it ready.

8 not stay a jot: *not wait a minute*

Exit an Attendant

How now! what art thou?

Kent

A man, sir.

Lear

What dost thou profess? What wouldst thou with us?

11 What does thou profess: *What is your occupation?*

Kent

I do profess to be no less than I seem, to serve him truly that will put me in trust, to love him that is honest, to converse with him that is wise, and says little to fear judgement, to fight when I cannot choose, and to eat no fish.

Lear

What art thou?

Kent

A very honest-hearted fellow, and as poor as the king.

Lear

If thou be as poor for a subject as he is for a king, thou art poor enough. What wouldst thou?

Kent

Service.

Lear

Who wouldst thou serve?

Kent

You.

Lear

Dost thou know me, fellow?

Kent

No, sir; but you have that in your countenance which I would fain call master.

24 countenance: *face*
25 fain: *gladly*

Lear

What's that?

Kent

Authority.

Lear

What services canst thou do?

Kent

I can keep honest counsel, ride, run, mar a curious tale in telling it, and deliver a plain message bluntly. That which ordinary men are fit for, I am qualified in; and the best of me is diligence.

29 keep honest counsel: *keep a secret*
29–30 mar a curious tale in telling it: *spoil an elaborate story by telling it plainly*
32 diligence: *persistence*

Lear

How old art thou?

Kent

Not so young, sir, to love a woman for singing, nor so old to dote on her for anything. I have years on my back forty eight.

Lear

Follow me; thou shalt serve me: if I like thee no worse after dinner, I will not part from thee yet. Dinner, ho, dinner! Where's my knave? My Fool? Go you, and call my Fool hither.

Exit an Attendant

Enter Oswald

You, you, sirrah, where's my daughter?

Oswald

So please you –

Exit

Lear

What says the fellow there? Call the clotpoll back.

Exit a Knight

Where's my Fool, ho? I think the world's asleep.

43 clotpoll: *dimwit*

Re-enter Knight

How now! Where's that mongrel?

Knight

He says, my lord, your daughter is not well.

Lear

Why came not the slave back to me when I called him?

Knight

Sir, he answered me in the roundest manner, he would not.

Lear

He would not!

Knight

My lord, I know not what the matter is, but to my judgement, your highness is not entertained with that ceremonious affection as you were wont. There's a great abatement of kindness appears as well in the general dependants as in the duke himself also and your daughter.

Lear

Ha! Sayest thou so?

Knight

I beseech you, pardon me, my lord, if I be mistaken, for my duty cannot be silent when I think your highness wronged.

Lear

Thou but rememberest me of mine own conception. I have perceived a most faint neglect of late, which I have rather blamed as mine own jealous curiosity than as a very pretence and purpose of unkindness. I will look further into it. But where's my Fool? I have not seen him this two days.

Knight

Since my young lady's going into France, sir, the Fool hath much pined away.

Lear

No more of that, I have noted it well. Go you, and tell my daughter I would speak with her.

Exit an Attendant

Go you, call hither my Fool.

Exit an Attendant

Re-enter Oswald

48 roundest: *firmest*

52 wont: *accustomed*
abatement: *lessening*

53 general dependants: *followers and servants*

58 conception: *impression*

60–61 very pretence and purpose: *real intention*

O, you sir, you, come you hither, sir.
Who am I, sir?

Oswald

My lady's father.

Lear

'My lady's father'! My lord's knave, you whoreson dog! you slave! you cur!

Oswald

I am none of these, my lord, I beseech your pardon.

Lear

Do you bandy looks with me, you rascal?

Striking him

Oswald

I'll not be struck, my lord.

Kent

Nor tripped neither, you base football player.

Tripping up his heels

Lear

I thank thee, fellow. Thou servest me, and I'll love thee.

Kent

Come, sir, arise, away! I'll teach you differences. Away, away! If you will measure your lubber's length again, tarry: but away! Go to! Have you wisdom?
So.

Pushes Oswald out

Lear

Now, my friendly knave, I thank thee: there's earnest of thy service.

Giving Kent money

Enter Fool

Fool

Let me hire him too; here's my coxcomb.

Offering Kent his cap

Lear

How now, my pretty knave! How dost thou?

Fool

Sirrah, you were best take my coxcomb.

73 cur: *worthless dog*

75 bandy: *swap*

77 base: *inferior*

80 lubber: *awkward fool*
tarry: *wait*

83 earnest: *a token payment*

85 coxcomb: *court jester's cap*

86 knave: *scoundrel*

87 Sirrah: *belittling form of address*

Kent

Why, Fool?

Fool

Why? For taking part that's out of favour. Nay, and thou canst not smile as the wind sits, thou'lt catch cold shortly. There, take my coxcomb. Why, this fellow has banished two on's daughters, and did the third a blessing against his will. If thou follow him, thou must needs wear my coxcomb. How now, nuncle? Would I had two coxcombs and two daughters!

Lear

Why, my boy?

Fool

If I gave them all my living, I'd keep my coxcombs myself. There's mine; beg another of thy daughters.

Lear

Take heed, sirrah, the whip.

Fool

Truth's a dog must to kennel. He must be whipped out when Lady Brach may stand by the fire and stink.

Lear

A pestilent gall to me!

Fool

Sirrah, I'll teach thee a speech.

Lear

Do.

Fool

Mark it, nuncle:

Have more than thou showest,
Speak less than thou knowest,
Lend less than thou owest,
Ride more than thou goest,
Learn more than thou trowest,
Set less than thou throwest,
Leave thy drink and thy whore,
And keep in-a-door,
And thou shalt have more
Than two tens to a score.

89–90 thou canst not...shortly: *if you cannot fawn, you will suffer from those who are in power*

94 nuncle: *uncle (common court jester address to his master)*

101 Lady Brach: *female hunting hound*

102 pestilent gall: *deadly irritation*

108 owest: *own*

109 goest: *walks*

110 trowest: *believe*

111 throwest: *gamble*

115 score: *twenty*

117 unfee'd: *not yet paid*

139 monopoly: *complete possession of*

Kent

This is nothing, fool.

Fool

Then 'tis like the breath of an unfee'd lawyer; you gave me nothing for it. Can you make no use of nothing, nuncle?

Lear

Why, no, boy. Nothing can be made out of nothing.

Fool

To Kent

Prithee, tell him, so much the rent of his land comes to: he will not believe a fool.

Lear

A bitter fool!

Fool

Dost thou know the difference, my boy, between a bitter fool and a sweet fool?

Lear

No, lad. Teach me.

Fool

That lord that counselled thee
To give away thy land,
Come place him here by me,
Do thou for him stand:
The sweet and bitter fool
Will presently appear;
The one in motley here,
The other found out there.

Lear

Dost thou call me fool, boy?

Fool

All thy other titles thou hast given away; that thou wast born with.

Kent

This is not altogether fool, my lord.

Fool

No, faith, lords and great men will not let me. If I had a monopoly out, they would have part on it – and ladies too, they will not let me have all fool to myself; they'll be snatching. Give me an egg, nuncle, and I'll give thee two crowns.

Lear

What two crowns shall they be?

Fool

Why, after I have cut the egg i' the middle, and eat up the meat, the two crowns of the egg. When thou clovest thy crown in the middle, and gavest away both parts, thou borest thy ass on thy back over the dirt. Thou hadst little wit in thy bald crown when thou gavest thy golden one away. If I speak like myself in this, let him be whipped that first finds it so.

Singing

Fools had never less wit in a year;
For wise men are grown foppish,
They know not how their wits to wear,
Their manners are so apish.

Lear

When were you wont to be so full of songs, sirrah?

Fool

I have used it, nuncle, ever since thou madest thy daughters thy mothers: for when thou gavest them the rod and put'st down thine own breeches,

Then they for sudden joy did weep,
And I for sorrow sung,
That such a king should play bo-peep,
And go the fools among.

Prithee, nuncle, keep a schoolmaster that can teach thy fool to lie: I would fain learn to lie.

Lear

An you lie, sirrah, we'll have you whipped.

Fool

I marvel what kin thou and thy daughters are: they'll have me whipped for speaking true, thou'lt have me whipped for lying, and sometimes I am whipped for holding my peace. I had rather be any kind o' thing than a fool. And yet I would not be thee, nuncle. Thou hast pared thy wit

145 clovest: *divided*
147 borest: *carried*
152 foppish: *foolish*
154 apish: *silly*
156 used: *practised*
158 breeches: *trousers*
161 bo-peep: *a childish game*
164 fain: *gladly*
170 pared: *cut away*

on both sides, and left nothing in the middle. Here comes one of the parings.

Enter Goneril

Lear

How now, daughter! What makes that frontlet on? You are too much of late i' the frown.

Fool

Thou wast a pretty fellow when thou hadst no need to care for her frowning. Now thou art an O without a figure: I am better than thou art now; I am a fool, thou art nothing.

To Goneril

Yes, forsooth, I will hold my tongue, so your face bids me, though you say nothing.

Sings

Mum, mum!
He that keeps nor crust nor crumb,
Weary of all, shall want some.

Pointing to Lear

That's a shealed peascod.

Goneril

Not only, sir, this your all-licensed fool,
But other of your insolent retinue
Do hourly carp and quarrel; breaking forth
In rank and not-to-be endured riots. Sir,
I had thought, by making this well known unto you,
To have found a safe redress, but now grow fearful,
By what yourself too late have spoke and done.
That you protect this course, and put it on
By your allowance; which if you should, the fault
Would not 'scape censure, nor the redresses sleep,
Which, in the tender of a wholesome weal,
Might in their working do you that offence,
Which else were shame, that then necessity
Will call discreet proceeding.

Fool

For, you trow, nuncle,
The hedge-sparrow fed the cuckoo so long,
That it's had it head bit off by it young.
So, out went the candle, and we were left darkling.

172 parings: *shavings*
173 frontlet: *frown*
176 O: *worthless*
183 shealed peascod: *empty pea-pod*
184 all-licensed: *unrestrained*
185 insolent retinue: *rude followers*
186 carp: *complain continually*
187 rank: *foul, unpleasant*
189 safe redress: *sure remedy*
191 put it on: *support it*
193 redresses: *remedies*
194 weal: *state*
197 discreet proceeding: *proper action*
198 trow: *know*
201 darkling: *in the dark*

Lear

Are you our daughter?

Goneril

Come, sir,
I would you would make use of that good wisdom,
Whereof I know you are fraught; and put away
These dispositions, that of late transform you
From what you rightly are.

Fool

May not an ass know when the cart draws the horse?
Whoop, Jug! I love thee.

Lear

Does any here know me? This is not Lear:
Does Lear walk thus? speak thus? Where are his eyes?
Either his notion weakens, his discernings
Are lethargied – Ha! waking? 'Tis not so.
Who is it that can tell me who I am?

Fool

Lear's shadow.

Lear

I would learn that; for, by the marks of sovereignty, knowledge, and reason, I should be false persuaded I had daughters.

Fool

Which they will make an obedient father.

Lear

Your name, fair gentlewoman?

Goneril

This admiration, sir, is much o' the savour
Of other your new pranks. I do beseech you
To understand my purposes aright:
As you are old and reverend, you should be wise.
Here do you keep a hundred knights and squires;
Men so disordered, so deboshed and bold,
That this our court, infected with their manners,
Shows like a riotous inn; epicurism and lust
Makes it more like a tavern or a brothel
Than a graced palace. The shame itself doth speak

205 fraught: *filled with*

206 dispositions: *tendencies, moods*

208 ass...horse: *the order is wrong*

209 Whoop...love thee: *ironic reference to Goneril's previous declarations of love for Lear*

212 discernings: *good judgement*

213 lethargied: *asleep*

226 deboshed: *morally corrupted*

228 epicurism: *gluttony*

233 disquantity: *lessen*
train: *retinue, followers*

235 besort: *suits*

238 Degenerate: *unnatural*

248 kite: *bird of prey*

249 choice: *excellence*
rarest parts: *unusual accomplishments*

251 in the most exact regard: *with the utmost care*

254 engine: *destructive machine*
wrenched: *violently pulled*

256 gall: *annoyance*

For instant remedy: be then desired
By her, that else will take the thing she begs,
A little to disquantity your train;
And the remainder, that shall still depend,
To be such men as may besort your age,
And know themselves and you.

Lear

Darkness and devils!
Saddle my horses; call my train together:
Degenerate bastard! I'll not trouble thee.
Yet have I left a daughter.

Goneril

You strike my people; and your disordered rabble
Make servants of their betters.

Enter Albany

Lear

Woe, that too late repents –

To Albany

O, sir, are you come?
Is it your will? Speak, sir. Prepare my horses.
Ingratitude, thou marble-hearted fiend,
More hideous when thou showest thee in a child
Than the sea-monster!

Albany

Pray, sir, be patient.

Lear

To Goneril

Detested kite! thou liest.
My train are men of choice and rarest parts,
That all particulars of duty know,
And in the most exact regard support
The worships of their name. O most small fault,
How ugly didst thou in Cordelia show!
That, like an engine, wrenched my frame of nature
From the fixed place, drew from heart all love,

And added to the gall. O Lear, Lear, Lear!
Beat at this gate, that let thy folly in

Striking his head

And thy dear judgement out! Go, go, my people.

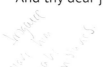

Albany

My lord, I am guiltless, as I am ignorant
Of what hath moved you.

Lear

It may be so, my lord.
Hear, nature, hear; dear goddess, hear!
Suspend thy purpose, if thou didst intend
To make this creature fruitful!
Into her womb convey sterility!
Dry up in her the organs of increase;
And from her derogate body never spring
A babe to honour her! If she must teem,
Create her child of spleen, that it may live,
And be a thwart disnatured torment to her!
Let it stamp wrinkles in her brow of youth;
With cadent tears fret channels in her cheeks;
Turn all her mother's pains and benefits
To laughter and contempt, that she may feel
How sharper than a serpent's tooth it is
To have a thankless child! Away, away!

Exit

Albany

Now, gods that we adore, whereof comes this?

Goneril

Never afflict yourself to know the cause,
But let his disposition have that scope
That dotage gives it.

Re-enter King Lear

Lear

What, fifty of my followers at a clap!
Within a fortnight!

Albany

What's the matter, sir?

Lear

I'll tell thee.

To Goneril

Life and death! I am ashamed
That thou hast power to shake my manhood thus,
That these hot tears, which break from me perforce,

265 increase: *breeding*
266 derogate: *deviant, degraded*
267 teem: *give birth*
268 spleen: *bad temper*
269 thwart: *baffling*
disnatured: *unnatural*
271 cadent: *falling*
fret: *wear away*
278 disposition: *natural character*
scope: *opportunity*
279 dotage: *weak old age*
280 a clap: *one stroke*
285 perforce: *against my wishes*

287 untented woundings: *untreated injuries*
288 fond: *foolish*
291 temper: *moisten, soften*
295 flay: *whip*
visage: *face*
296 shape: *appearance of a king*
300 partial: *unfair*
303 knave: *scoundrel*
304 tarry: *wait*
308 halter: *hangman's noose*
310 counsel: *advice*
311 politic: *wise*
312 At point: *armed and ready*
313 buzz: *rumour*
314 enguard: *safeguard, protect*

Should make thee worth them. Blasts and fogs upon thee!
The untented woundings of a father's curse
Pierce every sense about thee! Old fond eyes,
Beweep this cause again, I'll pluck ye out,
And cast you, with the waters that you lose,
To temper clay. Yea, is it come to this?
Ha! Let it be so. I have another daughter,
Who, I am sure, is kind and comfortable.
When she shall hear this of thee, with her nails
She'll flay thy wolvish visage. Thou shalt find
That I'll resume the shape which thou dost think
I have cast off for ever. Thou shalt,
I warrant thee.

Exeunt Lear, Kent and Attendants

Goneril

Do you mark that, my lord?

Albany

I cannot be so partial, Goneril,
To the great love I bear you –

Goneril

Pray you, content. What, Oswald, ho!

To the Fool

You, sir, more knave than fool, after your master.

Fool

Nuncle Lear, nuncle Lear, tarry and take the Fool with thee.
A fox, when one has caught her,
And such a daughter,
Should sure to the slaughter,
If my cap would buy a halter.
So the Fool follows after.

Exit

Goneril

This man hath had good counsel! A hundred knights!
'Tis politic and safe to let him keep
At point a hundred knights? Yes, that, on every dream,
Each buzz, each fancy, each complaint, dislike,
He may enguard his dotage with their powers,
And hold our lives in mercy. Oswald, I say!

Albany

Well, you may fear too far.

Goneril

Safer than trust too far.
Let me still take away the harms I fear,
Not fear still to be taken. I know his heart.
What he hath uttered I have writ my sister
If she sustain him and his hundred knights
When I have showed the unfitness –

Re-enter Oswald

How now, Oswald!
What, have you writ that letter to my sister?

Oswald

Yes, madam.

Goneril

Take you some company, and away to horse.
Inform her full of my particular fear,
And thereto add such reasons of your own
As may compact it more. Get you gone,
And hasten your return.

Exit Oswald

No, no, my lord,
This milky gentleness and course of yours
Though I condemn not, yet, under pardon,
You are much more ataxed for want of wisdom
Than praised for harmful mildness.

Albany

How far your eyes may pierce I cannot tell:
Striving to better, oft we mar what's well.

Goneril

Nay, then –

Albany

Well, well, the event.

Exeunt

327 compact: *strengthen, bolster*

329 milky: *mild, gentle*

331 ataxed: *disapproved of*
want of wisdom: *lack of good sense*

332 harmful mildness: *dangerous tolerance*

334 mar: *spoil*

336 the event: *only time will tell*

Analysis

Loyal Kent (lines 1–81)

At the start of the scene, Kent explains that he has returned, disguised ('I razed my likeness'), to enlist in Lear's service. He also shows genuine respect for the king's authority, even when Lear is behaving irrationally. Kent takes Lear's part against Goneril's insolent servant, Oswald, and the king immediately rewards him: 'there's earnest of thy service'. Throughout the play, Kent will be the personification of loyalty.

The self-important monarch (lines 8–75)

Lear returns from the hunt with his followers and demands attention straightaway: 'Let me not stay a jot for dinner'. He behaves less like a guest in Albany's palace than as a reigning monarch who still has all the trappings of kingship. The king continues to act as if he were master, hiring Kent and imperiously asking for his Fool. Oswald irritates the king by his disrespectful behaviour: 'Why came not the slave back when I called him?' It is obvious to Lear that his authority is being undermined.

The king tries to reassert his influence by confronting Goneril's servant: 'Who am I, sir?' Oswald's reply, that Lear is 'My lady's father', is predictably infuriating. Now that power has changed hands, Lear is being defined in relation to his children. Enraged by so much deliberate insolence, the ageing king can control himself no longer and begins to beat Oswald – exactly the confrontation Goneril had hoped to provoke. Albany's palace is rapidly descending into uproar. Despite all the signs, however, the autocratic Lear refuses to accept that his position has changed significantly.

The truthful Fool (lines 68–183)

Throughout this scene, Lear repeatedly asks for his Fool. This colourful character is a traditional court jester and entertainer, but he also alerts the king to the truth. The Fool is unhappy because of Cordelia's banishment and will not let Lear forget about the injustice of his rash behaviour. He uses sarcasm, simple rhymes, and songs to point out the king's faults. This adds further pathos to Lear's tragic story. In conversation with the Fool, Lear accidentally echoes Cordelia's words with his comment that 'Nothing can be made out of nothing'.

The Fool believes that the world has gone mad because Lear has given away all his other titles except that of fool, 'that thou wast born with'. He recounts the story of the stupid man who bore his ass on his back to be kind, and he thinks Lear is equally foolish in giving away his kingdom: 'Thou hadst little wit in thy bald crown when thou gavest thy golden one away'. He is miserable that Lear now depends completely on Goneril and Regan: 'thou madest thy daughters thy mothers'. The Fool is in a privileged position, permitted to make critical comments which would not be accepted from anyone else at court.

An angry daughter and a confused father (lines 184–220)

The conflict between Lear and Goneril is caused by her complaints about his 'all-licensed fool'. She also launches into a rant against her father over the behaviour of his followers who 'hourly carp and quarrel'. Lear is so shocked that he pretends that Goneril must not really be his daughter: 'Your name, fair gentlewoman?' His own sense of self is clearly disappearing. Finally, he asks, 'Who is that can tell me who I am?' The Fool answers that he is a pale reflection of his former self, 'Lear's shadow'. This simple metaphor provides an insightful glimpse into the king's mental breakdown.

Rows and regrets (lines 221–282)

When Goneril abruptly demands that Lear should dismiss half his followers, her father is forced to accept that he is no longer in control, and he decides to go to Regan. The significance of his earlier rashness begins to dawn on him: 'Woe, that too late repents'. Albany attempts to calm him, but he will not be restrained and accuses Goneril of lying.

He is beginning to realise that he over-reacted to Cordelia's 'small fault' and that he has left himself exposed to danger, 'wrenched my frame of nature/ From the fixed place'. This marks the first small step on his road to self-enlightenment. As the conflict between father and daughter escalates, Lear issues a terrible curse on Goneril: 'Dry up in her the organs of increase'. If she is to ever give birth, he hopes that she will have a 'child of spleen'.

At this stage, Lear appears to see himself as the centre of a universe where the only gauge of goodness or wickedness is loyalty to himself. However, Goneril sneeringly dismisses this outburst as just another sign of her father's 'dotage'.

Sorrow and anger (lines 283–309)

Lear explains to Albany that fifty of his followers are due to be dismissed. He is ashamed that he has been moved to tears by Goneril's heartless behaviour. It seems clear that Albany is naturally concerned for the king's welfare, but he lacks the strength of character to challenge his wife. Meanwhile, Lear is caught between sorrow and bitter anger ('hot tears'). He plans to 'resume' his rightful position by moving to Regan's palace – hoping she will be 'kind and comfortable' – still not accepting that he has lost his former status as king.

Fears (lines 310–336)

Goneril is worried that Lear has too strong a power base with 'his hundred knights'. She is also uneasy in case Regan might indulge their father when she has dismissed him. Albany tries to get her to realise that she may be fearing the worst unnecessarily, but Goneril ignores him and sends her trusted servant Oswald to make sure her sister understands what is to be done. Like Edmund, she is assuming control of her family.

As well as being the more assertive sister, Goneril is the stronger partner in her marriage. She does not hesitate to remind Albany that she disapproves of his 'milky gentleness'. Shakespeare has reversed the traditional roles of male and female. Goneril is much more aggressive than Albany. She openly scorns her husband's 'harmful mildness' and bluntly dismisses his advice to be reasonable and cautious, 'Striving to better, oft we mar what's well'.

your insolent retinue
Do hourly carp and quarrel

Goneril
Act 1 Scene 4, l.185–6

Key Quotes

Quote	Comment
Let me not stay a jot for dinner. Go get it ready (Lear) l.8	A haughty Lear demands refreshments at once in his host's household. He is behaving as if he still had all his royal power and expects to be obeyed immediately.
My lady's father (Oswald to Lear) l.71	Oswald has been instructed by Goneril to treat the old king with disrespect and to antagonise him. The servant refers to Lear in relation to Goneril rather than in his own right – a calculated snub.
All thy other titles thou hast given away; that thou wast born with (Fool to Lear) l.135–6	The Fool tries to help Lear to see the disastrous error he has made by giving away all his power. His role is to remind the king of his foolishness in relinquishing his destiny to rule Britain.
your insolent retinue/ Do hourly carp and quarrel (Goneril to Lear) l.185–6	Goneril is frustrated by the rowdy behaviour of Lear's followers, who constantly complain and fight. She is obviously looking for excuses to reduce Lear's retinue and further diminish what little power he has left.
Does any here know me? (Lear) l.210	The Fool introduces the idea of Lear's identity. The old king is still shocked at the blatant challenge to his usual authority. He is used to being obeyed without question. He has not yet understood the full significance of surrendering power.
Dry up in her the organs of increase (Lear's prayer to Nature) l.265	Lear curses his eldest daughter, invoking the powers of nature to sterilise her. Some critics have found his loathing for Goneril shocking and unnatural. He is still behaving like a tyrant as he did towards the disobedient Cordelia.
I have another daughter,/ Who, I am sure, is kind and comfortable (Lear to Fool) l.292–3	The audience is aware that Goneril and Regan are in agreement that Lear needs to be restricted. He is still unaware of this and foolishly believes that he will be treated differently if he goes to Regan's household.
This milky gentleness (Goneril to Albany) l.329	Goneril is openly critical of her mild-mannered husband, Albany. She already appears to see him as weak and tells him that he is often condemned for his placid approach to life.

Act 1
Scene 5

INTRODUCTION

- Lear instructs Kent to go to Regan's palace to announce the king's imminent arrival.
- The Fool continues to remind Lear about how he treated Cordelia.
- Lear is unsure about Regan's love and is increasingly fearful of insanity.

Courtyard in front of Albany's palace

Enter Lear, Kent and Fool

Lear

Go you before to Gloucester with these letters. Acquaint my daughter no further with anything you know than comes from her demand out of the letter. If your diligence be not speedy, I shall be there afore you.

Kent

I will not sleep, my lord, till I have delivered your letter.

Exit

Fool

If a man's brains were in his heels, were it not in danger of kibes?

7 kibes: *chilblains*

Lear

Ay, boy.

Fool

Then, I prithee, be merry; thy wit shall not go slip-shod.

9 thy wit shall not go slip-shod: *your brain doesn't need slippers (you don't have a brain)*

Lear

Ha, ha, ha!

Fool

Shalt see thy other daughter will use thee kindly, for though she's as like this as a crab's like an apple, yet I can tell what I can tell.

11 kindly: *according to her nature*

12 crab: *sour apple*

Lear

Why, what canst thou tell, my boy?

Fool

She will taste as like this as a crab does to a crab. Thou canst tell why one's nose stands in the middle on's face?

Lear

No.

Fool

Why, to keep one's eyes of either side's nose, that what a man cannot smell out, he may spy into.

Lear

I did her wrong –

Fool

Canst tell how an oyster makes his shell?

Lear

No.

Fool

Nor I neither; but I can tell why a snail has a house.

Lear

Why?

Fool

Why, to put his head in, not to give it away to his daughters, and leave his horns without a case.

Lear

I will forget my nature. So kind a father! Be my horses ready?

Fool

Thy asses are gone about 'em. The reason why the seven stars are no more than seven is a pretty reason.

Lear

Because they are not eight?

Fool

Yes, indeed, thou wouldst make a good fool.

Lear

To take it again perforce! Monster ingratitude!

Fool

If thou wert my fool, nuncle, I'ld have thee beaten for being old before thy time.

Lear

How's that?

Fool

Thou shouldst not have been old till thou hadst been wise.

Lear

O, let me not be mad, not mad, sweet heaven
Keep me in temper: I would not be mad!

Enter Gentleman

How now! are the horses ready?

Gentleman

Ready, my lord.

Lear

Come, boy.

Fool

She that's a maid now, and laughs at my departure,
Shall not be a maid long, unless things be cut shorter.

Exeunt

26 case: *protective covering*

29 asses: *fools of servants*

33 perforce: *by force*

39 in temper: *of sound mind*

43 maid: *virgin*

Analysis

Lear makes plans (lines 1–5)

Lear is worried about his future and not at all confident about Regan's true feelings for him. He sends Kent to deliver a letter to her, announcing his arrival, but asks him not to tell her anything about the earlier row with Goneril: 'Acquaint my daughter no further with anything'. Presumably Lear wants to give Regan his own version of Goneril's cruel behaviour. As always, Kent (now disguised as Caius) shows his unconditional loyalty to the king.

Sharp comments (lines 6–26)

The Fool continues to make sarcastic comments about Lear's poor judgement. He tells him that the two older sisters are almost identical 'as a crab does to a crab'. Lear is unlikely to be treated any better at Regan's palace than he was at Goneril's. The Fool also reminds Lear of the importance of having a secure home, remarking that even the lowly snail has to have one 'to put his head in, not to give it away to his daughters'.

Once again, he is pointing out Lear's stupidity: 'thou wouldst make a good fool'. The distracted king is lost in his own thoughts, however, and slowly coming to some understanding of what he has done to Cordelia: 'I did her wrong'. For a moment, he even wonders if he can regain his throne by violent means.

Lear's fears (lines 27–44)

The elderly king also obsesses over Goneril's thanklessness, 'Monster ingratitude'. Lear has a terrifying fear of insanity: 'O, let me not be mad, not mad, sweet heaven'. Audiences are likely to be shocked and dismayed because they know he is heading from one unhappy state of affairs with Goneril into a similar situation with Regan. We can identify with his predicament and sympathise with his fear.

She will taste as like this as a crab does to a crab

The Fool
Act 1 Scene 5, l.15

Key Quotes

She will taste as like this as a crab does to a crab (Fool to Lear) l.15	The Fool continues to advise Lear, now telling him that his daughters Goneril and Regan are alike, just as one sour apple is to another.
I did her wrong (Lear to himself) l.20	Lear is finally beginning to regret his mistreatment of Cordelia when he banished her for refusing to flatter him in public.
I can tell why a snail has a house (Fool to Lear) l.23	The Fool is trying to get Lear to realise the vulnerable position he has put himself in, relying on the hospitality of his daughters rather than having his own independence.
Thou shouldst not have been old till thou hadst been wise (Fool to Lear) l.37	In another poignant reminder, the Fool tells Lear that he should have gained wisdom through his long life, rather than ending up old and foolish.
O, let me not be mad, not mad, sweet heaven/ Keep me in temper (Lear to himself) l.38–9	Lear now fears for his own sanity due to the strain of recent events. His volatile behaviour could push him into the abyss of madness. The repetition of 'mad' and the frantic tone reflect his distress.

Key Points | Act 1

Scene 1

- King Lear has abdicated his power and plans to divide his kingdom between his three daughters, Goneril, Regan and Cordelia.
- His youngest daughter, Cordelia, refuses to take part in Lear's 'love test'.
- Cordelia is disinherited by her angry father.
- Kent is banished for defending Cordelia.
- The hypocritical daughters, Goneril and Regan (with their husbands, Albany and Cornwall), become the new rulers of Britain.

Scene 2

- The sub-plot is introduced, focusing on the Earl of Gloucester and his two sons – Edgar (his legitimate heir) and Edmund (a son born outside marriage).
- Edmund plans to dispossess Edgar and seize his inheritance.
- He tricks Gloucester into believing that Edgar wants to murder him.
- Edmund easily deceives his older brother into believing that he has upset Gloucester and must go into hiding.

Scene 3

- Lear is a guest in Goneril's household, but there is immediate conflict between them.
- Goneril becomes furious at Lear and his followers' disorderly behaviour.
- She commands her servant, Oswald, to be disrespectful to Lear in order to provoke him.
- Goneril sends a message to Regan to encourage her to behave in a similar fashion.

Scene 4

- The ever-loyal Kent, now disguised, offers his services to Lear and is employed as a servant.
- Oswald is rude to the king. He is struck by Lear and tripped up by Kent.
- The Fool continues to remind Lear of his error in leaving himself dependent on the good will of his daughters.
- Goneril is determined to take Lear's remaining power base away by reducing the number of his followers.
- Lear curses Goneril with sterility and departs for Regan's palace.

Scene 5

- Kent delivers a letter to Regan, informing her of Lear's impending arrival while the Fool tries to warn his master that both daughters share the same attitude towards him.
- Lear is slowly growing in self-awareness, but fears that he may lose his sanity.

Act 2
Scene 1

INTRODUCTION

- Edmund learns of possible conflict between Albany and Cornwall.
- He tricks his brother Edgar into fleeing from Gloucester's castle.
- Gloucester condemns Edgar to death and makes Edmund his heir.
- Cornwall and Regan welcome Edmund into their service.

The Great Hall of Gloucester's castle, at night

Enter Edmund and Curan, separately

Edmund

Save thee, Curan.

Curan

And you, sir. I have been with your father, and given him notice that the Duke of Cornwall and Regan, his Duchess, will be here with him this night.

Edmund

How comes that?

Curan

Nay, I know not. You have heard of the news abroad – I mean the whispered ones, for they are yet but ear-kissing arguments?

Edmund

Not I. pray you, what are they?

Curan

Have you heard of no likely wars toward, 'twixt the Dukes of Cornwall and Albany?

Edmund

Not a word.

Curan

You may do, then, in time. Fare you well, sir.

Exit

Edmund

The duke be here to-night! The better, best.
This weaves itself perforce into my business.
My father hath set guard to take my brother,
And I have one thing, of a queasy question
Which I must act. Briefness and fortune, work!
Brother, a word; descend: brother, I say!

Enter Edgar

My father watches: O sir, fly this place.
Intelligence is given where you are hid;
You have now the good advantage of the night.
Have you not spoken 'gainst the Duke of Cornwall?
He's coming hither, now, in the night, in the haste,
And Regan with him. Have you nothing said

1 Save thee: *God save you*

15 perforce: *inevitably*

17 queasy question: *difficult nature*

Upon his party 'gainst the Duke of Albany?
Advise yourself.

Edgar

I am sure on 't, not a word.

Edmund

I hear my father coming. Pardon me,
In cunning I must draw my sword upon you.
Draw, seem to defend yourself. Now quit you well.
Shouting
Yield! Come before my father! Light, ho, here!
Aside
Fly, brother – Torches, torches!
So, farewell.
Exit Edgar
Some blood drawn on me would beget opinion –
Wounds his arm
Of my more fierce endeavour. I have seen drunkards
Do more than this in sport. Father, father!
Stop, stop! No help?
Enter Gloucester, and Servants with torches

Gloucester

Now, Edmund, where's the villain?

Edmund

Here stood he in the dark, his sharp sword out,
Mumbling of wicked charms, conjuring the moon
To stand auspicious mistress.

Gloucester

But where is he?

Edmund

Look, sir, I bleed.

Gloucester

Where is the villain, Edmund?

Edmund

Fled this way, sir. When by no means he could –

Gloucester

Pursue him, ho! Go after.
Exeunt some servants
By no means what?

Edmund

Persuade me to the murder of your lordship,
But that I told him, the revenging gods

27 Advise yourself: *Think carefully*

30 quit you well: *perform well*

34–5 beget...endeavour: *suggest that I have been involved in a fierce struggle*

40 conjuring the moon: *calling on the moon goddess*

41 auspicious mistress: *guiding light*

47 parricides: *killers of fathers*
bend: *aim*
48 manifold: *numerous*
49 in fine: *finally*
50 loathly opposite: *violently opposed*
51 in fell motion: *with a sudden lunge*
52 prepared sword: *unsheathed weapon*
53 unprovided; *unarmed*
lanced: *wounded*
55 Bold in the quarrel's right: *confident in the justice of my cause*
56 gasted: *frightened*
59 dispatch: *put to death*
60 arch: *lord*
66 pight: *firm, determined*
68 unpossessing: *incapable of inheriting*
71 faithed: *believed*
Tucket: *trumpet call*

'Gainst parricides did all their thunders bend,
Spoke, with how manifold and strong a bond
The child was bound to the father; sir, in fine,
Seeing how loathly opposite I stood
To his unnatural purpose, in fell motion,
With his prepared sword, he charges home
My unprovided body, lanced mine arm;
But when he saw my best alarumed spirits,
Bold in the quarrel's right, roused to the encounter,
Or whether gasted by the noise I made,
Full suddenly he fled.

Gloucester

Let him fly far,
Not in this land shall he remain uncaught;
And found, dispatch. The noble duke my master,
My worthy arch and patron, comes to-night.
By his authority I will proclaim it,
That he which finds him shall deserve our thanks,
Bringing the murderous coward to the stake;
He that conceals him, death.

Edmund

When I dissuaded him from his intent,
And found him pight to do it, with curst speech
I threatened to discover him. He replied,
'Thou unpossessing bastard! dost thou think,
If I would stand against thee, would the reposal
Of any trust, virtue, or worth in thee
Make thy words faithed? No; what I should deny
(As this I would, ay, though thou didst produce
My very character) I'd turn it all
To thy suggestion, plot, and damned practise;
And thou must make a dullard of the world,
If they not thought the profits of my death
Were very pregnant and potential spurs
To make thee seek it.'

Gloucester

O strange and fastened villain
Would he deny his letter? I never got him.

Tucket within

Gloucester

Hark, the duke's trumpets! I know not why he comes.
All ports I'll bar, the villain shall not escape,

The duke must grant me that. Besides, his picture
I will send far and near, that all the kingdom
May have the due note of him – and of my land.
Loyal and natural boy, I'll work the means
To make thee capable.

86 capable: *able to inherit*

Enter Cornwall, Regan, and Attendants

Cornwall

How now, my noble friend! since I came hither,
Which I can call but now, I have heard strange news.

Regan

If it be true, all vengeance comes too short
Which can pursue the offender. How dost, my lord?

Gloucester

O, madam, my old heart is cracked, it's cracked!

Regan

What, did my father's godson seek your life?
He whom my father named? Your Edgar?

Gloucester

O, lady, lady, shame would have it hid!

Regan

Was he not companion with the riotous knights
That tended upon my father?

96 tended: *waited*

Gloucester

I know not, madam: 'tis too bad, too bad.

Edmund

Yes, madam, he was of that consort.

98 consort: *group*

Regan

No marvel, then, though he were ill affected:
'Tis they have put him on the old man's death,
To have the expense and waste of his revenues.
I have this present evening from my sister
Been well informed of them, and with such cautions,
That if they come to sojourn at my house,
I'll not be there.

99 ill affected: *false*

100 put him on: *encouraged him to cause*

104 sojourn: *temporarily stay*

Cornwall

Nor I, assure thee, Regan.
Edmund, I hear that you have shown your father
A child-like office.

108 bewray his practice: *reveal his mischievous intent*

113 strength: *authority*

120 threading: *travelling with great difficulty through*

121 poise: *importance*

126 attend dispatch: *wait to return*

129 craves the instant use: *needs to be dealt with immediately*

Edmund

'Twas my duty, sir.

Gloucester

He did bewray his practise, and received
This hurt you see, striving to apprehend him.

Cornwall

Is he pursued?

Gloucester

Ay, my good lord.

Cornwall

If he be taken, he shall never more
Be feared of doing harm. Make your own purpose,
How in my strength you please. For you, Edmund,
Whose virtue and obedience doth this instant
So much commend itself, you shall be ours.
Natures of such deep trust we shall much need,
You we first seize on.

Edmund

I shall serve you, sir
Truly however else.

Gloucester

For him I thank your Grace.

Cornwall

You know not why we came to visit you –

Regan

Thus out of season, threading dark-eyed night?
Occasions, noble Gloucester, of some poise,
Wherein we must have use of your advice.
Our father he hath writ, so hath our sister,
Of differences, which I best thought it fit
To answer from our home. The several messengers
From hence attend dispatch. Our good old friend,
Lay comforts to your bosom and bestow
Your needful counsel to our businesses,
Which craves the instant use.

Gloucester

I serve you. Madam
Your Graces are right welcome.

Flourish. Exeunt.

Analysis

Edmund the opportunist (lines 1–27)

Due to Lear's disastrous decision to divide his kingdom, there is growing tension between his two sons-in-law, 'likely wars toward, 'twixt the Dukes of Cornwall and Albany'. Edmund is quick to exploit their rivalries. He is also pleased to receive news of Cornwall's expected arrival and immediately uses it to his own advantage. Edmund tricks Edgar by suggesting that there are rumours about him: 'Have you not spoken 'gainst the Duke of Cornwall?'

Deception (lines 28–44)

Edmund then says that he hears Gloucester coming and pretends to be concerned about Edgar's safety. He is a very convincing liar and advises Edgar to go into hiding for his own good. As always, Edgar suspects nothing and does everything his brother asks. Meanwhile, Gloucester has already condemned the innocent Edgar and asks, 'Where is the villain?' In turn, Edmund plays to his father's superstitious nature by pretending that Edgar has been using 'wicked charms'. An incensed Gloucester immediately sends servants to find Edgar: 'Pursue him, ho!' He is horrified that the natural bonds between parent and child have been broken. Such a vulnerable father – and an honest brother – are no match for the treacherous Edmund.

Edmund prospers (lines 45–86)

Not only does Edmund ruin Edgar's reputation with the slur of attempting to kill Gloucester, he also depicts himself as the loving son who tried to stop his brother from doing wrong: 'I told him, the revenging gods/ 'Gainst parricides did all their thunders bend'. Gloucester accepts Edmund's distorted version of events unquestioningly, while the audience watches in horrified fascination as he calls for Edgar's execution: 'Not in this land shall he remain uncaught;/ And found, dispatch'.

This is exactly like Lear's earlier rejection of Cordelia after being fooled by his hypocritical daughters. Edmund continues to poison his father's mind, so that Gloucester no longer accepts Edgar as his son: 'I never got him'. The old earl also decides to make his 'Loyal and natural boy' Edmund the heir to all his property. Audiences must decide for themselves whether Edmund is a villain or a victim – or both. At any rate, his rise to the top has been rapid.

In this scene, the main plot and sub-plot merge. The evil characters are uniting to suit their common purposes. By contrast, the honourable ones (Cordelia, Kent and Edgar) are in exile.

Edmund's promotion (lines 87–104)

Cornwall and his wife arrive at Gloucester's castle after hearing rumours about Edgar's 'treachery'. Like Edmund, Regan is an opportunist, and she uses everything she can to her own advantage. Gloucester admits that he has been shocked by Edgar's plot against him and that his 'old heart is cracked'.

Regan suggests that Edgar is friendly with Lear's followers: 'Was he not companion with the riotous knights/ That tended upon my father?' She then asks if these same knights might be responsible for turning Edgar against his father. It's clear that, just like Goneril, she does not intend to have Lear's followers as guests in her castle.

Seeking advice (lines 105–130)

Ironically, Cornwall believes that Edmund has behaved as a devoted son should, having 'shown your father/ A child-like office'. He offers to take him into his service: 'you shall be ours'. Is there anything concerning about this new alliance between the two of them?

Regan is strong-willed and domineering. She interrupts Cornwall and speaks of her hazardous journey 'threading dark-eyed night'. This trip was undertaken because they had received two letters: one from Goneril, and another from Lear which spoke of a quarrel ('differences').

The audience can sense the deep unease Regan feels. She seeks advice from Gloucester about the best way to proceed with this delicate matter. Fortunately for her, she is now conveniently away from her own palace and does not have to receive Lear and his knights. Has she already decided how she will act?

Key Quotes

Have you nothing said/ Upon his party 'gainst the Duke of Albany? *(Edmund to Edgar) l.25–6*	Edmund tries to convince his brother that he is in danger from the approaching Duke of Cornwall, so that Edgar will flee and Edmund can then arouse Gloucester's suspicions.
In cunning I must draw my sword upon you *(Edmund to Edgar) l.29*	Edmund tells his brother that he must pretend to fight him because everyone suspects Edgar of plotting against Cornwall.
I told him, the revenging gods/ 'Gainst parricides did all their thunders bend *(Edmund to Gloucester) l.46–7*	The deceitful Edmund pretends to Gloucester that he has been advising Edgar not to kill his father.
I never got him *(Gloucester to Edmund) l.79*	Edmund's plan has worked and he has succeeded in convincing Gloucester of Edgar's guilt. The gullible old man now disowns his honest son.
What, did my father's godson seek your life? *(Regan to Gloucester) l.92*	The opportunistic Regan seizes the moment to blacken Edgar's name by implicating him in Lear's activities.
For you, Edmund,/ Whose virtue and obedience doth this instant/ So much commend itself, you shall be ours *(Cornwall to Edmund) l.113–15*	Edmund has also succeeded in fooling the Duke of Cornwall with his story, and is taken into his service.

Act 2
Scene 2

INTRODUCTION

- The disguised Kent quarrels with Oswald, Goneril's messenger.
- Cornwall punishes Kent by having him placed in the stocks.
- Gloucester's attempts to calm the situation are unsuccessful.
- Kent receives a letter from Cordelia, who is concerned about her father.

Gloucester's castle entrance

Enter Kent and Oswald, separately

Oswald

Good dawning to thee, friend. Art of this house?

Kent

Ay.

Oswald

Where may we set our horses?

Kent

In the mire.

Oswald

Prithee, if thou lovest me, tell me.

Kent

I love thee not.

Oswald

Why, then, I care not for thee.

Kent

If I had thee in Lipsbury pinfold, I would make thee care for me.

Oswald

Why dost thou use me thus? I know thee not.

Kent

Fellow, I know thee.

Oswald

What dost thou know me for?

Kent

A knave, a rascal, an eater of broken meats, a base, proud, shallow, beggarly, three-suited, hundred-pound, filthy, worsted-stocking knave; a lily-livered, action-taking whoreson, glass-gazing, super-serviceable finical rogue; one-trunk-inheriting slave; one that would be a bawd in way of good service, and art nothing but the composition of a knave, beggar, coward, pander, and the son and heir of a mongrel bitch, one whom I will beat into clamorous whining, if thou deniest the least syllable of thy addition.

4 mire: *mud*

8 Lipsbury pinfold: *in my grasp*

13 eater of broken meats: *humble servant*

14 three-suited: *a servant's suit allocation for a year*

15 worsted-stocking: *mock gentleman*
action-taking: *litigious*

16 glass-gazing: *vain*
super-serviceable: *over-anxious*
finical: *affected, fussy*

17 bawd: *procurer, pimp*

19 pander: *go-between in illicit dealings*

21 addition: *titles*

Oswald

Why, what a monstrous fellow art thou, thus to rail on one that is neither known of thee nor knows thee!

Kent

What a brazen-faced varlet art thou, to deny thou knowest me! Is it two days ago since I tripped up thy heels, and beat thee before the king? Draw, you rogue! For, though it be night, yet the moon shines. I'll make a sop o' the moonshine of you,

Drawing his sword

you whoreson cullionly barber-monger, draw.

Oswald

Away! I have nothing to do with thee.

Kent

Draw, you rascal! You come with letters against the King and take Vanity the puppet's part against the royalty of her father. Draw, you rogue, or I'll so carbonado your shanks. Draw, you rascal! Come your ways!

Oswald

Help, ho! murder! help!

Kent

Strike, you slave! Stand, rogue, stand! You neat slave, strike.

Beating him

Oswald

Help, ho! Murder! Murder!

Enter Edmund, with his rapier drawn

Edmund

How now! What's the matter? Part!

Kent

With you, goodman boy, if you please! Come, I'll flesh ye; come on, young master.

Enter Cornwall, Regan, Gloucester and servants

Gloucester

Weapons? Arms? What's the matter here?

24 varlet: *rogue*

29 cullionly barber-monger: *foolish, vain person*

32 Vanity the puppet's part: *a reference to Goneril, who acts like a conceited doll*

33 carbanado your shanks: *slit your legs*

40 goodman boy: *arrogant youth*

Cornwall

Keep peace, upon your lives.
He dies that strikes again. What is the matter?

Regan

The messengers from our sister and the king.

Cornwall

What is your difference? Speak.

Oswald

I am scarce in breath, my lord.

Kent

No marvel, you have so bestirred your valour. You cowardly rascal, nature disclaims in thee: a tailor made thee.

49 disclaims: *denies responsibility*

Cornwall

Thou art a strange fellow – a tailor make a man?

Kent

A tailor, sir, a stone-cutter or painter could not have made him so ill, though he had been but two years at the trade.

Cornwall

Speak yet, how grew your quarrel?

Oswald

This ancient ruffian, sir, whose life I have spared at suit of his gray beard –

54 at suit: *in pity*

Kent

Thou whoreson zed! thou unnecessary letter! My lord, if you will give me leave, I will tread this unbolted villain into mortar, and daub the wall of a jakes with him. Spare my gray beard, you wagtail?

56 whoreson zed: *useless creature*
57 unbolted: *effeminate*
58 daub: *paint*
jakes: *toilet*
59 wagtail: *jerky bird*

Cornwall

Peace, sirrah!
You beastly knave, know you no reverence?

Kent

Yes, sir, but anger hath a privilege.

Cornwall

Why art thou angry?

66 holy cords: *marriage and family bonds*

67 intrinse: *tightly knotted*
smooth: *flatter*

70 Renege: *deny*
halcyon: *kingfisher*

71 vary: *change of mood*

73 epileptic visage: *convulsed face*

75 Sarum: *Salisbury*

76 Camelot: *legendary home of King Arthur*

89 constrains: *distorts*

Kent

That such a slave as this should wear a sword,
Who wears no honesty. Such smiling rogues as these,
Like rats, oft bite the holy cords a-twain
Which are too intrinse t'unloose; smooth every passion
That in the natures of their lords rebel,
Bring oil to fire, snow to their colder moods,
Renege, affirm, and turn their halcyon beaks
With every gale and vary of their masters,
Knowing nought, like dogs, but following.
A plague upon your epileptic visage!
Smile you my speeches, as I were a fool?
Goose, if I had you upon Sarum plain,
I'd drive ye cackling home to Camelot.

Cornwall

Why, art thou mad, old fellow?

Gloucester

How fell you out? Say that.

Kent

No contraries hold more antipathy
Than I and such a knave.

Cornwall

Why dost thou call him a knave? What is his fault?

Kent

His countenance likes me not.

Cornwall

No more, perchance, does mine, nor his, nor hers.

Kent

Sir, 'tis my occupation to be plain.
I have seen better faces in my time
Than stands on any shoulder that I see
Before me at this instant.

Cornwall

This is some fellow,
Who, having been praised for bluntness, doth affect
A saucy roughness, and constrains the garb
Quite from his nature. He cannot flatter, he,
An honest mind and plain, he must speak truth!

An they will take it, so; if not, he's plain.
These kind of knaves I know, which in this plainness
Harbour more craft and more corrupter ends
Than twenty silly-ducking observants
That stretch their duties nicely.

Kent

Sir, in good sooth, in sincere verity,
Under the allowance of your great aspect,
Whose influence, like the wreath of radiant fire
On flickering Phoebus' front –

Cornwall

What mean'st by this?

Kent

To go out of my dialect, which you discommend so much. I know, sir, I am no flatterer. He that beguiled you in a plain accent was a plain knave, which for my part I will not be, though I should win your displeasure to entreat me to it.

Cornwall

What was the offence you gave him?

Oswald

I never gave him any.
It pleased the king his master very late
To strike at me, upon his misconstruction,
When he, compact and flattering his displeasure,
Tripped me behind; being down, insulted, railed,
And put upon him such a deal of man
That worthied him, got praises of the king
For him attempting who was self-subdued;
And, in the fleshment of this dread exploit,
Drew on me here again.

Kent

None of these rogues and cowards
But Ajax is their fool.

Cornwall

Fetch forth the stocks!
You stubborn ancient knave, you reverend braggart,
We'll teach you.

Kent

Sir, I am too old to learn.

95 silly-ducking: *cringing attendants*

96 stretch their duties nicely: *perform their work with too much bowing and scraping*

97 verity: *truth*

100 Phoebus' front: *sun-god's forehead*

101 dialect: *way of speaking*

107 very late: *recently*

108 misconstruction: *misinterpretation*

109 compact: *allied*

111 deal of man: *show of bravery*

113 self-subdued: *did not fight back*

114 fleshment: *elation*

116 stocks: *wooden frame used to incarcerate criminals*

121 small respect: *discourtesy*

129 self-same colour: *exactly the same type*

Call not your stocks for me. I serve the king,
On whose employment I was sent to you.
You shall do small respect, show too bold malice
Against the grace and person of my master,
Stocking his messenger.

Cornwall

Fetch forth the stocks!
As I have life and honour,
There shall he sit till noon.

Regan

Till noon? Till night, my lord, and all night too.

Kent

Why, madam, if I were your father's dog,
You should not use me so.

Regan

Sir, being his knave, I will.

Cornwall

This is a fellow of the self-same colour
Our sister speaks of. Come, bring away the stocks.

Stocks brought out

Gloucester

Let me beseech your grace not to do so.
His fault is much, and the good king his master
Will check him for't. Your purposed low correction
Is such as basest and contemn'd wretches
For pilferings and most common trespasses
Are punished with. The king must take it ill,
That he, so slightly valued in his messenger,
Should have him thus restrained.

Cornwall

I'll answer that.

Regan

My sister may receive it much more worse,
To have her gentleman abused, assaulted,
For following her affairs. Put in his legs.

Kent is put in the stocks

Come, my good lord, away.

Exeunt all but Gloucester and Kent

Gloucester

I am sorry for thee, friend; 'tis the duke's pleasure,
Whose disposition, all the world well knows,
Will not be rubbed nor stopped. I'll entreat for thee.

Kent

Pray, do not, sir. I have watched and travelled hard.
Some time I shall sleep out, the rest I'll whistle.
A good man's fortune may grow out at heels.
Give you good morrow!

Gloucester

The duke's to blame in this; 'twill be ill taken.

Exit

Kent

Good king, that must approve the common saw,
Thou out of heaven's benediction comest
To the warm sun!
Approach, thou beacon to this under globe,
That by thy comfortable beams I may
Peruse this letter! Nothing almost sees miracles
But misery. I know 'tis from Cordelia,
Who hath most fortunately been informed
Of my obscured course, and shall find time
From this enormous state, seeking to give
Losses their remedies. All weary and o'er-watch'd
Take vantage, heavy eyes, not to behold
This shameful lodging.
Fortune, good night. Smile once more, turn thy wheel.

Sleeps

145 rubbed: *stopped*
entreat for thee: *ask for you*

151 saw: *proverb*

154 under globe: *earth*

160 enormous state: *outrageous situation*

161 o'er-watched: *exhausted*

Analysis

Loyalty and contempt (lines 1–38)

Kent is already furious at Oswald's disrespect towards the old king and immediately picks a fight, calling him the 'son and heir of a mongrel bitch'. However, Oswald fails to recognise the disguised Kent, saying 'I have nothing to do with thee'. But loyalty to Lear is Kent's only concern and he continues to abuse Goneril's messenger. He is also angered that Oswald is delivering 'letters against the King' and carrying out the wishes of Goneril 'against the royalty of her father'.

Unruly events (lines 39–99)

The brawl between Kent and Oswald creates uproar in Gloucester's castle. Cornwall demands to know the cause of the quarrel, but Kent continues his scathing insults. Oswald's true character is evident when he blatantly lies that he spared Kent's life because he is elderly. Cornwall tries unsuccessfully to calm Kent and restore order: 'know you no reverence?' But there seems to be no stopping Kent's fierce tirade of abuse towards Oswald, whom he accuses of being a rogue who 'wears no honesty'.

It's obvious that Kent takes pride in his own outspokenness: 'Sir, 'tis my occupation to be plain'. He dares to insult everyone around him: 'I have seen better faces in my time'. Cornwall is astonished at such insolence and instinctively suspects Kent's bluntness, regarding it as an act, 'in this plainness/ Harbour more craft and more corrupter ends'.

Consequences (lines 100–130)

The argument between Kent and Cornwall says much about both their characters. Cornwall seems to believe that nobody ever tells the truth. Kent mocks Oswald's elaborate use of language and makes the point that he himself is 'no flatterer'. However, Cornwall has had enough of Kent's rudeness and calls for the stocks to punish Lear's messenger. In response, Kent insists that he cannot change his behaviour: 'I am too old to learn' and reminds Regan: 'I serve the king'.

Cornwall treats Kent like a common criminal by placing him in the stocks. This public humiliation of the king's personal messenger is also a calculated insult to Lear himself.

Shakespeare reveals more of Regan's vindictive nature when she doubles the length of the punishment. Kent protests that 'if I were your father's dog,/ You should not use me so'. Cornwall promptly asserts his authority and refers to Goneril's letter, in which she complains of the unruly behaviour of Lear's followers, 'of the self-same colour/ Our sister speaks of'. It is clear that political power in Britain has now changed. Kent has been severely punished for his blunt speech, just as Cordelia was when she refused to take part in Lear's 'love test'.

Ineffective intervention (lines 131–150)

Gloucester is horrified at the disrespect being shown to Lear by imprisoning his messenger: 'The king must take it ill'. But his mild objection is dismissed by an arrogant Cornwall: 'I'll answer that'. Like the former king, Gloucester is losing all authority within his own household. The playwright shows a more sympathetic side to Gloucester's character as he promises Kent that he will continue to plead with Cornwall on his behalf.

Kent's soliloquy (lines 151–164)

Left alone, Kent reads a letter from Cordelia, who has learned of his disguise and will undoubtedly act to help her father: 'shall find time/ From this enormous state'. Kent resolves to join forces with her in her plan to restore the country to order. He trusts that everything will eventually improve: 'Smile once more, turn thy wheel'. Shakespeare uses one of the oldest images in Western culture – the goddess Fortune with her wheel which turns constantly – to give the audience some sense of balance about what is about to happen.

Kent's closing comments reflect on Lear's fall from power, but having received a letter from Cordelia, he still hopes for better days to come.

Key Quotes

Quote	Comment
A knave, a rascal, an eater of broken meats *(Kent to Oswald) l.13*	A furious Kent insults Oswald by saying that he only eats scraps. Oswald has been disrespectful to Lear and has brought Regan a letter which is against the king's interests.
Sir, 'tis my occupation to be plain *(Kent to Cornwall) l.84*	Kent has no time for flattery. He prides himself on his honesty and bluntness.
Ajax is their fool *(Kent to Cornwall) l.116*	Unable to control himself, Kent further offends the Duke by comparing Oswald to the self-important Greek commander who was known for his brawn rather than his brains.
I am too old to learn *(Kent to Cornwall) l.118*	Kent is not going to change his behaviour even if he is punished. Is he brave or foolhardy?
The king must take it ill *(Gloucester to Cornwall) l.136*	Gloucester feebly attempts to intervene on Kent's behalf by reminding Cornwall and Regan that Lear will be insulted at this poor treatment of his messenger.
Smile once more, turn thy wheel *(Kent) l.164*	In his soliloquy, a stoical Kent reflects that life goes on and circumstances change, sometimes from worse to better.

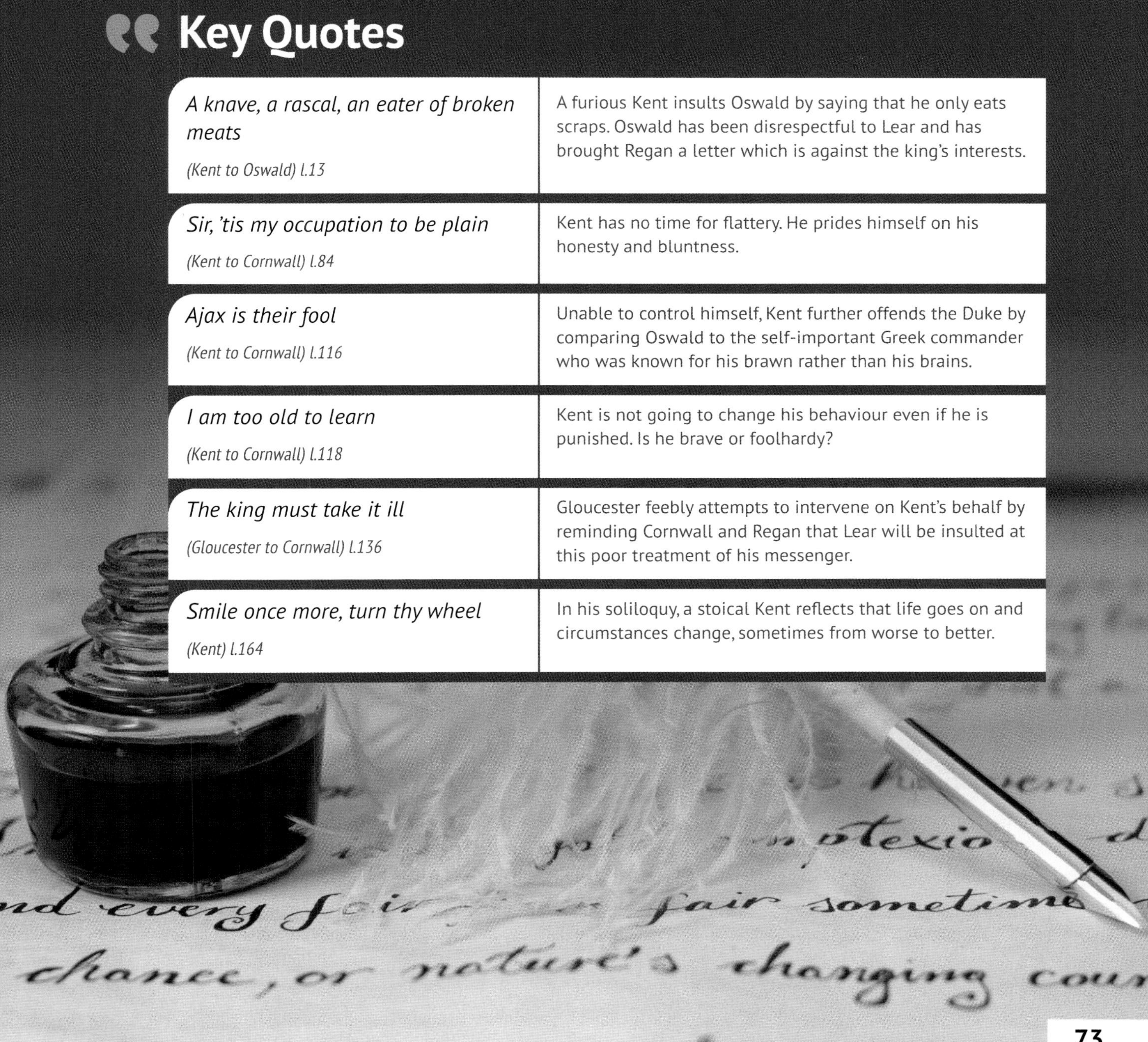

Act 2
Scene 3

INTRODUCTION

- Edgar reveals plans to escape his death sentence.
- He intends to go into hiding and disguise himself as a deranged beggar.

Open countryside near Gloucester's castle

Enter Edgar

Edgar

I heard myself proclaimed,
And by the happy hollow of a tree
Escaped the hunt. No port is free, no place
That guard and most unusual vigilance
Does not attend my taking. Whiles I may escape,
I will preserve myself, and am bethought
To take the basest and most poorest shape
That ever penury, in contempt of man,
Brought near to beast. My face I'll grime with filth,
Blanket my loins, elf all my hair in knots,
And with presented nakedness outface
The winds and persecutions of the sky.
The country gives me proof and precedent
Of Bedlam beggars, who with roaring voices,
Strike in their numbed and mortified bare arms
Pins, wooden pricks, nails, sprigs of rosemary;
And with this horrible object, from low farms,
Poor pelting villages, sheep-cotes, and mills,
Sometime with lunatic bans, sometime with prayers,
Enforce their charity. 'Poor Turlygod! Poor Tom!'
That's something yet. Edgar I nothing am.

Exit

1 proclaimed: *declared an outlaw*

4 most unusual vigilance: *exceptional watchfulness*

8 penury: *poverty*

10 elf: *twist*

14 Bedlam: *mad*

15 mortified: *unresponsive, insensitive*

18 pelting: *insignificant*

19 lunatic bans: *insane curses*

20 Enforce their charity: *beg for money* 'Poor Turlygod! Poor Tom!': *Edgar is practising the whine of a beggar*

Analysis

In disguise (lines 1–21)

Due to Edmund's scheming, Edgar is now fleeing from Gloucester and the court. He has been declared an outlaw and cannot escape: 'No port is free'. To survive, he decides to disguise himself as a mad beggar, 'To take the basest and most poorest shape/ That ever penury, in contempt of man/ Brought near to beast'.

In Shakespeare's time, people in the mental institution Bethlehem in London (Bedlam) were often released with a licence for begging. They roamed around the countryside, sometimes uttering wild curses in their attempts to receive charity. Edgar plans to adopt their wild appearance, soiling his face and knotting his hair. Like Kent, he is now forced to demean himself. This foreshadows Lear's tragic situation.

Throughout the soliloquy, Edgar's frantic tone reflects his desperate circumstances. He imitates the whining voice of the professional beggar: 'Poor Turlygod! Poor Tom!' For the present, his old identity is gone: 'Edgar I nothing am'. There are now two characters in disguise: Kent as an old serving man, and Edgar as a demented vagrant.

Shakespeare develops the theme of appearance and reality by presenting honourable characters who are increasingly at odds with the hypocritical, hostile society that has developed in Britain since Lear's abdication. As Poor Tom, Edgar is an impoverished social outcast – a poignant symbol of this new chaotic world.

Key Quotes

Quote	Comment
I heard myself proclaimed *(Edgar) l.1*	Alone on the heath, Edgar reveals he has heard himself declared an outlaw.
am bethought/ To take the basest and most poorest shape *(Edgar) l.6–7*	Edgar's assumed madness prepares the audience for what will happen to Lear later in the play. Shakespeare is also introducing the theme of 'unaccommodated man' and political responsibility.

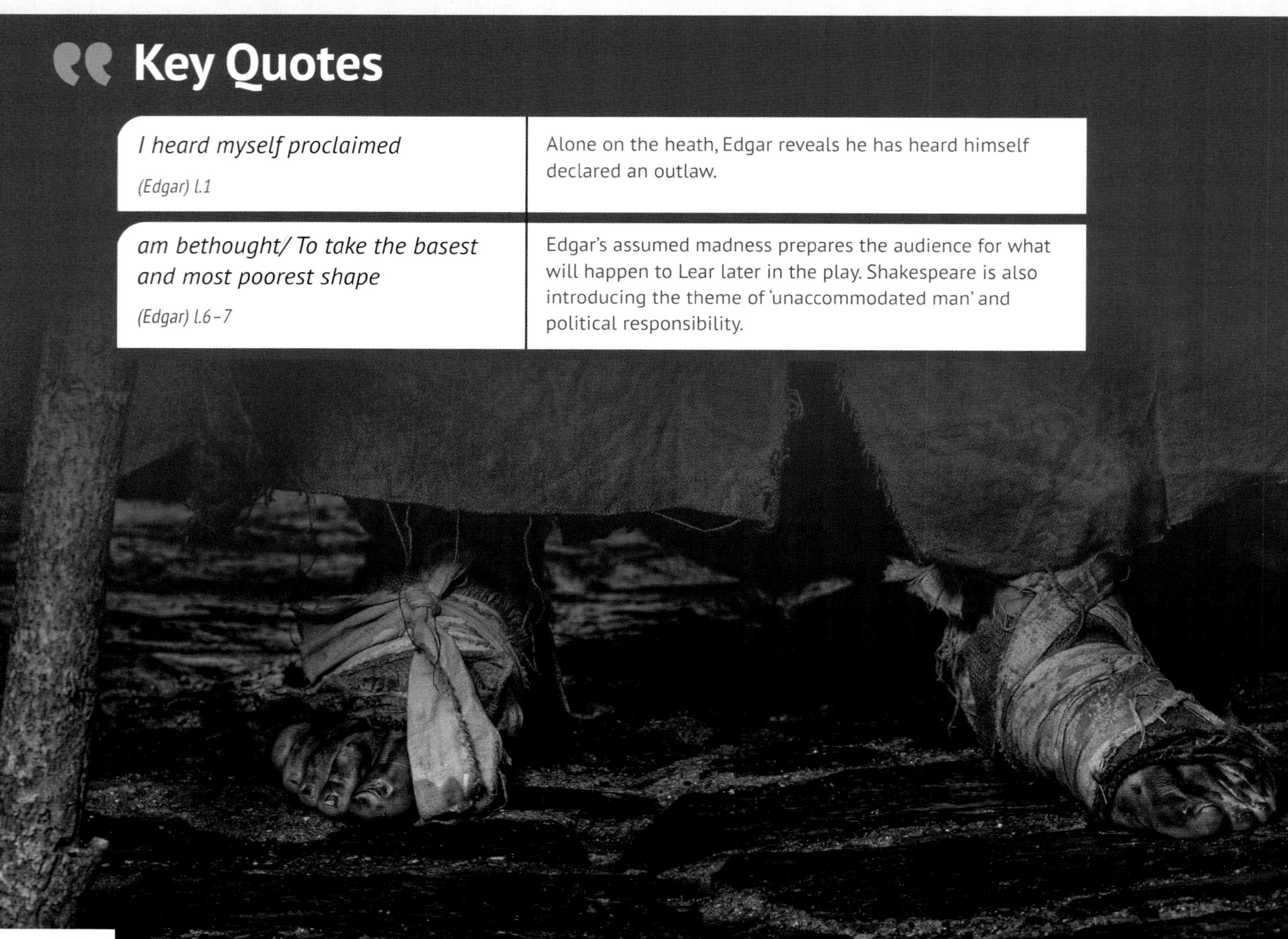

Act 2
Scene 4*

INTRODUCTION

- Lear is shocked by the sight of his messenger imprisoned in the stocks.
- He cannot believe that Regan and Cornwall would disrespect his authority.
- Goneril and Regan insist on reducing the number of their father's knights.
- Enraged and fearing for his sanity, Lear ventures into the stormy night.

*** This key scene requires close, detailed study.**

Before Gloucester's castle

Enter Lear, the Fool and a Gentleman

Lear

'Tis strange that they should so depart from home,
And not send back my messenger.

Gentleman

As I learned,
The night before there was no purpose in them
Of this remove.

Kent

Hail to thee, noble master!

Lear

Ha!
Makest thou this shame thy pastime?

7 Makest thou this shame thy pastime?: *Are you joking?*

Kent

No, my lord.

Fool

Ha, ha! he wears cruel garters. Horses are tied by the heads, dogs and bears by the neck, monkeys by the loins, and men by the legs: when a man's over-lusty at legs, then he wears wooden nether-stocks.

10 over-lusty: *too passionate*

11 wooden nether-stocks: *restraints*

Lear

What's he that hath so much thy place mistook
To set thee here?

12 thy place mistook: *disrespectful of your position as my messenger*

Kent

It is both he and she,
Your son and daughter.

Lear

No.

Kent

Yes.

Lear

No, I say.

Kent

I say, yea.

Lear

No, no, they would not.

Kent

Yes, they have.

Lear

By Jupiter, I swear, no.

Kent

By Juno, I swear, ay.

Lear

They durst not do it:
They could not, would not do it. 'Tis worse than murder,
To do upon respect such violent outrage.
Resolve me with all modest haste which way
Thou mightst deserve or they impose this usage,
Coming from us.

Kent

My lord, when at their home
I did commend your highness' letters to them,
Ere I was risen from the place that showed
My duty kneeling, came there a reeking post,
Stewed in his haste, half breathless, panting forth
From Goneril his mistress salutations;
Delivered letters spite of intermission,
Which presently they read. On those contents,
They summoned up their meiny, straight took horse;
Commanded me to follow, and attend
The leisure of their answer, gave me cold looks;
And meeting here the other messenger,
Whose welcome, I perceived, had poisoned mine –
Being the very fellow that of late
Displayed so saucily against your highness –
Having more man than wit about me, drew.
He raised the house with loud and coward cries.
Your son and daughter found this trespass worth
The shame which here it suffers.

Fool

Winter's not gone yet, if the wild-geese fly that way.
Fathers that wear rags
Do make their children blind,

21 Jupiter: *ruler of the gods in Roman mythology*

22 Juno: *wife of Jupiter*

25 Resolve me: *give me a reason why*

28 commend: *deliver*

30 reeking post: *sweating messenger*

33 spite of intermission: *despite interrupting my business*

35 meiny: *retinue, followers*

41 Displayed: *acted*

42 more man than wit: *more courage than common sense*

46 Winter's not gone yet: *there's more trouble in store*

48 blind: *indifferent*

49 bear bags: *have money*

56 Hysterica passio: *mounting madness*

But fathers that bear bags
Shall see their children kind.
Fortune, that arrant whore,
Ne'er turns the key to the poor.

But, for all this, thou shalt have as many dolours for thy daughters as thou canst tell in a year.

Lear

O, how this mother swells up toward my heart!
Hysterica passio! Down, thou climbing sorrow,
Thy element's below. Where is this daughter?

Kent

With the earl, sir, here within.

Lear

Follow me not. Stay here.

Exit

Gentleman

Made you no more offence but what you speak of?

Kent

None. How chance the king come with so small a number?

Fool

And thou hadst been set in the stocks for that question, thou'dst well deserved it.

Kent

Why, fool?

Fool

We'll set thee to school to an ant, to teach thee there's no labouring in the winter. All that follow their noses are led by their eyes but blind men, and there's not a nose among twenty but can smell him that's stinking. Let go thy hold when a great wheel runs down a hill, lest it break thy neck with following it. But the great one that goes upward, let him draw thee after. When a wise man gives thee better counsel, give me mine again; I would have none but knaves follow it, since a Fool gives it.

That sir which serves and seeks for gain,
And follows but for form,
Will pack when it begins to rain,
And leave thee in the storm,

But I will tarry; the fool will stay,
And let the wise man fly;
The knave turns fool that runs away;
The fool no knave, perdy.

81 perdy: *by God*

Kent

Where learned you this, fool?

Fool

Not in the stocks, fool.

Re-enter Lear with Gloucester

Lear

Deny to speak with me? They are sick, they are weary,
They have travelled all the night? Mere fetches;
The images of revolt and flying off.
Fetch me a better answer.

85 fetches: *ruses, tricks*

86 revolt and flying off: *rebellion and desertion*

Gloucester

My dear lord,
You know the fiery quality of the duke,
How unremovable and fixed he is
In his own course.

89 unremovable: *determined*

Lear

Vengeance! plague! death! confusion!
Fiery? What quality? Why, Gloucester, Gloucester,
I'd speak with the Duke of Cornwall and his wife.

Gloucester

Well, my good lord, I have informed them so.

Lear

Informed them! Dost thou understand me, man?

Gloucester

Ay, my good lord.

Lear

The king would speak with Cornwall, the dear father
Would with his daughter speak! Commands – tends – service!
Are they informed of this? My breath and blood!
Fiery? The fiery duke? Tell the hot duke that –
No, but not yet. Maybe he is not well.
Infirmity doth still neglect all office
Whereto our health is bound. We are not ourselves

102 Infirmity: *sickness*
office: *duty*

When nature, being oppressed, commands the mind
To suffer with the body. I'll forbear;
And am fallen out with my more headier will,
To take the indisposed and sickly fit
For the sound man. Death on my state! Wherefore

105 forbear: *have some patience*
106 headier will: *headstrong impulse*
107 sickly fit: *unwell person*

Looking on Kent

Should he sit here? This act persuades me
That this remotion of the duke and her
Is practice only. Give me my servant forth.
Go tell the duke and his wife I'd speak with them,
Now, presently. Bid them come forth and hear me,
Or at their chamber-door I'll beat the drum
Till it cry sleep to death.

110 remotion: *distance, aloofness*
111 practice: *performance, trickery*

Gloucester

I would have all well betwixt you.

Exit

Lear

Oh me, my heart! My rising heart! But down.

Fool

Cry to it, nuncle, as the cockney did to the eels when she put 'em i' the paste alive; she knapped 'em o' the coxcombs with a stick, and cried 'Down, wantons, down!' 'Twas her brother that, in pure kindness to his horse, buttered his hay.

119 paste: *pastry*
knapped: *rapped*
120 wantons: *badly behaved creatures*

Enter Cornwall, Regan, Gloucester and Servants

Lear

Good morrow to you both.

Cornwall

Hail to your grace!

Kent is set at liberty

Regan

I am glad to see your highness.

Lear

Regan, I think you are. I know what reason
I have to think so. If thou shouldst not be glad,
I would divorce me from thy mother's tomb,
Sepulchring an adultress. *[To Kent]* O, are you free?
Some other time for that. Beloved Regan,

128 Sepulchring; *containing within*

Thy sister's naught. O Regan, she hath tied
Sharp-toothed unkindness, like a vulture, here –
Points to his heart
I can scarce speak to thee – thou'lt not believe
With how depraved a quality – O Regan!

Regan

I pray you, sir, take patience. I have hope
You less know how to value her desert
Than she to scant her duty.

Lear

Say, how is that?

Regan

I cannot think my sister in the least
Would fail her obligation. If, sir, perchance
She have restrained the riots of your followers,
'Tis on such ground, and to such wholesome end,
As clears her from all blame.

Lear

My curses on her!

Regan

O sir, you are old.
Nature in you stands on the very verge
Of her confine. You should be ruled and led
By some discretion, that discerns your state
Better than you yourself. Therefore I pray you,
That to our sister you do make return;
Say you have wronged her, sir.

Lear

Ask her forgiveness?
Do you but mark how this becomes the house?
'Dear daughter, I confess that I am old;
Kneeling
Age is unnecessary. On my knees I beg
That you'll vouchsafe me raiment, bed, and food.'

Regan

Good sir, no more. These are unsightly tricks.
Return you to my sister.

130 naught: *evil*

136 scant: *minimise*

144 confine: *limit*

149 house: *the royal household of which I am head*

151 Age is unnecessary: *old age has few needs*

152 vouchsafe: *grant me*
raiment: *clothing*

153 unsightly: *ugly*

155 abated me of: *dispossessed me of*

159 top: *head*
young bones: *unborn child*

160 taking: *malignant*

163 fen-sucked: *marsh-soaked*

167 tender-hefted nature: *gentler personality*

171 scant my sizes: *reduce my allowances*

172 oppose the bolt: *shut the door*

174 offices: *responsibilities*

175 Effects: *accomplishments*

Lear

Rising

Never, Regan.
She hath abated me of half my train,
Looked black upon me, struck me with her tongue,
Most serpent-like, upon the very heart.
All the stored vengeances of heaven fall
On her ingrateful top! Strike her young bones,
You taking airs, with lameness!

Cornwall

Fie, sir, fie!

Lear

You nimble lightnings, dart your blinding flames
Into her scornful eyes! Infect her beauty,
You fen-sucked fogs, drawn by the powerful sun
To fall and blister.

Regan

O the blest gods!
So will you wish on me when the rash mood is on.

Lear

No, Regan, thou shalt never have my curse:
Thy tender-hefted nature shall not give
Thee o'er to harshness. Her eyes are fierce, but thine
Do comfort and not burn. 'Tis not in thee
To grudge my pleasures, to cut off my train,
To bandy hasty words, to scant my sizes,
And in conclusion to oppose the bolt
Against my coming in. Thou better know'st
The offices of nature, bond of childhood,
Effects of courtesy, dues of gratitude;
Thy half o' the kingdom hast thou not forgot,
Wherein I thee endowed.

Regan

Good sir, to the purpose.

Lear

Who put my man i' the stocks?

Tucket within

Cornwall

What trumpet's that?

Regan

I know't, my sister's. This approves her letter,
That she would soon be here.

Enter Oswald

Is your lady come?

Lear

This is a slave, whose easy-borrowed pride
Dwells in the fickle grace of her he follows.
Out, varlet, from my sight!

Cornwall

What means your grace?

Lear

Who stocked my servant? Regan, I have good hope
Thou didst not know on't. Who comes here? O heavens,

Enter Goneril

If you do love old men, if your sweet sway
Allow obedience, if yourselves are old,
Make it your cause! Send down, and take my part!

To Goneril

Art not ashamed to look upon this beard?
O Regan, wilt thou take her by the hand?

Goneril

Why not by the hand, sir? How have I offended?
All's not offence that indiscretion finds
And dotage terms so.

Lear

O sides, you are too tough!
Will you yet hold? How came my man i' the stocks?

Cornwall

I set him there, sir. But his own disorders
Deserved much less advancement.

Lear

You? Did you?

Regan

I pray you, father, being weak, seem so.
If, till the expiration of your month,
You will return and sojourn with my sister,
Dismissing half your train, come then to me.

179 approves: *endorses, confirms*

181 easy-borrowed: *effortlessly put on*

182 fickle grace: *changeable approval*

186 sway: *power*

192 indiscretion: *rashness*

193 dotage: *foolish old age*

198 expiration: *end*

199 sojourn: *stay*

204 abjure: *reject*

205 enmity o' the air: *terrible storm*

207 Necessity's sharp pinch: *the pain of being in need*

208 dowerless: *without property or wealth on her marriage*

212 sumpter: *drudge, pack-horse*

220 embossed carbuncle: *swollen tumour*

221 corrupted: *diseased*

223 thunder-bearer: *Jupiter, armed with thunderbolts*

I am now from home, and out of that provision
Which shall be needful for your entertainment.

Lear

Return to her, and fifty men dismissed?
No, rather I abjure all roofs, and choose
To wage against the enmity o' the air;
To be a comrade with the wolf and owl –
Necessity's sharp pinch. Return with her?
Why, the hot-blooded France, that dowerless took
Our youngest born – I could as well be brought
To knee his throne, and, squire-like, pension beg
To keep base life afoot. Return with her?
Persuade me rather to be slave and sumpter
To this detested groom.

Pointing at Oswald

Goneril

At your choice, sir.

Lear

I prithee, daughter, do not make me mad.
I will not trouble thee, my child. Farewell.
We'll no more meet, no more see one another.
But yet thou art my flesh, my blood, my daughter,
Or rather a disease that's in my flesh,
Which I must needs call mine. Thou art a boil,
A plague-sore, an embossed carbuncle,
In my corrupted blood. But I'll not chide thee;
Let shame come when it will, I do not call it:
I do not bid the thunder-bearer shoot,
Nor tell tales of thee to high-judging Jove.
Mend when thou canst, be better at thy leisure:
I can be patient, I can stay with Regan,
I and my hundred knights.

Regan

Not altogether so.
I looked not for you yet, nor am provided
For your fit welcome. Give ear, sir, to my sister,
For those that mingle reason with your passion
Must be content to think you old, and so –
But she knows what she does.

Lear

Is this well spoken?

Regan

I dare avouch it, sir. What, fifty followers?
Is it not well? What should you need of more?
Yea, or so many, sith that both charge and danger
Speak 'gainst so great a number? How, in one house,
Should many people, under two commands,
Hold amity? 'Tis hard, almost impossible.

Goneril

Why might not you, my lord, receive attendance
From those that she calls servants or from mine?

Regan

Why not, my lord? If then they chanced to slack you,
We could control them. If you will come to me
(For now I spy a danger) I entreat you
To bring but five and twenty. To no more
Will I give place or notice.

Lear

I gave you all –

Regan

And in good time you gave it.

Lear

Made you my guardians, my depositaries,
But kept a reservation to be followed
With such a number. What, must I come to you
With five and twenty, Regan? said you so?

Regan

And speak't again, my lord. No more with me.

Lear

Those wicked creatures yet do look well-favoured,
When others are more wicked. Not being the worst
Stands in some rank of praise.
To Goneril
I'll go with thee.
Thy fifty yet doth double five and twenty,
And thou art twice her love.

232 well spoken: *the proper way to address a father*

233 avouch it: *declare it to be true*

235 charge: *expense*

238 amity: *friendly relations*

241 slack: *show disrespect*

247 depositaries: *custodians*

Goneril

Hear me, my lord.
What need you five and twenty, ten, or five,
To follow in a house where twice so many
Have a command to tend you?

Regan

What need one?

Lear

O, reason not the need! Our basest beggars
Are in the poorest thing superfluous.
Allow not nature more than nature needs,
Man's life's as cheap as beast's. Thou art a lady;
If only to go warm were gorgeous,
Why, nature needs not what thou gorgeous wear'st,
Which scarcely keeps thee warm. But, for true need –
You heavens, give me that patience, patience I need.
You see me here, you gods, a poor old man,
As full of grief as age, wretched in both!
If it be you that stir these daughters' hearts
Against their father, fool me not so much
To bear it tamely. Touch me with noble anger,
And let not women's weapons, water drops,
Stain my man's cheeks. No, you unnatural hags,
I will have such revenges on you both,
That all the world shall – I will do such things –
What they are, yet I know not, but they shall be
The terrors of the earth. You think I'll weep
No, I'll not weep.

Storm and tempest

I have full cause of weeping, but this heart
Shall break into a hundred thousand flaws
Or ere I'll weep. O fool, I shall go mad!

Exeunt Lear, Gloucester, Kent, and Fool

Cornwall

Let us withdraw, 'twill be a storm.

Regan

This house is little. The old man and his people
Cannot be well bestowed.

262 superfluous: *extra*

282 flaws: *pieces*

286 bestowed: *housed*

Goneril

'Tis his own blame; hath put himself from rest
And must needs taste his folly.

Regan

For his particular, I'll receive him gladly,
But not one follower.

Goneril

So am I purposed.
Where is my lord of Gloucester?

Cornwall

Followed the old man forth. He is returned.

Re-enter Gloucester

Gloucester

The king is in high rage.

Cornwall

Whither is he going?

Gloucester

He calls to horse, but will I know not whither.

Cornwall

'Tis best to give him way; he leads himself.

Goneril

My lord, entreat him by no means to stay.

Gloucester

Alack, the night comes on, and the bleak winds
Do sorely ruffle. For many miles about
There's scarce a bush.

Regan

O, sir, to wilful men,
The injuries that they themselves procure
Must be their schoolmasters. Shut up your doors.
He is attended with a desperate train,
And what they may incense him to, being apt
To have his ear abused, wisdom bids fear.

Cornwall

Shut up your doors, my lord. 'Tis a wild night,
My Regan counsels well. Come out o' the storm.

Exeunt

287 put himself from rest: *is the author of his own discomfort*

289 For his particular: *for his sake*

298 ruffle: *unsettle*

302 desperate: *rowdy*

303–4 apt...abused: *inclined to listen to lies*

Key Scene Analysis

Disrespect (lines 1–27)

An incredulous Lear cannot understand the disregard shown by Regan and Cornwall towards him. First, they are unexpectedly absent from home. He then finds that his servant, Kent, has been imprisoned in the public stocks. Naively, he thinks there must be some reasonable explanation because they 'durst not do it' to a royal messenger. Lear is still in denial and does not yet understand the effects of abdicating royal power.

This powerful scene marks a defining moment for Lear. He is directly challenged by his two daughters. Goneril and Regan display their common interest in taking action against him.

The first shock (lines 27–59)

Kent explains that when he was about to deliver Lear's letter, Oswald interrupted him with a letter from Goneril. Immediately, Regan and her husband set off, commanding Kent to follow. Kent realised that the letter Oswald had delivered had 'poisoned' his. He drew his sword and was placed in the stocks for his actions.

The Fool uses his satirical song to warn Lear that good luck usually favours the wealthy: 'Fathers that wear rags/ Do make their children blind', while rich fathers tend to have caring offspring: 'But fathers that bear bags/ Shall see their children kind'.

Faced with the truth about his family relationships, Lear begins to experience the first symptoms of hysteria, which was believed to originate in the stomach: 'Down, thou climbing sorrow,/ Thy element's below'. The condition caused a choking sensation and a feeling of suffocation. In this unstable state, Lear continues to worry about his mental well-being.

Unrest and confusion (lines 60–96)

The Fool tells Kent of the stupidity of following a leader without power: 'Let go thy hold when a great wheel runs down a hill, lest it break thy neck with following it'. He warns against fair-weather friends who 'Will pack when it begins to rain'. Like the ever-loyal Kent, however, the Fool will not desert Lear.

Lear is faced with the new reality of his own importance. He is stripped of dignity and compelled to accept the shocking consequences of surrendering his power.

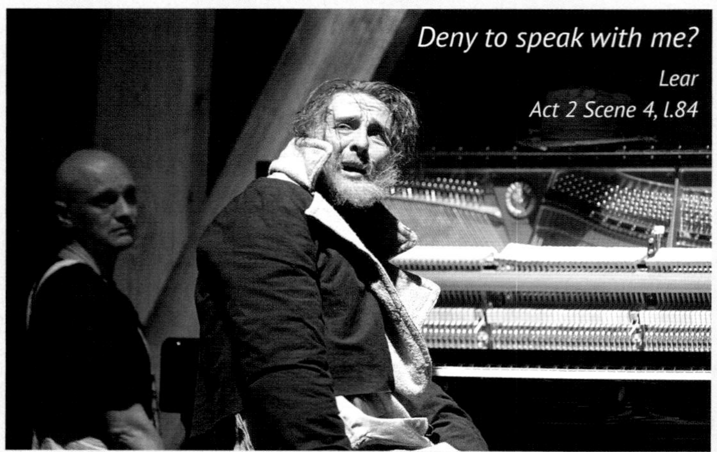

Deny to speak with me?
Lear
Act 2 Scene 4, l.84

The king re-emerges with Gloucester, furious that he will not be received by Regan and Cornwall. He regards their excuses as 'Mere fetches'. Gloucester attempts to calm Lear by reminding him of Cornwall's 'fiery quality'. But Lear still insists on speaking to them. Unlike the former king, Gloucester understands that there is a new political order in the country.

There is growing tension as Lear becomes more desperate. Lear is increasingly confused, behaving like a furious old man who has lost everything and left himself dependent on the goodwill of his children. It is impossible to have authority without power: 'Informed them! Dost thou understand me, man?'

Impulsive behaviour (lines 97–122)

Lear starts to display several mood swings. At first, he is angry at Regan and her husband: 'My breath and blood!' Then he starts to make excuses for them: 'Maybe he is not well'. When he looks again at his stocked messenger, however, he realises that Regan and Cornwall are not being honest with him. Lear frantically issues a series of commands: 'Give', 'Go', 'Bid'. As usual, Gloucester wants peace between all the parties: 'I would have all well betwixt you'. Lear greets his daughter and son-in-law sarcastically, 'Good morrow to you both'. He knows that they have deliberately left him waiting until evening.

Meanwhile, the Fool continues his sharp analysis of Lear's true situation by telling the comic story of a kind-hearted cockney girl who foolishly put live eels in a pie because she could not bear to kill them and was then surprised when they would not stay there. She had an equally silly brother who smeared butter on his horse's hay to improve the taste. Through customary random humour, the Fool is warning Lear about his misguided kindness and that he can no longer play the role of a strict father. Despite everything, Lear still does not fully realise the truth of his position.

The second shock (lines 123–180)

Regan and Cornwall's formal greeting suggests that Lear is foolish to hope for sympathy from them: 'Hail to your grace', 'I am glad to see your highness'. In contrast, Lear warmly embraces his second daughter, 'Beloved Regan'. He immediately begins to describe the wrongs done to him by Goneril, using the recurring image of predatory animals: 'Sharp-toothed unkindness, like a vulture, here'.

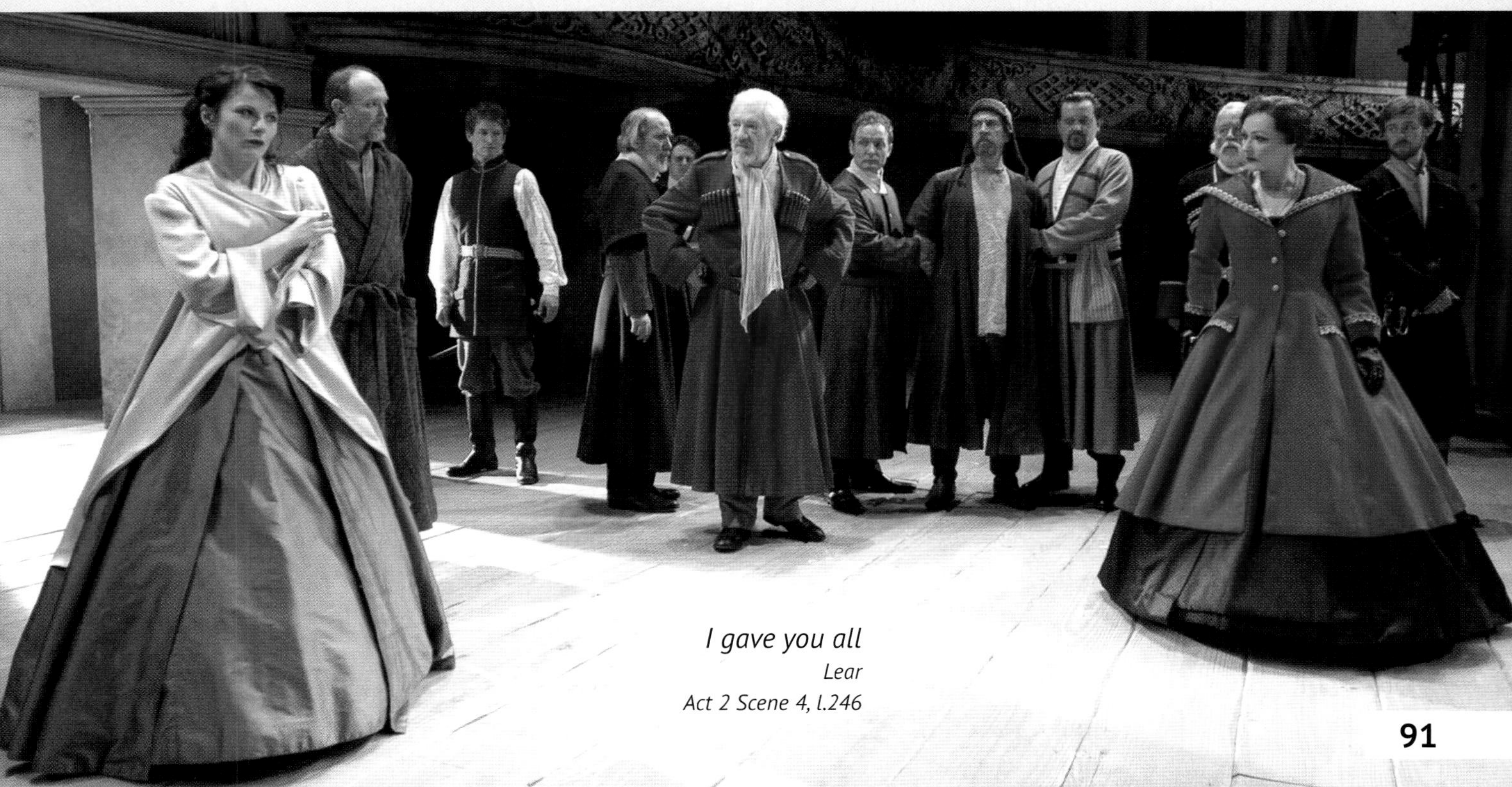

I gave you all
Lear
Act 2 Scene 4, l.246

But Regan quickly interrupts him, urging 'patience'. Lear is bewildered and when she says that Goneril was right to reduce Lear's followers, he flies into a rage and vehemently curses his oldest daughter. Regan then points out that Lear is old: 'Nature in you stands on the very verge/ Of her confine'. She urges him to return to Goneril and beg her forgiveness.

Lear mocks her suggestion and asks her, 'Do you but mark how this becomes the house?' Is Lear acting ironically when he falls to his knees to beg Regan for food and shelter? Is it true that 'Age is unnecessary'? Lear viciously curses Goneril: 'Infect her beauty,/ You fen-sucked fogs'. He is still blind to reality and just as he arithmetically divided his kingdom at the start of the play, he continues to measure love numerically ('cut', 'scant', 'half'). He remains fully convinced that Regan knows the 'dues of gratitude'.

Lear falls to his knees, aiming to show how inappropriate it is for him to have to lower himself to anyone. However, his melodramatic gesture is dismissed by Regan as just another of his 'unsightly tricks'.

The third shock (lines 181–306)

Although surrounded by people, Lear is becoming increasingly isolated. To his astonishment, Goneril is warmly greeted by her sister: 'O Regan, wilt thou take her by the hand?' Lear has no idea that his daughters have formed an alliance against him. Once again, he begins to lose control: 'O sides, you are too tough!' Regan tells Lear that she is not ready to receive him and that he must return to Goneril – but with fewer followers: 'half your train'. However, Lear swears to sleep in the open rather than go back, 'I abjure all roofs, and choose/ To wage against the enmity o' the air'.

Just as the king had carved up his kingdom, Lear's two daughters now dismantle what remains of his power. Regan decides that even fifty followers are too many. Goneril suggests that he can get all the service he needs from their servants. Pathetically, Lear reminds them, 'I gave you all'. Regan's response ('And in good time you gave it') is a telling reminder that he was reluctant to relinquish power.

Petulantly, Lear decides to go back to Goneril because she will allow him fifty followers whereas Regan will only entertain twenty-five: 'thou art twice her love'. Both sisters ritualistically work together to gradually decrease the number of his knights. They repeat their spell-like calculations until Regan finally asks her father: 'What need one?'

Lear's powerful response recounts how even the poorest beggars have a few things over and above what they actually need to survive: 'Are in the poorest thing superfluous'. He turns the argument back on his daughters by referring to their 'gorgeous' clothes which are for show and pleasure, and not merely for keeping them warm.

Overcome by sorrow, he asks the gods for 'noble anger' as opposed to tears. At this point, the audience is likely to identify with Lear's dilemma and even sympathise with a proud man who refuses to give in. Having been treated like a child, he resorts to vague – and pathetic – threats against his cold-hearted daughters: 'I will have such revenges on you both'.

The elderly Lear, now fearful of his ability to remain sane under such pressure ('I shall go mad!') rushes out into the wild night with Kent, Gloucester, a gentleman and the Fool. Goneril and Regan justify their treatment of their father: 'This house is little./ The old man and his people/ Cannot be well bestowed'. As the scene ends, the old king is locked out of the castle at the mercy of the storm. Cornwall commands, 'Shut up your doors ... 'Tis a wild night'.

Shakespeare's Dramatic Style

Symbols are objects, concepts or events that represent something else. **Symbolically**, the coming storm ('bleak winds/ Do sorely ruffle') reflects the growing disorder in Lear's mind. The elderly king loses control because of the callous treatment of his ungrateful daughters: 'my rising heart', 'O fool, I shall go mad!'

The **storm also symbolises the chaos that Lear's kingdom is beginning to experience** as a result of Lear's rash decision to hand over power. Serious divisions have already occurred within the families of Lear and Gloucester. In Shakespeare's time, people believed in a natural sense of order. The natural world mirrored human disorder and upheaval. In his growing despair, the old king resorts to nature for refuge.

Critical Analysis

'Lear is an isolated figure on a crowded stage.' Discuss this statement in relation to Act 2 Scene 4. Refer closely to the text in developing your response.

Sample Paragraph 1

I think Lear is an isolated figure because he does not really know what is going on. Regan and her husband left. Lear tries to accept their excuses. He thinks Regan will accept him not like her 'serpent' sister with his followers. But she won't. She is in agreement with Goneril that he is in his 'dotage'. Even Cornwall tells Gloucester to shut the doors against Lear. Lear is definitely isolated. He has Kent, but he is in disguise. The Fool is loyal to Lear but he keeps making smart remarks at Lear's expense. No real help. Gloucester comes back to his own palace after leaving Lear in the storm. Lear is on his own. *(115 words)*

Examiner's Comment

- Attempts to give some illustrations of Lear's isolation.
- Points are not developed.
- More effective use of supportive reference and quotation needed.
- Expression is note-like and repetitive in this basic-grade response.

Sample Paragraph 2

In this scene, Shakespeare presents Lear as a once-powerful king who ends up a humiliated old man. Surrounded by ruthless people, Regan, Cornwall and Goneril, a pathetic Lear stands alone. His followers, the disguised Kent, the Fool and Gloucester are no match for them. Lear's daughters remind him of reality, 'you are old', 'dotage'. I felt it was when he saw the agreement between his daughters, 'O Regan, wilt thou take her by the hand?', that Lear really faces defeat. This is a major step in his decline. Without power, he takes his chances on the heath. Even Gloucester leaves him and returns to the castle where he is ordered to shut the doors against Lear. Shakespeare highlights how the old king is left isolated. Even his sanity is beginning to desert him, 'O fool, I shall go mad!' *(140 words)*

Examiner's Comment

- Successful, focused response addresses the question, using apt reference.
- Good developed discussion, e.g. 'a major step in his decline'.
- Close interaction with the text ('he takes his chances on the heath').
- Fluent and assured expression adds to the quality of this top-grade answer.

Class/Homework Exercise

To what extent would you agree that Act 2 Scene 4 marks an important turning point in Lear's development as a character?

Write a paragraph (about 150 words), supporting your response with reference to the text.

Exam Focus

Act 2 Scene 4 can be used successfully in response to a range of examination questions about the play's central themes, characters, relationships and the playwright's dramatic style.

This **key scene** has important dramatic functions:

- Signifies a turning-point in Lear's relationships with his daughters.
- Marks the beginning of the king's path towards self-awareness.
- Develops themes of power, justice and injustice.
- Engages audience sympathy for the central character.
- Increases dramatic tension through conflict and foreshadowing.
- Storm imagery symbolises Lear's unstable mental state.

Key Quotes

Quote	Comment
They could not, would not do it *(Lear to Kent) l.23*	Lear cannot believe that Regan and Cornwall could be responsible for this insulting treatment of his servant, Kent. He does not realise that both his influence and his self-esteem are being stripped away.
Nature in you stands on the very verge/ Of her confine *(Regan to Lear) l.143–4*	Regan reminds her irate father that he has grown old and should now be led by others. Is she being sensible or merely cold-hearted?
dart your blinding flames/ Into her scornful eyes! *(Lear cursing Goneril) l.161–2*	Losing control, Lear behaves as he has done before, uttering terrible curses against his eldest daughter for her pitiless treatment of him.
The offices of nature, bond of childhood,/ Effects of courtesy, dues of gratitude;/ Thy half o' the kingdom hast thou not forgot *(Lear to Regan) l.174–6*	A forlorn Lear futilely attempts to tell Regan why she ought to behave well towards him. First, they share natural ties as father and daughter. Second, she should welcome him as a guest. Most important, he has recently given her half of his kingdom.
No, rather I abjure all roofs, and choose/ To wage against the enmity o' the air *(Lear to Goneril and Regan) l.204–5*	Lear is furious that his daughters are attempting to humiliate him by removing all his knights and followers. He decides that he will not seek shelter under either of their roofs and will instead endure the harsh elements out of doors.
And in good time you gave it *(Regan to Lear) l.246*	Regan's caustic comment reminds the audience that Lear selfishly held on to power until he was a very old man. She is not at all impressed by his self-pitying claim that he gave his daughters everything.

Key Points | Act 2

Scene 1

- There are rumours of growing tensions between Cornwall and Albany.
- Edmund tricks Edgar into flight and Gloucester into condemning Edgar.
- Regan is warned by Goneril of Lear's impending arrival. Wishing to avoid being at home to receive Lear, she goes to Gloucester's castle

Scene 2

- Kent abuses Oswald, knowing that the steward is delivering letters that are hostile to Lear.
- Kent insults Cornwall and is placed in the stocks like a common criminal.
- Gloucester tries to intervene on Kent's behalf because this treatment is an insult to the king. His efforts are unsuccessful.
- Cordelia has contacted Kent and he is preparing to co-operate with her in restoring order to the kingdom.

Scene 3

- Edgar is now a fugitive and has to survive by adopting the guise of a mad beggar, Poor Tom.
- He is a resilient character.

Scene 4

- Lear is shocked to see Kent in the stocks and seeks an explanation. Cornwall eventually admits that he put him there.
- The loyal Fool is still attempting to get Lear to realise his mistake in misjudging his daughters and giving up power.
- Regan and Cornwall initially make excuses not to meet Lear, who tries to excuse them.
- The former king believes that Regan will treat him better than Goneril did, but Regan tells him to return to her sister and apologise.
- Goneril arrives and Lear realises that the two sisters are working closely together as they reduce his followers to none.
- Lear threatens vengeance, but is powerless to effect it.
- The old king feels the first stirrings of mental breakdown due to the pressures imposed upon him.
- In anger, he leaves Gloucester's castle and ventures into a terrible storm on the heath. Regan and Cornwall order Gloucester to bar the doors of his castle against Lear, saying that he is now a danger to them.

Act 3

Scene 1

INTRODUCTION

- Kent searches for Lear on the heath.
- The deranged king and his fool have been seen in the storm.
- Cordelia's French army is on its way to Dover.

A heath

Enter Kent (disguised) and a Gentleman, separately

Kent

Who's there, besides foul weather?

Gentleman

One minded like the weather, most unquietly.

Kent

I know you. Where's the king?

Gentleman

Contending with the fretful elements:
Bids the winds blow the earth into the sea,
Or swell the curled waters above the main,
That things might change or cease; tears his white hair,
Which the impetuous blasts, with eyeless rage,
Catch in their fury, and make nothing of;
Strives in his little world of man to out-storm
The to-and-fro-conflicting wind and rain.
This night, wherein the cub-drawn bear would couch,
The lion and the belly-pinched wolf
Keep their fur dry, unbonneted he runs,
And bids what will take all.

Kent

But who is with him?

Gentleman

None but the Fool, who labours to out-jest
His heart-struck injuries.

Kent

Sir, I do know you,
And dare, upon the warrant of my note,
Commend a dear thing to you. There is division,
Although as yet the face of it be covered
With mutual cunning, 'twixt Albany and Cornwall,
Who have – as who have not, that their great stars
Throned and set high? – servants, who seem no less,
Which are to France the spies and speculations
Intelligent of our state. What hath been seen,
Either in snuffs and packings of the Dukes,
Or the hard rein which both of them have borne
Against the old kind king, or something deeper,

2 minded like the weather: *with a mind as disturbed as the weather*

4 Contending with: *struggling against*
fretful elements: *violent weather*

6 curled waters: *stormy seas*
main: *mainland*

12 cub-drawn: *hungry, drained of milk*

14 unbonneted: *hatless, unprotected*

16 labours to out-jest: *tries to make a joke of*

21 mutual cunning: *hiding it from each other*

23 seem no less: *appear to be*

26 snuffs and packings: *grudges and conspiracies*

27 hard rein: *cruel treatment*

Whereof perchance these are but furnishings;
But, true it is, from France there comes a power
Into this scattered kingdom, who already,
Wise in our negligence, have secret feet
In some of our best ports, and are at point
To show their open banner. Now to you:
If on my credit you dare build so far
To make your speed to Dover, you shall find
Some that will thank you, making just report
Of how unnatural and bemadding sorrow
The king hath cause to plain.
I am a gentleman of blood and breeding,
And, from some knowledge and assurance, offer
This office to you.

Gentleman

I will talk further with you.

Kent

No, do not.
For confirmation that I am much more
Than my out-wall, open this purse, and take
What it contains. If you shall see Cordelia –
As fear not but you shall – show her this ring;
And she will tell you who your fellow is
That yet you do not know. Fie on this storm!
I will go seek the king.

Gentleman

Give me your hand. Have you no more to say?

Kent

Few words, but, to effect, more than all yet:
That, when we have found the king – in which your pain
That way, I'll this – he that first lights on him
Holla the other.

Exeunt

29 furnishings: *pretexts*
31 scattered: *disunited*
33 at point: *ready*
38 bemadding: *infuriating*
39 plain: *complain*
45 out-wall: *outer appearance*
52 to effect: *in importance*
53 your pain: *your task, effort*
54 lights on him: *finds him*
55 Holla: *stop*

Analysis

Support for Lear (lines 1–55)

The gentleman (probably one of Lear's knights) meets Kent and tells him how the old king is battling against the raging storm on the wild heath, 'Contending with the fretful elements'. Lear is clearly in a deranged state, ordering the wind to drown the earth, so that 'things might change or cease'. Is there something majestic about Lear's defiant efforts to assert his authority, even though he has yet to accept responsibility for his own downfall?

Throughout the scene, Shakespeare is commenting on the weakness of man in comparison to the savage world of nature. Lear is accompanied only by the Fool, who tries to ease his master's trauma with jokes and witticisms. Kent reveals that Cornwall and Albany are in secret conflict ('division') against each other, but concealing their disagreement with 'mutual cunning'. Is either of them entirely trustworthy?

In this short scene, there are disturbing reports of Lear's spiralling descent into madness. The king's antics in the storm build suspense for the wild events that lie ahead.

Meanwhile, French spies are active throughout Britain and Cordelia's army has secretly landed at Dover. Being very careful about his disguise, Kent gives the gentleman a gold ring by which Cordelia will recognise Kent when they next meet. At this point, audiences are likely to feel a little relief due to Kent's cautious optimism and the prospect of Cordelia's soldiers defeating the forces of evil.

Key Quotes

Contending with the fretful elements *(Gentleman to Kent) l.4*	One of Lear's knights graphically describes the hopeless actions of the old king on the windswept heath as he tries to challenge the raging storm. It is a pitiful reminder of Lear's powerlessness.
The lion and the belly-pinched wolf/ Keep their fur dry, unbonneted he runs *(Gentleman to Kent) l.13–14*	Using vivid imagery and energetic language, Shakespeare contrasts the sensible action of even the wildest animals with the madness of Lear's erratic behaviour.
There is division *(Kent to Gentleman) l.19*	There are renewed reports of imminent conflict between the rival Dukes. Is the growing animosity between Albany and Cornwall a good sign?
I will go seek the king *(Kent to Gentleman) l.50*	Kent's unconditional loyalty to the king is evident as he braves the fierce storm to find his master.

Act 3
Scene 2

INTRODUCTION

- Lear rages against the storm and his daughters' ingratitude.
- In his madness, he becomes obsessed with justice and punishment.
- Both the Fool and Kent advise him to reconcile with his daughters.
- For the first time, Lear begins to show concern for others.

The heath, storm

Enter Lear and the Fool

Lear

Blow, winds, and crack your cheeks! Rage! Blow!
You cataracts and hurricanoes, spout
Till you have drenched our steeples, drowned the cocks!
You sulphurous and thought-executing fires,
Vaunt-couriers to oak-cleaving thunderbolts,
Singe my white head! And thou, all-shaking thunder,
Smite flat the thick rotundity of the world!
Crack Nature's moulds, all germens spill at once,
That make ingrateful man!

Fool

O nuncle, court holy-water in a dry house is better than this rain-water out o' door. Good nuncle, in, and ask thy daughters' blessing. Here's a night pities neither wise man nor fools.

Lear

Rumble thy bellyful! Spit, fire! Spout, rain!
Nor rain, wind, thunder, fire, are my daughters.
I tax not you, you elements, with unkindness.
I never gave you kingdom, called you children,
You owe me no subscription. Then let fall
Your horrible pleasure. Here I stand, your slave,
A poor, infirm, weak, and despised old man.
But yet I call you servile ministers,
That have with two pernicious daughters joined
Your high engendered battles 'gainst a head
So old and white as this. O! O! 'tis foul!

Fool

He that has a house to put's head in has a good head-piece.

The cod-piece that will house
Before the head has any,
The head and he shall louse;
So beggars marry many.
The man that makes his toe
What he his heart should make
Shall of a corn cry woe,
And turn his sleep to wake.

1 crack: *puff out*
2 cataracts: *large waterfalls*
3 cocks: *weather-cocks*
4 sulphurous: *poisonous*
thought-executing: *mind-numbing*
5 Vaunt-couriers: *messengers*
oak-cleaving: *tree-splitting*
8 germens: *seeds*
10 court holy-water: *flattery*
18 subscription: *allegiance, loyalty*
23 high engendered: *heaven made*
32 corn: *painful blister*

For there was never yet fair woman but she made mouths
in a glass.

Lear

No, I will be the pattern of all patience.
I will say nothing.

Enter Kent

Kent

Who's there?

Fool

Marry, here's grace and a cod-piece; that's a wise man and a fool.

Kent

Alas, sir, are you here? Things that love night
Love not such nights as these. The wrathful skies
Gallow the very wanderers of the dark,
And make them keep their caves. Since I was man
Such sheets of fire, such bursts of horrid thunder,
Such groans of roaring wind and rain I never
Remember to have heard. Man's nature cannot carry
The affliction nor the fear.

Lear

Let the great gods,
That keep this dreadful pudder o'er our heads
Find out their enemies now. Tremble, thou wretch,
That hast within thee undivulged crimes,
Unwhipped of justice. Hide thee, thou bloody hand;
Thou perjured, and thou simular man of virtue
That art incestuous. Caitiff, to pieces shake,
That under covert and convenient seeming
Hast practised on man's life. Close pent-up guilts,
Rive your concealing continents and cry
These dreadful summoners grace. I am a man
More sinned against than sinning.

Kent

Alack, bare-headed?
Gracious my lord, hard by here is a hovel.
Some friendship will it lend you 'gainst the tempest.
Repose you there, while I to this hard house –
More harder than the stones whereof 'tis raised,

34 mouths: *pretty expressions*
36 pattern: *epitome*
42 wrathful: *angry*
43 Gallow: *alarm, terrify*
47 carry: *bear*
48 affliction: *distress*
49 pudder: *chaos*
52 Unwhipped: *untouched by*
53 perjured: *false*
simular: *fake*
54 Caitiff: *wretch*
55 seeming: *pretence, appearances*
57 Rive: *burst through*
57–58 cry...grace: *beg for mercy*
60 hovel: *makeshift shelter*

66 scanted: *mean, minimal*

Which even but now, demanding after you,
Denied me to come in – return, and force
Their scanted courtesy.

Lear

My wits begin to turn.
Come on, my boy. How dost, my boy? Art cold?
I am cold myself. Where is this straw, my fellow?
The art of our necessities is strange,
That can make vile things precious. Come, your hovel.
Poor Fool and knave, I have one part in my heart
That's sorry yet for thee.

Fool

Singing

He that has and a little tiny wit
With heigh-ho, the wind and the rain,
Must make content with his fortunes fit,
For the rain it raineth every day.

Lear

True, my good boy. Come, bring us to this hovel.

Exeunt Lear and Kent

Fool

78 courtesan: *prostitute*

This is a brave night to cool a courtesan. I'll speak a prophecy ere I go:

When priests are more in word than matter,
When brewers mar their malt with water,
When nobles are their tailors' tutors,
No heretics burned, but wenches suitors,
Then shall the realm of Albion
Come to great confusion.
When every case in law is right,
No squire in debt, nor no poor knight,
When slanders do not live in tongues,
Nor cutpurses come not to throngs,
When usurers tell their gold i'the field,
And bawds and whores do churches build,
Then comes the time, who lives to see it,
That going shall be used with feet.

89 cutpurses: *thieves*

90 usurers: *money-lenders*

94 Merlin: *legendary wizard*

This prophecy Merlin shall make, for I live before his time.

Exit

Analysis

Lear's rage (lines 1–24)

Exposed to the harshest natural elements, the old king defies the fury of the raging storm. His own volatile mental state is reflected in the list of violent verbs: 'Blow', 'Rage', 'Singe', 'Smite', 'Crack'. Entirely self-obsessed, Lear is still deluded and believes that he is the country's supreme ruler, even capable of commanding the weather. In his frustration, he wants the whole world destroyed: 'Smite flat the thick rotundity o' the world!/ Crack Nature's moulds'.

The audience is likely to admire Lear's fighting spirit as he refuses to be intimidated by both his daughters and the fierce tempest. His anger is not against the elements since they owe him no loyalty, unlike his 'pernicious daughters'. However, in his self-pitying state, he believes that both human nature and elemental nature are out to destroy him. The former king is beginning his journey towards self-awareness with the recognition that he is only a 'poor, infirm, weak, and despised old man'.

The Fool's common sense (lines 25–35)

The Fool has constantly pointed out Lear's weaknesses. He continues to mock his master's irresponsible behaviour and its consequences. Lear's foolishness has resulted in his own homelessness. The Fool also reminds Lear of the hypocrisy of women such as Goneril and Regan, who practise to deceive as they make faces in a mirror, 'For there was never yet fair woman but she made mouths in a glass'.

Signs of change (lines 36–59)

Lear struggles to control himself and to be 'the pattern of all patience'. This signals a growing change in his personality as he has often been prone to bursts of uncontrolled anger. He begins to consider wrong-doing and justice, listing some of the criminal types who can sometimes escape punishment – including perjurers, hypocrites and secret

Come on, my boy. How dost, my boy? Art cold? I am cold myself

Lear
Act 3 Scene 2, l.67–8

murderers. Significantly, Lear still regards himself as a victim, a 'man/ More sinned against than sinning', rather than someone who has brought about his own destruction.

Concern for others (lines 59–77)

All three outcasts on the heath show genuine concern for one another, unlike those occupying the comfort of palaces. The disguised Kent attempts to find Lear some shelter from the ferocious rainstorm: 'here is a hovel/ Some friendship will it lend you 'gainst the tempest'. The king remains aware that he is on the edge of madness ('My wits begin to turn') due to his daughters' abusive treatment.

The Fool's dry humour contrasts with Lear's self-pity, 'a man/ More sinned against than sinning'. This stark difference between the two characters heightens the play's dark tragedy.

However, he shows some concern for others besides himself, worrying about finding shelter for the Fool: 'I have one part in my heart/ That's sorry yet for thee'. This marks another critical turning point in Lear's painful path towards self-knowledge, and will inspire audience sympathy. Having experienced misfortune personally, he is finally becoming aware of the needs of others.

The Fool's prophecy (lines 78–94)

The Fool's 'prophecy' foretells of the tragedies about to happen in the kingdom ('Albion'). He warns of an age of corruption where nothing is as it should be; priests do not practise what they preach, beer is diluted, noblemen are only concerned with fashion, and blasphemers will not be punished – except for those with diseases.

This satirical account of all the faults of Elizabethan society would be appreciated and enjoyed by Shakespeare's audience. The Fool then predicts a surreal utopian future where criminals and sinners abandon their wicked ways. He rounds off by saying that Merlin, the wizard at the legendary court of King Arthur, will make the same prediction at a later time.

Key Quotes

Quote	Comment
Crack Nature's moulds, all germens spill at once,/ That make ingrateful man! *(Lear on the heath) l.8–9*	Raging against his daughters' callous behaviour, Lear rants against the storm, demanding that the world and all ingratitude should be destroyed. His fury is mirrored by the violence of nature.
Here I stand, your slave,/ A poor, infirm, weak, and despised old man *(Lear) l.19–20*	Lear is beginning to gain insight into the reality of his situation, at the mercy of both the fierce elements and his ungrateful daughters. But he is still egocentric, seeing himself as the victim rather than the architect of his own misfortune.
My wits begin to turn *(Lear) l.66*	The ageing king's great worry is that he will go mad, due both to the cruelty of his daughters and his own uncontrollable rages.
Poor Fool and knave *(Lear to the Fool) l.71*	Lear begins to show concern for somebody other than himself. This marks another important stage in his journey towards self-enlightenment.

Act 3
Scene 3

INTRODUCTION

- Gloucester tells Edmund of his plans to help Lear.
- He also confides in him about the French invasion.
- Edmund reveals his intention to betray his father to Cornwall.

A room in Gloucester's castle

Enter Gloucester and Edmund

Gloucester

Alack, alack, Edmund, I like not this unnatural dealing. When I desired their leave that I might pity him, they took from me the use of mine own house, charged me, on pain of perpetual displeasure, neither to speak of him, entreat for him, or any way sustain him.

Edmund

Most savage and unnatural!

Gloucester

Go to, say you nothing. There's a division between the dukes, and a worse matter than that. I have received a letter this night – 'tis dangerous to be spoken – I have locked the letter in my closet. These injuries the king now bears will be revenged home. There is part of a power already footed. We must incline to the king. I will seek him and privily relieve him. Go you and maintain talk with the Duke, that my charity be not of him perceived. If he ask for me, I am ill and gone to bed. If I die for it, as no less is threatened me, the King my old master must be relieved. There is some strange thing toward, Edmund; pray you, be careful.

Exit

Edmund

This courtesy, forbid thee, shall the Duke
Instantly know, and of that letter too.
This seems a fair deserving, and must draw me
That which my father loses – no less than all.
The younger rises when the old doth fall.

Exit

2 leave: *consent, permission*
4 perpetual: *eternal*
5 sustain: *maintain, help*
12 footed: *landed*
incline to: *take the side of*
13 privily: *stealthily, secretly*
14 perceived: *detected*
17 toward: *at hand*
19 courtesy: *kindness*
21 deserving: *reward*
draw: *win*

Analysis

Gloucester – loyal and naive (lines 1–18)

Gloucester is unhappy over the 'unnatural dealing' which Lear has received at the hands of his daughters. He shows his loyalty by deciding to help his old master: 'I will seek him and privily relieve him'. But without having the courage to directly confront Goneril and Regan, he will only act secretly.

However, Gloucester knows that he is putting himself at great risk: 'If I die for it'. He is not a truly heroic figure, but acts cautiously as he has always done. He requests that Edmund will keep his plans secret from Cornwall: 'If he ask for me, I am ill and gone to bed'. Gloucester continues to trust Edmund, little realising that he is handing his son the means by which he can betray his old father.

The play's sub-plot closely mirrors the main plot as the hypocritical child betrays the well-meaning but naive parent. Ironically, Gloucester still trusts the wrong son.

Conspiracy (lines 19–23)

The hypocritical Edmund lives by the laws of nature – the survival of the fittest – and is now close to achieving what he believes is his right to inherit Gloucester's wealth and position. He will conspire with Lear's enemies to betray his unsuspecting father and condemn him to certain death, so long as he himself can benefit: 'The younger rises when the old doth fall'.

Key Quotes

Quote	Analysis
Edmund, I like not this unnatural dealing *(Gloucester to Edmund) l.1*	Gloucester's naivety is evident. He disliked what happened to Lear at the hands of his unnatural daughters. Without knowing it, he is also giving his own son the means to act unnaturally and to destroy him.
There's a division between the dukes *(Gloucester) l.7–8*	Once again, the deep rivalry between the Albany and Cornwall is highlighted. Ironically, Lear handed over power to avoid turmoil in the country.
I will seek him and privily relieve him *(Gloucester) l.12–13*	Gloucester has a decent sense of justice, but he lacks the moral courage to act directly. This has always been a character flaw.
and must draw me/ That which my father loses *(Edmund) l.21–2*	Edmund is an opportunist who seizes every chance he gets to improve his situation. Here he decides to betray his father to the Duke of Cornwall so that he will be rewarded with Gloucester's title and lands.

Act 3
Scene 4*

INTRODUCTION

- On the wild heath, Lear is in a highly disturbed and fragile state.
- Poor Tom (Edgar in disguise) makes a deep impression on the former king.
- Lear develops a new social awareness and becomes more compassionate.
- Gloucester finally convinces Lear to take shelter from the storm.

*** This key scene requires close, detailed study.**

Outside a hovel on the heath

Enter Lear, Kent and Fool

Kent

Here is the place, my lord. Good my lord, enter.
The tyranny of the open night's too rough
For nature to endure.

Storm still

Lear

Let me alone.

Kent

Good my lord, enter here.

Lear

Wilt break my heart?

Kent

I had rather break mine own. Good my lord, enter.

Lear

Thou think'st 'tis much that this contentious storm
Invades us to the skin: so 'tis to thee.
But where the greater malady is fixed,
The lesser is scarce felt. Thou'dst shun a bear,
But if thy flight lay toward the roaring sea,
Thou'dst meet the bear in the mouth. When the mind's free,
The body's delicate. This tempest in my mind
Doth from my senses take all feeling else
Save what beats there. Filial ingratitude!
Is it not as this mouth should tear this hand
For lifting food to it? But I will punish home.
No, I will weep no more. In such a night
To shut me out? Pour on, I will endure.
In such a night as this! O Regan, Goneril!
Your old kind father, whose frank heart gave all –
O, that way madness lies; let me shun that;
No more of that.

Kent

Good my lord, enter here.

Lear

Prithee, go in thyself, seek thine own ease.
This tempest will not give me leave to ponder
On things would hurt me more. But I'll go in.

2 tyranny: *cruelty*

6 contentious: *furious*

8 malady: *sickness*
fixed: *established*

12 delicate: *sensitive*

21 shun: *reject*

24 leave: *a chance*

26 houseless poverty: *homeless outcasts*

29 bide: *endure*
pelting: *beating*

31 looped and windowed: *tattered*

33 physic: *medicine*
pomp: *powerful people, royalty*

35 superflux: *surplus*

37 Fathom: *six feet of water*

49 foul fiend: *evil devil (mad people were believed to be possessed by spirits)*

To the Fool

In, boy, go first. You houseless poverty –
Nay, get thee in. I'll pray, and then I'll sleep.

Fool goes in

Poor naked wretches, wheresoe'er you are,
That bide the pelting of this pitiless storm,
How shall your houseless heads and unfed sides,
Your looped and windowed raggedness, defend you
From seasons such as these? O, I have taken
Too little care of this! Take physic, pomp,
Expose thyself to feel what wretches feel,
That thou mayst shake the superflux to them,
And show the heavens more just.

Edgar

Within

Fathom and half, fathom and half! Poor Tom!

The Fool runs out from the hovel

Fool

Come not in here, nuncle, here's a spirit!
Help me, help me!

Kent

Give me thy hand. Who's there?

Fool

A spirit, a spirit! He says his name's poor Tom.

Kent

What art thou that dost grumble there in the straw?
Come forth.

Enter Edgar disguised as a madman

Edgar

Away! the foul fiend follows me! Through the sharp hawthorn blow the cold winds. Humh! Go to thy cold bed and warm thee.

Lear

Didst thou give all to thy daughters? And art thou come to this?

Edgar

Who gives anything to poor Tom? Whom the foul fiend hath led through fire and through flame, and through ford and whirlpool, o'er bog and quagmire, that hath laid knives under his pillow, and halters in his pew, set ratsbane by his porridge, made him proud of heart, to ride on a bay trotting-horse over four-inched bridges, to course his own shadow for a traitor. Bless thy five wits! Tom's a-cold! O do de, do de, do de. Bless thee from whirlwinds, star- blasting, and taking! Do poor Tom some charity, whom the foul fiend vexes. There could I have him now, and there, and there again, and there.

Storm still

Lear

What, have his daughters brought him to this pass?
Couldst thou save nothing? Didst thou give them all?

Fool

Nay, he reserved a blanket, else we had been all shamed.

Lear

Now, all the plagues that in the pendulous air
Hang fated o'er men's faults light on thy daughters!

Kent

He hath no daughters, sir.

Lear

Death, traitor! Nothing could have subdued nature
To such a lowness but his unkind daughters.
Is it the fashion that discarded fathers
Should have thus little mercy on their flesh?
Judicious punishment! 'Twas this flesh begot
Those pelican daughters.

Edgar

Pillicock sat on Pillicock Hill
Alow, alow, loo, loo!

Fool

This cold night will turn us all to fools and madmen.

Edgar

Take heed o' the foul fiend. Obey thy parents, keep thy word justly, swear not, commit not with man's sworn spouse, set not thy sweet heart on proud array. Tom's a-cold.

Lear

What hast thou been?

52 ratsbane: *rat poison*

53–54 ride...bridges: *ride over narrow bridges*

56 star-blasting: *diseases caused by stars*

57 taking: *bewitching*

60 pass: *plight*

66 subdued: *reduced*

70 Judicious: *sensible*

71 pelican: *young bird believed to feed on the flesh of its parents*

77 array: *fine clothing*

80 gloves in my cap: *love tokens from his mistress*
81 did the act of darkness: *had sex*
83 contriving: *planning*
85 out-paramoured: *had more lovers than*
86 sloth: *laziness*
90 plackets: *slits in petticoats*
98 three on'us: *Lear, Kent and the Fool*
99 Unaccommodated: *left without material possessions*
100 forked: *two-legged*
101 lendings: *clothes (which come from nature)*
103 lecher: *dirty old man*
106 Flibbertigibbet: *the dancing devil*
107 web and the pin: *cataracts*
108 mildews the white: *rots the ripe*

Edgar

A serving-man, proud in heart and mind, that curled my hair, wore gloves in my cap, served the lust of my mistress' heart, and did the act of darkness with her. Swore as many oaths as I spake words, and broke them in the sweet face of heaven. One that slept in the contriving of lust, and waked to do it. Wine loved I deeply, dice dearly, and in woman out-paramoured the Turk. False of heart, light of ear, bloody of hand; hog in sloth, fox in stealth, wolf in greediness, dog in madness, lion in prey. Let not the creaking of shoes nor the rustling of silks betray thy poor heart to woman. Keep thy foot out of brothels, thy hand out of plackets, thy pen from lenders' books, and defy the foul fiend. Still through the hawthorn blows the cold wind, says suum, hey, nonny. Dolphin my boy, my boy, sessa! Let him trot by.

Storm still

Lear

Thou wert better in thy grave than to answer with thy uncovered body this extremity of the skies. Is man no more than this? Consider him well. Thou owest the worm no silk, the beast no hide, the sheep no wool, the cat no perfume. Ha! Here's three on'us are sophisticated! Thou art the thing itself! Unaccommodated man is no more but such a poor, bare, forked animal as thou art. Off, off, you lendings! Come unbutton here.

Tearing off his clothes

Fool

Prithee, nuncle, be contented; 'tis a naughty night to swim in. Now a little fire in a wild field were like an old lecher's heart – a small spark, all the rest on's body cold. Look, here comes a walking fire.

Enter Gloucester, with a torch

Edgar

This is the foul fiend Flibbertigibbet. He begins at curfew and walks till the first cock. He gives the web and the pin, squints the eye, and makes the hare-lip, mildews the white wheat, and hurts the poor creature of earth.

Chants

Swithold footed thrice the wold,
He met the night-mare, and her nine-fold;
Bid her alight,
And her troth plight,
And, aroint thee, witch, aroint thee!

110 Swithold: *St Swithin*
wold: *open country*

114 aroint: *go away*

Kent

How fares your grace?

Lear

What's he?

Kent

Who's there? What is it you seek?

Gloucester

What are you there? Your names?

Edgar

Poor Tom; that eats the swimming frog, the toad, the tadpole, the wall-newt and the water; that in the fury of his heart, when the foul fiend rages, eats cow-dung for sallets, swallows the old rat and the ditch-dog, drinks the green mantle of the standing pool, who is whipped from tithing to tithing, and stock-punished, and imprisoned, who hath had three suits to his back, six shirts to his body

Horse to ride, and weapon to wear;
But mice and rats, and such small deer,
Have been Tom's food for seven long year.

Beware my follower. Peace, Smulkin! Peace, thou fiend!

122 sallets: *salads*

124 tithing: *parish*

129 Smulkin: *devil*

Gloucester

What, hath your grace no better company?

Edgar

The Prince of Darkness is a gentleman.
Modo he's called, and Mahu.

131 Prince of Darkness: *devil*

132 Modo...Mahu: *other names for the devil*

Gloucester

Our flesh and blood is grown so vile, my lord,
That it doth hate what gets it.

134 gets: *produced*

Edgar

Poor Tom's a-cold.

Gloucester

Go in with me. My duty cannot suffer
To obey in all your daughters' hard commands.

135 suffer: *allow me to*

137 injunction: *order*

141 philosopher: *deep thinker*

144 Theban: *Greek scholar*

148 Importune: *urge*

149 His wits begin to unsettle: *He is starting to go insane*

154 outlawed from my blood: *disinherited*

Though their injunction be to bar my doors,
And let this tyrannous night take hold upon you,
Yet have I ventured to come seek you out,
And bring you where both fire and food is ready.

Lear

First let me talk with this philosopher.
What is the cause of thunder?

Kent

Good my lord, take his offer; go into the house.

Lear

I'll talk a word with this same learned Theban.
What is your study?

Edgar

How to prevent the fiend, and to kill vermin.

Lear

Let me ask you one word in private.

Kent

Importune him once more to go, my Lord.
His wits begin to unsettle.

Gloucester

Canst thou blame him?

Storm still

His daughters seek his death. Ah, that good Kent!
He said it would be thus, poor banished man!
Thou say'st the king grows mad. I'll tell thee, friend,
I am almost mad myself. I had a son,
Now outlawed from my blood; he sought my life,
But lately, very late. I loved him, friend,
No father his son dearer. True to tell thee,
The grief hath crazed my wits. What a night's this!
I do beseech your Grace –

Lear

O, cry your mercy, sir.
Noble philosopher, your company.

Edgar

Tom's a-cold.

Gloucester

In, fellow, there, into the hovel: keep thee warm.

Lear

Come let's in all.

Kent

This way, my lord.

Lear

With him.

I will keep still with my philosopher.

Kent

Good my lord, soothe him, let him take the fellow.

Gloucester

Take him you on.

Kent

Sirrah, come on; go along with us.

Lear

Come, good Athenian.

Gloucester

No words, no words: hush.

Edgar

Child Rowland to the dark tower came,
His word was still 'Fie, foh, and fum,
I smell the blood of a British man'.

Exeunt

167 Athenian: *Greek philosopher*

169 Child Rowland: *legendary knight*

170–1 'Fie, foh...man': *refrain from the children's rhyme 'Jack and the Beanstalk'*

Key Scene Analysis

A distraught father (lines 1–22)

While Kent encourages his master to take shelter, Lear explains why the storm has so little effect on him; he has a greater affliction with which he is concerned: 'This tempest in my mind/ Doth from my senses take all feeling else/ Save what beats there. Filial ingratitude!' Lear regards himself and his daughters as part of one body which they have violated by turning against him. He is acutely aware that by thinking obsessively about what has been done to him, he is in danger of losing his mind – 'that way madness lies; let me shun that'.

Filial ingratitude!

Lear
Act 3 Scene 4, l.14

This climactic scene presents the audience with a stark vision. Poor Tom's wretched nakedness symbolises the essence of humanity.

Lear's great prayer (lines 23–36)

The king eventually goes into the hovel, thankful that the storm will 'not give me leave to ponder/ On things would hurt me more'. He displays a more considerate side to his character, ushering in the Fool, 'In, boy, go first'. His new-found humility is expressed in a powerful prayer which addresses society's 'Poor naked wretches'.

Graphic description reveals Lear's awareness of their suffering almost as if he is seeing them for the first time: 'houseless heads and unfed sides'. He imagines their 'looped and windowed raggedness' and the vulnerability of homeless people. The uncharacteristically sympathetic king now accepts that he has taken 'Too little care of this' in the past. Lear is conscious that if the rich and powerful were to be exposed in this way, there would be a more equal sharing of wealth, 'shake the superflux to them'.

Views of madness (lines 37–93)

In his confusion, Lear thinks that Poor Tom's madness has been caused by a foolish error of judgement: 'Didst thou give all to thy daughters?' He is now so completely obsessed with ingratitude that he refuses to accept any other explanation. When Kent points out that Tom 'hath no daughters', we see a momentary flash of the old domineering Lear: 'Death, traitor!'

We are presented with the heart-breaking sight of the once-noble Lear descending headlong into mental collapse, absolutely convinced that all Tom's troubles are due to his 'pelican daughters'. In contrast, there is some amusement at the surreal antics of Poor Tom, 'whom the foul fiend vexes'.

Ironically, Lear is profoundly moved by Tom's presence whereas the Fool's barbed comments have been less effective. As the professional madman in this memorable scene, the Fool is a helpless bystander who is left to articulate the ominous conclusion: 'This cold night will turn us all to fools and madmen'.

Much of the scene's remarkable tragedy comes from the confrontation between the pathetic figure of the genuinely insane Lear and Edgar, who is only pretending to be mad.

Man's basic nature (lines 94–171)

As Lear watches Poor Tom reciting nursery rhyme nonsense and his own jumbled version of the ten commandments, he suddenly experiences a clear moment of insight into the natural essence of man: 'Unaccommodated man is no more but such a poor, bare, forked animal as thou art'.

Unaccommodated man
Lear
Act 3 Scene 4, l.99

The elderly monarch wishes to reduce himself to the same naked state and begins to remove his own clothes: 'Off, off, you lendings!' His royal robes are worthless to him now. The inability to distinguish himself from the wretched beggar is yet another symptom of Lear's utterly confused mind. He still views everything almost entirely through the lens of his own experiences. Gloucester arrives, intent on helping the old king. He is appalled that Lear is attended only by his Fool, an apparent peasant (Kent), and a wild lunatic whom he fails to recognise as Edgar.

Appearance and reality are interwoven throughout this chaotic scene. We are being shown a world where the correct order and stability of man and nature is in chaos.

Gloucester laments the alleged treachery of his son, Edgar: 'Now outlawed from my blood; he sought my life'. Ironically, this same son (disguised as Poor Tom) listens to his father's sorry story. Like the king, Gloucester also regrets the break-up of his family: 'The grief hath crazed my wits'.

As the scene ends, there is a sense that nothing is as it should be. Lear thinks Tom is an educated philosopher whom he needs to consult. Everything goes from bad to worse for all these desperate characters who huddle together in the remote hovel, listening to the deafening sounds of the storm and Poor Tom's madcap commentary.

Shakespeare's Dramatic Style

In the powerful 'Poor naked wretches' speech, Shakespeare allows the audience to experience Lear's emerging insight through his use of effective **poetic language**. The old man is seeing poverty and its dire consequences for the first time. Harsh, explosive 'p' sounds echo the repetitive beating of rainfall, 'the pelting of this pitiless storm'. **Alliteration** draws attention to the plight of those without shelter ('houseless heads').

My duty cannot suffer
To obey in all your daughters' hard commands

Gloucester
Act 3 Scene 4, l.135–6

Graphic clothing imagery highlights the miserable defences that the poor have against such harsh elements: 'looped and windowed raggedness'. At the height of Lear's madness and shocked by the half-naked Bedlam beggar, the old king tears symbolically at his clothes, 'Off, off, you lendings'. His great insight into the true essence of humanity is also couched in clothing terms – 'poor, bare, forked animal'. Shakespeare's emphatic use of language adds to the intensity of the drama, involving the audience in the experiences of characters in turmoil.

Critical Analysis

'In Act 3 Scene 4, Shakespeare makes effective use of a variety of dramatic techniques that evoke a wide range of responses from the audience.'

Discuss this view with reference to at least two dramatic techniques used by the playwright in this key scene. Develop your answer with reference to the text.

Sample Paragraph 1

Shakespeare makes use of a variety of dramatic techniques that evoke a wide range of responses from the audience. The scene is on the heath and Lear is totally insane, but he shows sympathy for a beggarman, acted by Edgar. Shakespeare uses this to show another side to Lear in this scene. The king has lost it because of how the two evil daughters treated him badly. Kent is another effective dramatic character technique. He keeps trying to get Lear to see reason. He points out that Edgar who is in a disguise as Tom, the mad beggar, does not have daughters, 'he has no daughters'. But Lear keeps talking about daughters and their ingratitude until he gets our sympathy. This is a repetition technique. Kent eventually gets Lear to go into the hovel, to 'soothe' him. Shakespeare also uses contrast between these different characters. *(145 words)*

Examiner's Comment

- An uneven response which is poorly organised.
- Two possible techniques – characterisation and contrast – need clearer development.
- More use of suitable reference and quotation expected.
- Weak control of language and expression in this basic-grade answer.

Sample Paragraph 2

Shakespeare uses a terrifying setting, the fierce storm on the heath, to mirror the confusion Lear is experiencing after the callous treatment of his daughters: 'Filial ingratitude'. The audience has sympathy with the old man when he says, 'Your old kind father, whose frank heart gave all'. But I feel Shakespeare really shows the power of language to move an audience in Lear's famous prayer about the 'naked wretches'. We can imagine the shocking consequences of extreme poverty. Alliteration emphasises the reality of their 'houseless heads'. The audience reaction varies from compassion to dark humour to grim realisation in hearing the absurd conversation between three mad men: Lear, the genuinely mad, Poor Tom pretending to be mad and the Fool. Their insane discussion reflects the real state of a basic human being, 'a poor, bare, forked animal'. This pitiful image makes audiences agree with Lear that we too 'have taken too little care of this'. *(155 words)*

Examiner's Comment

- Well-written, focused paragraph that responds directly to the question.
- Coherent points, effectively developed and supported.
- Excellent language control, e.g. 'Alliteration emphasises the reality'.
- Top-grade standard that includes some good personal engagement.

Class/Homework Exercise

From studying Act 3 Scene 4, to what extent do you think that Lear himself is to blame for how Goneril and Regan are treating him?

Write a paragraph (about 150 words), developing your response with reference to the text.

Exam Focus

Act 3 Scene 4 can be used successfully in response to a range of examination questions about the play's central themes, characters, relationships and the playwright's dramatic style.

This **key scene** has important dramatic functions:

- Reveals the changing, more compassionate Lear.
- Storm setting intensifies the dramatic experience.
- Develops themes of power, justice and personal responsibility.
- Scenes of madness heighten the dramatic tension.
- Powerful language and imagery engage the audience.

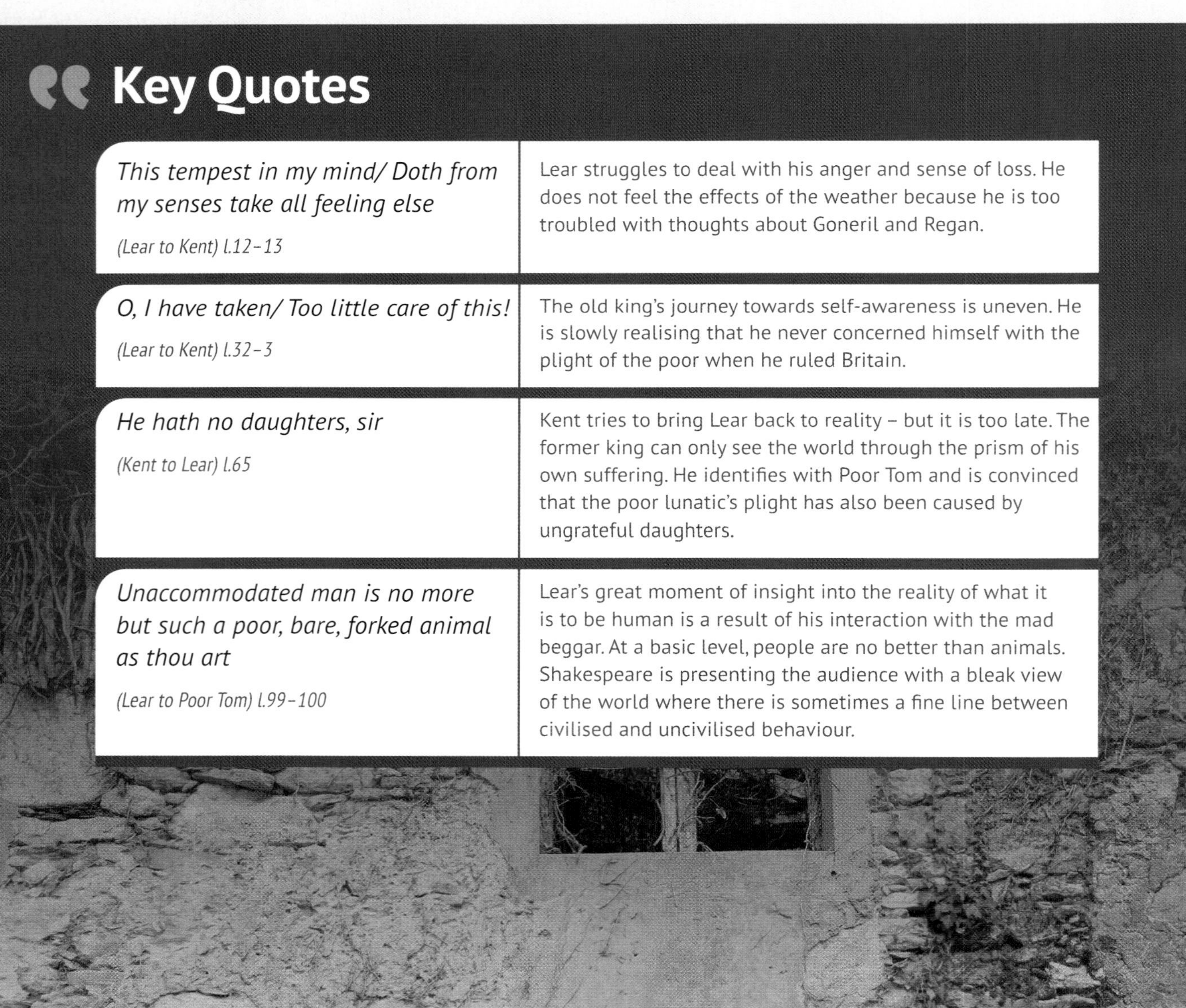

Key Quotes

This tempest in my mind/ Doth from my senses take all feeling else (Lear to Kent) l.12–13	Lear struggles to deal with his anger and sense of loss. He does not feel the effects of the weather because he is too troubled with thoughts about Goneril and Regan.
O, I have taken/ Too little care of this! (Lear to Kent) l.32–3	The old king's journey towards self-awareness is uneven. He is slowly realising that he never concerned himself with the plight of the poor when he ruled Britain.
He hath no daughters, sir (Kent to Lear) l.65	Kent tries to bring Lear back to reality – but it is too late. The former king can only see the world through the prism of his own suffering. He identifies with Poor Tom and is convinced that the poor lunatic's plight has also been caused by ungrateful daughters.
Unaccommodated man is no more but such a poor, bare, forked animal as thou art (Lear to Poor Tom) l.99–100	Lear's great moment of insight into the reality of what it is to be human is a result of his interaction with the mad beggar. At a basic level, people are no better than animals. Shakespeare is presenting the audience with a bleak view of the world where there is sometimes a fine line between civilised and uncivilised behaviour.

Act 3
Scene 5

INTRODUCTION

- Edmund tells Cornwall that Gloucester is trying to help Lear.
- He shows him the letter which implicates his father in the French invasion.
- Cornwall awards Edmund his father's title and lands.

A room in Gloucester's castle

Enter Cornwall and Edmund

Cornwall

I will have my revenge ere I depart his house.

Edmund

How, my lord, I may be censured, that nature thus gives way to loyalty, something fears me to think of.

Cornwall

I now perceive, it was not altogether your brother's evil disposition made him seek his death, but a provoking merit, set a-work by a reprovable badness in himself.

Edmund

How malicious is my fortune, that I must repent to be just! This is the letter he spoke of, which approves him an intelligent party to the advantages of France. O heavens! That this treason were not, or not I the detector!

Cornwall

Go with me to the duchess.

Edmund

If the matter of this paper be certain, you have mighty business in hand.

Cornwall

True or false, it hath made thee Earl of Gloucester. Seek out where thy father is, that he may be ready for our apprehension.

Edmund

Aside

If I find him comforting the king, it will stuff his suspicion more fully. I will persevere in my course of loyalty, though the conflict be sore between that and my blood.

Cornwall

I will lay trust upon thee and thou shalt find a dearer father in my love.

Exeunt

2 censured: *judged*
nature: *family feelings*
3 loyalty: *allegiance to the state*
5–6 provoking merit: *just reason*
6 reprovable badness: *disgraceful evil*
8 approves: *proves*
16 apprehension: *arrest*
17 stuff: *intensify*
18 persevere: *carry on*
19 blood: *family*

Analysis

Cold-blooded hypocrisy (lines 1–21)

Edmund knows that Gloucester is facing severe punishment when the Duke of Cornwall declares, 'I will have my revenge ere I depart his house'. He has always been inventive in controlling those around him. Edmund has already achieved much, but he is impatient to claim his inheritance and is now prepared to sacrifice his father.

Not for the first time, Edmund uses the device of an incriminating letter. His skill as a manipulator is seen as he pretends to be torn between allegiances to his own family and duty to Cornwall: 'that nature thus gives way to loyalty'. The audience will be in no doubt that his latest performance is for the benefit of Cornwall.

This short scene focuses on unnatural dealings. An ambitious son plots to destroy his naive father and a ruthless duke seeks revenge for disloyalty.

The only true words Edmund speaks are in the aside: 'If I find him comforting the king, it will stuff his suspicion more fully'. He is utterly cold-blooded and wants to damn Gloucester as much as he possibly can. His treachery is rewarded when Cornwall tells him, 'thou shalt find a dearer father in my love'.

In an unstable kingdom where almost nothing is certain, Gloucester's cunning son knows the importance of having a powerful supporter. Edmund finally succeeds in taking over Gloucester's title and lands. He replaces his natural father with the influential Duke of Cornwall.

Key Quotes

Quote	Comment
I will have my revenge ere I depart his house *(Cornwall to Edmund) l.1*	Edmund has shown Cornwall the letter about the planned French invasion and implicates Gloucester. Characteristically violent, Cornwall is determined to punish Gloucester as soon as possible.
If I find him comforting the king, it will stuff his suspicion more fully *(Edmund) l.17–18*	In an aside, the opportunistic, self-serving Edmund reveals that he hopes to find his father with Lear so that the old man will be further compromised.
I will persevere in my course of loyalty, though the conflict be sore between that and my blood *(Edmund to Cornwall) l.18–19*	Always duplicitous, Edmund continues his charade that he is torn between loyalty to the Cornwall and duty to his own family. The audience is aware of the dramatic irony of this situation and will have no sympathy for Gloucester's treacherous son.

Act 3
Scene 6

INTRODUCTION

- Lear insists on conducting a mock trial of Goneril and Regan's crimes.
- He now sees both daughters for what they truly are.
- Gloucester has news that Cornwall is seeking to have Lear killed.
- The king is advised to go to Dover and join Cordelia.

A farmhouse near Gloucester's castle

Enter Kent, Gloucester

Gloucester

Here is better than the open air. Take it thankfully. I will piece out the comfort with what addition I can. I will not be long from you.

Kent

All the power of his wits have given way to his impatience. The gods reward your kindness!

Exit Gloucester

Edgar

Frateretto calls me, and tells me Nero is an angler in the lake of darkness. Pray, innocent, and beware the foul fiend.

Fool

Prithee, nuncle, tell me whether a madman be a gentleman or a yeoman.

Lear

A king, a king!

Fool

No, he's a yeoman that has a gentleman to his son, for he's a mad yeoman that sees his son a gentleman before him.

Lear

To have a thousand with red burning spits
Come hizzing in upon 'em!

Edgar

The foul fiend bites my back.

Fool

He's mad that trusts in the tameness of a wolf, a horse's health, a boy's love, or a whore's oath.

Lear

It shall be done. I will arraign them straight.

To Edgar

Come, sit thou here, most learned justicer.

To the Fool

Thou, sapient sir, sit here. Now, you she foxes!

2 piece out: *add to*

4 impatience: *frenzy*

6 Frateretto, Nero: *more names for demons*

7 innocent: *the Fool*

10 yeoman: *farmer*

14 spits: *splutters*

19 arraign them straight: *put them on trial immediately*

21 sapient: *wise*

Edgar

Look, where he stands and glares!
Wantest thou eyes at trial, madam?
 Come o'er the bourn, Bessy, to me –

Fool

 Her boat hath a leak,
 And she must not speak
 Why she dares not come over to thee.

Edgar

The foul fiend haunts poor Tom in the voice of a nightingale. Hopdance cries in Tom's belly for two white herring. Croak not, black angel. I have no food for thee.

Kent

How do you, sir? Stand you not so amazed. Will you lie down and rest upon the cushions?

Lear

I'll see their trial first. Bring in the evidence.

To Edgar

Thou robed man of justice, take thy place.

To the Fool

And thou, his yoke-fellow of equity,
Bench by his side.

To Kent

You are o' the commission,
Sit you too.

Edgar

Let us deal justly.
 Sleepest or wakest thou, jolly shepherd?
 Thy sheep be in the corn;
 And for one blast of thy minikin mouth,
 Thy sheep shall take no harm.
Pur! the cat is gray.

Lear

Arraign her first. 'Tis Goneril. I here take my oath before this honourable assembly, she kicked the poor king her father.

Fool

Come hither, mistress. Is your name Goneril?

23 eyes: *witnesses*
24 bourn: *river*
29 Hopdance: *evil spirit*
35 yoke-fellow of equity: *partner in fairness*
36 bench: *judges' bench*
37 o' the commission: *one of the commissioned, a King's Justice of the Peace*
42 minikin: *little, shrill*
44 gray: *devil's and witches' cats were grey*
45 arraign: *accuse, bring to trial*

Lear

She cannot deny it.

Fool

Cry you mercy, I took you for a joint-stool.

Lear

And here's another, whose warped looks proclaim
What store her heart is made on. Stop her there!
Arms, arms, sword, fire! Corruption in the place!
False justicer, why hast thou let her escape?

Edgar

Bless thy five wits!

Kent

O pity! Sir, where is the patience now,
That thou so oft have boasted to retain?

Edgar

Aside

My tears begin to take his part so much,
They'll mar my counterfeiting.

Lear

The little dogs and all – Tray, Blanch, and Sweetheart –
see, they bark at me.

Edgar

Tom will throw his head at them. Avaunt, you curs!
Be thy mouth of black or white,
Tooth that poisons if it bite,
Mastiff, grey-hound, mongrel grim,
Hound or spaniel, brach or lym,
Or bobtail tyke or trundle-tail,
Tom will make them weep and wail
For with throwing thus my head,
Dogs leap the hatch, and all are fled.
Do de, de, de. Sessa! Come, march to wakes and fairs and market-towns. Poor Tom, thy horn is dry.

Lear

Then let them anatomise Regan, see what breeds about her heart. Is there any cause in nature that makes these hard hearts?

To Edgar

50 joint-stool: *low wood stool (possibly representing Goneril at the mock-trial)*

51 another: *Regan*
warped: *twisted, unnatural*

52 store: *substance*

59 counterfeiting: *pretence*

62 Avaunt: *get away*

65 Mastiff: *large guard dog*

66 brach: *bitch-hound*
lym: *bloodhound*

67 bobtail tyke: *short-tailed dog*
trundle-tail: *long-tailed dog*

72 dry: *empty, thirsty*

73 anatomise: *dissect*

You sir – I entertain for one of my hundred, only I do not like the fashion of your garments. You will say they are Persian attire, but let them be changed.

78 Persian: *exotic*

Kent

Now, good my lord, lie here and rest awhile.

Lear

Make no noise, make no noise; draw the curtains, so, so.
We'll go to supper in the morning.

Fool

And I'll go to bed at noon.

82 go to bed at noon: *play the fool*

Re-enter Gloucester

Gloucester

Come hither, friend: where is the king my master?

Kent

Here, sir; but trouble him not, his wits are gone.

Gloucester

Good friend, I prithee, take him in thy arms.
I have o'erheard a plot of death upon him.
There is a litter ready, lay him in 't,
And drive towards Dover, friend, where thou shalt meet
Both welcome and protection. Take up thy master.
If thou shouldst dally half an hour, his life,
With thine, and all that offer to defend him,
Stand in assured loss. Take up, take up
And follow me, that will to some provision
Give thee quick conduct.

87 litter: *small coach*

92 assured: *certain*

Kent

Oppressed nature sleeps.
This rest might yet have balmed thy broken senses,
Which, if convenience will not allow,
Stand in hard cure.
To the Fool
Come, help to bear thy master;
Thou must not stay behind.

95 balmed: *soothed*

96 convenience: *circumstances*

Gloucester

Come, come, away.

Exeunt all but Edgar

Edgar

When we our betters see bearing our woes,
We scarcely think our miseries our foes.
Who alone suffers, suffers most in the mind,
Leaving free things and happy shows behind:
But then the mind much sufferance doth o'er skip,
When grief hath mates, and bearing, fellowship.
How light and portable my pain seems now,
When that which makes me bend makes the king bow,
He childed as I fathered. Tom, away!
Mark the high noises, and thyself bewray
When false opinion, whose wrong thought defiles thee,
In thy just proof repeals and reconciles thee.
What will hap more to-night, safe 'scape the king!
Lurk, lurk.

Exit

100 woes: *sorrows*

104 sufferance: *endurance*
o'er skip: *avoid*

105 mates: *companionship*

108 childed: *Lear bore disloyal children*
fathered: *Edgar had a disloyal father*

109 bewray: *reveal*

110 defiles: *taints*

111 repeals: *revokes*

113 lurk: *lie in wait*

Analysis

Three madmen (lines 1–15)

At a farmhouse near Gloucester's estate, Lear, the Fool and Poor Tom are brought together in a mesmerising scene of hellish madness. Although each character is trapped in his own separate world, they occasionally communicate with one another.

Kent declares that Lear is now completely insane: 'All the power of his wits have given way to his impatience'. Tom rants about demons ('Frateretto calls me'), while Lear's Fool continues to remind his old master of his rash decision to make his daughters superior to him in wealth and power.

There is a stark contrast between the earlier strength of Edmund and Cornwall and the frantic behaviour of Lear, the Fool and Poor Tom in this scene. The characters who represent evil seem invincible while the forces of good appear weak.

The 'mock trial' (lines 16–72)

Lear busies himself, carefully organising a judicial trial for Regan and Goneril: 'I will arraign them straight'. He calls on the Fool and Poor Tom to act as judges. At no stage does it occur to him that his daughters are not actually present. Seeing the world through his own suffering, he has already pronounced sentence on the two accused even before the trial begins: 'a thousand with red burning spits/ Come hizzing in upon 'em!'

As the atmosphere becomes increasingly surreal, Lear's absurd interrogations begin. He uses formal judicial language, yet still has a jester and a lunatic beggar as court justices. Straightaway, Lear accuses Goneril of the symbolic crime against him: 'she kicked the poor king her father'.

The Fool's response ('Cry you mercy, I took you for a joint-stool') is typically comic, but the fact that such dark humour comes from Lear's painful madness adds to the poignancy. Like the audience, the Fool recognises his master's tortured mental state.

Kent also tries to console Lear, reminding him, 'where is the patience now,/ That thou so oft have boasted to retain?' However, it is too late to help the old king, who is lost within his own fantasy world, and the audience can only observe the tragic grandeur of Lear's torment.

Lear is preoccupied with vengeance against Goneril and Regan. Their mock trial is a distorted reminder of the earlier 'love test'.

Edgar is genuinely overcome by the pitiful state of the once all-powerful king and he feels he cannot continue the charade: 'My tears begin to take his part so much,/ They'll mar my counterfeiting'. Lear continues to hallucinate, imagining that he sees his own pet dogs, 'Tray, Blanch, and Sweetheart'. Associating them with his own children, he even pictures them barking viciously at him as though he were a stranger.

Beyond reach (lines 73–94)

Lear urges the judges to find out what can make his daughters so cruel and to 'anatomise Regan' to see 'what breeds about her heart'. He desperately hopes that someone can explain why she is so cold-blooded and does not love him.

This is the loyal Fool's final appearance. He has always tried to make his master see the irrationality of his ways. But Lear is now beyond reach and the Fool's function is at an end. His absurd parting words, 'I'll go to bed at noon', are an appropriate reflection of this tragic scene.

And I'll go to bed at noon

The Fool
Act 3 Scene 6, l.82

Meanwhile, Gloucester tells Kent that there is 'a plot of death upon' Lear and that they must get him to the safety of Dover. It is clear that the exhausted old king needs to rest. Yet even this will be denied to him. Lear is paying a terrible price for his former foolishness and arrogance. The forces of evil appear very strong against the small band of Lear supporters.

Shakespeare presents us with a disordered world. In his madness, Lear is caught between vengeance and a desire for justice. Britain is now on the verge of civil war.

A bleak conclusion (lines 94–113)

Kent notes that if Lear had had an undisturbed sleep, perhaps his mind would have settled: 'This rest might yet have balmed thy broken senses'. Edgar is left alone on stage to reflect on how his own sorrows now seem insignificant in comparison to those of the king: 'How light and portable my pain seems now'. However, he realises that both he and Lear are in the same situation: 'He childed as I fathered'.

Both are victims of hostile family members. Edgar's concluding soliloquy reminds the audience of his real character and suggests that he has the necessary qualities of a future king. Like all of Lear's followers, he shows compassion and an ability to think of others before any immediate self-interest.

Key Quotes

Quote	Comment
Where take my oath before this honourable assembly, she kicked the poor king her father *(Lear) l.45–7*	With a mixture of reserved judicial language and childish outrage, Lear formally accuses Goneril of abusing him. He still sees himself as a blameless victim.
My tears begin to take his part so much,/ They'll mar my counterfeiting *(Poor Tom/Edgar) l.58–9*	Poor Tom reverts to his true self, Edgar, overcome with sorrow at the terrible torment of Lear. He is concerned that he will not be able to keep up the charade of playing the poor, mad beggar.
How light and portable my pain seems now *(Edgar) l.106*	Edgar is aware that his own unhappiness seems easier to bear when he looks at the heavy weight of suffering the old king is experiencing.

Act 3
Scene 7

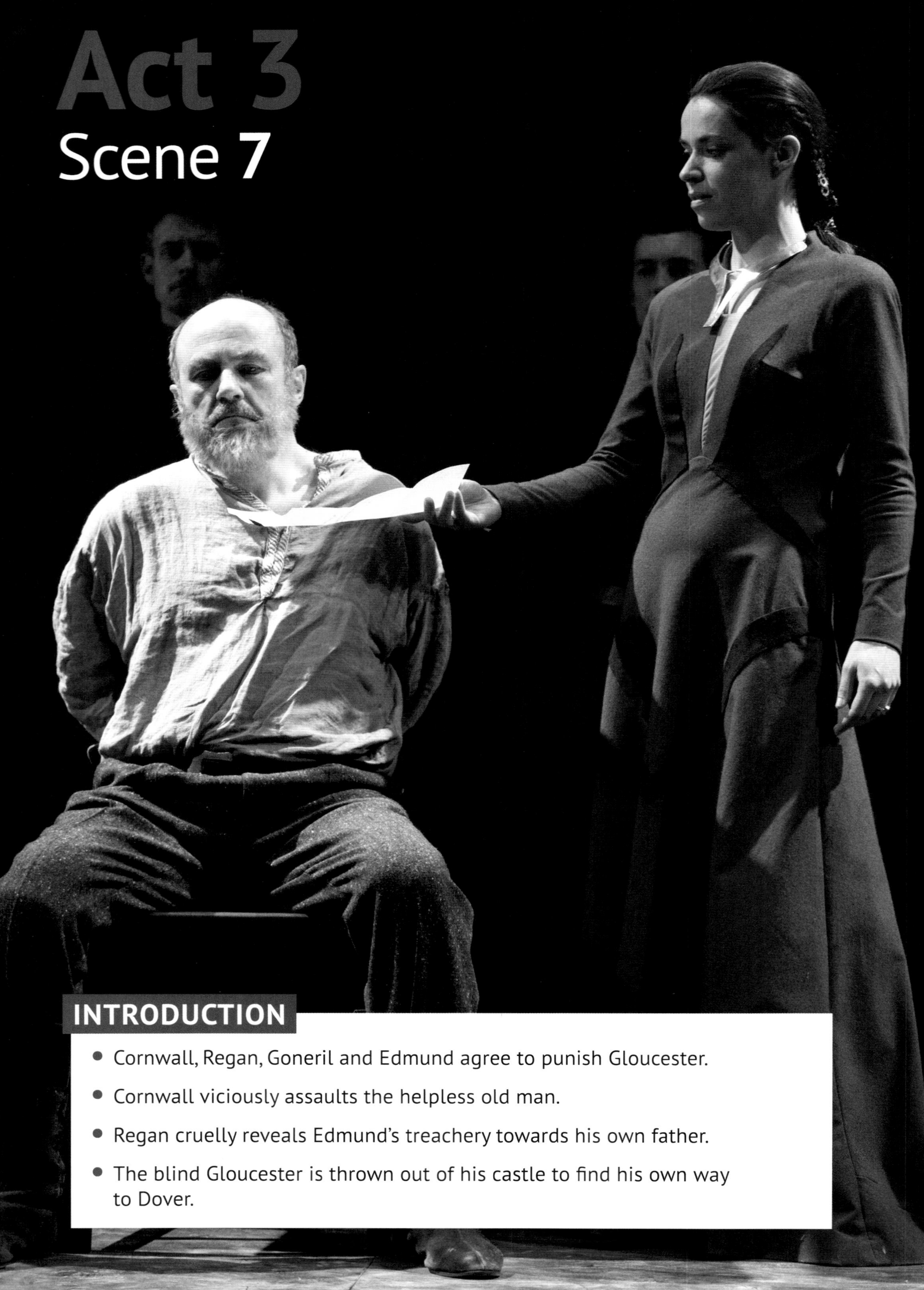

INTRODUCTION

- Cornwall, Regan, Goneril and Edmund agree to punish Gloucester.
- Cornwall viciously assaults the helpless old man.
- Regan cruelly reveals Edmund's treachery towards his own father.
- The blind Gloucester is thrown out of his castle to find his own way to Dover.

The Great Hall of Gloucester's palace

Enter Cornwall, Regan, Goneril, Edmund and servants

Cornwall

Post speedily to my lord your husband; show him this letter. The army of France is landed. Seek out the villain Gloucester.

Exeunt some servants

Regan

Hang him instantly.

Goneril

Pluck out his eyes.

Cornwall

Leave him to my displeasure. Edmund, keep you our sister company. The revenges we are bound to take upon your traitorous father are not fit for your beholding. Advise the duke, where you are going, to a most festinate preparation. We are bound to the like. Our posts shall be swift and intelligent betwixt us. Farewell, dear sister: farewell, my lord of Gloucester.

Enter Oswald

How now! Where's the king?

Oswald

My lord of Gloucester hath conveyed him hence.
Some five or six and thirty of his knights,
Hot questrists after him, met him at gate,
Who, with some other of the Lord's dependants,
Are gone with him towards Dover; where they boast
To have well-armed friends.

Cornwall

Get horses for your mistress.

Goneril

Farewell, sweet lord, and sister.

Cornwall

Edmund, farewell.

Exeunt Goneril, Edmund and Oswald

Go seek the traitor Gloucester;
Pinion him like a thief; bring him before us.

Exeunt remaining servants

1 Post: *ride*

4 him: *Gloucester*

8 traitorous: *treacherous (to the new regime of the Dukes and their wives)*

9 festinate: *hasty*

10 bound to the like: *prepared to do the same*

16 Hot questrists: *followers urgently seeking Lear*

24 Without the form of justice: *without a formal trial*
25 do a courtesy to: *yield to*
28 corky: *shrivelled*
34 ignobly: *dishonourably*
36 Naughty: *wicked*
37 ravish: *tear*
38 quicken: *increase*

Though well we may not pass upon his life
Without the form of justice, yet our power
Shall do a courtesy to our wrath, which men
May blame, but not control. Who's there? The traitor?

Enter Gloucester brought in by two or three servants

Regan

Ingrateful fox! 'Tis he.

Cornwall

Bind fast his corky arms.

Gloucester

What mean your graces? Good my friends, consider
You are my guests. Do me no foul play, friends.

Cornwall

Bind him, I say.

Servants bind him

Regan

Hard, hard. O filthy traitor!

Gloucester

Unmerciful lady as you are, I'm none.

Cornwall

To this chair bind him. Villain, thou shalt find –

Regan plucks his beard

Gloucester

By the kind gods, 'tis most ignobly done
To pluck me by the beard.

Regan

So white, and such a traitor!

Gloucester

Naughty lady,
These hairs, which thou dost ravish from my chin
Will quicken, and accuse thee. I am your host.
With robbers' hands my hospitable favours
You should not ruffle thus. What will you do?

Cornwall

Come, sir, what letters had you late from France?

Regan

Be simple-answered, for we know the truth.

Cornwall

And what confederacy have you with the traitors
Late footed in the kingdom?

Regan

To whose hands have you sent the lunatic king?
Speak.

Gloucester

I have a letter guessingly set down,
Which came from one that's of a neutral heart,
And not from one opposed.

Cornwall

Cunning.

Regan

And false.

Cornwall

Where hast thou sent the king?

Gloucester

To Dover.

Regan

Wherefore to Dover? Wast thou not charged at peril –

Cornwall

Wherefore to Dover? Let him answer that.

Gloucester

I am tied to the stake, and I must stand the course.

Regan

Wherefore to Dover, sir?

Gloucester

Because I would not see thy cruel nails
Pluck out his poor old eyes; nor thy fierce sister
In his anointed flesh stick boarish fangs.
The sea, with such a storm as his bare head
In hell-black night endured, would have buoyed up,
And quenched the stelled fires.
Yet, poor old heart, he holp the heavens to rain.
If wolves had at thy gate howled that stern time,
Thou shouldst have said 'Good porter, turn the key,'

43 confederacy: *conspiracy*

48 neutral: *fair*

51 charged at peril: *warned on danger of your life*

53 stake: *pole*

56 anointed: *holy*
boarish: *crude*

58 buoyed up: *risen, swelled up*

59 stelled: *starry*

61 stern: *grim*

All cruels else subscribed. But I shall see
The winged vengeance overtake such children.

Cornwall

See't shalt thou never. Fellows, hold the chair.
Upon these eyes of thine I'll set my foot.

Gloucester

He that will think to live till he be old,
Give me some help! O cruel! O you gods!

Regan

One side will mock another – the other too.

Cornwall

If you see vengeance –

First Servant

Hold your hand, my lord!
I have served you ever since I was a child,
But better service have I never done you
Than now to bid you hold.

Regan

How now, you dog!

First Servant

If you did wear a beard upon your chin,
I'd shake it on this quarrel. What do you mean?

Cornwall

My villain!

They draw and fight

First Servant

Nay, then, come on, and take the chance of anger.

Regan

Give me thy sword. A peasant stand up thus!

Takes a sword, and runs at him behind

First Servant

O, I am slain! My lord, you have one eye left
To see some mischief on him. O!

Dies

Cornwall

Lest it see more, prevent it. Out, vile jelly!
Where is thy lustre now?

74 If you did wear a beard: *if you were a man*

78 stand up: *challenge, defy us*

82 lustre: *brilliance*

Gloucester

All dark and comfortless. Where's my son Edmund?
Edmund, enkindle all the sparks of nature,
To quit this horrid act.

Regan

Out, treacherous villain!
Thou call'st on him that hates thee. It was he
That made the overture of thy treasons to us,
Who is too good to pity thee.

87 overture: *first report*

Gloucester

O my follies! Then Edgar was abused.
Kind gods, forgive me that, and prosper him!

89 follies: *mistakes*
abused: *wronged*

Regan

Go thrust him out at gates, and let him smell
His way to Dover.

Exit one with Gloucester

How is't, my lord? How look you?

Cornwall

I have received a hurt. Follow me, lady.
Turn out that eyeless villain. Throw this slave
Upon the dunghill. Regan, I bleed apace.
Untimely comes this hurt. Give me your arm.

Exit Cornwall supported by Regan

Second Servant

I'll never care what wickedness I do,
If this man come to good.

Third Servant

If she live long,
And in the end meet the old course of death,
Women will all turn monsters.

Second Servant

Let's follow the old earl, and get the bedlam
To lead him where he would. His roguish madness
Allows itself to anything.

101 bedlam: *madman (Poor Tom)*

Third Servant

Go thou. I'll fetch some flax and whites of eggs
To apply to his bleeding face. Now heaven help him!

Exeunt separately.

104 flax: *linen*

Analysis

Evil triumphs (lines 1–20)

The dominance of evil characters seems invincible. Cornwall is stronger than ever in asserting his authority, acting decisively to stamp out any challenges. Regan's ferocity is even more frightening in its intensity.

The vicious sisters compete to outdo each other in venomous cruelty towards the captured Gloucester; Regan's call to 'Hang him instantly' is immediately matched by Goneril's suggestion: 'Pluck out his eyes'.

Cornwall takes control, ordering Edmund to leave so that he will not have to witness the punishments his father will receive – they 'are not fit for your beholding'. As the tension mounts, there seems to be no relief for Lear's loyal followers.

Perversion of justice (lines 21–49)

Although Cornwall cannot legally pass sentence of death on Gloucester without a trial, punishment can still be cynically inflicted at the whim of those in power without public approval, 'which men/ May blame, but not control'. The audience is well aware that it is Cornwall and his violent accomplices who are the evildoers as they treat the old man with the utmost disrespect: 'Bind fast his corky arms'. This is an obvious mockery of justice.

Since Lear's abdication, the natural order has been breaking down in the kingdom. Traditional values are rejected; guests no longer respect their host, and the young refuse to obey their elders. Edmund heartlessly betrays his father while Regan seems incapable of any compassion: 'Hard, hard. O filthy traitor!' She is just one example of how powerful people abuse their authority.

Moral courage (lines 50–84)

Although tied like an animal to a stake, Gloucester shows courage in pointing out how the natural order has been up-ended. He no longer hides his feelings and now stands up for Lear: 'I would not see thy cruel nails/ Pluck out his poor old eyes'. The audience can recognise a more noble – and even heroic – side to Gloucester, who paints a pitiful picture of the old king and criticises Regan for not offering shelter to her father.

Cornwall makes no effort to curb his viciousness and rips out one of Gloucester's eyes. Regan, not to be outdone in brutality, demands the gouging out of the other eye: 'One side will mock another – the other too'. Some fragile hope emerges when one of the servants, sickened by such casual cruelty, tries to put a stop to Cornwall's viciousness: 'now to bid you hold'. He even dares to challenge Regan, 'If you did wear a beard upon your chin,/ I'd shake it on this quarrel'. Cornwall draws on him and Regan stabs the servant from behind. The forces of evil remain in control.

More than anything else, imagery connected with sight and blindness makes the greatest impact in this grotesque scene. Just as Lear gained knowledge through madness, the blinding of Gloucester leads to his eyes being metaphorically opened to the truth about his two sons.

The servant calls for Gloucester to avenge him. But Cornwall, in another sickening act of unbelievable callousness, blinds Gloucester, 'Out, vile jelly'. Gloucester now cries out pathetically for vengeance: 'Edmund, enkindle all the sparks of nature,/ To quit this horrid act'. Of course, the audience already know that this same son is responsible for his torture. Through the use of dramatic irony, Shakespeare heightens the poignancy of this scene.

Bitter truths (lines 85–105)

Regan takes sadistic delight in informing Gloucester the awful truth about Edmund's treachery: 'It was he/ That made the overture of thy treasons to us'. Almost overwhelmed by the enormity of his mistake, the old earl must now accept that he banished his loyal son wrongly. Yet he retains some faith in divine justice and prays for pardon, 'Kind gods, forgive me that, and prosper him!' Throughout this harrowing scene, Gloucester has grown in moral stature. In contrast, Regan continues to diminish as she sinks further into mindless depravity: 'let him smell/ His way to Dover'.

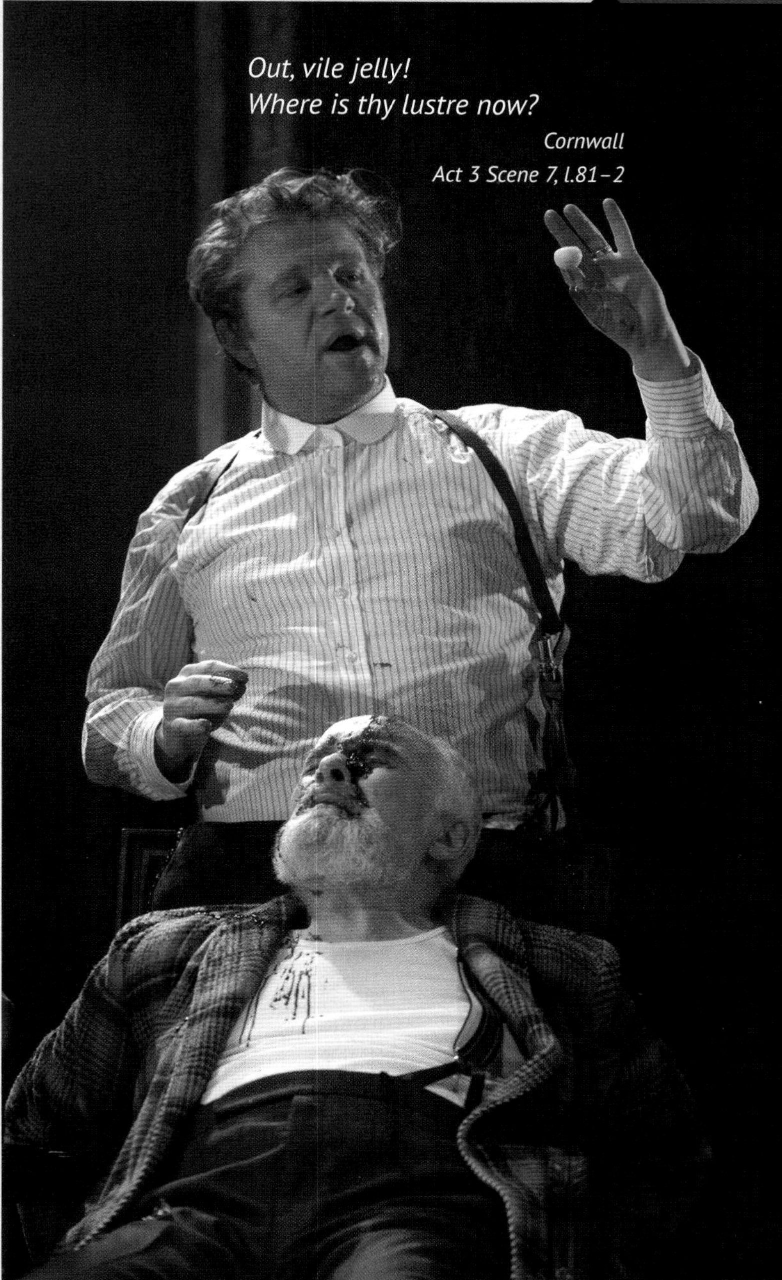

Out, vile jelly!
Where is thy lustre now?
Cornwall
Act 3 Scene 7, l.81–2

One of the most gruesome events in Shakespearean tragedy occurs in this scene. Shakespeare shocks us with a graphic portrayal of cruelty. Goneril and Regan reveal their vicious nature as they relish inflicting pain and suffering.

But the forces of evil are also facing a sharp truth. They are not entirely invincible. Cornwall has been wounded by the slain servant: 'I have received a hurt … I bleed apace'. Unlike Gloucester, however, who has learnt compassion through pain, Cornwall continues to abuse power. He orders the blind Gloucester to be flung out of his own castle ('Turn out that eyeless villain') and demands that the dead servant's body should be thrown 'Upon the dunghill'.

Gloucester's physical torture mirrors Lear's mental torment on the heath. Both men pay dearly for their lack of moral judgement. The playwright presents a dark vision of disorder and contempt for civilised behaviour.

In contrast to such inhumanity, this fast-moving act concludes with a further example of compassion when two other servants apply oils to soothe Gloucester's wounds. But after all the violence of the earlier scenes, audiences are left horrified and in a heightened state of tension.

Key Quotes

Quote	Comment
Pluck out his eyes (Goneril to Cornwall) l.5	Goneril is the dominant sister, and her malice knows no bounds. She revels in her savagery. Shakespeare makes effective use of onomatopoeia in the harsh-sounding verb.
our power/ Shall do a courtesy to our wrath (Cornwall to court) l.24–5	Corrupted by power, Cornwall is bent on revenge against the supposed traitor, Gloucester. His arrogance convinces him that he can act as he wishes.
I am tied to the stake, and I must stand the course (Gloucester to court) l.53	Gloucester has been tied to a chair and is being abused and baited by Cornwall and Regan. Bear baiting (where dogs attacked chained bears) was a common entertainment in Elizabethan times. Just like Kent, Gloucester is forced to endure harsh punishment for helping Lear.
Out, vile jelly!/ Where is thy lustre now? (Cornwall to Gloucester) l.81–2	At Regan's instigation, Cornwall gouges out Gloucester's second eye, leaving the old earl totally blinded. Gruesome imagery heightens the grisly deed.
O my follies! Then Edgar was abused (Gloucester) l.89	After hearing of Edmund's treachery, Gloucester is quick to acknowledge his great misjudgement of Edgar. Like Lear, he has suffered greatly for his mistakes.
let him smell/ His way to Dover (Regan on Gloucester) l.91–2	In an attempt to outdo her sister in cruelty, Regan ejects Gloucester from his own castle with this chilling remark. Her sadistic joke is further evidence of Regan's depraved inhumanity.

Key Points | Act 3

Scene 1

- One of Lear's knights informs Kent that the old king is running wild on the heath.
- The loyal Fool remains with Lear, trying to get him to see the error of his ways.
- Kent reveals rumours of a growing rift between Albany and Cornwall.
- A French army has landed to rescue Lear and challenge the forces of evil.

Scene 2

- On the heath, a wild storm reflects the chaos in Lear's mind and in society at large.
- Enraged and self-obsessed, Lear hopes that the entire universe will be destroyed.
- Lear's suffering teaches him the truth of his own situation. He shows compassion for the Fool.
- Out of concern, the Fool tries to get Lear to see that he himself is responsible for his downfall.
- The sympathetic Kent attempts to bring the old king to shelter.

Scene 3

- The Earl of Gloucester is concerned at how Lear is being treated.
- Gloucester confides in Edmund about the landing of the French in Dover.
- For the first time, Gloucester emerges as a man of strength, determined to help the king.
- Edmund's ruthlessness is evident when he betrays his father to further advance himself.

Scene 4

- Lear welcomes the storm as a diversion from his suffering.
- He is aware that his obsession with his daughters' ingratitude will drive him insane.
- Lear now recognises the effects of poverty and acknowledges his neglect of this when in power.
- His path to self-awareness is uneven. He thinks Poor Tom's plight is also due to filial ingratitude.
- Loyal Kent continues to try to shelter Lear.
- Gloucester also shows loyalty to the king, but is grief-stricken by Edgar's supposed crime.
- The Fool fears for the future.

Scene 5

- Edmund's callousness is seen in his relentless pursuit of wealth and power.
- The gullible Cornwall is easily manipulated by Edmund, who is given Gloucester's lands and title.

Scene 6

- The 'mock trial' of Lear's daughters reflects Lear's new-found interest in justice.
- Kent and Edgar are both moved by Lear's anguish.
- Gloucester has information about a plot to kill the king.
- On witnessing Lear's intense suffering, Edgar dismisses his own pain.
- With Cordelia's French forces in place at Dover, Britain now stands on the brink of war.

Scene 7

- In a travesty of justice, Gloucester is viciously blinded by Cornwall.
- Edmund's villainy is exposed by a gloating Regan.
- The servant's intervention on Gloucester's behalf offers a ray of hope.
- Gloucester's moral insight ironically comes at the expense of his sight.
- Two more servants show traces of humanity.
- Cornwall is fatally wounded. The forces of evil are not invincible.

Act 4
Scene 1

INTRODUCTION

- Edgar is shocked to see his blind father being led by one of his old tenants.
- There are signs that Gloucester is beginning to acknowledge his past mistakes.
- Left alone with his father, Edgar still pretends to be Poor Tom, the beggar.
- In despair, Gloucester asks to be brought to the edge of a cliff at Dover.

The heath

Enter Edgar

Edgar

Yet better thus, and known to be condemned,
Than still condemned and flattered. To be worst,
The lowest and most dejected thing of fortune,
Stands still in esperance, lives not in fear.
The lamentable change is from the best:
The worst returns to laughter. Welcome, then,
Thou unsubstantial air that I embrace!
The wretch that thou hast blown unto the worst
Owes nothing to thy blasts. But who comes here?

Enter Gloucester, led by an Old Man

My father, poorly led? World, world, O world!
But that thy strange mutations make us hate thee,
Life would not yield to age.

Old Man

O, my good lord,
I have been your tenant, and your father's tenant,
these fourscore years –

Gloucester

Away, get thee away. Good friend, be gone.
Thy comforts can do me no good at all;
Thee they may hurt.

Old Man

You cannot see your way.

Gloucester

I have no way, and therefore want no eyes.
I stumbled when I saw. Full oft 'tis seen,
Our means secure us, and our mere defects
Prove our commodities. O dear son Edgar,
The food of thy abused father's wrath!
Might I but live to see thee in my touch,
I'd say I had eyes again!

Old Man

How now! Who's there?

Edgar

Aside

4 esperance: *expectation, hope*

7 unsubstantial: *flimsy*

11 mutations: *changes, alterations*

12 yield to age: *accept old age and death*

14 fourscore: *eighty*

20 means: *belongings*
secure us: *make us careless*
defects: *disadvantages, shortages*
21 commodities: *opportunities*
22 wrath: *anger*

O gods! Who is't can say 'I am at the worst'?
I am worse than e'er I was.

Old Man

'Tis poor mad Tom.

Edgar

Aside

And worse I may be yet. The worst is not
So long as we can say 'This is the worst.'

Old Man

Fellow, where goest?

Gloucester

Is it a beggar-man?

Old Man

Madman and beggar too.

Gloucester

He has some reason, else he could not beg.
I' the last night's storm I such a fellow saw,
Which made me think a man a worm. My son
Came then into my mind, and yet my mind
Was then scarce friends with him. I have heard more since.
As flies to wanton boys are we to the gods.
They kill us for their sport.

36 wanton: *thoughtless, vicious*

Edgar

Aside

How should this be?
Bad is the trade that must play fool to sorrow,
Angering itself and others. *[Aloud]* Bless thee, master!

Gloucester

Is that the naked fellow?

Old Man

Ay, my lord.

Gloucester

Then, prithee, get thee gone. If, for my sake,
Thou wilt o'ertake us, hence a mile or twain,
I' the way toward Dover, do it for ancient love,
And bring some covering for this naked soul,
Which I'll entreat to lead me.

42 twain: *two*

43 ancient: *old*

Old Man

Alack, sir, he is mad.

Gloucester

'Tis the times' plague, when madmen lead the blind.
Do as I bid thee, or rather do thy pleasure;
Above the rest, be gone.

Old Man

I'll bring him the best 'parel that I have,
Come on't what will.

Exit

Gloucester

Sirrah, naked fellow –

Edgar

Poor Tom's a-cold. *[Aside]* I cannot daub it further.

Gloucester

Come hither, fellow.

Edgar

Aside

And yet I must. – Bless thy sweet eyes, they bleed.

Gloucester

Know'st thou the way to Dover?

Edgar

Both stile and gate, horse-way and foot-path. Poor Tom hath been scared out of his good wits. Bless thee, good man's son, from the foul fiend! Five fiends have been in poor Tom at once; of lust, as Obidicut, Hobbididence, prince of dumbness, Mahu, of stealing, Modo, of murder, Flibbertigibbet, of mopping and mowing, who since possesses chambermaids and waiting-women. So, bless thee, master!

Gloucester

Here, take this purse, thou whom the heavens' plagues
Have humbled to all strokes. That I am wretched
Makes thee the happier. Heavens, deal so still!
Let the superfluous and lust-dieted man,
That slaves your ordinance, that will not see
Because he doth not feel, feel your power quickly;

46 times' plague: *awful state of the present world*

49 'parel: *apparel, clothes*

51 daub it further: *pretend any more*

55 stile: *steps in a wall*

58–60 Obidicut, Hobbididence...Mahu... Modo...Flibbertigibbet: *names of devils*

66 superfluous and lust-dieted: *excessively wealthy and lustful*

67 ordinance: *law, divine rule*

So distribution should undo excess,
And each man have enough. Dost thou know Dover?

Edgar

Ay, master.

Gloucester

There is a cliff, whose high and bending head
Looks fearfully in the confined deep.
Bring me but to the very brim of it,
And I'll repair the misery thou dost bear
With something rich about me. From that place
I shall no leading need.

Edgar

Give me thy arm.
Poor Tom shall lead thee.

Exeunt

Analysis

Insights (lines 1–78)

In his opening soliloquy on the heath, Edgar wonders if his life as a homeless beggar can possibly get any worse. He then sees his unfortunate father being guided by an old man. Edgar is the victim of cruel irony. Everything is undoubtedly worsening for him.

Gloucester is finding wisdom late in life and is beginning to 'see' the truth since losing his eyesight: 'I stumbled when I saw'. Ironically, when he had his physical sight, he fell into moral blindness. His words echo those of the old king, who has also realised that power and self-importance can have a negative effect.

Like Lear, Gloucester admits that he has made mistakes as a parent: 'O dear son Edgar,/ The food of thy abused father's wrath!' He hopes desperately for them to be reconciled, 'Might I but live to see thee in my touch,/ I'd say I had eyes again!'

Edgar watches in agony and begins to think that there are no limits to human misery: 'The worst is not/ So long as we can say "This is the worst"'. Gloucester has an equally depressing view of humanity. He now believes that people have little or no control over their lives, 'As flies to wanton boys are we to the gods./ They kill us for their sport'. This idea of the gods' random cruelty recurs throughout the play, which is set in pre-Christian times.

When Gloucester decides to dismiss the old man and get Poor Tom to lead him to Dover, Edgar finds it hard to continue his pretence: 'I cannot daub it further'. Increasingly, Edgar's positive character traits are evident. Despite

Despite all his bad experiences, Gloucester's personal development continues. He shows genuine compassion for other people, insisting that clothing is provided for Poor Tom: 'bring some covering for this naked soul'.

the wrong he has suffered at Gloucester's hands, he shows his father nothing but caring forgiveness. But his continuing portrayal of himself as the Bedlam beggar often attracts criticism. Why is he still so reluctant to reveal his real identity?

It's clear that Gloucester is in despair and intends to die by suicide: 'There is a cliff ... Bring me but to the very brim of it'. Yet he still shows pity for the suffering of others: 'I'll repair the misery thou dost bear'. As Edgar, still disguised as Poor Tom, agrees to lead his father to Dover, we are left wondering if he will assist him in ending his life. Or is there a chance that he might behave like his brother Edmund? Has he cause? The scene ends on an uncertain note.

Key Quotes

Quote	Comment
The wretch that thou hast blown unto the worst/ Owes nothing to thy blasts *(Edgar) l.8–9*	Poor Tom/Edgar is in a more hopeful mood. He is a stoical character and remarks that the elements have done their worst. Yet, because he has nothing, he owes nothing.
I stumbled when I saw *(Gloucester to Old Man) l.19*	Gloucester admits that when he had the benefit of physical sight, he made mistakes. Ironically, now that he is blind, he has gained true sight and understands the world. This is a moment of epiphany for Gloucester, who has always been morally weak.
As flies to wanton boys are we to the gods./ They kill us for their sport *(Gloucester to Old Man) l.36–7*	The old earl paints a bleak picture of the universe and human existence. He compares human beings to insects, mere playthings that a heedless boy might kill just for fun. In the play's pre-Christian setting, the gods are characterised by their indifference to the plight of humanity.
'Tis the times' plague, when madmen lead the blind *(Gloucester to Old Man) l.46*	Another desolate view of the human condition is presented, suggesting that the world's great problems are due to lunatics controlling the visionless.
So distribution should undo excess/ And each man have enough *(Gloucester to Poor Tom) l.69–70*	Like Lear, Gloucester has come to understand that there must be a more even distribution of wealth, so that every individual can survive with dignity.

Act 4
Scene 2

INTRODUCTION

- Albany has changed and is now committed to the cause of justice.
- He confronts Goneril about her disgraceful treatment of her father.
- Rivalry develops between Goneril and Regan for Edmund's love.
- Albany promises to avenge Edmund's mistreatment of Gloucester.

Before the Duke of Albany's palace

Enter Goneril and Edmund

Goneril

Welcome, my lord. I marvel our mild husband
Not met us on the way.

Enter Oswald

Now, where's your master'?

Oswald

Madam, within, but never man so changed.
I told him of the army that was landed.
He smiled at it. I told him you were coming,
His answer was 'The worse'. Of Gloucester's treachery,
And of the loyal service of his son,
When I informed him, then he called me sot,
And told me I had turned the wrong side out.
What most he should dislike seems pleasant to him;
What like, offensive.

Goneril

To Edmund

Then shall you go no further.
It is the cowish terror of his spirit
That dares not undertake. He'll not feel wrongs
Which tie him to an answer. Our wishes on the way
May prove effects. Back, Edmund, to my brother;
Hasten his musters and conduct his powers.
I must change arms at home, and give the distaff
Into my husband's hands. This trusty servant
Shall pass between us. Ere long you are like to hear,
If you dare venture in your own behalf,
A mistress's command. Wear this, spare speech

Giving a favour

Decline your head: this kiss, if it durst speak,
Would stretch thy spirits up into the air.
Conceive, and fare thee well.

Edmund

Yours in the ranks of death.

Goneril

My most dear Gloucester!

Exit Edmund

1 mild: *soft, weak-minded*

2 Not met: *did not meet*

8 sot: *fool, drunkard*

12 cowish: *cowardly*

16 musters: *assembly of troops*

17 distaff: *symbol of female domesticity*

20 venture in your own behalf: *pursue your own interests*

favour: token of love, small gift

O, the difference of man and man!
To thee a woman's services are due:
My fool usurps my body.

Oswald

Madam, here comes my lord.

Exit

Enter Albany

Goneril

I have been worth the whistle.

Albany

O Goneril!
You are not worth the dust which the rude wind
Blows in your face. I fear your disposition:
That nature, which contemns its origin,
Cannot be bordered certain in itself;
She that herself will sliver and disbranch
From her material sap, perforce must wither
And come to deadly use.

Goneril

No more; the text is foolish.

Albany

Wisdom and goodness to the vile seem vile:
Filths savour but themselves. What have you done?
Tigers, not daughters, what have you performed?
A father, and a gracious aged man,
Whose reverence even the head-lugged bear would lick,
Most barbarous, most degenerate! Have you madded.
Could my good brother suffer you to do it?
A man, a prince, by him so benefited!
If that the heavens do not their visible spirits
Send quickly down to tame these vile offences,
It will come,
Humanity must perforce prey on itself,
Like monsters of the deep.

Goneril

Milk-livered man!
That bear'st a cheek for blows, a head for wrongs,
Who hast not in thy brows an eye discerning
Thine honour from thy suffering, that not know'st

28 fool usurps my body: *my foolish husband does not deserve me*

29 worth the whistle: *worth looking for*

32 disposition: *nature*

33 contemns: *disdains*

35 sliver: *slice*

36 material sap: *what gives life*

37 deadly use: *will be burned*

38 the text is foolish: *what you are saying is senseless*

39 vile: *despicable*

40 savour: *relish, enjoy*

45 good brother: *Cornwall*
suffer: *allow*

50 perforce: *inescapably*

51 Milk-livered: *weak, childish*

53 discerning: *distinguishing*

Fools do those villains pity who are punished
Ere they have done their mischief. Where's thy drum?
France spreads his banners in our noiseless land,
With plumed helm thy flaxen biggin threats;
Whilst thou, a moral fool, sits still and cries
'Alack, why does he so?'

Albany

See thyself, devil!
Proper deformity seems not in the fiend
So horrid as in woman.

Goneril

O vain fool!

Albany

Thou changed and self-covered thing, for shame
Be-monster not thy feature. Were't my fitness
To let these hands obey my blood,
They are apt enough to dislocate and tear
Thy flesh and bones. Howe'er thou art a fiend,
A woman's shape doth shield thee.

Goneril

Marry, your manhood, mew –

Enter a Messenger

Albany

What news?

Messenger

O, my good lord, the Duke of Cornwall's dead,
Slain by his servant, going to put out
The other eye of Gloucester.

Albany

Gloucester's eyes?

Messenger

A servant that he bred, thrilled with remorse,
Opposed against the act, bending his sword
To his great master, who, thereat enraged,
Flew on him, and amongst them felled him dead,
But not without that harmful stroke, which since
Hath plucked him after.

58 flaxen biggin: *flaxen slayer*

61 deformity: *distortion*

74 thrilled: *deeply moved*

79 plucked: *killed*

80 nether: *worldly*

86–7 pluck...life: *force me to live with Albany*

88 tart: *bitter, disagreeable*

91 back: *on his way back*

Albany

This shows you are above,
You justicers, that these our nether crimes
So speedily can venge! But, O poor Gloucester!
Lost he his other eye?

Messenger

Both, both, my lord.
This letter, madam, craves a speedy answer.
'Tis from your sister.

Goneril

Aside

One way I like this well,
But being widow, and my Gloucester with her,
May all the building in my fancy pluck
Upon my hateful life. Another way,
The news is not so tart. – I'll read, and answer.

Exit

Albany

Where was his son when they did take his eyes?

Messenger

Come with my lady hither.

Albany

He is not here.

Messenger

No, my good lord; I met him back again.

Albany

Knows he the wickedness?

Messenger

Ay, my good Lord. 'Twas he informed against him;
And quit the house on purpose, that their punishment
Might have the freer course.

Albany

Gloucester, I live
To thank thee for the love thou show'dst the king,
And to revenge thine eyes. Come hither, friend.
Tell me what more thou know'st.

Exeunt

Analysis

Surprises (lines 1–28)

Edmund and Goneril arrive at her husband's palace to be greeted only by a servant: 'I marvel our mild husband/ Not met us'. Oswald then tells her of the radical change that has come over Albany, who appears to be pleased at the arrival of Cordelia's French army, and is highly critical of Edmund's abuse of Gloucester.

Another surprise occurs when Goneril gives Edmund a token of her love. Her behaviour towards the young, handsome nobleman suggests more exciting times to come: 'this kiss, if it durst speak,/ Would stretch thy spirits up into the air'. Edmund swears complete loyalty to her: 'Yours in the ranks of death'.

The audience must wonder at his sincerity – particularly as he has already betrayed his father and brother. However, Goneril continues to fantasise about Edmund, 'To thee a woman's services are due', and she contrasts him with her dull husband: 'O, the difference of man and man!'

Confrontation (lines 29–78)

When Albany appears, she immediately criticises him for not welcoming her: 'I have been worth the whistle'. Albany responds angrily, telling Goneril that she is not 'worth the dust which the rude wind/ Blows in your face'. He is shocked at her mistreatment of Lear, regarding it as unnatural for a child to cut themselves off from a parent: 'She that herself will sliver and disbranch ... must wither/ And come to deadly use'. Goneril dismisses his remarks, still seemingly unaware of how changed he has become.

However, Albany is a match for his domineering wife and launches into a harsh critique of her many faults. In attacking Goneril, he uses images of nature ('Tigers', 'monsters of the deep') to describe her 'vile' character. Albany cannot believe that Cornwall would allow her to act like this: 'Could my good brother suffer you to do it?' Ironically, he does not yet know that it was Cornwall who blinded Gloucester.

Albany considers Goneril to be worse than a devil: 'Proper deformity seems not in the fiend/ So horrid as in woman'. In turn, she calls him a 'Milk-livered man' and a 'vain fool'. Her arrogance echoes Lear's spiteful behaviour in the early scenes of the play. But worse is to come when a messenger brings news of Cornwall's death. Albany now knows that Goneril, Regan, Cornwall and Edmund are all implicated in horrifying deeds.

Cornwall's death marks a new phase in the restoration of order within the kingdom. Albany's transformation also gives the audience hope.

Justice (lines 79–98)

Albany regards the death of Cornwall as proof that there is some justice and integrity in this world: 'This shows you are above,/ You justicers'. For the moment, he is mainly concerned with his wife's cruelty towards Lear and her brutal punishment of Gloucester. As yet, he is unaware of her feelings for Edmund.

Meanwhile, Goneril is concerned that Regan ('being widow') might upset her plans to make Edmund her lover. After further reflection, she considers that Cornwall's death now makes it possible for her to take over as the country's single ruler. At the same time, she knows that Edmund is becoming even more powerful.

Albany's transformation, along with Cornwall's death, begins to balance the influence of good and evil in the play. Goneril's estranged husband has become an important figure. As leader of the British troops, he has no choice but to fight against the invading French troops. Despite this, it's evident that Albany is primarily aiming to restore justice and order after all the trauma suffered by Lear and Gloucester.

Key Quotes

Quote	Comment
It is the cowish terror of his spirit/ That dares not undertake (Goneril to Oswald) l.12–13	Goneril's contemptuous remark about her mild-mannered husband clearly suggests that Albany's lack of response to the news that French forces have landed in Britain is due to cowardice.
Ere long you are like to hear,/ If you dare venture in your own behalf,/ A mistress's command (Goneril to Edmund) l.19–21	Outspoken and determined, Goneril has decided that Edmund, a man of action, suits her much more than her weak, placid husband, Albany. Used to taking charge, she lets Edmund know of her feelings for him.
She that herself will sliver and disbranch/ From her material sap, perforce must wither/ And come to deadly use. (Albany to Goneril) l.35–7	No longer the gentle, cautious man of previous scenes, Albany roundly criticises Goneril for her cruel treatment of Lear, using imagery from nature. He warns her that the branch which is cut off from the tree that bred it will surely die.
Tigers, not daughters, what have you performed? (Albany to Goneril) l.41	A deeply incensed Albany continues the searing attack on his wife, likening her and Regan's behaviour to that of wild animals. His essential sense of common decency and morality is now evident.

Act 4
Scene 3

INTRODUCTION

- Kent learns that the King of France has returned to his homeland.
- Cordelia is now in command of the French army near Dover.
- She has been severely shocked by her sisters' cruelty to their father.
- Lear's shame over his treatment of Cordelia prevents him from meeting her.

The French camp near Dover

Enter Kent and a gentleman

Kent

Why the King of France is so suddenly gone back know you the reason?

Gentleman

Something he left imperfect in the state, which since his coming forth is thought of, which imports to the kingdom so much fear and danger that his personal return was most required and necessary.

Kent

Who hath he left behind him general?

Gentleman

The Marshal of France, Monsieur La Far.

Kent

Did your letters pierce the Queen to any demonstration of grief?

Gentleman

Ay, sir. She took them, read them in my presence,
And now and then an ample tear trilled down
Her delicate cheek. It seemed she was a queen
Over her passion, who, most rebel-like,
Sought to be king o'er her.

Kent

O, then it moved her.

Gentleman

Not to a rage. Patience and sorrow strove
Who should express her goodliest. You have seen
Sunshine and rain at once. Her smiles and tears
Were like a better way. Those happy smilets,
That played on her ripe lip, seemed not to know
What guests were in her eyes, which parted thence,
As pearls from diamonds dropped. In brief,
Sorrow would be a rarity most beloved,
If all could so become it.

Kent

Made she no verbal question?

Gentleman

'Faith, once or twice she heaved the name of 'father'
Pantingly forth, as if it pressed her heart.
Cried 'Sisters! sisters! Shame of ladies! sisters!
Kent! father! sisters! What, i' the storm? i' the night?

3 imperfect: *unfinished*

9 the Queen: *Cordelia*

12 trilled: *trickled*

19 smilets: *little smiles*

25 heaved: *sighed, whispered*

Let pity not be believed!' There she shook
The holy water from her heavenly eyes,
And clamour moistened, then away she started
To deal with grief alone.

Kent

It is the stars,
The stars above us, govern our conditions.
Else one self mate and mate could not beget
Such different issues. You spoke not with her since?

Gentleman

No.

Kent

Was this before the king returned?

Gentleman

No, since.

Kent

Well, sir, the poor distressed Lear's in the town,
Who sometime, in his better tune, remembers
What we are come about, and by no means
Will yield to see his daughter.

Gentleman

Why, good sir?

Kent

A sovereign shame so elbows him: his own unkindness,
That stripped her from his benediction, turned her
To foreign casualties, gave her dear rights
To his dog-hearted daughters, these things sting
His mind so venomously, that burning shame
Detains him from Cordelia.

Gentleman

Alack, poor gentleman!

Kent

Of Albany's and Cornwall's powers you heard not?

Gentleman

'Tis so, they are afoot.

Kent

Well, sir, I'll bring you to our master Lear,
And leave you to attend him. Some dear cause
Will in concealment wrap me up awhile.
When I am known aright, you shall not grieve
Lending me this acquaintance. I pray you, go
Along with me.

31 clamour moistened: *cries of grief softened by her tears*

33 conditions: *characters, feelings*

35 issues: *children*

39 tune: *mood*

41 yield: *agree*

42 elbows: *jostles, reminds*

43 benediction: *approval*

44 casualties: *losses*

46 venomously: *bitterly*

48 powers: *armies*

51 Some dear cause: *an important reason*

Analysis

Concern and hope (lines 1–55)

Just when it seemed that the forces of good were gaining strength, the King of France has had to return home unexpectedly. His army officers remain to help Cordelia lead the defence for her father. Kent wonders if Cordelia showed any emotion ('demonstration of grief') at hearing the latest news about Lear. His concern reminds the audience that Cordelia's earlier weakness was an inability to outwardly express her feelings.

However, the reports of Cordelia's response indicate how much she has changed, 'now and then an ample tear trilled down/ Her delicate cheek'. The gentle language reflects her sensitivity. Cordelia is described as a reserved person who chooses to 'deal with grief alone'.

Shakespeare highlights the remarkable contrast between the characters of Lear's daughters. Goneril and Regan's hypocritical displays of love have turned out to be exactly what Cordelia had feared – a way of hiding their cruelty.

Although she has been wronged, Cordelia shows deep compassion: 'she heaved the name of "father"'. Meanwhile, Kent's comment that 'The stars above us, govern our conditions' echoes Gloucester's belief that destiny controls our lives. Kent questions how the same parents could have such different children as Lear's daughters. Meanwhile, the old king is so ashamed of how he treated Cordelia that he is reluctant to meet her, 'A sovereign shame so elbows him'.

Throughout this scene, Cordelia is shown in an idealised way – as an almost angelic figure. The audience is led to believe that Lear's suffering will soon be relieved.

As always, Kent continues to act on Lear's behalf. He is the vital link between Cordelia and her father, relaying information and attempting to reunite them. This tender scene is a startling contrast to the earlier tension and savagery in the play. For the moment at least, selfishness and deceit have been replaced by concern and self-control. The audience can now hope that Lear might find some relief through the sincere efforts of Cordelia and Kent.

Key Quotes

O, then it moved her *(Kent to gentleman) l.15*	A steadfastly loyal Kent is relieved that Cordelia has been so affected by her father's plight. This contrasts with the callous treatment of Lear by her sisters and also shows the change in Cordelia's character. She can now express her true feelings.
You have seen/ Sunshine and rain at once *(Gentleman to Kent) l.17–18*	Again, we hear of Cordelia's tender reaction to her father's dilemma, described appropriately through a beautiful natural image. The language differs sharply from the portrayal of her two sisters, who are often associated with savage, animal imagery.
There she shook/ The holy water from her heavenly eyes *(Gentleman to Kent) l.29–30*	Cordelia is closely linked with holiness that brings grace and forgiveness to sinners. Her character is often described as Christ-like or representative of divine goodness.
these things sting/ His mind so venomously *(Gentleman to Kent) l.45–6*	Dramatic imagery from nature is used to show the bitter regret Lear is experiencing over how badly he treated his youngest child. He had heartlessly disowned her because she had refused to participate in his public 'love test'.

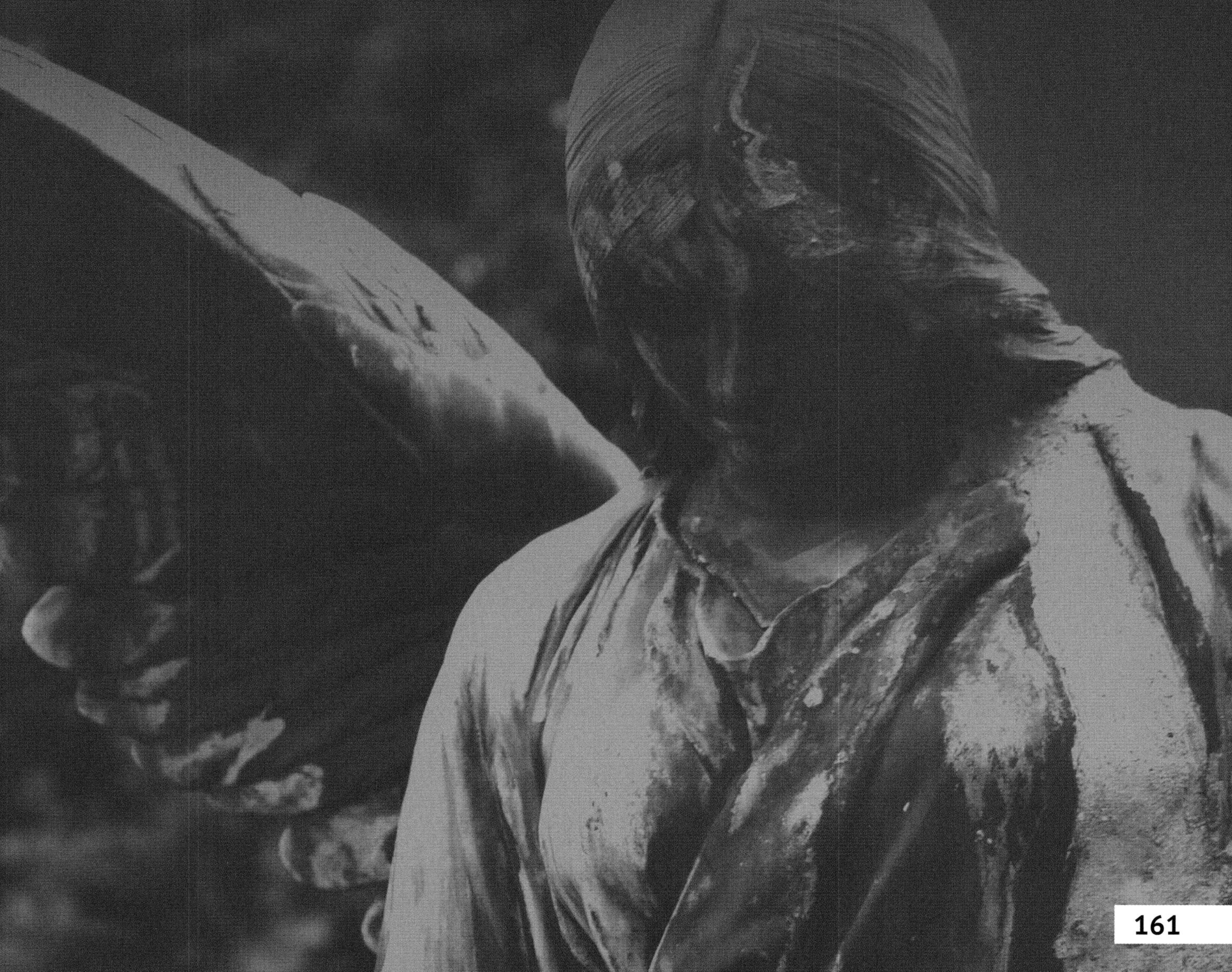

Act 4
Scene 4

INTRODUCTION

- Cordelia orders the French soldiers to search for her father.
- She explains that she has returned out of love and not political ambition.
- A doctor assures her that Lear's insanity may be curable.
- Meanwhile, her sisters' British troops are marching towards the French army.

The French camp near Dover

Enter, with drum and colours, Cordelia, Doctor and Soldiers

Cordelia

Alack, 'tis he. Why, he was met even now
As mad as the vexed sea, singing aloud,
Crowned with rank fumiter and furrow-weeds,
With hardocks, hemlock, nettles, cuckoo-flowers,
Darnel, and all the idle weeds that grow
In our sustaining corn. A century send forth.
Search every acre in the high-grown field,
And bring him to our eye.

Exit an Officer

What can man's wisdom
In the restoring his bereaved sense?
He that helps him take all my outward worth.

Doctor

There is means, madam.
Our foster-nurse of nature is repose,
The which he lacks. That to provoke in him,
Are many simples operative, whose power
Will close the eye of anguish.

Cordelia

All blest secrets,
All you unpublished virtues of the earth,
Spring with my tears! Be aidant and remediate
In the good man's distress! Seek, seek for him,
Lest his ungoverned rage dissolve the life
That wants the means to lead it.

Enter a Messenger

Messenger

News, madam.
The British powers are marching hitherward.

Cordelia

'Tis known before. Our preparation stands
In expectation of them. O dear father,
It is thy business that I go about.
Therefore great France
My mourning and important tears hath pitied.
No blown ambition doth our arms incite,
But love, dear love, and our aged father's right:
Soon may I hear and see him!

Exeunt

3–5 fumiter...Darnel: *poisonous weeds growing in ploughed soil*

6 century: *a hundred soldiers*

9 bereaved: *bereft, robbed*

10 outward worth: *wealth*

12 repose: *sleep*

17 aidant: *helpful*
remediate: *restorative*

19 ungoverned: *uncontrolled*

20 means: *reason*

21 powers: *military forces*

27 blown: *inflated*
incite: *rouse*

Analysis

Recovery (lines 1–29)

Cordelia is concerned with finding her father, who is reported to have wandered off wearing a crown of wildflowers, 'As mad as the vexed sea, singing aloud,/ Crowned with rank fumiter and furrow-weeds'. She is also hoping that Lear can be cured of his insanity: 'What can man's wisdom/ In the restoring his bereaved sense?'

The doctor is confident of recovery, but only if the king has 'repose'. Cordelia is anxious that Lear's uncontrolled passions may cause him to harm himself, 'Lest his ungoverned rage dissolve the life/ That wants the means to lead it'. She is well aware of his feverish character.

Nature imagery in this scene conveys the confused state of Lear's mind ('all the idle weeds'). He wears a useless crown of poisonous wildflowers. In symbolic terms, this replaces the powerful crown he gave away.

After a messenger informs Cordelia that the British army is close by, she remains self-controlled in the face of such danger: 'Our preparation stands/ In expectation of them'. This is in striking contrast to her two hot-tempered sisters. Cordelia makes it clear that it is not personal ambition but natural concern for Lear that brings her bearing arms: 'But love, dear love, and our aged father's right'.

This short scene again illustrates the difference between Cordelia's selflessness and the ruthless self-interest of her sisters. Unlike Regan and Goneril, Lear's youngest daughter has 'No blown ambition'.

Key Quotes

Quote	Comment
As mad as the vexed sea *(Cordelia) l.2*	Cordelia describes her father's state of mind through vivid nature imagery. His emotional turmoil is like a raging ocean, boiling and fuming.
He that helps him take all my outward worth *(Cordelia) l.10*	Lear's youngest daughter shows the clear difference between herself and her two sisters. She is willing to give all her material wealth to cure her ailing father, unlike her sisters, who want all the riches and power they can get.
No blown ambition doth our arms incite *(Cordelia) l.27*	Unlike the over-ambitious Edmund and her self-interested sisters, Cordelia has not come to seize land, but simply to aid her sick father, Lear.

Act 4
Scene 5

INTRODUCTION

- Oswald arrives with a letter from Goneril for Edmund.
- Regan is curious about what her sister has written.
- She is intensely jealous, and believes she is a more suitable partner for Edmund.
- Oswald agrees to kill Gloucester to prove his loyalty to Regan.

Gloucester's castle

Enter Regan and Oswald

Regan

But are my brother's powers set forth?

Oswald

Ay, madam.

Regan

Himself in person there?

Oswald

Madam, with much ado:
Your sister is the better soldier.

2 with much ado: *with a great deal of protest*

Regan

Lord Edmund spake not with your lord at home?

Oswald

No, madam.

Regan

What might import my sister's letter to him?

6 import: *signify, be the meaning of*

Oswald

I know not, lady –

Regan

'Faith, he is posted hence on serious matter.
It was great ignorance, Gloucester's eyes being out,
To let him live. Where he arrives he moves
All hearts against us. Edmund, I think, is gone,
In pity of his misery, to dispatch
His nighted life. Moreover, to descry
The strength of the enemy.

12 dispatch: *end*

13 nighted: *darkened, despairing*
descry: *discover*

Oswald

I must needs after him, madam, with my letter.

Regan

Our troops set forth to-morrow. Stay with us.
The ways are dangerous.

Oswald

I may not, Madam.
My lady charged my duty in this business.

18 charged: *emphasised, warned me about*

Regan

Why should she write to Edmund? Might not you
Transport her purposes by word? Belike –
Some things – I know not what – I'll love thee much –
Let me unseal the letter.

Oswald

Madam, I had rather –

Regan

I know your lady does not love her husband –
I am sure of that – and at her late being here
She gave strange oeillades and most speaking looks
To noble Edmund. I know you are of her bosom.

Oswald

I, madam?

Regan

I speak in understanding. You are! I know't.
Therefore I do advise you, take this note.
My lord is dead. Edmund and I have talked,
And more convenient is he for my hand
Than for your lady's. You may gather more.
If you do find him, pray you, give him this
And when your mistress hears thus much from you,
I pray, desire her call her wisdom to her.
So, fare you well.
If you do chance to hear of that blind traitor,
Preferment falls on him that cuts him off.

Oswald

Would I could meet him, madam! I should show
What party I do follow.

Regan

Fare thee well.

Exeunt

20 Transport: *carry*
Belike: *perhaps*

25 oeillades: *loving glances*

26 of her bosom: *in her confidence*

31 convenient: *suitable*
hand: *in marriage*

38 Preferment: *promotion*

Analysis

Intrigue and disloyalty (lines 1–40)

Goneril worries that because Regan is now widowed, she will appear a more attractive partner for the highly ambitious Edmund. She is right to be concerned. Regan questions Oswald about Albany's troops and he informs her that the duke has divided loyalties and that her sister is 'the better soldier'. Regan is particularly keen on finding out what is in the letter from Goneril to Edmund and tries to delay it from being delivered: 'Stay with us./ The ways are dangerous'.

In Gloucester's castle, the atmosphere is filled with jealousy and hatred – a stark contrast to the previous scene in the French camp near Dover. Oswald reports that Albany is leading the British troops, but with some reluctance.

Regan's vindictiveness knows no bounds. She and Goneril are now bitterly divided by their rivalry for Edmund's love. As always, family ties mean nothing to either of these ruthless women.

Regan has also concluded that it was a tactical error to allow Gloucester to live because people who have heard of his cruel treatment have begun to turn on her: 'Where he arrives he moves/ All hearts against us'. In another act of deliberate hypocrisy, she claims that Edmund has been so moved with pity at Gloucester's suffering that he has gone 'to dispatch his nighted life' and put him out of his misery.

The sisters are now in open competition for Edmund's attentions. Regan is less confident – and almost paranoid at times – about Goneril. This is conveyed in her broken speech patterns: 'Belike –/ Some things – I know not what'. Edmund, the expert manipulator, plays the two sisters as pawns in his desire for absolute power. Regan lets Oswald know that 'Edmund and I have talked,/ And more convenient is he for my hand/ Than for your lady's'.

Her murderous instincts surface again as she calls for the killing of Gloucester, promising promotion to whoever succeeds: 'Preferment falls on him that cuts him off'. Oswald's corrupt nature is evident throughout the scene. Untroubled by any sense of honesty, he has no difficulty serving two mistresses when it suits him. Without a moment's hesitation, Oswald accepts Regan's offer of reward for killing the old earl. 'Would I could meet him, madam! I should show/ What party I do follow'.

Key Quotes

Quote	Comment
It was great ignorance, Gloucester's eyes being out,/ To let him live *(Regan to Oswald) l.9–10*	Because of her involvement in the blinding of Gloucester, public opinion has turned against Regan, who is now convinced that the old earl should have been killed.
stay with us./ The ways are dangerous *(Regan to Oswald) l.16–17*	Both of Lear's daughters are in love with Edmund, so Regan is doing everything possible to delay the letter from Goneril reaching him.
She gave strange oeillades and most speaking looks/ To noble Edmund *(Regan to Oswald) l.25–6*	A jealous Regan is furious that her sister flirted with Edmund. She remembers how Goneril tried to seduce him with inviting glances.
I should show/ What party I do follow *(Oswald to Regan) l.38–9*	Always a weak and entirely unprincipled individual, Oswald quickly accepts Regan's request to kill Gloucester.

Act 4
Scene 6

INTRODUCTION

- Edgar saves his blind father from taking his own life.
- Lear is still confused and grief-stricken.
- The battle between the British and French forces is beginning.
- Edgar learns that Goneril hopes that Edmund will kill her husband, Albany.

The countryside near Dover

Enter Gloucester and Edgar (dressed like a peasant)

Gloucester

When shall I come to the top of that same hill?

Edgar

You do climb up it now. Look how we labour.

Gloucester

Methinks the ground is even.

Edgar

Horrible steep.
Hark, do you hear the sea?

Gloucester

No, truly.

Edgar

Why, then, your other senses grow imperfect
By your eyes' anguish.

Gloucester

So may it be, indeed.
Methinks thy voice is altered, and thou speak'st
In better phrase and matter than thou didst.

Edgar

You're much deceived. In nothing am I changed
But in my garments.

Gloucester

Methinks you're better spoken.

Edgar

Come on, sir, here's the place. Stand still. How fearful
And dizzy 'tis, to cast one's eyes so low!
The crows and choughs that wing the midway air
Show scarce so gross as beetles. Half way down
Hangs one that gathers samphire, dreadful trade!
Methinks he seems no bigger than his head.
The fishermen, that walk upon the beach,
Appear like mice, and yond tall anchoring bark,
Diminished to her cock, her cock, a buoy
Almost too small for sight. The murmuring surge,
That on the unnumbered idle pebbles chafes,

6 anguish: *pain*

13 choughs: *(pronounced chuffs) red-billed crows*

15 samphire: *rock-plant*
trade: *activity*

18 bark: *ship*
19 cock: *small boat*
buoy: *float*
20 surge: *sea*
21 chafes: *rubs*

Cannot be heard so high. I'll look no more,
Lest my brain turn, and the deficient sight
Topple down headlong.

Gloucester

Set me where you stand.

Edgar

Give me your hand. You are now within a foot
Of the extreme verge. For all beneath the moon
Would I not leap upright.

Gloucester

Let go my hand.
Here, friend, is another purse; in it a jewel
Well worth a poor man's taking. Fairies and gods
Prosper it with thee! Go thou farther off.
Bid me farewell, and let me hear thee going.

Edgar

Now fare you well, good sir.

Gloucester

With all my heart.

Edgar

Why I do trifle thus with his despair
Is done to cure it.

Gloucester

Kneeling

O you mighty gods!
This world I do renounce, and, in your sights,
Shake patiently my great affliction off.
If I could bear it longer, and not fall
To quarrel with your great opposeless wills,
My snuff and loathed part of nature should
Burn itself out. If Edgar live, O, bless him!
Now, fellow, fare thee well.

He falls forward

Edgar

Gone, sir. Farewell.

Aside

And yet I know not how conceit may rob
The treasury of life, when life itself
Yields to the theft. Had he been where he thought,
By this, had thought been past. – Alive or dead?

23 turn: *become dizzy*
deficient: *failing*

30 Prosper: *increase, multiply*

33 trifle: *play, mislead*

39 opposeless: *inescapable*

40 snuff: *old age*

43 conceit: *imagination*

45 where he thought: *(beneath the cliff)*

46 past: *dead*

50 gossamer: *fine threads*
51 precipitating: *falling headlong*
52 shivered: *splintered*
54 at each: *one on top of the other*
55 fell: *fallen*
58 chalky bourn: *edge of Dover cliff*
59 shrill-gorged: *harsh-sounding*
64 beguile: *cheat*

(to Gloucester)
Ho, you sir! Friend! Hear you, sir? Speak –
Aside
Thus might he pass indeed. Yet he revives –
(to Gloucester)
What are you, sir?

Gloucester

Away, and let me die.

Edgar

Hadst thou been aught but gossamer, feathers, air,
So many fathom down precipitating,
Thou'dst shivered like an egg. But thou dost breathe,
Hast heavy substance, bleed'st not, speak'st, art sound.
Ten masts at each make not the altitude
Which thou hast perpendicularly fell.
Thy life's a miracle. Speak yet again.

Gloucester

But have I fallen, or no?

Edgar

From the dread summit of this chalky bourn.
Look up a-height. The shrill-gorged lark so far
Cannot be seen or heard. Do but look up.

Gloucester

Alack, I have no eyes.
Is wretchedness deprived that benefit,
To end itself by death? 'Twas yet some comfort,
When misery could beguile the tyrant's rage,
And frustrate his proud will.

Edgar

Give me your arm.
Up – so. How is 't? Feel you your legs? You stand.

Gloucester

Too well, too well.

Edgar

This is above all strangeness.
Upon the crown o' the cliff, what thing was that
Which parted from you?

Gloucester

A poor unfortunate beggar.

Edgar

As I stood here below, methought his eyes
Were two full moons. He had a thousand noses,
Horns whelked and waved like the enridged sea.
It was some fiend. Therefore, thou happy father,
Think that the clearest gods, who make them honours
Of men's impossibilities, have preserved thee.

Gloucester

I do remember now. Henceforth I'll bear
Affliction till it do cry out itself
'Enough, enough,' and die. That thing you speak of,
I took it for a man. Often 'twould say
'The fiend, the fiend' – he led me to that place.

Edgar

Bear free and patient thoughts. But who comes here?

Enter Lear, fantastically dressed with wild flowers

The safer sense will ne'er accommodate
His master thus.

Lear

No, they cannot touch me for coining. I am the King himself.

Edgar

O thou side-piercing sight!

Lear

Nature's above art in that respect. There's your press-money. That fellow handles his bow like a crow-keeper. Draw me a clothier's yard. Look, look, a mouse! Peace, Peace! This piece of toasted cheese will do 't. There's my gauntlet; I'll prove it on a giant. Bring up the brown bills. O, well flown, bird! I' the clout, i' the clout! Hewgh! Give the word.

Edgar

Sweet marjoram.

Lear

Pass.

Gloucester

I know that voice.

72 whelked: *spiralled, twisted*
enridged: *grooved*

74–75 make them...impossibilities: *gain respect by performing miracles*

77 Affliction: *suffering*

82 safer sense: *sane mind*
accommodate: *dress*

84 coining: *counterfeiting*

86–87 press-money: *soldier's pay*

88 clothier's yard: *full extent*

90 gauntlet: *glove (thrown down in challenge)*

91 I' the clout: *directly on target*

93 Sweet marjoram: *herb used as a medicine*

99 divinity: *religious sign*

104 ague-proof: *immune from sickness*

105 trick: *distinctive sound, tone*

110 gilded: *golden*

115 luxury, pell-mell: *uncontrolled lechery*

117 face...presages snow: *appearance predicts frigidity*

120 fitchew: *pole-cat (slang for prostitute)*
soiled: *well-fed*

122 Centaurs: *half man, half horse (mythological creature)*

128 civet: *perfume*
apothecary: *shopkeeper*

Lear

Ha! Goneril, with a white beard! They flattered me like a dog, and told me I had white hairs in my beard ere the black ones were there. To say 'ay' and 'no' to every thing that I said 'ay' and 'no' to was no good divinity. When the rain came to wet me once and the wind to make me chatter, when the thunder would not peace at my bidding, there I found 'em, there I smelt 'em out. Go to, they are not men o' their words. They told me I was everything. 'Tis a lie, I am not ague-proof.

Gloucester

The trick of that voice I do well remember.
Is 't not the king?

Lear

Ay, every inch a King.
When I do stare, see how the subject quakes.
I pardon that man's life. What was thy cause?
Adultery? Thou shalt not die. Die for adultery! No:
The wren goes to 't, and the small gilded fly
Does lecher in my sight.
Let copulation thrive; for Gloucester's bastard son
Was kinder to his father than my daughters
Got 'tween the lawful sheets.
To 't, luxury, pell-mell, for I lack soldiers.
Behold yond simpering dame,
Whose face between her forks presages snow;
That minces virtue, and does shake the head
To hear of pleasure's name –
The fitchew, nor the soiled horse, goes to 't
With a more riotous appetite.
Down from the waist they are Centaurs,
Though women all above.
But to the girdle do the gods inherit,
Beneath is all the fiend's.
There's hell, there's darkness, there's the sulphurous pit – burning, scalding, stench, consumption! Fie, fie, fie! Pah, pah! Give me an ounce of civet, good apothecary, to sweeten my imagination. There's money for thee.

Gloucester

O, let me kiss that hand!

Lear

Let me wipe it first; it smells of mortality.

Gloucester

O ruined piece of nature! This great world
Shall so wear out to nought. Dost thou know me?

Lear

I remember thine eyes well enough. Dost thou squiny at me? No, do thy worst, blind Cupid! I'll not love. Read thou this challenge; mark but the penning of it.

Gloucester

Were all the letters suns, I could not see one.

Edgar

I would not take this from report. It is;
And my heart breaks at it.

Lear

Read.

Gloucester

What, with the case of eyes?

Lear

O, ho, are you there with me? No eyes in your head, nor no money in your purse? Your eyes are in a heavy case, your purse in a light; yet you see how this world goes.

Gloucester

I see it feelingly.

Lear

What, art mad? A man may see how this world goes with no eyes. Look with thine ears. See how yond justice rails upon yond simple thief. Hark, in thine ear. Change places and, handy-dandy, which is the justice, which is the thief? Thou hast seen a farmer's dog bark at a beggar?

Gloucester

Ay, sir.

Lear

And the creature run from the cur? There thou mightst behold the great image of authority. A dog's obeyed in office.
Thou rascal beadle, hold thy bloody hand!
Why dost thou lash that whore? Strip thine own back;

131 mortality: *death*

132 ruined piece of nature: *spoiled masterpiece*

134 squiny: *squint*

135 blind Cupid: *the god of love was blind*

136 challenge: *summons to fight a duel*

138 report: *rumour*

141 case of eyes: *eye sockets*

145 feelingly: *with other senses*

147 rails: *censures, criticises*

149 handy-dandy: *easy-peasy (children's phrase)*

152 creature: *human*
cur: *animal*

153 obeyed: *is given status*

154 beadle: *parish officer, constable*

157 usurer: *moneylender*
cozener: *petty thief*
159 Plate: *cover*
161 pigmy's straw: *small weapon*
165 scurvy: *cheating*
168 matter and impertinency: *sense and foolishness*
174 wawl: *bawl, wail*
175 Alack, alack the day: *Gloucester uses an old expression of sorrow*
177 block: *possibly refers to the 'hat' of flowers on his head*
178 stratagem: *plot*
179 felt: *matted cloth*
put it in proof: *test it*
180 stolen: *crept up*
185 natural fool: *born idiot*

Thou hotly lusts to use her in that kind
For which thou whipp'st her. The usurer hangs the cozener.
Through tattered clothes small vices do appear;
Robes and furred gowns hide all. Plate sin with gold,
And the strong lance of justice hurtless breaks.
Arm it in rags, a pigmy's straw does pierce it.
None does offend, none, I say, none; I'll able 'em:
Take that of me, my friend, who have the power
To seal the accuser's lips. Get thee glass eyes.
And like a scurvy politician, seem
To see the things thou dost not. Now, now, now, now!
Pull off my boots. Harder, harder – so.

Edgar

Aside

O, matter and impertinency mixed!
Reason in madness!

Lear

If thou wilt weep my fortunes, take my eyes.
I know thee well enough, thy name is Gloucester.
Thou must be patient. We came crying hither.
Thou know'st, the first time that we smell the air,
We wawl and cry. I will preach to thee: mark.

Gloucester

Alack, alack the day!

Lear

When we are born, we cry that we are come
To this great stage of fools. This a good block;
It were a delicate stratagem, to shoe
A troop of horse with felt. I'll put it in proof,
And when I have stolen upon these sons-in-law,
Then, kill, kill, kill, kill, kill, kill!

Enter a Gentleman, with Attendants

Gentleman

O, here he is. Lay hand upon him. Sir,
Your most dear daughter –

Lear

No rescue? What, a prisoner? I am even
The natural fool of fortune. Use me well.

You shall have ransom. Let me have surgeons,
I am cut to the brains.

Gentleman

You shall have anything.

Lear

No seconds? All myself?
Why, this would make a man a man of salt,
To use his eyes for garden water-pots.
Ay, and laying Autumn's dust.

Gentleman

Good sir –

Lear

I will die bravely, like a smug bridegroom.
What! I will be jovial. Come, come; I am a king.
Masters, know you that?

Gentleman

You are a royal one, and we obey you.

Lear

Then there's life in't. Come and you get it, you shall get it by running. Sa, sa, sa, sa.

Exit running, attendants follow

Gentleman

A sight most pitiful in the meanest wretch,
Past speaking of in a king! Thou hast one daughter,
Who redeems nature from the general curse
Which twain have brought her to.

Edgar

Hail, gentle sir.

Gentleman

Sir, speed you: what's your will?

Edgar

Do you hear aught, sir, of a battle toward?

Gentleman

Most sure and vulgar. Everyone hears that
Which can distinguish sound.

Edgar

But, by your favour,

189 seconds: *supporters*

189 salt: *tears*

197 life: *hope*

202 twain: *the two sisters, General and Regan*

205 sure and vulgar: *definite and widely known*

208 main descry...thought: *their main forces are expected soon*

218 Am pregnant...pity: *have learned to show sympathy*

219 biding: *safe haven*

220 benison: *blessing*

221 boot: *further reward*
proclaimed prize: *outlaw with reward for capture*

222 framed flesh: *born*

How near's the other army?

Gentleman

Near and on speedy foot; the main descry
Stands on the hourly thought.

Edgar

I thank you, sir: that's all.

Gentleman

Though that the Queen on special cause is here,
Her army is moved on.

Edgar

I thank you, sir.

Exit Gentleman

Gloucester

You ever-gentle gods, take my breath from me.
Let not my worser spirit tempt me again
To die before you please!

Edgar

Well pray you, father.

Gloucester

Now, good sir, what are you?

Edgar

A most poor man, made tame to fortune's blows,
Who, by the art of known and feeling sorrows
Am pregnant to good pity. Give me your hand,
I'll lead you to some biding.

Gloucester

Hearty thanks.
The bounty and the benison of heaven
To boot, and boot!

Enter Oswald

Oswald

A proclaimed prize! Most happy!
That eyeless head of thine was first framed flesh
To raise my fortunes. Thou old unhappy traitor,
Briefly thyself remember. The sword is out
That must destroy thee.

Gloucester

Now let thy friendly hand
Put strength enough to't.

Edgar intervenes

Oswald

Wherefore, bold peasant,
Darest thou support a published traitor? Hence,
Lest that the infection of his fortune take
Like hold on thee. Let go his arm.

Edgar

Chill not let go, zir, without vurther 'casion.

Oswald

Let go, slave, or thou diest!

Edgar

Good gentleman, go your gait, and let poor volk pass. An chud ha' bin zwaggered out of my life, 'twould not ha' bin zo long as 'tis by a vortnight. Nay, come not near th' old man; keep out, che vor'ye, or I'se try whether your custard or my ballow be the harder. Chill be plain with you.

Oswald

Out, dunghill!

Edgar

Chill pick your teeth, zir. Come, no matter vor your foins.

They fight, and Edgar knocks him down

Oswald

Slave, thou hast slain me. Villain, take my purse.
If ever thou wilt thrive, bury my body,
And give the letters which thou find'st about me
To Edmund, Earl of Gloucester. Seek him out
Upon the British party. O, untimely death!

Dies

Edgar

I know thee well. A serviceable villain,
As duteous to the vices of thy mistress
As badness would desire.

Gloucester

What, is he dead?

227 published: *proclaimed*

230 Chill: *I will*
zir: *sir*

232 go your gait: *go on your way*

233 zwaggered: *bullied*

235 che vor'ye: *I warn you*
custard: *apple head*

236 ballow: *cudgel, stick*

238 foins: *thrusts (of Oswald's weapon)*

244 serviceable: *useful*

Edgar

Sit you down, father; rest you.
Let's see these pockets. The letters that he speaks of
May be my friends. He's dead. I am only sorry
He had no other deathsman. Let us see.
Leave, gentle wax; and, manners, blame us not
To know our enemies' minds, we'ld rip their hearts,
Their papers, is more lawful.

Reads

'Let our reciprocal vows be remembered. You have many opportunities to cut him off. If your will want not, time and place will be fruitfully offered. There is nothing done, if he return the conqueror. Then am I the prisoner, and his bed my gaol. From the loathed warmth whereof deliver me, and supply the place for your labour.
Your (wife, so I would say)
Affectionate servant,
Goneril.'

O undistinguished space of woman's will!
A plot upon her virtuous husband's life,
And the exchange my brother! Here, in the sands,
Thee I'll rake up, the post unsanctified
Of murderous lechers, and in the mature time
With this ungracious paper strike the sight
Of the death-practised duke. For him 'tis well
That of thy death and business I can tell.

Gloucester

The king is mad. How stiff is my vile sense,
That I stand up, and have ingenious feeling
Of my huge sorrows! Better I were distract,
So should my thoughts be severed from my griefs,
And woes by wrong imaginations lose
The knowledge of themselves.

Drum far off

Edgar

Give me your hand.
Far off, methinks, I hear the beaten drum.
Come, father, I'll bestow you with a friend.

Exeunt

250 deathsman: *executioner*
251 wax: *wax seal on the letter*
254 reciprocal: *mutual*
255 cut him off: *kill Albany*
264 undistinguished: *boundless*
267 rake up: *cover thinly*
post unsanctified: *evil messenger*
268 murderous lechers: *Goneril and Edmund*
269 ungracious paper: *evil letter*
270 death-practised duke: *Albany, the intended target*
271 thy: *Oswald's*
272 How stiff...sense: *difficult it is to express what I feel*
273 ingenious: *fully conscious*
274 distract: *mad*
276 wrong imaginations: *insanity*
279 bestow you: *find you safe lodgings*

Analysis

Deception and hope (lines 1–80)

As Gloucester struggles with his increasing despair, Edgar is determined to save him from suicide. Still in disguise, he describes what he can 'see' in front of him in an effort to convince his father that they are close to a cliff that is 'Horrible steep'. He continues his vivid portrayal of the imaginary coastal scene and even mimics the sound of the waves, 'The murmuring surge'. Gloucester kneels and, in his anguish, he blesses Edgar, not knowing whether he is alive or dead.

Edgar is no longer the easily deceived brother who believes everything he hears. He assumes a more active role and demonstrates considerable skill and cunning when he introduces himself to the fallen Gloucester as a countryman who has just witnessed what has happened. In this new disguise, Edgar must pretend that he does not know Gloucester is blind, urging him, 'Do but look up'. He even refers to Poor Tom, 'what thing was that/ Which parted from you?'

Edgar insists that Gloucester's survival can only be described as 'a miracle'. Once again, he reveals his faith in divine justice, 'the clearest gods'. Edgar's efforts bring about a significant change in Gloucester, who is now prepared to accept that the gods have saved him. He now promises to endure life as best he can: 'Henceforth I'll bear/ Affliction'.

Is the audience relieved that Edgar is showing signs that he will soon challenge his unscrupulous brother? Or is all the deception unconvincing?

Surreal wisdom (lines 81–219)

Edgar is shocked by the sudden appearance of Lear, fantastically clothed in weeds, a 'side-piercing sight'. The king seems to have has lost all touch with real life, hallucinating wildly and speaking in jumbled phrases about money, justice and archery. He imagines seeing an arrow hit its mark, imitating its whooshing sound. Suddenly there is a glimmer of reality as Gloucester recognises his master: 'I know that voice'.

The main plot and the sub-plot intermingle in this scene. Two old men meet, each brought down by their own character flaws. Both of them have been betrayed by ungrateful children, but have gained wisdom through suffering.

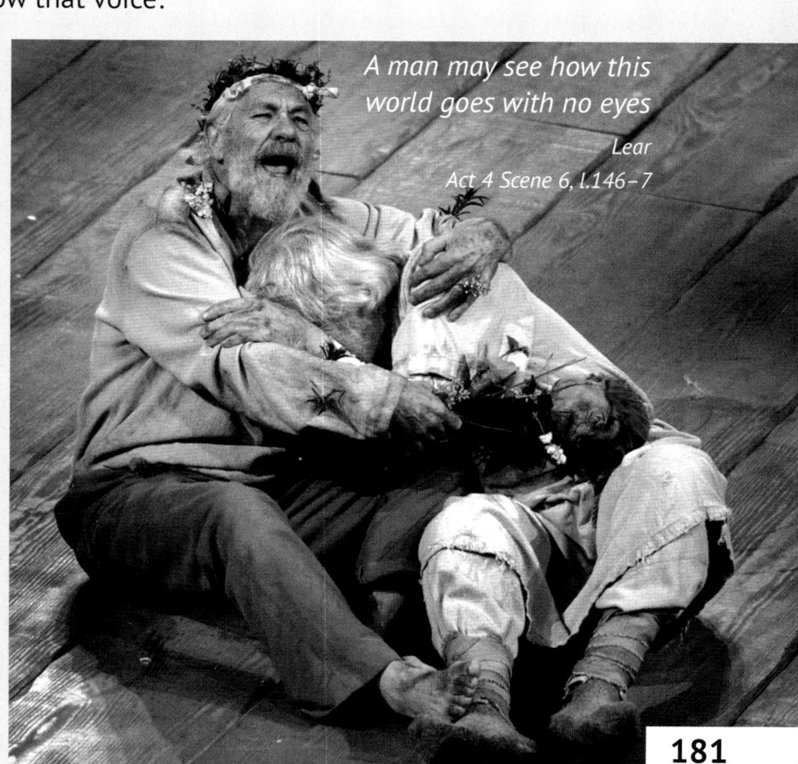

A man may see how this world goes with no eyes

Lear
Act 4 Scene 6, l.146–7

Lear's disturbed state of mind is evident in his obsessive repetition of his treatment at the hands of his elder daughters: 'They flattered me like a dog'. Another step on his road to self-knowledge is taken with his concluding realisation that he is not all-powerful after all: 'I am not ague-proof'.

The depth of Lear's hatred of humanity is expressed in his disgust with female sexuality. His comments on adultery and sex reflects his inner turmoil: 'The wren goes to 't and the small gilded fly'. Critics sometimes find his remarks offensive, but usually recognise the likely relevance to Goneril and Regan's treachery.

Lear is a pathetic presence who is simply overwhelmed by his suffering, madness, and loss of faith in life itself. He even imagines using strong perfume to sweeten his imagination.

Shakespeare often regards the world as a performance where human beings are at the mercy of cruel forces. In his madness, Lear is convinced that all of life is absurd. He speaks of the moment of birth, when a child arrives in this imperfect world: 'we cry that we are come/ To this great stage of fools', revealing his negative outlook, and his disillusionment with human beings and their motives. His opinion of his fellow human beings is a direct consequence of his own foolishness.

When Cordelia's followers find Lear, they are shocked at the state of the once-powerful monarch: 'A sight most pitiful in the meanest wretch,/ Past speaking of in a king'. He is completely unsettled by their arrival and behaves as if he were playing a children's game of hunt and hound.

There are occasional moments of insight for Lear as he recalls his former royal authority, using powerful language: 'Ay, every inch a King./ When I do stare, see how the subject quakes'. Despite his insanity, it is also clear that he has finally learned that power is control: 'A dog's obeyed in office'.

In contrast, Gloucester has at least found some peace of mind – thanks to the supportive influence of Edgar. He prays to the 'ever-gentle gods' that they should 'take my breath from me' if he is tempted by thoughts of suicide again. Edgar is naturally pleased at this outcome. It is also likely to leave audiences hoping that Cordelia may have a similarly positive effect on her father.

Fragile hope (lines 220–279)

It becomes clear why Edgar thought it necessary to remain in disguise as a countryman. Danger appears in the form of Oswald who – on Regan's orders – tries to kill Gloucester, a 'proclaimed prize'. As always, Oswald's only motive is personal advantage, and he is outraged that a peasant should support someone who has been declared a traitor. However, Edgar is ready to defend his father at all costs.

Oswald's death is a significant blow to the forces of evil. It also shows that Edgar is gaining confidence and beginning to correct some of the wrongs in Lear's kingdom.

Oswald is fatally wounded by Edgar. With his dying breath, he still tries to fulfil his duty to deliver Goneril's letters to Edmund. But Edgar refuses to forgive the 'serviceable villain'. Instead, he rips open the letters and discovers Goneril's involvement with his brother.

Edgar is left reeling with shock at the revelations and is determined to disclose the letter's details to Albany.

Meanwhile, Gloucester longs to be mad like Lear, so that he would be unaware of all the terrible things happening around him: 'Better I were distract'. To the ominous sounds of the approaching drums of battle, Edgar leads his father to the safety of the French camp at Dover. Once again, the scene ends on an edgy and uncertain note. What will happen next? Will good or evil triumph?

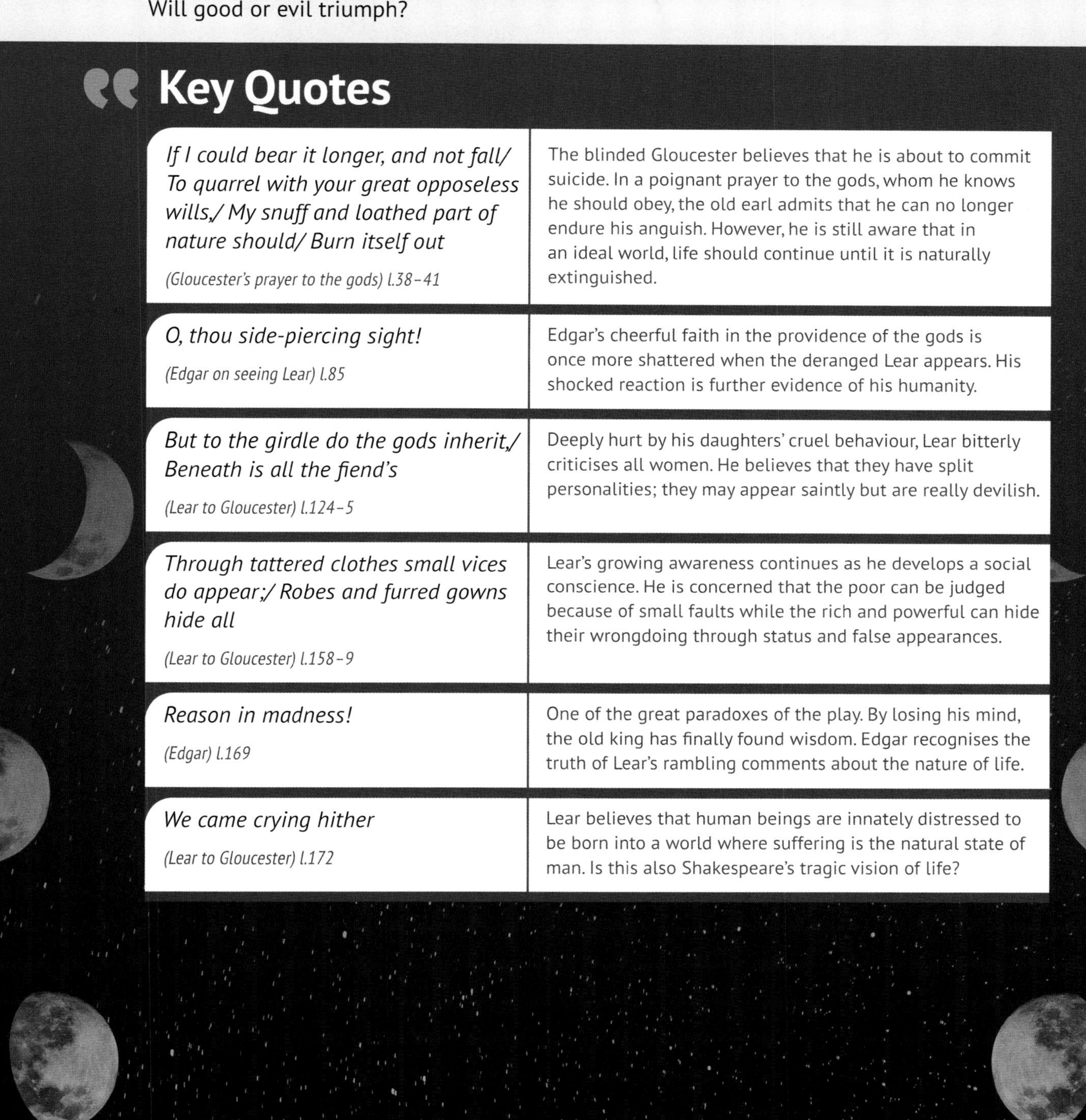

Key Quotes

Quote	Comment
If I could bear it longer, and not fall/ To quarrel with your great opposeless wills,/ My snuff and loathed part of nature should/ Burn itself out (Gloucester's prayer to the gods) l.38–41	The blinded Gloucester believes that he is about to commit suicide. In a poignant prayer to the gods, whom he knows he should obey, the old earl admits that he can no longer endure his anguish. However, he is still aware that in an ideal world, life should continue until it is naturally extinguished.
O, thou side-piercing sight! (Edgar on seeing Lear) l.85	Edgar's cheerful faith in the providence of the gods is once more shattered when the deranged Lear appears. His shocked reaction is further evidence of his humanity.
But to the girdle do the gods inherit,/ Beneath is all the fiend's (Lear to Gloucester) l.124–5	Deeply hurt by his daughters' cruel behaviour, Lear bitterly criticises all women. He believes that they have split personalities; they may appear saintly but are really devilish.
Through tattered clothes small vices do appear;/ Robes and furred gowns hide all (Lear to Gloucester) l.158–9	Lear's growing awareness continues as he develops a social conscience. He is concerned that the poor can be judged because of small faults while the rich and powerful can hide their wrongdoing through status and false appearances.
Reason in madness! (Edgar) l.169	One of the great paradoxes of the play. By losing his mind, the old king has finally found wisdom. Edgar recognises the truth of Lear's rambling comments about the nature of life.
We came crying hither (Lear to Gloucester) l.172	Lear believes that human beings are innately distressed to be born into a world where suffering is the natural state of man. Is this also Shakespeare's tragic vision of life?

Act 4

Scene 7*

INTRODUCTION

- Lear is still confused, but begins to recover his senses.
- He recognises Cordelia and begs forgiveness.
- Cordelia pardons him unconditionally.
- Edmund, the new Earl of Gloucester, leads the British troops.

*** This key scene requires close, detailed study.**

A tent in the French camp near Dover

Enter Cordelia, Kent (disguised) and Doctor

Cordelia

O thou good Kent, how shall I live and work,
To match thy goodness? My life will be too short,
And every measure fail me.

Kent

To be acknowledged, madam, is o'erpaid.
All my reports go with the modest truth,
Nor more nor clipped, but so.

Cordelia

Be better suited.
These weeds are memories of those worser hours.
I prithee, put them off.

Kent

Pardon me, dear madam.
Yet to be known shortens my made intent.
My boon I make it, that you know me not
Till time and I think meet.

Cordelia

Then be it so, my good Lord.

To the Doctor

How does the king?

Doctor

Madam, sleeps still.

Cordelia

O you kind gods,
Cure this great breach in his abused nature!
The untuned and jarring senses, O, wind up
Of this child-changed father!

Doctor

So please your majesty
That we may wake the King. He hath slept long.

Cordelia

Be governed by your knowledge, and proceed
I' the sway of your own will. Is he arrayed?

5 modest truth: *genuine reality*
6 clipped: *understated*
7 weeds: *ragged clothes (Kent's disguise)*
9 shortens my made intent: *interferes with my plans*
10 boon: *request, favour*
16 breach: *wound*
17 untuned: *disturbed, unsettled*
jarring: *harsh*
18 child-changed: *changed (to madness) by his cruel daughters*
21 sway: *judgement*
arrayed: *dressed*

Gentleman

Ay, madam. In the heaviness of his sleep
We put fresh garments on him.

Doctor

Be by, good madam, when we do awake him,
I doubt not of his temperance.

Cordelia

Very well.

Doctor

Please you, draw near. Louder the music there!

Cordelia

O my dear father! Restoration hang
Thy medicine on my lips, and let this kiss
Repair those violent harms that my two sisters
Have in thy reverence made!

Kent

Kind and dear Princess!

Cordelia

Had you not been their father, these white flakes
Had challenged pity of them. Was this a face
To be opposed against the warring winds?
To stand against the deep dread-bolted thunder?
In the most terrible and nimble stroke
Of quick, cross lightning? To watch, poor perdu,
With this thin helm? Mine enemy's dog,
Though he had bit me, should have stood that night
Against my fire. And wast thou fain, poor father,
To hovel thee with swine, and rogues forlorn,
In short and musty straw? Alack, alack!
'Tis wonder that thy life and wits at once
Had not concluded all. He wakes. Speak to him.

Doctor

Madam, do you; 'tis fittest.

Cordelia

How does my royal lord? How fares your majesty?

Lear

You do me wrong to take me out o' the grave.
Thou art a soul in bliss, but I am bound

25 temperance: *mood, self-control*

31 white flakes: *snow-white hair*

35 nimble stroke: *sharp bolt*

36 poor perdu: *lost sentry*

37 thin helm: *scant covering of hair*

39 fain: *gladly*

40 hovel: *stay in a dirty shack*

47 soul in bliss: *angel*

Upon a wheel of fire, that mine own tears
Do scald like molten lead.

Cordelia

Sir, do you know me?

Lear

You are a spirit, I know. When did you die?

Cordelia

Still, still, far wide!

Doctor

He's scarce awake. Let him alone awhile.

Lear

Where have I been? Where am I? Fair daylight?
I am mightily abused. I should e'en die with pity,
To see another thus. I know not what to say.
I will not swear these are my hands. Let's see,
I feel this pin prick. Would I were assured
Of my condition!

Cordelia

O, look upon me, sir,
And hold your hands in benediction o'er me.
No, sir, you must not kneel.

Lear

Pray, do not mock me.
I am a very foolish fond old man,
Fourscore and upward, not an hour more nor less,
And, to deal plainly,
I fear I am not in my perfect mind.
Methinks I should know you, and know this man,
Yet I am doubtful for I am mainly ignorant
What place this is, and all the skill I have
Remembers not these garments, nor I know not
Where I did lodge last night. Do not laugh at me,
For, as I am a man, I think this lady
To be my child Cordelia.

Cordelia

And so I am, I am.

48 a wheel of fire: *hellish torment*
49 molten: *smelted*
59 benediction: *blessing*
62 Fourscore and upward: *over eighty*

Lear

Be your tears wet? Yes, 'faith. I pray, weep not.
If you have poison for me, I will drink it.
I know you do not love me, for your sisters
Have, as I do remember, done me wrong.
You have some cause, they have not.

77 some cause: *a reason*

Cordelia

No cause, no cause.

Lear

Am I in France?

Kent

In your own kingdom, sir.

Lear

Do not abuse me.

79 abuse: *mock*

Doctor

Be comforted, good madam. The great rage,
You see, is killed in him. And yet it is danger
To make him even o'er the time he has lost.
Desire him to go in, trouble him no more
Till further settling.

84 settling: *calmness*

Cordelia

Will't please your highness walk?

Lear

You must bear with me. Pray you now, forget and forgive.
I am old and foolish.

Exeunt all but Kent and Gentleman

Gentleman

Holds it true, sir, that the Duke of Cornwall was so slain?

Kent

Most certain, sir.

Gentleman

Who is conductor of his people?

90 conductor: *leader*

Kent

As 'tis said, the bastard son of Gloucester.

Gentleman

They say Edgar, his banished son, is with the Earl of Kent in Germany.

Kent

Report is changeable. 'Tis time to look about. The powers of the kingdom approach apace.

Gentleman

The arbitrement is like to be bloody. Fare you well, sir.

Exit

Kent

My point and period will be throughly wrought,
Or well or ill, as this day's battle's fought.

Exit

94 powers: *military forces*

96 arbitrement: *outcome*

97 point and period: *purpose in life*
throughly: *thoroughly*

Key Scene Analysis

Loving kindness (lines 1–87)

Lear is now recovering at the French camp. Cordelia thanks Kent for his loyalty to her father and asks him to take off his ragged disguise ('weeds'), as they are reminders of a darker time when he was banished from Lear's court. However, Kent has other plans and says that he still needs to maintain his disguise.

Cordelia's natural sense of decency and justice is evident throughout, and her only concern now is the well-being of her 'child-changed father'. The mood is one of calmness and tenderness as the old king sleeps, surrounded by loyal supporters and a loving daughter: 'let this kiss/ Repair those violent harms'. Cordelia is greatly changed from the stubborn and distant girl she was in the play's opening scene. She addresses the sleeping Lear, but seems slightly hesitant about speaking to her father directly, suggesting that she still finds it hard to express her feelings openly.

This warm reunion between Lear and his youngest daughter is in striking contrast to the many scenes of unbearable cruelty and sadness earlier in the act. Cordelia's sincere compassion demonstrates her absolute love for her father.

When Lear wakens, he is highly confused at first and feels tormented: 'I am bound/ Upon a wheel of fire'. As he comes to his senses, it's clear that he is haunted by shame and regret: 'mine own tears/ Do scald like molten lead'. Although he recognises his daughter, he thinks she is a spirit in heaven: 'Thou art a soul in bliss'. In response, Cordelia asks for his blessing and gets upset when he attempts to beg for forgiveness: 'No, sir, you must not kneel'.

Lear imagines that Cordelia is an angel who has saved him from eternal suffering. The wheel of fire is a well-known metaphor for hell and is appropriate for the ageing king who has now been rescued from a hellish existence on earth.

Now humble and restrained, Lear becomes much more self-aware, declaring himself 'a very foolish fond old man,/ Fourscore and upward'. He is also conscious that he may not have regained all his senses: 'I fear I am not in my perfect mind'. But like Cordelia, he has been transformed from the time of the 'love test', when he behaved as the tyrannical ruler who expected to be obeyed unquestioningly.

Lear offers to drink poison because he knows that he wronged Cordelia by disowning her: 'You have some cause'. However, he still refuses to accept responsibility for Goneril and Regan. Yet order has returned to Lear's life and his regeneration continues under the caring attention of his loving daughter.

The former king has learned many important lessons. He no longer sees himself as all-powerful and makes no mention of royalty. Instead, he acknowledges that Cordelia has every right to hate him.

Dark forces (lines 88–98)

We are reminded that the threat of evil has not disappeared. Talk of the coming conflict casts a shadow over the quiet scene of redemption. Kent and a gentleman discuss the killing of Cornwall by Edmund at Goneril's insistence, after Cornwall had made him Earl of Gloucester and rewarded him with his father's lands. Edmund now leads the British forces, and the scene concludes uneasily as final arrangements are made for battle.

Shakespeare's Dramatic Style

This gentle scene includes **interesting contrasts**. An appreciative Cordelia sets the positive tone: 'good Kent'. But just as the audience begins to settle, Shakespeare introduces a dark, ironic note when Cordelia unwittingly declares, 'My life will be too short,/ And every measure fail me'.

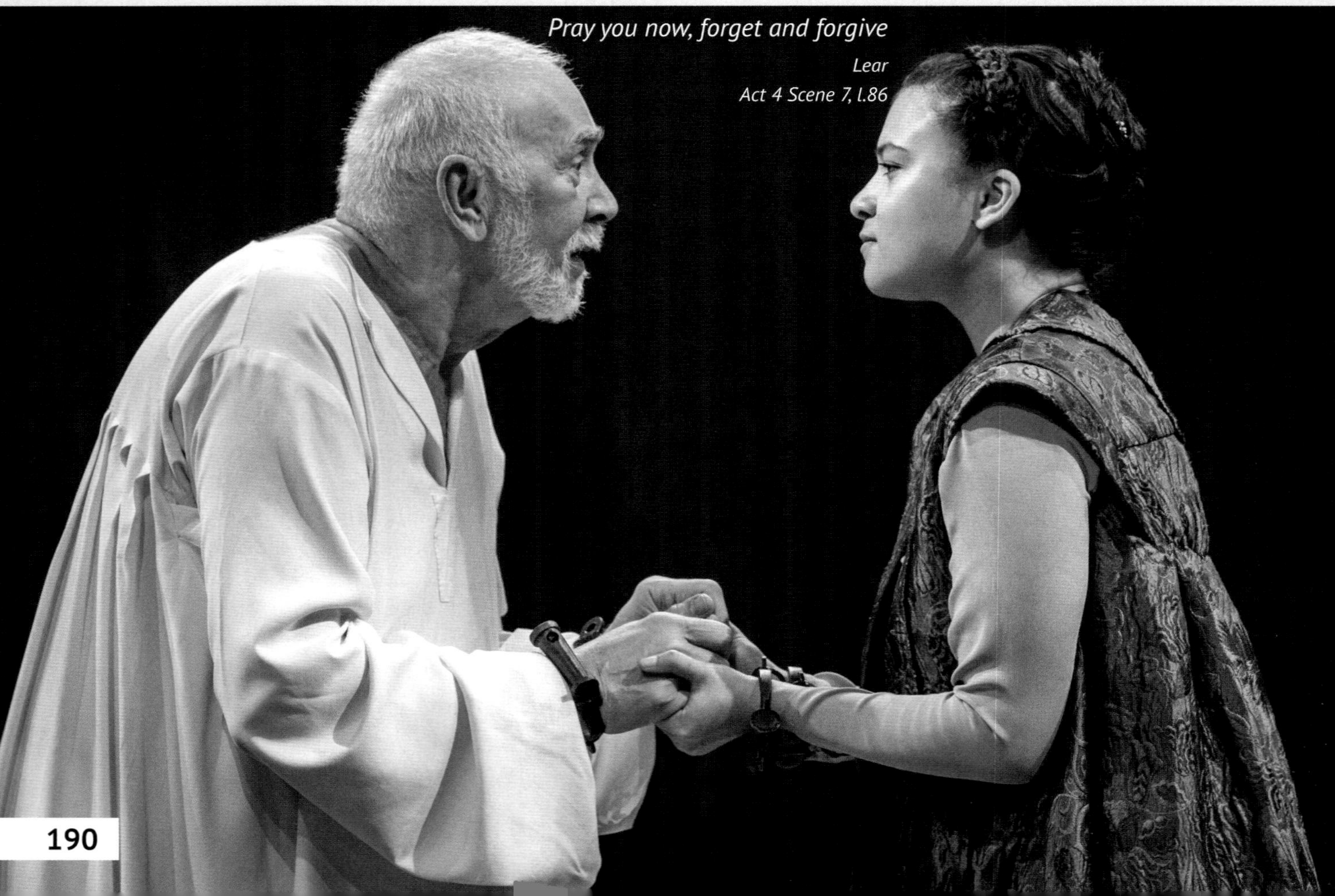

Pray you now, forget and forgive

Lear

Act 4 Scene 7, l.86

Another contrast is the expressive words of affection the formerly restrained Cordelia articulates to a sleeping Lear: 'Restoration hang/ Thy medicine on my lips'. **Animal imagery reflects sympathy**, not savagery: 'Mine enemy's dog/ Though he had bit me, should have stood that night/ Against my fire'. This is the exact opposite to the inhumane treatment of Lear by his two other daughters.

Throughout this scene of pathos and renewal, Shakespeare uses **simple language appropriate to the moving reconciliation** between the repentant father and his forgiving daughter; 'hold your hands in benediction o'er me', 'I am old and foolish'. Their emotional dialogue is more powerful because of its directness, with the phrase 'forget and forgive' emphasising the harmony between the now calm Lear and his gentle daughter.

Critical Analysis

'Act 4 Scene 7 highlights a transformation in Lear's character.' To what extent do you agree or disagree with this view? Develop your answer with suitable reference to the text.

Sample Paragraph 1

Lear totally highlights his transformation in the scene. He used to be proud. Regan and Goneril talked about the 'infirmity of his old age'. Since he's well over eighty. He was never totally fully in control – but totally 'rash' and especially mad on the heath scene. He wanted the winds to 'blow and crack their stormy cheeks'. He is still nearly mad to a degree. He thinks Cordelia's a ghost. Madness is Lear's natural state of mind. He thinks he is in hell 'scalded' by his own tears. But he still gets totally angry, especially with Kent. He does not like being told he is in his kingdom, and he does not like being 'abused'. I think we can highlight a transformation this scene. Cordelia has totally redeemed him and he is now humble and calm. He is transformed by suffering which is totally down to him and nobody else. *(150 words)*

Examiner's Comment

- A basic-grade standard that touches on some aspects of Lear's changing character.
- Points are somewhat disjointed, lacking development.
- Some inaccurate quotations – and over-use of 'He' and 'totally'.
- More careful control of expression would improve the standard.

Sample Paragraph 2

A different Lear emerges in this scene to the bullying king earlier. There is no sign of the 'the dragon and his wrath'. A more humane Lear is seen: 'The great rage you see is killed in him'. Lear has gained self-knowledge after terrible pain: 'I am a very foolish fond old man'. How different to the old king who 'hath ever but slenderly known himself'. He is no longer egotistical, but begs Cordelia: 'do not mock me'. Lear is ready to take poison because he feels he deserves punishment for his attitude to Cordelia. He even attempts to kneel before her – unlike when he first disowned her: 'I disclaim all my paternal care'. A simple phrase contains his deep sense of regret: 'forget and forgive'. As the scene ends, Lear admits: 'I am old and foolish'. He is transformed. *(140 words)*

Examiner's Comment

- Some clearly focused discussion points – well developed.
- Effective use of accurate quotes show engagement with the play.
- Good control of language throughout.
- A successful top-grade response.

Class/Homework Exercise

To what extent does Act 4 Scene 7 mark a significant turning point in the relationship between Cordelia and her father?

Write a paragraph (about 150 words), developing your response with reference to the text.

Exam Focus

Act 4 Scene 7 can be used successfully in response to a range of examination questions about the play's central themes, characters, relationships and the playwright's dramatic style.

This **key scene** has important dramatic functions:

- Illustrates the development in the characters of Lear and Cordelia.
- Emphasises their close father–child bond.
- Advances themes of appearance and reality, reconciliation and family love.
- Compelling, intense drama engages the audience.
- Contrasts happy reconciliation with looming conflict.
- Marks a significant turning point in the play.

Key Quotes

Quote	Comment
O thou good Kent, how shall I live and work,/ To match thy goodness? (Cordelia to Kent) l.1–2	This reunion scene begins on an optimistic note. Lear's youngest daughter greets the ever-loyal Kent warmly and wonders how she can live up to his good services to her distressed father.
Cure this great breach in his abused nature! (Cordelia's prayer) l.16	Cordelia's only concern is to restore her traumatised father to full health after the appalling treatment he has received from Goneril and Regan.
Had you not been their father, these white flakes/ Had challenged pity of them (Cordelia) l.31–2	The callous abuse of their father is denounced by an appalled Cordelia. She also castigates her sisters' lack of humanity and respect for Lear's age.
If you have poison for me, I will drink it (Lear to Cordelia) l.74	A contrite Lear acknowledges that he should be punished for his mistreatment of Cordelia.
Do not abuse me (Lear to Kent) l.79	Kent has assured the confused Lear that he is still in his own kingdom. However, the former king now knows that he gave away his power a long time ago, hence his bitter reply.
I am old and foolish (Lear to Cordelia) l.87	Lear has finally acknowledged his true state. He has come a long way on his torturous journey to self-knowledge.

Key Points | Act 4

Scene 1

- Edgar, still masquerading as Poor Tom, is shocked to meet his blinded father led by an old man.
- As Gloucester achieves personal growth, he has developed a social conscience.
- A despairing Gloucester wishes to commit suicide at Dover and asks the disguised Edgar to lead him there.

Scene 2

- The Duke of Albany has changed and is no longer willing to regard Lear and Cordelia as enemies or to see Edmund as loyal.
- Albany believes in divine justice and swears to avenge Gloucester's blinding. He condemns Goneril and Regan.
- Goneril has fallen in love with Edmund. She anticipates competition from Regan, who is now a widow.

Scene 3

- Cordelia is deeply distressed by her father's sufferings.
- Like Gloucester, the Earl of Kent believes in the stars' influence on the affairs of man.

Scene 4

- Cordelia orders a search for Lear, who is wandering the countryside.
- She announces that she is not in Britain for her own ambition but simply to aid her distressed father.

Scene 5

- The rivalry between Goneril and Regan increases.
- A jealous Regan attempts to read Goneril's letter to Edmund.
- Her instruction to Oswald to kill the blinded Gloucester if he should meet him is further evidence of her completely amoral character.
- Oswald proves himself to be as treacherous as the two sisters he serves.

Scene 6

- Edgar deceives his father to prevent him from committing suicide.
- Plot and sub-plot merge with the meeting of the unhinged Lear and the blind Gloucester.
- Lear's condemnation of corruption displays insight into the power of money and social status to influence the judicial system.
- Goneril sends a letter to Edmund and encourages him to kill her husband.
- Oswald attempts to kill Gloucester as Regan had instructed. He is slain by Edgar, who finds Goneril's incriminating letter.

Scene 7

- Lear is reconciled with his devoted daughter, Cordelia.
- Cordelia is presented as a symbol of goodness.
- Lear's lucid moments convey his personal journey to wisdom and self-knowledge.

Act 5
Scene 1

INTRODUCTION

- Edmund has doubts that Albany can be relied upon to fight the French invaders.
- Goneril and Regan's jealousy over Edmund intensifies.
- Both sisters are unaware that Edmund is using them cold-heartedly.
- He also plans to execute Lear and Cordelia after the battle.

The British camp near Dover

Enter, with drum and colours, Edmund, Regan, Gentlemen, and Soldiers

Edmund

Know of the duke if his last purpose hold,
Or whether since he is advised by aught
To change the course. He's full of alteration
And self-reproving. Bring his constant pleasure.

To a Gentleman, who goes out

Regan

Our sister's man is certainly miscarried.

Edmund

'Tis to be doubted, madam.

Regan

Now, sweet lord,
You know the goodness I intend upon you.
Tell me, but truly, but then speak the truth,
Do you not love my sister?

Edmund

In honoured love.

Regan

But have you never found my brother's way
To the forfended place?

Edmund

That thought abuses you.

Regan

I am doubtful that you have been conjunct
And bosomed with her, as far as we call hers.

Edmund

No, by mine honour, madam.

Regan

I never shall endure her. Dear my lord,
Be not familiar with her.

Edmund

Fear me not:
She and the duke her husband!

Enter, with drum and colours, Albany, Goneril and Soldiers

2 aught: *anything*

3 course: *plans*
alteration: *change*

4 self-reproving: *guilt, self-criticism*
constant pleasure: *final decision*

5 sister's man: *Oswald*
miscarried: *has met with harm*

10 brother: *Albany*

11 forfended place: *Goneril's bed*
abuses you: *does you no credit*

12 conjunct: *intimate*

Goneril

Aside

I had rather lose the battle than that sister
Should loosen him and me.

Albany

Our very loving sister, well be-met.
Sir, this I hear, the King is come to his daughter,
With others whom the rigour of our state
Forced to cry out. Where I could not be honest,
I never yet was valiant. For this business,
It touches us, as France invades our land,
Not bolds the king, with others, whom, I fear,
Most just and heavy causes make oppose.

Edmund

Sir, you speak nobly.

Regan

Why is this reasoned?

Goneril

Combine together 'gainst the enemy;
For these domestic and particular broils
Are not the question here.

Albany

Let's then determine
With the ancient of war on our proceedings.

Edmund

I shall attend you
Presently at your tent.

Regan

Sister, you'll go with us?

Goneril

No.

Regan

'Tis most convenient. Pray you, go with us.

Goneril:

Aside

O, ho, I know the riddle.– I will go.

As they are going out, enter Edgar disguised

19 loosen: *separate*

20 well be-met: *welcome*

22 rigour of our state: *harshness of our administration*

23 cry out: *complain, rebel*

25 touches us: *deeply concerns us*

26 bolds: *encourages to oppose*

30 domestic and particular broils: *personal arguments*

33 ancient of war: *experienced officers*

37 the riddle: *her true intentions*

Edgar

If e'er your grace had speech with man so poor,
Hear me one word.

Albany

I'll overtake you. Speak.

Exeunt all but Albany and Edgar

Edgar

Before you fight the battle, ope this letter.
If you have victory, let the trumpet sound
For him that brought it. Wretched though I seem,
I can produce a champion that will prove
What is avouched there. If you miscarry,
Your business of the world hath so an end,
And machination ceases. Fortune love you.

41 ope: *open*

44 champion: *defender, witness*

45 avouched: *disclosed*
miscarry: *fail*

47 machination: *plot, manoeuvring*

Albany

Stay till I have read the letter.

Edgar

I was forbid it.
When time shall serve, let but the herald cry,
And I'll appear again.

Albany

Why, fare thee well.
I will o'erlook thy paper.

Exit Edgar

Re-enter Edmund

Edmund

The enemy's in view. Draw up your powers.
Here is the guess of their true strength and forces
By diligent discovery, but your haste
Is now urged on you.

53 guess: *estimate*

54 diligent discovery: *painstaking monitoring*

Albany

We will greet the time.

55 greet the time: *be prepared*

Exit

Edmund

To both these sisters have I sworn my love;
Each jealous of the other, as the stung
Are of the adder. Which of them shall I take?
Both? One? Or neither? Neither can be enjoyed,
If both remain alive. To take the widow

57 jealous: *suspicious*

58 adder: *venomous snake*

Exasperates, makes mad her sister Goneril
And hardly shall I carry out my side,
Her husband being alive. Now then we'll use
His countenance for the battle, which being done,
Let her who would be rid of him devise
His speedy taking off. As for the mercy
Which he intends to Lear and Cordelia,
The battle done, and they within our power,
Shall never see his pardon. For my state
Stands on me to defend, not to debate.
Exit

64 countenance: *power*
65 devise: *arrange, concoct*
66 taking off: *murder*
69 state: *situation, plan*
70 defend: *act*

Analysis

Uncertainty and intrigue (lines 1–37)

In the British camp, Edmund is unsure of Albany's intentions: 'He's full of alteration/ And self-reproving'. Although he is leader of the British forces, Albany's sympathies lie with Lear and Cordelia. Regan is filled with suspicion about Edmund's feelings for Goneril. She shows signs of paranoid insecurity: 'Dear my lord,/ Be not familiar with her'. Edmund assures her that he will not be intimate with Goneril. The audience will find his promise less than convincing.

At the start of the play, Goneril and Regan were united against Lear and subsequently opposed him. Now that the sisters are divided due to jealousy over Edmund, they are more concerned with personal relations than political affairs.

Goneril is equally obsessed with Edmund and declares, 'I had rather lose the battle than that sister/ Should loosen him and me'. While Albany is debating the rights and wrongs of Lear's struggle against the new leaders of Britain, the sisters are engaged in a game of manoeuvres as they struggle against each other for Edmund's love.

Preparing for battle (lines 38–70)

Edgar appears in disguise, determined to deliver Goneril's incriminating letter to Albany. His mood has changed from the optimism of earlier scenes to a much more fatalistic attitude. He offers to 'produce a champion' for Albany if the British are successful in the battle. Edgar's painful experiences have made him a stronger character and he is now prepared to fight Edmund.

Gloucester's illegitimate son, Edmund, has always been excluded from society and so he recognises no authority. Everyone he encounters must give in to his selfish needs.

Edgar's arrival builds suspense towards the play's climax. The scene is filled with urgency, not only because of the impending battle, but also because of the competition between the sisters and Edmund's mistrust of everyone around him. Meanwhile, Edmund focuses on his long-term prospects, heartlessly considering which of Lear's daughters he will he choose: 'Both? One? Or neither?' He completely disregards their feelings and continues to act by the laws of nature – where the strongest always win.

In his soliloquy, Edmund promises to use Albany's support ('countenance') to help him win the battle against Cordelia's French army. He hopes that Goneril herself will find some way of killing Albany: 'Let her who would be rid of him devise/ His speedy taking off'. While constantly instigating terrible cruelty, Edmund never actually involves himself directly. He resolves that he will not adhere to Albany's plan to spare the lives of Lear and Cordelia after the war: 'they within our power,/ Shall never see his pardon'.

For Edmund, decisive action is now needed if he is to succeed: 'For my state/ Stands on me to defend, not to debate'. The scene concludes on a brisk, purposeful note. Shakespeare again leaves a mood of heightened expectancy. Will Lear's supporters be powerful enough to take on the ruthlessly determined British forces?

Key Quotes

Quote	Comment
Do you not love my sister? *(Regan to Edmund) l.9*	Now that she is a widow, Regan hopes to marry Edmund and her infatuation with him has made her increasingly neurotic. Here she directly confronts Edmund about his feelings for Goneril. She is suspicious that they are lovers.
I had rather lose the battle than that sister/ Should loosen him and me *(Goneril) l.18–19*	Goneril is equally obsessive, fearing that Edmund will favour her widowed sister over herself, who is still married to Albany. She is no longer primarily concerned with political matters, only personal affairs.
Neither can be enjoyed,/ If both remain alive. *(Edmund) l.59–60*	Edmund has always put his own interests before anything else. With chilling cynicism, he debates the true state of affairs in this triangle of lust.
we'll use/ His countenance for the battle *(Edmund) l.63–4*	Audiences are left in no doubt about Edmund's contempt for Albany. Always coolly rational, he will gladly benefit from the duke's authority on the battlefield and then discard him.
For my state/ Stands on me to defend *(Edmund) l.69–70*	Unlike Albany, the ambitious Edmund has no moral scruples about the impending battle. At the beginning of the play, he set out to advance his position and power. He now goes off to war to protect what he has gained.

Act 5
Scene 2

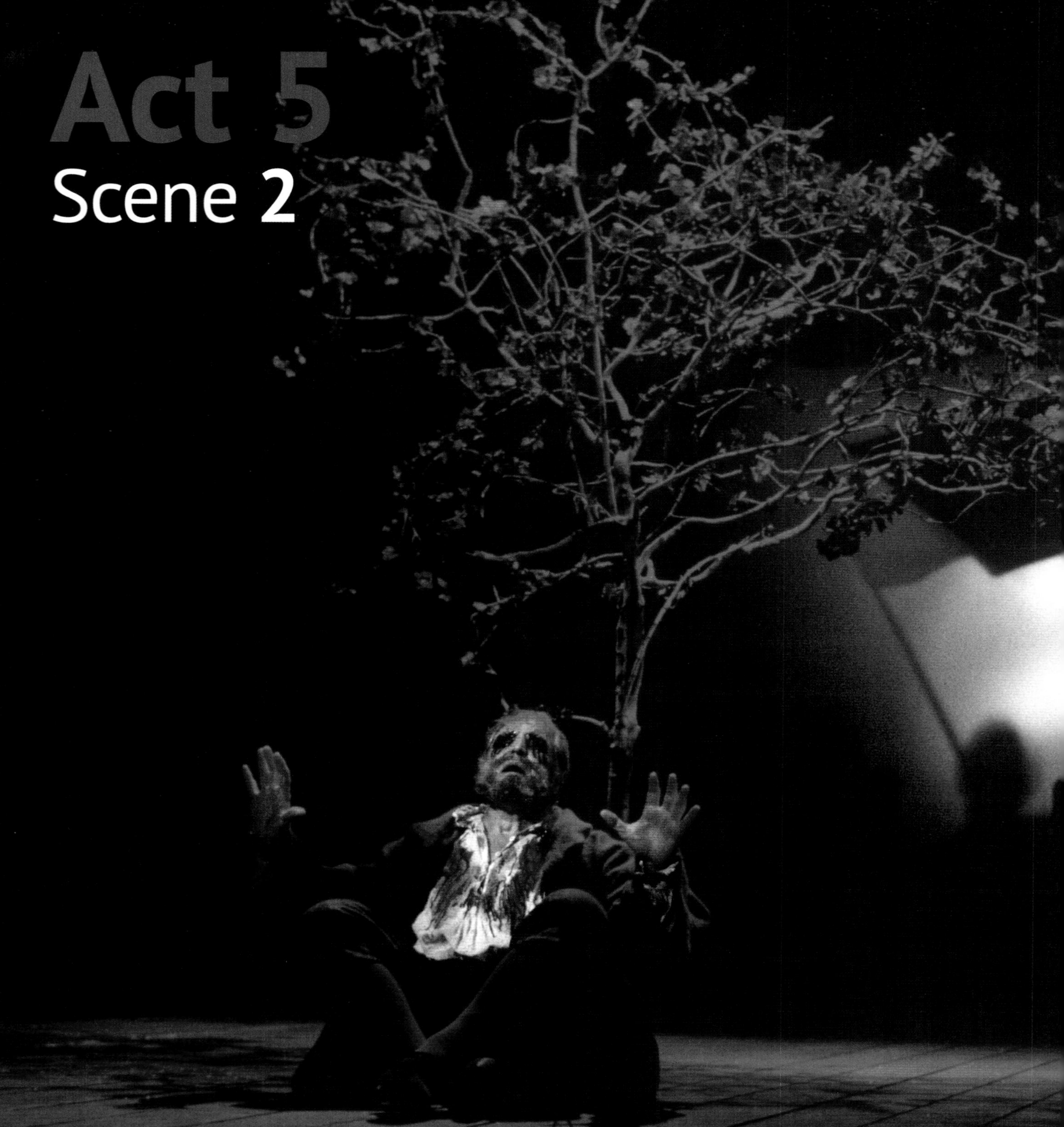

INTRODUCTION

- Edgar leads his father to safety for the last time.
- He soon returns with news that Cordelia's army has been defeated.
- Gloucester is plunged into deep despair once more.

A field between the two camps

Alarum within. Enter, with drum and colours, Lear, Cordelia and Soldiers, over the stage, and exeunt

Enter EDGAR and GLOUCESTER

Edgar

Here, father, take the shadow of this tree
For your good host. Pray that the right may thrive.
If ever I return to you again,
I'll bring you comfort.

Gloucester

Grace go with you, sir!

Exit Edgar

Alarum and retreat within. Re-enter Edgar

Edgar

Away, old man. Give me thy hand! Away!
King Lear hath lost, he and his daughter ta'en.
Give me thy hand; come on.

Gloucester

No farther, sir. A man may rot even here.

Edgar

What, in ill thoughts again? Men must endure
Their going hence, even as their coming hither.
Ripeness is all. Come on.

Gloucester

And that's true too.

Exeunt

8 father: *a general term of respect*

2 host: *place of shelter*
thrive: *win*

6 ta'en: *captured*

8 rot: *perish*

11 Ripeness: *maturity, readiness*

Analysis

Defeat (lines 1–11)

In this short scene, Shakespeare is more interested in the consequences of the battle than showing the actual fighting on stage. Edgar has brought his blind father to a place of safety before joining the conflict. He still believes in seeking the power of divine help: 'Pray that the right may thrive'. However, he soon returns with dire news that the battle has been won by Edmund and Albany's British troops who have captured Lear and Cordelia. Gloucester is filled with despair and becomes suicidal again: 'A man may rot even here'.

With the defeat of Cordelia's French forces, the earlier sense of hope and renewal has faded. Only Edgar is determined not to be overwhelmed by this setback. He remains strong and resilient, expressing his view that life's hardships and disappointments must be accepted: 'Men must endure/ Their going hence, even as their coming hither'. Human beings cannot choose their own deaths any more than their births.

Edgar's comment that 'Men must endure' reflects the commonly held Christian belief of Shakespeare's time that people should accept suffering and endure God's will. Therefore, everyone should be realistic about the inevitability of death.

Edgar is now transformed from the naive character who was so easily deceived in the play's opening scenes. Unlike his father, he regards dying as a natural part of the cycle of life and believes that people cannot change their destiny. Here we see a wiser, strong-willed man displaying admirable staying power.

Key Quotes

Men must endure/ Their going hence, even as their coming hither./ Ripeness is all *(Edgar to Gloucester) l.9–11*	The stoical Edgar reminds his pessimistic father that there is an order to the human life cycle and it has to be obeyed. It is natural to live, grow and die. Birth and life's other experiences must be accepted – and also death in the fullness of time.

Act 5
Scene 3*

INTRODUCTION

- Goneril poisons Regan and then kills herself.
- A disguised Edgar fatally wounds Edmund, who then confesses his guilt.
- Edgar reveals his true identity and the news of Gloucester's death.
- Lear dies, holding Cordelia's lifeless body in his arms.
- Edgar is left to establish law and order in Britain.

*** This key scene requires close, detailed study.**

The British camp near Dover

Enter, in conquest, with drum and colours, Edmund, Lear and Cordelia as prisoners, Captain, Soldiers

Edmund

Some officers take them away. Good guard,
Until their greater pleasures first be known
That are to censure them.

Cordelia

We are not the first
Who, with best meaning, have incurred the worst.
For thee, oppressed King, I am cast down;
Myself could else out-frown false fortune's frown.
Shall we not see these daughters and these sisters?

Lear

No, no, no, no! Come, let's away to prison.
We two alone will sing like birds i' the cage.
When thou dost ask me blessing, I'll kneel down,
And ask of thee forgiveness. So we'll live,
And pray, and sing, and tell old tales, and laugh
At gilded butterflies, and hear poor rogues
Talk of court news, and we'll talk with them too –
Who loses and who wins; who's in, who's out –
And take upon's the mystery of things,
As if we were God's spies. And we'll wear out,
In a walled prison, packs and sects of great ones,
That ebb and flow by the moon.

Edmund

Take them away.

Lear

Upon such sacrifices, my Cordelia,
The gods themselves throw incense. Have I caught thee?
He that parts us shall bring a brand from heaven,
And fire us hence like foxes. Wipe thine eyes,
The good-years shall devour them, flesh and fell,
Ere they shall make us weep. We'll see 'em starve first.
Come.

Exeunt Lear and Cordelia, guarded

1 Good guard: *keep strict watch*
3 censure them: *pass sentence on them*
4 meaning: *intention*
incurred: *suffered*
6 false: *fickle*
7 daughters and these sisters: *Goneril and Regan*
16 mystery of things: *divine truth of the universe*
18 packs and sects: *plots and groups*
21 throw incense: *worship*
caught thee: *convinced you*
24 good-years: *plagues*
fell: *skin*

Edmund

Come hither, Captain. Hark.
Take thou this note.

Giving a paper

Go follow them to prison.
One step I have advanced thee. If thou dost
As this instructs thee, thou dost make thy way
To noble fortunes. Know thou this, that men
Are as the time is. To be tender-minded
Does not become a sword. Thy great employment
Will not bear question. Either say thou't do 't,
Or thrive by other means.

Captain

I'll do 't, my lord.

Edmund

About it! And write happy when thou hast done.
Mark – I say, instantly; and carry it so
As I have set it down.

Captain

I cannot draw a cart, nor eat dried oats;
If it be man's work, I'll do't.

Exit

Flourish. Enter Albany, Goneril, Regan, another Captain and Soldiers

Albany

Sir, you have shown to-day your valiant strain,
And fortune led you well. You have the captives
That were the opposites of this day's strife.
I do require them of you, so to use them
As we shall find their merits and our safety
May equally determine.

Edmund

Sir, I thought it fit
To send the old and miserable king
To some retention and appointed guard;
Whose age has charms in it, whose title more,
To pluck the common bosom on his side,
And turn our impressed lances in our eyes

28 note: *death warrant on Cordelia and Lear*

40 draw a cart...: *be a horse*

42 valiant strain: *courage*

44 opposites: *opponents*

46 their merits: *what they deserve*

47 equally: *fairly*

49 retention: *place of confinement*

51 common bosom: *people's sympathy*

52 impressed lances: *conscripted soldiers*

56 session: *court sitting*

58 the heat: *times of anger*

62 patience: *permission*

63 brother: *equal*

63 list: *like*

64 pleasure might have been demanded: *wishes should have been consulted*

67 The which immediacy: *that association*

69 exalt: *promote*

70 addition: *title*

71 compeers: *equals*

74 a-squint: *distorted*

77 patrimony: *property inherited from my father*

Which do command them. With him I sent the Queen,
My reason all the same; and they are ready
Tomorrow, or at further space, to appear
Where you shall hold your session. At this time
We sweat and bleed. The friend hath lost his friend,
And the best quarrels, in the heat, are cursed
By those that feel their sharpness.
The question of Cordelia and her father
Requires a fitter place.

Albany

Sir, by your patience,
I hold you but a subject of this war,
Not as a brother.

Regan

That's as we list to grace him.
Methinks our pleasure might have been demanded,
Ere you had spoke so far. He led our powers,
Bore the commission of my place and person,
The which immediacy may well stand up,
And call itself your brother.

Goneril

Not so hot!
In his own grace he doth exalt himself,
More than in your addition.

Regan

In my rights,
By me invested, he compeers the best.

Goneril

That were the most, if he should husband you.

Regan

Jesters do oft prove prophets.

Goneril

Holla, holla!
That eye that told you so looked but a-squint.

Regan

Lady, I am not well; else I should answer
From a full-flowing stomach. General,
Take thou my soldiers, prisoners, patrimony;

Dispose of them, of me. The walls are thine.
Witness the world, that I create thee here
My lord and master.

Goneril

Mean you to enjoy him?

Albany

The let-alone lies not in your good will.

Edmund

Nor in thine, lord.

Albany

Half-blooded fellow, yes.

Regan

To Edmund

Let the drum strike, and prove my title thine.

Albany

Stay yet; hear reason. Edmund, I arrest thee
On capital treason; and, in thine attaint,
This gilded serpent.

Pointing to Goneril

For your claim, fair sister,
I bar it in the interest of my wife
'Tis she is sub-contracted to this lord,
And I, her husband, contradict your banns.
If you will marry, make your loves to me,
My lady is bespoke.

Goneril

An interlude!

Albany

Thou art armed, Gloucester. Let the trumpet sound.
If none appear to prove upon thy head
Thy heinous, manifest, and many treasons,
There is my pledge.

Throwing down a glove

I'll prove it on thy heart,
Ere I taste bread, thou art in nothing less
Than I have here proclaimed thee.

Regan

Sick, O, sick!

81 let-alone: *power to prevent*

82 half-blooded: *illegitimate*

85 attaint: *impeachment*

86 gilded serpent: *Goneril*

89 sub-contracted: *promised in marriage*

90 contradict: *forbid*
banns: *marriage arrangements*

92 bespoke: *promised*

92 interlude: *sham, farce*

95 heinous: *monstrous*

Goneril

Aside

If not, I'll ne'er trust medicine.

Edmund

There's my exchange.

Throwing down a glove

101 What in the world he is: *whatever rank he holds*

What in the world he is
That names me traitor, villain-like he lies.
Call by thy trumpet. He that dares approach,
On him, on you, who not? I will maintain
My truth and honour firmly.

Albany

A herald, ho!

Edmund

A herald, ho, a herald!

Albany

107 single virtue: *courage*

Trust to thy single virtue, for thy soldiers,
All levied in my name, have in my name
Took their discharge.

Regan

My sickness grows upon me.

Albany

She is not well; convey her to my tent.

Exit Regan, led

Enter a Herald

Come hither, herald – Let the trumpet sound,
And read out this.

Captain

Sound, trumpet!

A trumpet sounds

Herald

Reads

115 quality: *degree of nobility (only those of noble birth could challenge)*

117 manifold: *multiple*

'If any man of quality or degree within the lists of the army will maintain upon Edmund, supposed Earl of Gloucester, that he is a manifold traitor, let him appear by the third sound of the trumpet. He is bold in his defence.'

Edmund

Sound!

First trumpet

Herald

Again!

Second trumpet

Herald

Again!

Third trumpet

Trumpet answers within

Enter Edgar armed

Albany

Ask him his purposes, why he appears
Upon this call o' the trumpet.

Herald

What are you?
Your name, your quality? And why you answer
This present summons?

Edgar

Know, my name is lost,
By treason's tooth bare-gnawn and canker-bit.
Yet am I noble as the adversary
I come to cope.

126 bare-gnawn: *bitten away*
canker-bit: *withered, worm-eaten*

128 cope: *contest, challenge*

Albany

Which is that adversary?

Edgar

What's he that speaks for Edmund Earl of Gloucester?

Edmund

Himself. What say'st thou to him?

Edgar

Draw thy sword,
That, if my speech offend a noble heart,
Thy arm may do thee justice. Here is mine.
Behold, it is the privilege of mine honours,
My oath, and my profession. I protest,
Maugre thy strength, youth, place, and eminence,
Despite thy victor sword and fire-new fortune,
Thy valour and thy heart, thou art a traitor;
False to thy gods, thy brother, and thy father;
Conspirant 'gainst this high-illustrious prince.

133 it: *despite*

135 Maugre: *my sword*

136 victor sword: *recent success in battle*
fire-new fortune: *newly minted luck*

142 toad-spotted: *stained with treason*
143 my best...bent: *all my determination*
146 outside: *appearance*
147 say: *sign*
148 nicely: *carefully*
149 disdain: *scorn*
152 glance: *skim*
156 practice: *duplicity*
158 opposite: *opponent*
159 cozened and beguiled: *cheated and deceived*
164 arraign: *charge*

And, from the extremest upward of thy head
To the descent and dust below thy foot,
A most toad-spotted traitor. Say thou 'No,'
This sword, this arm, and my best spirits, are bent
To prove upon thy heart, whereto I speak,
Thou liest.

Edmund

In wisdom I should ask thy name;
But, since thy outside looks so fair and warlike,
And that thy tongue some say of breeding breathes,
What safe and nicely I might well delay
By rule of knighthood, I disdain and spurn.
Back do I toss these treasons to thy head,
With the hell-hated lie o'erwhelm thy heart,
Which, for they yet glance by and scarcely bruise,
This sword of mine shall give them instant way,
Where they shall rest for ever. Trumpets, speak!
Alarums. They fight. Edmund falls.

Albany

Save him, save him!

Goneril

This is practice, Gloucester.
By the law of arms thou wast not bound to answer
An unknown opposite. Thou art not vanquished,
But cozened and beguiled.

Albany

Shut your mouth, dame,
Or with this paper shall I stop it. *[To Edgar]* Hold, sir.
[To Edmund] Thou worse than any name, read thine own evil.
[To Goneril] No tearing, lady. I perceive you know it.
Gives the letter to Edmund

Goneril

Say, if I do, the laws are mine, not thine.
Who can arraign me for it.

Albany

Most monstrous! oh!
[To Edmund] Know'st thou this paper?

Edmund

Ask me not what I know.

Exit

Albany

Go after her. She's desperate; govern her.

Edmund

What you have charged me with, that have I done,
And more, much more; the time will bring it out.
'Tis past, and so am I. But what art thou
That hast this fortune on me? If thou'rt noble,
I do forgive thee.

Edgar

Let's exchange charity.
I am no less in blood than thou art, Edmund.
If more, the more thou hast wronged me.
My name is Edgar, and thy father's son.
The gods are just, and of our pleasant vices
Make instruments to plague us.
The dark and vicious place where thee he got
Cost him his eyes.

Edmund

Thou hast spoken right, 'tis true.
The wheel is come full circle. I am here.

Albany

Methought thy very gait did prophesy
A royal nobleness. I must embrace thee.
Let sorrow split my heart, if ever I
Did hate thee or thy father!

Edgar

Worthy prince, I know it.

Albany

Where have you hid yourself?
How have you known the miseries of your father?

Edgar

By nursing them, my lord. List a brief tale.
And when 'tis told, O, that my heart would burst!
The bloody proclamation to escape,
That followed me so near – O, our lives' sweetness!
That we the pain of death would hourly die
Rather than die at once – taught me to shift
Into a madman's rags, to assume a semblance

167 desperate: *in a state of despair*

171 fortune: *advantage*

172 charity: *forgiveness*

176 pleasant vices: *vicious acts that give us pleasure*

178 got: *begot, conceived you*

180 full circle: *Edmund is back where he started*

181 gait: *walk, body language*

189 proclamation: *warrant for his arrest*

192 shift: *change*

194 habit: *disguise*
195 rings: *eye sockets*
196 new: *lately*
202 flawed: *weak, broken*
204 passion: *emotion*
207 as: *as though*
210 period: *end*
211 another: *another story*
212 amplify: *increase it*
213 top extremity: *go beyond what is tolerable*
214 clamour: *grief*
217 so endured: *lived as Poor Tom*
219 him: *himself*
222 puissant: *powerful*
224 tranced: *dazed*

That very dogs disdained, and in this habit
Met I my father with his bleeding rings,
Their precious stones new lost; became his guide,
Led him, begged for him, saved him from despair;
Never – O fault – revealed myself unto him,
Until some half-hour past, when I was armed.
Not sure, though hoping, of this good success,
I asked his blessing, and from first to last
Told him my pilgrimage. But his flawed heart,
Alack, too weak the conflict to support!
'Twixt two extremes of passion, joy and grief,
Burst smilingly.

Edmund

This speech of yours hath moved me,
And shall perchance do good. But speak you on;
You look as you had something more to say.

Albany

If there be more, more woeful, hold it in.
For I am almost ready to dissolve,
Hearing of this.

Edgar

This would have seemed a period
To such as love not sorrow; but another,
To amplify too much, would make much more,
And top extremity.
Whilst I was big in clamour came there in a man,
Who, having seen me in my worst estate,
Shunned my abhorred society. But then, finding
Who 'twas that so endured, with his strong arms
He fastened on my neck, and bellowed out
As he'd burst heaven; threw him on my father;
Told the most piteous tale of Lear and him
That ever ear received. Which in recounting
His grief grew puissant and the strings of life
Began to crack. Twice then the trumpets sounded,
And there I left him tranced.

Albany

But who was this?

Edgar

Kent, sir, the banished Kent, who in disguise
Followed his enemy king, and did him service
Improper for a slave.

Enter a Gentleman, with a bloody knife

Gentleman

Help, help, O, help!

Edgar

What kind of help?

Albany

Speak, man.

Edgar

What means that bloody knife?

Gentleman

'Tis hot, it smokes.
It came even from the heart of – O! She's dead!

Albany

Who dead? Speak, man.

Gentleman

Your lady, sir, your lady, and her sister
By her is poisoned. She hath confessed it.

Edmund

I was contracted to them both. All three
Now marry in an instant.

Edgar

Here comes Kent.

Albany

Produce their bodies, be they alive or dead.
This judgement of the heavens, that makes us tremble,
Touches us not with pity.

Exit Gentleman

Enter Kent

O, is this he?
The time will not allow the compliment
Which very manners urges.

Kent

I am come

227 Improper: *unworthy of*

234 contracted: *engaged*

235 marry: *united in death*

240 compliment: *greeting*

241 manners: *courtesy*

To bid my king and master aye good night.
Is he not here?

Albany

Great thing of us forgot!
Speak, Edmund, where's the king? And where's Cordelia?
See'st thou this object, Kent?

The bodies of Goneril and Regan are brought in

Kent

Alack, why thus?

Edmund

Yet Edmund was beloved.
The one the other poisoned for my sake,
And after slew herself.

Albany

Even so. Cover their faces.

Edmund

I pant for life. Some good I mean to do,
Despite of mine own nature. Quickly send,
Be brief in it, to the castle, for my writ
Is on the life of Lear and on Cordelia:
Nay, send in time.

Albany

Run, run, O, run!

Edgar

To who, my lord? Who hath the office? Send
Thy token of reprieve.

Edmund

Well thought on. Take my sword,
Give it the captain.

Albany

Haste thee, for thy life.

Exit Edgar

Edmund

He hath commission from thy wife and me
To hang Cordelia in the prison, and
To lay the blame upon her own despair,
That she fordid herself.

245 object: *this awful sight*
248 after slew: *later killed*
252 writ: *death warrant*
255 office: *task*
256 reprieve: *pardon*
259 commission: *command*
262 fordid: *killed*

Albany

The gods defend her! Bear him hence awhile.

Edmund is borne off

Re-enter Lear with Cordelia dead in his arms, Edgar, Captain and others following

Lear

Howl, howl, howl, howl! O, you are men of stones.
Had I your tongues and eyes, I'd use them so
That heaven's vault should crack. She's gone for ever!
I know when one is dead, and when one lives,
She's dead as earth. Lend me a looking-glass.
If that her breath will mist or stain the stone,
Why, then she lives.

Kent

Is this the promised end?

Edgar

Or image of that horror?

Albany

Fall, and cease!

Lear

This feather stirs. She lives! If it be so,
It is a chance which does redeem all sorrows
That ever I have felt.

Kent

Kneeling

O my good master!

Lear

Prithee, away.

Edgar

'Tis noble Kent, your friend.

Lear

A plague upon you, murderers, traitors all!
I might have saved her! Now she's gone for ever!
Cordelia, Cordelia! Stay a little. Ha!
What is it thou say'st? Her voice was ever soft,
Gentle, and low, an excellent thing in woman.
I killed the slave that was a-hanging thee.

266 vault: *dome, sky*

271 image of that horror: *vision of Doomsday*

283 falchion: *curved sword*

285 crosses: *troubles*

287 she: *fortune, fate*

289 dull sight: *sad spectacle*

291 Caius: *Kent's name when in disguise*

295 I'll see that straight: *I'll attend to that in a moment*

296 first of difference and decay: *beginning of the abdication and banishment*

299 fordone: *destroyed*

Captain

'Tis true, my lords, he did.

Lear

Did I not, fellow?
I have seen the day, with my good biting falchion
I would have made them skip. I am old now,
And these same crosses spoil me. Who are you?
Mine eyes are not o' the best. I'll tell you straight.

Kent

If fortune brag of two she loved and hated,
One of them we behold.

Lear

This is a dull sight. Are you not Kent?

Kent

The same, your servant Kent.
Where is your servant Caius?

Lear

He's a good fellow, I can tell you that;
He'll strike, and quickly too. He's dead and rotten.

Kent

No, my good lord. I am the very man –

Lear

I'll see that straight.

Kent

That, from your first of difference and decay,
Have followed your sad steps.

Lear

You are welcome hither.

Kent

Nor no man else. All's cheerless, dark, and deadly.
Your eldest daughters have fordone themselves,
And desperately are dead.

Lear

Ay, so I think.

Albany

He knows not what he says, and vain it is
That we present us to him.

Edgar

Very bootless.

Enter a Captain

Captain

Edmund is dead, my lord.

Albany

That's but a trifle here.
You lords and noble friends, know our intent.
What comfort to this great decay may come
Shall be applied. For us we will resign,
During the life of this old majesty,
To him our absolute power.

To Edgar and Kent

You, to your rights.
With boot, and such addition as your honours
Have more than merited. All friends shall taste
The wages of their virtue, and all foes
The cup of their deservings. – O, see, see!

Lear

And my poor fool is hanged! No, no, no life!
Why should a dog, a horse, a rat, have life,
And thou no breath at all? Thou'lt come no more,
Never, never, never, never, never!
Pray you, undo this button. Thank you, sir.
Do you see this? Look on her, look, her lips,
Look there, look there!

Dies

Edgar

He faints! My lord, my lord!

Kent

Break, heart; I prithee, break!

Edgar

Look up, my lord.

Kent

Vex not his ghost. O, let him pass! He hates him
That would upon the rack of this tough world
Stretch him out longer.

302 bootless: *in vain*

303 a trifle: *of little consequence*

305 this great decay: *wretched situation (Lear's tragedy)*

310 boot: *something added*

312 wages: *rewards, honours*

313 deservings: *due punishments*

314 fool: *Cordelia*

322 pass: *pass away*

Edgar

He is gone, indeed.

Kent

The wonder is, he hath endured so long.
He but usurped his life.

Albany

Bear them from hence. Our present business
Is general woe.

To Kent and Edgar

Friends of my soul, you twain
Rule in this realm, and the gored state sustain.

Kent

I have a journey, sir, shortly to go.
My master calls me, I must not say no.

Edgar

The weight of this sad time we must obey;
Speak what we feel, not what we ought to say.
The oldest hath borne most. We that are young
Shall never see so much, nor live so long.

Exeunt

326 usurped his life: *lived too long*

327 Bear them: *carry their bodies*

328 general woe: *shared grief and mourning*

330 gored state sustain: *care for this damaged country*

333 weight: *sadness*

Key Scene Analysis

Brief reunion (lines 1–41)

Edmund's soldiers have captured Lear and Cordelia. For a moment, the frail king looks forward to being imprisoned with the daughter he loves: 'We too alone will sing like birds i' the cage'. In his fantasy, he imagines them having time to 'laugh/ At gilded butterflies, and hear poor rogues/ Talk of court news'. Lear believes that they will now be safe from the power struggles and intrigue going on around them.

Lear imagines that he and his youngest daughter will also experience the 'mystery of things' – the true meaning of what is most important in life, enjoying simple things and being in each other's company.

Cordelia is much more realistic than her father and does not share his dream. She cares nothing for herself but is disheartened at her army's defeat: 'We are not the first/ Who, with best meaning, have incurred the worst'. This calm sense of acceptance sets the bleak tone for the tragedy's conclusion, which is already overshadowed by Edmund's wish that Lear and Cordelia will be put to death against Albany's wishes and 'Shall never see his pardon'.

The reality of their dismal situation is highlighted by Edmund's decisive actions. Not content with victory on the battlefield, he bribes one of his officers with 'noble fortunes' to execute Cordelia. He is more confident than ever and in no mood to waste time: 'Thy great employment/ Will not bear question'. Little does Lear know that his hopes of happiness will be cruelly dashed.

Disagreement and division (lines 42–92)

In a tense encounter, Albany acknowledges Edmund's bravery in the battle, 'your valiant strain'. But when he asks for custody of Lear and Cordelia, the request is refused. In the confrontation that follows, Albany reminds Edmund of his inferior position: 'I hold you but a subject of this war,/ Not as a brother'. This enrages Regan, who hints that she may marry Edmund. She also claims that he already has equal rank to Albany because he represented her in the battle: 'That's as we list to grace him …/ He led our powers'.

The two jealous sisters continue to argue about Edmund. In the presence of her husband, Goneril brazenly asserts that Edmund has no need of Regan's title: 'In his own grace he doth exalt himself,/ More than in your addition'. The degrading personal quarrel illustrates how the two sisters have now lost almost all sense of dignity.

As Regan begins to feel the effects of Goneril's poison, she entrusts everything she has to Edmund: 'I create thee here/ My lord and master'. Albany intervenes, harshly reminding Edmund of his illegitimacy, calling him a 'Half-blooded fellow'. As the atmosphere becomes increasingly edgy, Albany charges Edmund with 'capital treason' and challenges him to defend himself against the charge in a public duel. Albany then sounds the trumpet, calling for his champion to represent him.

A fight between brothers (lines 93–154)

Edmund accepts the challenge, promising to defend his 'honour'. Meanwhile, both sisters have sunk to a new low in their obsessive love for the same man. In an aside, Goneril reveals that she has poisoned Regan to prevent her from being with Edmund: 'If not, I'll ne'er trust medicine'. The repeated trumpet sound increases the audience's unease as they await the arrival of Edgar.

The duel between Gloucester's sons is an obvious metaphor for the struggle between good and evil. The two brothers fight, and Edmund is fatally wounded. He is finally paying for his cold-blooded corruption. Does this signify the return of order and justice in Britain?

Edmund stays true to form as he prepares for the swordfight, still refusing to act by the rules. He is entitled to know the name of his opponent but does not even bother asking. Edgar lists the charges against Edmund: 'False to thy gods, thy brother, and thy father'. Although Edmund does not have to fight this unnamed champion, he is filled with confidence after his success against Cordelia's army: 'In wisdom I should ask thy name ... By rule of knighthood, I disdain and spurn'.

Punishment and justice (lines 155–235)

Albany confronts the fatally wounded Edmund with Goneril's damning letter. Not for the first time, she defies her husband: 'the laws are mine, not thine'. In a frantic temper, she rushes away and Albany sends an officer after her in case she becomes suicidal. Edmund then admits his wrong-doing, but is keen to find out who defeated him. Still full of his own importance, he offers conditional forgiveness: 'If thou'rt noble,/ I do forgive thee'. At last, his estranged brother reveals himself, 'My name is Edgar, and thy father's son'.

For Edgar, all the suffering and tragic events that have happened are part of a natural order. In a lengthy speech, he describes his own experiences as Poor Tom, forced to 'assume a semblance/ That very dogs disdained'. His distress is evident when he speaks of Gloucester's death after the old man's heart 'Burst smilingly' between the 'two extremes of passion, joy and grief'.

Most monstrous!
Albany
Act 5 Scene 3, l.164

Edgar believes in divine justice: 'The gods are just, and of our pleasant vices/ Make instruments to plague us'. He reaches the same moral conclusion as Lear and Gloucester over the course of the play, as the sins of the fathers come back to haunt their children.

Somewhat surprisingly, Edgar's words even affect Edmund: 'This speech of yours hath moved me'. In his final moments, Edmund decides that he will now 'perchance do good'. At this point, a servant arrives with news that Goneril has died after confessing that 'her sister/ By her is poisoned'.

Horror and tragedy (lines 236–326)

Albany takes control of the traumatic situation. He orders that the bodies of Goneril and Regan be brought in, though he feels no emotion for their deaths: 'Touches us not with pity'. The arrival of Kent prompts Albany to remember Lear and Cordelia: 'Great thing of us forgot'. In the panic that follows, Edmund observes the bodies of the dead sisters, commenting before his death, 'Yet Edmund was beloved'.

His warped relationship with Regan and Goneril appears to have affected him deeply. Is he sneering at these two foolish women who gave up everything for him? Or might this be the first time that Edmund has actually experienced love? Are we to believe that he is finally showing a humane side to his character and even reflecting on his own immoral actions?

In his last moments, it is ironic that Edmund thinks of love. Does this suggest that his evil behaviour was due to insecurity, after being rejected by his father and society? Is Shakespeare saying that compassion, loyalty and respect are the most important things in life?

Edmund has always seemed to be at ease with his own villainy. But just before he dies, he acknowledges his past selfishness: 'Some good I mean to do,/ Despite of mine own nature'. Confessing that he has ordered his soldiers to kill Lear and Cordelia, he makes a last-minute attempt to save them. Albany urgently sends a messenger to halt the execution – but time is slipping away.

Just as Edmund's body is removed, Lear appears, carrying Cordelia in his arms.He is overcome by grief and echoes his former self when he raged against the storm on the heath. The pathetic repetition of his agony in the words, 'Howl, howl, howl, howl! O, you are men of stones!' reflects his overwhelming sorrow.

As the old king sinks again into madness at the devastating loss of the daughter he loves, he rages against the justice of the gods, that 'heaven's vault should crack'. For a moment, he confronts the grim finality of death: 'She's gone for ever!'

Lear clings desperately to the vain hope that Cordelia might still show some signs of life. He asks for a mirror, 'Lend me a looking-glass', to check if she is still breathing. Unable to accept the truth, the panic-stricken father retreats into fantasy: 'This feather stirs'. This self-delusion makes his suffering all the more poignant. It seems as though, even in death, Lear is still anxiously searching for the love he never fully achieved in life.

Edgar and Kent are also very distressed by what they are witnessing. This is not the 'promised end' they had hoped for. Lear is too preoccupied with his youngest daughter to respond to Kent when his old friend's true identity is revealed. Instead, he curses everyone around him for Cordelia's death: 'A plague upon you'. He believes that he can hear her voice, 'ever soft,/ Gentle, and low'.

She's gone for ever!
Lear
Act 5 Scene 3, l.266

Kent tries to connect with the distraught king to tell him what has happened to his other two daughters, but it is impossible to communicate with Lear now, when 'All's cheerless, dark, and deadly'. Edmund's death is announced, but it is of little consequence to Albany: 'That's but a trifle here'.

Lear is caught between denial and acceptance of Cordelia's death: 'Thou'lt come no more'. Edgar attempts to revive him, but Kent knows that Lear has already endured too much 'upon the rack of this tough world' and advises, 'let him pass'. Having 'endured so long', Lear dies, either deluded with overwhelming love or enraged by injustice.

Order restored (lines 327–336)

Albany requests the removal of the dead, before turning to Kent and Edgar to ask them to help rule 'the gored state'. Is the same mistake being made again? The appointing of twin rulers over one country? But Kent declines the offer, choosing to join his king in death: 'My master calls me, I must not say no'. The closing mood is solemn and purposeful. Albany's concern is to establish law and order after the turmoil which has divided Britain. Edgar is equally focused, and his quiet sense of resignation is appropriate to the occasion.

Edgar's final words indicate that he will be the country's next king. The hope is that because of all he has experienced, he will be a wiser, more humane ruler. He has learned that life, no matter how awful, must be endured: 'The weight of this sad time we must obey'.

If Edgar is true to his word, his reign will be open and honest: 'Speak what we feel', unlike the old, corrupt court where things were never as they seemed, 'not what we ought to say'. This is a direct reference to the lies told during Lear's rash 'love test', and to Edmund's countless deceptions. Edgar also acknowledges that the 'oldest hath borne most'. Lear and Gloucester have endured the worst of the appalling tragedy – and they have been punished out of all proportion to their crimes.

At the end of this disturbing drama, we are left with much to consider. Were Lear and Gloucester 'More sinned against than sinning'? Is there really divine justice in this harsh universe? Shakespeare's great tragedy leaves its audience with many soul-searching questions.

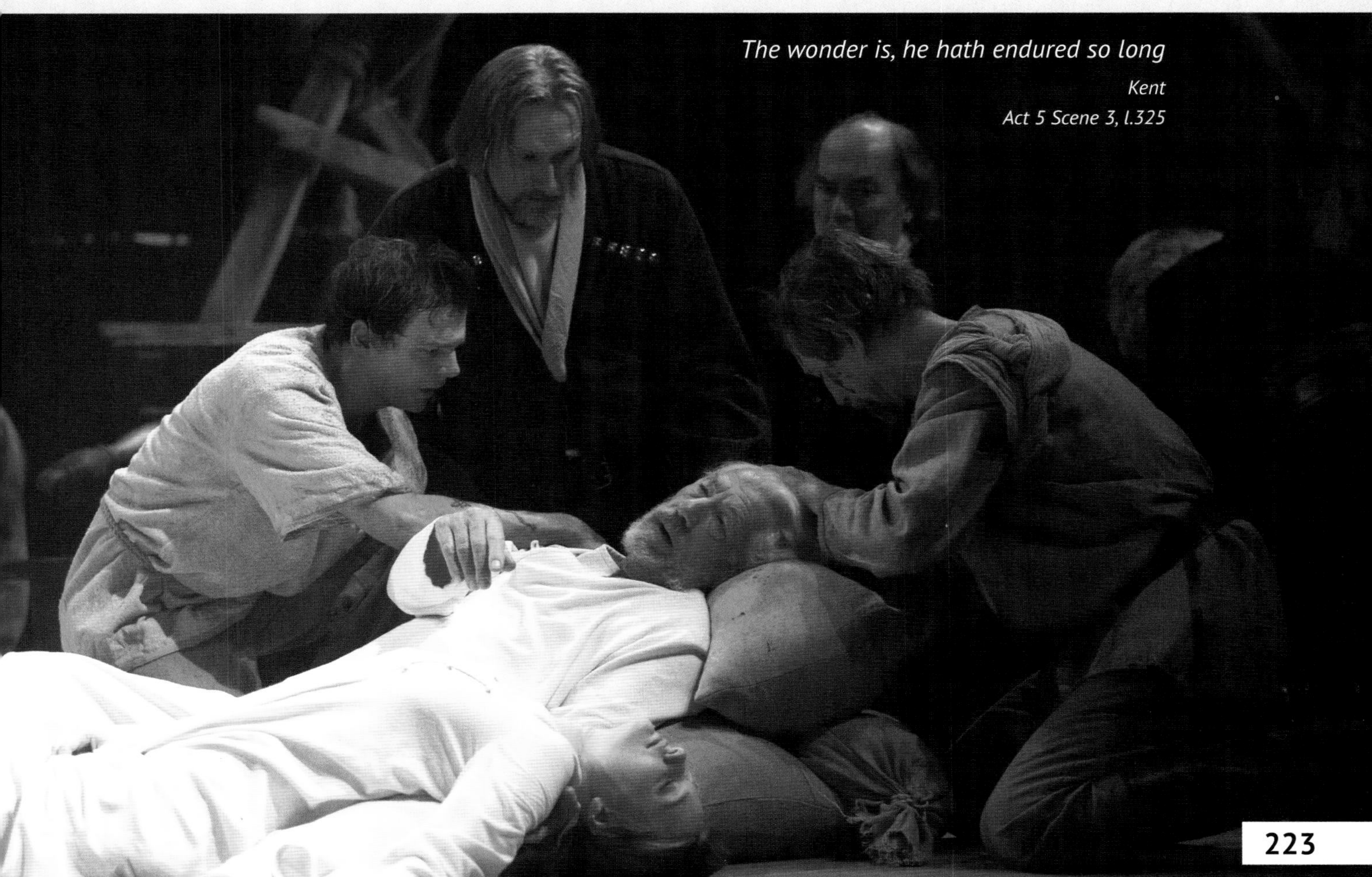

The wonder is, he hath endured so long

Kent

Act 5 Scene 3, l.325

Shakespeare's Dramatic Style

The **heightened language** of Act 5 Scene 3 has powerful emotional impact. Shakespeare forces the audience to confront the uncomfortable reality of human experience at its worst. There is no escaping the atmosphere of loss and grief – particularly in Lear's struggle to accept Cordelia's death. Effective repetition (of emotive words, including 'howl', 'dead', 'no', 'look', 'life' and 'never') emphasises the distress and anguish.

Irony is used effectively in this scene to show that well-meaning individuals, such as Cordelia, can sometimes experience 'the worst'. The evil characters also make ironic comments. Goneril – who is filled with lust and rage over Edmund – describes her unhappy marriage to Albany as an 'interlude'. Little does she know that it is her death, not Albany's, which will end their loveless relationship.

This key scene includes many **violent images** to describe the universe. Albany refers to the kingdom as a 'gored state'. Kent wishes for Lear's release from 'the rack of this tough world'. Lear himself kills Cordelia's executioner with his 'good biting falchion' while Goneril ends her life with a 'bloody knife'. Gloucester died when his heart 'Burst smilingly'. Towards the end of the play, Edgar states that the gods 'of our pleasant vices/ Make instruments to plague us'.

Throughout the scene, **animal imagery** is used to highlight Lear's fantasy of the carefree life he and Cordelia will share when they are safe in prison: 'We two alone will sing like birds i' the cage'. Albany describes his murderous wife Goneril as a 'gilded serpent'. But it is Lear's anguish at the death of Cordelia which results in the most vivid use of references to animals when he poignantly asks, 'Why should a dog, a horse, a rat, have life,/ And thou no breath at all?' Shakespeare leaves the audience with a deep sense of Lear's unbearable sorrow at what he sees as life's injustice.

Critical Analysis

'As a result of their personal flaws, the central characters in *King Lear* experience horrific suffering and learn bitter lessons.'

To what extent do you agree with this view? Develop your response with particular reference to Act 5 Scene 3. Refer to one central character in your answer.

Sample Paragraph 1

Lear himself suffers most. Cordelia lies dead after all the fighting. I don't think he learns that much because he goes mad again and halucinates thinking she could of been breathing as normally. Edgar tries to save Lear, because he always looks on the bright side and thinks you just have to put up with things and carry on. Some characters experience suffering on the heath and others learn lessons. Poor Tom is homeless, but Lear made the biggest mistake, he has most to learn on account of his flaw in having no clue about his own family and who to trust in the first place. Lear definately pays for giving away total power to the two worst daughters – 'in good time you gave it too' as Goneril tells him. They drove him mad Goneril and Regan and it took a lot of suffering before he eventually copped on that Cordelia was the one he should of handed power to. *(160 words)*

Examiner's Comment

- Basic-grade standard that strays from discussing one central character.
- Some reasonable commentary on Lear's flaw and its consequences.
- Lack of effective reference to support and develop points.
- Note-like expression, slang and misspellings ('halucinates', 'definately').

Sample Paragraph 2

In Act 5 Scene 3, Edmund gets the punishment he deserves as the personification of selfishness and cruelty. But when he hears about Regan and Goneril dying because of him, he completely changes: 'Yet Edmund was beloved'. He is still very caught up in himself, but he now decides to do some good, 'despite of mine own nature'. He makes a very late effort to cancel the order he gave to have Lear and Cordelia executed. The idea that he was loved by two women, rather than humiliated because of being illegitimate, has brought out his hidden potential to be decent for once. Edmund had many faults, but I think the question remains – if he had not been excluded early on in life, especially by his father, Gloucester, could he have been a force for good? Flawed people like Edmund have, through suffering, learned such qualities as thinking of others and behaving as decent human beings. *(155 words)*

Examiner's Comment

- Solid high-grade answer showing understanding of the scene.
- Central points about Edmund are developed, using suitable reference.
- Identifies some sense of 'horrific suffering' and learning 'bitter lessons'.
- Expression is clear and well-controlled throughout.

Class/Homework Exercise

'Act 5 Scene 3 of *King Lear* leaves audiences in no doubt that good overcomes evil.' To what extent would you agree with this statement?

Write a paragraph (about 150 words), developing your response with reference to the text.

Exam Focus

Act 5 Scene 3 can be used successfully in response to a range of examination questions about the play's central themes, characters, relationships and the playwright's dramatic style.

This **key scene** has important dramatic functions:

- Completes the tragic hero's downfall due to his flaw of misjudgement.
- Shows a final brief glimpse of Lear as a loving parent.
- Emphasises the triumph of good over evil – after turmoil and suffering.
- Brings the dramatic tension to a climax, engaging audience sympathy.
- Highlights development of the honourable characters, Edgar and Albany.
- Presents another view of Edmund as the possible victim of exclusion.
- Rounds off the tragedy, leaving questions about family, justice and fate.

Key Quotes

Come, let's away to prison./ We two alone will sing like birds i' the cage *(Lear to Cordelia) l.8–9*	Lear is so overjoyed to be reunited with Cordelia that he is quite happy to be imprisoned with her, and envisages an ideal existence where they are safe from all the intrigues of court. His comment is an echo of his former wish to spend his life in her 'kind nursery'.
Half-blooded fellow *(Albany on Edmund) l.82*	Albany's new assertiveness leads him to challenge Edmund with this barbed reference to his birth circumstances. He has never been as easily duped by Edmund as Cornwall was.
What safe and nicely I might well delay/ By rule of knighthood, I disdain and spurn *(Edmund to Edgar) l.148–9*	From the outset of the play, Edmund had vowed to act by the laws of nature (where the strongest survive) and he continues in this manner, rejecting the rules of duelling. He could refuse to fight the unnamed champion but he remains overbearing and scorns to do so.
The gods are just, and of our pleasant vices/ Make instruments to plague us *(Edgar to Edmund) l.176–7*	Edgar is a staunch believer in divine retribution and informs Edmund that we are corrected by the gods for our wrong-doing. He now realises that the poor judgement shown by both Lear and Gloucester has come back to haunt them.
The wheel is come full circle *(Edmund) l.180*	Edmund ruefully admits that despite all his scheming to advance his position in life, he is back where he started, without power or influence. Destiny is often depicted as a wheel which keeps turning as a way of explaining the fluctuating fortunes of human beings.
I was contracted to them both. All three/ Now marry in an instant *(Edmund) l.234–5*	When the deaths of Goneril and Regan are announced, Edmund reveals that he was engaged to them both. With a dark sense of humour, he imagines their imminent reunion when they will all be joined together in death.
Had I your tongues and eyes, I'd use them so/ That heaven's vault should crack *(Lear) l.265–6*	In a paroxysm of grief, Lear wonders why all the onlookers are not voicing their great sorrow so loudly that the heavenly clouds would be shattered. There is a suggestion of an earlier speech when the enraged king roamed around the heath and implored the gods to destroy the human race: 'Crack nature's moulds'.
Is this the promised end? *(Kent) l. 270*	Kent is horrified at the tragic turn of events. He had hoped to save Lear and Cordelia, and to restore the king to power. His heartfelt question reflects the audience's feelings of shock and dismay.
Speak what we feel, not what we ought to say *(Edgar) l. 334*	Edgar ends the play by introducing hope of a fresh start, with a different set of values in place. He wishes to restore Britain to a new order, declaring that people should speak plainly and honestly, acknowledging their true feelings rather than allowing appearances to disguise reality.

Key Points | Act 5

Scene 1

- Edmund is doubtful about Albany's objectives. Albany's personal sympathies lie with Lear and Cordelia, but his duty is to resist the French force that has recently invaded English soil.
- Intense rivalry between Goneril and Regan over Edmund threatens the union of the English force.
- Edgar gives Albany Goneril's letter to Edmund and offers to produce a champion after the battle to verify the letter's incriminating contents.
- Edmund's soliloquy reveals his cold-blooded ambition. He has sworn his love to both sisters. He even expects Goneril to organise the murder of her husband. But he will use Albany to ensure that the battle is won. Meanwhile, Edmund plans to have Lear and Cordelia executed after the battle.

Scene 2

- The forces of good (represented by Lear's supporters and Cordelia's army) are defeated.
- Lear and Cordelia are captured and imprisoned.
- Gloucester loses hope again and becomes deeply depressed.
- The stoic Edgar resiliently bears life's fluctuating fortunes.

Scene 3

- Edmund organises the execution of Lear and Cordelia because they might be a rallying point for popular support and become a threat to his political aspirations.
- Goneril and Regan argue openly over Edmund.
- Albany arrests Goneril and Edmund for treason.
- Edgar arrives disguised as a champion to validate the contents of Goneril's letter to Edmund.
- During their duel, Edmund is killed by Edgar, who finally reveals his true identity. The brothers are reconciled.
- After fatally poisoning Regan, Goneril commits suicide.
- As he lies dying, Edmund tries to redeem himself and sends a countermanding order to prevent the execution of Lear and Cordelia. He appears to be motivated by the fact that Goneril and Regan died for love of him.
- Lear enters carrying the lifeless body of Cordelia. He is completely consumed by grief.
- Edgar reveals his true identity to his father shortly before Gloucester's death.
- Lear dies from a broken heart, hoping in vain that Cordelia might still be alive.
- With Albany's support, Edgar is left to establish a new order of honesty and justice in the kingdom.

Character Studies

King Lear

TRAGIC HERO

- Introduced at height of power
- Fatal character flaws lead to tragic downfall
- Makes serious error of judgement
- Unleashes forces beyond his control
- Gains insight through tremendous suffering
- Audience response – sympathy and fear
- New order established
- Conclusion brings a sense of release

First Impressions

> *'we will divest us both of rule,*
> *Interest of territory, cares of state'*
>
> ***(Act 1 Scene 1, l.45–6)***

- Shakespeare introduces Lear as an **almost superhuman figure**. The elderly ruler of ancient Britain decides to abdicate his responsibilities as king and hand over power to his three daughters. In Shakespeare's time, this would be considered shocking as most people believed that the reigning sovereign was God's appointed ruler.
- **Lear is obviously an arrogant man whose only concern is for himself.** While maintaining that he wants to give up the responsibilities of ruling, he still wants to 'retain/ The name, and all the additions to a king'. This important decision to step away from the throne, yet still hold on to the benefits of kingship, shows how unaware Lear is of the reality of political power.

> *'Which of you shall we say doth love us most?'*
>
> ***(Act 1 Scene 1, l.47)***

- **Lear's arrogance has been driven by a long career of absolute power.** He demands not only agreement to his wishes, but displays of flattery. He insists on a public 'love test' and calls on his daughters to express their love for him before he rewards them with a share of his kingdom.

Lear is presented as a vain man who values cheap displays of emotion over real feeling. The ageing king is deceived by appearance over reality, impressed by what someone says rather than their actions. He fails to understand that words and actions do not always match.

- In front of the assembled court his eldest daughter, Goneril, makes an extravagant declaration, 'I love you more than words can wield the matter'. This **flattery delights the foolish king** who then turns to his second daughter. Regan tries to outdo her sister and uses equally poetic language: 'I am alone felicitate/ In your dear highness' love'. Her father is highly impressed by what she says.

King Lear: a victim of his own excessive power

- But Cordelia, Lear's youngest daughter, refuses to take part in what she believes is a hypocritical farce: 'I cannot heave/ My heart into my mouth'. In response, the enraged king immediately disinherits her: 'thy truth, then, be thy dower'. He also disowns Cordelia: 'I disclaim all my paternal care'. **Lear has cruelly humiliated his daughter** in front of her two suitors, the Duke of Burgundy and the King of France. When his loyal courtier, Kent, tries to prevent this 'hideous rashness', he also becomes the target of Lear's rage: 'Come not between the dragon and his wrath'. Kent is then banished by the volatile king, 'Out of my sight!'

Lear is unpredictable and vindictive. Goneril and Regan give an accurate, if cynical, assessment of his character: 'the best and soundest of his time hath been but rash'. They believe he has become worse with age, 'infirm and choleric years'.

Lear's Character Development

- Over the course of the story, Shakespeare gradually shows us some of Lear's better character traits, so that audiences can look beyond his failings. He employs the disguised Kent because he likes him. He openly discusses his trouble with the Fool, asking him, 'Teach me'. The playwright wants audiences to concentrate on **the horrific impact Goneril and Regan had on the old king through their 'Filial ingratitude'**.

Lear believes that feelings can be measured and thinks that because Goneril will let him have fifty of his knights instead of Regan's twenty-five, then she is 'twice her love'. Regan turns on him: 'What need one?'

- But Lear can still be cruel. He curses Goneril, his 'thankless child'. Yet he begins to understand his own weaknesses and realises that Cordelia's silence was a 'most small fault'. He becomes increasingly terrified that he will crack under the pressure and lose all control, 'O let me not be mad'. Shakespeare is encouraging us to see Lear as 'A man/ More sinned against than sinning'.
- Lost on the windswept heath, with his mind in turmoil from the effects of his daughter's ingratitude, **Lear suffers physically, emotionally and spiritually**. At first, he is defiant. The old tyrannical king attempts to control the elements, ordering the storm to destroy the universe, 'Smite flat the thick rotundity of the world!'
- As Lear becomes more and more deranged, **he begins to develop a social conscience** and considers the needs of others. He asks the Fool, 'Art cold?' He regrets his earlier lack of concern for the 'Poor naked wretches' of his kingdom. Lear's great prayer on behalf of 'houseless poverty' shows genuine concern for the less fortunate in society. He admits, 'I have taken/ Too little care of this'.

'a man
More sinned against than sinning'

(Act 3 Scene 2, l.58)

- When Lear meets Edgar (disguised as Poor Tom), the king identifies himself with the Bedlam beggar. Dressed only in a blanket, the beggar represents for Lear a compelling image of humanity reduced to its necessities. In his insanity, **Lear can distinguish between appearance and reality**.

Lear understands that a man with no possessions ('Unaccommodated man') is reduced to the level of a beast, no more than 'a poor, bare, forked animal'. The loss of Lear's sanity is reflected in Shakespeare's language which changes from poetry to prose.

- When Lear meets the blinded Gloucester, the elderly king provides an insightful analysis of legal and political corruption. He **understands that appearances can hide the truth**. Unlike the poor, the rich and privileged can escape justice, because 'Robes and furred gowns hide all'. Lear is now aware of his own mistakes and the injustice of the world, 'Reason in madness'. A new man has emerged, more thoughtful and sensitive. For the first time, he recognises the fine line between civilised and uncivilised behaviour on 'this great stage of fools'.

Lear flees into the storm as a child flees

Overview

> *'I am a very foolish fond old man'*
>
> ***(Act 4 Scene 7, l.61)***

- Lear's tender reconciliation with Cordelia at Dover reveals his development as a human being. He is **deeply ashamed of his past behaviour** and acknowledges who he really is: 'a very foolish fond old man'. His focus is now on the importance of his relationship with his daughter, Cordelia. He begs her to 'forget and forgive'. She readily forgives: 'No cause, no cause'.

The reunion scene shows Lear at his most dignified, and finally aware of the importance of true feelings rather than flattery. Shakespeare has taken a flawed old man of over eighty and shown how he has matured and become a better person through suffering.

- The old monarch is no longer concerned with political power and intrigue. He and Cordelia have been imprisoned by the victorious Edmund, who has defeated France's army, but Lear is content. He dreams of the joys that await them: 'We two alone will sing like birds i' the cage'. **Lear's unconditional love for Cordelia has redeemed him** and the audience can sympathise with him.
- Yet **traces of the old Lear remain**. When Cordelia is executed, his temper is once again unleashed. He seeks revenge: 'I killed the slave that was a-hanging thee'. In an echo of his previous behaviour, he curses all present: 'A plague upon you, murderers, traitors all!' Shakespeare concludes the play with the aged father still in denial, desperately trying to convince himself that Cordelia lives, 'This feather stirs'. He rails against her unjust death: 'Why should a dog, a horse, a rat, have life,/ And thou no breath at all?'

Lear dies of a broken heart: 'O, let him pass'. The playwright has left his audience without a complete sense of release from the central conflict. A new order will be restored – but has Lear been fully reformed?

- Shakespeare's heart-breaking story leaves audiences reeling from the sheer waste of the potential for good, caused by the actions of a reckless old man. Is it possible to reject Lear's moral blindness and unrestrained fury, yet remain deeply sympathetic to his tragic life?

LEAR'S QUALITIES

- courageous
- inspires loyalty
- heroic
- compassionate
- acknowledges mistakes
- asks forgiveness
- gains insight

LEAR'S FLAWS

- arrogant
- rash
- foolish
- unstable
- irresponsible
- self-centred
- vindictive

The Earl of Gloucester

SIMILARITIES BETWEEN GLOUCESTER AND LEAR

- **Gloucester believes dishonest son, Lear believes dishonest daughters**
- **Gloucester disowns honest son, Lear disowns honest daughter**
- **Both fathers are betrayed by their dishonest children**
- **Gloucester and Lear recognise their character flaws**
- **The two men gain insight through suffering**
- **Gloucester is reunited with loyal son, Lear is reunited with loyal daughter**

First Impressions

'We have seen the best of our time'
(Act 1 Scene 2, l.104)

- The Earl of Gloucester is a rich and loyal subject of King Lear. In many ways, he is a mirror image of the king, although he lacks the vitality and energy of the old monarch. Gloucester brags about Edmund's illegitimate birth, even when his son is present: 'there was good sport at his making'. Edmund's resentment is understandable. Shakespeare has introduced us to **an insensitive and irresponsible man**.
- In contrast to Kent, **Gloucester does not challenge Lear's reckless division of Britain**, nor the disowning of his daughter, Cordelia. He does not speak up for what is right but chooses to behave cautiously and diplomatically, and, unlike Kent, he keeps his position. Is Shakespeare suggesting that evil flourishes when ineffective men like Gloucester fail to speak out?

'It is a letter from my brother'
(Act 1 Scene 2, l.36)

- **Edmund uses a forged letter to trick his 'credulous' father and ruin Edgar's reputation.** Gloucester immediately accepts Edmund's word and his 'evidence', without giving Edgar a chance to defend himself. Naively, he even asks Edmund to 'Find out this villain'. The superstitious earl does not believe in taking personal responsibility, but instead blames the chaos around him ('son against father ... father against child') on the movements of the stars, 'These late eclipses in the sun and moon'.

Gloucester allows Cornwall and Regan to take over his castle. While he lacks courage, some sense of morality emerges in his faint-hearted protests over Kent's punishment in the stocks.

'I like not this unnatural dealing'
(Act 3 Scene 3, l.1)

- Gloucester does not protest against Kent's punishment in the stocks, even though he knows it isn't appropriate. Although he regards the stocks as a 'low correction', fit only for petty criminals, **he does not dare to object**. He is aware that Lear will be furious, 'The king must take it ill', but is clearly afraid of the 'fiery' Cornwall and remains helplessly neutral, saying, 'I would have all well betwixt you'.

Gloucester's Character Development

'I must stand the course'
(Act 3 Scene 7, l.53)

- Over the course of the play, **Gloucester undergoes a transformation from an easy-going, gullible man to one who puts duty and loyalty above self-interest**. Shocked by Cornwall's heartless instruction to him to 'Shut up your doors' against Lear, he tries to help, but does so secretly: 'my old master must be relieved'. Unfortunately, the earl

Gloucester: initially blind to reality

tells all this to his treacherous son, Edmund. Still lacking moral courage, he even asks his son to lie on his behalf if Cornwall asks for him: 'I am ill and gone to bed'. These confidences will soon come back to haunt him.

- After Edmund betrays his father to Cornwall and Regan, Gloucester is arrested and harshly interrogated about Lear's whereabouts. Realising that he is trapped, he stoically accepts his fate: 'I am tied to the stake, and I must stand the course'. **Finally, he speaks up on Lear's behalf, condemning the harsh treatment he has received**: 'I would not see thy cruel nails/ Pluck out his poor old eyes'.
- Cornwall inflicts the horrific punishment of gouging out one of Gloucester's eyes, egged on by Regan, 'the other too'. When Gloucester calls out for Edmund, Regan delights in inflicting emotional pain on the blinded earl by revealing that it was actually Edmund who betrayed him. **Gloucester now realises the terrible mistake he has made**: 'O my follies! Then Edgar was abused.'
- This shocking scene marks the **emergence of a more noble Gloucester**. He prays for pardon, 'Kind gods, forgive me that, and prosper him!' At last, the old earl accepts responsibility for his actions rather than blaming his own mistakes and other unfortunate events on the stars.

Overview

> *'Men must endure*
> *Their going hence, even as their coming hither.*
> *Ripeness is all'*
>
> ***(Act 5 Scene 2, l.9–11)***

- The blinding of Gloucester is another example of devastating irony. The old man acknowledges his earlier misjudgements, 'I stumbled when I saw', and **he continues to grow in compassion**. Like Lear, he is developing a social conscience and starts to consider other people. Meeting Edgar, now disguised as Poor Tom, he reflects on how unequal society is and thinks that wealth should be more evenly shared, that 'distribution should undo excess'.

Gloucester eventually realises that he was blind to the truth when he still had his eyes and was mistaken in how he judged his two sons.

- **Gloucester's overall view of human existence is terrifyingly bleak**: 'As flies to wanton boys are we to the gods./ They kill us for their sport'. He decides to die by suicide: 'This world I do renounce'. In Shakespeare's time, it was believed that taking one's own life would mean eternal damnation for the soul. He is saved by Edgar, however, and accepts that it is the gods, not man, who will decide the time of a person's death.
- Gloucester's reconciliation with the son he wronged takes place off-stage. But it is reported that he dies of a 'flawed heart', overcome with mixed emotions of 'passion, joy and grief'. His death **parallels Lear's journey towards self-awareness and insight** into the reality of the human condition. Throughout the play, the old earl has suffered greatly because of his morally weak nature. Once again, Shakespeare leaves audiences to consider whether Gloucester's punishment was in proportion to his crimes.

GLOUCESTER'S QUALITIES

- loyal
- compassionate
- courageous
- well-intentioned
- stoical
- social conscience
- moral integrity
- gains insight

GLOUCESTER'S FLAWS

- morally weak
- tactless
- impulsive
- naive
- self-interested
- superstitious
- passive
- pessimistic

Cordelia

CORDELIA'S ROLE IN *KING LEAR*

- **Symbol of goodness and loyalty**
- **Mirror image of obstinate Lear**
- **Contrast to hypocritical sisters**
- **Parallel to good son Edgar**
- **Signifies hope in an evil world**
- **Forgives and redeems her father**
- **Innocent victim of evil**

First Impressions

> *'Love, and be silent'*
>
> ***(Act 1 Scene 1, l.59)***

- **Cordelia is Lear's youngest daughter, whom he loved 'most'.** She plays a central role in the tragic story and her influence is immense, even though she appears in only four scenes. Cordelia is the essence of goodness and provides a startling contrast to her evil sisters. However, Cordelia is much more than a timid figure or passive victim. She shares her father's capacity for tenderness and stubborn pride.

> *'Unhappy that I am, I cannot heave*
> *My heart into my mouth'*
>
> ***(Act 1 Scene 1, l.88–9)***

- At the start of the play, Lear has established a public 'love test' for his daughters to decide on the amount of his kingdom each shall inherit when he hands over power to them. His two older daughters eagerly take part, flattering the old king with 'glib and oily art'. He rewards them handsomely. **But Cordelia stubbornly refuses to humour her self-indulgent father.** Instead, she chooses to 'Love, and be silent' even though her love for her father is 'More ponderous than my tongue'. She just cannot bear to stand before the assembled court and publicly declare her personal feelings. Lear's command, 'Speak', draws a one-word response from her: 'Nothing'.
- **Cordelia's self-righteous pride, coupled with Lear's arrogance, results in a series of terrible events.** The king's youngest daughter is a mirror image of Lear, whose abdication is a refusal to take responsibility for his country. Cordelia's refusal to be part of the 'love test' can also be seen as a withdrawal of her responsibility as a daughter to show her elderly father affection: 'So young, and so untender'. Should Cordelia have indulged him?

> **Lear is now humiliated in public. He warns Cordelia, 'Nothing will come of nothing'. She replies in legal terms. She loves him 'According to my bond; no more nor less'. Cordelia speaks the truth, but her reply lacks warmth. Is she brave or misguided?**

- **There is no doubt that Cordelia is not a submissive character.** She tries hard to show Lear that her self-centred sisters are using empty words to please him: 'Why have my sisters husbands, if they say/ They love you all?' She challenges Goneril and Regan directly: 'I know you what you are'. Cordelia also dismisses her suitor, the Duke of Burgundy, when he reveals he is more interested in her dowry than he is in her: 'respects of fortune are his love,/ I shall not be his wife'.
- Cordelia insists that Lear clear her good name: 'It is no vicious blot ... No unchaste action ... That hath deprived me of your grace and favour'. Her other suitor, the King of France, **recognises her flaw as shyness**, 'a tardiness in nature' – something which can easily be misinterpreted as cold-heartedness. He is happy to marry her despite her lack of a dowry, 'Most choice, forsaken'. Cordelia leaves with France, issuing a warning to her hypocritical sisters, 'Use well our father'.

Cordelia: civilised behaviour in a brutish world

Cordelia's Character Development

> *'No blown ambition doth our arms incite,*
> *But love, dear love, and our aged father's right'*
> ***(Act 4 Scene 4, l.27–8)***

- Kent is very much aware of Cordelia's inability to express emotion. He asks a gentleman if she has shown 'demonstration of grief' over Lear's misfortune. The reply that her face was like 'Sunshine and rain at once. Her smiles and tears' shows how much **she has changed**. Out of genuine concern for Lear, Cordelia returns to Britain to rescue her wronged father.

For audiences shocked by barbaric cruelty in earlier scenes, Cordelia is a symbol of civilised behaviour. She thanks Kent for his selfless loyalty to her father, 'how shall I live and work,/ To match thy goodness?'

- The scene where Cordelia is reunited with Lear highlights their close relationship. She prays for him as he sleeps, 'O you kind gods,/ Cure this great breach in his abused nature'. **The caring daughter redeems the old king with unconditional love and forgiveness**: 'let this kiss/ Repair those violent harms that my two sisters/ Have in thy reverence made'. When her father awakens, Cordelia becomes slightly shy again, but her feelings for Lear are overwhelming. As he gradually begins to recognise her, 'I think this lady/ To be my child Cordelia', she responds simply, 'And so I am, I am'.
- Cordelia comforts her frail father as he admits that he wronged her, 'No cause, no cause'. Nor does she allow Lear to take all the blame for what has happened: 'you must not kneel'. **She is willing to give everything, 'all my outward worth', to help him.** This is a telling contrast to her sisters, who wanted all Lear's power and wealth.

Overview

> *'For thee, oppressed King, I am cast down;*
> *Myself could else out-frown false fortune's frown'*
> ***(Act 5 Scene 3, l.5–6)***

- Following the defeat of the French army, father and daughter are imprisoned. But **Cordelia shows her strength of character** and is able to endure all that has happened: 'We are not the first,/ Who, with best meaning, have incurred the worst'. However, she continues to be primarily concerned about the 'oppressed King'. When Lear speaks of how they will live idyllically in prison, 'We two alone will sing like birds', gossiping about court affairs, the realistic daughter does not answer. She is only too aware that if they survive, they pose a continuing threat to their enemies.
- Cordelia's **death is one of the most poignant and upsetting moments in all of Shakespeare's tragedies.** The cries of the old king that his beloved daughter will 'come no more,/ Never, never, never, never, never!' are heart-rending. Shakespeare does not present his audience with an entirely positive ending where the good live happily ever after when evil has been defeated. Instead, the playwright shows a world where wickedness is given a chance to flourish because of a break in the natural order.

Cordelia represents dignity and genuine love. She has always been true to herself and had the moral courage to say exactly what she believed. This makes her an exceptional character within a world of corruption and hypocrisy in Lear's court.

- Although Edgar and Albany establish a new order in Britain based on justice and humanity, the audience is left to wonder about Cordelia's role in the play. Had Lear recognised the truth from **his honest daughter**, rather than being swayed by the empty words of his deceitful daughters, could the horrific events have been prevented? If Cordelia had indulged her aged father a little, and spoken lovingly, would this tragedy have concluded as it did?

CORDELIA'S QUALITIES

- truthful
- courageous
- loving
- selfless
- forgiving
- stoical

CORDELIA'S FLAWS

- stubborn
- insensitive
- distant
- cruel

Edmund

–opportunist
= Goneril / Regan

First Impressions

'this knave came something saucily into the world'

(Act 1 Scene 1, l.17–18)

- Edmund is 'the villain' in *King Lear* and one of Shakespeare's more fascinating characters. Gloucester's illegitimate son is handsome, intelligent and charming. But appearances can be deceptive. He is also ruthless, amoral and completely focused on his own interests. **Edmund places no value on anyone else.** He is a natural opportunist, prepared to destroy anyone who stands in his way: 'All's with me's meet that I can fashion fit'.

Edmund has no respect for anything – family, friendship, religion or country. Gloucester, Edgar, Cornwall, Albany, Goneril, Regan and Cordelia are all victims of this clever manipulator. 'My practices ride easy'.

- Gloucester makes crude references to Edmund's birth in his presence: 'the whoreson must be acknowledged'. These slurs hurt Edmund, who does not accept that he is inferior: 'My mind as generous, and my shape as true,/ As honest madam's issue?' He **deeply resents the country's laws that prevent him from inheriting** his father's wealth, simply because he was not born within marriage.

'Why bastard? wherefore base?'

(Act 1 Scene 2, l.6)

- Edmund despises his older brother, 'Legitimate Edgar', who will take over their father's estate and is determined to 'have your land'. But Edmund realises that **he can only rely on himself to prosper**: 'my state/ Stands on me to defend'. He therefore dedicates himself to 'nature', to the law of the survival of the fittest.

- Shakespeare has given Edmund plausible reasons to feel hurt, so audiences sometimes see him as **a victim.** They can feel some sympathy for the young man who has been the subject of his father's thoughtless cruelty and society's exclusion.

'my invention thrive'

(Act 1 Scene 2, l.20)

- However, approving of Edmund's **corrupt and devious actions** is a very different matter. He mocks his father's superstitious beliefs as 'the excellent foppery of the world' and feels nothing but contempt for those who blame their misfortunes on the stars. Edmund believes in taking responsibility for shaping his own life, by devising an ingenious plan to get what he wants.
- He forges a letter and passes it off as though it has been written by Edgar. As a result, gullible Gloucester is easily convinced that his legitimate son is seeking his life, so his trust in Edgar is immediately destroyed. The earl not only believes Edmund, but decides to reward him, 'To make thee capable' of inheriting. This **ensures that Edmund will receive all of his father's lands.**

Edmund's Character Development

'The younger rises when the old doth fall'

(Act 3 Scene 3, l.23)

- While Edmund's fortunes rise, his **character descends further into the depths of wickedness**. His ambitions have increased and he now seeks Gloucester's title: 'must draw me/ That which my father loses'. When he betrays his father to Cornwall, Edmund pretends to be sorry that to be a loyal subject, he is forced to behave like an unnatural son: 'How malicious is my fortune, that I must repent to be just'. Cornwall is deceived by the persuasive deception and even promises to be 'a dearer father' to this unscrupulous villain.

Edmund: master schemer

Goneril and Regan are both attracted to Edmund, but he treats the two women with heartless contempt, 'Which of them shall I take?/ Both? One? Or neither?' His sights are now set on a much bigger goal, the throne of England. However, he realises that he will not succeed in this ambition while Goneril's husband, Albany, is alive.

- Edmund decides to use Albany in the battle against France and Cordelia's army. He also hopes that Goneril will arrange her husband's murder, 'devise/ His speedy taking off'. As usual, Edmund cleverly protects himself by **having others carry out his villainy**. Worried that the captured Lear and Cordelia might arouse sympathy from the ordinary people of Britain, he instructs an army captain to execute them.

Overview

'Yet Edmund was beloved'

(Act 5 Scene 3, l.246)

- Following the defeat of the invading French forces, Edmund informs Albany that he has sent Lear and Cordelia to prison in case they stir up sympathy from the people. Albany sharply reminds Edmund that he is merely 'a subject' and not 'a brother'. **Edmund's arrogance and his contempt for following rules** is shown when he does not bother to find out the name of the challenger in their final public duel.
- The disguised Edgar fatally wounds Edmund. As he lies dying, **Edmund suddenly surprises us**: 'Some good I mean to do'. He makes an attempt to prevent his ordered execution of Lear and Cordelia by sending a message to the prison. The late change in his character appears to be because he realises that 'Edmund was beloved'. Lear's two older daughters have died for love of him. Regan is poisoned by Goneril, who dies by suicide.

Edmund's personality is that of the typical Shakespearean villain – bitter, selfish, ruthless and sadistic. Yet audiences often empathise with him. We ask if he has always had some potential for good. Did the playwright believe that nobody is completely bad, but that we are the product of upbringing or circumstance?

- **Edmund has always clearly known himself.** He admits that he is now acting 'Despite of mine own nature'. But his gesture fails, and Cordelia is hanged. We are left to wonder at Edmund's true motives. Was he really transformed by the twisted love of Goneril and Regan? Or is he still trying to put himself at the centre of the action? Even as he dies, Edmund's dark sense of humour about his relationship with the two sisters is evident: 'All three/ Now marry in an instant'. Shakespeare has created a puzzling villain, charismatic and appealing, but one who takes great delight in the evil he does.

EDMUND'S QUALITIES

- courageous
- clever
- vulnerable
- appealing
- believable
- stoical

EDMUND'S FLAWS

- hypocritical
- evil
- manipulative
- opportunistic
- heartless
- self-centred

Edgar

when he sees his father blind → he shows compassion, understanding and acceptance of his father's flaws.

FIVE DIFFERENT EDGARS

- Trusting victim of Edmund's treachery
- Poor Tom, insane Bedlam beggar
- Peasant who prevents Gloucester's suicide
- The challenger in the duel with Edmund
- Commentator on tragic events

First Impressions

> *'a brother noble'*
>
> ***(Act 1 Scene 2, l.165)***

- Edgar is the Earl of Gloucester's elder son, 'Legitimate Edgar', so is due to inherit his father's wealth and title. Because of this, Edgar is despised by his younger half-brother Edmund, who is illegitimate and has no legal inheritance rights. Edgar is **a symbol of goodness** throughout the play and the treacherous Edmund exploits his 'foolish honesty'.
- When Edmund tells Edgar that their father is full of 'rage' against him, Edgar believes that 'Some villain hath done me wrong', but **never suspects that it is his own brother** who has forged a damning letter implicating him in treachery against their father. Instead, he hastily accepts Edmund's advice to 'away'. Naive and short-sighted, Edgar doesn't even consider discussing the matter with Gloucester.

Edgar: always fair-minded

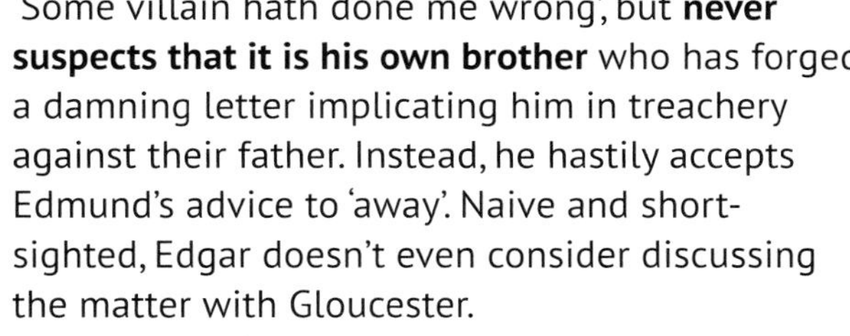

Shakespeare presents Edgar as a trusting and honourable character who sees no alternative but to stoop to deceit by disguising himself. Deception is something that is associated with many of the characters in the play.

- Edgar is now proclaimed a traitor and hunted down as a fugitive. To survive, he realises that he must adopt a disguise – the insane Bedlam beggar, Poor Tom. He denies his own true identity: 'Edgar I nothing am'. For the audience, his **impulsive decision** reinforces the sense of panic and fear in Britain since Lear's sudden abdication.

Edgar's Character Development

> *'basest and most poorest shape'*
>
> ***(Act 2 Scene 3, l.7)***

- In desperation, Edgar now shelters inside a hovel on the windswept heath. He displays resourcefulness in his disguise as Poor Tom, crying, 'the foul fiend follows me'. His shocking image makes a huge impact on Lear, who gains insight into the human condition: 'Is man no more than this?' Tom is a human being stripped to the essentials, 'a poor, bare, forked animal'. Like the king, **Edgar also grows in moral awareness**, realising that his own suffering is 'light and portable', in contrast to the aged king's trauma.

- **Edgar is an emotional individual who finds it hard to continue his pretence** when he meets his blinded father: 'I cannot daub it further'. Gloucester gives money to Poor Tom to lead him to a high hill. In utter despair, he has decided to end his life. Such an act would have been seen as a great sin during Shakespeare's time, when it was widely believed that anyone who died by suicide was condemned to hell for eternity.
- While disguised as the mad Bedlam beggar, **Edgar continues to develop his ability to deceive**, not just as a means of survival, but as a way of saving his father's soul. He now pretends to be an old peasant who describes the steep hill overlooking the sea to the blinded Gloucester. In reality, it is only a small mound, so Gloucester survives after throwing himself off what he thinks is a cliff. Still in disguise, Edgar consoles his father that 'the clearest gods' have 'preserved thee'.

The wronged Edgar, unlike Edmund, treats his flawed father with compassion and unconditional love. His motives are always well-intentioned. His disguises and deception aim to 'cure' Gloucester's despair.

- Edgar also **acts as a chorus, commenting on the events in the play**. Shakespeare uses him as a moral guide. He does his best to support his vulnerable and agitated father: 'The worst is not/ So long as we can say "This is the worst"'. Always considerate, he reacts sensitively to the insane Lear as 'thou side-piercing sight'.

Overview

'The weight of this sad time we must obey;
Speak what we feel, not what we ought to say'

(Act 5 Scene 3, l.333–4)

- In their public duel, **Edgar confronts his younger brother's treachery**: 'False to thy gods, thy brother, and thy father'. His defeat of Edmund clearly symbolises the triumph of good over evil. Although Edgar fatally wounds Edmund, he offers his dying brother who cruelly wronged him 'charity'.
- Edgar **represents civilised behaviour against corruption**. He has always acted with compassion towards the father who ill-treated him. Towards the end of the play, a confident Edgar (in contrast to his earlier mild character) expresses his personal beliefs clearly, 'The gods are just, and of our pleasant vices/ Make instruments to plague us'. He now understands how people's weaknesses and vices haunt them. Edgar realises that Lear's foolishness and his father's irresponsibility have caused great harm.
- It is left to Edgar and Albany to restore order to the 'gored state' of Britain. Edgar acknowledges the tremendous suffering of Lear and Gloucester, 'The oldest hath borne the most'. He is **determined to establish a kingdom of transparency and truth**: 'Speak what we feel, not what we ought to say'. Is there a suggestion that Cordelia should have initially shown her deep love for Lear?

Shakespearean audiences would regard Edgar as the hero of the play. He is 'noble' and has committed no crime. He believes in human justice and in the good will of the powers controlling man's destiny on earth. Edgar never doubts the triumph of good over evil.

- Edgar's role in the sub-plot is similar to Cordelia's in the main plot. The misjudged child redeems the misguided father through unconditional love and forgiveness. However, at the play's conclusion, Shakespeare leaves his audience guessing. **Is Edgar a strong enough character to rule the country successfully?** Or is he just a convenient dramatic device symbolising the forces of justice?

EDGAR'S QUALITIES

- trusting
- honest
- inventive
- courageous
- heroic
- loving
- selfless
- authoritative

EDGAR'S FLAWS

- gullible
- indecisive
- pitiful
- ineffective

Goneril and Regan

First Impressions

> *'let's hit together'*
>
> ***(Act 1 Scene 1, l.300)***

Goneril and Regan: symbols of human depravity

- Lear uses a pubic 'love test' to divide the kingdom of Britain between his **three daughters** so 'that future strife/ May be prevented now'. Ironically, **this decision will set each sister not only against their father, but also against each other**. The ambitious elder sisters, Goneril and Regan, are happy to take part in their father's foolish plan and they tell him exactly what he wants to hear. Goneril swears, 'I love you more than words can wield the matter'. Regan flatters the old king just as much, 'I find she names my very deed of love'.
- **Cordelia is disgusted by their 'glib and oily' hypocrisy**: 'I know you what you are'. The older sisters are as aware of Cordelia's character as she is of theirs, 'with what poor judgement he hath now cast her off'. They also know their ageing father very well and have a realistic attitude towards him: 'The best and soundest of his time hath been but rash'. They decide they will have to act quickly together 'in the heat' because of the likely dangers that might result from his 'unconstant starts'.

> **As King of Britain, Lear breaks the natural order by deciding to abdicate. Is he also a bad father? He showed obvious favouritism towards Cordelia. How might this have contributed to the 'Filial ingratitude' of his other daughters? Goneril also questions his judgement.**

- **Regan and Goneril immediately start to undermine the old king.** Goneril complains that his knights are boisterous 'rabble' turning her home into a 'riotous inn'. She encourages her servants to act disrespectfully towards Lear with 'weary negligence'. They are to regard him with contempt: 'Old fools are babes again'. In a reversal of the usual family roles, the father is now the child, while the child is the parent – the natural order is shattered.

Goneril and Regan's Character Development

> *'Is there any cause in nature that makes these hard hearts?'*
>
> ***(Act 3 Scene 6, l.74–5)***

- Audiences find it hard to excuse Regan and Goneril's increasingly bad conduct. Both women are cold-hearted realists. Regan reminds Lear that he did not hand over power until he was very old: 'in good time you gave it'. Although he gave 'all', it came with conditions. He would live with each daughter in turn month by month. He also demanded to have one hundred knights as his personal guard.

- Shakespeare **associates Goneril and Regan with vicious animal imagery** to highlight their inhumane behaviour. The image of a 'gilded serpent' reflects Goneril's deceitful character. The sisters' ingratitude to their father is described as being 'sharper than a serpent's tooth'. When Gloucester attempts to help the king, their instinctive reaction is, 'Hang him instantly', 'Pluck out his eyes'.
- In the play's most horrific scene, **Regan descends into depths of almost unimaginable cruelty**. Not only does she insist that Gloucester must be completely blinded, 'the other too', but she also takes pleasure in telling him that Edmund betrayed him. 'It was he/ That made the overture of thy treasons to us'. She dismisses the old earl heartlessly: 'Let him smell/ His way to Dover'.

Regan and Goneril have achieved success using cool calculation and teamwork. But they only co-operate when it suits them. They quickly turn against each other because of their uncontrollable feelings for Edmund.

- Goneril despises her 'Milk-livered' husband and plots with Edmund to kill him. When she realises that her sister is also attracted to Edmund, she acts decisively and murders Regan by poisoning her. However, after Edmund is killed by Edgar, she loses her ambition to rule and dies by suicide. Ironically, the **two sisters' pursuit of power has been destroyed by uncontrollable passion for a man who cared nothing for either of them**: 'Which of them shall I take?/ Both? One? Or neither?'

Overview

'Is this the promised end?'

(Act 5 Scene 3, l.270)

- In the final scene, the dead bodies of Goneril and Regan lie onstage, symbols of **good triumphing over evil**. Shakespeare has used the two sisters to reveal how corruption and immorality flourish when the natural bonds of family and country are broken. Lear's ill-judgement and the resulting 'Filial ingratitude' have had tragic consequences.

In Shakespeare's time, the audience would have been horrified that two women could behave so viciously and violently. Even today, Goneril and Regan are disturbing symbols of human evil.

- The playwright leaves us with some puzzling questions. Not only are the two wicked daughters dead, but their innocent younger sister, who had acted out of love, has also lost her life. When evil is set loose, does it destroy everyone in its path? **Are Goneril and Regan evidence of divine justice?**

GONERIL AND REGAN'S QUALITIES

- rational
- realistic
- independent
- strong-willed
- clever

GONERIL AND REGAN'S FLAWS

- hypocritical
- vindictive
- vicious
- unreliable
- cunning

The Duke of Albany

First Impressions

> *'Striving to better, oft we mar what's well'*
>
> ***(Act 1 Scene 4, l.334)***

- Lear has decided on his 'love test' to prevent 'future strife' between Cornwall and Albany. There is already court gossip about 'a division between the dukes'. At the beginning of the play, Goneril's husband, **Albany, appears cautious, an ineffective bystander** to events. He is dominated by his strong-willed wife, who regards their marriage as 'An interlude'. Albany protests that he is unaware of the reason Lear is in such a violent rage: 'I am guiltless, as I am ignorant/ Of what hath moved you'.
- Yet one of the knights comments that Albany's less than enthusiastic reception for the king is an 'abatement of kindness' on Albany's part. The duke does make a half-hearted protest against Goneril when Lear decides to leave, but she dismisses his 'milky gentleness'. Goneril regards her husband as a harmless, **dull-spirited man who wants to leave well alone**.

Albany: presides over the restoration of order

Albany's Character Development

> *'never man so changed'*
>
> ***(Act 4 Scene 2, l.3)***

- Like Lear and Gloucester, **Albany grows in moral strength** as the play progresses. He is shocked by Gloucester's cruel blinding, a punishment carried out by Cornwall, Regan and Goneril – and he now confronts his evil wife: 'See thyself, devil!' He also promises Gloucester that he will 'revenge thine eyes'.
- Albany sees Goneril as a 'gilded serpent', but her insults no longer scare him. **He has matured** from the 'Milk-livered man' he once was. Albany now answers Goneril in her own brutal language, declaring that his hands are ready 'to dislocate and tear/ Thy flesh and bones'.

Overview

> *'Our present business*
> *Is general woe'*
>
> ***(Act 5 Scene 3, l.327–8)***

- In the final scene, the duke emerges as a moral leader. Faced with the problem of Cordelia's French army landing in Britain, he has to decide whether to fight them or let his sympathies for Lear take priority. He **decides on the more rational course of action** and joins forces with Edmund to defeat the invaders.

After the victory over the French, Albany demands custody of Lear and Cordelia, who were being held captive by Edmund. While acknowledging Edmund's bravery on the battlefield, the **newly self-confident Albany** puts Edmund in his place: 'I hold you but a subject of this war,/ Not as a brother'. Shortly afterwards, he charges him with 'capital treason'.

- Albany and Edgar are the forces of good who intend to restore order to the 'gored state'. The duke takes control, ordering that the bodies of the two evil sisters be produced. 'This judgement of the heavens, that makes us tremble,/ Touches us not with pity'. Albany has emerged as **a stronger and more compassionate man**, interested in establishing law and order after the chaos which has led to so many deaths.

ALBANY'S QUALITIES	ALBANY'S FLAWS
• honourable	• indecisive
• well-meaning	• weak
• dignified	• dull
• moral	• ineffective
• matures	• lacks foresight

Albany and Cornwall: division between the dukes

The Fool

The Fool: reason in an absurd world

First Impressions

> *'all-licensed fool'*
>
> ***(Act 1 Scene 4, l.184)***

- Lear's court jester is **not a character in the ordinary sense**. The Fool was employed to amuse the king and court with jokes, riddles, songs and dances, but he also served a more serious purpose – to keep the king informed of what was happening behind the scenes in his court.
- The 'all-licensed fool' also had a special position. He was **able to speak the truth without fear of punishment**. Shakespeare's audiences enjoyed the Fool's antics and clever wordplay: 'Speak less than thou knowest,/ Lend less than thou owest'.

> *'This is not altogether fool'*
>
> ***(Act 1 Scene 4, l.137)***

- From his earliest appearance, **the Fool exposes the stupidity of Lear's decision to abdicate**: 'Thou hadst little wit in thy bald crown when thou gavest thy golden one away'. He openly disapproves of the king's elder daughters: 'they will make an obedient father'. Through non-stop mockery, he tries to get his master to see what he has done: 'thou art an O without a figure'. The Fool also knows who Lear is now without his crown: 'thou art nothing'.
- While the Fool does not develop as a character, he has important functions, **acting as the king's conscience** and making him feel guilty about his disastrous errors of judgement. He warns the audience of the dangers of a corrupt society, where nothing is as it should be. In return, Lear also uses the Fool as a confidant, telling him that he is afraid of going insane. Desperate for help, he begs the Fool, 'Keep me in temper: I would not be mad!'
- The Fool is a **steady source of support for Lear** in this chaotic world where the natural order has been turned upside down: 'May not an ass know when the cart draws the horse?' He focuses on the old king's lack of common sense. Lear believed in appearances rather than reality during his absurd 'love test'. The king's jester echoes the evil sisters' advice that a person must look out for their own interests.
- However, the Fool himself decides to act foolishly and unselfishly when he remains by Lear's side: 'the fool will stay/ And

let the wise man fly'. **The Fool supports Lear through the painful transition from arrogant selfishness to an understanding of humanity.** The Fool's vulnerability gives the insane monarch someone else to care for when they are on the heath. 'Take physic, pomp,/ Expose thyself to feel what wretches feel'.

Overview

> *'I would not be thee'*
>
> ***(Act 1 Scene 4, l.170)***

- **The Fool protects Lear until Cordelia can return** to help him. He then disappears suddenly, exiting for the last time with a typically surreal comment, 'I'll go to bed at noon'. His final comment reinforces the disordered world which has emerged since Lear's abdication.
- In a strange way, the old king seems to have turned into the Fool at this point. He no longer needs anyone else to remind him of his foolishness. Later, in the heart-breaking scene where Lear carries Cordelia's lifeless body, he cries, 'And my poor fool is hanged!' Shakespeare is reminding the audience that in this cruel world, when people do not act in their own selfish interests, the cost can be high. Like Cordelia, **the Fool chose to love and be loyal to Lear** in this uncertain world.

THE FOOL'S QUALITIES	THE FOOL'S FLAWS
• loyal	• inconsiderate
• honest	• pitiable
• independent	• bitter
• wise	• hurtful
• entertaining	• frivolous

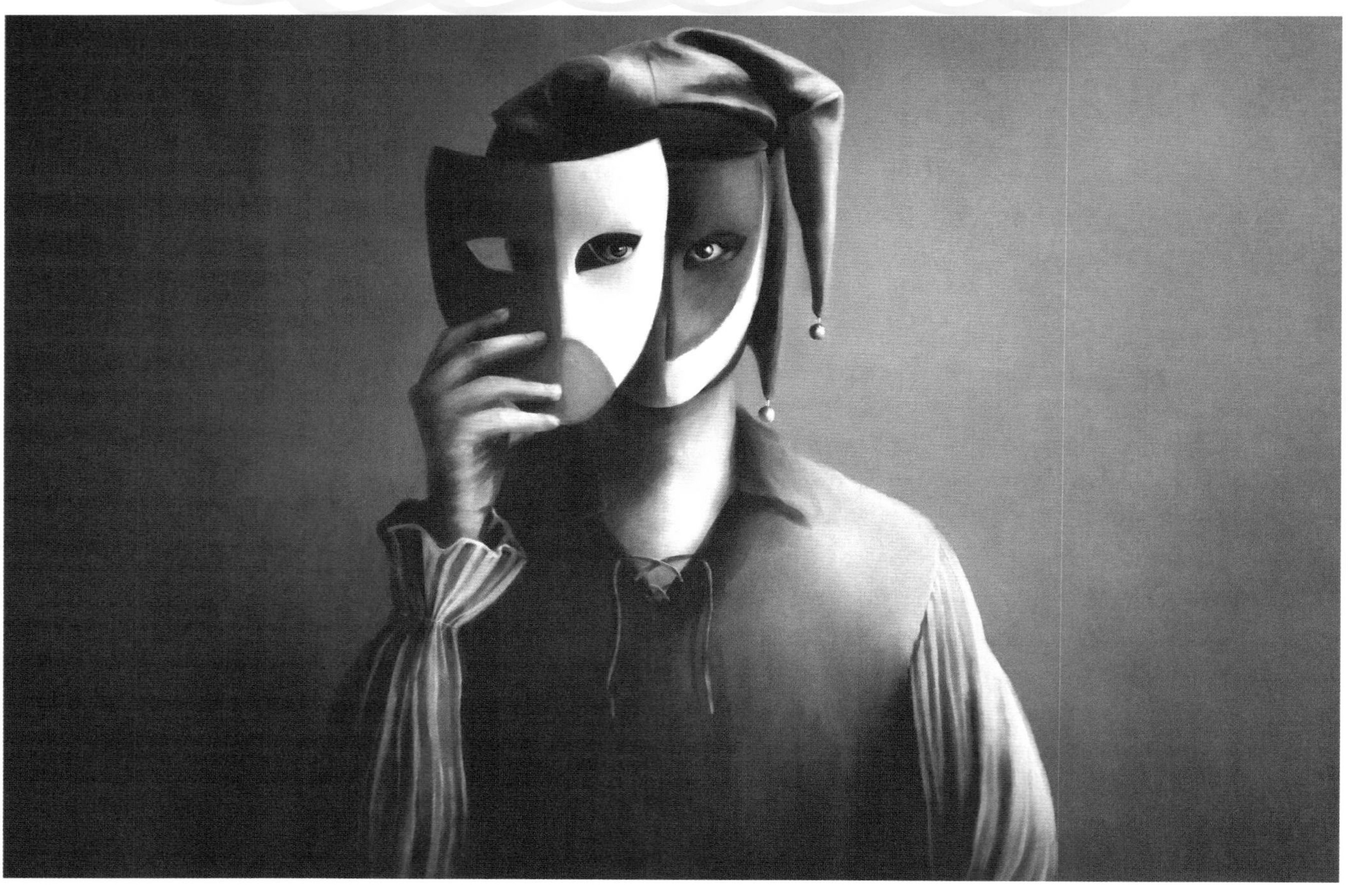

The Earl of Kent

First Impressions

> *'See better, Lear'*
>
> ***(Act 1 Scene 1, l.155)***

- The Earl of Kent is defined by his loyalty to Lear. He is an old man who has served the king faithfully for years. Unlike other courtiers, **Kent is honest and outspoken.** He expresses his outrage at Lear's banishment of Cordelia, 'I'll tell thee thou dost evil'. For his efforts, Lear banishes the 'recreant'. But Kent disguises himself as Caius and enters Lear's service once more. His only role in life is to protect the ageing king from his enemies. Kent is not swayed by Goneril and Regan's 'large speeches'. Indeed, he is one of the few characters in the play who can see the truth about others from the beginning.
- Kent is punished by being placed in the stocks by Cornwall following an angry exchange with one of Goneril's servants. He **accepts his punishment patiently**, waiting for fortune to 'turn thy wheel'. Shakespeare uses Kent's character as a part of Lear's journey towards self-knowledge. The king is forced to recognise that he is no longer respected as he has given up his throne. Nobody fears him because he is no longer in office: 'How came my man i' the stocks?'
- In the chaos on the heath, Kent is **the only voice of sanity.** When the old king places the blame for Poor Tom's troubles on his ungrateful daughters, Kent calmly reminds him, 'He hath no daughters'. He helps Lear escape to Dover and also stays in touch with Cordelia through an exchange of letters, keeping her up to date with developing events.
- When Lear enters with the dead Cordelia and is overcome with trauma, it is Kent who declares, 'O, let him pass'. **He feels that the aged king has suffered enough** in this wicked world: 'All's cheerless, dark, and deadly'. He also refuses Albany's offer to share joint rule of the kingdom with Edgar.
- In the final scene, Kent is restored to his former nobility. However, his purpose in life has finished with Lear's passing and so he now awaits his own death: 'My master calls me'. Although Kent plays a small part in the play, it is an important one. Shakespeare has created a character of **unswerving loyalty, honour and duty.** From the opening scenes to the end of the play, the audience sees a minor character who represents many of the values that the playwright himself believed in.

KENT'S CHARACTER TRAITS

- **honest**
- **outspoken**
- **loyal**
- **tactless**
- **honourable**
- **selfless**
- **philosophical**

Kent: unconditional devotion

The Duke of Cornwall

First Impressions

> *'How unremovable and fixed he is*
> *In his own course'*
> ***(Act 2 Scene 4, l.89–90)***

- The Duke of Cornwall is married to Lear's second daughter, Regan. When the old monarch transfers royal power to his daughters and their husbands, Cornwall becomes ruler of half of Britain. He is an **ambitious, hot-tempered man** – in contrast to Goneril's husband, the mild-mannered Albany.
- Cornwall judges by appearances and is easily deceived. When Edmund reveals Gloucester's hidden letter, he declares, 'I will lay trust upon thee', without investigating the matter any further. There are **many examples of the duke's cruel character**. He disrespects Lear by putting Kent in the stocks. He also orders Gloucester to lock the king out of the castle, 'Shut up your doors, my lord ... My Regan counsels well'.
- Shakespeare uses **Cornwall's character to show the depths of evil to which a human being can sink** when he believes he is beyond the law.

Cornwall's violent behaviour has a sadistic edge, and he clearly enjoys causing pain. In the play's most horrific scene, he gouges out Gloucester's eye as a punishment for helping Lear. Encouraged by his wife, he then scrapes out the other eye: 'Out, vile jelly!/ Where is thy lustre now?'

- Even after being fatally wounded by an outraged servant, Cornwall gives one last despicable order – to evict Gloucester, 'Turn out that eyeless villain'. The **'fiery duke' dies as he lived, by the sword**. Shakespeare's audience would have regarded the killing of Cornwall as natural justice, as he was the personification of evil.

CORNWALL'S CHARACTER TRAITS

- **hot-blooded**
- **ambitious**
- **scheming**
- **violent**
- **naive**
- **sadistic**
- **abuses power**
- **fails to mature**

Cornwall: violence and villainy

Key Themes in *King Lear*

Introduction

What is a theme?

A theme is an issue or idea that is central to the drama.

> **CENTRAL THEMES IN *KING LEAR***
>
> **Appearance and reality, justice, love, madness, revenge, power, relationships, self-knowledge, etc.**

All of these themes – and many others in the play – are closely interlinked.

Key themes are presented through the main characters and are reflected in the play's language and imagery.

What kinds of questions are asked on themes?

Leaving Certificate exam questions usually include several elements. Some questions focus on multiple themes and their dramatic impact, e.g. **'Deceit and dishonesty are used to great effect throughout Shakespeare's play *King Lear*.' Discuss this statement, developing your response with reference to the play.**

Another type of question combines a key theme with the dramatic style of the play.

'In the play *King Lear* Shakespeare makes effective use of a variety of dramatic devices to explore the tragic consequences of deception.' Discuss this statement, developing your answer with reference to the play.

How do I approach the question?

- Study the wording of the question closely to identify the various aspects to be considered.
- Decide on your opinion (agree, disagree, partially agree). Be prepared to challenge aspects of the question.
- Plan your answer. Each paragraph should be a step in your developed argument which is firmly rooted in the text.
- Avoid general summary, i.e. telling the story of the play.
- Aim for around 800 words written over 60 minutes.

> **Expand your vocabulary to vary expression**
>
> **Deception** – false appearance, deceit, hypocrisy, cunning, dishonesty, treachery, disloyalty, etc.
>
> **Truthfulness** – reality, sincerity, openness, etc.

Appearance and Reality

— sight, blindness

Lear's essential flaw is his failure to distinguish the difference between reality and appearance

Deception in the play's main plot

In the deceptive, 'gilded' world of King Lear's court, **nothing is as it first appears**. Appearance and reality is a central theme. There is a sharp difference between what seems to be true and what is really true. Goneril, Regan and Edmund appear caring to their fathers, but all three of them are resentful and ruthlessly ambitious. In contrast, honourable characters, such as Cordelia and Kent, are punished for telling the truth.

At the start of the play, Shakespeare presents Lear as a foolish old man who is easily fooled by appearances. He insists on a 'love test' as a way of dividing his kingdom between his daughters. Their inheritance depends on a public declaration by each daughter about how much they love him. Regan and Goneril appear to be loyal and loving towards their father. They exaggerate their feelings for him through **lavish praise and deceptive language**. Goneril declares, 'Sir, I love you more than words can wield the matter'.

Yet Lear welcomes her flattery. She has publicly told him what he wants to hear, whereas **Cordelia, his youngest daughter, is sincere – but stubborn**. She refuses to play the game which requires her to 'heave' her heart into her mouth, and simply says that she loves Lear according to their 'bond' as father and daughter. However, this is not good enough for the egotistical king, who does not appreciate her honesty. In a sudden fit of rage towards Cordelia, Lear disinherits and banishes her.

Kent, his loyal servant, tries to make the headstrong king think again about this 'hideous rashness'. For this, he is also banished. **Lear's major flaw is his inability to distinguish between reality and appearance.** He refuses to see human existence as it is, preferring life as he wishes it to be. He simply does not want to 'See better'.

Throughout the opening scene, Shakespeare shocks the audience by revealing the evil depths of deception to which human beings will stoop. **Lear's reckless decisions increase the dramatic tension.** Hypocrisy and family conflicts intrigue us from the start. What is likely to happen next as a result of the old king's poor judgement? Have we seen the last of Cordelia and Kent? Will Goneril and Regan live up to all their loving words?

> **Remember!**
>
> Examination questions test your understanding of the play. Answers should demonstrate your ability to analyse the story, rather than merely summarise.
>
> Discuss the playwright's treatment of a theme where appropriate.

Deception in the play's sub-plot

Gloucester also allows himself to be taken in by dishonesty. His younger son, Edmund, pretends to hide a letter, knowing that his father will be eager to see it. Edmund has forged this letter about a conspiracy to kill Gloucester. He gives the impression that his elder brother, Edgar, is responsible, 'It is his hand'. **Like Lear, Gloucester accepts without question what is put in front of him.** He calls Edgar a 'villain' without giving him an opportunity to defend himself. Edmund intensifies his dishonesty by pretending to be concerned for Gloucester's reputation. He even advises his father not to act 'violently' against Edgar.

Later on, Edmund pretends to be a loyal subject to Cornwall when he betrays Gloucester's efforts to help Lear. Cornwall reacts by gouging out Gloucester's eyes. Ironically, it is only when he is blind that Gloucester gains wisdom and insight: 'I stumbled when I saw'. He finally realises the truth, that he has misjudged Edgar. In the sub-plot, **Shakespeare develops the theme of appearance and reality**, highlighting the dangers of acting rashly without considering the consequences.

> **Writing effectively about themes**
>
> When discussing themes, consider the playwright's viewpoint. In which scene is the theme first introduced? How does Shakespeare treat the theme? What is his attitude to it as the story develops? What points is he making about deception, power, love, justice, etc.?

use to hide reality Edgar – "Poor Tom"

Disguise and revelation

The playwright also makes **effective use of disguises to reveal the truth**. While Edgar is hiding from his father he pretends to be 'Poor Tom', a mad beggar, in order to survive. When Lear meets this 'poor, bare, forked animal' on the stormy heath, he begins to understand more about basic humanity. Tom's confused display helps the old king to empathise with the most vulnerable people in society.

Edgar adopts two other disguises. Pretending to be a peasant, he tries to save Gloucester from dying by suicide. His third disguise, near the end of the play, is that of an unnamed challenger to take on Edmund in a duel, calling him out as 'a traitor'. He is determined to expose his brother's treachery.

Shakespeare shows that honourable characters sometimes deceive in order to do good. Banished **Kent disguises himself as Caius** to continue protecting the king. Yet again Lear displays his lack of judgement when he fails to recognise his loyal servant, despite Kent's heavy hint that he can 'deliver a plain message bluntly'. The self-centred monarch has become obsessed with 'Filial ingratitude' as a result of his treatment by his daughters Goneril and Regan.

The Fool appears to be a mere clown, but in reality he is very wise. Through humour, songs and rhymes, he dares to mock the king's foolishness. He tries again and again to get Lear to see how his decision to hand over power to his daughters has been disastrous. He cannot be king if others hold power. Lear has reversed the natural order: 'May not an ass know when the cart draws the horse?'

Only when Lear descends into madness does he begin to recognise that Goneril and Regan 'flattered me like a dog'. He also **realises that he has misjudged Cordelia**: 'I did her wrong'. He has come to understand the hypocrisy of a society which protects the rich and powerful, 'Robes and furred gowns hide all'. Ironically, Lear has found 'Reason in madness'.

Towards the end of the play, Shakespeare presents Lear carrying his dead daughter Cordelia in his arms, still hoping to hear her voice, 'soft,/ Gentle, and low'. This is a bitter contrast to the opening scene when he dismissed her words. The playwright leaves his audience to question whether Lear has accepted life as it truly is, or **whether he is still trying to impose his version of reality**. Is the finality of death too hard to accept?

Through the playwright's treatment of deception of various kinds, other themes such as ambition, power, justice, truth and the cycle of life are explored. As a result, audiences come to a fuller understanding and appreciation of these issues. Over the course of the drama, **Shakespeare explores the value of truly seeing oneself and the real state of the world**.

Overview

Appearance and reality in *King Lear*

- This theme is used to show the true identity of certain characters.
- It exposes contrasts between good and evil.
- For Lear and Gloucester, failure to distinguish the difference is particularly damaging.
- Provides compelling moments of insight.
- Propels the story to its tragic conclusion.
- Intensifies the dramatic experience for the audience.

Justice

Shakespeare leaves the audience to consider the rights and wrongs of human justice

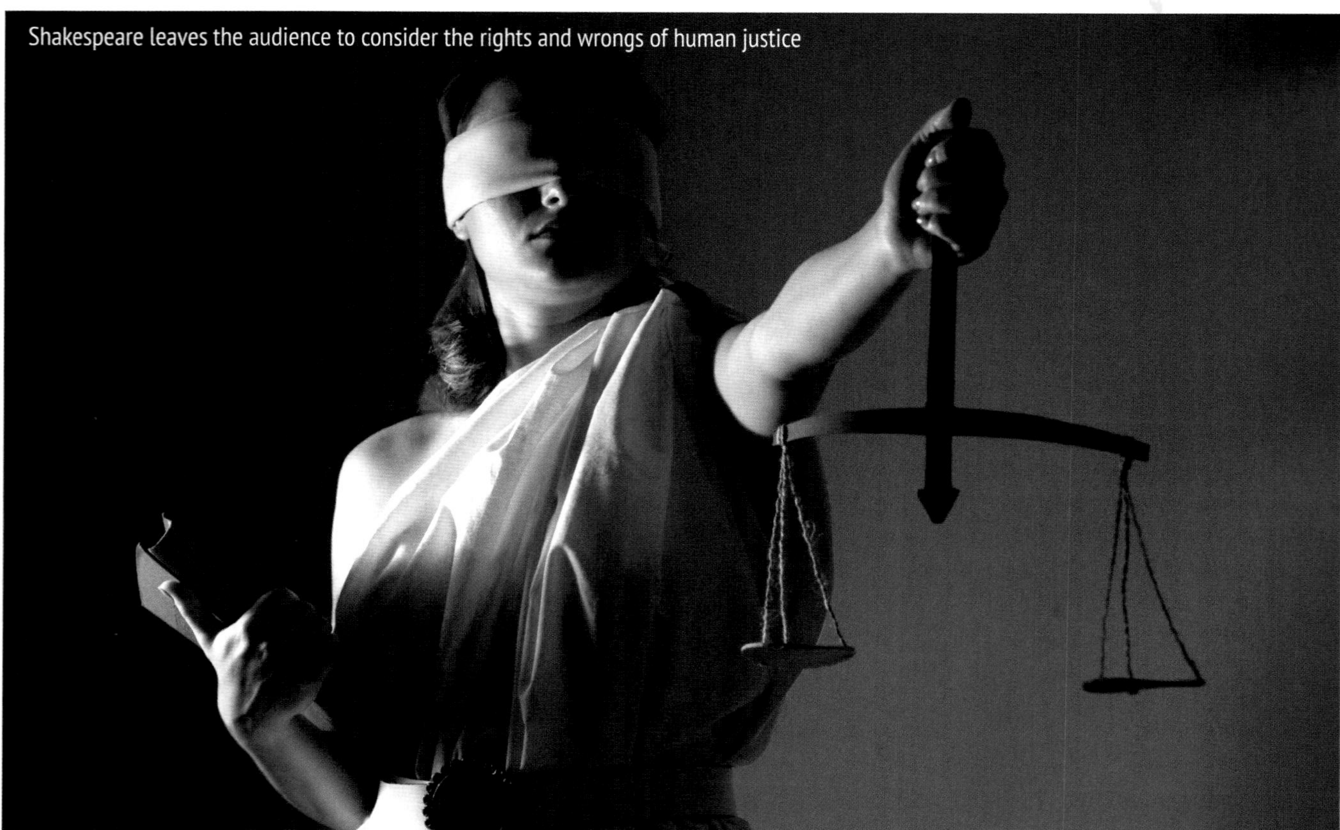

In *King Lear*, many characters struggle with the concept of justice. There is a strong emphasis on the question of whether there is in the world a moral power that guarantees appropriate punishment for crimes.

Justice generally means that **everybody will get what they rightly deserve**. Shakespeare explores the key theme of justice throughout the play. At the end Albany suggests that justice has triumphed: 'All friends shall taste/ The wages of their virtue, and all foes/ The cup of their deservings'. But is this really what has happened in *King Lear*?

Expand your vocabulary to vary expression

Justice – fairness, lawfulness, morality, integrity, even-handedness, etc.

Injustice – unfairness, prejudice, inequality, wrong, discrimination, etc.

Divine justice

Shakespeare wrote his plays during the Elizabethan era (1558–1603). At that time, religious leaders taught the people that they would be judged by God when they died. Divine justice meant that the virtuous would be rewarded and taken up to heaven, but the wicked would be condemned to hell. In *King Lear*, which is set in pagan times, the 'gods' are mysterious beings who govern the universe and control humanity. Shakespeare **presents contrasting views of divine justice**, both negative and positive.

Characters constantly appeal to the gods for help, but they are rarely successful. The blinded Gloucester believes the gods have little regard for humans: 'As flies to wanton boys are we to the gods./ They kill us for their sport'. Lear appeals to the gods, 'Send down, and take my part!' He is answered by Regan, who increases his suffering by demanding that he get rid of his one hundred knights. When the king begs, 'You see me here, you gods, a poor old man', he is deafened by the sounds of an approaching storm in which he will lose his sanity. This is the **negative view of divine justice** in the play.

In contrast, Edgar and Albany present a more **optimistic view of divine power**. Edgar believes that 'The gods are just'. As a fugitive, he adopts the disguise of Poor Tom, a deranged beggar. Yet he is convinced that life will get better: 'The worst returns to laughter'. He consoles his father, Gloucester, who has just tried to take his own life, 'the clearest gods ... have preserved thee'. Edgar accuses his treacherous brother, Edmund, of being 'False to thy gods'. The Christian view of suffering is that people become better when humbled; they gain insight. Gloucester admits he 'stumbled' when he saw. He eventually renounces his former negative view of the gods and finally understands that 'Men must endure'.

But a key question remains: **is the suffering out of proportion to the sin**? Both Gloucester and Lear have sinned – one out of lust, the other from pride. Both made serious errors of judgement, breaking the natural order by disowning their loyal children. Gloucester is blinded. Lear becomes insane. Yet both irresponsible fathers are reunited with the child they earlier rejected. There is an element here of divine justice.

At the end of the play, Edgar turns Edmund's disregard for rules against him and fatally wounds his brother in a duel. This clear sign of **good winning over evil is often seen by the audience as poetic justice**. Meanwhile, Cordelia, the rejected daughter, displays the flaw of stubbornness by refusing to take part in in Lear's 'love test'. Should she have been less 'untender' and indulged her old father? Her suffering and death far outweigh her character defect. Was she treated justly?

King Lear concludes with a stage cluttered with bodies. Some have deserved their deaths. Cornwall has been killed by his own servant. Goneril and Regan are destroyed by their jealous lust – one murdered, the other a suicide. But other characters can be seen as innocent victims of evil – Gloucester and Lear to some degree – and especially Cordelia. Has Shakespeare presented a divine justice which does not include mercy? **To what extent is there redemption?**

Shakespeare uses the theme of justice to raise questions about whether individuals get what they deserve. All through the play, justice is closely intertwined with other themes, including honesty, revenge, destiny, self-knowledge, and the use and abuse of power.

Human justice

At the beginning of the play, **Lear leads with absolute power**. But arrogance brings about his downfall. He wants to be king, but without the responsibilities which attend the role. Old and tired, he decides to divide the rule of his kingdom between his three daughters, according to their public declaration of love for him. When Cordelia refuses, he swiftly banishes her: 'I disclaim all my paternal care'.

When Kent, his servant, tries to reason with him, Lear banishes him as well. However, when he relinquishes his power to Goneril and Regan, all his royal authority is lost. He is deprived of his knights and servants, locked out and left to wander the heath in a storm. The way human justice works seems to reflect Lear's faults. Descending into madness, the elderly king begins to change and becomes aware of **the injustice of social inequality**.

Meeting Poor Tom, **Lear gains insight into how privilege for some creates deprivation** for many, 'Poor naked wretches'. He realises that having power does not always reflect the worth of the person who occupies it: 'A dog's obeyed in office'. Through his suffering, he begins to understand how wealth and privilege hide the sins of the rich, 'Through tattered clothes small vices do appear;/ Robes and furred gowns hide all'. Those who can afford to pay can avoid justice, 'Plate sin with gold'. Similarly, Gloucester also gains insight into social injustice through his suffering: 'distribution should undo excess,/ And each man have enough'.

Throughout the drama, various 'trials' show **how imperfect human justice is**. The ludicrous 'love test' clearly exposes flawed judgement. Justice is not done when Cornwall imprisons Kent in the stocks for his bluntness in loyally defending the king. Nor is it done when Gloucester is tried for treason by Cornwall, Goneril and Regan, and has his eyes gouged out. Lear becomes more and more obsessed with seeking justice and arranges a mock trial for Goneril and Regan. He is as eager to punish them as they were with Gloucester. He wants to blitz them with 'red burning spits'. All semblance of justice has been overturned.

The play ends with Britain under new leadership, and the hope that justice will be restored. Edgar promises that his rule will be defined by truth and openness: 'Speak what we feel, not what we ought to say'. But is there a chance that he might also be corrupted by power, just as Lear was? Shakespeare presents **thought-provoking questions about many aspects of justice** – divine justice, poetic justice, social justice, and the wider justice system – leaving audiences feeling unsure and uncomfortable.

Overview

Justice in *King Lear*

- The play offers different views on the possibility of divine justice.
- Undermines the idea of divine justice through the unjust death of Cordelia, and Lear's terrible suffering.
- Exposes social injustice, highlighting abuses of power and poverty.
- Leaves audiences questioning their beliefs in justice.

Is justice really served.!

Love

Shakespeare's play focuses on the power of love in its many forms

Love is a very **important theme** in *King Lear*. The tragic story is driven by the important question, 'Which of you shall we say doth love us most?' Lear's self-important 'love test' for his daughters results in tearing his family apart. The terrible storm on the heath mirrors this tragedy. The play explores child/parent love, the loyal love of a servant for his master, romantic love between men and women, and the universal love of humanity.

Expand your vocabulary to vary expression

Love – affection, tenderness, devotion, respect, warmth, passion, friendship, etc.

Hatred – detestation, dislike, resentment, distaste, contempt, disrespect, loathing, etc.

Family love

Lear's daughters

The starting point of this tragedy is Lear's foolish 'love test' which demands public expressions of his daughters' feelings for him before he decides on their inheritance. The two older daughters, Goneril and Regan, pretend to love their father in 'glib and oily' speeches. Goneril makes an obviously untrue statement: 'Sir, I love you more than words can wield the matter'. Yet Lear allows himself to be misled by her false flattery. Regan tries to outdo her sister: 'she comes too short'. **Both manipulative daughters are well rewarded for their dishonest displays of love.**

Cordelia refuses to take part in the absurd spectacle, preferring to 'Love, and be silent'. When forced to speak by her father, she states that she **loves him according to her 'bond'** – the natural tie between parent and child. Is she too honest for her own good, particularly in her choice of the legal term 'bond'? Lear is shocked by her 'untender' announcement. The king feels embarrassed before the whole court.

Rashly, he divides Cordelia's inheritance between her two sisters and publicly disowns her. He admits that he had hoped to spend his remaining years with Cordelia: 'I loved her most, and thought to set my rest/ On her kind nursery'. Is Cordelia as stubborn as her father in refusing to flatter the old king? **Should she exaggerate her love for him?** Is Lear being bad-tempered and petty when he disinherits and banishes Cordelia?

Ironically, Lear's youngest daughter represents true love – something he fails to recognise. She is not bitter towards her father and only becomes angry when she learns of her sisters' terrible treatment of him. Goneril and Regan turn him out of doors into a raging storm. 'Mine enemy's dog,/ Though he had bit me, should have stood that night,/ Against my fire'.

Just as her sisters understand Lear's faults, 'The best and soundest of his time hath been but rash', Cordelia is aware of their shameless hypocrisy: 'I know you what you are'. She represents honesty and loyalty. **Cordelia genuinely loves Lear and brings comfort to him in the later part of the play** when she returns from France. She acts out of 'dear love, and our aged father's right'.

The reunion of Lear and Cordelia takes place at Dover. Lear is humble but dignified: 'forget and forgive'. **Cordelia, unlike the Lear of old, does not measure love.** She refuses to let her father shoulder all the blame for what has happened: 'you must not kneel'. Shortly afterwards, when captured by Edmund, Lear fondly imagines their prison as a sanctuary: 'We two alone will sing like birds i' the cage'.

Cordelia's tears are the 'holy water' leading to Lear's redemption. She too has matured and has learned to 'Speak what we feel'. Kent, Lear's loyal servant, approves of this new expressive daughter, 'Kind and dear Princess'. **Had she been able to express her love earlier, could this tragedy have been avoided?**

Shakespeare explores various aspects of love over the course of the play. Within King Lear's family, it has both destructive and healing effects. Love is closely associated with other key themes including honesty, hypocrisy, self-pity, conflict and loyalty.

Gloucester's sons

The play's main plot – centred on Lear's family – is closely mirrored in the sub-plot of Gloucester and his sons, Edgar and Edmund. **Both Lear and Gloucester have misguided ideas about love.** Like the ageing Lear, Gloucester is fooled by a dishonest child. He also banishes a loyal child, and this rash action leads to terrible consequences. Edmund goes on to betray his father to Cornwall by showing a forged letter which claims that Gloucester wishes to help Lear. As a result, the earl is viciously punished and has his eyes gouged out.

He is eventually rescued by his loving son, Edgar, who also saves him from taking his own life. Once again, **Shakespeare is emphasising the redemptive power of genuine love within a family**. Gloucester, like Lear, begins to understand reality and accept his own lack of judgement in the past: 'I stumbled when I saw'.

Edgar's 'foolish honesty' is replaced by recognising the need to be cautious. He does not reveal who he is when he challenges his treacherous brother, Edmund, to a duel. Yet, like Cordelia, **he realises that people must 'Speak what we feel'**. While Edgar and Edmund exchange forgiveness and are reconciled, Cordelia and her sisters are not. In the end, Edmund acknowledges the justice of his own death at the hands of the loving brother he betrayed, 'The wheel is come full circle'.

Love and loyalty

Lear's loyal servants reveal represent selfless love in a cruel world. The Fool tries to get his master to see the truth and even follows Lear into the storm, always acting as a faithful protector. Honest Kent, who loved Lear 'as my father', also tries to advise the king to 'See better'. Shortly after being banished, Kent returns in disguise to continue to save Lear from harm. When the king collapses at the sight of the dead Cordelia, Kent insists that Lear has already suffered enough and should be allowed die: 'let him pass'. Right to the end, Kent's love is unconditional.

Other examples of love and loyalty are presented when Gloucester is helped by one of his old tenants. Elsewhere, a concerned servant courageously tries to stop Cornwall from tearing out Gloucester's second eye. There are **many moments of human compassion** in the play – evidence of true friendship and selfless love in a sinister world.

Romantic love

Love between men and women is also explored in *King Lear*. Cordelia had two admirers who wished to marry her. But the Duke of Burgundy changes his mind when she is disinherited. However, the King of **France understands true love** and is happy to 'take up what's cast away'. This contrasts with Goneril's marriage and her dismissive attitude to her husband. She despises Albany for his 'milky gentleness' and his lack of decision-making. In return, he acts swiftly when her adultery with Edmund is revealed. He now regards his unfaithful wife as 'not worth the dust which the rude wind/ Blows'.

Shakespeare also illustrates selfish love. Edmund is desired by both sisters, Goneril and Regan. His comment, 'Which of them shall I take?/ Both? One? Or neither?', makes it clear that he really only loves himself. Their love for him was soon spoiled by jealousy: 'The one the other poisoned for my sake,/ And after slew herself'. Yet Edmund, because he was 'beloved' by them, tries to cancel the death sentences placed on Cordelia and Lear. Unfortunately, he is too late. Not even the innocent can escape the cruel consequences of destructive selfish love.

Universal love

When Lear and Gloucester are separated from their families, they begin to feel concern for other vulnerable people. Their **social conscience develops**. As the deranged king wanders the storm-battered heath, stripped of his royal power, he starts to understand the reality of poverty: 'Poor naked wretches .../ How shall .../ Your looped and windowed raggedness, defend you/ From seasons such as these?' He regrets doing so little to help those in need: 'I have taken/ Too little care of this'. Lear now believes that the rich and powerful should 'Expose' themselves to poverty so that they can 'feel what wretches feel'.

The blinded Gloucester also appreciates the importance of love for others and comes to believe that wealth should be more evenly distributed, so that 'each man have enough'. Over the course of the play, Shakespeare engages the sympathy of the audience for both Lear and Gloucester, two flawed men who have finally gained insight and awareness through appalling suffering. The playwright shows that **redemption comes from selfless love** – loving service to parent, child, partner, master, and society at large.

Overview

Love in *King Lear*

- The play explores different types of love.
- Exposes the tragic consequences caused by the deceptive love of a treacherous child.
- Highlights the benefits of true love, care from a dutiful servant, and redemption through the love of a loyal child.
- Reveals how understanding and a love of humanity can develop as a result of terrible suffering.
- Leaves audience shocked that both the innocent and guilty suffer as a result of false emotional displays and jealousy.

Madness

Madness is a central theme in *King Lear*. Ironically, characters who pretend to be insane are among the wisest, whereas the sane characters often act in a foolish and unreasonable way. Much of **the tragedy comes from the constant tension between madness and sanity** in the play.

Shakespeare uses three characters to explore the theme of madness. Lear's madness is real. From the depths of self-delusion and uncontrolled anger, he gains new understanding and insight into the human condition. The banished Edgar adopts the disguise of a lunatic beggar, Poor Tom, to survive. His insanity is play-acted, but he helps the king to recognise social injustice. The Fool is a professional madman. He plays the part of the court jester who uses jokes to help the king become more aware of reality.

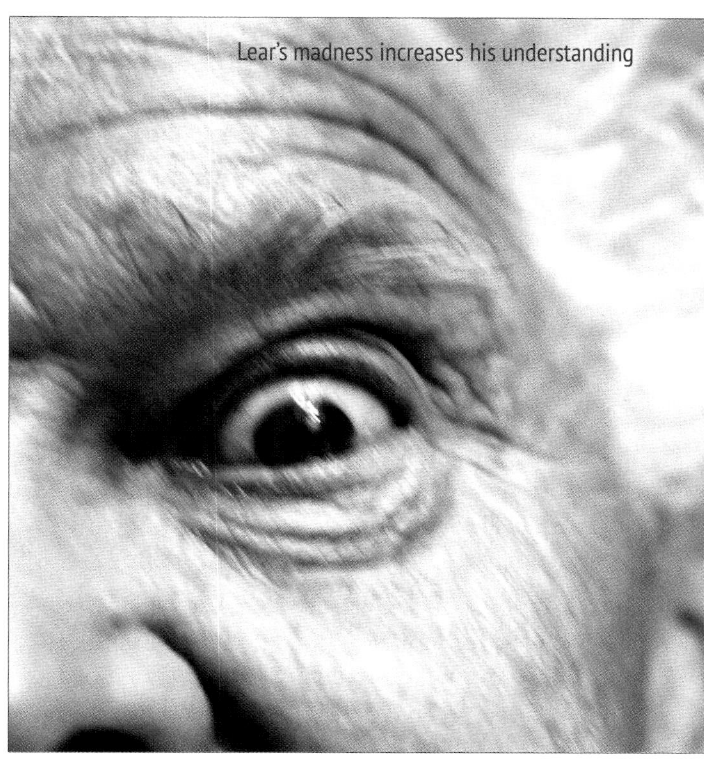
Lear's madness increases his understanding

Expand your vocabulary to vary expression

Madness – insanity, mental illness, foolishness, delusion, instability, hysteria, lunacy, etc.

Sanity – soundness of mind, mental health, stability, common sense, reason, level-headedness, etc.

Wisdom through insanity

Shakespeare presents the character of **Edgar** (as the insane beggar) to represent humanity stripped to its basic state, 'a poor, bare, forked animal'. This character allows the playwright to comment on social injustice and the shocking treatment of outcasts. Audiences can laugh at Poor Tom because they are aware, unlike Lear, that he is putting on an act. Yet, they are also moved, like Lear, to **an awareness of the reality of poverty** and homelessness: 'Unaccommodated man'. Poor Tom's dreadful condition makes a huge impact on the hysterical king. In a desperate attempt to be compassionate, Lear begins to remove his own clothes: 'Off, off, you lendings!'

The Fool holds a privileged position in the royal court. He is 'all-licensed' so that he can speak openly, without fear of punishment. Through jokes, songs and riddles, the Fool tries to get Lear to see what he has done by his hasty abdication and the disastrous division of his kingdom. 'Thou hadst little wit in thy bald crown when thou gavest thy golden one away'.

The 'sweet and bitter' Fool confronts his master with the stark truth: 'I am a fool, thou art nothing'. Both Edgar and the Fool – one a fake lunatic, the other a professional madman – **help Lear on his journey to self-discovery**. They encourage him to let go of his delusion that he is still a powerful ruler.

The playwright uses the theme of madness to show the tragic consequences of rash behaviour, and how mental suffering can lead to a real insight into the human condition. All through the play, madness is closely intertwined with other themes, including appearance and reality, loyalty, honesty, justice and self-knowledge.

Shakespeare presents Lear at the beginning of the play as **an arrogant, impulsive character** who is used to getting his own way: 'The best and soundest of his time hath been but rash'. Both Cordelia and Kent are dismissed for daring to disagree with his foolish decision to divide his kingdom on the basis of flattery in the reckless 'love test'. Lear finds it hard to admit that he **reversed the natural order** – and as the Fool reminds him, 'madest thy daughters thy mothers'.

The deluded old king blames everyone else for his predicament. He truly believes he is 'More sinned against than sinning' and is **obsessed with 'Filial ingratitude'**. When he meets his ungrateful daughter Goneril, he curses her viciously: 'Into her womb convey sterility!' He even assumes that Poor Tom's insanity must have been caused by his 'unkind daughters'.

Unable to cope with reality, the deranged monarch indulges his anger on the heath by challenging nature, which he thinks he can command: 'Blow, winds, and crack your cheeks!' Lear identifies with the storm. Both are out of control and creating devastation. **As Lear descends deeper into madness, however, his judgement begins to clear.** He realises he has mistreated Cordelia: 'I did her wrong'.

In the 'tempest' raging in his mind, **Lear finds sympathy for others**. He asks the Fool, 'Art cold?' He pities the 'Poor naked wretches' who have no homes and have to endure the 'pelting of this pitiless storm'. In his 'madness', he also begins to judge fairly, believing that the rich must not be allowed escape justice, 'Plate sin with gold'. His reunion with his estranged daughter Cordelia leads to his recognition of who he really is: 'a very foolish fond old man'.

Lear's madness not only represents his psychological suffering but also his **journey to self-awareness**. Tragically, the death of Cordelia leads him back into insanity. He deludes himself that she is alive, 'This feather stirs'. Both the audience and Kent want the old king's suffering to stop: 'O, let him pass! He hates him/ That would upon the rack of this tough world/ Stretch him out longer'.

Throughout the play, madness is associated with chaos – both in human society and in the natural world. Lear's insane act of dividing his kingdom unleashes devastation. The **natural order is broken by this unnatural act**. Storms rage, normal society collapses and evil flourishes. Yet out of disorder comes order. Shakespeare shows how true understanding of **what it means to be human can be gained through suffering**. He emphasises the need to be compassionate to others through the ramblings of three insane characters: 'Reason in madness'.

Overview

Madness in *King Lear*

- Madness is an important theme associated with both disorder and wisdom.
- Poor Tom's pretence of madness allows Shakespeare to comment on social injustice and the abuse of power.
- The Fool's professional madness enables Lear to negotiate his path to self-discovery.
- Lear's real madness is a symbol of the social disorder caused by the unnatural division of the kingdom.
- It allows Lear to gain a tragic vision of the world.

Dramatic Techniques in *King Lear*

Imagery

What is imagery?

Imagery is language that stimulates the senses. Shakespeare creates pictures in the minds of the audience by using descriptive language which appeals to the five senses: sight, hearing, touch, taste and smell. These vivid mental images deepen understanding of what is happening in the play and help to shape the audience's response.

What is the purpose of imagery?

The playwright uses imagery to:

- stir the audience's imagination about **themes**, e.g. power/powerlessness, justice/injustice, suffering, madness, order/disorder, etc. *(an empty eggshell signifies Lear's useless crown)*
- develop **characterisation** *(Goneril and Regan's evil is heightened through animal imagery)*
- create **moods** and atmospheres *(storm imagery represents Lear's disordered world)*
- add to the play's **emotional impact** *(broken family relationships: 'How sharper than a serpent's tooth it is/ To have a thankless child').*

Sight Imagery

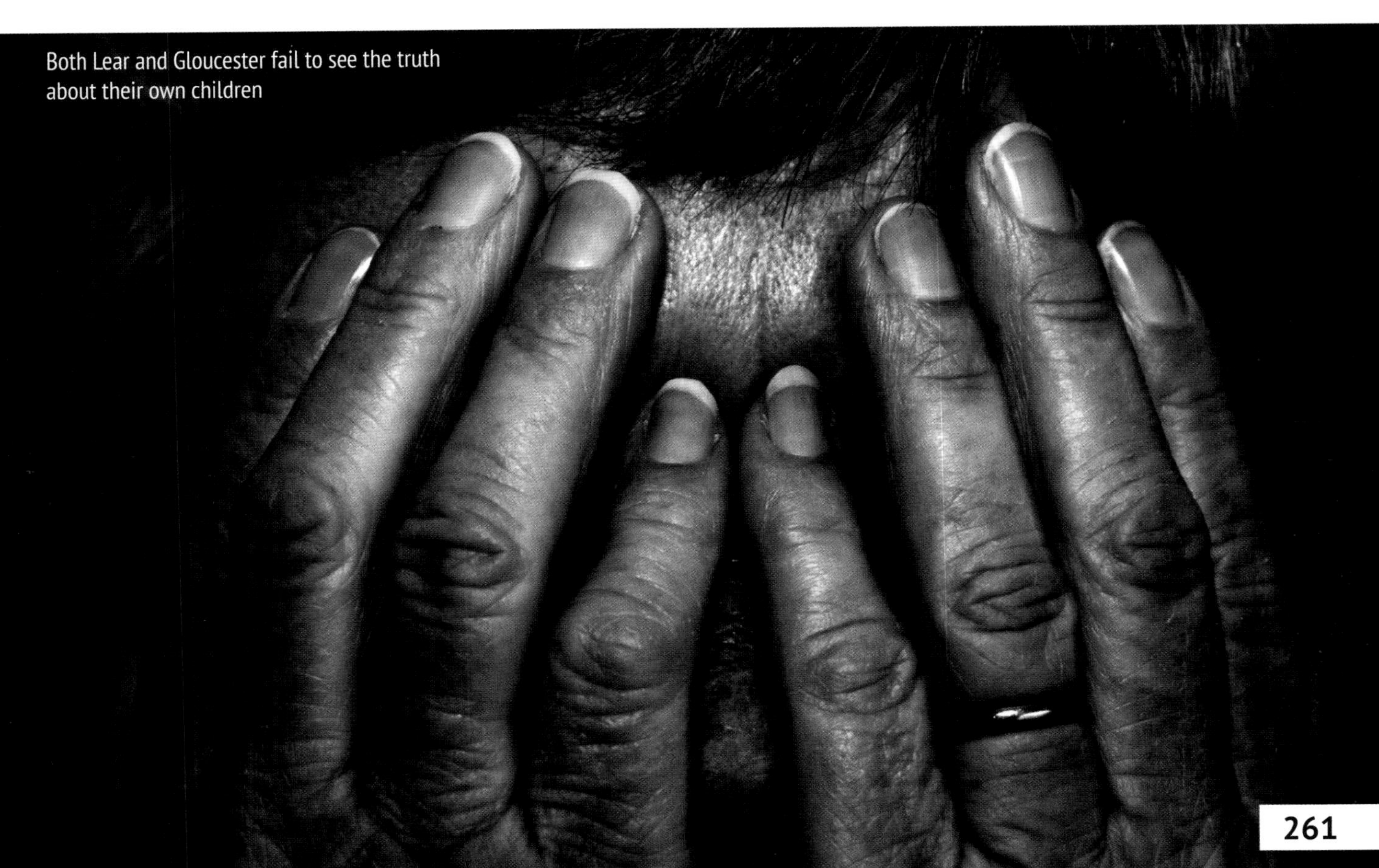

Both Lear and Gloucester fail to see the truth about their own children

> *'I stumbled when I saw'*
>
> ***(Act 4 Scene 1, l.19)***

King Lear is filled with images of sight and blindness. **Lear and Gloucester's inability to 'see' the truth prevents them from making correct decisions.** Both men are morally blind and out of touch with reality. They reward their wicked children and punish their loyal ones. Shakespeare's play illustrates how physical sight does not guarantee insight, the ability to know oneself and to see the world clearly.

Lear's blindness is particularly evident in the absurd 'love test' when he is fooled by Goneril's declaration of him being 'Dearer than eye-sight' to her. Lear is outraged by Cordelia's refusal to flatter him, so he banishes her: 'avoid my sight!' His loyal courtier, Kent, is also banished, 'Out of my sight', after warning him, 'See better, Lear'. **The pattern of sight imagery highlights the irony of his misjudgement.**

The Fool tries to get Lear to recognise the truth of the ridiculous situation he has created: 'Fathers that wear rags/ Do make their children blind'. His **sarcastic comments add to the sense of hopelessness, foreshadowing the suffering ahead**. The self-important monarch completely fails to recognise Goneril and Regan's plotting, Cordelia's genuine love, and his own foolishness. He does not see life as it is, but as he wants it to be.

Sight imagery is central to the play's most shocking scene, the blinding of Gloucester. Like Lear, this deluded father is viciously punished for helping the king: 'I would not see thy cruel nails/ Pluck out his poor old eyes'. Ironically, that is the precise punishment Cornwall, Goneril and Regan exact on Gloucester: 'Out, vile jelly'. Only in his blindness does the old man finally realise that 'Edgar was abused'. In the end, **both fathers achieve insight through suffering**. Both of them 'stumbled' when they saw.

Throughout the play, Shakespeare is using images of sight and blindness not only to reveal the truth about characters, but also to increase awareness of **the theme of appearance and reality**. Lear eventually concludes that 'A man may see how this world goes with no eyes'. He also begins to understand the reality of corruption in places of power: 'Get thee glass eyes,/ And like a scurvy politician, seem/ To see the things thou dost not'.

Just as the audience is desperate to see good triumph over evil, Lear appears, carrying Cordelia in his arms. He tries to convince himself and others that he sees her breathing: 'Look on her, look, her lips'. Does he die believing his daughter lives? Is he still not seeing life as it really is, but as he wants it to be? **Sight imagery increases the heart-breaking scene's emotional impact**, leaving the audience overwhelmed with sympathy and sorrow.

Animal Imagery

> *'Tigers, not daughters'*
>
> ***(Act 4 Scene 2, l.41)***

Images of wild, menacing creatures (wolf, boar, predatory birds, serpent, sea monster) with greedy appetites and cruel instincts invite audiences into the harsh world of the play. Both **Goneril and Regan are revealed through revolting animal imagery**. The violent Goneril is described in terms of birds of prey: 'Detested kite', 'like a vulture'. The sisters are portrayed as 'pelican daughters' who feed on their old father's generosity. Shakespeare's recurring imagery emphasises the viciousness of the two women.

Even Edmund, the object of their desire, describes their jealousy 'as the stung/ Are of the adder'. **Ironically, they are destroyed by their base animal instincts.** The mild-mannered Albany is disgusted by their callous treatment of their frail father: 'Tigers, not daughters'. He believes that if their brutality ('boarish fangs') is not stopped, the law of the jungle will triumph.

From the outset, **Lear's arrogant nature is obvious when he describes himself in striking animal imagery**. The enraged monarch warns Kent for daring to support Cordelia: 'Come not between the dragon and his wrath'. The fire-breathing mythical creature has biblical associations with the Devil, whose sin was pride. The Fool reminds the old king of his stupidity in suddenly expecting his daughters to act out of character and be kind to him: 'He's mad that trusts in the tameness of a wolf'.

As he descends further into madness, Lear eventually begins to recognise the falseness of authority: 'A dog's obeyed in office'. Anyone can be king – regardless of their qualities or faults – just as long as they officially hold power. Later on, Lear is presented as a more compassionate figure when he observes Poor Tom on the heath. In the **powerful image of 'a poor, bare, forked animal'**, the Bedlam beggar begins to signify humanity at its most basic.

At the end of the play, Lear dreams that he and Cordelia will find true happiness in prison: 'We two alone will sing like birds i' the cage'. They will laugh at the 'gilded butterflies', a reference to the overdressed royal courtiers. The **language reflects his new-found innocence**. But when his hopes are cruelly dashed by his daughter's execution, he cries out in anguish at life's unfairness, 'Why should a dog, a horse, a rat, have life,/ And thou no breath at all?'

Throughout the tragic story, Shakespeare makes effective use of **vivid animal imagery to expose the loss of society's rules** when the natural order is overturned. The thin veneer of civilisation is revealed.

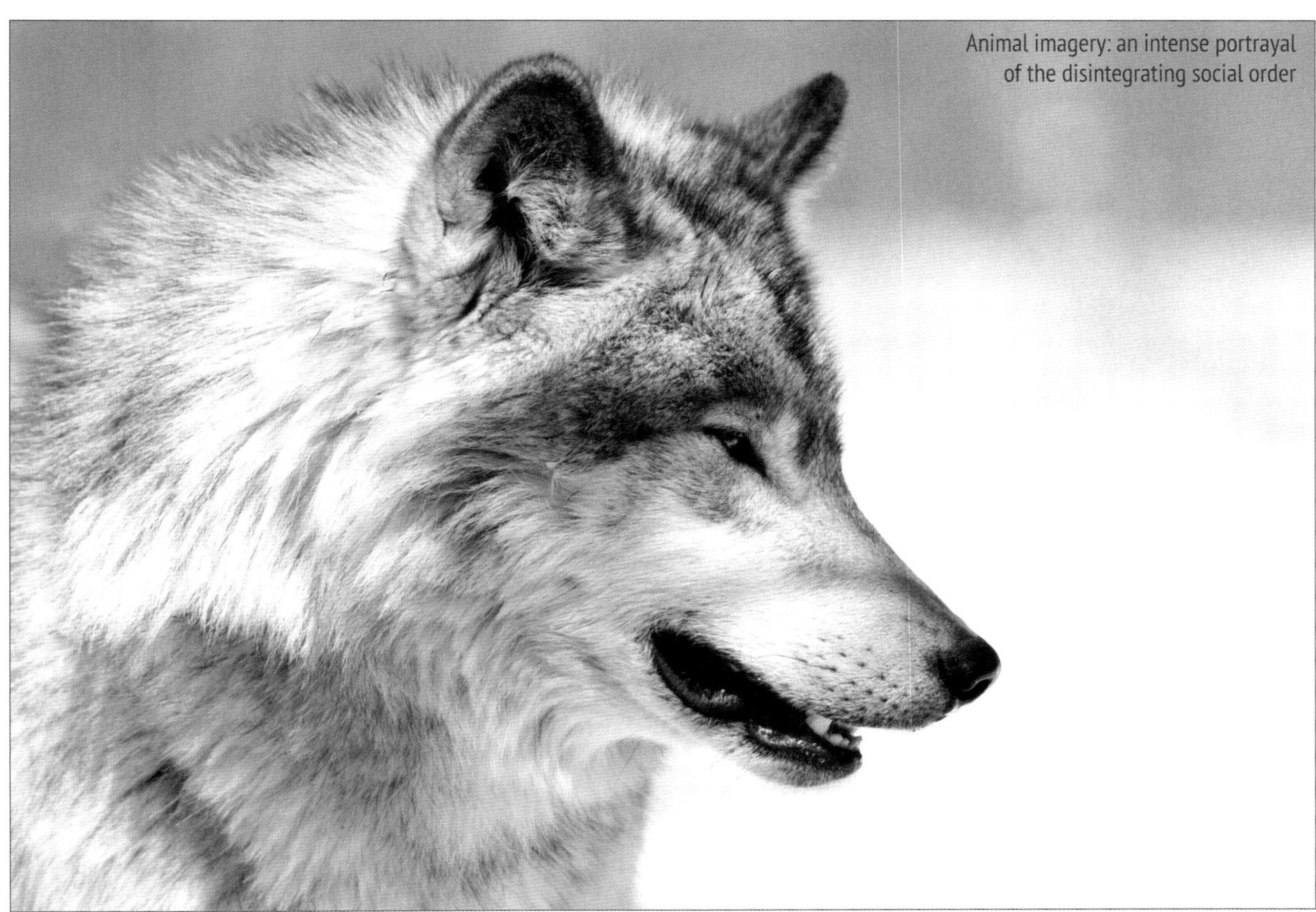

Animal imagery: an intense portrayal of the disintegrating social order

Nature Imagery

> *'Here I stand, your slave'*
>
> ***(Act 3 Scene 2, l.19)***

The **forces of good – Cordelia, Kent, Edgar and Albany – believe in a natural order**, a lawful king, justice and family responsibilities. Edgar is also convinced that 'The gods are just'. Cordelia loves her father, Lear, 'According to my bond'.

But Lear breaks this orderly system by rejecting his youngest daughter because she would not take part in his 'love test'. In her enraged father's mind, she suddenly becomes 'a wretch whom nature is ashamed/ Almost to acknowledge hers'. As a result, the self-indulgent king goes insane, 'let me not be mad', which is his greatest fear. Gloucester also disrupts the natural order by committing adultery and having an illegitimate son. Like Lear, he is severely punished.

Wild storm imagery symbolises Lear's mental upheaval as he begins to realise the truth about the daughters whom he trusted: 'Filial ingratitude'. The storm is also an outer symbol of the chaos unleashed on the kingdom by Lear's rash abdication.

Lear realises that he cannot rule the natural elements

Chaotic scenes on the windswept heath increase the audience's concerns for the frail king's well-being.

The **forces of evil – Goneril, Regan, Cornwall and Edmund – all believe in the law of nature**. For them, this means the survival of the fittest. They will do what is necessary to achieve their ambition. Edmund boasts that 'Thou, nature, art my goddess; to thy law/ My services are bound'. Since he is regarded by society as 'Half-blooded', he will pretend to accept society's rules while always looking out for himself: 'Legitimate Edgar, I must have your land'.

Throughout the play, imagery of the natural world emphasises the theme of right and wrong. It is ironic that **Lear's character only begins to develop when he is in the wilderness**. Here he finds 'Reason in madness'. For the first time, he recognises the falseness of royal court life, where 'Robes and furred gowns hide all'. When he meets Poor Tom, dressed only in a blanket, he finally understands that a man in nature is essentially 'a poor, bare, forked animal'.

King Lear presents an uncertain view of nature. The evil characters die, apparently confirming Edgar's belief that 'The gods are just'. But the playwright also presents another viewpoint, that nature has no real regard for human beings: 'As flies to wanton boys are we to the gods,/ They kill us for their sport'. The innocent Cordelia's death is not in line with natural justice. **Shakespeare leaves his audience to decide whether nature is just, or simply unmoved by the actions of man – good or bad.**

Plot and Sub-Plot: A Mirror Image

Similarities

- The main plot deals with Lear's downfall.
- The Gloucester sub-plot complements the main story, intensifying its dramatic effect.
- Both plots explore the miseries of human suffering.
- Lear and Gloucester both have ungrateful children who plot against them. Both fathers have a loyal child who saves them.
- The two men's suffering brings humility.
- They learn the truth about themselves and about life.
- Both men show heroism and strength in their suffering.
- Death provides a release for them from this harsh world.

Central characters

Lear and Gloucester are noble but flawed characters. They are both foolish and lack self-awareness. They each make poor decisions about their family because they believe without question what their disloyal children tell them. Lear trusts Goneril and Regan when they swear their undying love for him in 'glib and oily' speeches. Gloucester believes that the forged letter Edmund shows him is real and he judges his loyal son, Edgar, 'Abominable villain!' He disowns him: 'I never got him'. Lear also disowns his loyal daughter, Cordelia: 'Here I disclaim all my paternal care'.

Development

Both men **learn self-knowledge and compassion through suffering**. Lear recognises, 'I am a very foolish fond old man'. Gloucester realises, 'I stumbled when I saw'. Lear acknowledges that when he was king, he took 'Too little care' of the suffering of his unfortunate subjects. Gloucester also becomes more compassionate and gains a better understanding of life.

Contrasts

Lear's flaw is more complex than Gloucester's. It is psychological, both mental and emotional. In his arrogance, he wants to be publicly flattered by his daughters: 'Which of you shall we say doth love us most?' His punishment will be harsh. He will have to endure the death of Cordelia. Gloucester's flaw is sensual – adultery. He is deprived of the sense of sight. Lear is a powerful, energetic king, who fights for what he believes to the very end. He even kills Cordelia's hangman: 'I killed the slave'. He also has a great command of language: 'Why should a dog, a horse, a rat, have life,/ And thou no breath at all?' Gloucester is a less heroic figure, a passive character who attempts to take his own life, and when faced with tragedy mumbles, 'alack the day'.

Purpose of sub-plot

The sub-plot parallels the main plot. The two storylines are skilfully intertwined and both deal with the common problems of handing over power from one generation to the next. The sub-plot highlights this universal experience. The two storylines emphasise how power corrupts and highlight how wisdom can come from painful experiences. Both plots end in redemption – but not for everyone. While Edgar concludes that 'The gods are just', the main plot ends on a less optimistic note with Kent's question, 'Is this the promised end?' Shakespeare leaves his audience to decide.

Dramatic Irony

What is dramatic irony?

Dramatic irony occurs when audiences know something the characters do not.

This can often heighten the dramatic experience.

It is highly ironic that Lear disowns Cordelia – the daughter who loves him most

Dramatic irony in *King Lear*

- Audiences are aware that Cordelia is loyal to her father, whereas her father believes that she loves him least, 'Love, and be silent'.
- Lear is deceived by the 'glib and oily' speeches of Goneril and Regan, while the audience hears them plotting against their father, 'We must do something, and in the heat'.
- We recognise that Lear is mistaken when he banishes his true servant, Kent, for daring to challenge him: 'See better, Lear'.
- We also know that Lear hires Kent back into his service as the disguised Caius.
- Gloucester's blinding leads to his ability to seeing the truth: 'Then Edgar was abused'.
- Lear gains 'Reason in madness', and accepts that he is 'a very foolish fond old man'.

Impact of dramatic irony

- Intensifies the audience's involvement in the play's tragic events.
- Increases the suspense. Will Lear discover the error of his ways?
- What will happen to the evil characters?
- Audiences expect the evil characters to taste 'The cup of their deservings'.
- Will good triumph in the end?

Soliloquies

What is a soliloquy?

- A soliloquy is a speech that a character in a play speaks out loud.
- It can only be heard by the audience.
- Soliloquies reveal the character's thoughts and feelings.
- Audiences are made aware of secrets which the other characters do not know.

Soliloquies in *King Lear*

Edmund

- Edmund reveals his anger and insecurity about his illegitimate birth, 'wherefore base?'
- He admits his secret ambition: 'Legitimate Edgar, I must have your land'.
- His belief in survival of the fittest rather than society's rules is shown: 'Now, gods, stand up for bastards!'
- His cold-hearted ambition to be king is disclosed, 'Which of them shall I take?' when he considers who to marry.

Impact

- Audiences are now prepared for Edmund's secret schemes.
- We have some sympathy for this villain because of the injustice over his birth.
- We look on in horror as Edmund easily tricks Gloucester and Edgar: 'My practices ride easy'.
- Ironically, he tries to do good by preventing the execution of Lear and Cordelia, 'Despite of mine own nature'.
- Do we still have some sympathy for the 'Half-blooded' villain at the play's conclusion?

Lear

- In a soliloquy on the storm-battered heath, Lear still believes he is absolute ruler.
- He even tries to command the weather, 'Blow, winds, and crack your cheeks!'
- We are made aware that Lear's power no longer exists due to his abdication.
- When Lear looks at Poor Tom, he realises that 'Unaccommodated man' without wealth or possessions is reduced to 'a poor, bare, forked animal'.

Impact

- Audiences feel pity for the powerless old man, who is still deluded.
- We are shocked that Lear's wisdom comes too late to do anything about the 'Poor naked wretches' whom he did not care for when he was king.

Throughout the play, Shakespeare uses powerful monologues and soliloquies to let characters reveal the truth about themselves

Exam Focus

Successful *King Lear* Leaving Certificate answers will be assessed on four basic criteria:

- knowledge and understanding of the play
- developing focused and relevant discussion points
- effective use of suitable reference and quotation
- quality of written expression.

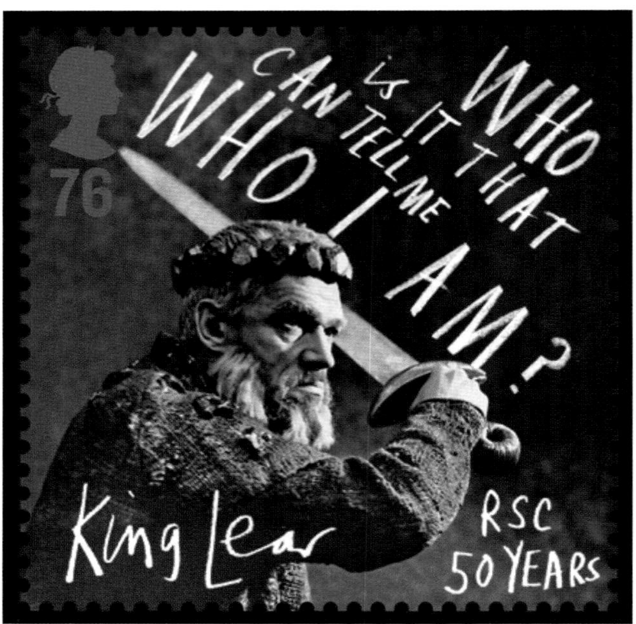

Reading Questions

The wording of questions should be studied carefully to identify the various elements that you are being asked to discuss. In both sample questions below, the three key terms (highlighted in bold) need to be addressed over the course of your answer.

Q. 'In the play *King Lear*, Shakespeare presents **a powerful vision** of **human endurance and strength** in a **world of evil and injustice**.'

To what extent do you agree with this statement? Develop your response with reference to the play.

Q. 'Shakespeare's play *King Lear* is filled with **images and symbols** that **intensify our experience** of the **tragic drama**.'

Discuss the above statement, developing your response with reference to the text.

Planning Answers

- Take at least five minutes to plan your main essay points **based on revealing scenes** from the play.
- Effective critical literacy skills and incisive **analysis will be well rewarded**.
- **Avoid unfocused narrative** or general summary. Refer to key scenes or specific moments that are relevant to the question.
- Arguments should be supported by reference to the play to develop your viewpoint.
- **Be prepared to challenge** aspects of a question, perhaps disagreeing with some parts or even with the entire premise.

Paragraphing Guide

- A paragraph is a unit of writing that usually focuses on **one main idea**. This central idea (or discussion point) is simply what the paragraph is about.
- It may be introduced in a **topic sentence** (often early in the paragraph), or it may be so obvious that it is just implied.
- An **effective paragraph develops the main idea** and advances your argument or viewpoint, using relevant reference to the play.
- Most paragraphs consist of at least five or six sentences which build on the topic sentence and **develop the analysis**.

- The examiner needs to understand your train of thought, so **what you write should always be clear and coherent**.
- Since Single Text examination essays are around 800 words in length, it's useful to plan five or six key points (paragraphs). While **a paragraph can be any length**, depending on its purpose, many are 130–150 words on average. Introductions and conclusions tend to be shorter.
- Your own language skills are very important. Aim for **controlled expression that is fresh, varied and assured**. Avoid repeating key words from the question in an attempt to show relevance. Alternatives to phrases in the question will invigorate your writing, e.g. a character's 'admirable qualities' can also be described as 'personal attributes', 'attractive features', 'appealing traits', etc.
- It's usual to take a **new paragraph**:
  - after ending your introduction
  - to begin a new discussion point
  - when contrasting key ideas
  - at the start of your conclusion.
- Aim to **structure your paragraphs** in the same way as a full essay, with a short introduction, main body, and brief conclusion:
  - introduce the paragraph's main point
  - develop and support the point
  - show the significance of the point you are making.

Quoting Effectively

As a general guide, quotations should be **accurate, brief and relevant**. Quotes should always support discussion points.

Words taken directly from the play should be placed within **quotation marks**, e.g. 'A dog's obeyed in office'.

A short accurate quotation aids discussion of theme, character/s and style. Apt quotes, derived from a close knowledge of the play, will help to develop your analysis.

Try to **integrate quotes** into your own sentences, e.g. Goneril flatters Lear, saying that she loves him more 'than eye-sight, space, and liberty'.

You will be penalised for mechanical errors, so **take great care** with spelling, grammar and punctuation. Remember – examiners award marks for 'quality of language'.

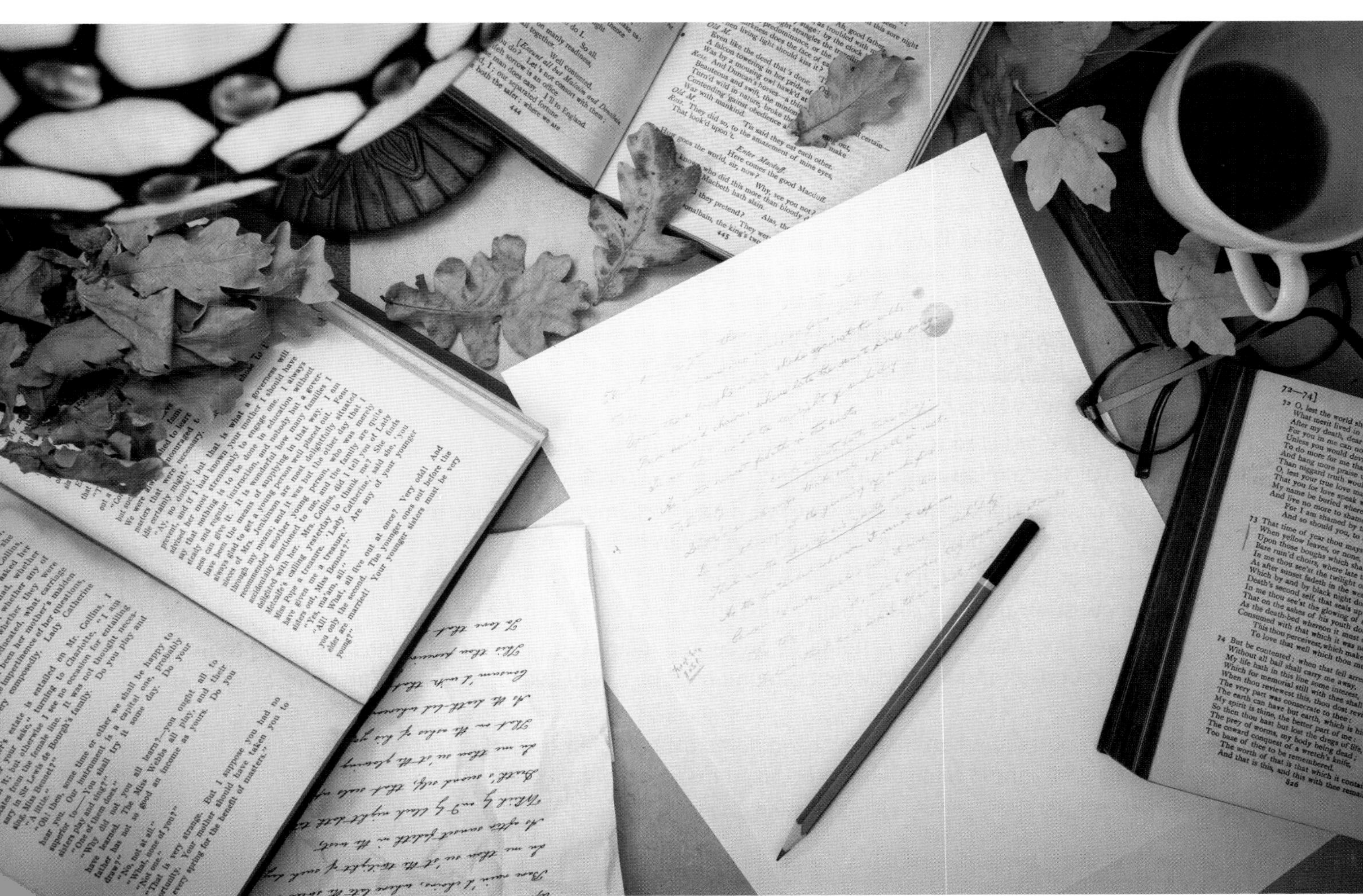

How the Single Text Shakespeare Question Is Marked

The Single Text English (Higher Level) question is allocated 60 minutes in the exam and worth **60 marks** in total. These are awarded by reference to the **PCLM** criteria for assessment (i.e., 3 x 18 marks for each of P, C and L, plus 6 marks for M):

P = Clarity of **Purpose**:	18 (30%)
C = **Coherence** of Delivery:	18 (30%)
L = Efficiency of **Language** Use:	18 (30%)
M = Accuracy of **Mechanics**:	6 (10%)

P

In assessing 'Clarity of Purpose', examiners will judge how successfully the candidate has addressed the question and engaged with the set task. This refers to the quality of engagement, relevance, focus, originality and understanding of the appropriate genre.

The marks awarded for 'Coherence of Delivery' and 'Efficiency of Language Use' will not normally be higher than 'Clarity of Purpose'.

C

In awarding the marks for 'Coherence of Delivery', examiners will assess how well the candidate has sustained the response and developed the entire answer. This refers to the quality and management of ideas, supporting points, sequencing, and engagement with texts.

L

Marks for 'Efficiency of Language Use' are awarded for the management and control of language. This refers to the quality of language used to achieve clear communication in terms of vocabulary, paragraph structure, syntax, punctuation, fluency, style and expression.

Marks for 'L' are awarded in so far as the candidate's answering is considered 'appropriate to the delivery of the task'.

The standard of both 'Coherence of Delivery' and 'Efficiency of Language Use' informs the marks awarded for 'Clarity of Purpose'.

M

Marks awarded for 'Accuracy of Mechanics' refer to spelling and grammar appropriate to the register. Marks for 'M' are essentially independent of 'P', 'C' and 'L' marks.

Chief Examiner's Report Observations

- It is the question set which must be answered.
- Students should be assisted to develop the skills needed to shape, manipulate and adapt their knowledge to produce measured, informed and reflective responses.
- Some examiners identified candidates who were able to demonstrate knowledge of a text ... but were less able to deliver this knowledge in a lucid and coherent fashion.
- It is essential that candidates fully engage with the terms of any question attempted, challenging the terms of the question, perhaps disagreeing with some part or the entire premise outlined.
- Examiners were impressed when candidates presented lucid responses to questions based on their knowledge and understanding of the texts, augmented by a well-reasoned argument, point of view or opinion.
- Examiners were pleased when they saw candidates trust in their own personal response and demonstrate a willingness to challenge the 'fixed meaning' of texts.
- Careless use of quotation served to undermine answers.

www.examinations.ie

Sample Essays on *King Lear*

Exam Advice

- In the Single Text *King Lear* question, you will be expected to engage with the question and show a close understanding of the play.
- Avoid prepared essays or formulaic approaches.
- Time management is important: 60 minutes are allocated for the question, so you should spend about five minutes planning your response.
- Aim to write around 800 words in a developed answer.

Sample Essay 1

Q. 'Shakespeare's play *King Lear* is not only a tragedy about the breakdown of family relationships, but also a tragedy about the failure of kingship.'

Discuss the reasons why you agree or disagree with the above statement.

Develop your discussion with reference to the text.

STARRING FRANK LANGELLA IN WILLIAM SHAKESPEARE'S
KING LEAR
JAN 7—FEB 9, 2014 BAM HARVEY THEATER

Lear's tragic fate is to lose everything: judgement, family and power

Marking Scheme Guidelines

Candidates are free to agree and/or disagree but they should engage with both aspects of the statement, though not necessarily equally. Allow for a broad interpretation of 'tragedy'.

Indicative Material

- Lear fails initially in both his personal and public roles.
- Abuse of royal power has devastating consequences.
- Two dysfunctional families affected by pride, ambition and betrayal.
- Madness/suffering propels Lear to develop qualities as parent and king.
- Tragic pattern: powerful flawed characters pay for/learn from mistakes, etc.

1 In *King Lear*, the powerful King of Britain wishes to abdicate his throne, but hold on to his title. Lear's tragic downfall occurs when he loses everything but gains an understanding of what is important in ordinary human life. Shakespeare explores this tragedy through broken family relationships and by exploring what it means to have power.

2 Lear is first presented as a powerful, well-respected monarch. He has been in power for so long that it has gone to his head and he decides to introduce a 'love test' to hand over the kingdom to his daughters, 'To shake all cares and business from our age'. This is his first step to tragic ruin. He will divide his kingdom between Goneril, Regan and Cordelia based on how they respond to his question, 'Which of you shall we say doth love us most?'

3 Cordelia his youngest daughter refuses to co-operate. In answer to her father's question, 'What do you say to draw a third more opulent than your sisters?', she replies, 'Nothing, my lord'. Publicly humiliated, Lear forces her and she then explains 'I love you according to my bond'. The father–daughter relationship shatters with terrible consequences for both. In anger, he disinherits her, 'thy truth then be thy dower' and banishes her, 'avoid my sight'.

4 Impulsively Lear divides his kingdom between Goneril and Regan. He has now left himself without power, yet believes he can still act as if king. But as Regan says, 'he has ever but slenderly known himself'. This is the basis of the tragedy in my opinion. Later on, the two daughters leave him abandoned in a violent storm accompanied only by the Fool and Kent. Lear's tragedy is seen in his regret and over his daughters' disrespect and ingratitude. Even when raging against the storm, he says, 'I never gave you kingdom'.

5 Later, as his 'wits begin to turn', Lear loses his sanity. But he also begins to really understand life. He starts to think of others, 'Poor Fool and knave, I have one part in my heart sorry for thee yet'. Gradually, he realises that things have changed, he is no longer the most powerful man in Britain, 'Does any here know me?' Tragically, we see a similar tragedy with Gloucester who has also failed his family.

6 Lear fails due to misjudgement both as a powerful king and a foolish father. He has lost not only his family and kingdom, but even his own identity, 'Who is it that can tell me who I am?' But it is not all tragedy. Lear learns from his mistakes. When he sees Edgar in the beggar's disguise of Poor Tom, he sees 'a poor bare, forked animal'. This is a human being stripped to the basics. Lear regrets past failures, 'I have taken too little care of this'. A king's duty was to protect his people and retain order. He did not.

7 When Cordelia returns with her army from France to help him, he can now face up to his failure towards his youngest daughter, 'If you have poison for me I will take it'. He realises how he has wronged her, and begs 'forget and forgive. I am old and foolish'. But the dream of the re-united father and daughter is not to happen. They will never live to 'sing like birds in the cage' because Cordelia is cruelly executed in prison. Her distressed father kills the executioner, but he himself is completely broken by her death, 'Why should a dog, a horse, a rat have life and you no breath at all!'

8 The play ends in tragedy with the unexpected death of Lear's innocent daughter. Both good and bad characters die. Lear's misjudgement has ruined his family, his country and himself. His basic faults of gross pride led to him being fooled by appearances. Lear abused power and caused his own downfall. Gloucester was equally arrogant and failed as a father to both his sons, Edgar and Edmund. He suffered for his foolish irresponsibility.

9 Lear may have gained some insight into the mistakes he made but there is only a very slight sense of hope at the end of this heart-breaking story of family and kingship. 'The oldest has borne the most'. Gloucester and Lear made similar mistakes in not really knowing their own children well and they certainly paid for it.

(730 words)

Marking Scheme		
P	16	18
C	14	18
L	15	18
M	6	6
	51	60

GRADE: H2

Examiner's Comment

- Deals effectively with both elements of tragedy – family relationships and kingship.
- Paragraph 6 included a strong point about Lear's tragic flaw.
- Some development of Gloucester's tragic experience would have been welcome.
- Uses a wide range of apt references and (generally) accurate quotations.
- Controlled expression and impressive vocabulary throughout this solid H2 response.

Sample Essay 2

Q. 'The villainous characters hold much more fascination for audiences than the virtuous ones in Shakespeare's play *King Lear*.'

Discuss this statement with reference to at least one villainous and one virtuous character in the play.

Develop your answer with reference to the text.

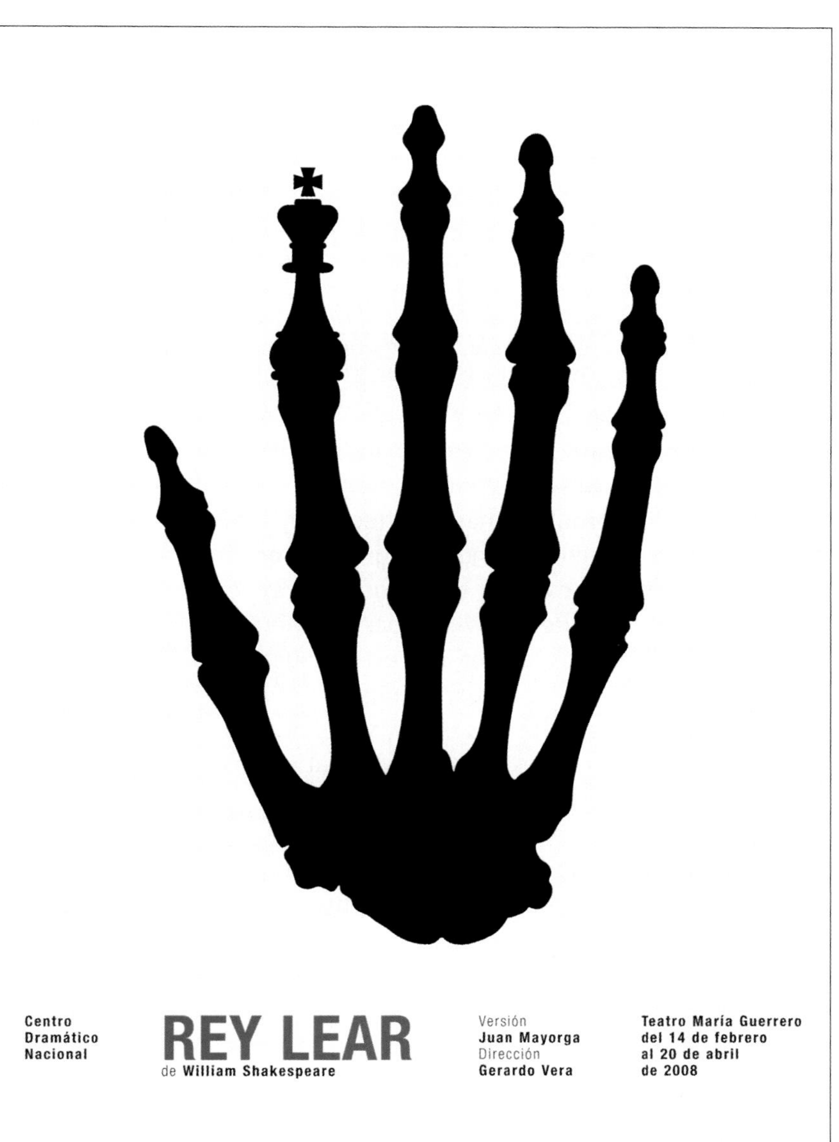

Centro
Dramático
Nacional
REY LEAR
de William Shakespeare
Versión
Juan Mayorga
Dirección
Gerardo Vera
Teatro María Guerrero
del 14 de febrero
al 20 de abril
de 2008

Evil characters – especially Edmund and Goneril – have always had a strange appeal for audiences

Marking Scheme Guidelines

Candidates are free to agree and/or disagree with the statement, but they must engage with both 'villainous' and 'virtuous', though not necessarily equally. Expect candidates to focus on at least one villainous and one virtuous character, and to offer a view/s on their appeal/fascination for the audience. Allow for a broad interpretation of 'fascination'.

Indicative Material

- Intriguing interaction between villainous and virtuous characters.
- Charismatic Edmund is more/less engaging than Edgar.
- Loyalty of good/virtuous characters is appealing/unappealing.
- Goneril, Regan and Cornwall are more/less credible than Cordelia and Kent.
- Fascinating traits of good/evil characters, etc.

1 In *King Lear*, all the evil characters, Goneril Regan, Edmund and Cornwall, with their hypocrisy and brutality really fascinate the audience. The virtuous characters, Edgar, Cordelia and Kent, ought to be admired for their honesty and loyalty but are often too dull to be of interest. We watch to see that justice is done, that the evil are punished and the good rewarded.

2 Goneril is larger than life, the most disgraceful character in the play. Regan is no less evil, but it is Goneril who is the dominant sister. She initiates most of the cruel schemes against Lear, humiliating him in a cold, calculating manner, complaining of his 'insolent retinue' and 'all-licensed fool'. She disrespects his old age, 'dotage'. This amazingly cruel but fascinating woman shows no compassion for the indignant king remarking, 'he must needs taste his folly'.

3 Regan soon equals her. She demands Kent's time in the stocks be extended, 'all night too'. This barbarous woman, unaffected by the cruelty of her husband's gouging out of Gloucester's eye, calls for his second eye to be pulled out too, 'One side will mock another; the other too'. Regan is also of interest because she speaks the truth about Lear's kingship – which he held onto until he was eighty years of age, 'and in good time you gave it'. But what is most fascinating about her is that she is always on the verge of doing something violent. Audiences are spellbound and shocked that people can be capable of such cruelty.

4 But it is Edmund who is the most amazing of the evil characters. Shakespeare uses Edmund's soliloquy to inform us of his deep hurt at the unequal treatment he receives because he is illegitimate and is denied any inheritance, 'Why brand they us with base?' His questioning emphasises his deep resentment at this injustice. He captures the audience's sympathy and we admire him, 'Now gods, stand up for bastards!' Edmund will not bend beneath the force of society's expectations. He adopts the laws of nature, the survival of the fittest, since society excludes him.

5 When Edmund's 'credulous' father confides in Edmund that the French have landed on British soil and that he is going, secretly, to aid the king, Edmund decides to betray Gloucester, 'This courtesy, forbid thee, shall the duke instantly know'. Gloucester is now to be sacrificed for Edmund's self-interest. Shakespeare has portrayed this evil character with energy and an amazing capability of opportunism. He also has a wicked sense of humour. When dying he looks at the two sisters who sacrificed themselves for his love and remarks, 'I was contracted to them both. All three now marry in an instant'.

6 Kent is Lear's friend and loyal supporter. He is interesting at first when he stands up to the king and supports Cordelia. But after he is banished and returns in disguise as Caius, he becomes one-dimensional and does not develop at all as a character. Kent is amazingly loyal for sure, but doesn't actually change Lear or show any of his early energy. Even the Fool keeps pointing out Lear's mistakes and is interesting for his mad humour, but I found Kent to be dull and defeatist, overall.

7 Cordelia is the symbol of love and tenderness in the play. This is shown by her actions, in contrast to the false words of her sisters in the 'love contest'. Cordelia expresses her love for Lear tenderly, 'let this kiss repair those violent harms that my two sisters have in thy reverence made!' But this is said to a sleeping Lear who cannot hear her.

8 Even in the final moments of the play, the old king is pleading with her to speak, 'What is it thou sayst?' Lear recognises that 'her voice was ever soft, gentle and low', there is a deep awareness that if she could have given a little of what her foolish father wanted in the first scene, a public show of love, this awful tragedy might have been avoided. Shakespeare shows the consequences of not clearly saying what one feels or means. Cordelia, to me, is not appealing, but infuriating.

9 Shakespeare has created evil characters with tremendous energy. Their savagery and hypocrisy fascinates the audience who can't quite believe the depths of evil to which humans can sink. The evil characters show determination and ingenuity. However, the good characters like Cordelia, do not display the same vigour and do not engage the audience, despite their integrity and kindness.

(750 words)

Marking Scheme

P	17	18
C	16	18
L	16	18
M	6	6
	55	60

GRADE: H1

Examiner's Comment

- Good H1 response that shows close understanding of characters.
- References and suitable supportive quotations are effectively used.
- Effectively developed points on Edmund and Cordelia.
- Overall expression is good, apart from some repetition.
- Clear analysis and informed approach – a top-grade response.

Sample Essay 3

Q. 'The plot and sub-plot mirror each other in interesting ways throughout Shakespeare's play *King Lear*.'

Discuss the reasons why you agree or disagree with the above statement.

Develop your discussion with reference to the text.

Marking Scheme Guidelines

Candidates are expected to explore the ways in which the plot and sub-plot mirror/do not mirror each other in interesting ways.

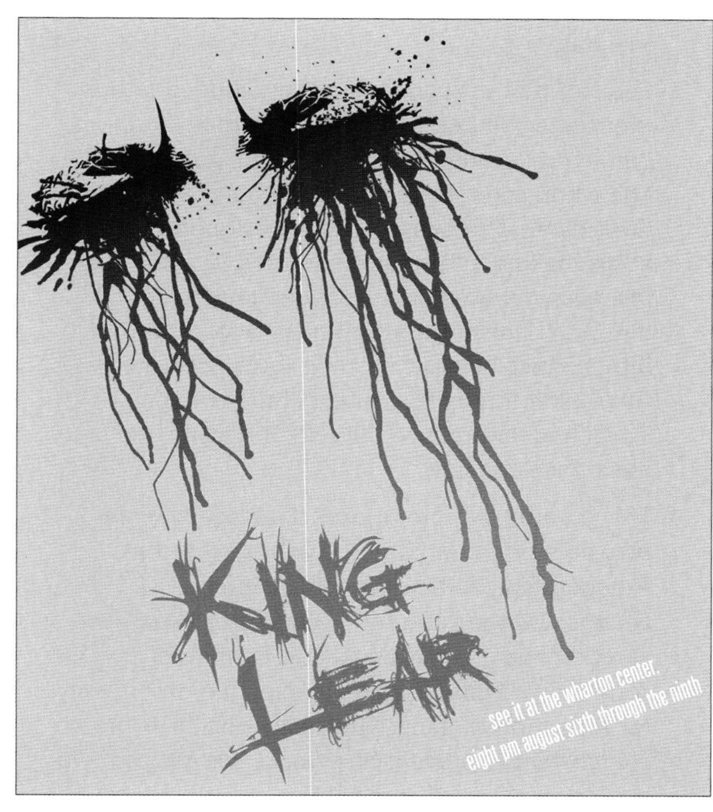

Lear and Gloucester share many tragic experiences – and these are heightened by the parallel plots

Indicative Material

- Thought-provoking similarities/differences in both stories.
- Lear's misjudgement is/is not matched by Gloucester.
- Both characters develop/do not develop morally through suffering.
- Double plot heightens/lessens drama and sense of tragedy.
- Emphasises key themes of family, power, ambition, justice/injustice, etc.

1 The plot and sub-plot of *King Lear* reflect each other while the audience watches the unfolding drama which has resulted from 'hideous rashness'. Two storylines develop together, as Lear and Gloucester gain insight and self-knowledge, concluding with the deaths of these main characters.

2 Lear is a self-important king who sets up a childish 'test' asking his daughters to publicly flatter him, 'Which of you shall we say doth love us most?' This arrogant ruler is about to indulge his ego in the excessive flattery of Goneril and Regan and is completely fooled by their 'glib and oily art'. When Cordelia responds with the simple truth, 'Obey you, love you, and most honour you', that is seen as insufficient by the self-centered father who flies into a terrible rage. Rashly he disowns her, 'as a stranger to my heart and me, hold thee from this for ever.' This catastrophic mistake acts as a starting point for the subsequent tragic events and suffering in the play.

3 The sub-plot introduces another deluded father, Gloucester. He describes his illegitimate son, Edmund, in crude terms in the son's presence, 'the whoreson must be acknowledged'. Gloucester even boasts, 'There was good sport at his making'. Gloucester, imitating Lear's rashness, disowns his son, Edgar, 'I never got him', and banishes him, 'Let him fly far'. Both fathers have now cut off their loyal children. Gloucester totally trusts his delinquent son, 'Loyal and natural boy, I'll work the means to make thee capable'.

4 This parallel sub-plot makes the tragedy more plausible. The main plot – Lear's family – has exaggerated characters and very intense actions. But the sub-plot – Gloucester, Edgar and Edmund – is more realistic. Edmund's soliloquy provides a credible explanation for his actions against Gloucester. His birth circumstances prevent him from inheriting so he decides to act, 'Let me, if not by birth, have lands by wit'. Gloucester also has a slightly more believable reason for banishing Edgar. Copying the events of the main plot in the more realistic sub-plot, Shakespeare is showing the truth that children sometimes fool their gullible parents for personal gain, 'there's father against son'.

5 Shakespeare's themes are reinforced through two emphatic storylines. Both fathers have children who despise them. Goneril and Regan are vicious in their attacks on Lear's old age, 'the unruly waywardness that infirm and choleric years bring with them'. They are full of contempt for their father, 'Old fools are babes again'. Edmund is equally dismissive of Gloucester's belief in superstition, 'These late eclipses in the sun and moon portend no good to us'. He rejects this as the 'excellent foppery of the world' where people blames disasters on 'the sun, the moon and the stars'. These two corresponding events are thought-provoking. Truth can be hard to accept.

6 The redemption of each flawed father is achieved through the selfless actions of a once-favoured child. Cordelia was closest to Lear, 'I loved her most'. Gloucester also loved his son Edgar, 'that so tenderly and entirely loves him'. But now the playwright has the good characters perform what might seem as questionable actions in order to do good. Edgar deceives his father and Cordelia invades Britain. Cordelia returns with her husband's army from France, explaining that she has acted entirely on Lear's behalf, 'It is thy business I go about'. Edgar also aids his father by preventing him from dying by suicide. Together, both plots emphasise good characters realising that in this imperfect world it is not sufficient to be good, one must act, and sometimes use unusual methods.

7 Both fathers were blind wrongdoers. Lear was dictatorial, Gloucester was irresponsible. Each man gains self-knowledge through horrific suffering. But Shakespeare intensifies the dramatic experience by matching the suffering to the sin. Lear suffered mental torment by descending into what he dreaded – insanity, 'O let me not be mad'. Gloucester was also brutally punished. Shakespeare is drawing attention to how there can be retribution, people do get 'The cup of their deservings'.

8 The play's conclusion has all the evil characters dead and there is a sense of a new order emerging. Although Edgar is ready to restore a more honest, government system, 'Speak what we feel, not what we ought to say', Shakespeare presents us with the truly horrific spectacle of Lear carrying his executed daughter. The startled audience hears his frightful cry ring out, 'Howl, howl, howl, howl'. The awful finality of death is presented, 'She's gone for ever'. The main plot again emphasises the sub-plot's observation that 'As flies to wanton boys are we to the gods, they kill us for their sport'.

9 While the Gloucester story concludes in the usual tragic way, with the main character killed and a new order about to be restored, the main plot provokes the audience into considering whether 'The gods are just'. If this is 'the promised end?' then why have the good characters died? The plot and sub-plot structure leave unanswered questions and much to consider.

(825 words)

Marking Scheme		
P	18	18
C	17	18
L	16	18
M	6	6
	57	60

GRADE: H1

Examiner's Comment

- Focused approach to the question throughout.
- Effective developed discussion point paragraphs (e.g. 4, 5 and 8).
- Good range of detailed references and accurate quotations.
- Generally well-controlled expression and varied vocabulary throughout.
- Confident H1 response showing a close knowledge of the play.

Sample Essay Plan

Q. 'Shakespeare's *King Lear* is filled with images and symbols which heighten the dramatic experience of the play.'

Discuss this statement, developing your answer with reference to the text.

Marking Scheme Guidelines

Candidates are expected to explore the ways in which images/symbols heighten the dramatic experience of the play.

- Address the question directly
- Adopt a stance (agree, disagree, partially agree)
- Discussion points (sight/blindness, nature, animal and clothing imagery, symbols of storm, tears)
- Impact of language (engaging audiences, revealing characters/relationships, developing themes, etc.)

INTRODUCTION

Agree – **images and symbols enhance the dramatic experience** of the play. Animal imagery, sight/blindness, clothing, etc. intensify audience response to events and characters.

POINT 1

Powerful animal imagery associated with evil characters ('wolfish visage', 'Tigers, not daughters') **increases audience's horror at their inhumanity**. Images intensify satisfaction at their downfall.

POINT 2

Clothing imagery reinforces for the audience the difference between appearance and reality. Audience shocked that good characters are forced to adopt a disguise to survive (Edgar, Kent). Develops understanding that appearances can conceal wrong-doing ('Robes and furred gowns hide all').

POINT 3

Images of sight and blindness deepen audience's understanding of two deluded fathers. Lear's banishment of two loyal characters, Cordelia and Kent ('avoid my sight'). Gloucester's realisation of his mistake in believing Edmund ('I stumbled when I saw').

POINT 4

Audience shocked that evil characters see reality so clearly. Goneril knows Lear, 'The best and soundest of his time hath been but rash'. Edmund describes Gloucester and Edgar, 'A credulous father and a brother noble.'

POINT 5

Tears as a symbol of redemption console the audience. Cordelia shows a genuine expression of affection for her father's troubles because of her evil sisters' actions, 'she shook/ The holy water from her heavenly eyes'. Lear responds, 'Be your tears wet?'

CONCLUDING PARAGRAPH

Vivid images and symbols increase awareness of a range of emotions (horror, shock, relief, etc.). This heightens the dramatic experience, so audiences form new insights into Lear's world, 'Speak what we feel, not what we ought to say'.

Sample Leaving Certificate Questions on *King Lear*

Note: 60 marks/60 minutes. Aim for around 800 words.

1. 'Deceit and disguise are used to great effect throughout Shakespeare's play *King Lear*.'
   To what extent do you agree with the above statement? Develop your response with reference to the text.
2. 'In the play *King Lear* Shakespeare makes effective use of a variety of dramatic techniques to explore various aspects of justice and injustice.'
   Discuss this view, with reference to at least two dramatic techniques used by Shakespeare in the play. Develop your answer with reference to the text.
3. Discuss the view that Shakespeare's play *King Lear* is both a horrifying as well as an inspiring experience. Develop your discussion with reference to the text.
4. A production of Shakespeare's *King Lear*, in which the characters of Kent and the Fool do not appear, has been proposed.
   Discuss the reasons why, in your opinion, the removal of each of these characters would or would not diminish the play. Develop your response with reference to the text.
5. 'Lear and Gloucester have much in common and share a similar tragic fate, but Lear emerges as the more admirable and heroic figure in Shakespeare's play *King Lear*.'
   Discuss the above statement, developing your response with reference to the text.
6. Discuss how Shakespeare uses language and imagery to heighten the dramatic tension and add a tragic quality to his play *King Lear*.
   Develop your answer with reference to the text.
7. 'The balance between power and powerlessness in Shakespeare's *King Lear* heightens our experience of the play.'
   To what extent do you agree with this view? Develop your answer with reference to the text.
8. Discuss how Shakespeare skilfully creates moments of heightened dramatic intensity in his play *King Lear*. Develop your discussion with reference to at least three moments of heightened dramatic intensity evident in the text.
9. 'Various aspects of Edmund's character in Shakespeare's *King Lear* are both disturbing and intriguing.'
   Discuss the reasons why you agree or disagree with the above statement. Develop your discussion with reference to the play.
10. 'Contrasting scenes of suffering and tenderness are used to great effect in Shakespeare's play *King Lear*.'
    Discuss the above statement, developing your response with reference to the text.

Using *King Lear* as a Comparative Text

Introduction

- The Leaving Certificate Comparative Study section is worth **70 marks** out of the 400 total.
- In the Comparative section, plays, novels and films are all referred to as **texts**.
- A **mode** of comparison is simply a framework in which to explore a text.

There are **four** Higher Level modes:

1. The Cultural Context
2. Theme or Issue
3. Literary Genre
4. The General Vision and Viewpoint.

You are required to study **at least two** of the three modes prescribed each year.

Only **two** of these three modes will appear on the exam paper.

Each mode that appears on the paper will have a choice of **two** questions.

These questions take two forms. Either:

- An **essay-type question** comparing three texts for 70 marks
  OR
- A **question divided into two parts**
  - Part (a) requires discussion of **one text** (30 marks)
  - Part (b) requires comparison of **two other texts** (40 marks)

You are allocated 70 minutes for the Comparative section. Aim to write about 900 words in the single 70-mark answer.

For the two-part question, aim to write about 350 words for Part (a) and about 550 words for Part (b).

When answering Comparative questions, candidates may compare and/or contrast, i.e. address similarities and/or differences in both the subject matter and style of their chosen texts.

Note: At Higher Level, a play by Shakespeare **must** be one of the texts chosen. This play can be studied on its own (for the Single Text section) or as one of the three Comparative texts.

1. The Cultural Context

Dysfunctional family relationships, and the use and abuse of power are central to the 'world' of the play

The cultural context is often described **as the society or 'world' of the text**. It refers to the social setting, values, attitudes, and day-to-day practices.

Our understanding of a text is enriched by knowing about the culture in which the story is set.

FAMILY	How does family impact on characters and their actions? Does it nurture or restrain the characters? (Obedience, love, duty, guilt, confidence, etc.)
SOCIETY/ CLASS STRUCTURE	How does the type of society affect the characters and their actions? Does it empower or restrict characters? (Power, money, status, education, etc.)
MEN/WOMEN	Who has power, men or women? (Patriarchy, matriarchy.) How does this influence the central character's life?
RELIGION	Is religion a comforting or inhibiting force? (How does it affect marriage, sex, social change, the happiness of characters?)
VIOLENCE	Is the violence physical, emotional or intellectual? Who is the offender and who is the victim? What is the impact of violence on society and individuals?
POVERTY	How does poverty affect the progress of characters? (Lack of opportunity, helplessness, disease, honour, pride, etc.)

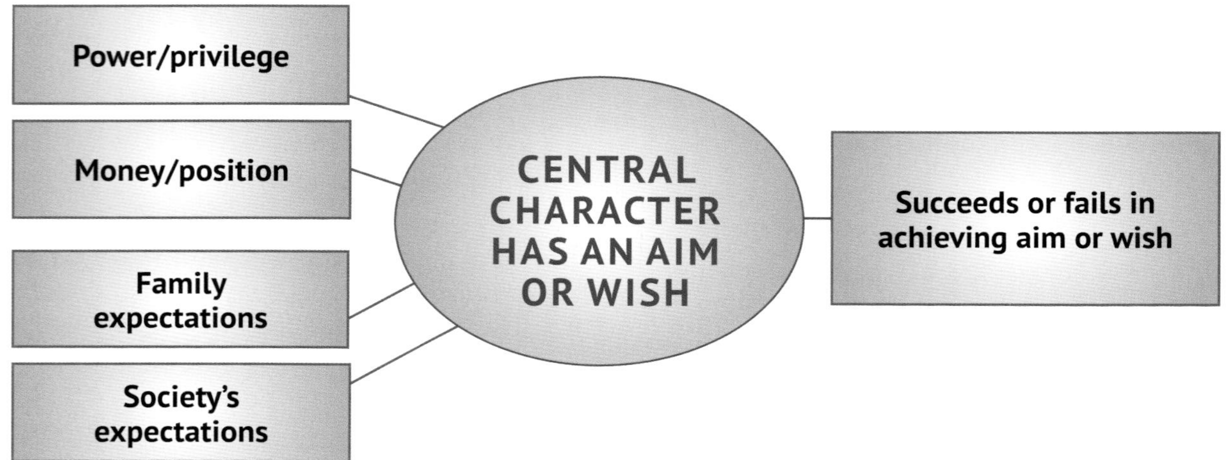

The Cultural Context in *King Lear*

Shakespeare chooses to set his tragedy in pre-Christian Britain. Paganism and self-interest rule in this largely uncivilised society. **The desire for power creates a world of political intrigue**, treachery and betrayal. Lear's Britain is a tightly organised society. It demands that respect is shown to the wealthy, the powerful and to parents and the elderly. In this distorted society, religion is replaced by superstition. Ageing fathers like Lear and Gloucester are at the mercy of their ruthless children. The playwright shows a social and moral order so fragile that it is easily destroyed.

Family values

The audience is introduced to **a world where parent–child relationships, succession and political power are distorted**. Lear's abdication, 'To shake all cares and business from our age', overthrows the natural order for the transfer of power – the death of the monarch. His 'love test' where he demands public declarations of love from his daughters in order to decide the division of his kingdom is a misrepresentation of his role as father. 'Which of you shall we say doth love us most?'

Family values have a negative influence in this world. The three dishonest children, Goneril, Regan and Edmund, overthrow the normal order of society in their relentless pursuit of power: 'We must do something, and in the heat'.

Gloucester and Lear are betrayed and suffer devastating consequences. Lear goes mad and Gloucester is blinded. Neither father knows their children's true characters. Both punish their loyal children and reward the deceitful ones. However, **family can also have a positive impact**. Cordelia and Edgar still love their parents. They are also prepared to suffer for what they believe is right: 'The weight of this sad time we must obey'.

A patriarchal society

Lear's Britain was **a man's world** where Gloucester's eldest legitimate son, Edgar, would inherit his title and property. His other son, Edmund, was not born from Gloucester's marriage, so he will not inherit: 'fine word, legitimate'. In this macho world, an old man can make jokes about his 'whoreson' and boast that 'there was good sport at his making'.

Young women were financially dependent on their families at this time. They needed their family to provide a rich dowry so that they could attract a suitable marriage partner. When Kear disinherits Cordelia, she loses the Duke of Burgundy as a suitor: 'you must lose a husband'.

Shakespeare reverses the normal roles of this male-dominated society. The women in *King Lear* are very powerful. All three daughters act in a way to contradict the social order of their society. Goneril and Regan will do whatever it takes to break down the old king: 'let's hit together'.

Cordelia represents another kind of **female power**. She courageously leads the French army to challenge the rule of her two ruthless sisters: 'I know you what you are'. Unlike Lear, Cordelia does not measure love. Instead, she redeems her father through her capacity for forgiveness, 'let this kiss/ Repair'.

The importance of royalty

The monarch is the head of his own family and of the state in Lear's Britain. He is regarded as God's representative on earth. **When Lear chooses to divide his kingdom among his daughters, he loses his authority.** He has bowed to 'flattery', yet he still believes he can hold on to 'The name, and all the additions to a king'.

It is only when the audience witness his terrible suffering that they realise his capacity for compassion, justice and courage. In his madness, Lear criticises **hypocrisy and corruption in society**. He believes that those living in luxury should distribute their excess, 'the superflux'. The tragedy is that he himself no longer has power to effect social change, having foolishly given it away: 'I do invest you jointly with my power'.

Religion and superstition

Shakespeare presents **contradictory views of the universe**. Gloucester is highly **superstitious**: 'These late eclipses ... portend no good'. He also sees man as a victim of an unpredictable and spiteful God, 'As flies to wanton boys are we to the gods'. Lear also calls on primitive magic when he disinherits Cordelia, 'by the sacred radiance of the sun/ The mysteries of Hecate'.

Edmund's goddess is nature. In contrast, Edgar believes **'The gods are just'**. He even regards them as kind, 'the clearest gods ... have preserved thee'. When Edmund repents and tries to prevent Lear and Cordelia being put to death, Albany prays, 'The gods defend her'. The prayer is answered by the horrific sight of Lear carrying his dead daughter in his arms. Is the playwright suggesting that the gods do not interfere in man's affairs? **Or that people should take responsibility for their own lives?**

Social outsiders

Three scenes are set on the heath in a raging storm which mirrors not only the madness infecting Lear's mind, but also the **corruption in society** that is at the centre of the tragic drama. Order, morality and mental well-being have been torn asunder – here the norms of civilised society do not apply. Everything is stripped to its essence. Man is 'a poor, bare, forked animal', no longer wearing the 'furred gowns' of the royal court.

Three apparent madmen, Lear, the Fool and Poor Tom, conduct a mock trial in this lawless place. This **perversion of justice** has Lear as judge, jury and executioner. He is angry at the ingratitude of his daughters: 'I gave you all'. He gives out the sentence before the trial takes place, 'red burning spits/ Come hizzing in upon 'em'. This trial mirrors the injustice of Lear's 'love test' and Cornwall's trial of Gloucester.

Ironically, the **three outcasts in the hovel show concern for each other**. This is in stark contrast to the self-serving residents of the comfortable palaces who plot and scheme against one another. In the tumult of the storm and his madness, Lear begins to gain insight. He admits that he took 'Too little care' of the 'Poor naked wretches' when he was king.

In this great tragedy, **the playwright has turned the norms of society upside down**. Wise, caring parents are now arrogant, deluded fathers. Loyal, dutiful children become power-hungry monsters. Hypocrisy and brutality beat down truth and compassion.

While a new order, under Edgar and Albany, emerges from the chaos, the heart-breaking sight of Lear carrying his beloved dead Cordelia makes a huge impact on audiences. Has the punishment been out of proportion to the crime? **To what extent have the values of Lear's Britain determined this great tragedy?**

Sample Part (a) Question

Q. 'The opening scene (or scenes) of a text can reveal valuable insights into the impact that the cultural context of a narrative is likely to have on the outcome of the story'.

Develop your response with reference to the text. *(30 marks)*

Indicative Material

The opening of a text can show:

- social/political setting
- family relationships/expectations
- attitudes to power, gender/marriage
- revealing language, imagery, etc.

This question requires you to address the mode and the question only. No comparison is needed.

Sample Answer

King Lear opens in the corrupt political world of the royal palace. Lear wants to divide his kingdom among his three daughters using a public 'love test'. Drunk on power, the old king believes this will decide who 'doth love us most', and so he will divide the kingdom among Goneril, Regan and Cordelia. This is a foolish method of transferring power which is open to corruption. Goneril and Regan flatter their father with deceiving words, 'Dearer than eye-sight, space and liberty'.

Lear is taken in by their smooth talk. He makes the foolish decision to hand over control to his two dishonest daughters: 'I do invest you jointly with my power'. The political setting of Lear's court, in which an unnatural handover of power occurs, will set in motion a tragic series of events for the characters.

The first scene exposes a deeply divided family. Lear obviously does not know his own children very well. When his youngest daughter, Cordelia, refuses to take part in the 'love test', Lear calls her 'young, and so untender'. He fails to recognise her honesty. He becomes angry that she will not flatter him publicly like her dishonest sisters. Rashly, he disinherits her, 'thy truth, then, be thy dower'. His abuse of his power as a parent suggests a bad outcome for himself and his 'most loved' daughter. 'The best and soundest of his times hath been but rash'.

Attitudes to marriage vary in this opening scene. Cordelia's two suitors who are proposing marriage have two very different reactions to her being disinherited. Burgundy blatantly refuses to marry her 'now her price is fallen'. This reflects the mercenary atmosphere of the court where money mattered most. However, the King of France decides to 'seize upon' her. Cordelia and France provide an exception to the dark disturbing world of Lear's court.

In *King Lear*, Shakespeare shows up some of the worst examples of human behaviour. A reckless king and father, unreliable daughters, a corrupt son, love of money, as well as the abuse of power. All these come together to present a shocking insight into an unstable disturbing world in which the good characters seem overwhelmed. *(360 words)*

Examiner's Comment

- Sustained focus on the question and mode throughout.
- Good points on the unstable political setting and likely outcome of the 'love test'.
- Expression is clear, varied and controlled.
- Overall, a well-supported top-grade response.

Sample 70-mark Question

Q. 'The way in which social forces affect the freedom of central characters can broaden our understanding of the cultural context of a text.'

Compare the way in which the effect of social forces on the freedom of central characters broadened your understanding of the cultural context when studying **three texts** on your comparative course. Develop your response with reference to your chosen texts.

Indicative Material

- Individuals can be freed/restricted by power, class, race, money, religion, etc.
- Impact of family expectations, relationships, marriage and traditional gender roles on characters' liberty.
- Effect of law, violence and tensions between power and freedom impact liberty of central characters.
- Freedom expressed through setting, narrative voice, language, symbols, music, etc.

Prompt!

The purpose of the 70-mark question is to address the three key elements (question, comparison, mode):

- to examine how social forces affect the freedom of central characters in your chosen texts (**question**)
- to show differences and similarities (**comparison**)
- evidence of understanding the Cultural Context (**mode**).

Sample Draft Plan

The following draft plan uses *King Lear* as one of the comparative texts.

INTRODUCTION

Opening of *King Lear* focuses on Cordelia, who is subject to various social, family, and patriarchal pressures. Attitudes to Edmund's illegitimacy have a negative effect on his freedom. *Similar/different situations exist in my other two texts ...*

POINT 1

Cordelia and Edgar are both excluded, victims of various social forces beyond their control. Lear's own independence is increasingly threatened by Goneril and Regan. *In contrast/similarly, my second text ...*

POINT 2

Frustrated family expectations of loyalty reduce the liberty of parent and child – Gloucester, Edgar and Edmund. *Equally revealing moments in my third text echo/do not echo ...*

POINT 3

As the story develops, central characters (Lear and Gloucester) find wisdom/truth despite/because of their loss of freedom. *There are some unexpected similarities/contrasts in my other texts ...*

POINT 4

Instructive insights into social behaviours in Act 5 of the play when Cordelia and Lear are reunited. *This is like/unlike the ending my second text ...*

CONCLUDING PARAGRAPH

All three texts show the range and influence of cultural influences. *King Lear* explores a hostile world where personal freedom is always threatened. *My knowledge of how society affects individuals was broadened by my other two texts ...*

Sample Paragraph: **POINT 2**

In the sub-plot of *King Lear*, Gloucester's family showed me how freedom is cut short when family expectations aren't met. A son expects to inherit from his father's estate. A father expects loyalty from his child. Neither hope is fulfilled. Gloucester's son, Edmund, is illegitimate and forbidden by law to inherit from his father. He feels his basic human rights are blocked 'by the plague of custom'. He fools his father into believing his legitimate son Edgar is plotting against him. Gloucester is then betrayed by Edmund to Cornwall who has his eyes gouged out. Edmund is unable to benefit from his father's estate. Gloucester has been deceived by his dishonest son and Edgar is on the run. All normal hopes have been dashed. This increased my understanding of how, when normal family expectations have been dashed, terrible consequences develop. *Equally interesting moments in my third text echo/do not echo ... (140 words)*

Examiner's Comment

- Addresses the question directly and focuses on the cultural context mode.
- Developed discussion on family expectations.
- Overall expression is good, but slightly repetitive.
- High-grade response uses effective reference and relevant quotation.
- Comparative approach evident at the end.

Class/Homework Exercise

Choose **one** of the other points in the Sample Draft Plan and write a paragraph of your own in response to the question above. (Aim for 140 words.)

2. Theme or Issue

Love, in its many forms, is one of the play's central themes

A theme or issue refers to a **central idea or message in a text**. The theme should not be confused with the plot or storyline, which is the sequence of events in a text. There will usually be a number of themes in a text, such as power, madness, relationships, nature, identity, conflict, justice, etc.

Why does a theme have special meaning for you?

The author's presentation of a key theme or issue often **challenges the reader** or audience to think about human nature and to distinguish between right and wrong. We often learn that struggling to do what is right can be difficult.

How do we respond to the author's treatment of a theme?

Comparing how different authors treat a theme can **broaden or change our understanding** of that particular theme or issue.

We engage with central characters as we follow their efforts to overcome obstacles, such as growing up, learning to be independent, responding to crises, etc. When we identify with another character's experiences, we can sometimes **clarify our own reactions to challenges** and problems in our own lives.

The Theme of Power in *King Lear*

Shakespeare's play is set in a brutally savage pre-Christian world. Violence, torture and suffering are common. If there is **a break in the natural order, chaos erupts**.

King Lear examines many aspects of this key theme, including:

- desire for power
- use and abuse of power
- consequences of losing power

Absolute power

King Lear is arrogant, rash and intolerant. The old king, 'fourscore and upward', is used to reigning and being obeyed without question. At the start of the play, Lear has decided to abdicate, 'To shake all cares and business from our age'. In Shakespeare's time, this would have been seen as breaking from the natural order for the safe transfer of power.

The king organises a 'love test', a public show from his daughters of their feelings for him. He will decide 'who doth love us most' and will reward land in proportion to their declared love for him. He is furious when his youngest daughter, Cordelia, refuses to take part, so he disowns and disinherits her: 'I disclaim all my paternal care'. **Power has corrupted Lear**, and he only listens to those who say what he wants to hear.

When Kent, his loyal courtier, tries to stop the king's 'hideous rashness', Lear banishes him. **Shakespeare is exploring the terrible effects of absolute power.** The king is fooled by the false flattery of his elder daughters, Goneril and Regan, when they declare 'glib and oily' vows of love for him. Lear believes that his supreme authority brings superior judgement – and that he is always right in everything he does. This self-important, reckless attitude will have appalling consequences.

Loss of power

Lear transfers authority to Goneril and Regan after the 'love test': 'I do invest you jointly with my power'. Yet he still wants to possess the royal title and have his own knights. He proposes to spend his time between his daughters' two homes. **But Lear fails to realise that loss of power means loss of privilege and status.** Goneril regards him as an 'Idle old man'. When he issues orders to Oswald, her servant, he is completely ignored.

The Fool tries to point out the reality of the king's new situation: 'I am a fool, thou art nothing'. Shakespeare is showing his audience that **when a person occupies a position of authority, power is unchallenged**, 'A dog's obeyed in office'. Anyone will be obeyed, regardless of their personal qualities. But when individuals no longer hold important positions, their power vanishes.

The playwright also explores the devastating results of losing power. For Lear, it also means loss of identity: 'Who is it that can tell me who I am?' He is now a powerless former monarch: 'Lear's shadow'. Unable to cope, he begins to lose his mind. When the king was powerful, he cared little for the rights and interest of others. In his madness, he realises how poorly he exercised his power as king, ignoring the 'naked wretches'. But now that he has no authority, he is unable to do anything about social injustice.

Abuse of power

Shakespeare is asking us to consider **what happens when power falls into evil hands**. Goneril and Regan, now joint rulers of Britain, use their new power to destroy Lear's happiness and sanity. They humiliate him by stripping him of his knights ('not one follower') and they eventually lock him out of their homes, 'Shut up your doors'.

The two sisters lack morality and basic humanity. Goneril becomes more masculine, a mirror **image of her domineering father**. When she is confronted by her husband, Albany, over her plot to have him murdered, she declares, 'the laws are mine, not thine'.

Goneril assumes that she is above the law, that she can act as she pleases. Who will dare 'arraign' her for it?

Regan is equally corrupted by power, becoming more and more sadistic. She increases the length of time that Kent is to be imprisoned in the stocks, 'all night too'. She demands that Gloucester's 'other' eye be gouged out as punishment for helping the tormented king. Regan kills the servant who fatally wounded Cornwall, and takes great delight in telling Gloucester that he was betrayed by his own son.

Edmund is forbidden by the laws of society from inheriting because of the circumstances of his birth. In anger, he shuns all social laws and adopts nature as his 'goddess'. Edmund believes in the survival of the fittest and that the end justifies the means. **His desire for power causes him to exploit his 'noble' brother and 'credulous' father.**

Edmund cares only about himself and his own obsessive ambition. He takes pleasure in leading Goneril and Regan on. Both sisters desire him, 'Each jealous of the other'. **Edmund's disregard for rules leads him to become over-confident.** He waives his right to know who the anonymous challenger is in the final duel and is defeated by his disguised brother, Edgar.

Over the course of the play, Shakespeare reveals how abuse of power, whether inherited or seized, has catastrophic effects. Everyone suffers, innocent and guilty.

Power restored

As the play concludes, **order is restored through the good characters**, particularly Albany and Edgar. Both men have matured. Albany is transformed from the 'milk-livered' man so despised by his wife into a strong leader who defeats the French army. He changed as a result of his anger over Lear's brutal treatment by Goneril and Regan. He intends to return 'absolute power' to Lear, but is prevented from doing so by the king's death. He then hands over the kingship to Kent and Edgar: 'you twain/ Rule in this realm'.

Edmund also matures, when fatally wounded in the duel. Edgar urges him to do the right thing, 'Send/ Thy token of reprieve', to save the condemned Cordelia. Edmund confesses that 'Some good I mean to do/ Despite mine own nature'. However, just as Albany fails to give back power to Lear, Edmund fails to save Cordelia. Shakespeare is reminding us that **good intentions do not always succeed**.

At the end of the play, there are signs of hope in that civilised order will be established in Britain. Edgar will 'Rule in this realm, and the gored state sustain'. The playwright clearly indicates **how power should be used responsibly**, based on justice and humanity. Egotistical control and ruthless terror have brought nothing but tragedy and widespread suffering.

Sample Part (a) Question

Q. 'In many texts, a central theme or issue may not be resolved to the complete satisfaction of the reader.'

Discuss the extent to which a theme or issue is resolved to your satisfaction in **one** text on your comparative course. Develop your response with reference to the text. *(30 marks)*

Indicative Material

Exploration of theme or issue can lead to:

- a convincing or unconvincing conclusion
- realistic/unrealistic plot and/or characters
- expectations fulfilled or unfulfilled
- effective/ineffective use of imagery/ language, etc.

This question requires you to address the mode and the question only. No comparison is needed.

Sample Answer

Shakespeare explored the key theme of nature in his play *King Lear* through character and language. He examined not only the destructive aspects of nature, but also its generous side, 'unpublished virtues of the earth'. He paints a very convincing picture of how a breakdown in the natural bond between child and father can destroy both the guilty and innocent. Lear, in a fit of anger at Cordelia's behaviour in the 'love test', banishes the 'wretch'. The signs of a tragic outcome are there from the start.

Gloucester also banishes his loyal child, Edgar. He does not give him a chance to defend himself, instead he judges him to be an 'unnatural, detested, brutish villain'. The 'bond of childhood' is cut. Nature takes terrible revenge for this break of its natural laws. On the wild heath, the two unnatural fathers wander in the storm, an obvious symbol of chaos. Gloucester, now horrifically blinded, gains insight: 'I stumbled when I saw'. Lear, now insane, begins to understand the reality of the world and develops compassion for others less fortunate.

The use of animal imagery is really effective in exposing the evil characters, such as Regan and Goneril – 'pelican daughters', 'Tigers'. These ruthless women have adopted the wild laws of nature – which is based on the survival of the fittest. Like feral animals they turn on each other over their lust for Edmund. 'I had rather lose the battle than that sister/ Should loosen him and me'. Shakespeare resolves the theme of nature by turning their own evil against them in the last act.

The play ends with the calm after the storm. Cordelia represents all that is good in nature. Like Kent and Edgar, she reveals the redemptive power of nature. Cordelia brings comfort to the maddened king through forgiveness: 'let this kiss/ Repair'. I found the final scene where Lear is cradling his executed daughter in his arms uncomfortably true. The innocent are often the victims of evil. Shakespeare's exploration of the theme of nature is realistic but disturbing. *(340 words)*

Examiner's Comment

- Engages well with the question and the play.
- Good clear discussion of the treatment of nature.
- Developed points on natural bonds, nature imagery and redemptive nature.
- Effective use of supportive reference and quotation.
- Overall, a focused top-grade response.

Sample 70-mark Question

Q. Compare the reasons why you found the exploration of a theme or issue more, less, or equally engaging in the **three texts** on your comparative course. Develop your response with reference to your chosen texts.

Indicative Material

Examination of theme is more/less or equally engaging because:

- character/s and/or plot provide interesting/thought-provoking insights
- use of language shapes reader's emotions
- resolution of theme satisfactory/unsatisfactory
- impact of setting, author's approach, key moments, etc.

Prompt!

The purpose of the 70-mark question is to address the three key elements (question, comparison, mode):

- to examine and explain the extent to which a theme was/was not engaging in your chosen texts (**question**)
- to show differences and similarities (**comparison**)
- evidence of understanding of the Theme or Issue (**mode**).

Sample Draft Plan

The following draft plan uses *King Lear* as one of the comparative texts.

INTRODUCTION

King Lear is a tragedy which explores emotionally engaging themes. My chosen theme is personal growth and self-knowledge. *My other two texts presented similar/contrasting views ...*

POINT 1

Central characters, Lear, Gloucester, Albany, Cordelia and even Edmund, overcame challenges and achieved self-knowledge. I became very involved in the text. *My other two texts presented similar/contrasting views ...*

POINT 2

Minor characters, Edgar and Albany, learned to stand up for themselves and they matured, which I found fascinating. *The changes minor characters underwent in my second text were similar/different ...*

POINT 3

Lear's growing awareness in the storm on the heath had a strong impact on me through his use of dramatic language. *Such intense language was/was not used in my other texts ...*

POINT 4

Lear grows in compassion and self-knowledge on the heath. I found this very poignant because of the insights he gained about using power responsibly. *In my other texts the central character does/does not achieve this level of self-knowledge ...*

CONCLUDING PARAGRAPH

I found the central characters' journeys towards self-knowledge emotionally engaging in all my three texts, but Shakespeare's exploration of the theme of self-growth was the most disturbing, particularly the final scene where Lear carried the dead Cordelia.

***Sample Paragraph*: POINT 3**

Shakespeare uses dramatic language and imagery to show the storm on the heath. The alliterative 'pelting of this pitiless storm' reveals the brute force of nature at times. Lear begins to realise that some people in society, 'homeless heads', have to constantly put up with these dreadful conditions. His own self-awareness increases as he describes the condition of these poor unfortunates with their 'looped and windowed raggedness'. He also realises that these unfortunate people are often punished much more for their crimes than the rich. Powerful metaphors, 'robes and furred gowns hide all', show how privileged people can get away with what the poor cannot. I felt that not only Lear, but we, are growing in humanity as we look at life through the dramatic language and imagery of this rambling old man helplessly rushing around the heath. *In my other texts the central characters ...* *(140 words)*

Examiner's Comment

- General high-grade standard engaging with the personal growth theme.
- Some well-developed points about dramatic language.
- Expression is reasonably good, although slightly repetitive.
- Effective use of back-up textual reference.

Class/Homework Exercise

Choose **one** of the other points in the Sample Draft Plan and write a paragraph of your own in response to the question above. (Aim for 140 words.)

3. The General Vision and Viewpoint

The General Vision and Viewpoint mode refers to the **broad outlook** of a particular text.

For example, if an author is critical of a society, events or central characters, the vision of the text is likely to be dark and **negative**.

If the outlook in the text is **positive** and life-affirming, the writer or director might well be praising the courage and resilience of characters as they overcome or come to terms with their problems and circumstances.

> **NOTE**
>
> *You are not required to make a distinction between vision and viewpoint. Both terms refer to the overall outlook of a text.*

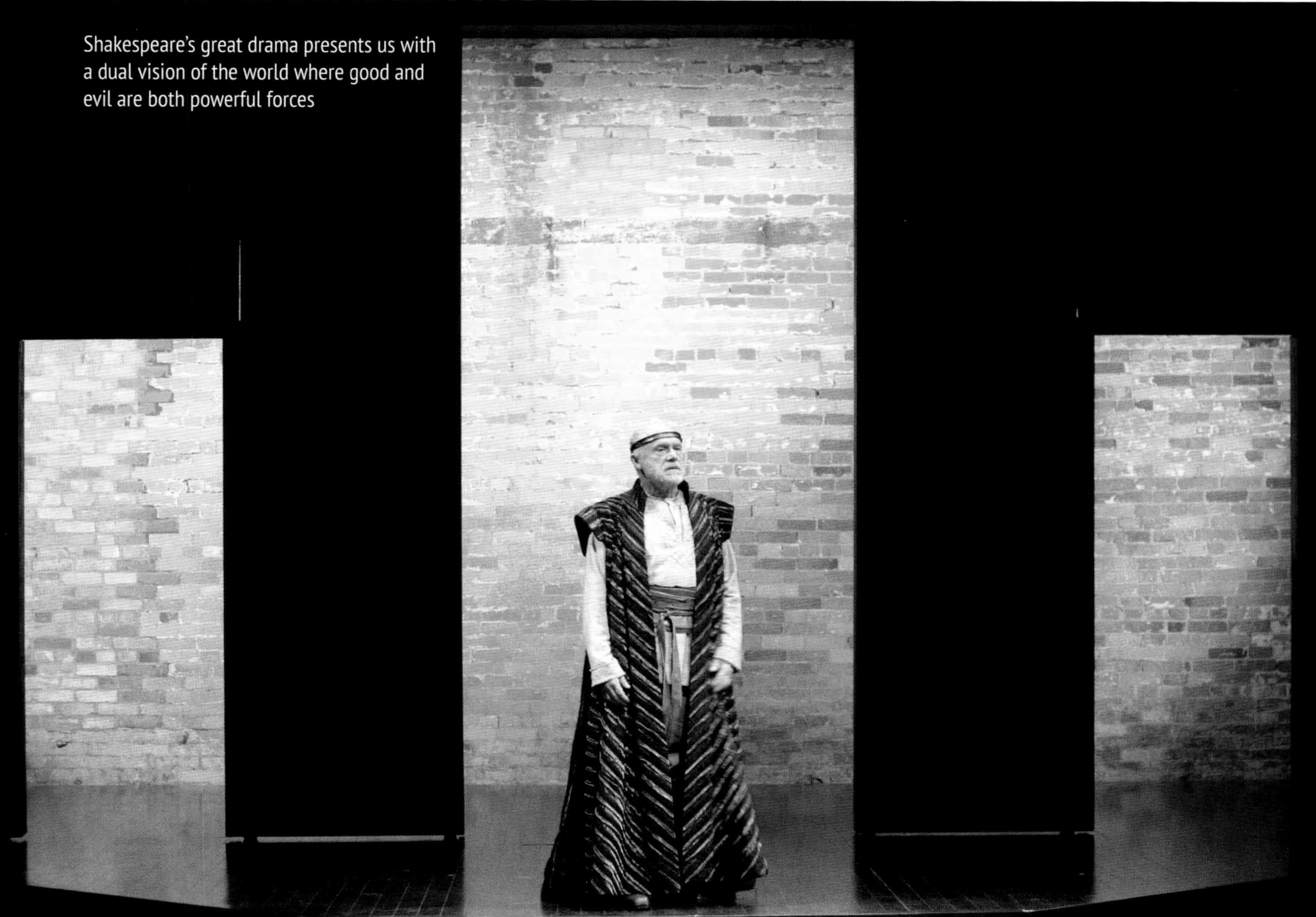

Shakespeare's great drama presents us with a dual vision of the world where good and evil are both powerful forces

Texts can usually be described as:

Optimistic – positive, bright, hopeful, inspiring

Pessimistic – negative, dark, hopeless, cynical

Realistic – credible, accurate, truthful, reasonable

Ambiguous – unresolved, unclear, contradictory, etc.

The ending of a story is very important in determining the viewpoint. Whether happy or sad (or a combination of both), readers usually expect the central conflict to have some kind of resolution. The ending has to be believable within the 'world' of the story.

Responding to the author's treatment of a theme

The viewpoint is likely to be pessimistic or tragic if the:

- plot focuses on suffering and failure.
- author's views are bitter or cynical.
- view of women is negative in a patriarchal society.
- detached language adds to the sense of hopelessness.

An optimistic outlook can be reflected by:

- the resilience of characters.
- enduring friendships and happy relationships.
- some sense of justice, redemption, etc.

A text can be seen as being balanced and realistic if:

- the future may not be bleak for every character.
- death is a release for some characters.
- we are given a true-to-life insight into a particular time and place.
- lyrical/descriptive language adds beauty.
- comic moments compensate for some of the unhappiness.
- the ending is credible within the context of the story.

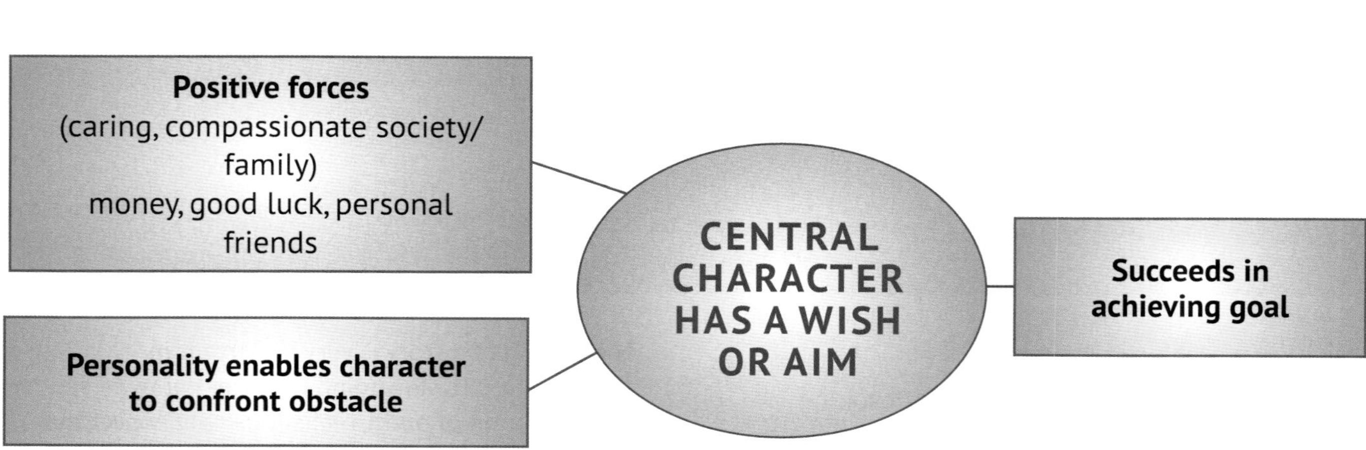

How is Vision and Viewpoint Established?

The broad outlook of a text is usually set by the writer's use of:

- character
- plot
- language
- narrative voice
- setting, atmosphere, etc.

> **NOTE**
>
> *Modes overlap. For example, the general vision and viewpoint is often shaped by the cultural context and literary genre.*

Shakespeare's vision

In *King Lear*, **Shakespeare presents a dual vision of the world, optimistic and pessimistic**. The view is bleak because the tragic story explores some of the worst things that can happen to an individual. Human happiness is shown as short-lived and fragile when faced with the forces of evil, 'As flies to wanton boys are we to the gods'.

However, **the outlook is also hopeful at times** because the play contains moments where decent people act bravely and compassionately. The playwright shows us characters who grow and mature through suffering, becoming better human beings.

How plot establishes the outlook in *King Lear*

The main plot, which concerns Lear and his daughters, is an epic **story of violence and suffering**. The sub-plot of Gloucester and his sons closely mirrors the main plot. Both storylines involve deluded fathers, deceitful and loyal children. Neither Lear nor Gloucester is aware of the true nature of any of their children. Lear is abandoned by Regan and Goneril, who view him as a troublesome guest in their homes.

The elderly king is locked out and left to wander the windswept heath 'unbonneted'. He becomes 'Unaccommodated man'. But **Lear is eventually saved** by his youngest daughter, Cordelia, who forgives him from disowning her: 'let this kiss/ Repair those violent harms that my two sisters/ Have in thy reverence made'. Gloucester is also betrayed by his favourite son, Edmund, and helped by Edgar, the son he misjudged.

Shakespeare presents a world where **evil consequences are caused by evil desires**. The playwright regards self-interest as man's greatest flaw. Edmund, Goneril and Regan are ruthless. They all hold society's rules in contempt and are blind to the rights or needs of others. As a result, Lear and Gloucester suffer terribly.

But evil destroys itself in the end. Edmund, Goneril and Regan are ultimately ruined because of their over-ambition and uncontrolled emotions. This is a **depressing world** where immoral behaviour – hypocrisy, corruption and violence – can be defeated, but only after great pain and suffering.

But there are also **acts of kindness and compassion which brighten the outlook** in the play. Shakespeare regards selfless, loving service to a parent, child, or society at large as the greatest virtue. During one of the darkest moments, as Gloucester's eyes are being gouged out by Cornwall, a servant intervenes. After drawing his sword and fatally wounding Cornwall, however, the servant is killed by Regan.

The **play's ending emphasises Shakespeare's dual vision** of life. Evil can be defeated, but only after a terrible price is paid, including the deaths of the innocent. This is illustrated in the heart-wrenching image of Lear carrying Cordelia in his arms: 'She's gone for ever'. At this stage, Kent, Lear's loyal knight, believes that the frail old king has suffered enough: 'let him pass'.

The **hope of a better future** is evident in the final victory of good over evil. Edgar and Albany establish a new order within the 'gored state'. They promise to replace selfishness and hypocrisy with truth and compassion, to 'Speak what we feel, not what we ought to say'.

Over the course of the tragedy, evil is punished, but good is not always rewarded. Shakespeare is not presenting a classic fairy-tale where everyone lives happily ever after. The **ending is neither totally optimistic nor totally negative**. Goneril and Regan die, but so does Cordelia. Innocence is no protection when evil is let loose.

The audience is left to consider whether or not 'The gods are just'. Edgar and Albany are establishing a more just society: 'All friends shall taste/ The wages of their virtue, and all foes/ The cup of their deservings'. But what is Shakespeare's view of human nature? Is he saying that life is always uncertain and unpredictable? And that 'Men must endure'? As always, we are left to decide for ourselves about the play's vision and viewpoint.

How characters establish the viewpoint

The playwright **uses characters to reveal a particular vision of life** while the audience listen to their comments on society or the problems they are facing. Edmund is furious because at this time, being born outside marriage means that he cannot inherit from his father. Edmund decides that if society is rejecting him, then he will reject society's laws, and embrace the laws of nature where only the fittest survives.

Relationships are shown as either destructive or nurturing. Shakespeare presents characters who are supported or prevented in their efforts to grow and achieve their goals. Dysfunctional families in both the main plot (Lear and his daughters) and the sub-plot (Gloucester's family) expose the playwright's dual vision.

Shakespeare makes audiences feel uncomfortable through the experience of observing how some children only value their parents for what they can give them: 'fathers that bear bags/ Shall see their children kind'. However, this **pessimistic view is counterbalanced by positive loyal relationships**.

The play's protagonist (central character) is capable of learning from his experiences and becoming a better person. Lear is genuinely loved by Cordelia, Kent and the Fool. However, he is a flawed character, arrogant and rash: 'Old fools are babes again'. He is blind to his faults and refuses to listen to well-meaning advice, so he makes disastrous choices. The enraged monarch banishes those who are truly loyal to him, Cordelia and Kent: 'Come not between the dragon and his wrath'. He then rewards those who will betray him, Goneril and Regan: 'he hath ever but slenderly known himself'. As a result, he suffers terribly. The tragic downfall of this once great king highlights **the story's bleak perspective**.

In Shakespeare's time, it was believed that if there was **a break in the natural order, civilisation would descend into chaos**. Lear's abdication and his foolish 'love test' weakened his society. Human beings turn against one another, 'Like monsters of the deep'. The play shows how a single break in society's natural order allows the forces of evil to enter and destroy: 'there's son against father ... there's father against child'.

Cruelty increases. Lear curses his daughter Goneril, 'Into her womb convey sterility'. Gloucester is blinded: 'let him smell/ His way to Dover'. The weather is in turmoil, reflecting the disorder in society: 'Such sheets of fire, such bursts of horrid thunder'. Lear's mental collapse due to 'Filial ingratitude' is mirrored in the fierce storm. **The world is out of control.**

But Shakespeare also shows how characters **learn through suffering**. Lear and Gloucester gain new insights into their own characters after undergoing horrific trials. Lear achieves 'Reason in madness'. He becomes sympathetic to the poor and admits that as king, he had 'taken/ Too little care of this'. Meeting the beggar, Poor Tom, he starts to understand 'Unaccommodated man'. A human being without possessions is reduced to a 'poor, bare, forked animal'.

The play's **positive outlook is also evident in Lear's attitude to justice**. He comes to understand that rich and influential people can hide their crimes, unlike the poor, 'Through tattered clothes small vices do appear;/ Robes and furred gowns hide all'. Both Lear and Gloucester eventually recognise the truth about their loyal children. Lear knows Cordelia's 'small fault' of silence did not deserve being disowned. Gloucester realises that his son 'Edgar was abused'. Like Lear, he becomes aware of the inequalities in society: 'distribution should undo excess,/ And each man have enough'.

The **dual vision of Shakespeare challenges audiences**. Good can defeat evil, but at a cost. People can improve through suffering. Resilience and love will eventually triumph, 'Ripeness is all'.

Remember!

Discussion points in the 30-mark Part (a) sample answer can also provide the basis for developed comparisons in the 40-mark Part (b) and 70-mark questions.

Sample Part (a) Question

Q. 'The extent to which a reader can relate a text to his or her experience of life helps to shape an understanding of the general vision and viewpoint of that text.'

Discuss this view in relation to your study of **one** text on your comparative course. *(30 marks)*

Indicative Material

The extent to which a reader can relate their experience of life to a text helps to shape an understanding of the vision and viewpoint through:

- personal response to characters
- key moments
- destructive/nurturing relationships
- setting and atmosphere
- impact of language, imagery, symbols, etc.

This question requires you to address the mode and the question only. No comparison is needed.

Sample Answer

I found the story of King Lear, Gloucester and Cordelia very upsetting. Lear foolishly insisted on his daughters declaring their love for him not only to gain power but to boost his ego. Cordelia decides to 'love silently'. The angry king banishes her. This leads to a series of catastrophes not only for the central characters, but for society as a whole. I related to this because I have already found that life, at times, is not very fair, not even for the innocent.

How often have we longed for a happy outcome in life and been disappointed? Lear is rejected by his two elder daughters to whom he gave 'all'. As a result, he loses his sanity and becomes a 'ruined piece of nature'. Reunited with his youngest daughter, Cordelia, he hopes that, even though imprisoned, 'We two together will sing like birds in the cage'. His and our hopes are cruelly dashed. Cordelia is executed. This unhappy ending led me to conclude that the vision in the play is extremely bleak and downbeat.

I found the family relationships in the play dysfunctional and toxic. Lear's ungrateful elder daughters, Goneril and Regan, abandoned the old man to run into a fierce storm on the heath. Lear also behaves badly as a father. He curses Goneril, asking nature to 'suspend thy purpose to make this creature fruitful'. Even the relationship between lovers is poisonous. Edmund is loved by both Regan and Goneril. He cynically wonders, 'Which of the two shall I take?' These destructive relationships reminded me of people who spend their time arguing and pulling each other apart. I formed a negative view of the vision in this text.

I feel when I look at the modern world and its cruelty, violence and lack of justice, I can understand the view expressed in the play, 'When we are born, we cry that we are come to this great stage of fools'. *(320 words)*

Examiner's Comment

- Addresses the question well and focuses on the mode throughout.
- Developed illustrations of the story's negative aspects.
- Some use of reference – although quotes are slightly inaccurate.
- Overall, expression is clear in this solid high-grade response.

Sample 70-mark Question

Q. 'Significant events in texts, and the impact they have on readers, often help to clarify the general vision and viewpoint of those texts.'

With reference to **three texts** on your comparative course, compare the ways in which at least one significant event in each text, and its impact on you, helped clarify the general vision and viewpoint of these texts.

Indicative Material

Significant events in texts influence the reader's understanding of the general vision and viewpoint through:

- impact of key scenes and moments of crisis
- hope, despair, joy, shock, etc. experienced by characters
- narrative voice, setting and atmosphere
- language, imagery, symbols, etc.

Prompt!

The purpose of the 70-mark question is to address the three key elements (question, comparison, mode):

- exploring how the outlook is clarified by key events and their impact in your chosen texts (**question**)
- to show differences and similarities (**comparison**)
- evidence of understanding of Vision and Viewpoint (**mode**).

Sample Draft Plan

The following draft plan uses *King Lear* as one of the comparative texts.

INTRODUCTION

The general outlook on life in my three comparative texts ranged from optimism to pessimism. Shakespeare's tragedy *King Lear* presented a dark, bleak view of the world although order was restored in the end. *My other two texts presented a similar/contrasting view ...*

POINT 1

In *King Lear* goodness is shown through the selfless love of two wronged children, Cordelia and Edgar. Evil is shown through the mercenary actions of the corrupt children, Goneril, Regan and Edmund. Even the innocent suffer from their wickedness. This shapes my negative view of the text. *My other texts reflect/do not reflect this point of view ...*

POINT 2

Shakespeare uses powerful language in key scenes to reveal his mixed feelings about the world. Lear's instability on the heath is reflected in his strength of spirit defying the storm and also his realisation that man is no more than a 'poor, forked animal' when stripped of possessions. This added to my dark vision of the text. *An equally revealing scene in my other two texts does/does not share ...*

POINT 3

The 'Trial Scene' where Lear is judge, jury and executioner allows the playwright to comment cynically on human justice and the ineffective legal system. This chaotic view of life is pessimistic. *This was like/unlike the view in my other two texts ...*

CONCLUDING PARAGRAPH

A play that has been dominated by pessimism, violence and corruption ends with healing, insight and hope. While a new order is established under the two good characters, Albany and Edgar, terrible suffering is inflicted on the innocent. Good triumphs but at a huge cost. I found this vision dark, rather than life-affirming. *With regard to the other texts ...*

Sample Paragraph: **POINT 2**

Strong language is used in the scene on the heath, adding to the chaotic atmosphere. Once powerful, Lear is now a pathetic outcast wallowing in self-pity, 'a poor, infirm, weak, and despised old man'. But he is also defiant, challenging nature to do its worst, 'Blow, winds, and crack your cheeks'. I see him as a victim of a merciless world. The king's madness brought on by 'filial ingratitude' is mirrored in the violence of the storm. In his delirious state, he curses his daughters, but his intense suffering brings new insight, 'Reason in madness'. Lear now understands the reality of human existence – without wealth and privilege, the ordinary human being is a 'poor, forked animal'. Sadly, he now has no power to help the 'naked wretches'. This added to the play's bleak vision. *I found an equally dark outlook in the novel ... (145 words)*

Examiner's Comment

- Focused top-grade response using supportive reference.
- Shows a good understanding of the vision and viewpoint mode.
- Developed discussion on the playwright's effective language use.
- Expression is excellent throughout.
- Comparative approach evident at the end.

Class/Homework Exercise

Choose **one** of the other points in the Sample Draft Plan and write a paragraph of your own in response to the question above. (Aim for 140 words.)

4. Literary Genre

Literary genre is a style of writing. It refers to **the way stories are presented**. Authors make effective use of various techniques in plays, novels and films. Our appreciation of a text is increased by being aware of the author's choice of literary and dramatic techniques.

NOTE

Modes overlap. For example, literary genre influences the general vision and viewpoint and can intensify our appreciation of themes and cultural context.

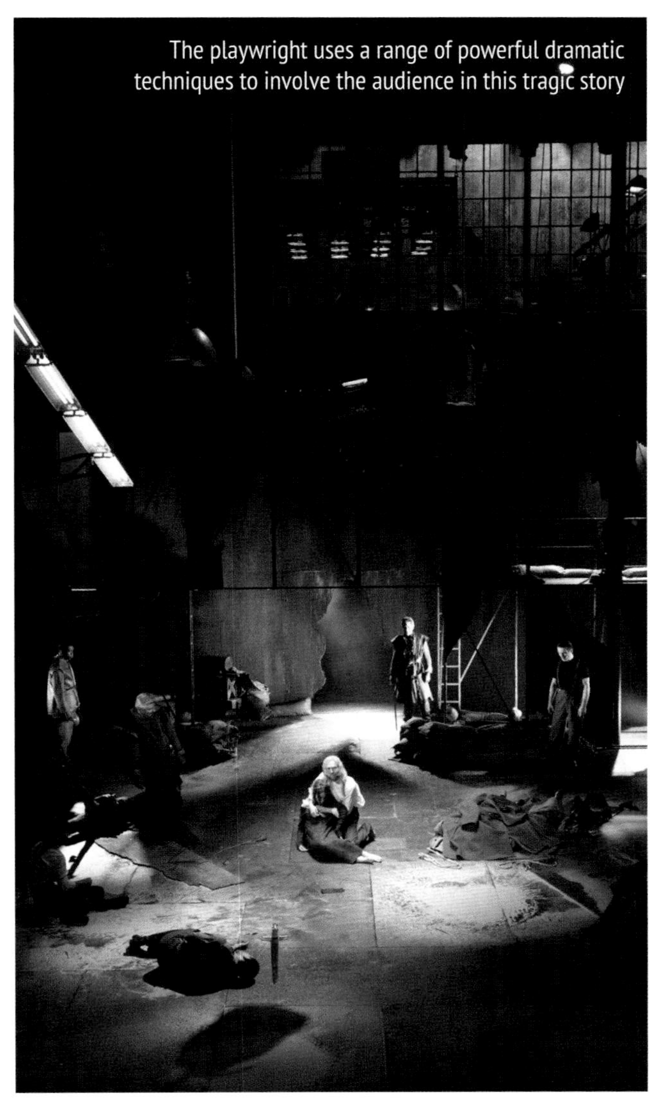

The playwright uses a range of powerful dramatic techniques to involve the audience in this tragic story

Responding to Texts

Our response to central characters and their actions is **influenced by how the author presents a character**. This can range from realistic three-dimensional characters with credible characteristics to stereotypical two-dimensional figures, such as heroes or villains.

The **shape of a story**, whether chronological (presenting events as they happen) or using flashback (moving back to the past), increases our understanding of why the narrative is developing in a particular way.

Symbols and images can enrich our engagement with a story and its characters.

Irony places readers and audiences in a privileged position. We know more than the characters and so we wait in anticipation to see how they will react to challenges.

The **title** can interest or excite the audience – what will happen to the characters in the story?

Genre also raises the audience's expectations. In a classical tragedy such as *King Lear*, the central character will die, but not before gaining self-knowledge. In modern tragedies the central character might not achieve self-knowledge. Socially realistic texts often show the good being defeated.

Setting is often used to make the story credible, adding to the positive or negative atmosphere in the text.

Dialogue also adds to the authenticity of a story. It not only conveys the personality of characters but also their socio-economic and educational status.

Soliloquies increase our understanding of a character's internal emotional struggles.

Conflict, tension and turning points heighten the reader's interest in the outcome of the story. Many of Shakespeare's central characters experience intense inner conflict throughout the play.

The **resolution** (whether the conflict is resolved happily, unhappily or is left open-ended) also strengthens the reader's engagement. Has the story concluded as expected?

Developing a Personal Response

Check the graphic below to aid your understanding of **common literary genre techniques**. Those on the right are specific to particular types of text. The techniques shape the response of readers and audiences towards central characters and their world.

> **NOTE**
>
> *A play makes use of stage directions to communicate the story. Novels use descriptive language to visualise the narrative. A film uses the camera to show its story.*

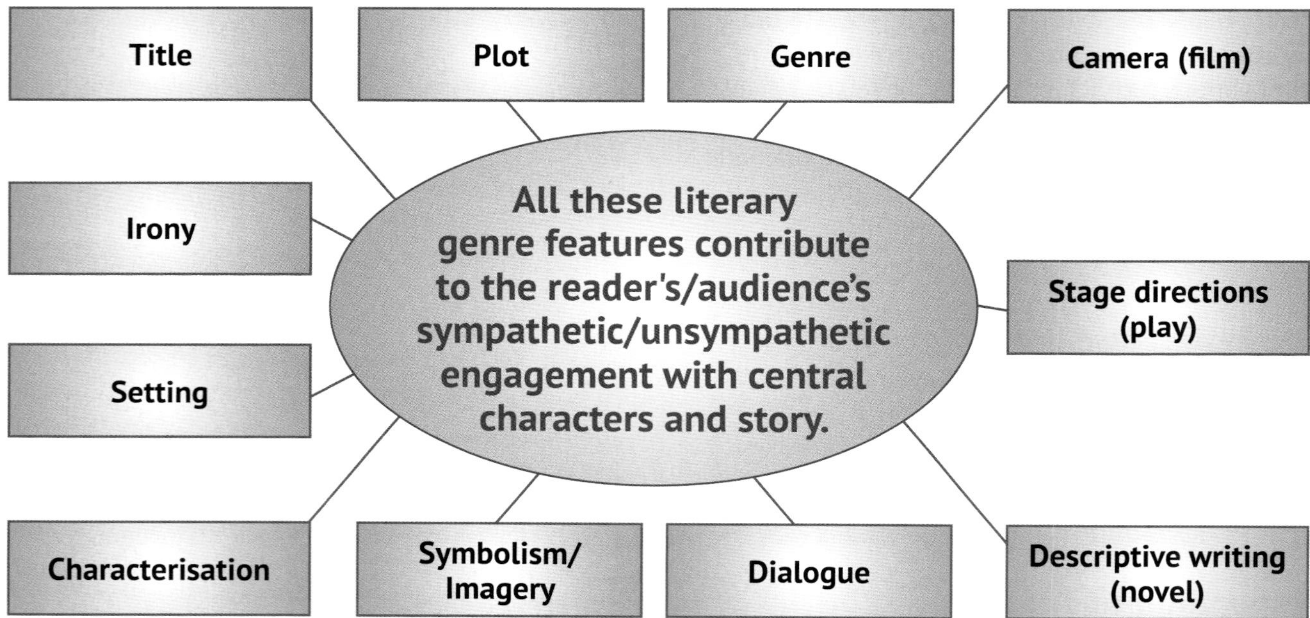

Literary genre in *King Lear*

Shakespeare's *King Lear* is **a tragedy in five acts**. In a tragedy, the hero has potential to be great, but fails to achieve this greatness because of a serious character weakness. This fault leads to the hero's downfall, with disastrous consequences for himself and others.

King Lear is a **political story** about the use and abuse of power. It is also a **moral tale**, showing the consequences of toxic family relationships. Those who flatter (Goneril, Regan and Edmund) at first succeed in their greed. But eventually, those who are wronged, yet remain loyal, redeem their deluded fathers.

Characterisation

Shakespeare's presentation of Lear reveals him as a flawed character. Arrogance and rashness are his greatest failings. After a long reign as king, he is unused to being challenged. When his youngest daughter refuses to take part in his 'love test', she is immediately disowned by him. This catastrophic misjudgement is a direct result of Lear's character defects.

The elderly monarch values appearance above reality. Not only does he believe the empty flattery of Regan and Goneril, he also thinks he can still be treated as king despite handing over power to his two daughters: 'He hath ever but slenderly known himself'. Lear's error was foolish rather than wicked. His poor judgement leads to his own death and a civil war in Britain. The **devastating consequences are out of proportion to his mistake**.

But **Lear develops as a character**, achieving insight through suffering, 'Reason in madness'. Gloucester also sees truth when blind: 'I stumbled when I saw'. His son Edgar learns to stop being naive and realises that he may have to adopt disguises when dealing with evil. Cordelia eventually understands the importance of showing her feelings and expresses her 'dear love' for her aged father. Albany learns to assert himself when, appalled at Goneril and Edmund's plot to have him killed, he joins the forces for good.

Lear's two older daughters display none of the usual feminine qualities, such as kindness or tenderness. Instead, Regan and Goneril try to outdo each other in cruelty: 'Hang him instantly', 'Pluck out his eyes'. But **they are instrumental in moving the plot forward**. Their jealousy over Edmund leads to their deaths.

While Shakespeare presents the extremes of good and evil in his characters, he also gives some of his characters depth. **Edmund is a fascinating villain.** He is presented as a clever manipulator who deceives his victims (a 'credulous' father and 'a brother noble') with ease. Angry that his illegitimate birth prevents him from inheriting, he decides to get Gloucester's lands 'by wit'. Edmund callously betrays his gullible father and exploits Lear's two daughters: 'To both these sisters have I sworn my love'. Shakespeare has created a monstrous villain.

Yet, **Edmund can also be seen as an engaging victim** with some cause to be angry. He is attractive, courageous. He scorns all rules and has a dry sense of humour: 'Which of them shall I take?' After being wounded by Edgar, he changes and tries to stop Cordelia's execution: 'Some good I mean to do/ Despite of mine own nature'. Shakespeare leaves the audience wondering if Gloucester had not humiliated Edmund about his birth, would his son have turned to evil? Is it fitting that his one attempt to do good ends in failure?

Soliloquies and asides

Shakespeare uses **soliloquy** as an important dramatic device in *King Lear*. The soliloquy requires that the character is alone on stage, as he reveals what he is thinking for the benefit of the audience. This develops dramatic irony and suspense, since the audience now know more than some of the characters in the story.

King Lear contains eleven soliloquies, with Edmund using this device most often to explain his motives to the audience. Edgar also uses soliloqiues several times, most notably when he explains why he will disguise himself as Poor Tom. This highlights the contrast between the two brothers.

Shakespeare also frequently makes use of the **aside**. This is where one character 'thinks aloud' and is not heard by other characters. The aside allows the audience to learn details that most of the characters on stage do not know. For example, Goneril's aside in Act 5 reveals that she has poisoned Regan.

Throughout *King Lear*, characters use soliloquies and asides to draw the audience into their own world and to express their true thoughts and feelings. Soliloquies also contain some of the play's most powerful language.

Dual plots

In *King Lear*, there are two plots, each with its own set of characters. The main plot deals with Lear and his three daughters – Cordelia, Regan and Goneril. Parallel to this is the sub-plot which focuses on the parent–child relationship between Gloucester and his two sons, Edgar and Edmund.

The double plot is another important dramatic device in this play. With two intertwined plots, Shakespeare can **explore and emphasise the tragic consequences that result when man's law is given precedence over natural law**. We see two variations on the theme of children turning against their parents. **The 'more realistic' sub-plot helps the audience to accept the 'fairy-tale' main plot.**

The Gloucester story intensifies our experience of the play's central action. The sub-plot illustrates some of the play's important themes. Gloucester's blindness, for example, clarifies Lear's suffering and his lack of awareness. Both men gain insight into the need to care for the poor, that 'each man have enough'. In his role as Poor Tom, Edgar shows the reality of homeless poverty at its worst.

The meeting of Lear and Gloucester brings the two plots together. Gloucester has committed adultery, a sin of the senses, and is then deprived of one of his senses – sight. Lear is punished on a greater level. Through madness he recognises his personal fault in condemning Cordelia, and his greater flaw that he has not taken care of 'naked wretches' when in power. He endures the shocking agony of losing Cordelia just when he had learned to truly love her.

Symbols and imagery patterns

The text is full of images of **sight**, and the word 'eye' (or 'eyes') is repeated throughout. Both Lear and Gloucester are morally blind, and it is only when Gloucester has lost his eyes that he is able to 'see' the truth: 'I stumbled when I saw'.

There are more than fifty different **animals** mentioned in the play. Such recurring animal imagery paints a vivid picture of the breakdown of the social order. It emphasises the savage instincts of Goneril, Regan and Edmund. There are many images of beasts of prey – wolves, tigers, wild boars, serpents and sea monsters – ripping, piercing and tearing their victims: 'In his anointed flesh stick boarish fangs'. There are images of the sharpness of their teeth, their claws, their talons. Lear believes Regan will 'flay' Goneril's 'wolfish visage' with her nails. All those images intensify the sense of torture and pain.

The sisters are compared to fiends and monsters. Goneril is 'sharp-toothed, like a vulture'. Lear curses her as a 'Detested kite'. The two sisters are 'Tigers, not daughters' who behave 'Like monsters of the deep'. They are cruel predators, 'pelican daughters', who want to see their father bleed.

There are **other references to animals which help us understand Lear's tragedy**. The Fool uses insightful imagery when he says to Lear: 'The hedge-sparrow fed the cuckoo so long/ That it's had it head bit off by it young'. This image highlights the old king's vulnerability. On the heath, Lear realises that man, when poor, is nothing more than 'a poor, bare, forked animal'. Animal imagery is used to show that nature's law, survival of the fittest, prevails. Eventually, reunited with Cordelia, he predicts that the two of them will 'sing like birds i' the cage'. For the first time we are presented with an attractive animal image.

Clothing imagery is used to show the contrast between appearance and reality. Lear comments, during his madness, how clothing as a symbol of wealth and class hides injustice. 'Through tattered clothes small vices do appear;/ Robes and furred gowns hide all'. Edgar, disguised as the beggar Poor Tom, is naked except for a blanket.

Lear tries to tear his clothes off to identify with those who are poor. He runs about in the storm 'unbonneted' and has descended to the level of his poorest subjects. He is filled with compassion: 'How shall your houseless heads and unfed sides,/ Your looped and windowed raggedness, defend you/ From seasons such as these?' When the old king regains his sanity, he is clothed in 'fresh garments', symbolising the new Lear.

Sample Part (a) Question

Q. 'The effective use of powerful imagery can help to create the atmosphere or mood in a text.'

Discuss how the effective use of powerful imagery helped to create the atmosphere or mood in **one** of the texts on your comparative course. *(30 marks)*

Indicative Material

Patterns of imagery:

- increase the dramatic power of particular scenes
- involve audiences in the play's essential tragedy
- add interest, shock, irony, humour and pathos
- intensify moods – tension, violence, tenderness, etc.

This question requires you to address the mode and the question only. No comparison is needed.

Sample Answer

King Lear opens with an uneasy atmosphere. Tension is created by the king's obvious instability: 'he hath ever but slenderly known himself.' The word 'nothing' is used by Cordelia in answer to Lear's demand that she publicly express her love for him. The Fool also uses this image when he tries to get Lear to see what he has done, 'now thou art an O without a figure'. He states, 'I am a fool, thou art nothing'. This use of the image of emptiness not only shows Lear's bad judgement but highlights the predicament he has put himself in because of his impulsive character. The imagery shows his personality.

Lear's language reveals a harsh side to his character. He commands Kent who is trying to prevent 'This hideous rashness', to 'Come not between the dragon and his wrath'. The shocking image of a creature spitting fire sums up the terrifying atmosphere in Lear's court. Animal imagery is being used to showcase Lear's hot temper. He has ruled in absolute power for a long time and is not used to being challenged.

Lear also uses animal imagery to describe his ungrateful daughters. He calls Goneril a 'sea-monster' and a 'detested kite'. His anger towards his daughters by cursing her with disease imagery: 'infect her beauty'. He describes Goneril as 'an embossed carbuncle'. This image highlights her wickedness and also emphasises his own unstable character. This creates an edgy mood. Anything might happen.

The wild atmosphere on the heath is reflected in powerful images. The storm imagery is also used to convey Lear's madness: 'Blow, winds'. Lear even refers to the 'tempest' in his mind. This is a very good symbol of Lear's suffering as a result of 'filial ingratitude'. In contrast, the ending of the play is much calmer. Reunited with Cordelia, Lear's mind is filled with religious images. He speaks of 'sins', 'praying' and 'mercy'. He has now regained his sanity and so he calls his youngest daughter 'a soul in bliss'. She, in turn, asks for his 'hands in benediction'. This reconciliation scene is heightened by this gentle imagery.

Shakespeare has used a wide range of imagery in *King Lear*. This creates a variety of moods which increase the audience's engagement with the characters and tragic events in the play. *(370 words)*

Examiner's Comment

- Engages well with the question and the play.
- Sustained and focused top-grade response.
- Developed discussion and good supportive reference.
- Expression is clear and well controlled.
- Effective points on key imagery – nothingness, nature, etc.

Sample 70-mark Question

Q. 'An engaging aspect of texts is that authors rarely tell their stories in exactly the same way.'

Compare the extent to which this statement applies to each of the **three texts** that you have studied on your comparative course.

Prompt!

The purpose of the 70-mark question is to address the three key elements (question, comparison, mode):
- to explain the extent to which different stories in your chosen texts were/were not engaging (**question**)
- to show differences and similarities (**comparison**)
- evidence of understanding of literary genre (**mode**).

Indicative Material

- Impact of distinctive storylines and central characters.
- Particular settings and key moments are/are not engaging.
- Contrasting atmospheres/moods affect engagement.
- Language, imagery and symbolism increase/lessen interest.
- Special effects heighten/reduce involvement.
- Effect of narrative voice, dialogue, voiceovers, etc.

Sample Draft Plan

The following draft plan uses *King Lear* as one of the comparative texts.

INTRODUCTION

The three texts on my comparative course are written in different genres, but have some aspects in common. *King Lear* uses the traditional five-act structure of a Shakespearean tragedy. *The other texts use different structures …*

POINT 1

The play is set in pre-Christian Britain, a harsh and violent place. A corrupt court and windswept heath invite the audience into this tough world. But a tender reconciliation scene in Dover introduces a more compassionate mood. *However, in my second text …*

POINT 2

Rich imagery is used to reveal character in the play. Repeated references to 'nothing' create a sense of loss and hopelessness. Animal imagery exposes evil, 'Tigers', 'pelican daughters'. *In contrast, my third text relies on dialogue to reveal character …*

POINT 3

Shakespeare uses dramatic soliloquies to show the inner lives of both Edmund and Lear. *A similar effect is achieved by the use of flashback in my other comparative text …*

POINT 4

Irony is used to devastating effect in the play. Both Lear and Gloucester gain insight through madness and blindness. *There are ironic moments in all three texts…*

CONCLUDING PARAGRAPH

The final act of *King Lear* is dominated by torment, death and a desperate hope for a better future. *This contrasted with …*

***Sample Paragraph*: POINT 3**

Shakespeare's soliloquies are important in *King Lear*. They really engage us with the tragic characters. Edmund confides in us when he demands, 'Now, gods, stand up for bastards'. He is furious that because he is illegitimate, he will be disinherited by Gloucester. His opening soliloquy makes it clear that he will do anything to manipulate his family to achieve his ambitions: 'All with me is meet that I can fashion fit'. Lear's powerful monologue to Goneril and Regan also packs an emotional punch. Having divided his kingdom between them, the two evil sisters intend to strip Lear of the last traces of his kingship. Angrily he challenges them: 'O reason not the need! Our basest beggars/ Are in the poorest thing superfluous'. Lear believes that reducing individuals to their basic needs is to treat them like animals. He is learning valuable life lessons. *Soliloquies played no part in my second text … (150 words)*

Examiner's Comment

- Well-written top-grade standard, directly tackling the question.
- Focused and developed discussion of two soliloquies.
- Good use made of suitable reference and quotations.
- Language use throughout is impressive.

Class/Homework Exercise

Choose **one** of the other points in the sample draft plan and write a paragraph of your own in response to the question above. (Aim for 140 words.)

The **When Saturday Comes** *Special No.3*

Editor: Andy Lyons

Assistant Editor: Bill Brewster

Design And Layout: Doug Cheeseman and Lance Bellers

Production: Mike Brady, Philip Cornwall, Harry Pearson, Jamie Rainbow

Contributors: Rupert Bassett, Stuart Bell, Graham Brack, Tim Bradford, Cathy Cassell, David Cleary, Ron Counte, Andy Corsham, David Davies, Churston Deckle, Mick Dickinson, Angela Galvin, Mariam Goldman, Joe Hennon, Ed Horton, Les Huson, Michael Irwin, Andrew Jackson, Simon Knott, John McLaughlin, Colin McPherson, Tim Newburn, Chris Power, Huw Richards, Fred Sedgwick, Alasdair Shaw, David Smales, David Smith, Matthew Symonds, Geddes Thomson, Roger Titford, Phil Town, Paul Tully, David Wangerin, Mike Wareing, Olly Wicken, Fawzi Zuberi

Illustrators: Tim Bradford, Paul Burns, Paul Miller, Robert Nancollis, Dave Robinson, Simon Smith

Thanks To: David Abbott at Hulton, Steve Brown, Ian Caldwell, Colorsport, John Duncan, Tim Maddox and Paul Tarrington at Fastpoint, Simon Parry, Mark Vernon, Jon Westbrook

A QUEEN ANNE PRESS BOOK

First published in Great Britain in 1991 by Queen Anne Press, a division of Macdonald & Co (Publishers) Ltd
165 Great Dover Street
London SE1 4YA

A member of Maxwell Macmillan Publishing Corporation

A CIP catalogue for this book is available from the British Library

ISBN 0-356-20317-4

Typeset by Fastpoint

Printed and bound in Great Britain by BPCC Hazell Books Ltd, Aylesbury and Paulton

Picture Credits

Colorsport: Front Cover and top 9, bottom 18-19, 36-37, top 38, 49-51, bottom 56, top 57, top 60, bottom 61, top 69, 70, bottom 71, top 83, 90-91; Hulton Picture Library: 4, 26-27, bottom 28, 68-69; Allsport: 25, 49-51, top 71; Mrs Camus: 5; Hamish Hamilton: top 6; Jonathan Cape: bottom 6; Hills Welsh Press: top 8; South Wales Evening Post: bottom 9; Colin McPherson: 10-12; John McLoughlin: 16-17 top 18-19; Zefa Picture Library: top 25; BBC: top 28, 88-89; Hull City: bottom 38; Oxford United: bottom 38; Tim Reder: bottom 38; Inpho: 38-39; Eoin Murphy: 58-59; Tim Reder: bottom 60, top 61; Bucks and Herts Newspapers Ltd: 62; Philip Cornwall: 63; Derby Telegraph: 65; ESPN: bottom 66, top 67; NME: bottom 67; Alastair Berg: 72-74, 92-94; Oxford and County Newspaper Group: 76-77;Sue Cunningham: 82-83; Joe Paine: 84-86.

Illustrations

Tim Bradford: 47, 48, 61, 79, 80; Dave Robinson: 3, 8, 14-15, 33-34, 48, 51, 54, 64, 76, 78, 87, 90; Paul Burns: 30-31, 32, 81; Robert Nancollis: 13, 35. Paul Miller: 7, 13, 29; Rupert Bassett: 92-94.

The Publishers have been unable to contact all the copyright holders of photographs published in this book. As we have no wish to infringe copyright, could any unacknowledged copyright holders please contact us at Fourth Floor, No 2 Pear Tree Court, London EC1R 0DS.

...by one of Britain's best-loved family entertainers, Monty 'Mind Your Syntax' Sinton.

Rightie-ho, my old muckers! That was my immediate reaction when asked to pen an introduction to this, the third *When Saturday Comes* Special. Of course, I jumped at the chance, being a mad keen footer fan of long standing.

Only the other day, I was on the golf course with a few chums from the round ball fraternity. Take it from me, if England's Number One striker ever asks to borrow your sand wedge, think twice before handing it over! Honestly, you wouldn't think metal could bend like that, which reminds me of another story I can't repeat here because there might be kiddies present!

Anyway, we were having a good old chinwag, putting the world to rights, as you do, when the subject of fanzines cropped up. Although, what with business, charity and family matters, none of us had actually got around to reading any, we agreed that they were a good thing. (And take it from me, agreement is never easy to come by when your group includes a certain Scottish manager with strong views on the game South of the border - and I don't mean Mexico - and a former England captain whose trophy cabinet is full of severed limbs taken off members of the Auld Enemy!)

The lads (and lasses!) at *When Saturday Comes* have spent all the hours God sends fiddling about with a John Bull Printing Set, and the fruits of their labours are presented in this here volume. *Late Tackle* contains the sort of interesting, madcap and just plain wicked material I know I'm going to enjoy reading, just as soon as I get my cheque!

No, but seriously, it's high time I stopped rabbiting and let you get on with the rest of the book. Otherwise the shop assistant might ask if you want to buy it!

Be good! And if you can't be good, be careful!

Cheerio!

Monty!

Literary

Speaking

SIMON KNOTT & FRED SEDGWICK *have unearthed so many cultural references to football that they could almost write a book on the subject, which is quite ironic really...*

THE COMPOSER SHOSTAKOVICH WAS absent-minded. On 22nd June 1941, the day German troops poured over the border into the Soviet Union, he went along as usual to the Kirov Stadium to watch Zenit Leningrad play, and sat there half an hour before he noticed that nobody else had turned up. Then it occurred to him that the game had been cancelled because of the invasion.

Shostakovich was nuts about football. As a reward for toeing the party line in the early Thirties, he was offered a lifetime season ticket to the team that was then called Stalin Leningrad.

But Stalin Leningrad were crap, and by 1940 the Soviet leader (crap himself, God knows, in a more serious way) decided that he didn't much fancy having his name associated with such a disaster. The team took on the name Zenit and Stalin forgot about them, which is probably why Shostakovich didn't lose his season ticket when he fell out of Stalin's favour.

In happier times, Shostakovich wrote a ballet about football. The Golden Age (1930) follows a Soviet team sent to the West as part of a trade delegation. The composer himself spent some time on the Suffolk coast with his friend Benjamin Britten. There's no evidence, but it seems likely that Shostakovich found his way 12 miles down the road to the excitement of Ipswich Town's great championship-winning season.

Indeed, a cadence in the second movement of the Thirteenth Symphony bears an astonishing resemblance to the Churchman's cry *"Come on you Bluuu-uuues!"*

Perhaps he even took his friends with him. We like to think of them, standing together in Churchman's; Shostakovich, Britten, Pears - as Crawford cracked home those goals against Aston Villa, bringing the trophy to East Anglia. (That is definitely the first time those surnames have appeared in the same sentence.)

Britten, inspired perhaps by the intensity and passion of that Saturday afternoon in the cauldron of Portman Road, began work on his opera *The Bruning Fiery Furnace*. Shostakovich went home and wrote a symphony about death, but he always was a miserable bastard.

> *"Shostakovich is a lone figure in his profession: classical composers with a passion for football are rare."*

Shostakovich is a lone figure in his profession: classical composers with a passion for football are rare. And jazz and football conflict to the extent that the results are coming up on Saturday afternoon as Jazz Record Requests begins on Radio 3: a reason why one of us has more than one radio in the house.

And it isn't very different in other art forms. Football hasn't a rich literary heritage (*What* literary heritage? Rich *what* heritage? Rich literary *what*?). The only reference in the *Everyman Dictionary of Quotations and Proverbs* is to a 16th Century saying: *"All fellows at football"*. It means that on the playing field all are equal. Good, eh?

Most writers ignore the game. Albert Camus kept goal for his university team in Algiers, but he never wrote about football. Unless, of course, The Plague is about Leeds United's followers, and *The Outsider* a triple-punning title for a book about Chris Waddle's playing position, his employment abroad, and his inability to hold down an England place.

The Fall is, of course, about Birmingham City.

The most famous evocation of football is JB Priestley's celebration of Huddersfield Town in *The Good Companions* (1929). Bruddersford United play at Manchester Road, and 35,000 people see them draw 0-0 with Bolton Wanderers. Michael Parkinson is always quoting the bit where Priestley says that *"for a shilling, Bruddersford United FC offer you conflict and art,"* but Priestley wasn't really a fan, and the book looks patronising these days.

The writer for children Bob Wilson (no, not that one) has written a delightful piece in stage-Northern verse (rather *Albert and the Lion* in style) about Huddersgate Albion beating a team of southern smartarses called the Spurs. This is worth seeking out, though mention of the book in an article alongside Primo Levi (wait for it) is probably in dubious taste.

● ***Albert Camus and friends***

One of us will eventually read JL Carr's novel *How Steeple Sinderby Wanderers Won The FA Cup* - and then write a better article. But this won't be soon.

Perhaps the best description of football in literature was actually written by an American. In *The Old Patagonian Express*, author Paul Theroux visits the Stadium Nacional in San Salvador to see El Salvador lose 6-1 to Mexico. He captures the exotic flavour of the event; the passion, the danger, the rioting, the blown-up condoms. Theroux, in *The Kingdom By The Sea* (1983), manages a five page scene about skinheads causing trouble on a train - without mentioning football once - a good man.

The Italian writer, Primo Levi, was a Juventus fan, and in *The Truce* (1963), his account of a survivor's return from Auschwitz, he has a Greek character who makes friends with the Italian contingent by not only speaking Italian, but knowing what to talk about: *"Girls and spaghetti, Juventus and lyrical music...wine, the black-market and motor bikes..."* Sounds like a normal Saturday afternoon's conversation at the Clock End. Oh, and the survivors naturally celebrate their freedom with a game of football.

Jock MacLeish, the hero of Alisdair Gray's novel, *1982 Janine* (1984), admits that the only time in his life he ever cried was that glorious day in 1977 when Scotland's victory over Wales ensured their presence in the Argentina World Cup.

But MacLeish goes on to say that he's never been to a football match, and since he spends the entire book masturbating in a Greenock hotel room, it doesn't look as though he'll be making it to Cappielow Park that afternoon. Who's a wanker?

The longer the bookshelf you look along, the more you begin to think that writers have thrown away glorious opportunities. George Orwell could have had the dissident Winston Smith in *1984* torn by his love for Airstrip One United. John Fowles' French lieutenant's woman in the book of that name might have been a secret Exeter City fan, which would have given dramatic irony to the way she stares out to sea in despair on the end of Lyme Cobb. And Franz Kafka's K would have enjoyed the alienation of standing alone at Dukla Prague's Stadion Juliska.

So, novels nil. And often the mentions in poetry are depressingly, even alienatingly, inadvertent - as when George Szirtes writes:

"Like a girl listening behind
A membrane for a football..."

It's clear that the unfortunate poet has been done over by a duff proof-reader, probably a Wimbledon supporter, and that he meant to write 'footfall'.

Samuel Beckett appears in *Wisden*, though we've never looked the entry up. Anyway, the obits showed he preferred rugby.

The poet Vernon Scannel, on the other hand, was a boxer.

The one sustained reference to football in twentieth century poetry is in a ballad by Leslie Norris, which begins: *"Outside Bristol Rovers' football ground..."* This is Eastville, not Twerton Park. Norris goes on to tell the story of how he saw a blind man begging outside the ground. He writes the most footballish lines in English poetry when he says"

"...having travelled the roads to watch Portsmouth in the Cup.
The Third Round, I believe..."

Anyway, he recognises the blind man - Billy Rose, the boxer he saw blinded twenty years before:

"I threw some frantic money, three treacherous pence -
And I cry at the memory - into his tray, and ran,
Entering the waves of the stadium like a drowning man..."

This is a rare example of modern art that readily accepts the language of football without someone satirizing it.

The only poems we know that are explicitly about football are by Wendy Cope, and they are for children: *Roger Bear's Football Poems*:

"Three cheers for Spurs!
They beat Stoke!
Glad I'm a football fan.
Glad I'm a bloke."

Clearly a few seasons old. Spurs/Stoke? Three cheers? *Bloke*?

Ian Crighton Smith has a nice poem about schoolboy footy (*"My gold and and purple strip/ fresh from the wash"*) ➡

"Paul Theroux, in The Kingdom By The Sea (1983), manages a five page scene about skinheads causing trouble on a train - without mentioning football once - a good man."

"In Ulysses (1916), James Joyce chronicles the complete activities of two men in the city of Dublin on one day: June 16th, 1904; but completely ignores the fact that on the evening of that day Shamrock Rovers took Bohemians apart, 5-1."

and in the same genre Kit Wright has a poem about a team called the Rovers who *"my Dad"* always goes to see. But they always lose. In fact, they've never scored. *"And sure enough/ They always stuff/ The Rovers."* A poem for Watford and Sheffield United last season, and Halifax and Hartlepool any year...

One of us thought that Auden's line

"About suffering they were never wrong:"

was about him watching York City, his home team, but the other felt you couldn't build a lifestyle on such a notion. Similarly,

"Everyone suddenly burst out singing
And I was filled with such delight..."

isn't an away goal at Anfield?

Well, you get the idea.

Other reps of the great and good have been fond of the game. Philosopher AJ Ayer supported Spurs; the Archbishop of Canterbury is an Arsenal man; Roy Hattersley makes a fraction of his living writing about Sheffield Wednesday in *The Guardian.* Prime Minister John Major supports Chelsea (Yes, we know: Great? Good?). But football is a no-go area as far as poets and novelists are concerned.

One reason might be that football arose as a mass spectator sport at the same time as literature was rejecting realism and romanticism in favour of modernism. The trouble is that all the great realist novels of the nineteenth century were written in the decade or so before the League was a twinkle in William McGregor's eye.

Otherwise, Dickens would have been a regular on the terraces of the Priestfield Stadium (with perhaps a box at White Hart Lane to keep up appearances, and for when he wasn't home in Kent). Naturally, all his characters would have supported their local teams: David Copperfield would have had a long walk to Ipswich Town once a fortnight, but Millwall was convenient for Little Dorrit. Mr Pickwick would follow West Ham on their tour of the South-East, and Thomas Gradgrind would try and take over the board of Manchester United.

Bill Sykes still *plays* for Millwall.

Anthony Trollope would have been a director of Barchester United, of course.

Many twentieth century writers were simply in the wrong place at the wrong time. There wasn't an Oxford United for Thomas Hardy's Jude the Obscure to follow, although Hardy himself was no doubt a secret fan of Dorchester Town.

Others had the opportunity and ignored it: DH Lawrence, for example, who perhaps surprisingly never fell for the bold and outstanding manhood of Notts County. Kipling referred to *"muddied oafs,"* and Housman to goalkeepers - in a banal way: *"The goal stands up, the goalkeeper/ Stands up to keep the goal."'*

Arthur Conan Doyle's Baker Street Irregulars never caused trouble at Stamford Bridge.

It's the same in Europe. In *A La Recherche Du Temps Perdu,* Marcel Proust doesn't bite into a cold meat pie and instantly recall the great Paris St Germain team of thirty years before.

After a while, you begin to wonder if there isn't some sort of conspiracy going on. In *Ulysses* (1916), James Joyce chronicles the complete activities of two men in the city of Dublin on one day: June 16th, 1904.

Joyce told friends that the book had absolutely everything in it, and it would keep the critics busy for years. *"I want to give a picture of Dublin so complete that if the city suddenly disappeared from the earth it could be reconstructed out of my book,"* he said. Leaf through it, and yes, the book contains virtually everything in the universe, including sport: you'll find horse racing, swimming, boxing, even motor racing.

But no football!

Joyce completely ignores the fact that on the evening of that day Shamrock Rovers took Bohemians apart, 5-1.

Back to the drawing board, Jim.

HE BLUES ARE MOST AGREEABLE

The Owls are not what they seem

Presented with a rare chance to cheer their favourites at Wembley, Wednesdayites savoured the day, as ANGELA GALVIN *recounts.*

NAPOLEON BONAPARTE, FRENCH TEAM boss of yore, once said: *"An army marches on its stomach."* We take that sort of thing to heart in Sheffield. On April 21st, Atkinson's Barmy Army could have bounced down to Wembley. This is not a comment on Big Ron's girth - just an indication of the piles of sandwiches and sundries assembled in our house on the morning of the Big Day. There would be no rumbling bellies at the Rumbelows Cup Final.

Shortly after the whistle had blown to confirm the Owls' triumph over Chelsea in the semis, Global Village rumours started spreading around the Kop. Wednesday fans hadn't had cause to make the trip down Wembley Way for twenty-five years. None of us girls could help - we hadn't been to the sort of school that sends its young ladies to watch the women's hockey. As far as Wembley was concerned, we were in the dark and prey to the wildest gossip and suggestion:

"A mate of my mate went down there once. He started queuing for a meat pie before the kick-off and didn't get served till the penalty shootout..."

"Meat pie? Nay lad, my mate's uncle's mate says it's all prawn cocktails and caviar at twenty quid a shot, tha' knows..."

We were leaving nothing to chance. We saw the sun rise buttering piles of bread, filling vacuum flasks and shining apples. In a world of uncertainties, we knew we could at least out-eat the fans of Manchester United.

Having loaded up the hatchback, we squeezed ourselves in amongst the comestibles and set out on what was to become the Longest Day. An 8.30 start for a three-hour drive may seem a little excessive in hindsight, but you can't be a Wednesdayite if you don't have Doubt. We doubted we'd get to the Rumbelows Final, despite taking a 2-0 lead from Stamford Bridge to the Hillsborough leg of the semis. Comfortable? We were all too nervous to eat our teas that evening. Talk was of previous meetings where a 3-0 lead had been turned to defeat. Was that 1898 or 1985? Who knows. The fact was, it had happened. And having made it to the Final, we wondered when the next time would be. We were going to make the most of this one, just in case.

Under the 'Been there, done that 100 times before' gazes of United fans, we held a photo session down Wembley way and checked our tickets as we had done every hour since they'd arrived. The seat numbers were the same, but the kick-off time that had once seemed so distant was creeping up on us. There were more than a few members of the Barmy Army whose stomachs were not fit for marching.

Through the turnstiles and the air was buzzing with South Yorkshire tones, *"Ow much?"* The cry was taken up in succession as each new fan at the head of the queue was stung for a slice of pizza or a mini-bottlette of beer. I'm not a great drinker, but £2 seemed a small price to pay for a slug of lager to calm the nerves. Fifteen minutes to kick-off and Judi decides that Wedenesday's fortunes will be decided by her half-time consumption. She's got a bag-full of sandwiches, but they won't do. It's got to be a Mars Bar. *"It's always worked at Hillsborough,"* she declares. What's worse, we believe her. Should I die before my three score year and ten, I shall attribute it directly to the nervous tension and trauma caused by hunting down a confectionery stall in a jungle of pizza and burgers. Just as despair reared its ugly head, just as the weight of responsibility for an imminent defeat pressed upon us, we found one. Three Mars Bars for £1.50. It seemed like a bargain at the time.

We reach our seats in time to hear the military band - or at least to catch a few notes each time they passed by a microphone. Then two sets of Subbuteo figures are presented to someone in turquoise. David Icke? No, it's Tracey Bateman, Rumbelows' Employee Of The Year. Jimmy 'In My Day That Would've been A Goal' Greaves thinks the lads would rather have met royalty. He doesn't know Sheffield.

The match? The Man In Front (who thought Judi's knee was a hand-rest) gave me a Chinese burn when Sheri scored; Cathy kissed the Man Behind; I ate a Mars Bar at half-time and my fingernails in the last fifteen minutes. And we won. Nothing has ever sounded so sweet to my ears as that final whistle. I dried my eyes on the nearest banner and felt the first pangs of hunger.

Seven hours later we were still on the M1, still singing and still eating peanut butter sandwiches. They call it the Wednesday Diet. They called us Atkinson's Burly Gurlies.

The Rivals No.1

HUW RICHARDS *has seen an indecently large number of Cardiff-Swansea matches over the years, but his enthusiasm for the fixture remains undimmed...*

LAST BOXING DAY, WE GOT UP LATE, drove the fifty or so miles to Stoke after lunch and watched a decent game in pleasant surroundings, perfectly climaxed when a bizarre aberration by their 'keeper allowed Jimmy Gilligan to slam home a last minute penalty for a well-deserved 2-2 draw.

But there was something missing. Boxing Day isn't supposed to be like that. Not if you're a Swansea supporter living in the Midlands. What you expect to do is get up at an obscene time in the morning, drive 120 miles, park your car in unreclaimed swamps, enter *Stalag Luft* Ninian in time for the kick-off set by the local *Geheime Staatspolizei* and watch a match that goes a long way to explaining the enduring popularity of Rugby Union in South Wales.

This will probably be goalless until the final minute. Then a characteristically ill-directed Cardiff cross, taking what the *Western Mail* will inevitably term a wicked deflection - has anyone ever seen a morally equivocal deflection? - is bundled past your suddenly stone-clad defence and 'keeper by a previously laughably inept opposition striker. Suitably uplifted, you go home.

As everybody except TV schedulers knows, League derby matches are among the activities that should only take place in private before audiences of consenting adults. Cup ties are a bit different. But imagine the ghastliness of most televised North London and Merseyside set-tos with considerably less talented players and you've some idea of the product offered by Swansea and Cardiff over the past decade or so.

These cultural exchanges are also characterised by the mutual affection and respect displayed by rival fans. Among the enduring favourites in the North Bank Male Voice Choir's repertoire is a version of 'Hark The Herald Angels' relating to the alleged flight of Cardiff fans on New Year's Day. New Year's Day 1980, that is.

> **“League derby matches should only take place in private before audiences of consenting adults.”**

Growing up in the Midlands, far from the centre of the action, failed to make me immune to West Walian attitudes to Cardiff. In my family, supporting the Swans is a genetic disorder passed down the male line, carrying with it the full weight of disdain for our so-called capital city and associated sporting organisations.

Hence my delight when travel writer Ian Nairn called Cardiff *"an unexplained malfunction between Swansea and Newport"* and unequalled hilarity when an American contributor to the *Book of Lists* rated it among the world's top twelve places to avoid - listed between Calcutta and Cartagena. The only thing that spoiled winning promotion to the First Division was that beating Preston kept Cardiff up.

So it was a little bit of a culture shock to arrive there as a student in 1981 and find that it was quite a tolerable place to live in. Not that this altered attitudes to Cardiff City.

Anyone with pictures of the crowd at Ninian Park the day they were relegated following defeat by Luton Town can identify me easily - the one grinning like a loon amidst a sea of desolation.

The fans and manager had spent much of the year moaning about the supposed deficiencies of Dave Bennett, acquired from Manchester City. The real reason for this was that the other ten were crap and the highly-talented Bennett was understandably discouraged.

This rather defined the style for the 1980s. Cardiff always had one or two decent players but they were either ex-Swansea (Alan Curtis), passing through in rather a hurry (Kevin Bartlett, Jimmy Gilligan and what odds on Nathan Blake staying?) or just so much like garden gnomes in appearance that they were hard to take seriously (Nigel Vaughan).

They were epitomised by Phil Dwyer. Phil, a centre-half generally termed 'uncompromising', had been the centre of one of Welsh football's better jokes in the late 1970s when, presumably to win a bet, a satirically inclined manager chose him at centre-forward for Wales. The joke worked rather well - he 'put himself about a bit', jumped all over opposing stoppers, and actually scored a couple of goals.

By this time he had returned to his rightful place in the defence. A sort of thinking man's Neanderthal, he gave the vague impression that he had only just learnt to walk upright and had a frequently devastating effect on opponents' attempts to do the same. Yer actual ball-playing centre-half he wasn't, but unless confronted by one of the few ball-playing centre-forwards knocking about the lower divisions, his determination and ability to intimidate by aspect alone were equally effective.

Successors weren't quite in his class.

But for most of the 1980s, Cardiff provided a brilliantly funny parody of the British game as seen by censorious Continentals - unsophisticated and crude, but hard-running and committed.

The problem for Swansea was that this made them rather tricky opponents. The one thing Cardiff never lacked was sheer guts. Swansea normally have rather more going for them in the way of footballing sophistication, but were often, how shall I put it, rather delicate. This made them vulnerable to the ruffians up the road, who aided their cause with fiendish ingenuity, sending Swansea their direst players as saboteurs - *something* has to explain the signing of Paul Maddy and Roger Gibbins. Now the cunning swine are sending us their managers as well.

As the two declined together throughout the 1980s, derbies took on a regular pattern. Boxing Day was spent shivering in Ninian Park, Easter Monday in the rain at Vetch Field. Nobody won away and the series always ended level over two games. When they reversed the pattern in 1989-90, the teams were so confused that Cardiff won at the Vetch on Boxing Day, only for the Swans to take decisive revenge on Easter Monday. A Cardiff double would have relegated us rather than them.

But if results were pretty predictable, most matches had their share of bizarre events. There was John Toshack's solo goal at Cardiff on Boxing Day 1983 - running from halfway with the speed of a stampeding listed building. There were Dean Saunders' two goals four months later and Joe Allon's sending off in 1987 - both reminders of Swansea's impeccable judgment in spotting no-hoper strikers and giving them free transfers to lifelong obscurity. Saunders' two goals followed a half-time reshuffle that reincarnated sweeper Dudley Lewis as a devastatingly effective winger - a talent never displayed before or since.

In Second Division days, Cardiff specialised in the unexpectedly dangerous free-kick. John Lewis distinguished the New Year's Day 1980 game by a floater of such ineptitude that we were still laughing as it drifted past Glan Letheran, apparently bewitched by the admittedly nasty spectacle of Ronnie Moore seen suddenly from close range, into the left hand corner of the Swansea goal.

Twelve months later, John Buchanan was the villain, anticipating Gazza's Semi-Final efforts by a decade with a thirty-five yarder that completed a sixty-second fightback from 3-1 to 3-3. That Cardiff recovery had been made possible by an underhit back pass from centre-half Nigel 'Speedy' Stevenson, whose infamy was completed eight years and a free transfer later when he played the game of his life at the centre of the Cardiff defence to force a 1-1 draw at the Vetch after Terry Boyle had been sent off. A further mystery was the continuous effectiveness in derby games of Nicky Platnauer, a Cardiff player of no visible attributes save an extremely low centre of gravity.

But the real classic was Boxing Day 1985. It was very cold, and Ninian Park, never the same since they took the roof off the Grangetown End, was looking its vilest. My girlfriend, who didn't much like football and had been been persuaded to come on the reasonable premise that she wouldn't see any, was being introduced to the unique qualities of the South Wales derby. Two very bad Third Division teams, both destined for relegation, produced the sort of game that makes a point each seem ludicrous over-reward. And Cardiff won with a last-minute goal.

Yet this was only a week after the Swans had gone briefly out of existence. Collecting buckets were out and the names of those willing to help the club financially or otherwise were being taken. I added my name to the list (the last I heard of this appeal) and was surprised and touched to see people who were clearly Cardiff supporters doing the same.

● ***Left:* A Real Sociedad manager in the making. *Above:* Nigel 'Speedie' Stevenson. *Bottom:* The end product of a famous Toshack trundle.**

Last season I laughed when Cardiff were ejected from the FA Cup by Hayes, was delighted when Merthyr humiliated them in the Welsh Cup. Their inability to win a play-off place and challenge our status as the least dreadful team in Wales was one of the few bright spots of the season. But I was horrified at the possibility of their going out of business. I admit my name isn't on any list - there hasn't been a derby game for one thing, nor has Tony Clemo rung up to seek access to either my advice or my overdraft. But if asked, I'd happily fork out a few quid, as those Cardiff fans were willing to do six years ago.

Perverse? Hardly. The continued existence (and existence is as high as you hope after twenty-odd years supporting Swansea) of your own team is the most important thing to any fan. But almost as important to psychological well-being is a readily identifiable object of fear and loathing.

While you've been going to matches for the sheer pleasure of it, COLIN MCPHERSON *has been exploring the lower levels of Senior football in Scotland...*

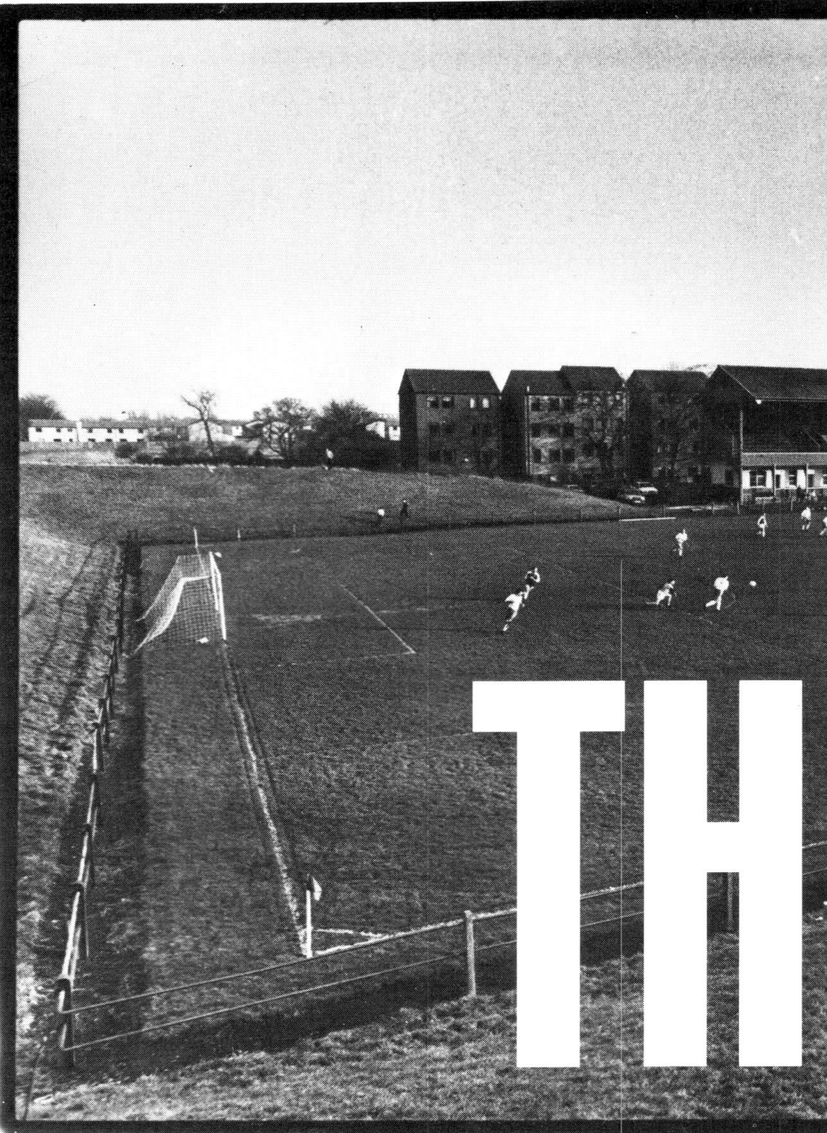

The particular ambiguity which exists in the set-up of Scottish football is nowhere better illustrated than in the little-publicised, closeted world of the East of Scotland League.

In status it is known as 'Senior', distinctly different and totally separate from the savage world of Junior football which thrives in nearly every region of mainland Scotland. Senior football exists only in the form of the Scottish League, and three regional competitions: the East of Scotland League; its weaker neighbour, the South of Scotland League; and the much-touted (not by me) Highland League. Were a system of promotion to the Scottish League ever devised, it's safe to assume that the clubs would be elevated from one of these august organisations.

Along with such illustrious individual clubs as Babcock & Wilcox and Burntisland Shipyard, it was the Seniors which stayed loyal to the SFA during the traumatic pre- and post-War ructions which split Scottish football into Junior and Senior camps and led to the present structure.

Born out of the primordial soup of the 1940s reconstruction, the EoSL originally catered for teams from the rugby-dominated Borders, recreational teams from various factories, offices and educational institutions in Edinburgh and a hotchpotch of reserve and third teams of Scottish League clubs from as far north as Tayside.

There have been plenty of comings and goings since those fledgling days. Gone are the wretched second strings and third XIs, while many of the recreational sides, aware during the 60s and 70s that the league was rapidly filling up with pot-hunters, streamlined their clubs. Some are now even renamed and have oriented themselves towards a more organised and - whisper it in a world where the only payment is expenses - 'professional' approach.

Many of the original Borders teams have since perished: football is monochrome without the likes of Chirnside United and Duns. Both these clubs even tasted the ultimate glory in their time - participation in the 'proper' rounds of the Scottish Cup.

Entry into the national competition is certainly the greatest carrot waved in front of many a donkey which plods aimlessly - but honestly - around the arid tundra wastelands of the EoSL. Although a club's ground has to be deemed fit (i.e. enclosed) to gain access to the Qualifying Cup (South) - the four semi-finalists then proceed to a potential glamour tie with the more powerful Highland participants or the sides at the rump of the Scottish Second Division - many EoSL grounds are little more than public parks with a rope flung around the playing surface. If you're ever in the vicinity of Home Park, Coldstream, witness the pandemonium caused by a few hundred slithering spectators clomping about ankle-deep in the *glaur,* while the players strive to play total football on a patch of ground about as smooth as the face of the moon.

The club names surely make this league one of the best-sounding collections this side of Burkina Faso.

one of the best-sounding collections this side of Burkina Faso). Their ground, Netherdale, is perched next to the dominant rugby club, but this hasn't prevented a programme of growth on top of an already strong base. A trim, recently upgraded stadium, which boasts Scotland's first cantilever stand, adds credence to a good record of achievement on the field.

Former player and manager Jim Jefferies is the glowing testament to the club at present. He is currently managing Falkirk with considerable aplomb after an eventful spell as boss at Berwick and Gala. While at Berwick there was talk of the Shielfield club moving its 'franchise' to Galashiels and introducing Scottish League football to the town. The plan fell through, but it was indicative of a new spirit within the game that such an idea was mooted at all. Jefferies was the local boy made good, having signed for Hearts from the Maroons in 1969 at the beginning of a fifteen-year career as a redoubtable defender.

He is, sadly, one of only a handful of players who initiated professional careers with EoSL clubs and went on to higher and better things. Another is Colin Campbell, now a sports shop proprietor but a one time cup-finalist with Hibs. Still remembered for a rather unfortunate miss in the initial drawn match, he nevertheless toils away with considerable guile and tenacity for Spartans, the team formed for ex-students of Edinburgh University. He emerged from a clutch of promising players who turned out for Edinburgh University in the late 1970s, and went some way to silencing the critics who argued that the inclusion of the University (and the perpetual losers from Heriot-Watt University) had demeaned the status of the EoSL to that of a fox hunt in which the fox is also blindfolded. Campbell is also thought to be the

be the last time

For all that, however, there are clubs with fine facilities, and although crowds for the average Tennents League match often fail to scrape into double, never mind treble, figures (and all this on the back of free admission), there are rumours of possible structural changes to the Scottish League to allow expansion into the uncharted territories to the North and in the relatively prosperous Borders. This has encouraged some clubs to expand and think bigger.

This ambition was aided in the mid-1980s when the EoSL was sub-divided into two compact divisions. New blood was introduced to make up the numbers, allowing the premier division standard to ascend rapidly.

The most progressive club is undoubtedly Gala Fairydean (the club names surely make this league only player in the history of the league to come from Benbecula in the Western Isles.

Quite what the catalyst for change and reshuffling was is difficult to say. Many point to the shock admission to the Scottish League of Edinburgh works side Ferranti Thistle in 1974. With the great reconstruction of the Scottish League into three divisions about to take place, it was suddenly realised that they were one club light. To the frothing chagrin of the vastly superior Highland League sides, the thirty-seven members voted in a team with a rented ground, an unconstitutional

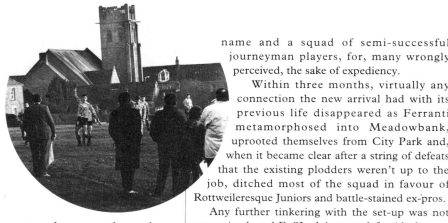

Thistle be the last time

> *At Whitestone Park you'll find one of the great characters, sporting garish tartan trousers, one of those hideous quilted rally jackets, a loud hat and an even louder ghettoblaster.*

name and a squad of semi-successful journeyman players, for, many wrongly perceived, the sake of expediency.

Within three months, virtually any connection the new arrival had with its previous life disappeared as Ferranti metamorphosed into Meadowbank, uprooted themselves from City Park and, when it became clear after a string of defeats that the existing plodders weren't up to the job, ditched most of the squad in favour of Rottweileresque Juniors and battle-stained ex-pros.

Any further tinkering with the set-up was not entertained, and EoSL clubs were left with the cup in which to make an impression.

Hitherto, the greatest moment of unparalleled effulgence came fully thirty years ago when, amidst much hauling and trawling, Eyemouth United made it to the quarter-finals of the cup. This isolated event was made even more remarkable in that 2900 fans packed the, er... slopey slopes of Gunsgreen Park, perched on the North Sea, to watch the Fishermen lose very narrowly to mighty Kilmarnock, at the time a giant of the Scottish game.

Despite other intermittent minor hiccups, most notably Vale of Leithen's superlative 4-1 demolition of Forfar in 1977, Scottish League teams usually view ties against East teams as a passport to progress without the unnecessary histrionics that occur in the English Cup. In fact, some teams even take time to rewrite their history books while beating East teams. Who would have thought, when Peebles Rovers scored against Hibs in 1960, that the scoreline would remain famous to this day? Well, they did concede fifteen, didn't they? And you have to admire Montrose's sense of symmetry while disposing of Vale of Leithen in 1975. Six in each half - a nice round dozen!

But pride of place went to Selkirk, who in 1985 managed to lose 20-0 (or [TWENTY] as they say in Teleprinterspeak) to Stirling Albion.

But to dwell on such one-offs would be to insult the current generation of players. Despite having to compete in an hermetically sealed environment where the genuinely ambitious seldom have the chance to compete at a higher level, they have still raised the profile and standard of the league almost beyond recognition.

One such opportunity comes in the yearly squabble for the East of Scotland, or City, Cup. An historic competition dating back to the last century, Berwick and Meadowbank compete against the finalists of the Qualifying Cup (East) for the dubious right to call themselves top dogs in the East. In the true spirit of friendly rivalry, Meadowbank regularly allow themselves to be humiliated by such soccer luminaries as Postal United (now less embarrassingly called Edinburgh City), Gala Fairydean, or, if all else fails and they reach the final, by Berwick Reserves, who are still members of the EoSL.

Indubitably the most successful team in terms of championships and cups over the last decade has been Whitehill Welfare, situated in an economic slough of despond just South of Edinburgh in an area more commonly associated with coal-mining and the Junior game. Formerly a juvenile team, the Rosewell side stepped up in 1977, and have since collected several notable scalps in the 'Scottish', including a thrilling victory over Albion Rovers and a draw at Stenhousemuir (never an easy feat in these uncertain times).

The league allows the casual spectator the chance to rediscover many of the long-lost joys of football, often against a backdrop of rolling hills and pleasant green scenery rather than drab housing schemes or grimy factories. And where the mad braying of Borders rugby types can also be kept at a safe distance. Places such as Kelso United, Annan Athletic and Hawick Royal Albert. There are no ugly offside traps at Kelso United, Annan Athletic or Hawick Royal Albert, and no centre-field punch-ups and baying fans ready for mindless assault.

Behind every slickly operated club apparatus, there is a phalanx of industrious committee men busy oiling the machinery. At Whitestone Park, Peebles, you'll find one of the great characters, usually sporting garish tartan trousers, one of those hideous quilted rally jackets, a loud hat and an even louder ghettoblaster, while actively bellowing *"Come on Rovers!"*

This is Maurice Gordon, self-made man with a heart of gold, who, it is claimed, lives off the profits from his stocks and shares. At one game I overheard Mo and a fellow-sufferer talking: *"I saw you speeding off to the Craigroyston game on Tuesday. A toute vitesse!"*

"No, no," came Mo's reply, *"It's a Mini Metro."* Legends are made thus.

If there is a bright future for the EoSL, it must lie in the belief that the Scottish League's closed shop is about to change under the increasing pressure from ambitious Highland clubs. Whether, say, Galashiels could support a team in the main body of the Kirk is, of course, debatable. Then again, East Stirlingshire have managed for God knows how long with thirty supporters. With the steady increase in sponsorship for clubs, the EoSL is in a comparatively healthy state, but progress in this country is always notoriously slow, so don't hold your breath in imminent expectation of Scottish League fixtures at Victoria Park, Innerleithen, or the like.

The EoSL may be an alien environment to most, but I cannot resist the charms of Kelso's rustic Springfield Park, Whitehill's Bovril served in a tea mug for 35p (including pie and free refills) and, if the 1934-35 League Handbook is to be believed, the fact that *"Each President shall on retiring be furnished with a Gold Badge and a Life-Member's Ticket, entitling him to admission to all Matches played by Clubs affiliated to this Association."* Me first!

This year, for sure, I'm going to a football match.....,

An Away Fan Writes

David Smales *hasn't been to a football match for over twenty years, a period of exile which may be about to end, as he explains...*

This year, for sure, I'm going to a football match. That might not seem like much of a statement to you, but if you hadn't been to a game in twenty-five years, you might be entitled to be excited too.

The last professional game I took in was Spurs *v* Arsenal in either 1964 or '65, followed by a few Enfield matches, before I left for Canada in October 1966.

For the first few years it was almost impossible to keep up with events in English football. There were a couple of shops that sold newspapers from around the world, but in 1970 would you have paid 50p for *The News Of The World*? There is also a radio show called *Calling All Britons* which gives the scores every Saturday evening, but without any background information they could be of no more than fleeting interest.

Quite often one of the local TV stations would carry the FA Cup Final. I once watched it with commentary in Spanish. I still don't know who won.

One year I dropped in on a friend who was watching a football match. He told me it was the FA Cup Final between Wimbledon and Liverpool. Of course, I was able to tell him that he was watching the *Amateur* Cup Final because, though Wimbledon had a useful non-paid team, the idea of them being in the full Cup Final was ridiculous. Obviously they were playing South Liverpool who must also have a good team. I certainly put him right. I know my football... don't I?

In Canada the major sports are ice hockey, American rules football, slightly amended, and baseball. I got caught up with all three. Contrary to popular belief outside Canada, ice hockey is not necessarily a sport for hulking backwoodsmen with a latent desire to commit mass murder. It does have craftsmen and artistes to compare with Rush, Lineker or Maradona. There are fewer and fewer of them, however, and I became increasingly disenchanted with the game. It didn't help that our local team, the Toronto Maple Leafs, are perennial losers and can't make the play-offs even when sixteen out of twenty-one teams are involved.

Baseball continues to excite the masses, and me, with the Toronto Blue Jays being one of the best. Most games are a sell-out well in advance, remarkable when you consider that the Skydome stadium has a capacity of 50,000 and that the Blue Jays play about eighty home games.

> **"Last time I went to White Hart Lane, it cost me 3s 6d. With inflation, will £1 11s and 3d get me a good seat?"**

With baseball now the only sport to interest me, I was stuck for something to do in the Winter. (Ski-ing was interesting until I arrived at some trees before I had expected to and they didn't forgive me.) Salvation came by way of the twenty-four-hour Sports Network with three hours of soccer per week hosted by the one-time Football League player, Graham Leggatt. At 10 am every Saturday morning I watch an English First Division game live. Slotted around this are highlights of the previous week's matches plus in-depth analysis of what's happening on the English soccer scene. The sports pages of the newspapers now also have more coverage, so I'm almost an expert. Almost. Before I go to my first game, I need the answers to a few questions:

1. Last time I went to White Hart Lane, it cost me 3s 6d. With inflation, will £1 11s and 3d get me a good seat?
2. Which cup is which? I assume the DAF Cup is what used to be the Welsh Cup but what is a Rumbelows? What are full members full of?
3. Where can I purchase tickets and replica kits for the Thames Valley Royals?
4. Most problematic of all for someone out of soccer for so long is the membership system. Will I be allowed in the home enclosure at Tottenham? Will my wife, who is Canadian, be allowed in? Are my children, born in Canada but by virtue of their parentage entitled to British passports, to be allowed into the home enclosure or will they be dragged away from us by official 'supporter sorters'? I've always wanted to watch my Dad's old team, Hull City, at Boothferry Park. What status would I have there? Would they even let me in? My maternal grandfather was a Leeds United fan. See the problem? You would if you were following soccer from across an ocean.

Maybe I'll take in a brass band contest instead or stay in my hotel and watch *Coronation Street*. Do something that won't be different from 1966. I know. I'll go to a cricket match. Have England beaten Australia since 1966? Who owns The Dust or whatever it's called? That's it. Five days of cricket and I'll be glad to go home. My wife will never forgive me for not going to Florida.

PUA ASKA AP MUSTIKKI S

A keen fan from a remote part of Europe recounts the main events of his nation's football history. Translation by HARRY PEARSON.

Potya

MY COUNTRY IS THE PEOPLE'S DEMOCRATIC Republic of Potya. Do not be ashamed if you have not heard of it. Few people have. Potya is the most ignored country in Europe. This has been true throughout history. The Vikings rowed down Potya's rivers but never paused to pillage or plunder. Mongol hordes galloped across our plains without bothering to stop. The Ottomans took one look at our capital, Loruta, and pushed on to Vienna.

In 1884, Potya's insignificance was officially acknowledged. Or rather it wasn't. The Italian cartographer, Arturo Bellini, compiler of the definitive European Atlas, missed Potya out altogether. Confused by sketchy and contradictory reports of my country's existence and whereabouts, he distributed it evenly between its neighbours. Naturally enough, he got it wrong. Hungary is not one of our neighbours. The portion of Potya he awarded to Budapest was actually part of Croatia. A mistake that led, indirectly, to the Great War (the fact that the First World War was fought because the rest of Europe misplaced Potya is an irony not lost on my fellow countrymen).

The League of Nations, unaware of our existence, did not ask us to join. In 1940, the Germans occupied us but did not realise it. Four years later, the Russians liberated us without noticing. Finally, in the 1950s, an attempt was made to welcome Potya into the international fold. Tito invited us to join the Non-Aligned Movement. The head of Potya's government, Doktori Beeka, pointed out that there was something paradoxical about a group of non-aligned nations, and the offer was rejected. Nowadays, the only sign most of you ever see of Potya's existence is those little bottles of bilberries you come across in corner shops, when it's a rainy Sunday evening and you're looking for a light-bulb and a jar of horseradish sauce. But we are here, I assure you!

History records that soccer was introduced into our country by British sailors. But Potya has no coast! Ask a Potyani how British sailors came to be in our landlocked country, and he will shrug his shoulders and say, *"Pua aska ap mustikki succik?"* (*"Why is the bilberry sweet?"*) Attempt a rudimentary outline of photosynthesis, and after a few seconds he will yawn and turn away. Explanation is alien to most Potyanis. We are essentially a fatalistic people.

During the turn-of-the-century Balkan conflicts, Potya was visited by many British war correspondents. They instilled in Potyanis the belief that, *"It matters not who won or lost, but how you played the game."* In recent times, this has been refined by the apparatus of Potya's ruling Communist Party to produce a league (Potyani Footbaallki Laddi) which is unique throughout the world. There are no champions! At the end of each season, every team is presented with a trophy, all the players with winners' medals. In Potya we have no elitism!

Professori Yako Pitka, head of PIF (Potyani Instituti ak Footballki), explains the philosophy behind our system in typically Potyani fashion. *"It takes two teams to make a game of football,"* he says, and quotes Colonel Sappi, retired manager of Ihana 1934 Loruta and one of the most influential figures in the Potyani game: *"Ta ap Footballki Laddi, ap testi aska ap solda trumpita."* (*"In the Potyani Football League, the game is the only winner."*) When foreign visitors point out to Professori Pitka that the rest of the world functions with quite a different system, he smiles sadly before delivering an old Potyani proverb: *"Some men grow sweet bilberries, then pickle them!"*

IN 1911, MY ALREADY FOOTBALL-CRAZY country won its independence from the Turks (the Turks, naturally, did not know that they had colonised us!). The new nation decided to appoint a king. By a unanimous decision, the Potyani National Assembly voted in favour of offering the throne to the Sheffield United 'keeper, WJ 'Fatty' Foulke. Foulke gladly accepted. Unfortunately, when he sat on the throne it collapsed. A man of great sensitivity, Foulke was mortified with embarrassment and returned to England without delay. His letter about 'The Coronation Incident' hangs proudly in PIF headquarters. It reads:

Dear All,
Sorry about the business with the chair. I felt a right charlie.
Yours faithfully,
Foulke (Fatty).

This was accepted by my forebears as a letter of abdication, and the reconstructed throne was passed on to Vlafti Smirka, a popular lyric poet whose verse elegy *"Ha succik, Ha succik, Da matki klabatko"* (*"How sweet, How sweet, My mother's bilberry dumplings"*) was adopted as the lyrics of our national anthem.

Tactically, football here in Potya is very naive. A lack of outside influence has allowed our game to develop in its own peculiar fashion. In one of our few international matches, versus Estonia in 1937, the effects of our insularity were all too apparent. Writing of that contest in *Universal Footie*, Ernst Banter observed: *"The Potyanis, in their bilberry-blue shirts, seemed to have no strategy at all. Their only tactical ploy was to allow each individual the opportunity to perform his own particular party piece seemingly ad nauseam. In the case of Akhnai Sprit, this involved a rather mediocre display of ball juggling; goalkeeper Bordo Tippi, on the other hand, contented himself by making repeated belly-flops into a pool of water which had gathered near the penalty spot. These dives bore no relation to any attempts to make a save, indeed they seemed to increase in frequency when the ball went out of play."*

We lost 11-0.

Our national team's only triumph came when we beat Montenegro 2-0 in May 1914. Just as we prepared to make our mark on the world game with a team containing such household names as Glubb Notko, Haka Flug and Nippi Tirpitz, the Great War began. If you mention this to a Potyani soccer fan, he will grin before giving vent to the popular sentiment: *"You always find the juiciest bilberries when you're wearing your best white shirt!"*

Going to a match in Potya is quite an experience. Our supporters do not display their colours on banners or scarves, but on specially painted clogs. To register our appreciation for a good move, or agile save, we jump up and down in unison to produce a rhythmic clacking sound.

Foreign fans are always welcomed enthusiastically, usually with cries of *"Sik bika sa batti metallica noppla?"* (*"Do you wish to exchange metal badges?"*) Even overseas visitors who are reluctant at first change their minds when they see the impressive array of badges their Potyani companions have to offer! The badge of Tervey-Valmista-Ceramica Bikachuk (Ceramic Sanitaryware Workers Bikachuk), for example, portrays an attractive range of bilberry-coloured bathroom furnishings. I do not wish to sound nationalistic, but which top British club can boast such a badge?

The real hotbed of soccer in Potya is the northern city of Bobka. Bobka's two teams, Mustikki-Pullo (Bilberry Bottlers) and Mustikki-Salyketto (Bilberry Canners), have a fierce rivalry that is legendary throughout Potya. The clash between 'Ap Nokki-Pulla' ('The Blue Bottles') and 'Ap Tubi' ('The Tins') is very much our equivalent of the Old Firm game. At one time, the match used to spill over into violence, with gangs of rival fans pelting one another with their own bilberry-related product. Happily, the situation has calmed in recent years, due to escalating food prices and the true supporters' cooperation with the Internal Security Service (GUB). This alliance has lead football fans in other parts of Potya to taunt Bobkanis with the chant, *"Vik solda sotti kan vik'ku la pa trotti!"* (*"You only sing when you're with a policeman!"*)

Up until a few months ago, the biggest football star in Potya was Haka Haasu. Perhaps you have heard of him in another way? Because Haka is known to film fans the world over. He appeared as Nightshift Foreman Gluggi in Brob Mikano's movie *At The Jam Factory* and won a coveted Bauxite Spanner at the Novograd Cinefest. Recently, Haka has been replaced as the fans' favourite by Potya's first foreign import, Svenbo Larsen of Mustikki-Processio Tottia. Tottia used their trade links with Greenland to lure Svenbo here from HGV40. The big man is something of a playboy by Potyani standards, and his unusual lifestyle has earnt him a cult following amongst the nation's youth. A recent record about Larsen by 'New Wave' group Ap Tuppa Mustikka ('The Sexy Biberries') contained the memorable lyric *"Svenbo, Svenbo toit mikimok lappika/ Al dak al su a tuni sak mustikka/ Lutti, lutti Svenbo/ Cossu pa luttoten guy!"* (*"Svenbo, Svenbo always eating fishes/ He says he likes them more than bilberries/ Crazy, crazy Svenbo/ What a madcap guy!"*)

The arrival of Svenbo Larsen is the first sign that football in my country is about to come in from the cold. Fans here welcome this step. We long for a time when our national team, Ap Mustikki-Camissa, can test themselves against the best the world has to offer. But the end of isolation will bring changes too. Changes to the unique phenomenon that is Potyani Footballki. If you wish to see our game in its raw and undiluted state, you must come now. For as we Potyanis are fond of saying, *"Ap mustikki feci nyuk'i lassu ip ap shrubhi paposta!"* (*"The ripe bilberry does not remain on the bush forever!"*)

You are welcome!

Vik Solda Sotti Ka Vik'ku La pa trotti!

UCCIK?

T*ONY MADRID LOOKS LIKE ALL WINGERS SHOULD. HE is 5' 1" tall. He has the bandy legs of a Garrincha. And he has the tough, watchful glare of one hoping you will mistake his size for weakness so he can dribble you onto the over-confident seat of your pants.

In the Summer, Tony spends most evenings at a large fenced-in playground on Manhattan's East Side, watching the pick-up basketball games and the amateur softball teams from a park bench. Every so often, someone will show up with a soccer ball, and Tony will spring to his feet and join in. At fifty-one, he can still put the ball on your head from the left wing nineteen times out of twenty.

In his teens in his native Spain, Tony played for the Barcelona youth team. He says he soon realised he would never make it as a pro. The opposing defenders were bigger and harder with each passing year, and craftier at kicking him out of a game without alerting the referee. But he saw Di Stefano and Puskas, Kocsis and Gento up close. And he once shook hands with Kubala. Thirty years after he emigrated to America, he still talks about it.

New York is full of Tony Madrids, football aficionados who grow up with the game in their native lands and hold fast to their passion in their adopted home. The pattern is generally the same. Poor immigrants arrive and trace their compatriots to one of the city's less salubrious areas. There football, with religion and language, remains among the most potent forces in keeping the community together and preserving links with the mother country.

But it is only as strong as the forces that impelled the immigration in the first place. As immigration ebbs, and the first arrivals claw their way up the economic ladder and out of the ghetto, the community disintegrates. The next generation grows up eager to escape its past, and more American than any.

That means embracing American sports. It is no accident that baseball and American football are marketed *ad nauseam* as symbols and vital elements of the 'American Way of Life', witness the hymn to American military might that was last year's Super Bowl. Meanwhile, soccer in New York City stays marooned in its ethnic fastness, largely ignored, covered with a blend of condescension and bewilderment that dooms it just as surely to the status of a minority sport.

You would never know from reading the city's major dailies that soccer is, with softball, New York's biggest organised participation sport. Nor would you know that the leading Hispanic soccer association includes

"Football, with religion and language, remains among the most potent forces in keeping the community together."

The Brooklyn Italians are not even household names in their own houses, never mind the rest of the US. JOHN McLAUGHLIN *investigates the semi-professional football scene in New York...*

Manh

sixteen separate leagues and has close to 10,000 players. Ironically, the ethnic character of the game in New York may be its greatest strength, but it is also its greatest dilemma.

Immigration comes in waves. Of the 18.6 million immigrants into the US in the first thirty years of the century, 15.9 million were Europeans, who formed the basis of the US game in the early days. They included more than 300,000 Norwegians, among them the founders of New York's oldest continuously playing soccer team, Sporting Club Gjoa.

Gjoa was founded in 1911 by Norwegian sailors in Bay Ridge, hard by the Brooklyn docks. After a decade of dominating the local tug-of-war scene, a soccer team was started in 1921, with players drawn from the local community and from sailors passing through the port. Its best years were in the early Sixties, when it won the National Soccer League three years in succession. But of the teams it played in those far-off years - among them Brooklyn Celtics and Prague FC, Palermo and Turkish American, Malta United and Maccabi - few have survived.

Sigurd Samuelsen is the club's president and former goalie, and he bears as close a resemblance to a Viking warrior as you are likely to find in New York City. *"When I first arrived in 1960, the stores and churches around here were all Norwegian,"* he says, *"and there were thousands of first generation Norwegians. If the local Swedish team, which had more money than us, tried to lure away a player, we'd just get on the phone to his mother in Norway. And he'd get an outraged call from home the next day."*

Since then, the influx from Norway has slowed to a trickle and the make-up of the neighbourhood and the team has changed. The team photos in the glittering clubhouse trophy room move from blonde-on-blonde Norsemen between the 20s and Sixties to a more diverse ethnic mix since then. Unable to compete with the wealthier semi-pro clubs in the city as its community base has withered, Gjoa has also become incapable of holding onto the talent it develops in its strong youth programme. Mike Windischman, for one, who captained the 1990 US World Cup team, was developed by Gjoa but then poached by their one-time rivals and current city soccer powerhouse, Brooklyn Italians.

Gjoa now plays in the relative obscurity of the Second Division of the Cosmopolitan League, which was formed in the 1970s from a merger of the National League and the old and illustrious German-American League. Most of its teams have suffered the same fate as Gjoa.

For decades, the German-American League was among the strongest in the country. Between 1951 and 1983, teams from the German-American or Cosmopolitan Leagues won ➡

● *International football comes to New York. Dandy Town Hornets of Bermuda take on Brooklyn Italians in the 1991 CONCACAF Club Championsip.*

transfers

attan

transfers

Manhattan

● *Above: More action from Dandy Town Hornets v Brooklyn Italians.*
Below: René Higuita receives the news that he's Colombia's sexiest man.

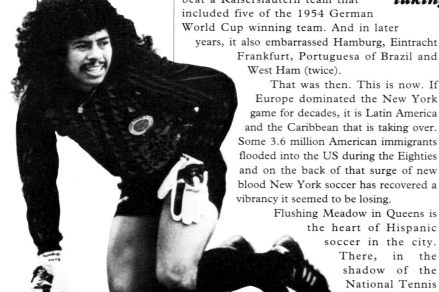

the National Open Cup, still as close as the US gets to a national championship, nineteen times. They included: German-Hungarian, a power in the 1950s until the knitting mills that sponsored it went out of business; Ukrainian, which was monied enough to fly former British pros from Canada for games; New York Hungaria, which included full and junior international players who had fled Hungary in 1956 when the Soviets moved in; and New York Hota, a club formed by German waiters working at the Waldorf Astoria.

At least until the early 1970s, the League was also powerful enough to hold its own, or at least go down fighting, against tough international opposition. In 1957, the League's all-star side beat a Kaiserslautern team that included five of the 1954 German World Cup winning team. And in later years, it also embarrassed Hamburg, Eintracht Frankfurt, Portuguesa of Brazil and West Ham (twice).

"If Europe dominated the New York game for decades, it is Latin America and the Caribbean that is taking over."

That was then. This is now. If Europe dominated the New York game for decades, it is Latin America and the Caribbean that is taking over. Some 3.6 million American immigrants flooded into the US during the Eighties and on the back of that surge of new blood New York soccer has recovered a vibrancy it seemed to be losing.

Flushing Meadow in Queens is the heart of Hispanic soccer in the city. There, in the shadow of the National Tennis Centre where the US Open is played, sit eight bone-hard pitches worn bald by overuse. On Summer weekends, games go on literally from dawn till dusk, observed with varying degrees of fervour by some 15-20,000 people, among them players and fans, and countless Hispanic families out for a day in the sun among their own.

Dino Dominguez, an Ecuadorian who came to the US in 1968, is president of Asoligas, an Hispanic Soccer Association which includes sixteen leagues and almost 400 amateur teams. He talks enthusiastically about the coming addition of a Bronx-based, forty-eight-team league next year to include the top amateur sides, and of a soccer camp organised this Summer with Latin American coaches that he expects to draw 300 kids.

"*We launched Asoligas in 1978,*" he says, "*and at first it was tough to keep the enthusiasm going. There was no press coverage, for one thing.*" But as the torrent of new arrivals continued unabated, and the Spanish-language press took up the cause, the association boomed. Colombians, Ecuadorians, Peruvians and, most recently, Salvadoreans flooded into the city and launched teams almost on hitting the tarmac.

This year, Smirnoff, seeing the potential, tied up a sponsorship deal with the thirty-team Hispano-American League that includes $15,000 for team kit, $3,000 for local Hispanic charities and more for events like table football tourneys in local bars and restaurants. Teofilo Cubillas, who still plays in another Smirnoff-sponsored Hispanic league in Florida, kicked off the new competition.

As Smirnoff obviously appreciates, the Hispanic teams are the best supported in the city and represent a potentially lucrative market. They also retain strong links with soccer in their home countries, whose professional clubs are just as appreciative of the exile dollar. So, when Colombian side Atletico Nacional of Medellin needed to raise some money last year to recoup losses suffered in the Copa Libertadores - they were forced to play its home games outside the country after death threats against a visiting referee - it sent René 'El Loco' Higuita to New York.

It's faith was rewarded. Some 4,000 Colombians came to see El Loco guest for a local side. There were five pitch invasions. The game took hours to complete. And Higuita was almost smooched to death by hordes of stout Colombian matrons no doubt mindful of his election by a Colombian mag as the country's sexiest man. But the most important thing for Atletico was that the club made thousands of dollars on the trip.

The fervour, and the cash power, of the Latin Americans is also beginning to force the two regional semi-pro leagues in the city - the North East Super League and the Hellenic League - to sit up and take notice, and for obvious reasons. Brooklyn Italians of the Super League are among the best teams in the country and one of two US representatives in this year's CONCACAF club tournament, the European Cup of Central America and the Caribbean. After seeing off Dandy Town Hornets of Bermuda in the first round, its next opponents were the hardened Mexican pros of Puebla, who play regularly in a World Cup stadium before tens of thousands of fans. The *Azzurri*, by contrast, play on the considerably less hallowed astroturf of a converted American football field, the pitch sloping gently upwards towards the middle. The slope and the plastic are good for drainage, they say, but murder on your ball control and knees. The team's 'clubhouse' is a dilapidated Brooklyn bar. There is scarcely an Italian player in the side. And it draws only a handful of diehards even for big games, compared with thousands in the glory years between the Fifties and the Seventies. The team may cost as much as $150,000 per year to run. The shortfall is made up by the group of local Italian businessmen that runs the club, and whose passion for the team has outlasted that of the community that spawned it.

Greek clubs have also been among the most successful in the city over the last thirty years, but they too have seen the crowds dwindle almost to nothing, forcing the merger of some teams and the disappearance of others. Until last year, the Hellenic League was exclusively Greek, but as new president Takis Moutis says, the dimensions of the crisis forced a re-assessment. "*We realised that immigration was dying off, and the teams with it. We had to take the league beyond the boundaries of the Greek stronghold in Astoria and out into other communities.*"

So, the league signed up Egyptian Star and the well-supported Peruvian Inka, which includes a number of ageing but still nimble past internationals in its ranks and a defender, Carlos Guido, who has just been called into Peru's squad for the Copa America. This year, Moutis also discovered a Salvadorean league on Long Island which attracted as many as 5,000 fans on a weekend. Drawing on that support, a Salvadorean select side is likely to join the league next year. The next step is a name-change for the league to reflect its new, ecumenical status.

The problem, particularly with the World Cup looming, is how to develop from here. Soccer in New York is still resolutely small time, its organisation haphazard, its disciplinary problems chronic. Fritz Marth remembers Cosmopolitan League games between Dalmatinec, sponsored by the Bank of Yugoslavia, and New York Croatia, some seven years ago where up to eight squad cars of police were needed to keep the rival fans apart. He adds that fans of New York Albanians frequently pack guns at games. "*The referee of one of their recent games just disappeared at half time after one of them fired a gun into the air.*"

● *Above: A questionable challenge in Smirnoff's Hispano - American League. Below: Teofilo Cubillas still playing in Florida.*

Dino Dominguez also concedes that Asoligas may throw some Salvadorean teams out of the association because of fan violence. "*They have just come out of a war zone, where it was kill or be killed,*" he says. "*They don't give a damn. A couple of beers before a game and they're supermen.*" Even in the semi-pro leagues, intimidation of referees from the sidelines is routine. And in May, a Mexican fan who had been in New York one week was shot dead in a post-game fight.

Still, there are signs that local soccer officials are beginning to impose greater discipline and more professional organisation on the game. And with the US Soccer Federation now looking at ways to launch a professional league, they are hopeful the ethnic leagues will find a place in the sun. The tale of New York Cosmos and the money men who ran it, dollar signs stencilled in their foreheads, was a lesson to everyone.

As Moutis says: "*You can't impose a team from above with a bundle of money and a big ad campaign. That's what they did with the Cosmos: they invested a few million dollars and when they saw it wasn't working they dismantled the whole thing and walked away. And meanwhile, we were still there in the background with our little community teams, still playing, still holding the game together in this country. You may not like the ethnic overtones of the game here, but you can use it as a base to expand, step by step from the bottom. As long as you have people who don't see the game coldly, as a money-maker. As long as you have people with a passion for soccer.*"

Non-League Northern

You're at a party and a clever clogs asks you who Blyth Spartans beat in the FA Cup First Round in 1977. Fortunately, you know the answer because you have read PAUL TULLY*'s article...*

THE NAMES WERE ALWAYS DOWN IN THE BOTTOM corner of the Football Special, in tiny print and with unreal scorelines from unreal places. Spartans would have beaten Synthonia 6-5 and you hadn't a clue where either side belonged.

But to a boy like me in 1964, the identity of the Northern League was mystical, almost mythical.

Where was Billingham, anyway? And how could Billingham find Blyth when, according to our classroom wall-map, no such place existed? And what was so special about Crook Town that they could play at Wembley which was in some place called London off the edge of the map which ended at some other place called Bishop Auckland who were also in the Northern League and did they really have bishops playing for them?

To a schoolboy still learning the agonising art of supporting Newcastle United, these teams belonged to another world of small-print reports in Sunday papers and inaccessible back streets in unexplored villages.

But after learning the whereabouts of ninety-two League teams on a bigger and better map, I started locating these mysterious little villages, and slowly but surely fell in love with the Northern League.

The serious obsession began when Blyth Spartans reached the First Round of the FA Cup in 1974. They were drawn at home to Preston North End. Bobby Charlton was in the Preston team and everybody went crackers, not least because Bobby Preston's late equaliser. No matter that Spartans were murdered in the replay at Deepdale - I was hooked, and from that day on Blyth Spartans have been *my* non-League team.

It's a unique atmosphere at Blyth; Croft Park always seems full, even when there are only 200 spectators. The pitmen standing in the shadow of the terrace roof are there every week, recalling the great Eddie Alder who became a cult hero in the 1970s, and every goal or near miss is greeted by a massive roar.

The clubhouse is where the heart of the Northern League beats. No club is complete without its bar, generally overlooking the pitch, which contains the inevitable collection of committee-men, yokels and eccentrics... some would say the same people belong to all three categories.

At Durham, there were always two crusty old souls who would watch the first five minutes and retreat into the clubhouse, never to be seen until last orders. But they could tell you everything that happened out on the pitch and, more importantly, what was going to happen next week.

As a young weekly newspaper reporter, I covered Durham City for a couple of seasons. There would always be a seat on the team bus for away games and adventures to places like Penrith in Cumbria, from where I returned at 4am one Wednesday and sat in the office taking five hours to type my six paragraphs before going off to the Magistrates' Court and falling asleep.

would be playing five miles from his Ashington 'hyem'.

So I endured a soaking wet night in Blyth to queue for my ticket, and rolled up again on the Saturday night with 8,500 others, clinging to the grass banks dotted with railway sleepers which remotely resembled terraces.

Micky Dagless banged in a free-kick for Blyth in the third minute and I was submerged in the delirium which lasted for more than an hour until

There was a match at Whitley Bay when the manager was so sorry for me sitting alone in the stand that he offered a seat in the dugout. There would be old Arthur Young, the secretary, who stood in exactly the same spot for every home match - over on the far side in glorious isolation, in hurricane or heatwave, sunshine or snowfall, steadfastly refusing to take up any other vantage point. And there was Willington, where I saw the worst game of football ever played, which inevitably ended 0-0 and where the

“The manager was so sorry for me sitting alone in the stand that he offered a seat in the dugout.”

Lights

twenty-seven spectators argued with the gateman to be allowed to go home at half-time.

Transcending all else was that magical 1977-78 season, when Spartans captured the hearts of the nation with a run to the Fifth Round of the FA Cup. There were 42,000 there when it all ended against Wrexham at St James' Park, but only 1,500 when they beat Burscough 1-0 in the First Round, and about 150 when Shildon were defeated in an early qualifier. They beat Chesterfield and Enfield, then Stoke City, and finally took 6,000 fans to Wrexham for the Fifth Round.

People who had never seen a Spartans home game were at the Racecourse Ground that freezing afternoon, and when Terry Johnson slipped the ball through Dai Davies's legs to open the scoring in the first half, complete strangers hurled themselves into each others' arms and wept tears of joy behind the visitors' goal. Wrexham equalised in the last minute with the help of a blind referee and a collapsing corner flag, and Spartans were denied the chance of meeting and beating Arsenal in the quarter-finals, but no-one within a 20,000 mile radius of Blyth will forget that year.

Today, it's a little different. The likes of Bishop Auckland and Whitley Bay, North Shields and Spennymoor have been attracted to other leagues because of the Northern's delay in joining the semi-professional pyramid system.

Now the Northern League has belatedly joined the pyramid, but things will never be the same again. It was an inevitable move, but it is a shame that so-called progress came along to split a competition whose century-old tradition was established on the unshakeable foundation of the same clubs year after year.

I know a bloke who for thirty years travelled the country watching Football League games only and who defiantly refused ever to attend a non-League game. When British Rail removed the late trains back to the North East from London, he decided to break with his lifetime's vow and attend a Northern League game near his East Durham home.

On Easter Monday 1991, he watched Bedlington Terriers beat Shotton Comrades 2-1 to complete his 'set' of Northern League grounds. He has no regrets. He still goes to League games, but now looks first to see if Easington Colliery or Shildon are at home before setting off for Leeds or Newcastle United.

Wherever he goes on a Saturday, he'll seek out a copy of the Football Special when he gets home to see how the games went.

And there are the results... down in the bottom corner in tiny print, with unreal scorelines from very real places.

Some things do change.

● Left: Bishop Auckland v Hendon. The 1955 Amateur Cup Final at Wembley.
Right: Blyth Spartans 1983.
Underlay: Bobby Charlton, Preston v Blyth 1974.

Paperback Writers

FORWARD WITH RANGERS
WILLIE HENDERSON

After a lifetime dedicated to reading footballers' autobiographies, TIM NEWBURN *is now able to select the definitive first eleven...*

The footballer's (auto) biography is a much maligned form of literature. Admittedly, there aren't many past or present pros who ever had a chance of making an impact on the world of letters. By the same token, however, neither is it the case that Graham Greene forfeited a career as the rock at the heart of Brighton's defence for quill and ink, or that Marcel Proust's sole reason for leaving his cork-lined room was to turn out for Paris St Germain. (The honourable exception to this rule is, of course, Alexei Sayle's favourite goalkeeper, Albert Camus.)

More often than not ghosted, repetitive and cliche-ridden, the football-biography is a dream read. Like slipping on old and comfy slippers, their worth may not be immediately obvious to the outside observer, but you know what you're getting and (apart from the occasional Eamonn Dunphy) you don't want it any other way. Despite the predictable format, biogs are a mine of information for the trivia enthusiast and a source of unlikely stories.

My favourite bit of the formula, the essential bit of padding, is the chapter (or two for those who are really struggling) in which our subject's 'All-time Top (substitute England, World, or League) Eleven' is described. Here the author can indulge himself, including in his side world-class players that he, like us, only saw on the television, together with patently under-qualified old lags that he owes money to from that last game of cards on the team coach.

Not one to miss an opportunity, what follows is an 'autobiography eleven'; players/writers in a 4-4-2 formation. This is not as easy as it looks, for there appears to be a complete embargo on autobiographies by left-sided defenders. Thinking of most of the left-backs I've seen over the past twenty-five years, it is a shame that their school teachers did not stop them from playing football as well as failing to teach them to write.

There is no shortage of choice for the green jersey, though. The place eventually goes to Gordon West (*The Championship in my Keeping*). Anyone brave enough to turn down the opportunity of a place in their country's World Cup squad because they don't fancy six weeks on the road with only footballers for company deserves a place in any side. Any doubts about his worthiness are dispelled when, with seemingly little concern for footballing stereotypes, he calmly reports having highly developed philatelic propensities (stamp collecting to you). This is just the sort of eccentric individuality we need at the back.

Brian Clough has recently taken to referring to his players by their trade, viz: *"Stuart Pearce, electrician"*. Sadly, Mr C doesn't make it into this side, although his message does via half-back and captain, Harry Johnston (*The Rocky Road to Wembley*). As uncompromising in prose style as in the tackle, he begins: "*My advice to all young footballers keen to take up the game professionally is GET A JOB.*" Just in case we youngsters don't get the message, Harry tells us how his newsagent, hairdressers' and general store helped him accompany Blackpool to three Cup Finals: "*I think the shop helps my football, just as plumbing helps Tom Finney.*" And now that you, reader, know where the modern game has gone wrong, you can begin to pick suitable careers for your favourite stars.

WITH JOHNSTON AT THE BACK IS STAN CULLIS, AUTHOR OF *All for the Wolves*. Stan gets the vote for his account of the way in which he retired from the game. Cullis' career was, like many before and since, punctuated and finally ended by injury. However, it was no dodgy knee, beloved of modern stars, for Stanley. No, it was headaches. His troubles started with an accidental collision in a League match in 1938 which resulted in five days in intensive care. One severe clash of heads and one piledriver shot to the chin later, he began to worry about his future. In the first season after the War, he collapsed after a match against Middlesbrough, having headed the icy leather ball once too often, and he retired almost immediately afterwards.

Putting the modern players to shame and the captain's advice to the test is our right-back, Bill Foulkes (more usually a centre-half, but Matt Busby says in the foreword that Foulkes would play anywhere, and who am I to disagree?). Foulkes (*Back at the Top*) was employed at the local colliery when he signed for Manchester United, and he continued working there right up until his one and only cap for England. He describes a daily routine of almost Pythonesque quality - got up at 6am, down pit by 6.30, worked

MY SOCCER STORY
BOBBY MOORE

"If I shaved before a game, the sting of sweat on my skin gave me a great deal of painful irritation."

2.30pm and then caught the train to Manchester for training, getting home, exhausted, to St Helens about half past ten at night. It was only some time later, after much cajoling by Busby, that he conceded that *"the lack of sleep was beginning to tell."* Quite clearly, just the sort of stubborn defender every side should have.

"More often than not ghosted, repetitive and cliche-ridden, the football-biography is a dream read."

At left-back - one of his original roles at West Ham - is Bobby Moore (*My Soccer Story*). An athletic and classy footballer to you and me, Moore was *"fatso"* or *"tubby"* to many of those who knew him as a youngster. Sadly, there are no photos of this pre-adolescent footballing Robbie Coltrane in the book, clearly proving Moore's point that these were indeed *"nicknames that can hurt a boy."* The other insight from the book worth preserving is the reason for his scruffy, designer-stubble look on matchday. Hands up all of you who thought this was an effort to look macho. Wrong - it was acne: *"If I shaved before a game, the sting of sweat on my skin gave me a great deal of painful irritation."*

On the left side of midfield is Willie Watson (*Double International*). Bobby Moore describes how he chose between two sports and reasoned that it was better *"to put all my eggs in one basket"* rather than risk *"falling between two stools."* Watson, whilst succeeding in playing for England at football and cricket, nevertheless had anxious times when the two clashed. In the summer of 1950, he was due to be a member of England's World Cup squad as well as playing county cricket. Consulting Yorkshire CCC about his predicament, he reports with a completely straight face that the County instructed him to play football because: *"Willie... it is England who need you."* Naturally, Watson wins his place to counterbalance our goalkeeper's international reticence.

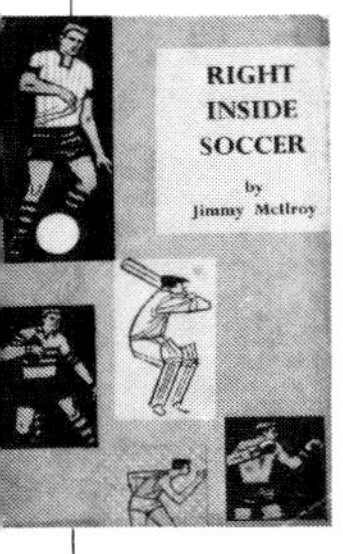

"The man with the whistle is nobody's friend."

Billy Bingham (*Soccer with the Stars*) gets his chance in midfield because of the robustness he displayed in an international tournament in New York in the early 1960s. The tournament was cosmopolitan to say the least, including an all-star side from Canada, teams from Germany, Romania and Brazil, and, naturally enough, Kilmarnock. Bingham seems a placid and gentle man. Even in the dark days when he was Everton manager in the 1970s, it was quite difficult to dislike him. It's not surprising to find, therefore, that when he was sent off in the opening game of the tournament it was the first dismissal of his career. Not content with this, Bingham, who seemed to develop a taste for violence quite quickly, left the pitch early again in the next match in the competition, having punched the opposing Brazilian left-wing so hard *"he went down for a count of about twenty."*

On the right side of an attacking midfield are Burnley's Jimmy McIlroy (*Right Inside Soccer*), a contemporary and team-mate of Bingham, and the diminutive Scot, Willie Henderson (*Forward With Rangers*). McIlroy gets the vote not just for his cracking chapter headings (*"Footballer or bricklayer... a teenager's problem"*; *"The man with the whistle is nobody's friend"*), but for managing to have in his background all those hackneyed features which are essential to the aspiring player: a sporting family, a football for Christmas, hours of practice with a tennis ball (the Xmas present is obviously only of symbolic importance), a sense of destiny, together with, and this is crucial, considerable innate sexism (he describes, for example, his disappointment when his Mother gave birth to another member of the *"petticoat brigade"* rather than a brother).

Willie Henderson, our right-winger, is included for further tales of aggressiveness and for another interesting career-threatening injury. He describes a Cup-Winners' Cup game in which, having taken considerable punishment, he retaliated and punched his marker who was a good six inches taller than he was. Having realised what he'd done - and displaying the quick-thinking that gets him into the side - he ran half the length of the pitch and hid behind his goalkeeper until things had cooled down. The injury which he sustained later in his career, and which he describes as necessitating surgery, a plaster-cast, three months out of the game and the prospect of never playing again, was a *bunion*. Unfashionable now, the bunion seems to have gone the way of the icy leather ball, knee-length shorts and, with the exception of Mr Clough's boys, having a trade.

UP FRONT, WE HAVE TWO TALL TARGET MEN: DEREK DOUGAN (*The Sash He Never Wore*) and Mike Channon (*Home and Away*). Dougan, it appears, would never have found his way into Brian Clough's heart. Although he had worked as an apprentice at Harland and Wolff before moving to Portsmouth, a club with a shipyard, his first decision on reaching the mainland was to become a full-time pro. Nevertheless, he lovingly reports his times at the docks, especially the practical jokes played by the old hands. He was caught out by the old lunch-box nailed to the floor trick, but, displaying the mobility that was to frustrate defenders for years to come, was never trapped by the old ploy of welding steel work-boots to the ship's deck.

Channon, by contrast, seems to have been involved in football in order to while away hours that couldn't be spent racing horses or dogs. As a writer , however (well, let's *pretend* he wrote it), he's an automatic selection for his distinguished and untiring use of cliche. Beginning with the old-chestnut *"Football's a funny game"*, he works his way through *"No game is easy anymore, especially on the international scene"*, which leads almost inevitably to *"We've got to keep working away and do what we're good at ... we've got to do it our way"*. He's under stiff competition from his team-mates, however, for McIlroy chips in with *"It can often be dangerous to be candid with the press"* and *"I play for the greatest club in England (Burnley)"*. My personal favourite is a veritable Freddie Trueman of a quote from Harry Johnston: *"Without trying to appear an old fogey, I do think our football has slipped and there aren't as many personalities in the game as there were before."* Looking at this writers' eleven, I think he might just have something there.

"I play for the greatest club in England (Burnley)."

Amazon Grace

DAVID CLEARY

delivers the first article your likely to read about Amazonia that doesn't once mention defoliation.

IF YOU'RE WORRIED ABOUT THE FATE OF THE Amazonian rain forest, there's no shortage of media coverage. If you're worried about the state of Amazonian football, on the other hand, you'll look for media guidance in vain.

In football, like everything else, Amazonia is Brazil's poor relation. If the Rio and Sao Paolo teams are the Liverpools and Arsenals of Brazilian football, the best Amazonia has to offer are the Halifax Towns. It's hardly surprising when you consider the practical difficulties of organising leagues in an area larger than Western Europe, where trips to away matches take days, even when the rivers are navigable. No Amazonian team has ever qualified for the national playoffs that decide the championship, and the only real claim to fame Amazonia has in football terms is the great Doctor Socrates: he was born in Belém, on the mouth of the Amazon, but his family moved south before the great man was old enough to kick a ball. All the same, Amazonians are as bitten by the footballing bug as any other Brazilians, and they do have their own teams, fierce rivalries, and a couple of fine stadia.

Amazonian football is divided into state leagues, of which the best is Para - about Fourth Division standard, with the rest barely even Vauxhall Conference. The capital of Para, and the heart of football in the region, is the city of Belém: home to about 1,500,000 people, Amazonia's three major football teams and an international class stadium called The Big Mango

Tree, of which more later. To call Belém football incestuous is putting it mildly; the nearest place big enough to support even an Amazonian equivalent of Kidderminster Harriers is about as far away as London is from Marseille. So the Para State Championship boils down to the three city teams playing each other incessantly in what are laughingly called *classicos*, more because of the historical longevity of the fixtures than the quality of the football.

Once upon a time the city divided up behind its teams on ethnic lines, but those days are long gone. The classiest team, in the social if not the footballing sense, is Remo, literally 'Rowing Club',

which was how it started off in the 1940s. Belém's microscopic middle class at the time thought sculling less proletarian, and there was no shortage of river to practise on, but the club's finances soon depended so much on spectator income from its footballing offshoot that Remo switched its attention to dry land.

Remo's colours are the famous red and black hoops of Flamengo, but you could never confuse the two on the pitch. Their dominance is challenged by Tuna-Luso; nothing to do with canned fish, but with the local Portuguese community who founded the club at the same time as Remo. The rivalry is the nearest Amazonia comes to an Old Firm, even extending to Tuna-Luso choosing the colours of Fluminense, Flamengo's Auld Rio Enemy, to emphasise it. Tuna-Luso's main claim to fame in Belém is a splendid leisure complex with clubhouse on the *Almirante Barroso* highway, built in the Forties and looking incomplete without men lounging around in white suits and Panama hats. Unfortunately, their stadium a few hundred yards down the road is falling to pieces, although its compactness gives the drums an echo effect and the atmosphere can be good. Final pretender to the throne are Paissandu, who have enjoyed more success lately than either of their rivals, without quite getting a grip on Belém's footballing affections.

No guide to Amazonian football would be complete without a mention of the sport's politics, because without it the state of most of the region's footballing facilities would be incomprehensible. Even in Belém, crowds rarely go into five figures, and the population is so poor that turnstile rates of more than 50p would be unthinkable. Surprising, then, that the city has a magnificent international-class stadium with a capacity of 85,000, all sweeping concrete curves and ramps reminiscent of the best Italian structures. Smaller but equally classy stadia are to be found in other Amazonian cities. So where does the money come from? There are two answers.

The first is local politicians: step forward Alacid Nunes, governor of Para State in the Seventies and all-purpose political string-puller ever since. He it was who hit on the idea of building a stadium worthy of the city, for which cost was no object. Building it bankrupted the state government, but enriched the construction companies Nunes owned, as is the Brazilian way. Unfortunately, the stadium wasn't completed in Alacid's term, and the project was immediately killed by his successor, a sworn enemy - which is why it still lacks the upper third of its terracing. This design flaw is actually a boon, as it lets the breezes in, which makes all the difference in a city where the temperature rarely dips below 30 degrees, even at night. Political warfare erupted over the stadium's name; although everyone calls it the Alacid Nunes Stadium, successive governments have tried to rename it the *Mangueirao* - the Big Mango Tree - without ever making it stick.

The only real claim to fame Amazonia has in football terms is the great Doctor Socrates: he was born in Belém, on the mouth of the Amazon

Top Left: The Amazon. An out-of-town site to beat them all.
Left: The Belém stadium half finished but still roomy.

The second source of funds is the CBF - *Confederacao Brasileira de Futebol* - which gave Joao Havelange to the world. Being President of the CBF is a high-profile job and provides an automatic passport to the big time in real Brazilian politics.The four-yearly elections for the presidency of the CBF are hard-fought, with the seven Amazonian state football associations providing a crucial bloc of votes. This explains the generous subsidies and other goodies the CBF steers to Amazonia as sweeteners. In 1986 the CBF election swung on the single vote of the western Amazon state of Acre, whose president was rumoured to have made $20,000 and ensured the building of a state headquarters for changing his vote at the last minute, all on live TV. An expectant nation was rewarded by the sight of him being flattened by a punch to the stomach as he unwisely walked past the ex-president on his way back to his seat.

It was Para's turn to cash in in 1990, when a promise to stage an international in Belém won its vote. The boys duly turned up in November to take on Chile, where a packed Big Mango Tree saw a post-World Cup side packed with new faces draw 0-0, in a disappointingly dull game where the only rockets were fired from the manager's bench (currently occupied by Falcao, he of glorious memory, in an Armani suit, fresh from his triumph of being voted 'Brazil's Best Dressed Man, 1990'). The crowd applauded every mis-directed pass in a stumbling Brazilian performance, terrified that jeers would offend the CBF and ruin chances of future internationals. They needn't worry: when the World Cup comes to Brazil, the CBF's tangled politics will ensure that Belém gets a Group. Gazza may play the Big Mango yet.

Class Distinctions

“ A comeback’s always around the corner, but so’s the Receiver. ”

The near definitive study of the League’s class system and the tenuous connection between Man Utd and Joan Collins, exposed by ROGER TITFORD.

“ ...typified by power, money and silverware. ”

“Class endures, divisional status is mere ephemera,” as sharp-shooting Brett Engels may have advised his Southend team-mates in the close season. If he did, he was making a serious and valid contribution to the way in which we should consider Football League teams. And even if he didn’t, we won’t be the last to put words in his mouth.

It is easy to take divisional status too seriously. Over the past forty years there has been a plague of promotions and relegations. Last season there were over three times as many promoted teams as in 1951. Divisions are now a good mechanism for mixing up the footballing classes. They are no longer indicative of the type of team you follow.

Unfortunately this observation seems lost on those intent on immobilising and preserving in aspic, or money, the current First Division as the new Premier League. In essence they are looking to replace a useful and mobile class structure with a stultifying and self-serving caste system.

Their natural opponents, ‘the Second Division clubs’, don’t know where to look for a counter-argument largely because they cannot recognise a common cause. They have none. In two years time half of them will be in another division. But they are still likely to be in the same class (and still likely to feel, along with forty two others, that their rightful place is in the Premier Division!).

What then is this underlying class structure that the more eagle-eyed readers have already spotted on the next page?

Derived from decades of close observation and minutes of further thought, it groups similar teams together on the basis of background, wealth, support, home ground and status.

Within the three broad levels of upper, middle and lower class there are some refined sub-divisions. For the sake of amplification and interest, the current 92 League clubs have each been assigned to a class. Of course, it’s highly subjective and arguable. It may not be capable of keeping up with the latest changes. Are West Brom still ‘respectable’? Have Hartlepool found some money? The important point is the class system as a whole rather than who exactly is where.

The characteristics of the classes themselves are described in greater detail on the following pages. It could be fancifully conjectured, a process not unknown in football writing, that the difference in characteristics may lead to a different type of relationship between club and supporter.

Just to illustrate and further annoy, female stereotypes have been selected to represent each class. No offence is intended to the clubs involved. Or, indeed, the ladies. If you haven’t already done so, now is the time to read ahead.

Of course clubs migrate between the classes as they do the divisions of the League, but rather more slowly. Problems of their class may be more similar than the problems offered by divisional status. With the advent of a Super League or other exclusion zones they may need to band together for support and for setting up alternative divisional structures.

In the past it has certainly enlivened fixture lists to have a richer mix of different classes within the divisions. That mixture is perhaps what lends the Second Division its interest in recent seasons. The likes of Aston Villa, Wolves or Sheffield Wednesday would always be welcome back in the Third Division. However, it seems Luton, Wimbledon and Oxford were not so welcome in the First.

No-one has had the right previously to be a First Division club for all time or, indeed, a first

THE HONOURABLES

Arsenal	Liverpool
Aston Villa	Manchester City
Chelsea	Manchester United
Everton	Nottingham Forest
Leeds	Tottenham Hotspur

THE HOTBEDS

Derby	Sheffield Utd
Middlesbrough	Sheffield Wed
Millwall	Sunderland
Newcastle	West Ham
Portsmouth	Wolves

THE RESPECTABLES

Barnsley	Luton
Blackburn R	Notts County
Bolton W	Oldham Ath
Bristol City	Plymouth Argyle
Charlton	Southampton
Coventry	Swindon
Leicester	WBA

THE NOUVEAU RICHE

Brighton	Oxford
Crystal Palace	QPR
Ipswich Town	Watford
Norwich	Wimbledon

THE HARD-TIMERS

Birmingham	Fulham
Blackpool	Huddersfield
Burnley	Preston
Cardiff	Stoke

THE JOURNEYMEN

The Rest of the Football League

THE STRUGGLING POOR

Aldershot	Maidstone
Chester City	Rochdale
Doncaster	Scarborough
Halifax Town	Torquay
Hartlepool	Wigan
Hereford	Wrexham

"...lean on pedigree and keen on revenue."

● Top left, left and above: Elsie Tanner, Joan Collins and Samantha Fox, representing the Hard-Timers, the Honourables, and the Nouveau Riche.

class club. An examination of the record book shows a greater and continuing degree of mobility than might be expected. Though the post-war consistency of the Big 5 clubs has to be acknowledged, they have had their weak periods.

Based on a weighted scoring system for domestic and European honours, finishing in the top ten of the First Division and reaching the last eight of the FA Cup, the top ten League clubs in each era/decade have been calculated, (see table over page). Even amongst this select group, and ten may not always have been the appropriate number to take, there is a substantial amount of change with new clubs continually coming to the fore, from Man Utd (pre-war), Huddersfield (1920's), Portsmouth (1930's), right up to Wimbledon. Some clubs come back: Forest (1890's and the late 1970's) or Derby (every third decade or so). In all, over a third of League clubs are represented on this table, suggesting that the top echelons of the game, certainly in Divisional and sometimes in class terms, have never been, and still are not, a closed shop.

With so many promotion and relegation places on offer within the League, real progress can only be measured by moving up and down the class system. To offend or inspire your opponents with your background and pedigree is the true measure of democracy within each division of the League and it will be a sad day for all if we have to draw a thick black line below the first eighteen or twenty occupants of Division One beyond which none, no matter how worthy or different, shall pass. As Brett's ancestor might have quipped: *"They have nothing to lose but their delusions."*

De Brett Angell's Guide to Club Class

THE HONOURABLES - typified by power, money and silverware. Rarely found outside metropolitan areas but inspire mad love from far-away ten-year-olds. Recover easily from lapses of character, (Man Utd 1974, Spurs 1977 and 1991, Man City passim).
Represented by: **JOAN COLLINS**
Strengths: The TV bosses, the newspaper headlines and an awful lot of seats.

THE HOT BEDS - typified by passion, tragedy and unrealised potential.
Great and grim football factories filled with disproportionately large and disorderly support. Prone to relegation, betrayal and striped shirts.
Represented by: **CARMEN**
Strengths: The past, the future, vocal support.

RESPECTABLE MIDDLE CLASS - typified by a pre-Great War honours list or always finishing 'thereabouts' these days. The solid, provincial backbone of the League, uncertain of confident behaviour in the First and ashamed of occasional bouts in the Third. On good days, still capable of pulling 15,000 world-weary cynics saying of current internationalists: *"Of course, he was crap when he played for us."*
Represented by: **RACHEL HEYHOE-FLINT**
Strengths: Scouts, men on the 'right' committees, grounds fit to stage Under-21 internationals.

The League's Top Ten Down The Ages

1890s	Pre-War	1920s	1930s	1945-56	1956-66	1966-76	1976-85	1985-91
Aston Villa	Newcastle	Huddersfield	Arsenal	Man Utd	Man Utd	Leeds Utd	Liverpool	Liverpool
Preston NE	Aston Villa	Bolton W	Man City	Arsenal	Spurs	Liverpool	Nott'm F	Arsenal
Sunderland	Everton	Aston Villa	Everton	Wolves	Wolves	Arsenal	Man Utd	Everton
Everton	Sheffield W	Liverpool	Sunderland	Newcastle	Burnley	Man City	Everton	Nott'm F
Blackburn	Sunderland	Newcastle	Portsmouth	Blackpool	Liverpool	Man Utd	Aston Villa	Man Utd
Wolves	Sheff Utd	Arsenal	Preston NE	Portsmouth	Aston Villa	Spurs	Ipswich	Spurs
WBA	Blackburn	Cardiff	WBA	Spurs	Everton	Chelsea	Arsenal	Wimbledon
Derby Co	Man Utd	WBA	Huddersfield	Liverpool	West Ham	Derby Co	Spurs	Luton
Sheffield Utd	Liverpool	Man City	Derby Co	Burnley	Leicester	Everton	West Ham	Coventry
Nott'm F	Man City	Spurs	Wolves	Charlton	Sheffield W	Newcastle	Southampton	Norwich

Based on Domestic and European honours, top ten in Division One, last eight in FA Cup.

Class Distinctions

NOUVEAU RICHE - typified by ground-sharing plans, re-building works and the occasional Cup Final. A post-Seventies phenomenon, lean on pedigree and keen on revenue. Slick of tongue Chairmen often the most prominent feature and thus not acceptable to the Hotbeds and the RMC's. Hence the Super League. Surprisingly, no Essex clubs represented - yet.
Represented by: **SAM FOX**
Strengths: A sure understanding of database marketing, landlord and tenant legislation and the potential for American football if the next deal goes pear-shaped.

HARD TIMERS - typified by Gothic grounds, grumbly old blokes saying *"I remember when..."* and an air of crisis that seems to have lasted since August 1939. Old Hotbeds gone lukewarm and middling clubs with no class left. Still add spice to a Fourth Division fixture list. Much favoured by TV features departments when they have to cover the lower division because of ready access to Hovis-style footage. A comeback's always around the corner, but so's the Receiver.
Represented by: **ELSIE TANNER**
Strengths: Period terracing, tawdry glamour, an entry form for the ZDS.

THE JOURNEYMEN - typified by working hard, getting nowhere and being patronised for it. Teams from solid, unpretentious, (some might say dull), towns for for which their place on the coupon is the biggest claim to fame. Used to be described on occasional TV appearances as *"a fine advertisement for......"* but best chance of a mention these days is embroidered across a Union Jack hanging on the fences in Malaysia, Paraguay or wherever.
Represented by: **PAULINE FOWLER**
Strengths: Heavy pitch, native cunning and staying power.

"...working hard, getting nowhere and being patronised for it."

● Above and right: Pauline Fowler and Hilda Ogden, representing the Journeymen and the Struggling Poor.

THE STRUGGLING POOR - typified by excellent tea-huts, sympathy from Radio 5 and imminent demise. Clubs that never quite made it in the Third, or the Fourth really for that matter. Not being in what one would call footballing areas, their crowds are tiny but devoted and charitable. 'Fighting Fund' Car Park bigger than Players' Car Park and rightly so.
Represented by: **HILDA OGDEN**
Strengths: The existence of The 92 Club and other groundhoppers, intimidating dressing rooms, the demand for modern warehousing developments.

Collectors Cornered

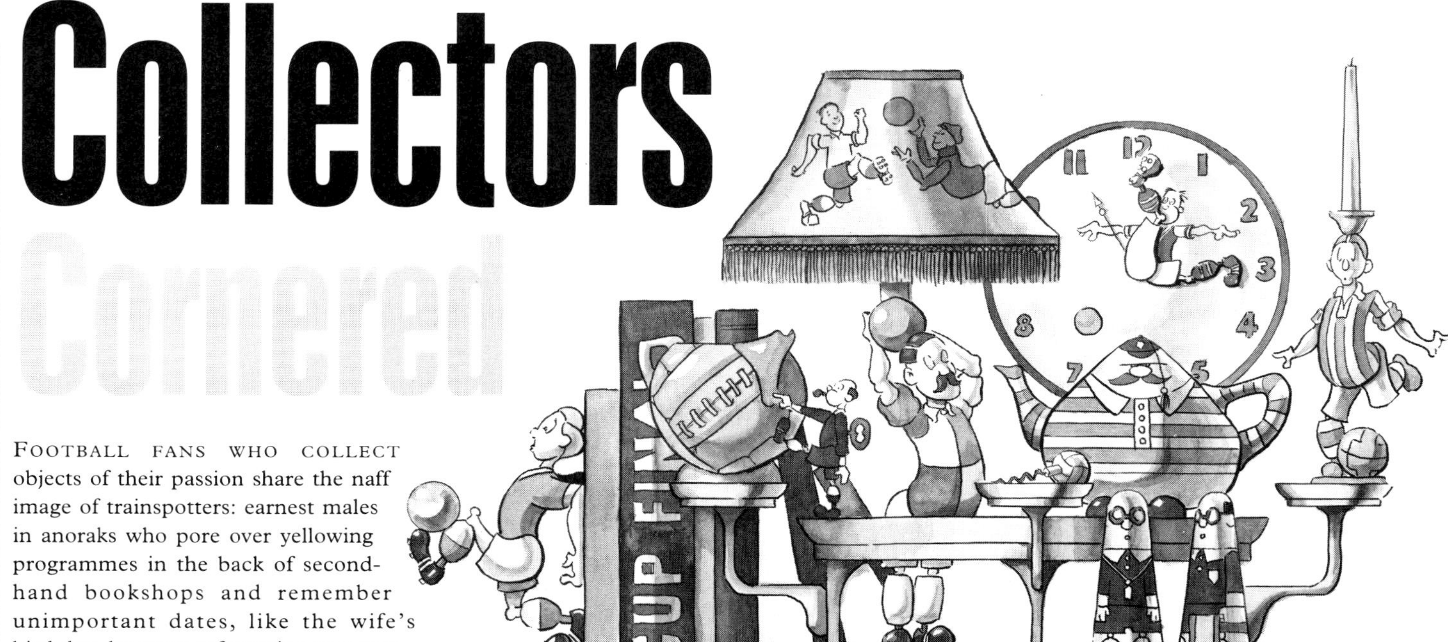

It begins with sticker cards or metal badges, but can expand to commemorative plates and oil paintings. Football collecting is big business, as MARIAM GOLDMAN *found out...*

FOOTBALL FANS WHO COLLECT objects of their passion share the naff image of trainspotters: earnest males in anoraks who pore over yellowing programmes in the back of second-hand bookshops and remember unimportant dates, like the wife's birthday, by cross-referencing to a vast mental databank of football facts and figures.

So it's refreshing to find Final Whistle, an Aladdin's Cave of selective footie memorabilia, tucked away amidst the oriental rugs and connoisseurs' murmurs at Alfie's Antique Market, a network of *objets d'art* emporia off the Edgware Road in North London.

You will find few anoraked statisticians with stained fingers to taint the museum-like air of Final Whistle, where sepia-tinted photos of Edwardian team groups look down on rare collectors' items - a pair of brass firestands in the shape of footballers, circa 1880, a brass car bonnet mascot in the shape of a player, circa 1920.

The Lovejoy of football is one John Trice, 32, a Wolves fan who describes his three-year-old shop as *"a hobby that got out of hand."* John travels the country, pouncing on pre-war decorative objects, prints, paintings and any interesting knick-knacks, whatever their age, with a footy theme. He also stocks a wide variety of books, from esoteric club histories to great philosophical tracts by exponents of the game - *The Dave Beasant Story* and *Crazy Horse* to name but too many. To date, John has sold three sets of *Association Football and the Men Who Made It*, an ancient four-volume work which he says *"you'd be lucky to get now for £350." The News of the World*'s 1896 tome, *Famous Footballers,* would set you back a piffling £250.

John is not so much targeting collectors, as the punter who genuinely hankers after a Sheffield United porcelain plate circa 1971 to love, admire and eat cheese toasties off, in the best tradition of practical antiques. *"Oddly enough, anything to do with Sheffield Wednesday is snapped up in a couple of days,"* says John, *"but there isn't much interest in Liverpool."*

His customers are mostly middle-aged men, with a healthy quota from abroad, including dealers from France, America and Italy. John reckons the attraction lies in the fact that the majority of prints and paintings from the 1840s to the early 1900s came from Britain, at a time *"when the British shaped and exported the game."*

Some dealers are attracted by a piece for its own sake. John once possessed a FIFA anniversary plate, made by Royal Crown Derby in the 1940s, which proved to be more valuable to a plate dealer than a football collector. Other items are equally rarefied: you might fancy a Longines silver watch, engraved with balletic player, for a cool £450; an inscribed silver pen presented to Glasgow Rangers manager William Struth in 1946, for £85; or you might plump for a crescent-shaped sweetie box for a mere tenner. Some of the thingies deserve a bit of Arthur Negus savvy to unravel their thinginess - make what you will of a *"stunning Victorian etched glass eperque, circa 1880s"*.

John's own passion is for paintings, prints and cartoons. He has pen and ink drawings mounted on silk, postcards from the first decade of this century and *"marvelously graphic"* drawings of the game in action, at a time when photography was largely limited to stills and the sketch pad was mightier than the microphone. Many of the prints come from the heyday of graphic design in the 1920s and '30s, perhaps best known through London Underground posters of the period.

Last summer, John visited Rome for an exhibition of football-related paintings, with some football tournament as a side-issue. *"You find a much larger range of art devoted to football on the Continent and in South America. Football there is relatively classless. You can walk into a top jewellers in Rome and see Cartier brooches with a footballing theme. Over here, decorative items have tended to be associated with 'gentlemanly' sports like golf - although that's changing."*

There are three priceless works that John dreams of owning. The first is Picasso's *Les Footballeurs* - to the uninitiated, a trio of gingerbread men executed in haste by a toddler with a wobbly crayon, but to the discerning eye, a masterly depiction of the flow and simplicity of the game. Then there's JM Turner's *The Night Before the Game,* nothing to do with brawls outside night clubs, but a charming cameo of a woman at an ironing board preparing kit for the morrow's fray. Thirdly, and least explicably, John has a yen for the life-size bronze statue of Sir Stanley Matthews that graces Stoke-on-Trent. Perhaps he's better off investing in Gazza's used hanky collection.

As everyone knows, Dalry Thistle are the greatest team in the universe. We tracked down GEDDES THOMSON, *who explains why...*

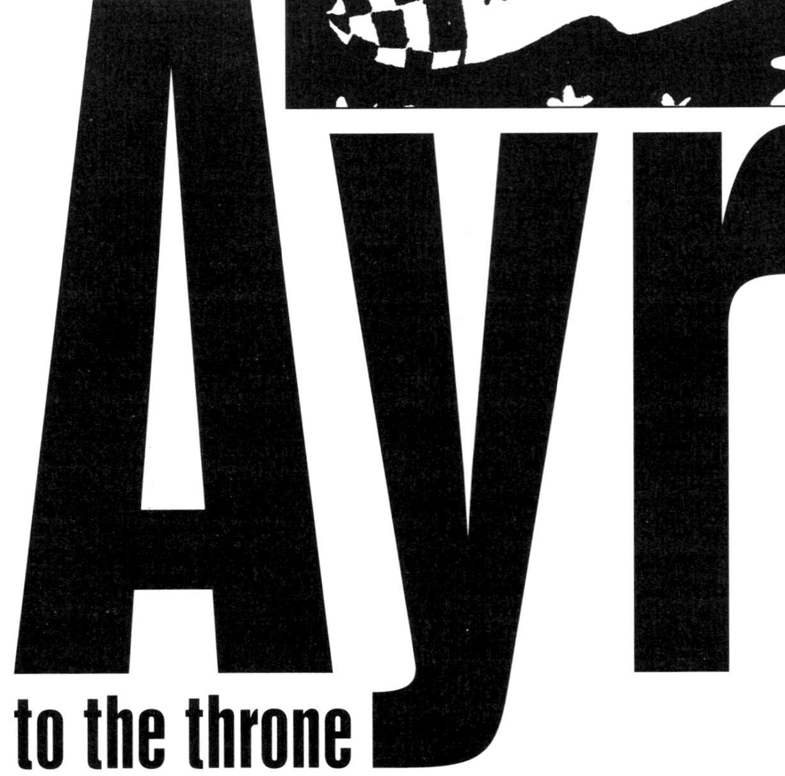

Ayr to the throne

IT IS... WELL... QUITE A FEW YEARS AGO IN AYRSHIRE. By an amazing coincidence, the greatest football team in the entire universe play in the town where I was born - Dalry. Or, to give it its full address, as I used to do surreptitiously on the inside back pages of my school jotters - Dalry, Ayrshire, Scotland, Britain, Europe, Earth, The Solar System, the Milky Way, the Universe - INFINITY! If you wrote this on the front page, you got the belt from Miss Pringle.

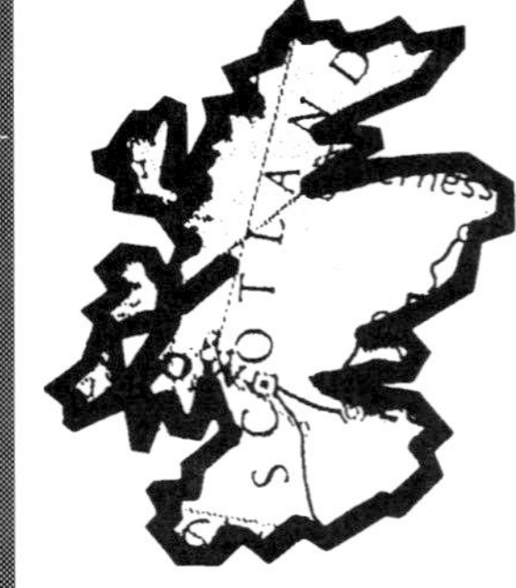

Anyway, to business. Dalry Thistle are the greatest team in the history of the universe, but no-one seems to know this except me and possibly my father. On matchdays I hang about outside Merkworth Park, literally hours before proceedings are due to start, in an agony of anticipation. Old men look upon me with pity and pull out their watches to measure the extent of my lunacy. *"The game's no' till this afternoon, son,"* they say, before hobbling up the street for a pint or two.

I am quite unshaken by this mysterious sangfroid in my elders. I know that with the inevitability of the rising sun, the game will happen eventually and the greatest team in the universe (who play in dark blue Scotland strips) will engage in battle with the forces of evil from a couple of miles up or down the road, ie Kilbirnie Ladeside, Irvine Meadow, or Kilwinning Rangers.

Kilbirnie Ladeside are the arch-enemies, possibly because they are the closest geographically. One of my uncles comes from there, an unfortunate blemish in an otherwise blameless individual. I remember once asking him, *"How does it feel to come from Kilbirnie?"*

He looked at me, unsmiling. *"Okay,"* he said, *"it feels okay. How does it feel to come from Dalry?"*

Kilbirnie teams are known for their physical commitment; the sods never seem to know when they are beat. They are also adept at off-the-ball antics and time-wasting, so much so that when the ball is kicked right out of the park, a not infrequent occurrence in Ayrshire football in those days, the cry goes up of *"Kilbirnie play!"* This expression supposedly comes from the occasion when a Kilbirnie supporter shouted *"Never mind the baw, get oan wi the game!"* when the only match ball, kicked by a Kilbirnie full back, landed in the back of a passing lorry and was wheeched away to Glasgow for ever and ever. By the way, if any Kilbirnie supporters are reading this, I *still* think you're a bunch of dirty cluggers.

Inside the ground I stand beside the old men, in quest of the secrets of the universe which I am convinced they will one day utter. Their judgments on players are at once definitive and delphic. For example: *"Needs tae take the padlock off his arse"* = slow and one-paced. *"A wee crapbag"* = a small player who shirks fifty-fifty tackles, almost certainly from Kilbirnie. *"Tanner-baw player"* = skilful but ineffective, probably from the tenements of Glasgow.

But the worst thing a player could do was to get married. That was even worse than being born in Kilbirnie. The oldsters would then remove pipes from mouths, spit solemnly and say, *"He got married last week. That's him finished. He'll never last the ninety minutes. The legs are away from him."* They would then nod sagely.

I could never fathom the apparently deadly connection between marriage and declining football ability, and when I enquired I was answered with sad shakings of heads and the cryptic observation, *"You'll know one day, son. You'll know one day."*

Since I was determined to play centre-forward for Scotland one day, I reckon my subsequent faith in the doctrine of the incompatibility of football and females retarded my social and sexual development by almost a decade.

At five to three the moment arrives. Dalry Thistle, the greatest team in the universe, run out purposefully in disciplined single file. When they reach the edge of the 'home' penalty area, the file bursts apart into individual players sprinting, jumping and whacking footballs venomously into the net. This is sometimes, well quite often, the high point of the game. Strips are pristine, confidence is high, the score is nothing each.

The other lot appears rather sheepishly to a ragged volley of abuse from those who have left the pub early enough to catch the kick-off. Surely they're too ugly to beat us... Aren't they?

I am not prepared to discuss what quite often happens in the next ninety minutes.

Our best player is Billy Walker, a centre-forward for all seasons. Billy is a big barrel-chested bruiser who uses his left foot for standing on and who needs an airfield to turn round in. Opposition fans are apt to shout scornfully *"Opin the gates and let him run out the park!"* when he starts off on one of his distinctly unmazy runs. Quite often he trips over his own feet inside the six yard box, or contrives to scoop the ball over the bar from impossible positions. Impossible-not-to-score positions, that is.

But Billy is a ninety-minute trier, and there are other afternoons when he thunders in drives and headers to the tune of three or four goals. He is picked several times for Junior Scotland and has many an offer to turn senior, but Billy remains faithful to Dalry Thistle, his home town team. By the end of his career he has accumulated more goals than other player in the history of the Scottish Junior game.

"The worst thing a player could do was to get married. That was even worse than being born in Kilbirnie."

At five past three, just as the players are breaking sweat, The Whumper appears. He is a rotund, red-faced, bespectacled individual with a voice like a spring buffalo's mating bellow. His presence is announced by a stentorian *"C'mon the Rye!"* and the Dalry players pick up the pace immediately.

The Whumper is a living legend in his own drinking time. It is said that he is never without a brown flat cap crammed atop that round red face. The rumour is that he even sleeps with it on, and my father maintains that once he required a hospital operation to remove it before he could have a haircut.

I remember coming back on the Thistle supporters' bus from an away cup tie in deepest southern Ayrshire. These return journeys could take quite a while, because of calls at various hostelries for liquid refreshments. On this occasion, we made an unscheduled stop beside a field to ease aching bladders. In the field was an Ayrshire bull of impressive proportions, which came trotting over to investigate, attracted, no doubt, by the strong whiff of ammonia.

The Whumper took instant deep offence, as befitted a Dalry man interrupted in the discharge of his natural bodily functions. He stripped down to his best braces and trousers (I thought for a moment that he was even going to remove the cap), climbed laboriously over the gate and challenged the bull to catch him. The beast seemed puzzled at first, but when The Whumper waved a crumpled red hanky it got the idea. Three exciting circuits of the field then followed, with the bull gaining all the time. I thought The Whumper's last hour had come, but he managed to scramble over the gate to safety at the end of the third circuit to the cheers of his fellows fans.

"He reminds me o' that dirty big bastard that plays centre half fur the Meadow," The Whumper wheezed in explanation of his bull-baiting adventure, as we piled him back on the bus.

You will see from all this that my young football days were passed in a world of legendary heroes. Later the magic faded rather brutally, and I will not spare you the details. The Milky Way galaxy, formerly a part of Dalry's universal address, became two chocolate bars. Billy Walker had a bust-up with the management and went to play for Largs Thistle, while The Whumper suffered a stroke which rendered him speechless. I myself grew bigger and discovered that I didn't really care that consorting with girls would stop you playing centre-forward for Scotland.

Platypus in boots

Who is PLATYPUS PETE, *where is he going and why don't his records sell?* HARRY PEARSON *sought some answers...*

DURING THE WEEK DES DOWSON, 'THE BIG D', hosts his own music show, on Sound Of The Salt Marsh Radio, Romney. But on Saturdays he joins that small band of hard-working individuals who are battling to transform the image of English soccer. For Des, in the shape of his duck-billed alter ego, Platypus Pete, is one of the herd of men-in-animal-suits who are bringing the families back to football grounds.

"Why a platypus? Well, why not, I guess! But seriously... Basically, I was looking for an animal which didn't carry too much negative baggage around with it. And it had to be fresh, too. At one time I was toying with a wombat. Then one night I'm home alone watching TV. Naturally, I'm very much into wildlife programmes. I think the world we live in, our environment, is really, really important.

So, I'm watching this programme and suddenly an animal comes on the screen and it was just, pow! I instantly knew that this incredible creature was perfect. I was staring at it, eyes on stalks kind-of-thing, and right there and then the name 'Pete' and his theme jingle just came to me:

"I come from Oz
I've got webbed feet
Strewth mate, I'm fond of water
I'm Platypus Pete from Ramsay Street
Soccer's number one supporter!"

Unbelievable. But true, I swear.

Later, thinking back on it, I could see my subconscious at work. I mean, look at the duck-billed platypus: it's a marsupial, it lays eggs, it suckles its young, it's got a beak, it's got fur. There's something here for everyone! It's like a symbol. It's as if nature was saying 'Look, guys, ladies, no matter what you believe in, no matter which team you support, we can still live together. We can get on.' Because the platypus is the living embodiment of that concept, basically. Which is terrific.

And another thing. It's Australian. And you only have to look at TV and the charts to see that for the kids the hot news at the moment is coming from 'Down Under'. Which was important to me, too. Because I wanted my creature, the animal I was inhabiting, to be one the kids could really relate to.

OK, so my mind's made up. Next problem, the costume! We're talking mega-headache time here. Because it turns out British theatrical costumers don't do duck-billed platypus suits. So it was very much a case of improvisation. The head from a Donald Duck outfit, the body of a gorilla, frogman's flippers on my hands and feet. It's never going to fool David Attenborough, but basically it's accurate. The total cost? £125. *"Just stick it on the bill, love,"* I said. Wicked, I know. But you have to be a wee bit crazy to work in local radio.

Now the guys who work with me at 'SOS' will tell you I'm a fanatic for detail. In the case of 'Pete', I think that attitude's brought its own reward. Because, you know, I've studied literally hours of film of duck-billed platypuses, and I'm pretty certain that if any of these literally fabulous creatures did ever parade a football pitch throwing toffees to the kids, they'd do it exactly the way 'Pete' does. And I don't think you can say that about everyone in my line of work. You know, I don't mean to criticise anyone - that's not my style. And if I do tread on toes, then, guys, it's meant constructively. Because it seems to me that there are too many cowboys in animal suits in British soccer these days. I mean, would a giant panda really re-adjust its head every time it took a penalty? Would a moose's horns wave about when it charged out of the tunnel with the team? Would a *real* robin run into the goal to collect the ball and get tangled up in the netting? I don't think so.

Maybe I'm speaking out of turn here, but it seems to me that those fellas haven't been working on their act hard enough. And in my book, that's not professional. Because, you know, if anyone out there is thinking of dressing up as an animal and getting into football entertainment, then I'd give them two words of advice. Accuracy and integrity. It's going to make life a lot harder for you. But in the end, the kids'll respect you for it. And that, take it from me, is what this game's all about."

Escort Service

Whilst most people prefer to relax on a sunny beach, RON COUNTE *likes nothing more than spending a wet day in Stockport...*

I LIKE TO THINK THAT I am the kind of person who learns by his mistakes. Having once been stranded in darkest Coventry by a minibus, I resolved in future to travel to all football matches in the safety and comfort of a car.

I obtained the use of a sleek, black, Ford Rally Sport Turbo, complete with electric windows, Ricaro seats and graphic equalizer. Not for me the horrors of a BR buffet car, or the indignity of queueing up for a BR loo used by those apparently lacking basic toilet training. I was to travel in style. Pausing only to slot my Yngwie Malmsteen cassette into the high-powered stereo system, I set off from London with my friend Bill to see Grimsby's crunch promotion clash at Stockport County. It was the Saturday of the Easter weekend.

Bad Trips No. 1

Three hours, two hundred miles and four Yngwie Malmsteen albums later, the sleek, black, Ford Rally Sport Turbo, complete with electric windows, Ricaro seats, graphic equalizer, Bill and myself, stormed into the outskirts of Stockport. We parked outside a row of terraced houses having a combined value almost equal to that of the car itself and before long were inside the converted bus shelter where Stockport play their home games. Perching on the 'seats' apparently designed for the unibuttocked among us, we awaited the kick-off, smiling sweetly at the police video cameraman who seemed to be taking rather a shine to us.

The game itself was fairly predictable. Stockport had a player sent off in the first minute for head-butting. Grimsby went into a 2-0 lead, Stockport's ten men levelled to 2-2, but were finally finished off by two late goals. The game was only marred by the female Stockport County fan sitting in the row behind us who insisted on shrieking at the top of her voice for most of the game. Even after three hours of Yngwie Malmsteen, this was rather trying.

Before long, Bill and I were back in the sleek, black, Ford Rally Sport Turbo (with electric windows, Ricaro seats and graphic equalizer), threading our way through the outskirts of Stockport towards the motorway. It was at this stage that cruel fate intervened. Whilst stationary at traffic lights, the sleek, black, Ford Rally Sport Turbo simply stopped. No bang. No flash. No anything. It just stopped.

We pushed the car over to the side of the road and I lifted the bonnet. The engine was still there. Having now exhausted my knowledge of mechanics, I closed the bonnet.

We surveyed the bleak industrial landscape. Fortunately, we were across the 

Escort
Service

We pushed the car over to the side of the road and I lifted the bonnet. The engine was still there. Having now exhausted my knowledge of mechanics, I closed the bonnet.

road from what appeared to be the only habitable building for miles around. It was a dark, gloomy pub which I went to investigate. It was closed.

After three or four minutes of sustained knocking, a gloomy face appeared at one of the windows. The owner looked old enough to be Albert Tatlock's dad and said simply: *"We're closed mate, bugger off."* Undeterred, I shouted through the letter box that my car had broken down. Eventually, I was allowed in. It took so long to unbolt, unlock and unchain the door that I began to wonder whether they had Salman Rushdie holed up in the back room. The old man issued a series of grunts and pointed towards the telephone.

As luck would have it, the pay 'phone was out of order. I gingerly went around the bar and knocked on the door marked 'Private'. It was opened by a strange, pimply youth of breathtaking ugliness. I explained the situation. *"Mmm,"* he said, *"sounds like the cam belt, that'll be expensive."* He lead me into a Steptoe-like dump which I assume constituted the landlord's living room. There I was confronted by a barmaid of staggering proportions whom I suspected of having been the role model for Stan Ogden in her youth. They would have no fear of football hooligans in this pub. She appeared perfectly capable of going the distance with Mike Tyson. I felt like an extra on the set of *Eraserhead.* (You know, the one about the alienated misfit trapped in a nightmare of disturbing visions set against a bleak, decaying industrial landscape. Driven on by psychotic depression, isolation and despair, he eventually murders the vile, inhuman offspring of his retarded, freakish girlfriend in a sickening orgy of nauseating imagery. It was a big hit in Stockport).

Wiping enough grease from the earpiece to fry a small turkey, I eventually managed to speak to the RAC representative. *"Well,"* he said, *"sounds to me like the cam belt, that'll be expensive. Someone should be with you in about thirty minutes."* Not wanting to push my luck by asking for a drink, I legged it back to the car. By now, Bill had carefully studied the owner's manual and could recline his seat at will, not to mention operate the cigarette lighter. I was impressed.

An hour later, having read the Stockport County match day programme four times, I was relieved to see the RAC van drive up. By now, Bill had mastered the electric wing mirrors.

Within a couple of minutes the expert had given his diagnosis. It was the cam belt. It would be expensive. He couldn't fix it. One-and-a-half hours later, with the Stockport County match day programme now reduced to a crumpled mass, the tow truck arrived. Bill had now progressed to adjusting the rear seat belts.

"What's the problem then?" said the driver cheerfully.

"Cam belt," said I.

"Mmm," he said, *"that will be expensive. Where do you want towing to?"*

"London," I said. He looked at me blankly, snorted like a pig choking on half a cabbage and stood motionless. An eerie silence descended over us to be broken only by a rasping belch from the pub across the road. Judging by its resonance and longevity, it can only have come from the barmaid.

Finally he spoke: *"That'll be expensive. I doubt that we'll get authorisation for that."*

After a brief conference, it was decided that we would get towed to Grimsby, where I know a friendly garage.

The sleek, black, Ford Rally Sport Turbo, with electric windows, Ricaro seats and graphic equalizer, was dragged unceremoniously onto the back of the tow truck and we were off. *"I wouldn't like to go on a rally in that bugger,"* he said, *"that'd be expensive."*

"Quite," I said.

It's a long, dull journey from Stockport to Grimsby, especially in a tow truck driven by someone with an extensive library of Country and Western tapes.

Late into the evening, the tow truck finally deposited the sleek, black, Ford Rally Sport Turbo onto the garage forecourt. Leaving the electric windows closed, the Ricaro seats empty and the graphic equalizer strangely silent, we disappeared for some sleep.

It was, of course, a bank holiday weekend and no-one was available to do any work on Sunday and Monday. On Tuesday, the garage started work. Sure enough, it was the cam belt. Sure enough, it was expensive. Furthermore, it would take a couple of days to strip down the engine, obtain the replacement parts and re-build it.

By a rare stroke of good fortune, Grimsby were at home to Scunthorpe on Tuesday evening, and the club kindly put out an announcement at half time on our behalf, asking for a lift back to London. In a crowd of almost 12,000, the Grimsby tannoy system can be clearly heard by at least two hundred people. Nevertheless, we did find a fellow London Mariner to take us back.

And so it was that I arrived in the metropolis in the early hours of Wednesday morning, minus the sleek, black, Ford Rally Sport Turbo, with electric windows, Ricaro seats and graphic equalizer. The round trip had taken ninety hours at an estimated cost to the RAC and the insurance company in excess of six hundred pounds. Could even British Rail compete with this?

Review

In New York chasing up a world exclusive for WSC, HARRY PEARSON *hailed a cab driven by* CHARLIE PALOOKA, *who has some forthright views on life, love and literature...*

"I GOTTA TELLYA, I USED TO THINK this soccer thing was strictly for wimps an' long-hairs, but since I read *The World Cup Murder* I ain't so certain. Sure, like Pele (that's the guy that wrote the book. He's some kinda big-shot in the Brazilian soccer game, an' I gotta say that for a Spanish speaker he don't write American too bad either), like Pele says, *"Football is theoretically a low contact sport,"* played by little guys (I figure this because *"Jason Benjamin, at six-two, was the tallest man in soccer."*), but the action off the field, boy, that's another story. These soccer fans are crazy! I mean, like the guy who's the hero of the book, Marc Burr, says when a groupa Bulgarians have tried to cripple the Brooklyn Booters in the World Cup Semi-Final: *"If this had happened in Palermo or Glasgow or Buenos Aires, the fans would have burned the stadium down with the referee in and then gone on to do some* really *bad things."* (Only one thing is puzzling me here. Later on Burr says there's *"three referees in ... zebra-striped shirts."* So how come when these loony Latinos torch the stadium there's only one stripey guy in it? I dunno, maybe I missed sump'n back there.)

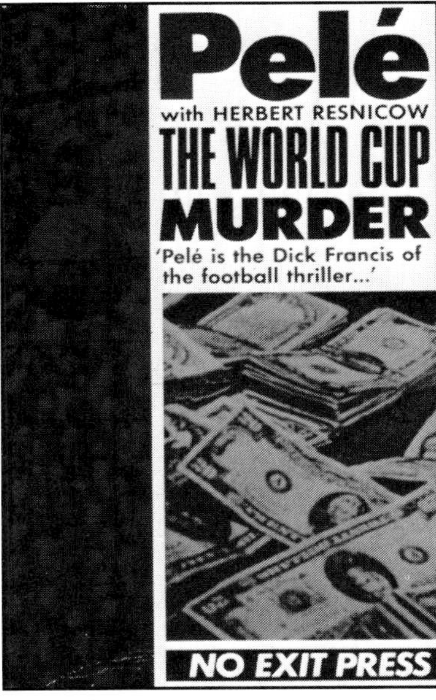

● ***The World Cup Murder* by Pele (with Herbert Resnicow) is published by No Exit Press in softback and priced £3.99.**

I guess I shoulda said at the outset that *The World Cup Murder* is set someplace in the future, when the World Cup soccer contest's taking place right here in New York City (kinda prophetic, huh?), which I guess is why Pele's hired this Herbert Resnicow guy - to help him out with all the shit about NYC, such as what a subway is, an' stuff. The US entry's the Brooklyn Booters. They get to the final by beating those cheating sons-of-bitches Bulgaria. In the final they gotta play another set of red bastards, East Germany. An waddaya know, the referee's from Hungary! So now you're getting the picture, right? We got a commie opponent, a commie official, an' the commies we just beat injured three of our star players 'cos the referee in that game didn't give us no protection. An' I ain't offering odds against anybody guessing where he came from. Right on the button. Russia!

So, you're getting the idea that what Pele's telling us is there's this pinko plot to stop the US winning the World Cup. An' I gotta say that when you look at the history-a this thing, an' see that it's always getting won by some buncha deadbeat Krauts or Spics, an' never by the US, you gotta concede that maybe the guy's got a point.

OK. So you got all this political stuff. But what makes this book really good is, like it says on the dust wrapper, *"Pele's depiction of the poetry and mathematical precision of the game."* I mean, I gotta tellya bud, I ain't no blubberer normally, but when I read stuff like this I gotta reach for the Kleenex: *"To tackle a dribbler who was approaching your goal, driving the ball ahead of him with both feet alternately, meant judging his intended course accurately without getting faked out or caught off balance, getting the proper foot against the ball to wedge it against the dribbler's foot, and then, at precisely the right instant, to knock him off balance by the force of your shoulder against his chest without being called for roughness."*

An' then on top of all that you got the slaying itself, which is perpetrated on this guy named Gregor Ragusic. This guy Ragusic's the Yugoslav owner of the Booters, an' like Pele says, *"Serbians did not conceal their emotions. On the other hand they were known to lie."* Which is maybe why the guy gets wasted. But I gotta say that in spite-a all this an' the fact that *"his breath... smelled of garlic even this early in the morning,"* I took kinduva shine to old Gregor. The guy's an immigrant who's made good by hard work, right? An' he's got a lotta wise thoughts in that tough Slavic skulla his: *"Look, when iron is hot, you can make it how you like. When iron is cold, you can only break your teeth."* I'm gonna copy that one out an' stick it right here on the dashboard, for reference, y'know?

Well, Gregor gets whacked on the head an' the whole Booters squad is suspects, an' Marc Burr too. But I guess if this is where you're going, this is where I gotta dropya, right? That's thirteen-fifty. An' I gotta say pal, there's a lotta people here don't think nothing of soccer, but since I read *The World Cup Murder,* I ain't one of 'em. Have a nice day."

New Zealand

Will football ever become a popular sport in New Zealand? MICHAEL SMITH *has his fingers crossed...*

KIWI GO

Kiwi go, Kiwi go..

IN A COUNTRY WHERE BEING AN EX-ALL BLACK IS considered a useful pre-requisite for election to Parliament; a controversial no-scrum rugby match is the first-up, shock item on the six o'clock news; and where Eamon Dunphy is known as U2's biographer and not as the author of *Only A Game?*, it's no wonder that football continues to have a low profile.

True, the rugby, racing and beer culture has been in decline since civilisation finally arrived in New Zealand - more gentle pursuits were introduced to schools, the numbers game, Lotto, squeezed out the turf industry and wine was discovered - but football has been slow to make an impression. Although the game sits above underwater hockey, radio-controlled yachting and, that most peculiar of indigenous sports, marching, in numbers participating, spectator apathy remains a pressing problem for the New Zealand FA.

Of course, success on the field has a lot to do with it: witness the 20,000+ crowds at home games for the 1982 qualifiers. The NZFA then blew their chance by bathing in the glory of qualification for the next year and a half, with the All Whites nowhere to be seen. As 1990 came around, the home tie *v* Australia, in theory the needle match on the international calendar, drew a paltry 5,000. And this in Auckland, population 900,000.

This sorry state of affairs hasn't been helped by the NZFA's decision to award exclusive domestic coverage rights to TV3, a private channel currently in receivership and still struggling to beam its signal nationwide. Telecasts to date have bordered on the pathetic: a weekly five-minute report on the national league (one game only), with a wobbly, hand-held camera; a broadcast in full of the local cup final marred by a hyperactive commentator who gave the impression he was watching a South American derby; and often-delayed screenings of internationals involving the All Whites in which skilfully placed cameras attempt to search out areas of the ground where ten or more spectators have gathered.

Compounding football's image problem was TV3's late withdrawal from what was presumably going to be a comprehensive effort to cover the 1990 World Cup - severe financial constraints and all that. Into the breach stepped TVNZ, the state corporation, whose obsession with the oval ball knows no bounds (they'll even take you to obscure third division games in remote locations where the sheep are rounded up prior to the kick-off).

On condition that the general populace should feel ever so grateful, TVNZ agreed to show

● *Above: The mighty All Blacks. Below: The modest All Whites.*

highlights only to the quarter-finals and then the remaining games in full (eight in all, count 'em). This induced an orgy of letter writing, the likes of which hadn't been seen since the 1981 Springbok tour, and rather pointedly demonstrated that Kiwis will watch football as long as it doesn't involve some sort of NZ content. Protests were staged outside TVNZ studios and South American immigrants proclaimed that Brazilian football was a gift to the world and should be on our screens. Fair enough, too, although with hindsight what we saw was just about sufficient.

Further holding back football here is the popular stereotype of its domination by expatriate Brits as they attempt to create a little England. The bash-a-Pom syndrome of the 1970s and the trade-unionists-with-Northern-accents-holding-the-country-to-ransom myth have all but disappeared, but the hangover remains. Still, twenty years ago you'd be leafing through a match programme trying desperately to find the 'born in NZ' bio details. These days, the locals are in a majority.

In addition, coaches here still favour the long ball, that wonderfully nebulous concept, 'workrate', and lumbering centre-backs who specialise in mistimed tackles. Crowds here have been conditioned to the quick, no-nonsense approach - should the back four start to stroke it around excessively, a restless shuffle will soon permeate through the 250 gathered in the stand.

Also a little unnerving, and no doubt a reminder of 'home', is the half-time PA entertainment. Organisers have yet to heed the maxim that there are only two types of music - good music and Country & Western.

"Skilfully placed cameras attempt to search out areas of the ground where ten or more spectators have gathered."

Yet more indicative of the British presence is the number of imports playing in the national league. This peripatetic band of lily-whites (literally) spend their dislocated lives in permanent Winter, commuting between hemispheres in economy class and on standby. There are Third and Fourth Division rejects and over 30s, apprentices from higher up the scale sent out for experience (anyone remember Steve Elliott and Bryan Gunn?) and journeymen from the Vauxhall Conference and Highland League.

The clubs give them some pocket money, a sponsor's car if they're lucky, free board at the reserve team coach's house, and in return they are expected to work a bloody miracle on the pitch. Many decide to stay, some making the All Whites, who all eventually go on to become air-conditioning installers and insurance salesmen.

A recent NZFA move to clear up the guest player rule - any player who lives here for twelve months or more to no longer be regarded as an import or guest - may well mean more of this hardy breed appearing in the national league.

If NZ football is really serious about coming out of the doldrums, the real saviour has to be a Summer season. The former NZFA Chairman and current President of the Oceania Football Confederation, Charlie 'Football is my life' Dempsey, says we are being left behind by playing in the mud. This could well be construed as a knee-jerk reaction to the 6-0 drubbing our juniors copped from their Aussie counterparts, but he does have a point. Playing *"on top of the ground,"* as he puts it, would certainly improve technique. It would also bring football here in line with our neighbours across the Tasman (now in their third year of a Summer national league), and make our players match-fit for future internationals. The sport's overall profile would also be helped by not having to compete for bums on seats with that other Winter code - we already have to watch games at the arse end of Sunday to avoid clashing with the national preoccupation.

And if these things don't improve, there's always the chance to wallow in nostalgia over the glory days of the 1982 World Cup, the All Whites' only Finals appearance to date. What a way to make it: a record fifteen qualifying games, including 13-0 over Fiji (no smirking); a win and a draw against the Aussies, who played beautiful possession football but then got lost in the last third; and a miraculous win in which five were needed for a play-off with China, six to go through automatically. 5-0 at half-time with the nation proverbially pinching itself; then total frustration as the second half ground to a close. Never mind, 2-1 over China and the rest was history.

Those aforementioned ➡

Kiwi go...

bumper home crowds (at Mt Smart, venue for the 1990 Commonwealth Games, since the unofficial national stadium - Newmarket Park - had quite literally gone down the gurgler in a landslip), and even our very own World Cup song, 'Heading For The Top', signalled that the All Whites had indeed arrived. (A brief mention here for the guest singer who helped the squad - an Eastender from way back and now a cabaret star 12,000 miles from home, sort of a Kiwi Tony Orlando.)

The 1986 and 1990 campaigns never really cut it in comparison with that earlier effort, although in the latter great delight was taken in stuffing Australia's moneyed operation with a 2-0 win. Unfortunately, that result, in a roundabout way, meant the Oceania spot came down to Israel *v* Colombia. FIFA, ever anxious to promote the concept of football as *the* world game, recognises Oceania as a confederation (in name only and more truthfully as a non-entity, especially considering its exclusion from certain key FIFA committees), throws some coaching money its way, but has yet to guarantee it a place in the World Cup.

For '94, the qualification route hasn't improved - in fact, it's marginally worse. True, the two teams that no-one wants but which Oceania always seems to get are on their way: Israel could well be joining UEFA, thus ending our pilgrimage to Tel Aviv, and Taiwan would appear to be back in the Asian fold. That, however, is where the good news ends.

At FIFA's December 1990 meeting, it was decided that following the straight fight among the true Oceanians (Australia, NZ, Fiji and possibly Tahiti), the winner would then head off on a convoluted journey to play the CONCACAF (North and Central American Zone) runner-up, with the victor of that contest meeting the fourth-placed South American nation for a Finals' berth.

The only worrying aspect apparent is the number of Jasons coming up through the grades - the so-called 'Peter Wyngarde' effect.

Surprised and bemused NZFA officials were expecting a play-off against the third Asian team or a highly placed European side (as in Australia *v* Scotland in 1986), but now face a far greater task. Oceania's 'They are expendable' tag seems more relevant than ever before.

Player exodus from the national league is a further reflection of harsh realities - those with a bit of quality aspire to more than just part-timing it (paying the bills with the match bonus). Australia's semi-professional league is the next step up, followed by the lower reaches of the Football League, where the current role of honour reads: Heremiah Ngata (Hull City), Chris Zoricich (Leyton Orient), Perry Cotton (Scunthorpe United) and NZ's top defender, Ceri Evans (Oxford United).

A notch higher up is forward Wynton Rufer, working hard at Werder Bremen (young men still talk about his wonder goal *v* Napoli in the UEFA Cup). Add his brother Shane (Servette Geneva) and Fred de Jong (with Fortuna Sittard in Holland), and these overseas players could combine in an All White team that might make waves in the lower reaches of the Second Division.

Continental drift will always sap our playing strength, but the domestic game is in reasonable shape. Participation levels in junior football are healthy, and schools of excellence for promising youngsters are having a definite effect on technique, reducing aerial ping-pong and improving the first touch.

The only worrying aspect apparent is the number of Jasons coming up through the grades - the so-called 'Peter Wyngarde' effect. Over twenty-fives will recall the TV series *Department S* from the 1970s (at least that's when it was shown in NZ, remembering we're often three years behind significant trends), and Wyngarde's dandy-ish Jason King character. Parents were so taken with this chap that they began naming their male offspring after him, a move somewhat reluctantly accepted by registrars of births at the time.

Unbelievable stories aside, the local scene recently received a timely boost with the revival of provincial football. The 1990 final, although watched by a mere 1,000, nevertheless gained some valuable media exposure and turned out to be an entertaining affair - not least because of a Jehovah's Witness convention on a neighbouring ground. Being a Sunday, this raised an interesting heretical dilemma - should the sports watchers have been at the game or doing their best to become one of the chosen few? Risking a cliche, it could be said that football was the winner.

The reactions of journalists to the new beast of provincial football have generally been positive, although many continue to be preoccupied with criticising the administrative and promotional side of the game. Of course, they're right, but their often glib dismissals of football's entertainment value just don't hold up. Because there is so little at stake, the lads play with natural freedom.

Under-financing has always been rife - with a population of just three million, there can be no miracles. 'Come on the amateurs' is a familiar cry from the wooden stands/ open patch of ground whenever money can be smelled (ie a physio on the bench, an away team's courtesy bus, more than three practice balls). The limitations have been accepted for a long time now.

● *Left: New Zealand v China World Cup qualifying play-off 1982.*
Below: Three New Zealanders who know better than to play rugby: (left to right) Chris Zoricich (Orient); Ceri Evans (Oxford); Heremiah Hgata (Hull).

WHEN SATURDAY COMES

ONE PENNY

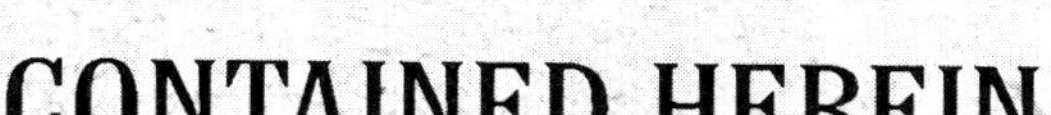

CONTAINED HEREIN:

Newton Neurotics - A Right Royal Arsenal
Nelson's Riddle - Leicester Fosse Be With You

"OLD ETONIANS refine their shooting technique in preparation for the forthcoming season."

Planning a breakaway? Why not visit

The

PREMIER HOTEL, DARTMOOR

The ideal meeting place for go-ahead **football clubs** - secrecy guaranteed. Press leaks optional. Utilise our two spacious drawing rooms - **'The Big Five'** and **'Top Eighteen'** European guests welcomed. Scenic and wholly unrealistic views provided.

Write for BROCHURE to:
Edwards (Fils), Little Berlusconi-on-the-Take, Lancs.

The Publishers of this paper respectfully desire to draw the attention of the sporting public to their recently introduced

MR S BASTARD'S REFEREEING JODHPURS

These WATERPROOF garments are manufactured from finest waxed INDIAN COTTON and are guaranteed free of all deleterious matter. MR BASTARD, referee of the recent Football Association Cup Final, says "I am delighted to approve this Empire-made attire, which has proved entirely satisfactory in every particular."

Available in all sizes. 10/6 per pair. Fitting service if desired.

Lines written upon reaching the Third Round of the FA Challenge Cup by Alfred, Lord Tennyson

But Lo! the swallow cometh with the spring
And all about the blossom bursts anew:
So man takes out his velvet bag and balls
And celebrates the ending of Round Two.

What's this? The shiny arboreal orb
Doth nestle in the Secretary's hand:
And soon the whispered numbers 'Four' and 'Two'
Are happily translated through the land.

Brave Chatham, who, in lengthy struggle fair,
Hath dealt defeat to Nottingham Forest, then
Await the spheres' blind pleasure, and delight
To find that they are drawn at home again.

But who shall visit? Whose the awful fate
The giant-killers' prowess to essay?
Fate's fickle finger ambles down the list
And comes to rest at 'WBA'.

West Bromwich! famed exponents of the art
And holders of the FA Challenge Cup;
Small Heath and Burnley vanquished in their wake:
Shall these almighty titans now slip up?

The day is come; all Chatham is *en fete*.
The fabled Throstles in their train arrive:
These demi-gods, their deeds in lightning writ
Or shall dark ashes loom by ten to five?

Around the park the teeming thousands press
And take their stance on hillock, slope or mound;
Amongst the trees the adolescents sit
And local worthies now seek out the ground.

At three o'clock the oscillating pea
Vibrates within the whistle loud and long:
The teams advance in fearsome conflict joined
And victory awaits the pure and strong.

No more the fiery rhetoric and boasts!
No more the need to threaten or cajole!
They now must serve who only stand and wait
And watch the ball retrieved from Chatham's goal.

Ah, luckless Chatham, how thou art deceived!
All present hopes of glory soon are gone.
West Bromwich show no mercy to their foe
And Chatham end up stuffed by ten to one.

And so, in distant time, when men are told
How Chatham once the mighty Baggies faced.
They'll hear how might defeated right once more,
But lowly Chatham never were disgraced.

No 54 - PJ Paravicini

The match versus Scotland on 10th March 1883 was a black day indeed for English football. It marked the last international appearance of the cultured Cambridge University and Old Etonians full-back, PJ de Paravacini. Paravacini was a fast athletic player, a good kick with either boot, and not averse to heading the ball. A staunch guardian of his line and a devoted club player, there are some who consider that he was made a scapegoat when Scotland's left half-back, Mr Fraser, scored the winning goal on that fateful day. Our special correspondent was fortunate enough to secure an personal interview with Mr de Paravacini recently, which is reproduced below.

Q: *Mr de Paravacini, your international career seems to have been stalled for some time now. Do you entertain any hopes of regaining your position in the England XI?*

A: No

Q: *May I ask why not?*

A: Chiefly because I don't play football anymore.

Q: *That has not been a hindrance to your friend, WE Bromley-Davenport! (Laughter)*

A: Brommers is a forward, and as such will never lose his skill and shot. For a defender, I fear lack of practice will prove an insuperable obstacle.

Q: *Do you feel unfairly treated by the selectors?*

A: By no means. You must recall that I appeared in no less than three international matches. I was the first right full-back to play in successive internationals since England's first two games.

Q: *Nevertheless, the England team did not concede a goal in your first two campaigns.*

A: No, though I should hardly arrogate all praise for myself in this regard. HA Shepstone of Pilgrims was a first-class goalkeeper, and Macrae of the Notts club also played in all three games with me.

Q: *Do you consider that the present England team is the equal of those in which you played a part?*

A: I should be inclined to say not. In fact, I am coming increasingly to believe that the prohibition on hacking has damaged our game considerably. Football is a manly pursuit; of course, it is possible by the adoption of such Scottish methods as dribbling and passing to achieve some temporary success, but the English game was always based upon stern physical effort of which hacking was a vital component. Until it is restored I fear we shall endure difficulties. We may even lose to the Irish.

Q: *Surely you exaggerate?*

A: I think not. The last match was won by only four clear goals.

Q: *Do you think football will become popular outside these islands?*

A: The British are taking this magnificent game wherever they go, but it does not appeal to the Latin temperament. I am of the opinion that it will not be adopted by the French or Italians, despite our best efforts.

Q: *Yet you have, I believe, some Italian blood yourself. But you have been a singular exponent of the modern game.*

A: I believe I inherited this facility from my mother, who was a noted player of shuttledore and an accomplished lady wrestler.

Q: *The latest England XI excluded AM and PM Walters, the noted Corinthian full-backs. Do you think that the gentleman amateur's day is past?*

A: There is undoubtedly some animus against the amateur and a movement in favour of the professional. But I cannot believe that a man playing for money will ever be able to produce the artistic results achieved by those who play for love of the game alone.

At this point our correspondent thanked Mr de Paravacini and left him to enjoy his collection of monogrammed boots.

Next issue: The Rev A Kirke-Smith

FANZINES FOR SALE

Not So Jolly Boating Weather (Old Etonians): Send twopence in postage stamps to the Hon AF Kinnaird, Westminster.

Armed To The Heath (Small Heath FC): Apply to the club.

Ardwick, 'Ard Times, 'Ard Luck (Ardwick FC): To be had at all superior newsagents in the Manchester area, or by post upon application to: The Alderman Longley Home For Distressed Gentlefolk, Ardwick, Manchester.

Darwenism (Darwen): Available for purchase in the vicinity of the Coal In The Bath public house, Darwen, Lancs.

Bootle On The Other Foot (Bootle): Obtainable for a farthing from the club. All proceeds donated to the Young Men's Christian Association.

Time For A Swift Half (Burton Swifts): A joint-issue with **Metal Fatigue** (Middlesbrough Ironopolis) in commemoration of the teams' splendidly robust encounter in the final of the Forbes Philipson-Masters Trophy.

Vale Of Leven On A Jet Plane (Vale Of Leven): An imaginative (some might say fanciful), futuristic work written and edited by a Mr HG Wells.

FOOTBALLS

The **VARSITY** ball is made of best **bison** hide (*subject to availability) with welted seams.

Match Size, 10/6 Post Free.

Predominantly **circular** in shape.

One ton in weight when soaked. Not to be struck with the head under any circumstances. **Match size 10/6.**

SPECIAL OFFER:

"WORKING MAN'S match ball 2/6 - similar to above in every particular save one.

Made of top quality bauxite. Unlikely to be affected by prevailing winds.

CHARLTON'S Used at Lansdowne Road, Dublin; Abbey Stadium, Cambridge; Old Trafford, Manchester (formerly utilised at the Baseball Ground, Derby) **GRASS** Guaranteed For One Week, Minimum. Free Bags of Finest-Quality Sand with Every Purchase **SEEDS**

BLINDFOLD FOOTBALL

A REPORT OF A MATCH INVOLVING THE LATE GENERAL GORDON

It is perhaps not realised that Charles George Gordon was something of a sportsman, *writes Brig. Arbuthnot Arbuthnot-Arbuthnot*. In his youth, Gordon was a noted pigsticker, and often practised with his native servants in the compound at Foochow. The ability of the Chinese to run at high speed on all fours should not be underestimated, and a keen eye and steady hand are required if they are to be speared. Both these talents Gordon had in abundance.

He was over fifty years of age when he first played Association Football. The recent heavy defeat of the Aberdeen club in the Scottish Football Association Challenge Cup at the hands of Queen's Park FC demonstrates the gulf between the Northerners and their Glasgow counterparts. It was this inequality that led to the wager of which I now write.

In the Mess one evening, Lt Huntley Palmer remarked that the Queen's Park XI could beat any other team with their eyes shut. A stickler for terminological exactitude, Gordon asked Palmer if he were prepared to back that assertion with a small wager. I regret to say that the gallant lieutenant - alas no longer with us after a disaster with an Indian Railways timetable - had imbibed rather freely of the water of life and maintained his position, not without some indelicacy of language. Gordon accepted the challenge and a fixture was arranged. The General organised exercises to be held in secret on the Gordon estates. The best ten players were selected, and Gordon himself went so far as to read a book on the subject of football, and practised shoulder-charging with his devoted wife every evening after dinner.

The terms of engagement were these. Each side staked a pair of grouse shot that morning. The Queen's Park XI were blindfolded by an eye specialist and led on to the field of play. The Aberdeen team played without blindfolds. If, at the end of the game, Queen's Park were not leading, Gordon won his bet.

GALA VARIETY PERFORMANCE

IN CELEBRATION OF THE 20th ANNIVERSARY OF THE FA Cup

BLOCK-BOOKINGS

NOW AVAILABLE

The extravaganza will feature a cast of thousands including:

Raucous music-hall duo ***WELSBY*** and ***NEWBON*** ('The Smarmers')

Popular songsmith ***TERENCE VENABLES*** ('The Dagenham Piper')

The jokey blokey ***ALBERT MILLICHIP*** and his performing spaniel, 'Kelly'

Those death-defying acrobats, the ***FLYING FUTCHER BROTHERS*** ('Brave, Bold and Balding')

Bamboozling magician ***BONNY RONNIE ATKINSON*** - he makes your money disappear!

THE NEWTON HEATH PLAYERS with selected scenes from the much acclaimed play 'Georgie Best Is Unwell'

A large crowd had gathered when the captains came together. The Queen's Park skipper called 'Heads', the coin was tossed, and Gordon instantly selected the town end. Some pedant in the crowd attempted to start an argument, claiming that Gordon had caught the coin in mid-air and pocketed it, but it is unwise to argue with a man wearing a Webley pistol and ammunition belt over his jersey.

It was soon clear that the Glasgow club presented a formidable challenge.

By careful calling and a meticulous attention to planned moves they mounted a succession of attacks, and the Aberdeen select were at sixes and sevens. Before long the black and white flags were flying proudly as their favourites held a two-goal lead. At the interval General Gordon addressed his team. I was close enough to hear his inspiring words.

"Men," he said, putting his finger right at the nub of the matter as usual, *"we stand at the crossroads of a very great endeavour. I need not remind you that the enemy has the advantage, nor that a great deal is at stake. Our people are depending upon us to do our duty unflinchingly and diligently, and to succeed in carrying off the prize."*

A lump came to several throats, my own included. The General cleared his, and continued: *"McIntyre, Findon and Ross, you bunch of half-witted nancy boys, when the referee isn't looking, spin the opponent round so he gets dizzy. McGregor (R), Johnstone, Peebles and McGregor (T), you illegitimate offspring of a Siamese floozie and a Barbary ape, let's have more calling for the ball, especially when it isn't near you. Drown them out, chaps! Ness and Lomond, what are full-backs for if it isn't to bring down the opponent when he is nearing our goal? Get thee behind him, and slip thy boot between his ankles. Colquhoun, just because you're a goalkeeper, doesn't mean you can't get involved. Stand ten yards to the left of your goal and keep calling for it."*

The second half was soon underway, and the General's wise disposition of his troops paid ample dividends. At one point, three of the Queen's Park team were in the crowd, trying to find the pitch, Gordon having wisely counselled his tenants to 'Haad their whisht' if they wished to keep their crofts. This prevented the Glaswegians scoring, but there remained the matter of recouping the two-goal deficit.

An hour had passed when Gordon saw his chance. Arriving in the penalty area and finding himself faced by three strapping defenders, he rolled the ball gently against the foot of a full-back, quietly whispering *"Your throw, old chap."* When the defender picked up the ball, the referee instantly awarded a penalty kick. Against a blindfolded goalkeeper, even a complete duffer like McGregor (T) could hardly fail to score, and it was 2-1. The Aberdonians pressed forward, but could not mark their second, and there were only minutes remaining when Gordon struck. He regrouped his troops in their own half, forming a phalanx around him. In this formation, they trotted down the field, maintaining the strictest silence. As they passed halfway, Colquhoun left his goal on a noisy decoy run down the right wing, all the while screaming for a pass. The silent squaddies reached the opposing goalmouth undetected, then separated into an umbrella formation with Gordon at the centre. He steadied himself to shoot. His first effort rolled lamely to one side, but Gordon sent Ness to retrieve the ball for a second time. Ness caught the ball just inside the goal line.

It was then that Ness, for the only time in his life, disobeyed an order. Gordon could not yell at him for fear of alerting the opposition, so Ness sneaked around the back of the custodian. Triumphantly he nudged the ball over the goal-line, returning to the hearty congratulations of his fellows. Gordon frowned severely, and Ness came to attention in front of his captain.

"You are an indisciplined, untrustworthy, shifty brute," said Gordon, *"and I'm promoting you to Corporal forthwith. You are just the sort of chap the British Army needs."*

We enjoyed the grouse immensely, and Gordon made a particular point of sending some of the bones to his men. That is the sort of man he was.

OLD PECULIARS' CAMPAIGN ITINERARY

Details have been released of the **OLD PECULIARS'** annual summer tour which is to comprise of a series of exhibition matches at various venues throughout England. Their first match will be against a **Mill-Owners XXII** at Wolverhampton on **9th June**. The team will be:

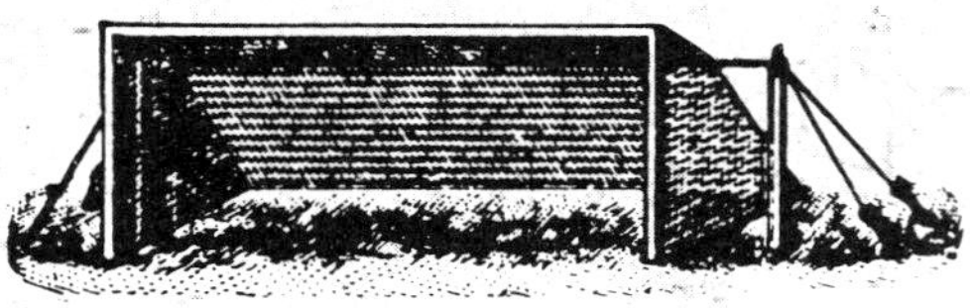

RIGHT.

Goal

x **JOHN SMITH**
Chequered cap, red and black stockings

Backs

x **REV. G. POSH**
Quartered cap, red and blue stockings

x **HON. E. LUBBOCK**
Blue and gold cap, fishnet tights

Half-Backs

x **HADLEIGH BAKERSHAFT**
Striped cap, Bakershaft's patented thermal socks

x **PROF. NORMAN PLANTAGENET**
Navy bearskin, khaki puttees

x **JA FEATHERSTONEHAUGH-WIBB**
Straw boater, Peek-A-Boo body stocking

Forwards

x **M.C.C. WILSON-PICKETT**
Maroon fez, blue suede shoes

x **CHRISTIAN PRINCIPLES**
Gold lame turban, mohair leg-warmers

x **AUBREY VON BISMARCK**
Prussian army helmet, rubber waders

x **MAJOR R.G. BARGY**
Feather headdress, Spandex trousers

x **CONSTANT GLANVILLE-SNOBBERY**
Tassled sombrero, Fibreglass FunniFeet (Reg. TM)

LEFT.

Match officials (supplied by the hosts):
Referee: **Col. Mustard-Leadpipe** *Linesmen*: **JR Hartley (yellow flag and blunderbuss)**
Duke of Clarence (orange flag and crossbow)

Thereafter, the remainder of the itinerary will be as follows:

11th June: v Sergeant Saunders' Small Heath/Aston Villa Select, Birmingham

13th June (pm) /14th June (am): High Spirits in the vicinty of Tamworth

15th June v Goalkeepers' XI, Chesterfield

17th -18th June: Expedition to the South Pole (inc. possible tourney involving Capt. Nemo's Irregular Penguins & Guests)

19th June: Horseplay in the Vicar's Arms, Sheffield

20th June v Mr W Fox's Lancashire Wrinklies XI, Blackburn

22nd June: Wrestling wild boar in the Forest of Bowland

23rd June: Visit to Rochdale Infirmary Casualty Dept. (optional)

25th June: v Seaside Landladies XI, Blackpool

26th June: Return Visit to Rochdale Infirmary Casualty Dept. (optional)

27-28th June: Expedititon to the Himalayas (inc. possible tourney involving Lieut. Pigeon's Light-Footed Abominables)

29th June: Amusing Japes on the outskirts of Carlisle

30th June: Sleep

LETTERS TO THE EDITOR

VOYAGERS

Sir,

I am a devoted supporter of Nottingham Forest Football Club, who are possibly the best team in the Empire. This season we have enjoyed a good run in the Challenge Cup competition, reaching the First Round proper, when we were drawn against the Linfield club of Belfast.

The first match being drawn 2-2, a replay in Belfast was necessary. We followers of the Forest club determined to travel to Ireland to encourage our favourites, and accordingly engaged a charabanc and a private train, taking the night ferry from Stranraer to Larne and then completing the journey by horse-omnibus. You will imagine, sir, our sentiments when we discovered upon arrival that the Linfield club had scratched from the competition!

A friendly fixture was hastily arranged, but this does not alter the matter. Are there no telegrams in Ireland? Was there no method by which this unnecessary journey could have been prevented? If this sort of nonsense cannot be remedied, I foresee a very short future for the FA Challenge Cup.

Yours faithfully,
Jas. Clough

VESTMENTS

Sir,

I write as a long-standing follower of Association Football, greatly disturbed by a recent development in the sport which, if unchecked, may lead to its ruin.

The source of my concern is the players' vestments. Until recent times, all the great footballing teams of this land, without exception, were identifiable by the distinctive, wholly original combinations of shirts and knickers worn on matchdays.

As I scarcely need remind you, Old Peculiars were known the world over for their chartreuse and lilac quartered shirts and cream knickers, Royal Fusiliers cut a fine dash in tan and scarlet stripes with beige culottes and Salopians were the very definition of manly athleticism in lime and chocolate.

Today, however, one rarely sees these fine sportsmen attired in traditional colours. Instead, they seize every opportunity to parade in utilitarian combinations of yellow and green, slate grey and navy blue, provided by a shadowy body of men, commonly referred to, I believe, as the 'kit manufacturers'.

Association football is being debased by these commercial travellers with their filthy lucre and their binding contracts. Are we to idly stand by while our sport prostrates itself before the tawdry demands of the mercantile class? They must be cast out like the money-lenders from the temple. Tradition is everything!

Yours faithfully,
Capt. JJ Coq-Sportif

OUTCASTS

Sir,

I would be very much obliged if someone would explain to me why the newly-formed 'Football League' does not include a team from the Metropolis. This doughty centre of our glorious Empire is home to a number of elevens, any one of which would have adorned the League. You will forgive me if I observe, sir, that the Old Carthusians are the equal of any in the land, and it is tragic that they have not been given the opportunity of proving their worth in fair competition!

I remain, sir,
your obedient servant
Salisbury, House of Lords

FOOTBALL ATTIRE OF YESTERYEAR

As worn by FRED, BARNEY and WILMA

As worn by PTOLEMY, KAHOTEK and TUTANKHAMUN

As worn by ACHILLES, ODYSSEUS and AGAMEMNON

As worn by ERIK, OLAF and KNUT

As worn by NANOOK OF THE NORTH (END)

As worn by IVANHOE, LANCELOT and ARTHUR

As worn by ATTILA, GENGHIS and TARAS BULBA

As worn by DRAKE, RALEIGH and ESSEX (the gent, not the county)

As worn by IVESON and the NEW MODEL ARMY side

As worn by SAMUEL PEPYS and his fellows

As worn by SPEKE, RHODES and MUNGO PARK

MORIATY & CO

For Complete

FOOTBALL OUTFITS

FOOTBALL SHIRT	BOYS'	MEN'S
Flannelette Double Sewn	2/1	2/3
All Wool Flannel	4/6	5/3

FOOTBALL KNICKERS

Best quality Heavy Milled 1/10 2/6Net

Catalogues Post Free

All orders over 10/- sent Carriage Paid

153-7 Pear Tree Court, London EC

MATTHEW SIMMONS *had a close encounter with a famous commentator and is keen to share his experience with you. Names have been flagrantly disregarded to protect the innocent, ie us.*

GOSH, IT'S TOP WELSH BROADCASTER SALVADOR DALI!
YES, THE STRANGE HATTED VERBLESS SURREALIST

Presenter Dilemma

SATURDAY 10TH FEBRUARY 1990, AND I FIND myself in the press box at the Vetch Field to cover the Swans *v* Fulham for my local freebie. The assembled hacks are all in position, customary jokes out of the way, and we await the start, writhing on our split plastic seats.

Suddenly the door opens and a portly, bespectacled, grey-haired man in the twilight of middle age, with a very silly hat, enters. He puffs and snorts and shakes the rain from his person, making as great a commotion as possible. The desired effect achieved, everyone turns round to look.

It is a legendary television commentator. Our man further announces his presence with a cheery, *"Swansea, Saturday afternoon, f****** impossible to drive."* Arses shift on tortuous seats as he squeezes in to occupy his centre front row berth. I stare agog. The great man is only inches away from me, a living legend in football journalism. I peer intently to discover the secret of his success. Ninety minutes later, and a packet of Embassy and Rothmans Football Yearbook are the only answers I can come up with.

He is unable to locate his free programme, so has to rely on others for identification of players. The steward shuffles round, flogging lotto tickets to the journos. *"Get my f****** programme then I'll buy some,"* our hero admonishes sternly. *"I'm shoeer I left sixteen yer, you-ers must b'yer somewhere, butt,"* mutters the steward sheepishly. That sixteenth programme burns in my hand as I stare fixedly out at the rain pelting down, avoiding a withering gaze.

Swans win 4-2. A Tommy Hutchison header and a Paul Chalmers hat-trick send everyone down memory lane. The legend gets into his stride. *"Last Swans hat-trick, Paul Raynor, Barry Town, Welsh Cup, Vetch Field, last year."* The familiar delivery steals the debate. The man really does talk without the benefit of verbs. Long-stored Seventies' commentary is reactivated in my brain. I savour the memory of Crystal Palace goals (*"Super drive, Steve Perrin, 1-0 Palace!"*) for a few heady moments.

The Vetch empties quickly as our man finishes yet another celebratory ciggie and shuffles off alone, looking for a quote or two in the vicinity of the bar.

I'm left with the abiding memory of a figure leaning out of the window in front of me attempting to identify the linesman at fault for Fulham's first goal. My view of the game mostly obscured by his bottom, the commentary uncalled for and unabated. *"Linesman, red flag, f****** hopeless!"* And I didn't even see his lips move.

Monty Sinton's Space Filler...

Popular First Names For Footballers Throughout History

9th century
Athelstan, Clovis, Ethelwulf, Theodoric

11th century
Olaf, Thor, Baldur, Ragnar

15th century
Leonardo, Michelangelo, Donatello, Raphael

1880s
Gervaise, Courtney, Piers, Roderick

1920s
Alf, Charlie, Bert, Wilf

1950s
Ken, Cliff, Ron, Len

1980s
Gary, Darren, Mark, Wayne

2010s
Lee, Bart, Chesney, Vanilla

23rd century
Alpha, Quantum, Astro, Gazza

Kenna Gowland Says...

“Well, I've had it confirmed now, like. I've had proof. The blokes in charge of our works are thicker than Foggon's waistline. I'm not kidding, if brains were passes, there's'd be in the Pat Heard class - totally misplaced.

We've got this new Personnel Director, haven't we? Loudmouth from down South. Doesn't wear a cap, like. Prefers an umbrella with a peak on it. Anyroad, he sends round this notice. It says - you should've bloody seen this, honest man - it says: *"Doughty-Laing is like Arsenal Football Club, we are working together as a team to produce a winning result!"* Our works like Arsenal! Oh aye. Only there's 800 men down our works and they still can't total as many driving endorsements.

"But just like Arsenal, Doughty-Laing can't go on being top of the table unless we keep our teamwork up to the same high standard. Just as it is vital to Arsenal's success that their players function as a unit, so it is vital here at Doughty-Laing that our departments inter-relate."

Italian champions? Oh very good. Inter Relate. Very droll, like. You should go on Bob Monkhouse, you. You could be the new Les Dennis.

So he started up this departmental football league, didn't he? I could've told him, me. If he'd bothered asking, like. I would've told him. But he never bothered.

First game. Welding Bay 'D' versus Accounts. Disaster? It was a bloody blood-bath, man. I seen the lad that ref-ed it next morning. I says, *"How did it go, like?"* He goes, *"Kenna, there was more fighting on that pitch than after the Boro v Darlo Cup replay,"* he says, *"I've never seen owt like it."* And he did his National Service in Korea that lad, mind.

So, after I'd talked to him I stuck my head in the Accounts office. There's only one little lass in there! I says, *"Where is everybody, pet?"* She goes, *"Mr Nesbitt's got concussion, Mr Hamilton's got double-vision and six stitches in his forehead, Gary's been kept in the Infirmary under observation, Colin's got..."* She just went on and on, like.

Well, when I came out of there I bumped into one of the welding foremen. I says, *"What's all this carry-on last night, like?"* He goes, *"I don't know, Kenna!"* he says, *"But I'll tell you what, they'll think twice before they bollock up our overtime money again."*

Ow! Pet! Hell. If I brewed my own I'd get a drink quicker.”

KENNA *was talking to* HARRY PEARSON

GAZZER THE CLOWN - AND BERNARD INGHAM!

There is nothing like a Dane

Something is written on the state of Denmark. (Shakespeare, adapted. Don't write in.). ANDREW JACKSON *has the details...*

CONTRARY TO POPULAR BELIEF, THE TALE of the ugly duckling was written not by Danny Kaye but by the Danish writer Hans Christian Andersen. The tale exemplifies the complex from which Danish football suffers, for in real life the beautiful swan has a habit of running into serious environmental hazards. Take the Danish side of 1983-87, which swept everyone but Spain before them. It turned out that by the time the ugly duckling found out it really was a swan, it was too old to fly. Take the case of current Danish champions, Brondby. Here the likely fate of the swan will be to end up decorating the tables of wealthy burghers further South. As for Danish football itself - well, ducks have such a hard life, don't they?

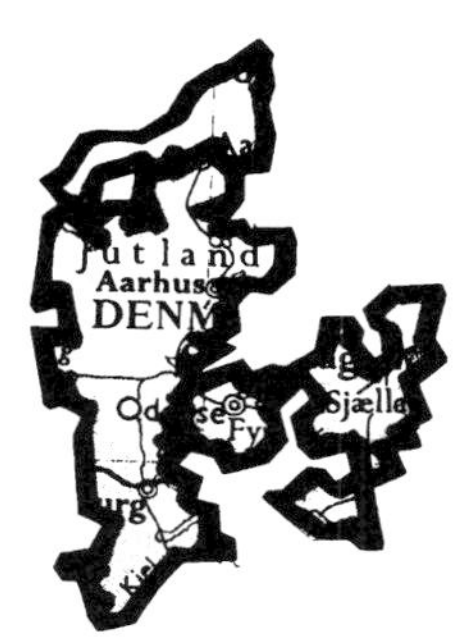

> **“Denmark's national side is looking about as likely as Derby County to lift any silver-ware.”**

Denmark's national side is looking about as likely as Derby County to lift any silverware. A year ago, the temperamental German trainer, Sepp Piontek (whose surname, as Slavic scholars will know, means 'Friday' in Polish), left in a huff after a tabloid newspaper had alleged certain irregularities in his tax position, a departure followed with what a suspicious mind might regard as an indecently hasty move to Turkey, where a contract to manage their national side awaited him.

There followed a scenario worthy of a *Carry On* film, in which the Danish FA, the DBU, amidst much trumpeting, presented Piontek's successor, the 'highly-esteemed' German coach, Horst Wohlers, who had guided mighty Bayer Uerdingen from mid-table Bundesliga respectability to, well, mid-table Bundesliga respectability in the space of three years. Why another German, queried the not-unpartisan popular press. They found an unlikely ally in the board of Bayer Uerdingen, who pointed out that Herr Wohlers was not contractually available. Egg was on just about everybody's faces. The DBU promptly gave the job to Piontek's long-suffering assistant, the mild-mannered and far-too-nice-to-be-a-football-manager Richard Moller Nielsen, whose main inheritance from his years at Piontek's side has been the acquisition of a German inflection in his softly-spoken Danish. They couldn't get another German so they settled for a Dane with a German accent.

The national side's results went from middling to depressing within months, culminating in what the less-

There is nothing like a

Dane

knowledgable press regards as a catastrophic 2-0 home defeat at the hands of Yugoslavia's superb side, a result which is likely to have ended Denmark's chances of qualifying for the 1992 European Championships in Sweden.

Following this, three leading players stated publicly that they no longer wished to play for their country: Michael and Brian Laudrup, because they couldn't get on with the new manager, and Jan Bartam, for more understandable reasons. He has a good academic education, and at the age of 29 couldn't see himself as part of Denmark's 1994 World Cup plans. (Bartram, a willing interviewee as long as he is asked intelligent questions, never made a go of it with Mr Souness in Glasgow. I wonder why?) The country still has a wealth of good players to choose from, but now that the somewhat egotistical Laudrup megastars have torpedoed the frail vessel of poor Moller Nielsen's credibility, it's difficult to see how he can stay on. Unless, of course, the suspicion that they can't afford to replace him is confirmed.

Meanwhile, the nation has adopted a new team. A friend of mine in his forties who comes from Copenhagen has told me that when he was a lad, Brondby was a marshy area South of Copenhagen where people on bicycle rides went to watch birds. Well, that's what he says they did. The transformation is partly due to the fact that Copenhagen in the post-War years has spread, as the English writer, Frank Kermode, once said of Manchester, *"like spilt beer,"* and partly due to the fact that the local club acquired a visionary chairman, Per Bjerregaard, who said of his then-non-league outfit that he expected them to be among Europe's elite one day.

"A crowd of over 5,000 is a rarity outside of four or five clubs"

Well, boys will be boys, and we've all had those thoughts, haven't we? Bjerregaard is, however, not one of the boys. He set about the job with a kind of ten-year plan, which culminated in Brondby's epic UEFA Cup run in 1990-91 in which they came to within two minutes of the Final only to be foiled by Roma and the appalling Rudi Voller. As Denmark's best football journalist, Per Hoyer Hansen, puts it: there are about six to eight top clubs in Europe, breathlessly pursued by about fifty others of about equal strength. Brondby now find themselves in the latter group, Europe's second division, and have the resources to remain there.

THE SPRING OF 1991 SAW THE MOST SIGNIFICANT innovation in Danish League football since the introduction of professionalism thirteen years ago (which Brondby followed up six years ago with full-time contracts). The ten clubs who made it through the eye of a needle to the Superliga at the end of last season will be feeling like the handful of POWs whom the Kommandant decided on a whim not to hang upside down in a pit of snakes. Their financial survival hangs on their sporting survival in the top flight, as Danish football, where a crowd of over 5,000 is a rarity outside of four or five clubs, simply does not have the cash flow to keep dozens of professional clubs above the breadline. The enigmatic Aab, from Aalborg, are the only club in Denmark to attract what might be called a fanatical, British-style following whatever they do on the pitch. Of the other nine, OB, from Odense, AGF, of Aarhus, Vejle BK and the Copenhagen club, B1903, are the last remnants of Danish football's aristocracy, while well-run smaller clubs like Silkeborg and Ikast are maybe better equipped to battle for UEFA Cup places together with Aab. The gulf between the others and the professional elite will only get wider.

The 1991 season, which in Denmark has always been March-October, is being used as a transition to a more 'normal' European season, to begin before the end of the year, with a Winter break. This will avoid the classic Nordic problem of a Championship-winning team being a year older and, in most cases, several players weaker by the time they get to

● ***Previous Page: Brian Laudrup. Below: Sepp Piontek fends off tricky questions about his tax affairs.***

compete in Europe. Brondby's wealth has already alleviated the latter problem as far as they are concerned. The question is now: can anyone prevent a permanent Brondby monopoly of the title? Even PSV Eindhoven, Rangers and Marseille are used to a bit of hot breath on the backs of their necks from time to time.

● ***Left to Right: Frank Arnesen; Preben Elkjaer (both now TV pundits); and Michael Laudrup (still playing but no longer for Denmark).***

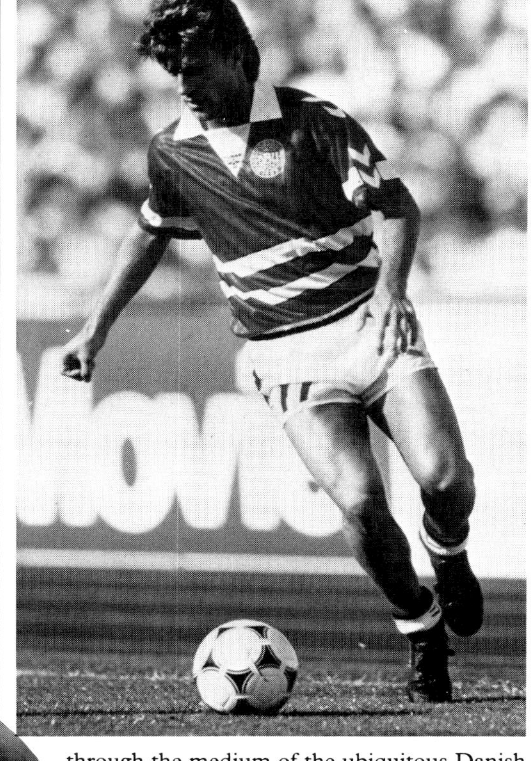

DANISH FANS ARE A FICKLE LOT. DURING THE heady mid-eighties, the entire world had an opinion as to whether Michael Laudrup should play up front or in midfield for Denmark and who should get the left-back spot. Now, Brondby are the national team and small boys would rather score goals as Bent Christensen than Fleming Povlsen. All of this is, of course, the result of media coverage, and while it's fine for those of you who live in London to be blase about TV football, it's a different matter if you live on a remote Baltic island eight hours by ferry from the nearest professional club. For some of us, television is all there is most of the time, and if the price for that is that diminutive goalscorers would often rather be Marco Van Basten than a Dane, then fair enough. The Danish football fan, especially in the windswept Baltic, is thrilled to get the chance to see Aston Villa play Luton live. Never mind the quality, feel the scarcity.

Televised football has progressed by leaps and bounds since the arrival three years ago of a second channel. DR (Danmarks Radio), the original purveyors of mass entertainment, were in a rut. Their football coverage was based on the extraordinary assumption that the only reason people might have been wanting to watch football was that they could bet on it through the medium of the ubiquitous Danish 'Tipskupon', which requires the punter to predict the results of 13 craftily chosen matches from the Danish League (Summer) and English League (Winter). This ingenious pools' system provides the justification for televising, on Saturday afternoons during the close season, a succession of wet and windy English games - with commentaries to match. DR actually do have one commentator, Svend Gehrs, who seems to appreciate that Ewood Park in January doesn't quite encourage the silky skills on show in Genoa in June, but most of the commentary is of the patronising 'typical-English-long-ball-up-the-middle' variety, even when the game on view isn't.

"The Danish football fan is thrilled to get the chance to see Aston Villa play Luton live. Never mind the quality, feel the scarcity."

DR had a flirtation with the Bundesliga a few years ago, until they discovered that a soggy pitch in Stuttgart didn't produce anything more watchable than a quagmire in Coventry. Then along came TV2. They cut the crap about betting providing the sole motivation for watching football and began to show live Italian games on Winter Sundays, punctuated by the odd gladiator battle from Spain as a late Saturday night thriller. They even hit on the innovatory idea of using proven professional football commentators, assisted by the wit and wisdom of ex-players like Frank Arnesen and Preben Elkjaer.

Even if the Danish game can only manage to sustain one or two more or less mangy birds in flight at the same time, there's a chance that widespread public appreciation of the game at grassroots level may begin to get off the ground. Then again, undue optimism in Denmark is a social taboo. There's no lack of justification for that.

Novel Approach

Masochism is alive and well and freely available in a bookshop near you. CHURSTON DECKLE *has been unable to resist the lure of the soccer novel, as he explains here...*

LET'S GET A FEW THINGS STRAIGHT FIRST. I WASN'T FORCED to do it, nobody put a gun to my head or anything of that sort. In fact, it was *my* idea. Mmm, football novels, I said. Now there's an interesting subject. Never been done before. Lots of scope. But, like Stretford Athletic, Scorton Rovers, Branton United and Manston Town, my cup runneth over. There is a limit to how many times a person can be expected to read the same story: poor boy from rough area signs for small club who, against all odds, get to the final of the FA Cup and win (the FA Cup can, in extenuating circumstances, be swapped for the League). Why is football literature so excruciatingly bad?

Perhaps the most compelling reason is that hoary old British chestnut: class. Most novelists and writers are from a background in which football does not loom as large as it does for 'ordinary' people. The fact remains that there are few working class authors, and this is reflected in the penurious state of football literature. But it runs much deeper than that, from author through to publisher. Most football novels are written for children, as are most football magazines. This is not to say that all football novels are *only* written for children or, indeed, that all football novels are bad. Perhaps the most surprising thing is that there have been some worthy, not to say successful, attempts at this maligned art form.

Ultimately, though, the real problem is that the soccer novel is held in such low esteem by the literati that it simply attracts the worst authors. There are a couple of men who have more or less devoted their lives to heightening the awareness of the novel: Michael Hardcastle and Brian Glanville. Hardcastle was something of a cult figure amongst kids growing up in the Seventies, as some of his dated prose suggests: *"No team in the land ever found it easy to win at Turf Moor."* At his most productive from the early Seventies right through to the early Eighties, he penned scores of books on the subject, some better than others, but with a dedication to the form that no-one else can match. Probably the best sequence of books is the Mark Fox series: a handy guide of how to become a footballer in 750 pages, though it didn't do me much good. Mark Fox lives in a Midlands town called Athletic, which is handy for naming the local team if nothing else. Like all heroes in football novels, he is destined to make it big. The same can't be said of these books.

When not rambling on about the Lobo-Solti Affair, the enigmatic, and occasionally batty, Brian Glanville can usually be found writing novels. Again, these books are principally aimed at the children's market: *Director's Wife*, *King of Hackney Marshes*, *Rise of Gerry Logan* and *Goalkeepers Are Crazy*. Having ploughed through a number of them, I can only deduce that it's not goalkeepers but publishers who are crazy.

One favourite ploy of book

publishers is to get a footballer to write a book with someone else who can do joined-up writing. To no avail, usually. A quartet of books by Norman Giller and Jimmy Greaves came out some time ago, starring a completely fictitious character called Jackie Groves. Jackie is an American striker, who scores lots of goals but isn't really liked by many of his team mates because he doesn't do any work (although sleeping with their wives may also have a bearing on things). His promiscuity stems from his having been sexually abused as a child, and he grows up in constant fear of 'becoming' homosexual. We grow up in constant fear that there may be additions to this series. It goes without saying that the books are absolute rubbish, but at least it kept Jimmy out of the pubs for a while in the late Seventies.

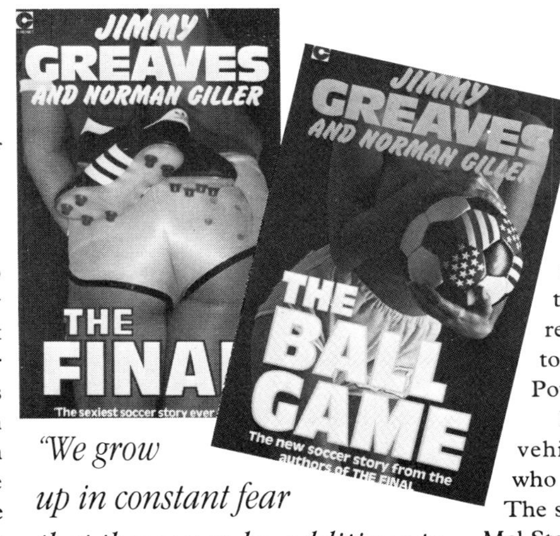

"We grow up in constant fear that there may be additions to this series."

That well-known Renaissance Man of Dagenham and creator of Hazell, Terry Venables, also had a stab at this lark with a laudable, but ultimately laughable, book called *They Used To Play On Grass,* written in 1971 with Gordon Williams, but set some time in the future, where players even earn as much as £200 per week. We know that it's fiction because Terry says: *"Scottish football has improved by leaps and bounds since that inspirational performance in the 1978 World Cup."* The less said about that, the better. The other main flaw (other than the fact that the book is crap) is that some of the characters talk in Cockney rhyming slang: Richards, Niagaras, orchestra stalls and cockles, to name but a few, all loom large throughout; and I'm still none the wiser.

Another book with a weird language (not to say story) is *Albion! Albion!* by Dick Morland, a futuristic tale set in an anarchistic England controlled by the Four Clubs: Wanderers, Athletic, United and Rovers. After two coach loads of Spurs fans are burned alive by Villa fans in 1982, football is banned. Before you know it, each club has a territory into which 'Supporters' of other Clubs don't tread on pain of death. The sleeve blurb says: *"Makes* Clockwork Orange *seem a gentle fantasy."* It also makes *Clockwork Orange* seem a very good book. The parallels are legion: both contain a glossary of words used in the story, *Clockwork Orange* is based on Russian, *Albion! Albion!* is based on football. For example 'nonleague' means below standard; finished. A 'striker' is an active member of the main security force of one of the Four Clubs, and so on. The only remotely prescient part of the book is the claim that Villa won the Championship in 1979; only two years out. Frank Keating, writing in *The Guardian* in 1975, claimed after witnessing a disturbance at a Luton *v* Chelsea game that *"it is not going too far to say that there was a frightening glimpse of what Morland was getting at."* It is also not going too far to say that this was a frightening glimpse of Frank Keating.

An honourable mention should also be made of the Richard Allen books, including such ideologically sound works as *Skinhead* and *Suedehead.* Growing up as a socially-warped misfit, these books seemed to me to encapsulate life itself. Re-reading them now, it is frightening to think that both they and Enoch Powell were once taken seriously.

Football appeares to be the ideal vehicle for wacky ideas, as anyone who has read *Danger Zone* will attest. The story, by Paul Gascoigne's solicitor Mel Stein, revolves around a week leading up to a Championship decider involving two clubs: Stretford Athletic and Thamesmead United. Naturally, there is a riot during the game, with most of South London being blown up as a result. Along the way we are treated to a couple of random killings by Stretford fans and a rape scene handled with all the sensitivity of a Gascoigne Cup Final tackle: *"...again [she] felt the thrill that she had so often promised herself alone in bed."* Mel Stein: Football's New Man, anyone?

A popular form of novel in the immediate post-war period was the football thriller, the doyen of these being the appropriately named Leonard Gribble. He wrote two, *They Kidnapped Stanley Matthews* and *The Arsenal Stadium Mystery,* both featuring ace dick, Anthony Slade. The *Arsenal* story is based on a typical day at Highbury: a well-known footballer drops dead shortly before half-time, in front of 70,000 witnesses. Superintendent Slade soon arrives with two pertinent questions: who was the mysterious girl who inquired after the murdered player, and where was 'Chopper' Harris when the player died?

In the same vein, but even more improbable, is *The White Hart Lane Mystery,* by Charles Hatton. A Hungarian scientist, Otto Kunniger, has developed a tactical theory (Plan K) which enables anyone who possesses it to, well, thrash all-comers. For no apparent reason, he gives the plan to Tottenham Hotspur, who just happen to be the favourite team of PC George Dixon (of Dock Green fame). As you may have guessed, the plans get stolen, as does Otto. PC Dixon, with a rat-a-tee-ta and an *"Evening all"*, sorts it all out. Spurs then use the plans to full effect by thrashing their next opponents (this *is* fiction, remember).

The modern equivalent of these bygone bibles of culture is the *Duffy* series, by Dan Kavanagh - aka Julian Barnes, the novelist and Leicester City supporter. The aforementioned Duffy is a bisexual private detective, who also plays in goal for a Sunday league team. The writing is superb, with some passages in the first book, *Duffy,* delightfully capturing the futile essence of amateur football.

If the reader hasn't lost the will to live, there are other genuinely good books, and one in particular stands out: *How Steeple Sinderby Wanderers Won The FA Cup,* by JL Carr. Unfortunately, the book is now out of print, which is perhaps an indication of the esteem that football literature is held in by publishers. Soaring prose, a gloriously improbable story told with wit and verve. Could anyone possibly ask for more?

Another fine attempt at overcoming the limitations of this tired category is the appallingly titled *Striker,* by Michael Irwin. Written in autobiographical form, the protagonist,

Vincent Gilpin, goes from park pitches to cup finals and back again. The story itself is routine football fare, but the most remarkable parts of the book are the passages concerning the on-the-field action. Despite the best efforts of ex-footballers at this caper, it is Irwin who comes nearest to conveying the feeling of actually being on the pitch with the player. No mean feat.

A third book which, surprisingly, is not at all bad is Derek Dougan's wittily titled *The Footballer*. The story, poor boy from rough area signs for club who, against all odds... yeah, you guessed. Anyway, this poor boy bears a remarkable resemblance to George Best, though I'm sure that is entirely coincidental. Okay, so three good novels might not send the Dewey Decimal library system into apoplexy, but they do at least prove that there is some life in the rotting corpse.

Probably the main reason that the football novel perpetually hovers around the potboiler level, rather than the glorious high-art status it surely deserves, is that it attracts potboiler authors rather than craftspeople of the quill. We are treated to a conveyor belt of fantastical stories wrapped in moribund prose rather than vice versa. In the absence of believable characters, we are left with empty stories about wonderful sportsmen, forever holding up cups and awards (unlike the authors).

Will they always remain 'books for kids', or will a publisher or author of standing have the nous and courage to commission or write *the* definitive book? There are several fine writers who either like football or who have made mention of it in their novels: Martin Amis, Julian Barnes, Alan Sillitoe, Stan Barstow, Arthur Hopcraft and Colin Dexter (plus the deceased Nabokov and Camus). There must be many more out there. Are you listening? ●

Thanks to the following for help with this article: John Earls, Keith Evans, Barney Williams, Steve Hanley, Nick Wright, Sarah Clark and Tony de la Fou

The Football Supporters' Guide To Opening Lines From Classic Literature.

"Hale knew, before he had been in Brighton three hours, that they meant to murder him. Steve Foster was out for revenge." - **Graham Greene's Brighton Rock**

"The past is a foreign country, they do things differently there. The England team play attractive, flowing football." - **LP Hartley's The Go Between**

"Hernia, hernia, hernia, hernia, hernia, hernia, hernia, hernia, hernia, hernia, hernia, hernia, hernia, HERnia, hernia, HERnia, hernia, hernia, hernia, hernia, HERnia, HERnia, HERnia, hernia, hernia, hernia, hernia, hernia, hernia, hernia, hernia, eight is the point, the point is eight, hernia, hernia, HERnia, hernia, hernia, hernia, hernia, all right, hernia, hernia, hernia, hernia, hard eight, hernia, hernia, hernia, HERnia, hernia, hernia, hernia, HERnia, hernia, hernia, hernia, HERnia, hernia, hernia, hernia, hernia. Ian Rush was having problems regaining fitness." - **Tom Wolfe's The Kandy-Kolored Tangerine-Flake Streamline Baby**

"The studio was filled with the rich odour of roses and when the light Summer wind stirred amidst the trees of the garden, there came through the open door the heavy scent of the lilac. Elton Welsby's Eau Savage was really getting on everyone's nerves." - **Oscar Wilde's Picture of Dorian Gray**

"The convict's outfit is pink and white striped. It is quite a contrast to the Arsenal red and white Adams is used to." - **Jean Genet's Thief's Journal**

"The night Vincent was shot he saw it coming. Jones's tackle on McMahon had seen to that." - **Elmore Leonard's Glitz**

"'I am back again after my absence of two weeks.' And so Mark Dennis returned after his third suspension of the season." - **Fyodor Dostoyesky's The Gambler**

"It was the best of times, it was the worst of times. No, let's be honest. It was another crap season for the Potters." - **Charles Dickens' A Tale of Two Cities**

FAWZI 'RASKALNIKOFF' ZUBERI & CHURSTON DECKLE

Hearing Problems

Graham Brack *could tell you a few stories about the strange things that happen at disciplinary hearings. In fact, here he comes now...*

Ten years have elapsed since I attended a Disciplinary Hearing. I started refereeing when I was fifteen, and my tutor told me that I should begin by enforcing the laws strictly, on the understanding that I could begin to relax them a little once I had some experience under my belt.

So it was that in my first season I sent off eighteen and cautioned sixty-six players. Before the second season, the FA wrote to us all demanding a tougher approach, so I did as I was told. By the time the pre-season friendlies came to an end, I already had five reports pending for sendings-off.

In my defence, I never sent anyone off without good cause, nor was any decision ever overturned by a disciplinary committee. In fact, one committee ticked me off in no uncertain manner for having been overly lenient and turning a blind eye to a momentary tiff between two players. Nevertheless, I found myself spending a lot of evenings at the Territorial Hall giving evidence.

The procedure varies a little from county to county, but a common pattern is as follows. At the end of the match, the official writes out his report and posts it to a Referee's Secretary. He sends a copy to the club, who decide if they want to ask for a personal hearing. Batches of these take place in any available committee-sized room with an anteroom available at little or no rent. If possible, cases relating to a single referee are taken together to keep his travelling expenses down.

There are numerous grounds for appeal but they may be classified thus:

1. Mistaken Identity. *"It was not Kev who kicked him, squire."* The chairman will then say *"Then who was it?"* The ritual reply is *"Person or persons unknown."* The chairman then says to the referee, *"Is it possible that you were mistaken?"* The wise referee says *"No, sir."* The chairman then says *"I thought not,"* and makes a mental note to add a week or two to the suspension.

2. Mountain Out Of A Molehill. *"Kev admits it may have looked like he roughed up the other guy, sir, but all he was doing was fending him off."* I once heard a player defend himself against a charge of kicking an opponent by claiming that he merely intended to kick the ball away, but missed and accidentally caught the other fellow's ankles. Both of them.

3. International Incident. If you ever take part in one of those Easter festivals where malcontents from the Continent play against good, wholesome English lads, be prepared for one of these. They come in two varieties: *"In France, such pushing of ze goalkeeper, she is not allowed and zat is why Pierre have complained at him."* (Pierre being a 6ft 2in centre-forward who head-butted his opposite number after a shoulder charge on his goalkeeper); and the English equivalent: *"These Eyeties fall on the floor if you look at them, we reckon the ref was taken in by a bit of clowning."* The full-back in question was taken in by an ambulance.

4. Extenuating Circumstance. In this defence, the offender admits absolutely everything and asks for the full penalty of the court. His manager then lets slip the nugget of information he was *"told"* to keep to himself. *"He's been under a strain since his wife ran off with our reserve team right-half,"* is a good one. *"He used to play rugby and this is only his second game of real football,"* is another. My own favourite came from the manager of a hotel side who had seen his inside-left take a long walk for attempted homicide thinly disguised as a tackle. *"He is a Spanish waiter, sir,"* he said, and sat down as if that were all the explanation needed.

5. Provocation. I never had a racially-motivated offence to deal with, but I did have a player who thumped another and protested that the striker kept trying to rub his bottom when they were close-marking. This is a very effective way for forwards to get a yard of space; very few defenders will stick as close as they should to someone who purrs when they push up against him. I suppose this is ungentlemanly conduct, but it is not easy to spot. A certain pub side in Southend were famed at one time for this sort of thing, and I wonder if it still goes on. A couple of women used to come along on Sunday mornings to support them, but left ten minutes from the end. I asked why this was and discovered that they were topless go-go dancers in the pub and their first show was at midday.

6. World Weariness. Once in a while you come across a player with a death wish. Perhaps his career is nearing a close and he wants to go out in a blaze of glory. These are the dangerous ones, because they may run amok if you cross them. I recall seeing one who had played for nearly twenty years without ever being cautioned who lost his head and started the mother of all punch-ups. I am pleased to say I wasn't the man in the middle that day.

7. Send For A Social Worker. Despite all the foregoing, there is always the odd individual who just likes getting sent off. Maybe it's a macho thing. Long years ago I refereed a certain youth club's game during which a player whom I shall call Kev (because that was his name) perpetrated some violence on an opponent. I took him aside and gave him a caution and two or three minutes of reasoned argument on his folly. After the match I was profusely thanked by the manager for not sending him off. It turned out this was the only match that month in which Kev had *not* been sent off. He was crushed by the whole experience, and sat in the corner of the dressing room for nearly an hour after the match without changing his kit. One of his team-mates told me, maliciously, that Kev was confused when I blew the final whistle because he had never been on the pitch at the end of a game before, and didn't know what he was supposed to do.

So, next time you bay for the red card, remember the poor ref and his writer's cramp. Wouldn't it be instructive if fans had to fill in a report after a sending-off?

Rep. of Ireland

Football has never been more popular in the Republic of Ireland than at present. JOE HENNON *examines the reasons why...*

Emerald

I GREW UP IN IRELAND DURING THE 1970s, when soccer there was very much a minority sport, only eight towns being represented in the League of Ireland. There were historical reasons for this. Soccer was a British sport introduced to Ireland at a time when the independence movement was very strong. The most popular field sports were Gaelic football and hurling, and the organisation which controlled these, the Gaelic Athletic Association, banned its members from playing or even attending 'foreign' games.

However, Gaelic games were not suited to confined spaces, and soccer was adopted by the urban working class. But it never managed to spread outside the towns until the mid-1960s, when a number of factors combined to begin a revolution which, by 1988, was to transform Irish soccer.

Firstly, the televising of the 1966 World Cup Finals in next-door England, the European Cup wins of Celtic and Man Utd and the beaming into Irish homes of English League games all helped to create a groundswell of interest in soccer. The result of this was a significant increase in the number of kids playing club football. Secondly, in 1972 the GAA removed the ban on its members playing 'foreign' games and, thirdly, FIFA's parental rule came into force allowing the children of Irish emigrants to play for Ireland.

Nonetheless, Ireland's principal spectator sport remained Gaelic football. Although I and my friends played street soccer and followed English clubs, the terraces we stood on most often were those of Croke Park, home of the Dublin County Gaelic football team. This was mostly because Dublin were an outstanding side that hardly ever lost. Furthermore, they were representing us, Dubliners, and they were doing so with style and power, unlike Shamrock Rovers, St Patrick's Athletic et al.

However, Gaelic games had no international outlet, which presented soccer with an obvious opportunity, but the national side would have to be either very successful or very stylish to convert Gaelic fans spoiled by a diet of fast-moving, high-scoring games. Unfortunately, it was neither. Many of our players were from the lower English divisions or the League Of Ireland, and the team rated on a par with Finland. For Irish soccer fans, the national team's history was one of unfulfilled promise, just a long series of disappointments.

In the mid-1970s, a crop of young players such as Brady, Stapleton and O'Leary appeared and, under the guidance of player-manager John Giles, Ireland at last began to win games and attract bigger crowds. Indeed, our form improved to the point where we were practically invincible at home. Attendances rose significantly and the team moved their matches from Dalymount (capacity 30,000) to Lansdowne Road (capacity 55,000).

Towards the end of the 1970s, one of the stars of the Dublin Gaelic football team, Kevin Moran, was dramatically signed by Manchester United and was soon capped for Ireland. This was Roy of the Rovers stuff and had a significant impact on the attitude to soccer among Gaelic supporters. Highly promising young players were continuing to emerge both at home - Whelan and McGrath - and among the Anglo-Irish - Lawrenson and Sheedy. However, qualification for the major championships eluded us. After Eoin Hand replaced Giles as manager, the team's performances deteriorated alarmingly, culminating in a disastrous campaign for the 1986 World Cup qualifiers. Support for the team dwindled and FIFA began to confuse us with Iceland for seeding purposes.

Fortunately, there were encouraging signs in other areas: the League of Ireland had by now been extended to two divisions and to parts of the country which had never been represented before, while the number of clubs at junior level was increasing at a steady rate. In 1985 our youth team (including one Niall Quinn) reached the semi-finals of the European Championships and, for the first time, the World Youth Cup Finals. We desperately needed the senior side to get its act together, and in 1986 our prayers were answered by the appointment of Jack Charlton as Ireland's first full-time professional manager.

It took him a year to get the team to play as he wanted. They were beaten four times in that

period, but in the subsequent four years would lose only three more games. Possession football was ditched as Ireland began to play each match as if they were losing 0-1 with five minutes left. Soccer was still a minority sport, but the draw for the 1988 European Championship Finals changed all that. On June 12th, 1988, Irish soccer made its quantum leap, *that* win over England sparking off celebrations that lasted for days. After a draw in which the USSR were outplayed, and a desperately unlucky defeat by the Dutch, the followers of other sports were hooked. The Gaelic supporters in particular appreciated the team's strong-running, hard-tackling, direct style of play. This was a team with an 'attitude', with plenty of skilful players, and which, above all, had shown that it could now compete with the best. They returned to Ireland to be mobbed by over a quarter of a million people. Every home game for the 1990 World Cup qualifiers was an instant sell-out, and we won them all, qualifying with four points to spare. When the re-match with England arrived, the country was in the grip of football fever. The national television station, RTE, broadcast a preview of the game which displayed scenes of manic anticipation in remote villages which three years previously had never heard of soccer. The tournament turned the team into a national institution. Only in Ireland was the hysteria of the Italians matched, with motorcades careering around the streets until the small hours after every game. When the team returned to Dublin this time, they would be greeted by half a million people - one seventh of the population of the country.

“This was a team with an ‘attitude’.”

Guile

Soccer now appears to have taken root in Ireland for good. The numbers playing the game in areas such as Munster - a hotbed of Gaelic games - increased by more than 70% over the last four years. A non-league side reached the FAI Cup Final in 1990, and five League of Ireland clubs were knocked out by such clubs in the first round this year - an indication of the growing strength of the game outside the league. In 1991 the Cup was won by Galway, the first time the trophy has ever gone West. Gaelic games and rugby supporters, Northern Irish nationalists and the emigrant Irish in Britain have all attached themselves to the team, and each Irish game for the last three years has been the occasion for an enormous party.

There is still work to be done, of course. Of the twenty-six counties in the Republic, only thirteen are represented in the League of Ireland, and we still await the club team capable of competing meaningfully in the European cups. Nor do we have a national soccer stadium. With regard to players, however, there are grounds for great optimism. It is significant that in the period between 1970 and 1986 almost all of the Irish-born players were Dubliners (imagine an English side consisting solely of players from London), whereas we now have players from Donegal, Dundalk and Cork in the first eleven. In contrast with our previous weakness, there are now First Division players who are not even within sight of the squad, and young talent such as Roy Keane continues to emerge. We fully expect to be involved in the shake-up for USA '94, and, with the support of forty million Irish-Americans, maybe we ain't seen nothin' yet...

Back in the days when Jackie Charlton was a player and Roy Keane was in nappies, football in the Irish Republic was synonymous with one name: Waterford. CHRIS POWER *recalls the team's finest moments...*

A friend of mine was 'reported' to the GAA after he'd been seen buying a programme outside a soccer ground. He didn't actually go to the game, but just wanted a souvenir of a friendly between Waterford and Manchester United.

Waterford, in the South-East of Ireland, has, like most former garrison towns, always been a soccer stronghold. It is the birthplace of Waterford Crystal, Jim Beglin, Mick McCarthy's father and, er, Val Doonican.

Situated on the outskirts of the town, Kilcohan Park is an unlikely sporting venue. In fact, it is hardly a ground at all, merely an undulating meadow with goalposts at either end, surrounded by a greyhound track. But here all comparisons with Wembley end. The venue is owned by the Irish Greyhound Board, although the soccer club has been in residence for the last sixty years or so. Between 1967 and 1973 - at this venue with no floodlights or terracing, with two stands of concrete steps, corrugated roofs and no seats - some of the best football ever seen in Ireland was played.

Waterford won six League of Ireland titles in those years. They invented the type of football made famous by the Brazilian team of 1970 - ten attackers and no defenders. My schoolfriends and I used to arrive at the ground at 1.30 for 3.30 kick-off to get a vantage point, standing on the benches lined along the back row of the main stand - the ground's only concession to consumer comfort.

By 2.30 the stand was usually full and at 3.30 the lions were fed to the Christians. Sligo Rovers were once beaten 9-0. Mick Lynch - inter-provincial amateur boxer, senior league rugby player, inter-county Gaelic footballer, scratch handicap golfer and Waterford's centre-forward - scored five. His fifth was particularly memorable. Mick was covered in so much mud that he was mistaken for a defender by the Sligo goalkeeper who threw the ball out to him. Mick nonchalantly chipped the ball over the bemused keeper's head and into the net.

We really loved the visit of English League clubs. Plymouth Argyle came, laughed at the state of our pitch, and lost 8-3. We allowed Bristol City to escape with a 2-2 draw and even permitted Leeds United to beat us 4-2, but this was merely an act of appreciation on our part for Gary Sprake's performance. In a European Cup game at Parkhead, we actually led Celtic 2-0 before losing 3-2.

For many Blues fans, the highlight of those years was a European Cup game against Manchester United in

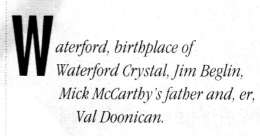

Waterford, birthplace of Waterford Crystal, Jim Beglin, Mick McCarthy's father and, er, Val Doonican.

Crystal Clear

September 1968 before a crowd of 55,000 at Lansdowne Road. United were holders of the Cup: Best, Law and Charlton all played and we held our own, losing 3-1. In the return leg, the Waterford team was applauded off the pitch, such was their sportsmanship in contrast with recent visitors Estudiantes. In the course of the game, Blues winger Al Casey was struck on a particularly sore place. Poleaxed, Al was surrounded by United players, some of whom started laughing when they realised his predictament, causing his reported reply: *"It's alright for you lot - you don't have to get up for work in the morning."*

Waterford had many fine players in that era. There was John O'Neill who could dominate a game without ever leaving the centre circle; Peter Bryan who once scored an own goal from near the halfway line; Johnny Matthews who never missed a penalty; and Alfie Hale, one of six members of the same family to play league football for Waterford, who scored consistently with his head - no mean achievement for a man of just 5ft 6. It would also be a mistake to assume that the highlight of Shay Brennan's career was winning a European Cup Winners' medal with Manchester United in 1968. His career took off shortly afterwards, when he became Waterford's player-manager and won a League Of Ireland medal. Having reached the pinnacle of his career he then retired.

One day in 1966 we heard that the club had signed a goalkeeper *"direct from the English First Division."* Peter Thomas, who had deputised for an injured Bill Glazier, was brought over from Coventry City. In his first game for Waterford, the nineteen-year-old Thomas saved a penalty. Over the next fifteen years, he was a hero in Waterford. To us schoolboys his ability seemed to defy the laws of physics and made us question our eyesight.

To stand behind his goal was to receive a lesson in the use of the English language. Supporters of other clubs thought Thomas saved his best performances for games at their own venue. He didn't - he played like that every week. Had he been a few inches taller than six foot instead of a few inches under it, he would surely have become one of the best keepers in England. As it was, he played for Ireland after becoming a naturalised citizen, his last game being a clean sheet against Poland on the Sunday after they had knocked England out of the 1974 World Cup.

● Left: Doing pennants. Shay Brennan and Billy McNeil, European Cup, 1970.
Underlay: Peter Thomas and Lou Macari can't bear to look.
Below: The 1972 squad looking pleased with themselves.

My favourite memory of all was the last League game of 1971-72. Waterford were two points ahead of Cork Hibernians and had to play them away in front of 35,000. We were down in the first minute, by half-time the score was 2-0, and we had been reduced to ten men through injury. With eleven minutes left, we got a consolation goal. Five minutes to go and a Cork defender handled the ball - 2-2. One of our defenders then did the same, but no penalty was awarded. The Cork fans went crazy and to rub more salt in their wounds, Alfie Hale then made it 3-2 and we'd achieved the greatest comeback since the resurrection.

"To stand behind Peter Thomas' goal was to receive a lesson in the use of the English language."

I still go to Kilcohan. Crowds are small, sometimes less than 100. You might get in free on your birthday. We have even fewer fans than my 'other' team, Stenhousemuir. Alfie Hale is manager, all the players are local and we scored eight against Longford Town a few seasons ago. We may never get the ground full on Sundays again - even with a good team there are too many counter-attractions. We may never win the League again either, but the few remaining fans go because we don't want to see League of Ireland football die in Waterford. And because we live in hope of beating Plymouth 8-3 again!

the Dire Tribe

Professor Granville Spivey is the most acclaimed sociologist resident in the Greater Rochdale area and a keen observer of professional football to boot. DAVID DAVIES *analyses one of his greatest works...*

ON FREQUENT TRIPS TO LONDON, I HAVE BEEN KNOWN TO burrow about in the musty book emporia of Charing Cross Road, in the usually fruitless hope of digging out and dusting off a literary footballing classic. Recently, however, I struck gold. The treasure I unearthed proved that the publishing of the Worst Football Book Ever Written - Desmond Morris' *The Soccer Tribe* - was an old school tie conspiracy of the grossest hue.

I can reveal that Morris nicked the whole idea from a vastly superior work. *Ballwatching,* by Professor (Rochdale Tech, Honorary) Granville Spivey, is the result of well over half a century of observations of the *"nomadic football-following folk of the North of England"* and of the invading hordes who have ventured into their territory weekly for eons.

The following is an inevitably brief look at Professor Spivey's work. The fulsome wealth of his ruminations would take every minute of a four-year university course to comprehend fully.

Tribal Followers

Professor Spivey has observed over the years that the dress and general appearance of football supporters can tell us something about their character.

Mr Morris calls this the *"costume language"* of the soccer fan, citing such obvious signals as which wrist the fan wears his scarf on, or whether he sports a Wrangler jacket or a beige Harrington. Spivey asserts that the signs are much more subtle than this, indeed that they would be almost invisible to the seasoned observer.

For example, with experience we might be able to ascertain the essential difference in character between a fan who taps one on the shoulder and says *"Excuse me, mate,"* as he negotiates his way past with a melting, plastic cup full of steaming Oxo (it's never really Bovril), and the one who plants a sharp blow behind your left ear and screams *"Outta me way, y'soft Southern poof,"* as he careers down the terraces with his confederates, without even stopping to check which side of Vicarage Road one hails from.

Dress is, of course, vitally important in identifying 'types' of fan. A satinised Tacchini leisure top with a Stanley knife peeping out of the pocket is the sign of a fan best avoided, while jam-jar bottom spectacles, brushed denim trousers with patch pockets on the front and a Millets' own-brand kagoul with a bunch of foil-wrapped Marmite butties nestling in the map pouch is less likely to be a cause for concern.

Then again, if the latter also has a Safeway carrier bag containing a rail pass and a softback copy of *The Football Grounds Of Great Britain,* it could be time to leave. We all, with the exception of Desmond Morris, know what that means.

Professor Spivey adds that another dead giveaway is that anyone who calls football 'soccer' is an impostor, probably struggling to shake off the effects of a 'rugby school' background (eg Desmond Morris, Russell Osman, anyone who has been involved in deciding the future of soc... football recently).

The subtlest of the subtle, however, is the Newcastle United fan. He blends in with his surroundings wherever he goes, and, as a result, is often to be found in: a) the away sections at St James's Park; b) the home sections of any other ground.

This does not really matter, because it is years since Newcastle fans have been known for practising hooliganism. Nevertheless, this freedom of movement isn't supposed to be allowed, so it is unfortunate that few policemen seem to be able to spot those, admittedly minuscule, peculiarities which set the Magpie apart from other fans, viz:

a) an accent which is not only impenetrable outside Tyne & Wear, Norway and Denmark, but, also, the speakers of which find completely impossible to either moderate or disguise.

b) a point-blank refusal, even in the interests of disguise, to wear anything on their torsos except (at the most) a t-shirt four sizes too small, even in pissing rain and especially if there is snow on the ground. As all Newcastle fans know, *"Ernly poofs wear curts."*

c) a maniacal predilection for Mars Bars, strong ale and dressing up in Batman/highwayman/chicken costumes for the entertainment of 'newspapers'. NB: This afflicts only a limited number of Newcastle devotees, although even being spotted by *"poncey teams from up London"* as a potentially world class footballing talent apparently does little to reduce the symptoms.

Tribal Chants

Professor Spivey is in no doubt that football chants evolved, as did most fans' habits, out of practical necessity. Early followers took an entirely individual approach to voicing their feelings, and their cries invariably took the form of offerings of practical advice. For example: *"Get thi' finger out, Ladysmith, yer big nosebleed!"*

As frustration set in, this turned to straightforward abuse, but initially only directed at the players: *"Hodgkiss, tha's abaht as much yoos as tits on a chickin!"*

Whether the shouts were designed to advise, encourage or insult, the packed grounds of the post-War football boom made it increasingly difficult for them to be heard, especially through a mouthful of glutinous meat and potato pie. It was then that crowds began to realise that if they shouted in unison their cries would be heard far and wide, and that these would serve to scold or bolster their team and to discourage the opposition.

They also discovered that it was much easier to call in unison, and coherently, if they followed a simple tune. The communal football chant was born. Furthermore, when both ends of the ground struck up a song, competitive chanting began, and from there it was a short step to the exchange of abuse between opposing fans as well as insults being hurled at players and opposing teams.

In *The Soccer Tribe,* Desmond Morris limited his research to chantings sampled at *"a number of matches in England during the 1978-79 season."* Most of the examples given referred to Oxford United, Oxford players or teams that had played at the Manor Ground that season. Professor Spivey agrees with me that this hardly constitutes a methodology worthy of a definitive history of chanting. The peculiarities and biases of individual crowds mean that a much wider sample needs to be taken to achieve statistical verity. Oxford United, for example, betray a possibly unique devotion to the stating of the obvious, witness: *"One Jason Seacole, There's only one Jason Seacole."*

Now that the Iron Curtain has been dismantled and Eastern Bloc football fans have a new-found right to such pleasures as Radio Lokomotiv Kosice or Arges Pitesti Clubcall, it is to be hoped that their songs and chants will survive the ravages of democratisation. Freedom of intellectual thought should never be allowed to whither such classics as *"Szombierki Bytom, Your Lacklustre Physical Efforts Are An Insult To The Heroes Of The International Class Struggle And Set A Shoddy Example For The Productivity Of The Noble Workers Of The Sczeczin Tractor Works Who Have Gone All Quiet Over There 'Cos They Only Sing When They're Winning!"* to the tune of the Polish national anthem.

This is somewhat removed from, but spine-tinglingly in tune with, the helpful interjections of the mufflered Sheffield foundrymen and Lancashire millworkers who first exercised their tonsils across a patch of fenced mud before the Great War.

Those days are irrevocably no more, but, given that singing with Pavarottian gusto is much harder to execute sitting than standing, the 'Bloke Behind All Of Us' could be about to rediscover a mass audience in much the same way as Dusty Springfield and the late, great Roy Orbison have done. Every cloud, as they say.

The Tribal Colours

"Although most clubs wear plain colours, some prefer a patterned costume. The designs are nearly always simple, the most common being a set of vertical stripes."

Thus wrote Desmond Morris. He detailed the practical purpose of the Tribal Colours as being: *"To give wearers a psychological advantage; to make them look different from their neighbours; to make them look different from their opponents."*

Psychological advantage? Of course. Wouldn't you feel inferior to a chap haring towards you with 'NOBO' written across his chest? And we all remember the effect of Huddersfield's small yellow and black checks at Maine Road. Was it 10-0 or 10-1?

Different from their near neighbours? Newcastle and Sunderland have worn black and white and red and white stripes with black shorts forever. Ditto Sheffield Wednesday and United (for black stripes read blue). Similarly, Barnsley, Doncaster and Rotherham are all in red and white.

Different from their opponents? Now you're talking. I miss the days when Man Utd and Man City trusted us to tell them apart when both wore white shorts. Did Utd really think that we couldn't identify them at Newcastle if they wore their mainly black socks?

I much prefer the more butch approach of Scottish clubs, who wear their colours like a badge and to hell with the other lot. The sea of green and white that is Hibs *v* Celtic is the classic example. I really admire the wit of Hibs wearing white shirts with green sleeves and shorts as their second-choice kit. Brilliant! Not for them the poncey concerns of English clubs thrown into a panic because the white Umbro logo on their socks clashes with the oppositions'.

The anthropological significance of this is nil. It just makes me bloody mad.

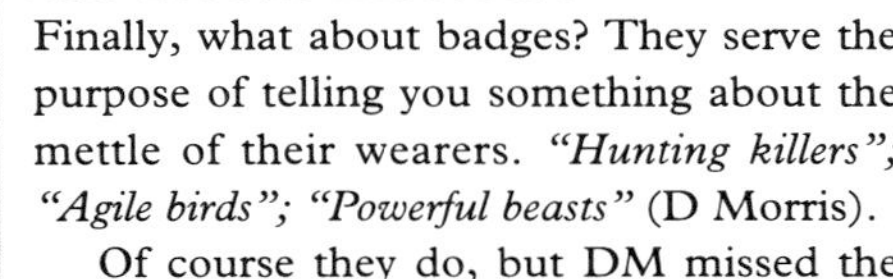

The Tribal Emblems

Finally, what about badges? They serve the purpose of telling you something about the mettle of their wearers. *"Hunting killers"; "Agile birds"; "Powerful beasts"* (D Morris).

Of course they do, but DM missed the best ones. Reading: the tenacity of an elm tree. Preston: the killer instinct of a reclining sheep. Shrewsbury: the universe-straddling power of the pygmy shrew. Chester: the sure-footedness of a sea-lion. Birmingham City: the world's on top of *us*. Coventry: the elephant that will never forget losing at Sutton.

Professor Granville Spivey is 107.

Non-League

The Bucks Stop

It's a soccer hotbed with two local teams always in contention for honours. That's right, we're talking about Buckingham. PHILIP CORNWALL *takes up the story.*

BUCKINGHAM IS NOT FAMOUS FOR ANYTHING; except, perhaps, indirectly, for having its Duke's townhouse taken over by the monarch. It has a county named after it, yet most people don't seem to know that there is a town of Buckingham. Boroughhood conferred by Alfred The Great, taken away by Ted Heath. Neatly on the boundaries of three TV regions, even if something did happen there no-one outside the town would ever find out, as no-one would know that it was they who were supposed to send cameras. When Oxford refused to give Maggie an honorary degree, it was the independent University of Buckingham that gave her her consolation; my consolation comes from knowing that nobody noticed.

Submerged by this tidal wave of media indifference and public ignorance, the town has somehow acquired two relatively successful non-League teams.

Unfortunately, leading members of the still more successful *Keep Buckingham Obscure* campaign sit on vital committees of both the Berks and Bucks FA and the Beazer Homes League. You've heard of stories of a side being denied promotion on a technicality before - but two, in one town, in one season?

Buckingham Town, aka 'The Robins', had twice been brought to national attention before this year. In 1984, a first round FA Cup tie *v* Orient yielded a five-second view of the ground on *Football Focus*, a comment from Bob Wilson that this was the prettiest ground in use that day and a 2-0 defeat. A couple of years later, *The Independent*'s sports diarist reported the occasion when our centre-forward of the time was arrested ten minutes before another Cup game, during the team-talk.

> **"Our centre-forward was arrested ten minutes before another Cup game, during the team-talk."**

Lower down the non-League pyramid, Buckingham Athletic play on a piece of open ground, briefly in view of those driving along the Stratford Road. Yet, deprived of both the oxygen of publicity by never having anyone arrested and the oxygen of the air by passing cars, they rose to a level where only their lack of facilities could prevent further progress up the non-League pyramid.

Athletic are not perceived as a threat to Town; the Tranmere/Liverpool relationship on a marginally smaller scale. My walk to Ford Meadow goes past their ground, and in Winter their lack of floodlights means a 1.45pm kick-off time, allowing me to linger a while without missing the main event. Even so, my knowledge of Athletic was mostly limited to what I read in the local paper. I can remember when they collected a goal difference of -77, and was surprised and delighted to see that they, like Town, were in danger of winning their league in March of this year.

A serious rivalry could do wonders for attendances; the thought that drawing them in a cup could see a crowd in excess of 300 simultaneously attempt to order drinks in the clubhouse after an imperious performance by the Robins filled me with anticipation.

Competing with this desire for fixtures new was a certain nervousness, however. Town's run to the FA Vase Quarter-Finals had seen Michael Whale of *Newsroom South East* make a return trip to North Bucks, six years after the Orient game. We were honoured that a TV company had laid claim to the story and found us on the map, but three minutes from time Guiseley scored their winner.

The Vase run and the weather had led to mass postponements, and eighteen league games were left on March 13th. Absolute deadline, May 4th. The danger that disappointment and exhaustion would lead to a repeat of 89-90 was imminent, when we missed promotion by just one point.

By the beginning of April, eight games had brought six wins - and two defeats by Salisbury, one of the sides still above us. But now we were playing the side bottom of the league: easy victims?

Our game against Corinthian was, without doubt, the worst match of the season. New heights of awfulness were reached that day. It was the kind of 0-0 draw which makes you understand what people see in Primal Scream Therapy.

British Rail enquiry staff had laughed at me when I'd explained why I needed to go to Sudbury and back in one evening; I treated this ignorance with a contempt usually reserved for Irthlingborough Diamonds fans.

After Corinthian, similar treatment would have seen me put the phone down in shame. The depth of the depression came when a lob from Steve

Jenkins, a centre-forward known for finishing rather than finesse, seemed certain to bring home three undeserved points, until the weather intervened. The ball stuck in a puddle, you think. Wrong. The wind blew it off course? Stili wrong. While the Summer of 1991 saw snow in Sussex in June, Spring saw drought warnings. The baked mud of Kent, instead of giving a little and letting the ball cross the line at knee-height, threw it skywards. It struck the crossbar and bounced well out. Not even a Russian linesman could have given that one. Yet I knew that justice had been done by the sun that day. At least Keith Baker (one League game in goal for Grimsby, in 1975) had kept a clean sheet.

Eight consecutive clean sheets later, and, on May 1st, a 2-0 win in our first competitive overseas match (Newport, Isle of Wight) gave us the title. That game had ended a spell of seven matches in just twelve days. Bad enough for League players, but this team didn't just have homes to go to, they had jobs the next day. Still, Town fans were in heaven; we knew Ford Meadow wouldn't pass the ground-graders, but a groundshare at a Conference-standard club (Aylesbury) was in the air. Athletic fans, however, were in Purgatory.

In order to gain promotion to the Key Consultants South Midlands League Premier Division, one step from the Vauxhall (now Diadora) League, Athletic needed to be a 'Senior' club, a qualification granted by the Berks and Bucks FA rather than the league; since records began, a formality. The 'no' Athletic received came from nowhere.

But when the *Buckingham Advertiser* went for a colour centre spread of the Robins' final game, a 2-0 defeat before the largest league crowd of the

Here

● ***Above: Terry Shrieves needs help against Canterbury City. Didn't their games teacher ever tell them not to crowd the ball? Below: Shrieves' fellow forward, Tony McGuinness, strikes a traditional pose.***

"You've heard of a side being denied promotion on a technicality before - but two, in one town, in one season?"

season, the headline on the rest of the sport was **Double joy for Athletic**. They could get the vital status through a groundshare with Town - who wouldn't be playing at Ford Meadow, but at Aylesbury - and had completed a league and league cup double. The world was once again a happy place. Until...

There was always the possibility that the league would reject the sharing plan, but I refused to believe that they would turn down a club using a ground of Aylesbury's standard while carrying out improvements at their home. Athletic's double joy became **Double blow rocks Robins**: Town's manager, Phil Lines, had gone to Premier Division Worcester, and the league had, indeed, defied common sense, natural justice and my prayers.

The Berks and Bucks FA, had welcomed Athletic's compromise. What the Beazer Homes League failed to realise was that the money needed to make the changes it deemed necessary could more easily be raised by a promoted team: promotion brings publicity, enthusiasm and larger crowds.

Dennis Strudwick, league secretary (voodoo dolls available on request), reasoned that it was necessary to have grounds improved to a certain level so that potential champions would not need to do too much work and so would not be denied promotion to the Conference, Dover's fate.

Logical enough. But Buckingham are as likely to win the Premier Division in the near future as Notts County are to win the First. And anyway, they were going to do the improvements while at Aylesbury. Groundshares are good enough next season for the First, Second, Third and Fourth Divisions, the Conference and the Key Consultants South Midlands League Premier Division, but not for the Beazer Homes League.

Keith Baker replaced the Worcester-bound Phil Lines; meanwhile, Athletic parted company with *their* championship-winning manager, in a row over player payments. But they can enjoy their promotion, and a change of heart by the league means that they'll even get to stay at Stratford Road. Next year, all we'll have is the championship pennant and memories of an outrageous season: Tom Pearson's injury-time hat-trick at Andover. He scored his first after 91 minutes. Seven minutes later, Tom had three, the five.

Then the four-times-postponed Vase game at Saffron Walden. Dark, wet, in the middle of nowhere, in front of 766. Goliath playing David in theory, but David had about 700 cheering him on. We led 1-0 from the 10th minute until the 87th; an equalizer brought 'You're not singing anymore' from the East Anglians... we weren't singing in the first place. A minute later, the winner, again from Tom, and now we really were singing.

But, best of all, club record goalscorer Terry Shrieves' rendition of 'Release Me' on the coach back from Newport, after he'd scored his first in the league since Christmas to win the title. 'The Last Waltz' was number one on the day I was born, but, whatever Dennis Strudwick says, there's only one Engelbert Humperdinck song for me now.

Monty Sinton's Space Filler...

Five Anagrams For People Who Hate Anagrams

1. Ten Ruined Matches (Manchester United)
2. Drown Stolen Bear (Bolton Wanderers)
3. I Cant Say Sew (Swansea City)
4. A Last Place Cry (Crystal Palace)
5. Brave Hand On Night Boil (Brighton And Hove Albion)

Five Titles That Were Nearly Used In This Book

1. Avenue Had Enough Of This Team? (Bradford rivalry)
2. Denmark, Get Set, Go (Danish football)
3. Ferranti Christ (East of Scotland League)
4. Wellington Boots (Football in New Zealand)
5. It's A Fair Copacabana (Brazilian stadia)

Kenna Gowland Says...

"Christmas? I've had a right carry on, me, like. I've went to the works' social at the Morrit Arms, Friday, haven't I. An' I've had a drink. To be honest like, I've had a few. I'm not kidding, there was more whisky in me than in Terry Cochrane's locker. Well, half as much anyway.

So it's two in the morning an' we're off back. I'm last out, cos I've just went to the toilet. Well, when I go through the door, the cold air hits me. I wasn't pissed, like. It was the cold air. I was disorientated.

I don't know what you're laughing at. Give over. You handle drink like Kevin Pole handles crosses. Badly.

I was disorientated. I see the headlights of the coach on the other side of the car park, so I head for them. An' I'm walking an' walking towards these headlights. An' walking an' walking.

Course when I get to them they're not headlights at all. They're two carriage lamps clagged either side of a farmhouse door. So I says, *"Oh Hell,"* an' I set off back to the Morrit. I'm right disorientated by this stage. My legs are going in all directions. I must've looked like Kernaghan trying for a volley. An' I'm walking an' walking.

Eventually I get back to the car park an' I sit down on this bench. I say to myself, *"I'll just wait here. An' when they realise they've went without us they'll come back. The bastards."*

So I sat on this bench and waited.

When I woke up, it's two thirty, Saturday afternoon an' I'm surrounded by this small crowd. I've only walked from Greta Bridge to West Auckland and fell asleep on a bench at Darlington Road Football Ground!

Well, as I was there, I thought I might as well stop on for the match.

I says to this bloke, *"Who're you playing?"*

He goes *"Evenwood,"* and says, *"Just think, one time we beat Juventus 6-1. An' now here we are, eighty years on, playing against a pit village in front of a few hundred people. It makes you sad."*

I says, *"It might make you sad, chief, but it's the thought that one day the same thing could happen to Sunderland that keeps a lot of us going."*

Ow, pet! When you can tear yourself away."

KENNA *was leaning on* HARRY PEARSON*'s shoulder*

GAZZER THE CLOWN – AND BERNARD INGHAM!

Entertainment U.S.A.

Wisconsin is not perhaps the best place to live if you are a football fan. DAVID WANGERIN *made the most of it, though, thanks to Mario Marchado and his cohorts...*

I don't suppose you could call me the typical American. I don't own a gun. I've never bought a Bruce Springsteen record. I don't insist on cold beer because I don't even like beer. And the activities of the British Royal Family are of no interest to me.

Take this a step further. I actually like to watch soccer. Living here in Britain has its advantages, particularly as I come from Wisconsin where no professional soccer team, however fleetingly, has ever set up shop. You don't get much exposure to English football in Wisconsin. You could count on the fingers of one hand the people in my hometown who had actually heard of Stanley Matthews. Growing up in the Seventies, raised on the World Series and Super Bowl, I'd never been introduced to the glory that is the FA Cup or the Third Division promotion race. I'd never been to England, never met anyone who had. For all I knew, Manchester United was a freight company and Geoff Hurst worked at the bank by the bridge. And yet, raised in a part of the world which didn't know Bobby Charlton from Charlton Athletic, I came to develop an affinity for English football. Rest assured this was not easy, given the wide variety of domestic sport available. In the Seventies, this included the North American Soccer League, even if Wisconsin newspapers had only vaguely heard of it and local television stations thought long and hard before showing its *Game Of The Week* in place of the documentary on the grazing habits of Patagonian beef cattle.

● Above: The irresistible charm of English football. Stoke City, Derby County and heaps of mud.

The NASL was of interest to me, but it was English football which ultimately commanded my attention. This I suppose begs the question: how does an American become a fan of English football?

Television takes full credit for my enlightenment. Just as a few brave TV executives dared to introduce something as radical as NASL soccer to American homes, a few even braver ones in charge of public television stations dared to bring us the glorious game that is English football.

The vehicle for this was, would you believe, *Star Soccer*. Not exactly the same 

Entertainment U.S.A.

Star Soccer you came to know and love over here. But fairly close. We had the same matches, the same cameras, the same carefully edited highlights, even the same, er, stirring theme music. In fact, there was only one difference: whereas you Britons had your own array of inimitable commentators, we in the States had the equally inimitable Mario Marchado.

I first came across *Star Soccer* whilst on holiday in Ohio late one summer evening in 1977. What a fascinating game it introduced me to, so unlike the American ones I had been reared on. The featured match that evening was Derby County at home to a team wearing stripes (Stoke?). I don't remember much about the match itself, except the name Archie Gemmill and a playing field completely devoid of grass. Make of that what you will.

What I do remember is supporters singing and chanting in unison, unprompted by Wurlitzer organs or scantily-clad cheerleaders. The rectangular-shaped ground, with fans in the front row close enough to pass on communicable diseases to players, the rather simple numbers sewn onto the backs of the players' shirts, and goalkeepers' plain green jerseys.

I was curious about nearly every facet of this completely foreign game. Why were the visitors wearing striped shirts, for example? Only referees wore striped shirts in the games I was familiar with. Why was the match commentator calling the home side 'Darby' and not 'Derby', as it was spelled, as in the famous Kentucky Derby horse race? And why did Derby play at the Baseball Ground when quite obviously its playing dimensions were wholly unsuitable for that American pastime? Did the English even play baseball?

I suppose the reason why I never so much as remembered the result of that first match was that I was too busy taking everything in. Here was a soccer match which didn't need the artificial excitement the NASL tried to generate, played in a stadium jam-packed full of fans who were there because they loved the game. Boring old soccer? Not in the least. The infamous low scores which annoyed my countrymen didn't bother these people - or me - one jot. Yes sir, this is the game as it was meant to be.

● Above: The unforgettable Archie Gemmill.
Below: The U.S. national team are not mentioned in this article, but we thought you'd like to see them playing Guatemala.

> *Four divisions, each with over twenty clubs, is rather different from the twenty-four clubs the NASL had in its heyday.*

Imagine my delight when *Star Soccer* came to my own local public TV station shortly thereafter. The only specific match I can recall was between Wolverhampton Wanderers and Nottingham Forest, at that time the two strangest names I'd ever heard for sports teams. Not the Chicago Stings versus the Dallas Tornado, certainly.

Such was the level of my knowledge of the game that I remember thinking it rather odd that an English League match was being held somewhere in France, where I assumed Molineux was. But wait - there was more. The pitch was covered in snow, yet the players were all wearing shorts. Behaviour like that where I came from led to two things: instant pneumonia in the arctic chill of a Midwestern Winter, and a quick despatch to the local giggling academy. Yet there they were, Wolverhampton Wanderers and Nottingham Forest, playing soccer. In the snow. With shorts on. This was too much!

Let's face it - English football couldn't be more dissimilar to American soccer. For starters, club names are not what your average American is used to. Aston Villa. Queen's Park Rangers. Bolton Wanderers. Crystal Palace. Tottenham Hotspur. Neither are the nicknames; West Bromwich Albion fans may feel quite comfortable with shouting 'come on you Baggies', but where I come from, baggies are what you put sandwiches into when you're packing a lunch.

There's more culture shock than you might imagine. The fact that a country with one-fourth of the population of the US could support a professional league of ninety-two clubs I found - and still find - quite remarkable. Four divisions, each with over twenty clubs, is rather different from the twenty-four clubs the NASL had in its heyday. And promotion and relegation is a completely alien concept to American sport. What was in it for the middle-of-the-division clubs at season's end, with no play-off berths and first round draft choices to vie for? And what in the hell was a 'local derby', anyway?

One week *Star Soccer* introduced me to West Ham United. Having never heard of the English city of Ham, I was mildly surprised to discover it was big enough to have had at least two clubs on the West side of town which had merged into one. And who ever heard of a team playing in 'claret', let alone claret and sky blue? As I watched the Hammers in action, my mother, half-listening to the programme from the kitchen, asks me why the crowd is singing 'I'm Forever Blowing Bubbles'. Do I know? I'm too busy looking for Ham on my *Atlas of Great Britain.*

Let me not overlook the action on the pitch, for there were plenty of moments of it which I, like any other fan, will not forget. Gary Bailey saving a penalty three times for Manchester United. Kenny Dalglish a yard in front of goal and putting his shot wide. Tottenham giving up seven at Anfield. But who was I to share these memories with? What was a Merseyside derby to my father? What did my friends know about bending free-kicks around walls? What memories did anyone else in town have of Mario Marchado, struggling to correctly pronounce the Third Division leaders Gillingham, exchanging pointless banter with 'guest' commentators (usually touring English rock stars or NASL cast-offs) and using his *"And... oh... yes... and it's a GOAL!"* to capture the frantic excitement of the game?

Looking back on it now, it's hard to believe *Star Soccer* lasted for the season or two that it did in my part of the world. And when soccer as a fad passed its sell-by date, public television pulled the plug on *Star Soccer* completely. German *fussball* would replace it. Poor Mario became Commissioner of the American Soccer League for about thirteen minutes in the late Seventies before it went under, and handled ABC-TV's twenty-seven seconds of soccer coverage during the 1984 Olympics. I last heard him several years ago, doing commentary on a few Argentinian league games which public television had bought the rights to. I wonder how long that lasted.

The development of cable television in the early Eighties gave birth to the phenomenon of the Sports Channel. One in particular, ESPN, picked up where *Star Soccer* left off in the Seventies. Their *Road to Wembley* series brought us the magic of the FA Cup. No Mario Marchado, though. John Motson had been unleashed on an unsuspecting America.

It all began with the 1980 FA Cup Final, shown one Sunday evening without much warning. I was busily switching channels, trying to find a station which wasn't airing a commercial. There it was: West Ham and Arsenal. Old friends. My family groaned. Not this crap again!

The following season, the rounds leading up to the Final were shown in hour-long instalments, with plenty of adverts thrown in. The peculiar transmission times did tend to infuriate me - one match was shown at 4 am on a weekday morning, and I confess to falling asleep after about ten minutes. It didn't matter how hard they tried to get me not to watch, though. I was there every time.

Of course, live English football on American TV was too good to be true, and ESPN gave up on it once they found out nobody was watching. Thus, Leicester City *v* Shrewsbury Town was replaced with more popular entertainment. Like kick-boxing and tractor-pulling.

By the time ESPN decided to pack it in, though, plenty of cable channels had sprung up, dealing in everything from home shopping to twenty-four hour weather (you don't believe me, do you?). What is more, the Football League had become wise to the marketing potential of its product and had packaged weekly hour-long programmes for export. Surely a few naive American programme planners would be interested in it as an alternative to the umpteenth Monster Truck extravaganza?

Live English football on American TV was too good to be true, and ESPN gave up on it once they found out nobody was watching.

They were. English football popped up on business channels, on rival sports channels, and probably on the odd rodeo channel in certain parts of Wyoming. Each time, though, it disappeared without trace. The audience was too small to measure.

The phenomenon persists to this day. Depending on where in America you happen to be, you can find English football on one cable station or another at some point during the week. You may have to stay up until the small hours of a Thursday morning, but it is still possible to follow the fortunes of Derby County and company, with Martin Tyler thrown into the bargain.

I've watched a few of these latest offerings myself. But it's impossible for me to pass any sort of judgment on them. English football has become Cold Hard Reality to me now, and teams like Nottingham Forest and Wolverhampton Wanderers don't hold the mystique they once did. I know all about Norman Hunter biting your legs and Ronnie Radford's goal against Newcastle. What is there left to fascinate me with?

Let this fascination be imparted to other Americans. Let us hope that the alleged magic of television will enable a few impressionable teenagers somewhere in middle America to go through the same sort of quasi-religious experience that I had. Times have changed, though. No doubt most kids just stumble upon the sport whilst fidgeting with the remote control. *"Ugh, soccer,"* they mumble, without a second's thought, before switching back to MTV. And Bruce Springsteen.

● ***Top: A selection of the equipment needed to pick up a televised football match in the States. Above : Britain's answer to Mario Marchardo.***

Paris matches

Paris is a sleepy backwater as far as football is concerned. ALASDAIR SHAW *looks into the reasons why.*

"F*rance, land of football - it's not just an image, it's authentic, living reality,"* trumpeted the country's official 1998 World Cup prospectus, and millions of Gallic chests swell with pride. FIFA, UEFA, the Nations Cup, the European Cup: *la France* was the prime mover of them all. Oh, and Jules Rimet created the World Cup.

But let's not get too misty-eyed over their rich heritage; consider this passing acknowledgement of the onset of modern, commercial living appearing further on in the same document: *"There is not the same attachment to clubs here as in England, Spain or Italy; but while we cannot pride ourselves on attendances comparable to those countries, the big games still attract the biggest TV audiences and our press is a point of reference both within and without our frontiers."* Quite. A subtle selling point to sway FIFA? Equally, in any case, a perfect resumé of why Paris has a perennial mobilisation problem when it comes to footballing support.

Sociologists could go gibberingly grey trying to decide why this is so, and while everyone might have their own theory, down on the ground the proof is there on Saturdays. Population: 2 million. Catchment area population: 9 million. Top level football clubs: 1 - Paris St Germain; average league gate: 17,000. Other considerations: two suburban second division teams and a small cluster of sleepy regional third division outfits. Enough overall to compare with, say, Oslo or, more aptly with the FIFA connection, Zurich. However, this second allusion is but a hollow one, insomuch as Grasshoppers regularly win things. Paris St Germain don't.

You get periodic campaigns for a 'great' football team for Paris like you get calls for the return of capital punishment, but potential investors feel it is simply too high-risk to guarantee any tangible dividend. There were two notable attempts, though. Firstly, fashion mogul Daniel Hechter took over the embryonic Paris St Germain shortly after its foundation in 1973 and put his money where his mouth was, though when it transpired that his mouth (to pursue this allegory) was uncomfortably close to a little jiggery-pokery in the ticket sales' office, he duly took his leave and plumped for more achievable objectives in menswear.

Floundering alongside Paris St Germain from 1982 to 1990 in this sea of mediocrity was a sickly playmate begotten of the Racing Club de France, conversely the nation's foremost sporting institution. Already the revamped version of a previous venture which first went under in the 1960s, Racing Club de Paris resurfaced to undergo two further drastic overhauls in the 1980s and then succumb to the awful realisation that even in a field of two you can still have also-ran.

When communications giant Matra rode over the hill with an open cheque book in 1986, irrational expectations rose that the blue and whites might somehow turn into world-beaters overnight. Soon, the first team bristled with international stars like

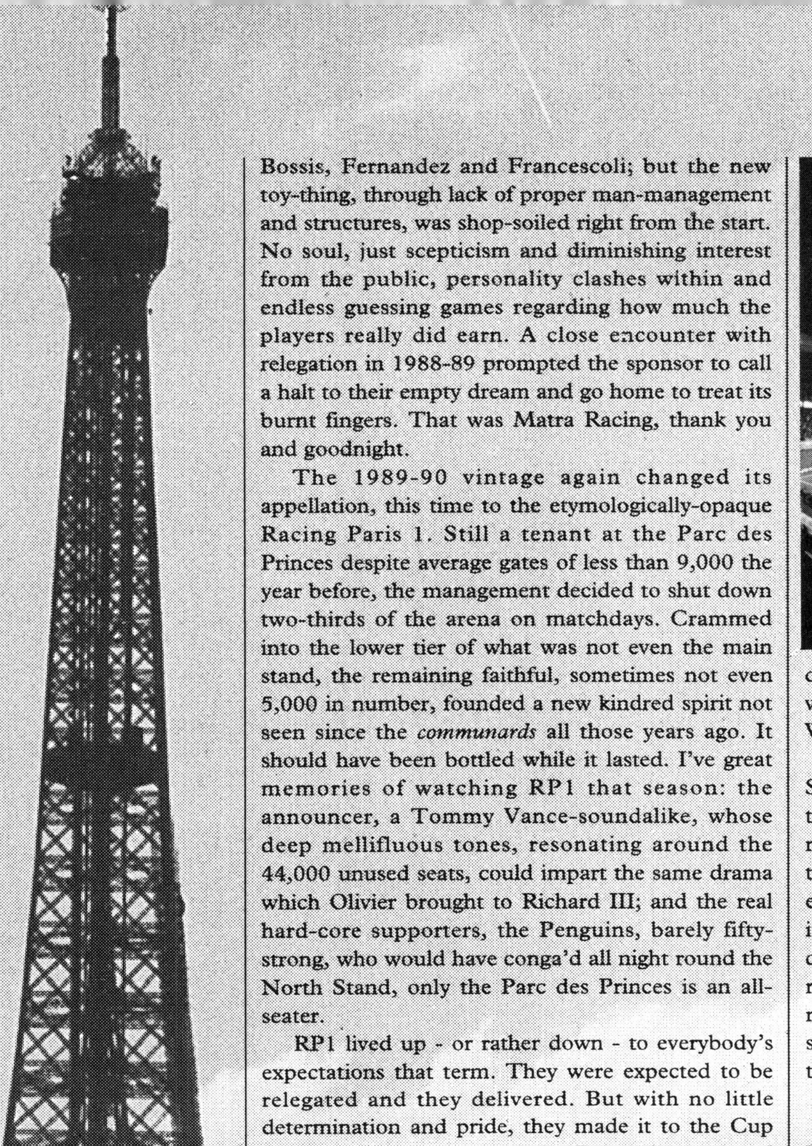

Bossis, Fernandez and Francescoli; but the new toy-thing, through lack of proper man-management and structures, was shop-soiled right from the start. No soul, just scepticism and diminishing interest from the public, personality clashes within and endless guessing games regarding how much the players really did earn. A close encounter with relegation in 1988-89 prompted the sponsor to call a halt to their empty dream and go home to treat its burnt fingers. That was Matra Racing, thank you and goodnight.

The 1989-90 vintage again changed its appellation, this time to the etymologically-opaque Racing Paris 1. Still a tenant at the Parc des Princes despite average gates of less than 9,000 the year before, the management decided to shut down two-thirds of the arena on matchdays. Crammed into the lower tier of what was not even the main stand, the remaining faithful, sometimes not even 5,000 in number, founded a new kindred spirit not seen since the *communards* all those years ago. It should have been bottled while it lasted. I've great memories of watching RP1 that season: the announcer, a Tommy Vance-soundalike, whose deep mellifluous tones, resonating around the 44,000 unused seats, could impart the same drama which Olivier brought to Richard III; and the real hard-core supporters, the Penguins, barely fifty-strong, who would have conga'd all night round the North Stand, only the Parc des Princes is an all-seater.

RP1 lived up - or rather down - to everybody's expectations that term. They were expected to be relegated and they delivered. But with no little determination and pride, they made it to the Cup final: their swansong at the Parc, the national stadium, fittingly the only time they ever filled it to the roof.

Nobody quite embodied the re-born identity of the team as much as madcap 'keeper Pascal Olmeta, at once a passionate and spectacular shot-stopper, a clown and a showman, and also a useful horseman and impromptu centre-forward. That balmy night in June 1990, it was announced that the match against Montpellier was to be his last for the locals. Just how would he mark it? Was he really to ride out to goal in the saddle as had been threatened? Or, more ominously, would he sport one of his, er, eyecatching designer outfits? In the event, his adoring fans were denied on each counts, the authorities clamping down and claiming that both the horse and the jersey might prove unnecessarily distracting. Olmeta, in his tawdry match sponsor's top, had a low-key game. As for the horse, it could have munched grass quite undisturbed in Montpellier's penalty box all night to no-one's

● *The Parc de Princes looking unusally full.*

discomfort. It was that sort of game. Montpellier won it, but our man had no cause for complaint. Within a few weeks he had signed for Marseille.

The entire professional staff also left RP1 that Summer, as the club, financially left for dead by the municipality, had to opt for voluntary relegation into the Third Division (East), which is tantamount to death by a thousand lashes. Now ensconced within Stade de Colombes and playing in front of crowds the size of a Monday morning queue in a DIY store, they have (incredibly) retained professional status in anticipation of a return to the good times, but one fancies that the still-faithful Penguins will have learned to fly before their club reaches the higher ground.

So then there were three...

They hung out the bunting at the office of PSG's supporters' club when the news filtered through. Logically, of the remaining major clubs in the area, theirs had most to gain. Immediately, a saturation programme was initiated, adverts proclaiming: *"PSG - I'm joining up (and I've got a free pin-on badge and phone card into the bargain - so beat that)."* The resultant sale of just 3,000 season tickets was the worst ever return.

This kind of promotion fights against the tide of history and of sociology: it's possibly the lack of tradition and trophies that undermines Paris in comparison with other French cities.

I suppose that in this most cultural of cities there exists more means of escapism than practically anywhere else, thus football is condemned to being mere entertainment. However, if it can associate itself with a little pomp and ceremony, with a really *big* match, the Parisian, above all others, tends to find the mix irresistible.

There were two top-of-the-billers in February 1991 at which this condition could be witnessed at first hand: two sell-out matches: the league clash between Paris SG and ➡

Paris matches

"Both teams contrive in equal measures to dull the senses of 1,120 remarkably patient spectators."

● *Top: The French Cup Final 1990 - Racing Paris' last game as a first division club. Above: Erstwhile Parisian Enzo Francescoli.*

Marseille, followed closely by the potentially decisive European Championship qualifier between France and Spain.

PSG - Marseille: the one and only match inscribed in countless pocket diaries when the fixtures are first published.

Visitors from across the Channel always have cause to comment on the disarmingly subdued proceedings on the way in. Tribal behaviour is not always easily discerned, a mandatory black jacket and face half-obscured by a club scarf the only concessions to the way the younger supporter would like to be. No chanting, no excited chattering, no pushing or shoving. The part-time punters realise it's only a game and we'll all be away from here in a couple of hours.

Once through the appointed gate, a *placeuse* will insist on escorting us to the correct seats and demand a tip for the privilege. Our places are right by the gate in any case, but that's incidental - it's her job.

To our right, the Boulogne Kop, home of the Boulogne Boys, the Headhunters and *Les Gavroches*, the lifeblood of PSG's support, permanently victimised by the CRS and, strangely, banned by their own club from parading banners. So they sing instead, French-style. Here's an extract from their version of 'When The Saints Go Marching In': *"Le PSG/ Le PSG/ Le PSG, oh, PSG..."* Repeat *ad nauseam.*

Out come the teams, and the Kop proceed to ignite several gaily-coloured smoke canisters that finally give a truly continental feel to the show. Several minutes later, the fog lifts and we are treated to a notable festival from our favourite ex-pat, the man everybody wants to see. A quite sumptuous juggle in the box right below us, an eventual cross and then a twenty-five-yard first time blast from his sidekick Jean-Pierre Papin expertly punched clear by fifty-times capped Joel Bats, still PSG's most consistent performer. Yup, Chris Waddle is making hay in France and, luckily for him, he meets defenders each week prepared to give him the room he thrives on: the only players who could stop him have all now been signed by Marseille.

That piece of action alone convinces our guests that at a trifling £14 a throw to sit by the corner flag, the tickets are a snip. Judging the match overall, it *was* special, because in the next hour the visitors play it calmly and clinically, the midfield battle-zone rapidly assuming the characteristics of a Ray Wilkins coach-in.

With twenty minutes to go, Marseille break their rhythm and score a goal which was never going to be anything other than the winner. Incongruously, a good 60% of those present rise to applaud and the secret is out. The same thing would have happened if the visitors had been St Etienne or Bordeaux. In Paris, more people support other teams than the local one. If this is what being a great team entails, Paris might as well admit defeat now. I can see no future for a supporters branch in Marseille...

The exit gates almost come off their hinges as the punters rush home to cotton wool their footballing alter egos for another year or so. We await the incontrovertible truth with the next home game, versus Metz, a fortnight later. A bright, sunny day, the season's absolute giveaway at 40 francs (£4) and the end of the goal-drought stretching back over four games, courtesy of a 60-yard mazy run and shot from emerging star Jocelyn Angloma. And all in front of just 8,000 people. Well, there's nowt so daft as folk, I must say.

No doubt as to where loyalties lie in between times on the date with destiny - 20th February, 1991 - at the top of Qualifying Group One. In TV land they hold their breath - out on site we're holding pocket-sized tricolours, distributed enterprisingly at the entrance. It's an uplifting evening as a technically inferior French side dispatch the Spanish by three goals to one. We almost mistake ourselves for Frenchmen, because apart from a slight confusion over lyrics for the National Anthem we know all the songwords. 'Les Bleus', 'La France' and that tireless old classic 'Pla-ti-ni' score particularly favourably in the audience poll tonight, and when Papin effects a magnificent scissor-kick to put *Les Bleus* 2-1 up, we confer with each other and reckon we can name that tune in *one.* And we are spot on. *"JPP, clap, clap ,clap, JPP..."*

It's been like the League of Nations around us tonight. While the CRS kept their arms folded, the French, the Spanish and the English have permitted themselves a little self-assertion and still maintained the balance. You can have a beer or two in the stadium, but there's no hint of disorder brewing.

. In-bred love for the game of football. Elusive within the city limits. Evident in the suburbs, though on a small scale, at the homes of the local delegates in the Second Division (North).

Creteil and Red Star 93 are two of the worst-supported clubs at this level, maybe partly explained by the difficulties getting there. Creteil lies South-East of Paris and could claim justifiably to be a University town, a dormitory town, a concrete ghetto and a mass development in one. It was in the last-named sector that the Stade Dominique-Duvauchelle rose over the desolate, flattened terrain.

Still, tonight's clash between second-bottom US Creteil and second-top Laval is all-ticket. Then again, *every* match is all-ticket. It's an indispensable part of the ritual to queue up for tickets and get it immediately torn in half. A place on a raised duckboard in the main stand costs £6, and it's an unusually good turnout. A fair few Lavallois have made the journey, equipped with optional extras such as tuba, trumpet, bass drum, sombrero and klaxon. If the ticket stubs they collect are the only means of determining the attendance, there's a fine opportunity of exaggerating the numbers a little. But they wouldn't do that at such an earthy place as this. There's a total of 437 paying spectators. Let the bells ring out.

It's a super little ground in fact, a well-appointed, all-purpose municipal athletics stadium. The side's best known player is Cameroon international Benjamin Massing, sadly missing from tonight's line-up. Sharing my bench is a genuine Creteil supporter who tells me that Massing is in dispute with the management after they blocked his projected move to Paris SG earlier in the season.

The first eighty-seven minutes offer only honest endeavour and tactical naivete from the local lads until Umpierrez - a Uruguayan and ex-Matra Racing - steps forward and unleashes an irresistible twenty-five-yard rocket. The little stand shakes to its foundations. Smiles and klaxons as second division obscurity flashes a dangerous grin. But then, in an improbable finish, Laval net twice, two and four minutes into injury time. My man laments: *"We needed to win to have a realistic chance of staying up."* One point adrift with eight games to go, but in France there's never a close season for sensationalism - it's *L'Equipe*'s watchword.

Battle weary after a long walk through what looked like the set for John Carpenter's *Escape From New York*, Red Star 93's stadium in St Ouen was everything I feared it would be. Uninspiring. And the fact that its name is Stade de la Porte de St Ouen (Stade Municipal du Docteur Bayer) only added to my travelling time when I stopped to ask for directions.

Red Star 93 was once the leading club in the Parisian basin, pre-eminent in football pre-war, but now content in its role as a kind of producing agent for the cream of local talent. The name of the team? Firstly, the '93' is not a gloomy portent of the vicissitudes in store for Racing Paris 1; it's merely a reference to the administrative code for the district. The first part relates to its Communist origins and perpetuation. Doubtless it was for this reason that it was able to procure two first-teamers from Spartak Moscow during 1991. The match, then, saw the visit of Niort and spoke volumes for the courage of ex-Luton and Caen man Brian Stein, who is now plying his trade at this level with Annecy.

A 1-1 bore draw is the right result, since both teams contrive in equal measures to dull the senses of 1,120 remarkably patient spectators. Personally, I am numb all over thanks to this breeze block I'm sitting on. The ever-resourceful authorities, simply by cementing a few together and painting on a few numbers, have turned building material into standard accommodation for home fans. The rest of the stadium is British in its hideousness and tight proximity to the pitch, a wanton collection of uneven corrugated bit-parts, some more disfiguring than others, and the open latrines behind the main stand would give Lord Justice Taylor palpitations.

Behind the goal, to the left, there's an irregular-shaped housing block coated in a gut-wrenching lemon and lime finish. Unsurprisingly, few people, if any, appear to be spectating from their living rooms. Directly below, we find a discreet plaque featuring a red star reposing between two laurel leaves and bearing the inscription: *"Association Sportive Red Star 93 - the Victory of Time."* The artist had been canny enough not to set out any time limit for the achievement of this 'victory', and it's not going to be tonight. In fact, their last league win was five months back.

In the last few moments of the game, the Red Star full-back attempts the Victory of Time with a ludicrously optimistic strike from forty yards which all but dislodges in its slipstream the supporters' club banner at the back of the terracing. The bugles and klaxons lament once again. The fans greet the passage of the meteor with a cry of *"Angleterre!"* the symbolism of which I still can't fathom.

This whistle-stop tour has failed to identify any hard and fast rule as regards the ideals of those who attend. No cross-section analysis could give the same result twice in a row in Paris. Here, football isn't about finding an identity or rallying to a cause. It's barely a sport. It's just entertainment and that's all, folks.

There's a promise of a brand new showpiece stadium for the region by 1998. Paris will be no closer to Marseille or Lyon at that time, so how it will capture the imagination of the populace remains to be seen. They'd maybe stand a better chance if they called it the Moulin Rouge, installed recliner seating, dressed the *placeuses* up accordingly and distributed free drinks and ice cream at the turnstiles. *Le culture Parisienne oblige...*

"Here, football isn't about finding an identity or rallying to a cause. It's barely a sport. It's just entertainment and that's all, folks."

● Above: Paris St. Germain the city's number 1 team (due to the lack of competition) take on Nantes.
Below: Montpellier fans with a surrealist banner at the 1990 French Cup Final.

New Latic

Wigan Athletic had been a major force in semi-professional football before being summoned to join the big boys in 1978. MIKE WAREING *watched their first forays in the Football League.*

NON-LEAGUE TEAMS HAVE IT FAR TOO EASY these days. For those in the GM Vauxhall Conference, the Fourth Division is just one good season away. But back in 1978, when men were men and the Northern Premier League wasn't the HFS Loans League, Division Four was about as obtainable as Nirvana.

Wigan Athletic hold the distinction of being the last club to gain entry to the Football League by being voted in. At the end of the 1977-78 season Southport were given notice to quit and Wigan took their place in Division Four. The following year the Northern and Southern Premier Leagues merged to form the Alliance: the first step on the road to Division Five and automatic promotion.

"The League - At Last"
Wigan Athletic 1978-79
Price £1.50

Looking back, it seems the most unlikely of times for the Football League to finally see sense and allow Wigan - undoubtedly *the* top non-League side for decades - to join their exclusive boy's club. And it was all because they lost to Birmingham 4-0 in the FA Cup. Then again, when did the Football League ever operate within the bounds of logic?

The technical requirements for admission to the League included things like a decent ground, healthy financial situation, proven track record of success in non-League football and good crowd-pulling potential. Apart from maybe the last of these, Wigan had satisfied the criteria for a good many years. As far as crowds are concerned, they have always been in the shadow of the town's more successful rugby league club, yet still pulled in decent crowds by non-League standards and, to this day, hold the record for the highest attendance for a match involving two semi-professional sides: 27,526 against Hereford in an FA Cup tie in 1953.

Although non-League football provided the basic framework for an application for League membership, it actually took spectacular giant-killing acts in the FA Cup to get taken seriously. It worked for Hereford and it worked for Wimbledon. Though less consistently successful than Wigan, both these clubs got their chance sooner thanks largely to Ron Radford's screamer against Newcastle and Dickie Guy's penalty saves against Leeds.

MANCHESTER CITY
versus
WIGAN ATHLETIC
F.A. CHALLENGE CUP—3rd Round
SATURDAY
2nd JANUARY, 1971
Kick-off 3-15 p.m.
NEWS 1/- 5p

The powers-that-be had ample opportunity to vote Wigan in over the years. In 1954, for example, when Newcastle - Jackie Milburn and all - needed a replay and a lucky 3-2 win to knock Wigan out of the FA Cup after being held to a 2-2 draw at St James's Park. Or in 1971 at Maine Road, when only a fluky Colin Bell goal took Manchester City through to the next round after the Wigan goalkeeper's boot had split as he took a goal-kick.

In both those seasons Wigan also won their championship and looked certainties to be playing League football the following year, but the authorities decided otherwise.

It seemed that the club would never escape the shadow of Wigan Borough, who went bust in 1931 and had to quit the old Third Division (North), thereby upsetting those sensitive League administrators. Although Athletic had no connection with the former club, other than the fact that they played at the same ground, it appeared that the Football League would always be suspicious of the

thrill

financial viability of professional football in a town where rugby league was such a big draw.

This, together with a general reluctance to admit Northern clubs, had conspired to freeze out our heroes for thirty-odd years. And so, at the end of of the 1977-78 season, more in hope than expectation, they went cap in hand to the League for the thirty-fifth time. There were several factors weighing against them. For a start, they had only managed to get their application through the back door. New regulations meant that only the winners of the Northern and Southern Premier Leagues could apply for League membership. That year's NPL champions were Boston Utd. However, since Boston's ground didn't come up to scratch, it was decided that Wigan, as runners-up, could go forward as the NPL's representatives.

The fact that Wigan had even managed to finish second that year was a bit of a surprise since they had just completed their worst two seasons ever in the NPL, finishing sixth and fourteenth. Before that they had never finished outside the top three.

By far the biggest obstacle was the fact that, just twelve months earlier, Wimbledon had been voted into the Fourth Division. The concept of admitting two new members in consecutive seasons was generally considered too vast for the tiny minds at the Football League to even begin to contemplate. Perceived wisdom has it that what finally swung things in Wigan's favour was the obligatory giant-killing cup run that duly materialised that season, although the 'giants' killed were Fourth Division York City and Third Division Sheffield Wednesday, then managed by Jack Charlton.

In the third round, Wigan were drawn away to Birmingham City, whose 4-0 win was due mainly to Trevor Francis' finishing and the fine goalkeeping of Jim Montgomery. Although well beaten, Wigan's players, supporters, and officials made a lot of friends that day and it's generally believed that Birmingham's influence (they did have some then, hard though it is to believe today) helped win the backing of the other Midlands clubs when it cam to the crunch.

The crunch came on 2nd June, 1978 at London's Cafe Royale, where the Chairmen of the First and Second Division clubs met to decide the fates of Wigan and Bath City, who were applying for League membership, and the four clubs seeking re-election. After the first vote York (49 votes), Rochdale (39) and Hartlepool (33) were all re-elected; Wigan and Southport tied on 26 votes and Bath were eliminated with 23. So a second ballot was required. Wigan had lost out once before on a re-vote but this time there was a difference. This time Southport just had to go, for I can now reveal that Wigan's ascension to the heady world of League football owed little to the good sense of the club chairmen who voted them in, nor did it depend much on anything the club did. It was in fact pre-ordained by the strange voodoo worked by me and my mate. Let me explain...

Back in those halcyon days of the NPL, we would slip up in the stand and, during particularly dour tussles against the likes of, say, Goole Town or Worksop, set up a chant which involved my mate shouting *"Southport!"* at the top of his voice, followed by my own cry of *"Workington!"*. Over and over we would repeat this strange incantation for reasons which escape me now. *"Southport!" "Workington!" "Southport!" "Workington!"* we'd go, to the bemusement of those around us.

Now, this is strange enough, but, unknown to ourselves, mysterious forces were at work and the fate of these two grim, workaday clubs was sealed as first Workington and then Southport were required to vacate the premises to make way for Wimbledon and Wigan respectively.

It is, of course, well known that the

New Latic Thrill

● ***Above: The Junior Latics caravan of love.***
Below: Current Wigan keeper Nigel Adkins

All those exotic faraway places: Rochdale, Doncaster, Crewe and... yes... even Torquay! Oh, the glamour of it all.

ordinary supporter can influence the outcome of a match by such methods as wearing that lucky kagoul, standing in a particular part of the ground or bringing along your mate from work who only goes to a couple of games a season but the team always win when he does. This, though, seemed to be taking things a little too far.

As the great and good of the Football League cast their votes for the second time, unseen forces were guiding their hands and the result was a foregone conclusion: Wigan twenty-nine votes; Southport twenty.

Wigan Athletic were in the League.

There then began the difficult task of transforming the club from a part-time operation into a full-time business within a few short months. For most of the players, it meant a drop in living standards as they gave up well-paid jobs for the uncertain world of the Fourth Division l. The manager, Ian McNeill, wisely decided to stick by the side that had won promotion. For the fans, the close season was a time of mounting excitement and anticipation as we perused the fixture list for the coming season: all those exotic faraway places with strange-sounding names, like Rochdale, Doncaster, Crewe and... yes... even Torquay! Oh, the glamour of it all.

At last the big day arrived: Wigan Athletic's first ever home League match. We'd had a couple of nice little warm-ups; Third Division Tranmere had been dispatched from the League Cup and Hereford had been held to a goalless draw on their own ground in a quietly impressive League debut.

This, though, was the start of our League adventure. Over nine thousand people turned up and the poor innocent little lambs to the slaughter were Grimsby Town. This was where we would announce our arrival to an unsuspecting football world in no uncertain terms. Unfortunately, Grimsby hadn't read the script. They pooped our party good and proper and gave us an uncomfortable lesson in League football. They won 3-0, a scoreline which, quite frankly, was highly flattering to Wigan. What a let down.

And there was worse to come. Wigan took one point from their first five League games as certain players sadly failed to make the transition from non-League to League.

The saddest of these was club skipper, Ian Gillibrand, for whom promotion had come a little too late. He managed just six games in League football, but did have the honour of leading the team out on their historic League debut. Gillibrand tragically died in 1989 at a ridiculously early age, but his name will be forever legend at Springfield Park.

Eventually the team found their feet and began climbing the table. In the end they finished a highly creditable sixth, just missing out on a spectacular first season promotion. There were many memorable matches. One in particular that stands out, was a a remarkable Good Friday game at home to Port Vale. At this stage in the season promotion was still a distinct possibility, but for the first seventy minutes Wigan were quite appallingly bad. Trailing 3-0, and without a hope of getting back into the game, McNeill finally made a substitution. By this time many fans had already left, so dire was the Wigan performance, and there are apocryphal stories of season tickets being found in the players' tunnel. Miraculously, though, the substitution worked. Wigan stormed back, scoring five times, including the club's first ever League hat-trick scored by Peter Houghton within the space of ten minutes. Incredibly, the final score was 5-3 to Wigan, and Port Vale, not to mention many of the fans, had to go and have a lie down in a darkened room. It was a comeback to rival that of the Holy Messiah himself.

All in all it had been well worth the wait and football in Wigan would never be quite the same again. For one thing we don't win as often as we used to and we've since been on the wrong end of giant-killing acts. From being a big fish in the non-League pond, regular winners of championships and trophies, we've had to adjust to our new role in the grand scheme of things as decidedly small fry indeed.

And, of course, we wouldn't have it any other way.

Futility test

In spite of both teams' best efforts, some matches are destined to remain goal-less. LES HUSON *recalls the numb feeling that overwhelms even the most-hardened supporter as a stalemate grinds on...*

If it's going to hit you at all, it will probably be about two-thirds of the way through the season. It'll be a cold, wet February night and a match you hadn't originally planned to see. You thought you'd be working late, but managed to get off at the last minute and, after all, a game is a game. Can't miss one without a cast-iron excuse.

You're a typical supporter. The heady days at the start of the season are over, the days when you basked in the glory, after the first game, of a home win and joint top place with about ten other clubs. Things went from bad to worse; your lads lost the next five games, and the manager signed an unknown Belgian Second Division defender, who lived up to all your worst nightmares. The club changed hands, bought by a 'local businessman' with interests in property development. The new team strip, arriving the obligatory few weeks late, proved to be a daring mixture of pink and yellow which, on sunny days, obliges you and the rest of the home terrace to wear shades in self-defence.

Yet here you are, loyal to the last, on said February evening, thinking that things couldn't get much worse, when it happens. Around thirty-seven minutes into the first half, it suddenly becomes clear that your lads aren't going to get the ball anywhere near the opposition goal-area, and that the visitors are content to stay in their own half, ten men back, grimly booting upfield every ball that comes their way. You realise, with dismay, as you shiver and freeze, drip and stamp your feet - it's going to be a 0-0 draw.

After months of endless tension, nail-biting, and raised blood-pressure, during which you've attempted to steer the ball into the net and push your team up the table by sheer will-power, the futility of it all is suddenly apparent. And, for tonight at least, you're lost. The game will have to watch itself. The lads will just have to manage without you for this match. You're going to retreat into the innermost recesses of your football-obsessed mind, a fantasy world where you control the game, rather than it controlling you.

> ***"You're going to retreat into the innermost recesses of your football-obsessed mind."***

You hang on for the last few minutes of the first half, but inevitably during the break your mind begins to wander. You gaze at the advertising hoardings on the opposite side of the pitch. You wonder what 'McArthur Fabrications' actually do. Perhaps they make it all up?

You're now well into dreamland. You could be anywhere. You remain blissfully unaware of the half-time tannoy announcements. All your rivals are 1-0 up at half-time, but you don't hear the news and don't have to curse and kick out at the nearest discarded plastic cup. For the only time in your life, your raffle ticket comes up, but you never get to claim the bottle of whisky. Your thoughts turn to other 0-0 draws you have known.

You're interrupted in your reverie at this point by the ref's whistle, as the second half kicks off, and for a moment you're back in the real world, shivering on the terrace at -2°C. The opposition No.10 taps the ball forward to No.7, whose pass directly back to his keeper is inch-perfect. The keeper stops the rolling ball with one hand, then for some unknown reason picks it up, throws it over the touchline, and collapses on the penalty spot, waving for the trainer. The ref stops the game and you're back in dreamland.

Some 0-0s are really exciting, you tell yourself. Can't actually think of any off-hand, but surely it must be so? Let's suppose your arch-rivals were second placed in the League needing a win to clinch the title. And let's suppose that their last game of the season is here, at your place! Now that would be a 0-0 to savour. Sod the beautiful game, let's go for a beautiful result! The mighty airborne kicks which usually earn your defenders a chorus of *"hee-haw"* would become exquisite 'lofted clearances', a perfectly respectable defensive tactic. Ten men back in your half seems an interesting, even innovative, line-up. Every second lost, every opponent thwarted, every ball cleared from the line would be lapped up. You mentally conjure up the scene. As the ball screams past your post for the twentieth time, their manager yells: *"Heads up, lads, it'll come!"* So will Christmas, but not till next season. They trudge from the pitch at the end, 0-0 and second place in the League.

And on cue, the final whistle goes in the real game. The one which made itself redundant in the thirty-seventh minute as your mental survival instinct switched you on to auto-pilot. 0-0, as you thought. You get home.

"Enjoy the game?" your partner enquires. *"Brilliant..."* you respond unthinkingly. *"Back there on Saturday?"*

"You bet...."

The Rivals No.2

Will Oxford United beat Swindon Town again before the end of the century? ED HORTON *has his doubts...*

LIVERPOOL? I THINK NOT. MANCHESTER? MY ARSE. The *greatest* derby match in world football was never played before 1965; it has never been a First Division fixture (or, for that matter, a Fourth Division game); and its protagonists are a small but thriving industrial town in Wiltshire (the villains) and a declining industrial city in Oxfordshire (the heroes). They are twenty miles apart, and most people don't realise the rivalry exists. If pushed to name Oxford United's local rivals, they might say *"Reading?"* After all, it is no further away than Swindon.

True, Reading think we *are* their local rivals. Not as far as we're concerned: after all, how can we take seriously a team who've finished above us just twice since 1967, not once in a higher division? Conversely, Swindon seem to take more interest in the proximity of Bristol City: links in a chain of resentment and ambivalence that starts in Aldershot and ends at Twerton Park. Why Swindon and not Reading? Take a look at the table: (*see facing page*)

This might be understandable, even acceptable, if the opponents were Liverpool. To have *played* them that many times would be a triumph: three actual wins are beyond imagination. But *Swindon*? In 1974-5 they came bottom of Division Two by miles. Dunphy goes on at satisfying length in *Only a Game* about how bad they were. No matter: a draw at home, defeat in Swindon. 1982 was almost as bad. They were going down, we were second, twelve games unbeaten, it was May, we'd beaten them 5-0 in April, unaided their players were doomed. The Town End showed their initiative.

Someone must have been in Paris in 1968, because, in homage to the CRS, a smoke bomb was thrown onto the pitch, strategically placed to obstruct our keeper... Roy Burton could see nothing. Swindon could see Paul Rideout, he could just about see the goal, he placed the ball therein and the referee let it stand. Hideous scenes followed on both sides of the perimeter fences, the most important thing being that we lost 3-2 and stayed down. After that, no more friendly rivalry. Swindon were a spectre, a lying awake at night, a furrow in the forehead, an obsession...

"Swindon were a spectre, a lying awake at night, a furrow in the forehead, an obsession..."

This climaxed a period when not only was defeat at Swindon inevitable, but 'clashes' (as they say) between supporters were not uncommon either. Newly recruited Robins appear unaware of this unpleasant tradition, to judge by the number of clean, new scarves being sported in Oxford last time out. However, their country cousins in uniform, Wiltshire Police, have forgotten nothing at all, and do their utmost to maintain a bitter and resentful atmosphere for fixtures at the County Ground. At times they appear more formidable opponents than the team themselves: they are frequently cited as the most important factor by people *"giving it a miss this year."*

The stories are legion: female fans have, for example, been body searched by male policemen, even after protests. I was put against a wall and threatened with refusal of entry... without having said a word: apparently my facial expression betrayed a dislike of having my coat and scarf roughly pulled around without a word of apology. Last season there were roadworks on the A420, causing a tailback not long before kick-off. In their wisdom, Plod saw fit to exacerbate the problem by operating a roadblock five miles out from Dodge City. Anything with a scarf was fair game: lads in minivans, families in cars, old ladies on supporters' coaches, all were taken from their vehicles and searched. By all accounts this was still happening as the game kicked off.

When you follow the U's, you can't help but think the Swindon game to be of overwhelming importance. Nor can you help noticing the appalling imbalance in results. So what do you do about it? You take refuge in imagined cultural superiority. Conjuring up a picture of straw-chewing smock-clad village idiots, we remind each other that whatever happens on Saturday afternoon, we will not spend the evening dragging the moon's reflection out of the village pond with a rake. Nor do we travel to the match on a tractor. Curiously, Swindon love the 'Moonraker' image, having given that title to a radio station and also a local pub. Their lack of concern has a solid base in complacency: maybe they can't read or write, but, when it really matters, counting skills are all they need.

In the near future, there may be a nastier edge to the rivalry. Oxford's decline (in every sense) is inseparable from the rundown of the Cowley car factory, once the bedrock of United's support as well as the local economy. Within a couple of years, it will all but close. Never mind, said the local press, you can get a job at Honda's new plant in Swindon. No, you can't, said Honda: we're not taking anyone from Cowley, due to their accumulation of nasty habits like trade union membership. Economic bitterness between Southern and Northern fans has been the cause of strife from a long time before Harry Enfield started waving his wad: it could easily be repeated in microcosm within the South Midlands. And worse. With their increased prosperity, they'll probably carry on holding the upper hand.

We did win at the County Ground once. Only once - in 1973: Roberts, Curran, Cassidy. We were so shocked that we didn't score again for a month. And what about the Manor? Home draws may be *de rigeur* at Elm Park, where they happen once a fortnight. But when, over sixteen seasons, we become the tipsters' friend and draw 75% of all your home games with a single team, it has to be something mental. Either that or God lives in Swindon and does the Treble Chance.

Speaking of psychological disorders, Chris Kamara has inflicted a permanent mental scar on Oxford's footballers. Undoubtedly, he would top any list of the most feared and hated players to visit the Manor. Hated, because of his preference for laying waste the bodies of the opposition. Feared, because he is also an exceptionally powerful player, and a very good one. Remarkable, with such a combination of power and malice, that he took fifteen years to make his way to Elland Road.

His finest hour was on Boxing Day 1977, when we led 3-0 at half-time and spent the last twenty minutes hanging on a for a draw after Kamara got two of Swindon's three goals. Kamara's birthday was the previous day, a coincidence often commented upon by Oxford fans (*"Chris Kamara? Jesus Christ!"*). Even after he left, he cast his shadow over the Manor Ground. I remember Dave Bennett as a small, moderately proportioned winger who won the Cup Final for Coventry. He played for Swindon in September 1990, and I didn't recognise him: he seemed to have sprouted enormous shoulders, as if a cartoon character had swallowed a chest expander. Other Oxford fans apparently had the same experience, and watched the game convinced they were witnessing the Return of Chris Kamara. It couldn't have been him, though, as three days later a thug from Darlington broke his leg with a vicious tackle. No-one would have dared do that to Kamara.

That's the sort of fascination that doubles the home attendance when Swindon come to visit. The Manor is not always the most atmospheric of grounds: on occasion the noise would not disturb the meditations of the Buddha. The two hours of passionate encouragement that accompany the visit of Swindon are scarcely muted by the failure of the team to respond, or by the precognition of inevitable failure.

OXFORD v SWINDON: LEAGUE

	P	W	D	L	F	A
Manor Ground	16	2	12	2	16	14
County Ground	16	1	4	11	9	30

(to the end of 1989-90)

Actually, we beat them in the League Cup in 1969, a feat all the more impressive for Swindon being the holders. But that was a problem in itself, for to talk about the triumph was to admit that they *had* won it, a burden gloriously lifted in 1986. And we did the double in 1972-3, the home win courtesy of Nigel Cassidy, riches and long life be upon him. Since then, nothing, in seventeen years and eighteen meetings, save for an extraordinary aberration in April 1982 which made George Lawrence a folk hero at the Manor. To the end of his days, George may do as he pleases: he can even score for Bournemouth at the Manor. He was on loan at the time and presumably nobody told him the rules: but he's forever The Man Who Beat Swindon Five-Nil.

Since our relegation in 1988 it's been a time of particular anguish. There was a 3-0 loss at the County Ground with two sendings-off and a linesman who gave offside direct from a throw-in. There was Swindon's late equaliser in 1988. There was 3-0 again the following season. But in the return, the gallants of Oxford strained every sinew. Steve Foster became the first Oxford centre-back *ever* to score twice in a game. Paul Kee performed so many miracles that he hasn't made a save since. And although we were played off the pitch, a one-goal lead was taken into the final minutes.

But back in Swindon, Wicker Men were burning, goats shrieked at the moment of slaughter. Entreaties were made to their pagan gods, and they were answered. A penalty was awarded. But all was not yet lost. Mike Ford knew a little about Paul Bodin. He hurried into the goalmouth, and several spectators overhead his advice. *"He puts them to the right,"* whispered Mike. And so he does, but to the goalkeeper's right rather than his own. Two-all, try again next year.

And so we did, courtesy of Brian Hillier, Lucky Lou and their several friends. *"We're going to win this time,"* said my mate down the pub. *"Ha!"* On the way to the ground I met the co-author of the club's history. *"I reckon this is our year,"* he told me. You should know better, I thought. Hardly had we squeezed in than David 'Bad' Penney put us ahead. Euphoria in the London Road. Then Paul Simpson burst through, Digby turned the shot aside and Martin Foyle, careering towards the home end, turned it in. Pandemonium: four minutes gone and we were 2-0 up.

From that moment we knew we were doomed. The wilderness is vast and we have grown well-accustomed to its mirages. This was a game in which we didn't even get a point.

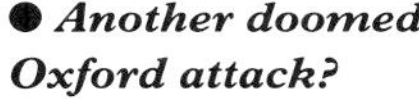

● ***Another doomed Oxford attack?***

Monty Sinton's Space Filler...

Gazzer the Clown – He's as daft as a brush!

Kenna Gowland Says...

"Hard man? Vinny Jones, man? Don't make me laugh. Vinny Jones, a hard man? You must be joking.

You're asking me? John Craggs, now we're talking hard, man. John Craggs. Eve of Boro *v* Liverpool, 1975. John Craggs goes down the Dragonara. He sinks twenty-eight pints of Jubilee black and tan, runs up to the sixth floor, dives off and lands, head first, in the Odeon car park, cracking a paving slab in half with the impact. He jumps straight to his feet, points to the paving slab and yells, *"Tommy Smith, you're next."*

Vinny Jones! You want to talk about hard men, you want to talk about Bobby Murdoch. I've seen Bobby in the Club Marimba, he's drunk ten pints of Snakebite and he's never been to the toilet once. Bladder like a blast furnace, man. Aye, first in the bar, last in the bog, that was Bobby Murdoch. He's working in a carpet shop now, like. Hell, imagine him coming round to tack down your shagpile.

Vinny Jones! I'm talking about hard men. I'm talking about Boro in the Sixties and Seventies: Whigham, Lugg, Craggs, Rooks, Foggon, Spraggon and Woof. Rock hard the lot of them. And everyone with a name that sounded like the Anglo-Saxon for an act of gross indecency.

Ow, pet! When you're ready!"

KENNA *was being helped off the floor by* HARRY PEARSON

Bernard Ingham – He's as daft as a brush!

Writers' Cramp

Writing a football novel can be a tortuous business, as MICHAEL IRWIN *discovered...*

SOME PEOPLE HAVE AN ACTIVE IMAGINATION AND SOME PEOPLE don't. I remember the surprise of a friend of mine, long ago, when I remarked that I couldn't run for a bus without fancying I was in the final of the Olympic 100 metres. I was equally surprised to learn that he never entertained any such fantasies. He thought I was a bit mad. I thought his life must be very sensible but strangely colourless. There's no right or wrong in this disagreement, and nothing can be done about it. If you don't have an imagination, you can't grow one. If you do have one, it's liable to keep working away aimlessly, like a gland.

In my own case it secretes, among other curiosities, a sort of endless drivel about football. Maybe at an early age there were fantasies about scoring a winning goal at Wembley, but it's a long time since things were that personal. My imagination may be childish, but it isn't egotistical. I find myself drifting as an observer into any one of several recurring stories, and the fancy rolls on unbidden. There's a nameless team, perhaps lying eighth in the Third Division, and they're away to Manchester United in the FA Cup, and they have a quick seventeen-year-old winger and a stubby midfield man recently recruited from a non-League club at the age of thirty, and it's a wet day with a strong wind swirling and the pitch cutting up, and United hit the bar in the first three minutes and... So the story can ramble on, pretty well of its own volition, even when I'd rather be thinking about something useful. I'll be lying in the bath brooding on some serious issue, when out will trot the imaginary footballers for yet another game. It can get very tedious.

So, one reason for trying to write a novel about soccer was a desire to divert this stream of fantasy into a useful channel. But when I got down to it, I encountered numerous technical difficulties.

To begin with, there's the problem of numbers. Football being a team game, you have a potential cast-list of at least fifteen (allowing for two substitutes, a coach and a manager) before a ball has been kicked. There won't be space to individualise that lot to a serious extent. The best hope is probably to give each one some little tag that might make him memorable - an unusual name, say, and some slight physical oddity. But unless you're careful you find you've created a team of freaks: 'Ginger' Aardvark in goal, Albert Hogswill, the seven-foot centre-back, 'Baldy' Bottomley in midfield and Lenny Xerxes, the albino striker. This may sound a facetious point, but it isn't. Names alone are hard enough. If you jot down an imaginary team it immediately looks all wrong. Smith, Jones, Thompson? Plausible names, but so ordinary that no reader will recall who's who. Haddock? Caesar? Shakespeare? Come on - *no* professional footballer could have a name like that.

Next question: in what league do you locate the leading character and his team? If it's entirely imaginary - Belchester versus Melchester - your hero is trapped inside a boys' comic. If it's the current English First Division, then you're in danger of childish name-dropping: *"Darting between Jan Molby and Steve Nicol, I flicked the ball deftly wide of Bruce Grobbelaar's groping right hand."* Even if you avoid the risk of libel - *"Vinny's studs raked blood from my thigh"* - you're dealing in soccer pornography. There are compromise solutions that will keep your story in touch with real life without attempting a furtive grope, but none is drawback-free.

The nastiest problem of all springs from the fact that a football novel is doomed to include numerous accounts of football matches. To describe a real match is difficult enough - which is why so few newspaper correspondents now attempt it, preferring to report on the post-match denunciations of the referee. To describe one that never took place is a ghostly business, a bit like eating an imaginary apple. Elsewhere in your novel you can have a reasonably clear idea as to who should do what, and why. But when the fictional match starts, you may know nothing in advance but the result. How is it to be achieved: a thirty-yard free-kick, a spectacular overhead volley or the goalkeeper punching a corner into his own net? Do such details matter, in terms of the larger story? Will the reader fall asleep? And in your next chapter there'll be another game...

If the novelist manages to steer round the road-blocks I've listed, his likely reward will be to end up in no-man's land. Roughly speaking, soccer fans don't read novels and novel readers are less than passionate about football. The generalisation may be dubious, but it's certainly true in the effective sense that *publishers* believe it. If you write a soccer novel, it had better be a labour of love.

Fortunately, football provides opportunities as well headaches for the novelist. A footballer's career is short and clear, and tells a story. It's likely to offer a nice mixture of triumph and disaster. Talent, luck and effort all play a part. Sex and drink may foul things up. There's an intriguing balance to be struck between what your man can do on his own and what he can accomplish as a member of a team. He may extend and over-reach his basic abilities by sheer force of will. There's the lurking theme of form: by what laws does it come and go? How can you lure it back? In these respects and a number of others, the life of the soccer star is a specialised, perhaps a usefully simplified, version of anybody's life. A good football novel won't merely be about football, any more than *Tess of the D'Urbevilles* is merely about milking cows.

Praise or Grumble?

CATHY CASSELL *explains why Radio Sheffield's football phone-in has such a large cult following...*

5.15 PM ON A SATURDAY AFTERNOON AND, tired of the predictable comments of the Stuart Halls of this world, you're ready for a more sophisticated analysis of your team's performance that day. It's time to listen to what the real experts have to say. In South Yorkshire, car-stereos, kitchen trannies and quadraphonic hi-fis alike all find themselves tuned into BBC Radio Sheffield's *Praise or Grumble* spot.

Football just wouldn't be the same without *Praise or Grumble*. Hosted by Robert Jackson, a friendly and very sensible man who sounds just like your favourite uncle, it's the sports supporters of South Yorkshire's chance to phone in and whinge or eulogise about their team. Robert supports all the local teams, or so he claims. Doncaster, Rotherham, Barnsley, Chesterfield and the two Sheffield teams, he wants them all to win. From anyone else such a claim would be ludicrously unbelievable, but from him, it makes sense.

WELL, IT'S A PRAISE FOR DONCASTER...

Your average caller phones up either to praise or grumble at their team. A typical call would go something like this:

"And it's Dean on line three, where are you Dean?"

"Rawmarsh, Bob."

"Praise or Grumble, Dean."

"It's a praise, Bob, praise for Rotherham United."

"But they lost 5-0 today, Dean."

"But it were a bad referee Bob, and the pitch were awful, our lads didn't have a chance."

Given the results of the day the calls are sometimes predictable, United fans will praise Sheffield United and make digs at Wednesday on the days they win, and vice versa. The unpredictable calls keep the programme lively: *"I'd like to praise Chesterfield, Bob, the lads played great today, but I need to grumble too, I want to grumble at me Mum, Bob, 'cos she wouldn't let me go."*

Or: *"I'd like to grumble, Bob, grumble at fellow Unitedites. It's not like me, Bob, but someone nicked me Blades shirt from the line this week. It cost me a lot that shirt did, I saved up for ages. It must have been a United fan, who else would want it?"* Needless to say, someone at Bramall Lane heard this plaintive cry and the lucky listener was sent a new shirt to replace the stolen one.

You don't actually have to be in South Yorkshire to phone *Praise or Grumble*. Numerous people phone up on their way home from the match, often from crackling car phones: *"I'm stuck in a traffic jam in London/Portsmouth/Bristol, Bob."* is a typical start to the conversation. You also get those on holiday: *"I'm in Florida/Corfu/Torremelinos, Bob, it's not on the tele here, how did Barnsley get on?"*

Evidence suggests that important people listen to *Praise and Grumble*. It is the one place where managers, players, directors and even local councillors are held publicly accountable or their actions. It's a place where fans can comment openly on their team's performance, can question decisions made by the board and can argue for change. Footballing careers may not be made or broken, but their progression is certainly influenced. If you want to know what local opinion is, then you listen in.

As the significance of *Praise and Grumble* increases, so does the importance of its callers. Rumour has it that Imre Varadi's wife phoned up in the days when Peter Eustace was in charge of Wednesday, to grumble about her husband being left out of the team. Reg Brealey, director of Sheffield United, phoned up from Calcutta, where he was on business, to explain about the prospective takeover bid planned for the club in response to calls from United fans worried about their future. Recently, after a number of Owls fans had praised Wednesday for their Rumbelows Cup win, a mysterious man by the name of Harry, with a distinctly Cock-ney accent, phoned to remind Robert and the listeners of the achievements of the Blades this season.

Towards the end of the season, *"Why haven't we got an open-topped bus, Bob?"* became a familiar cry from dejected United fans when the plans to celebrate Wednesday's cup-winning victory were announced. *"All them councillors are Wednesdayites, they're all biased, Bob,"* was a much-used refrain. Such calls prompted the Deputy Leader of Sheffield City Council to phone up to remind Unitedites of past civic receptions they had had, whilst gently commenting that they haven't won a cup this season and therefore wouldn't get an open-topped bus.

Perhaps it is a fitting tribute to *Praise and Grumble* that the latest Sheffield Wednesday song is based on callers' comments. Robert Jackson and the people of South Yorkshire have joined the ranks of New Order and Chas'n'Dave as music heroes with the classic, 'It's A Praise For Sheffield Wednesday'. What *Praise and Grumble* demonstrates most effectively is that if you let the ordinary fans have their say, not only do you get lively debate and more accountable local officials, but also good local entertainment.

Curl's talk

Our roving reporter chats to MR LARRY, *one of the many peripheral figures who play a vital part in this game we call soccer.*

LARRY COTTON IS THE owner of 'Mr Larry & Co' (Unisex; OAPs' concessions all day Monday). Watching him put the finishing touches to a wisteria rinse in his High Wycombe salon last Wednesday, it was hard to imagine that he had once been involved in football at the highest level. The impression, however, is misleading, for in 1970 'Mr Larry' took the exacting role of official hairdresser to England's World Cup Squad.

"I'll never forget the day I got the call. I'd just returned from a fortnight in Tenerife and I was sticking my 'Mr Larry Is Back!!!' poster in the window of the shop. I was chief stylist at 'Roma's of Venice' in East Finchley at that time. The caller was an old college chum, Alberto. He told me that that morning, while he'd been finger-drying Sir Alf Ramsey's hair (admittedly not a major task!) at 'Mane Street', Bayswater, the England supremo asked if he'd be prepared to accompany the squad to Mexico. Sir Alf saw hair as an integral part of player morale, and he was worried that the facilities wouldn't be up to scratch. (And how right he was! Mexico, quite frankly, was a hair-care nightmare. Conditioner stocks were limited and setting mousse non-existent. Also, you would have thought the world's leading exporter of avocados would have come up with a shampoo a little more adventurous than medicated Vosene! Not a bit of it... But I'm getting ahead of myself.) Anyway, Alberto was working on his own brand of hair products at that time, and was too preoccupied trying to squeeze essential oils out of his jojoba nuts to make the trip. Would I be interested? Naturally I jumped at the chance. 'Mr Larry' and sun go together like Fred and Ginger! I think there's a Roman legionary in a past life, I really do.

Being official team hairdresser meant I dealt directly with Sir Alf. He had terribly set ideas about coiffeur. For example, he didn't like blow-drying because he said it caused flaky skin problems. Nonsense, of course, but then as Alberto told me later, when he first took charge of Sir Alf's scalp 'the boss' was still washing it once a fortnight with carbolic soap. Can you imagine?

As you can guess, Sir Alf insisted that the boys have short hair. *"The heat,"* he said. I pointed out to him that the Arabs live in a hot climate, yet wear long flowing head dresses. And as for the Sikhs! Well, need I say more? But 'the boss' wouldn't hear of it. *"Hif hit was good henough for the Heighth Harmy, then hit's good henough for this lot,"* he snapped. I didn't argue. I abide by the maxim: 'The customer is always right' (Except in the case of a certain Chelsea forward. Straightener indeed! Who did he think he was, Diana Ross?). So it was Napoleon Solos all round. Except for poor Bobby and little Alan Ball. With them it was simply a case of making the best of what was available (which, in Alan's case, quite honestly, would have been a suede brush!).

Mexico, as I said before, was a wash-and-dry wasteland. I never thought I'd be glad to see a tub of Brylcreem, but I could've wept the day Geoff turned over his entire supply to me. Such a good team player, Hursty. I often wonder if Jimmy Greaves would have done the same thing in that situation.

The saddest part of the trip, naturally enough, was after the drama in Guadalajara. That evening, Peter came to me. He was distraught. Absolutely devastated. He wanted me to dye his hair white! I said, *"Peter, is it really that bad? Think about your loved ones."* He had such beautiful hair. Very dark. Very Marcello Mastroiani.

I eventually talked him down to grey streaks. His wife thanked me later, but it was the least I could do. Their daughter's an actress, you know."

As told to
HARRY PEARSON

Brazil

BRAZILIAN DOLLAR BABIES

The behaviour of Brazilian football fans is frequently more interesting than events on the pitch, as PHIL TOWN *reveals...*

AS SOON AS YOU SEE THE FLOODLIGHTS, IT'S TIME to park the car. Anywhere will do, but everywhere now is the domain of one of many of the illegal but tolerated 'car-ushers' who hanky-wave you into tiny spaces that will take you forever to get out of later. They charge you an arm and leg. If you don't pay, they break them. And your car. (No *"Look after you car for a tanner, mister?"* here.) So with your life intact, pocket a little lighter and beads of cold sweat on your brow, you look for a ticket. If it's a big game, there'll be a correspondingly big 'queue' milling around the ticket window, so you buy from a tout, ridiculously up-front, sometimes to the point of wearing a uniform. You pay maybe 25% over the odds - a snip. You find your gate and a grinning guard with a sub-machine gun gives you a going over. He finds your half-time apples. You can't take them with you when you go in, so you spend five minutes at the turnstiles munching away rather than chuck them. Then you're in.

Brazilian grounds are ostensibly all-seater and it's true, you can sit anywhere. But the majority of specs are unnumbered spots on deep-stepped concrete terracing - fine in the sun, nasty in the rain (and if you have a boney bum). But finding a good spec is rarely a problem. Despite the mad passion felt for the game traditionally and still bubbling away in the hearts of most Brazilians, attendances are meagre (except for important local derbies, Championship deciders and the Libertadores, the South American equivalent of the European Cup). There are many reasons for this: the economic crisis (until recently, inflation was 30% a month) which has seen football pricing itself out of the working- and under-class pocket; over-exposure on TV with three or four live games a week; an overcrowded season which lasts the best part of a year, what with the National and Regional Championship, plus Cup, plus Libertadores; and the talent drain to Europe.

So you find your spec. There are no programmes here. So for team news you take the morning paper (which doubles as a fan, sun/rain hat, seat cover), or your tranny which also supplies an hysterically incomprehensible commentary and confirmation of gooooool-scorers. Refreshments come round. There's beer-a-plenty, especially down the back of your neck as the vendor picks his way between legs and bodies. You can get whisky, too, from men in white waiter-jackets and bow-ties. Nothing dry about these grounds.

But there seems to be very little tribal violence in and around grounds. This has a lot to do, of course, with the vast distances between cities (Gremio *v* Bahia - 1600 miles) which means very little or no away support for a lot of games, but even for crunch local derbies, the emphasis seems to be more on out-shouting, out-drumming, out-flagging and out-fireworking the opposition support. Violence tends to be of a more insidious and indiscriminate kind: having a crowd of men shout *"puta"* (whore) at any girl that walks past; having a beer-cup full of piss thrown over you by some joker from the back when it's a big crowd and difficult to get to the toilets; having missiles whistle past your ear on their way to the linesman or opposition bench. (Transistor radio batteries are very smuggleable through the turnstiles.) The teams come out and there's bedlam. Tickertape, toilet rolls, fireworks and flags fill the air and the noise is deafening. But this is a small section of the crowd, and although these fans will carry on jumping and chanting throughout, verbal support from the majority is mostly reserved for the last ten minutes to force a final effort, or a more constant demand for the head of the right-winger, trainer or club president. They're probably the most fickle

fans on earth, the Brazilians. Shouts of *"Out! Out"* at two consecutive home games carry a lot of weight with the board, and the coach can start sending out his CV.

The quality of play on display rarely lives up to the expectations of an Englishman weaned on the smooth silkiness of Pele, Jairzinho, Rivelino, Zico et al. And it pales considerably against the stylish power and excitement of the Italian League, live on TV every Sunday morning. You get the impression that the hearts of a lot of players just aren't in it, not least, no doubt, because of the pittances earned by the players compared to their compatriots playing in Europe. It's only when a story breaks that some Italian or Portuguese club might be interested in a player that the bloke seems to raise his game a few notches. But there remains the pleasure of spotting budding Peles or Zicos - names to watch in the South, for example, are Assis of Gremio and Luis Fernando of Internacional, tricky midfielders both and destined for great things if it doesn't all go to their heads. Generally, though, you can't expect very dynamic stuff. Keep-footy is in, as is safety-first, and while this may invariably prove effective in terms of results, it doesn't exactly warm the cockles (witness Brazil's showing in Italy). You're left asking yourself how much this is based on Brazilian coaches' fear of failure and the sack and how much on the technical averageness of the current generation of players. Maybe a bit of both.

You find your gate and a grinning guard with the sub-machine gun gives you a going over.

But as you shuffle out at the end of a big game, tranny pressed to your ear for the post-match interviews (less hysterical, now, and almost comprehensible), you wonder at the buses crawling past with people hanging off the windscreen wipers and the smokey little barbecue stands doing a roaring trade in charred moggy and you think to yourself: *"Well, okay, it was 0-0 again, but I had a good spec, it didn't rain, the piss-throwers didn't get me today and that Assis is such a wonderfully beautiful passer of the ball that I think I'll be back next time."* And you will be.

Lone Rangers

To hell with the Maracana, Shielfield Park is the stadium to be seen in. STUART BELL *offers an indispensible guide to the sights and sounds of Berwick-on-Tweed.*

A strong contender for *the* most over-used football fact is that Berwick Rangers are the only English team who play their football in the Scottish League. Along with Berwick's famous demolition of the other Rangers in the 1967 Scottish Cup, this is the sum total of most fan's knowledge of the Borderers.

The club, though, has a colourful history and it is becoming more and more psychedelic all the time. At the moment there is no roof on the stand, no mileage left in the centre-half, no money in the bank, and not even a lizard in the bidet. Yet Alan Bowes, the club's Chief Executive, has confidently predicted Premier League status by 1995. Most 'Gers fans reacted to Mr Bowes' forecast by rupturing their eyebrow muscles, and checking on his relationship with David Icke. But St Johnstone and Dunfermline did it, so why not Berwick Rangers? The Berwick speedway team, operating out of a farmer's field in the middle of nowhere, are currently one of the biggest in the sport, all achieved through the owner's enthusiasm and money. Alan Bowes has the same enthusiasm for football, and as long as he is prepared to risk bankruptcy there is no reason why he and his Halifax instant access account shouldn't take us to new heights.

I'm often asked what Scottish Second Division football is like and usually respond by saying that it is just as exciting as watching Liverpool or Internazionale. Of course, this is to resort to

making swingeing cutbacks with the truth, and is like comparing a performance by Pavarotti with a Karaoke night in the back room of the Sunderland Leek Club. I tell anyone that's interested to find out for themselves, and actually join me in Berwick one Saturday, but they never do. So, for all those folk who are remotely interested, I'll try to describe a typical day out to watch a Berwick Rangers league match.

First of all, don't drive there. The A1 North and South of the town is a deathtrap. The thirty or forty miles of single-carriageway in both directions, liberally sprinkled with juggernauts, tractors and caravans, are likely to send your blood pressure through the sun-roof, and your car into a ditch. The train is much better, with fast and frequent services to the town on the East Coast main line. Your day should start, then, by telling the booking office clerk that you only want to travel on the train, not buy it. Obviously, she hasn't heard this witty remark for at least five minutes and will fall about laughing while you hand over a large chunk of your beer money to pay 50% more than you thought reasonably possible for your ticket.

Following a twenty-minute stop in a cutting (engineering works, Morpeth), you will soon be whizzing northwards towards the Tweed, through some very pretty countryside with frequent glimpses of the famed Northumberland coast. Your metabolic rate will now be slowing dramatically, and nothing will disturb this mystic feeling of peace and tranquillity until you sit next to a gang of drunken squaddies on the way home.

On arrival at Berwick, you must immediately buy the local weekly paper, *The Berwick Advertiser*, which will provide a good report of last week's match, the manager's increasingly feeble excuses and a photo of some ex-'Gers player who has just been picked as substitute for Blackburn Rovers reserves. Also, in the weekly record of borders' life, I can guarantee some hilarious stories in the 'In The Courts' section, and there is invariably someone in the letters page moaning about seagull shit. Don't bother reading the 'Women In The Community' column unless you're into gooseberry jam.

All English fans must at some point visit one of the town's chip shops and order a meat pie. This is an adventure anywhere in the country, but in Berwick there is an added and horrifying curiosity. In common with most of Scotland's chippies, your pie will not be pre-warmed, sat festering away on a dirty hot shelf; nor will it be tucked into a microwave for thirty seconds. You will be astonished and sickened to see your pie thrown in with the chips. This adds approximately 20,000 calories to your lunch, and explains how people in this part of the world can drink so much Younger's Tartan. It's the only chemical on the market strong enough to clear the grease from your tongue after a fried pie.

If you can still walk with fifteen gallons of oil swishing about in your stomach, it's time to head for the ground. Shielfield Park is in Tweedmouth on the South side of the river, and there are plenty of buses available. However, a twenty-minute walk is recommended so that you get a nice view of the old town from the bridge, and to give you a chance to reflect on some other fascinating facts of local history. For instance, up until 1990 the town was still at war with Russia. Apparently, at the outset of the Crimean War, Berwick (which used to be regularly swapped between England and Scotland) was specifically mentioned in the war declaration, but omitted from the peace treaty. This was all put right when three Russian jockeys, on some sort of exchange visit to Kelso races, were spotted in Berwick and whisked away to sign a hastily concocted document ending the war. *The Berwick Advertiser*, alerted to this historic event, published a marvellous photo of a beaming man in a suit (some local shopkeeper who had set it all up by pretending to be Henry Kissinger), and three totally bemused jockeys who had only popped into town for a hamburger.

Attendances average about 420, which means that the ground doesn't exactly buzz with excitement at 3pm.

● ***Left: Manager Ralph Callachan and assistant Jackie McNamara return from a successful trip to the launderette. Above: A face-pulling contest with Montrose. Below: Jock Wallace defies Rangers. (Unlikely but true.)***

At the end of the 1990-91 season, admission was a bargain £2 (standing). It's an even greater bargain if it's raining, when you see those who have paid twice as much to sit in a puddle with no shelter. Until the Main Stand roof is replaced (it was removed by a man with a tuppenny banger when it started bouncing in a fresh breeze), the ground looks awfully dilapidated. The pitch itself, though, is large, reputedly one of the best playing surfaces in the league, and would probably support quality football, given the chance.

Attendances average about 420, which means that the ground doesn't exactly buzz with excitement at 3pm. But although the atmosphere will feel distinctly odd, it is anything but unpleasant. There is usually enough juvenile humour from the motley crew under the Ducket Stand to remind you that you're at a football match, and if you're really out of luck, there may be enough away fans to sing a couple of verses of 'Flower Of Scotland'. Despite this regular aural assault, there is never even a hint of menace. Both policemen are quite capable of stopping that sort of nonsense.

Don't be surprised when neither goalkeeper ➡

Lone Rangers

● ***Right:* Work on Berwick's new stand. Some builders have dressed for the occasion.**
***Below:* Yet more balletic action from Berwick v Montrose.**

emerges with an arm missing or supported by a zimmer frame. Although there is the odd flapper around, most are good shot-stoppers and their handling is competent. Defences tend to rely on some crusty old centre-half (Berwick have two), such as Doug Rougvie at Montrose. They are normally flanked by a junior version of the same, and two full-backs who scurry up and down the touchline kicking anyone without a flag.

The forward line consists of an old bull-elephant, a headless chicken and a tricky young winger who can waltz past his man with ease but can't cross the ball. So, nothing different there, eh?

Don't be surprised when neither goalkeeper emerges with an arm missing or supported by a zimmer frame.

It is, in fact, the midfield which is primarily responsible for reducing many games to Greavsie fodder. They are essentially useless in terms of footballing skill, and can spend a full ninety minutes clattering into one another convinced they're having a good game. Any team that can find someone with the ability to trap the ball, turn quickly and play a decent pass behind the full-back will automatically be installed as promotion favourites.

Referees are generally okay, though they sometimes use the Second Division to practice their sending-off technique, but linesmen seem unusually fat and immobile, having probably been raised on a diet of fried pies.

Other attractions within Shielfield include a superb supporters' club shop, where there are lots of souvenirs and thousands of old programmes. The queueless tea hut is as squalid as anywhere else, and the programme is full of adverts - an unfortunate necessity for its survival.

The crusty centre-half and the bull-elephant centre-forward tending to cancel one another out, and with doubts over certain individuals' fitness and motivation leading to great swathes of open space, there are as many goals (if not more) than in any of the English divisions. Since there are no super-clubs around to buy up all the best players, sides are invariably evenly matched. The 1990-91 season saw nine or ten of the fourteen clubs still battling for promotion at Easter. If you are unlucky enough to catch a particularly dire match, or if you've tried all twenty-four pubs, Shielfield Park has a lovely grass embankment on which to lie down and have nightmares about thirty-yard Bovril queues, hordes of loud-mouthed nutters using your shoes as a toilet, and the various other delights of 'big-time' football.

Further aids to mental atunement are kindly provided by a golden retriever which does interesting things with an old tennis ball, and, away from home, such sights as Berwick's player-manager, Ralph Callachan (57), getting sent-off for dissent fifteen minutes from the end of a completely meaningless last match of the season at East Fife, which is almost as ridiculous as paying Cilla Black £500,000 a year for making excruciating TV shows. This means that you will still have a chance to see the geriatric genius plodding up and down Shielfield with the ball tied to his foot, as he can't possibly end his career on that note.

Well, chucky-eggs, what are you waiting for?

Bad Trips No.2

THIS PECULIAR TRIP HAS BEEN ENSHRINED FOR posterity in the form of a motion picture.

The film opens on an Orson Welles figure. Cloaked, he stands close-up to the camera in front of the main entrance at Ewood Park, Blackburn. Thunder rolls menacingly in the background, as heavy rain sweeps down through the darkness.

The man speaks portentously. *"Tonight, I want to take you on a journey. A journey through a man's subconscious mind. It is the story of a man's awakening. A man's awakening to beer."*

The man disappears, dissolving from view before our eyes, leaving us gazing at the rain-beaten main stand at Ewood.

The scene suddenly changes. It's a cold January afternoon in the paddock at Ewood Park, and the terraces are populated by faces registering extreme disinterest. We focus in on a fresh faced seventeen-year-old boy. He glances down at his watch - a gesture prompted by boredom rather than by any tension or anticipation - and smiles in relief as we hear the final whistle blowing.

but suddenly and momentarily clear to reveal the pub parrot in its cage. We see a hand flicking beer onto the bird and the bird stalks along its perch squawking: *"F**k off! F**k off!"*

Faces begin to appear haphazardly, swirling in and out of a mist. The bellowing landlord: *"One more pint! Ha! Ha! Ha!"* The parrot: *"F**k off!"* And now an octogenarian Matlock Town fan - bald, squinting, toothless and sporting an outsize blue rosette.

As the old man cackles, we see his rosette metamorphose into a plate of sausage and beans. One by one beans are inadvertently pushed off this plate as a trembly knife chases a sausage round and round to no avail.

And now the camera is staring up at the inside of a car roof. The roof is gently rotating and there's talk swirling round the ether - talk of times past, of bygone eras. Faintly we hear illustrious names being uttered reverentially: *"Brian Garvey... Walter Lees."*

Then, suddenly, a large plastic carrier bag rears up towards the camera. We cut to an external view of a Sierra alarmingly swerving over onto a motorway hard shoulder and stopping with a skid. The rear door opens and a bag of vomit is thrown out.

The screen fades to black, then fades up again to the view of the back of a lavatory door. A

Hops SKIP & DRUNK

The things people do for love don't begin to compare with what they'll do for Watford, as OLLY WICKEN *can testify...*

We now cut to a furious montage of images. The images appear surreal - in the style of a Dali print, Scorsese's *After Hours,* or a Calvin Klein's *Obsession* TV commercial - yet to one particular man they are true memories of his trip back from Blackburn.

The montage begins with the pub sign of the Station Hotel, Matlock, swaying sharply in the dark bluster of a winter's evening. Superimposed, we see the red-cheeked face of Keith, the jovial, ex-military landlord. Roaring with laughter under his handlebar moustache, he bellows: *"One more pint for the lad!"*

This cry echoes again and again, as we now see a hand-pump marked 'Old Peculiar' being pulled and pulled, again and again, faster and faster. The images begin to blur,

mother's voice beseeches: *"Wake up! Wake up! You don't want to spend the whole night in there, do you?"*

The montage of images has ceased and we're back with the Orson Welles figure. This time, he's standing outside the lavatory we've just seen, while in the background a flickering television shows highlights of a 3-3 draw between Charlton and Hull on *The Big Match.*

The man offers concluding words of wisdom: *"A true story. It is ironic, and yet perhaps fitting, that this man's awakening should end with him asleep on the toilet. But the moral is clear: beer and the Hornets make for a perfect match."*

Grandstand *finish*

The next time you're freezing on an open terrace, spare a thought for ANDY CORSHAM, *stuck at home in front of the fire finishing off the Milk Tray.*

I never thought I'd have to ask one of those ridiculous *Dr Who* fan types for help, but there you go: does anyone know when the yeti first terrorised those quasi-fascist troops in the London Underground? (Cue myopic, anoraked stereotypes discussing episode 29 in reverential tones, dissecting the outer details and the inner meaning, as though it really mattered a toss to anyone.) What *does* matter is that it was on early Saturday evening, filling the gap between *Grandstand* and *The Black and White Minstrels.*

Saturday afternoons back then meant mum and dad shopping, or mum shopping and dad at football. We kids were boarded out with our grandparents for the afternoon. This was great, because they had a colour telly and we didn't. And this set was very colourful - orange, turquoise and yellow, mainly.

Football itself didn't mean anything to me in those days - it was just another game to be played on Summer evenings until the light faded and it was so dark that you couldn't even tell which were you own feet. What's stuck with me from that time is the voice of the bloke who read the results on BBC1 - that sort of plummy, Northern received-English sound, resonant and liquid like a skilfully controlled dribble (yes, we're talking sputum here). I could be wrong, but I think the results board consisted of white lettering on a rich green background, with a black grid overlaying it. The whole thing wobbled when the results were pushed in from the side.

Whenever I watch the *"results sequence"* (as they call it in TV land), I'm transported back to my granny's sitting room in the late 1960's. It's dark outside, and inside the room is only lit by the TV. I'm full of cheese sandwiches, pickled onions, weak tea and as many chocolates as I could scoff before mum got back from the shops. Now we're just waiting for dad to get back from the match. The *"full time sequence"* (as they never called it then) begins. A few teams stick in the mind: *"Hamilton Academical"* (spit everywhere in the *Grandstand* studio); *"Workington nil"; "Arbroath"; "Raith Rovers... postponed".* Soon it will be time to cower behind the sofa as the yeti run amok. Then it's off home, the inside of the car all warm and smelling of leather seats and fish and chips, our Saturday night treat (not the smells, the fish and chips).

Now, these yearnings for childhood are all very well, but the problem is this: when I watch the results now, this uncontrollable tidal wave of nostalgia swamps me, and what makes it worse is that if I see the results, I haven't been to the game, so in addition to all the Chekhovian longing for youth, anguish at lost time and the essential meaninglessness of my existence, I'm racked with guilt about non-attendance.

If it's an away game it's not quite so bad: I can rationalise, create believable excuses - *"The car wasn't up to the trip"; "I thought the weather was going to turn nasty"; "I felt ill"; "My shoelace broke and I had to get a new one"* - anything but admit that I just plain couldn't be bothered. Admit that and you're not an 'away fan', not a part of that particularly cliquey breed who think that if you haven't attended every away fixture since 1977 and don't 'sing your heart out for the lads' you are somewhat devoid of testicles, if not all gendered bits.

Home matches are far, far worse. If I've decided not to go to the game, I'll set off for the shops at about half past one, just in case, on the off-chance, my brother tries to talk me into going along. So I run away. I'm safe, I think, wandering around the precinct. Then I suddenly find myself thinking: *"Jesus! Look at all these teenagers! What's the matter with them? Why aren't they at a match?"* At least at the match I'd have something in common with the whippersnappers - football. Out here on the street I'm just another sad, balding old fatty, with not even the unifying force of football to help me empathise. So even though I haven't gone to the game, I'm obsessed with it. Will Saturday afternoons ever be mine again?

There are special times. At two-fifty the strongest pang of guilt comes: now it's final - it's far too late to go now, even if I wanted to. At three o'clock a sense of depression settles on me - I'm a worthless, disloyal Quisling. I could have been there if I wasn't such a worm. I could have been there - smelling the wintergreen and the cigarette smoke, the wet grass, listening to the old git behind and slightly to the left of us (TOGBASTTLOU) who'd be slobbering his way through an apple, giving vent to his ignorant half-baked racist philosophy, and pushing us out of the way whenever we obscured his line of sight. Once, my brother turned round and pushed him back and received in return a lengthy, noisy and incomprehensible rebuke (not to mention a faceful of atomised apple pulp).

“Whenever I watch the ‘results sequence’ (as they call it in TV land), I'm transported back to my granny's sitting room in the late 1960's.”

At home, I turn the Teletext on. The Third and Fourth Divisions are on a series of scrolling pages. By the time your team comes round again, you've had time to build up high hopes. Your mind is full of *"Come on you reds. Come on!"*; you're ready for a fist-clenching *"Yiis!"*; but more often you settle for *"Christ! The useless, useless bastards"*, or the anti-climatic *"Still 0-0. That's good"*. Every once in a while something will be wrong with the Teletext computer, and your team's page will stay on the screen for 2 x 10 to the power of -2 seconds, leaving you with a fleeting glimpse of some unreadable figures, but the profound conviction that the score must have been worse than the last time around.

And you still hate yourself for not being there, despite this pathetic show of mock-interest. You're sitting with your fifth cup of coffee, feeling vacant and irritable, glued to the TV in a shameful, degrading act: trying to make amends for your lack of real loyalty and commitment. All the things you had planned to do this afternoon go out of the window in the face of your new-found determination to show solidarity and convince yourself (and everybody else) that you really *do* care.

FINAL SCORE

At 4.40 pm, the page reveals that the opposition have scored what must be the winner. The scattering electrons burn the terrible image into your brain. Your teeth clench and you breathe heavily through your nose. You think that if you get any angrier your head will explode. To ease the tension, you fetch a cup of tea and a handful of biscuits, catching up on the other scores, which seem suddenly important: *"If X draw and Y lose, we could still be in 10th place..."* Working the table out in your head, you vow that next week you'll be there, taking part in the whole football experience again, traipsing through the rain to enjoy a sweet away victory. A barren, football-less week stretches away interminably in front of you.

Somehow you know that by next week, lethargy will have overcome you and you'll have talked yourself out of the 150 mile trip up the motorway.

The final scores sequence comes on. It's all computer tarted-up now, not a patch on the wonky, hand-built results board they had when I was a lad.

The Rivals No.3

Two decades have passed since the Football League staged a Bradford derby match. MICK DICKINSON *remembers the last few encounters and looks to the future...*

AN EVENT OF PATHOS AND EMOTION TOOK PLACE before the start of season 1989-90, which has clearly rekindled old rivalries - the revival of Bradford City *v* Bradford Park Avenue derby matches.

I was brought up as a lad in West Bowling, very much Avenue territory. My Dad had always had a leaning towards City, as had his Dad before him, but my Grandma's second husband - 'Grandad' to me - was a staunch Leeds United fan, and more importantly, an Avenue-ite, and it was with him that I experienced my first taste of professional football. To be fair, my father, like a lot of people in those days, never travelled to away games, and therefore never developed an extreme partisan perspective. My Grandad was different. *"City are rubbish!"* he told me. *"Avenue 'ave allus 'ad a better side."* And he would regale me with tales of Albert Geldard and 'Pussyfoot' Shackleton.

Intuitively, though, I always felt more at home at Valley Parade, City's home ground. The people seemed friendlier. The players more rugged. But it was the strip that settled it. Those claret and amber stripes, the black shorts. No other team even remotely resembled them. In vain did my Grandad exhort me to *"stick wi' t'Avenue,"* and when we moved almost next door to Valley Parade later that season, Avenue never got a look in.

We lived in a little road called Spring Bank Place. I went on my own to games and imbibed the atmosphere of noise, humour, tobacco smoke and general excitement that was a Fourth Division game. I stood on the paddock yelling my heroes on. Bruce Bannister was one. John Hall another. In those days, my favourite was Ken Leek. My first City home game of which I have any real memory was the 1966 derby game against Avenue. Avenue were well beaten, 3-0. Derisive cries of 'bring on the draft dodgers' (a reference to the rumour that Avenue secured jobs for their players during the war, whilst City's fought for King and Country) greeted the appearance of the Avenue players, clad in an all-white strip with green edging. City routed them with a fine performance, despite the fact that they were in an inferior position in the League. By the end of the season, however, Avenue had won the return 5-1, finishing 11th with City a lowly 23rd.

> ***"Those claret and amber stripes, the black shorts. No other team even remotely resembled them."***

The following season, 1966-67, was my first as a fully-fledged City fan. I was a 'paddock lad' and I grew to love the narrow stretch of terracing in front of the old main stand that was so tragically swept away in the fire of 1985. I used to lean on the old stone wall and thump the roof of the dug-outs with the best of them. Occasionally you would hear a superb comment such as that shouted by one supporter at Jim McAnearney: *"Waken up, you're rubbish!"* To which he replied, *"Aye, but I'm not ugly."* And once I had the pleasure of seeing an old age pensioner throw a meat pie at a referee, hitting him fair and square between the shoulder blades.

But across town, life was not so rosy. This was the season when Avenue said goodbye to goal-wizard Kevin Hector, who went to Derby County for £40,000, a reluctant sale for a now-struggling club. He'd scored two in the previous season's City game and had helped Avenue win their first four League games of the present one, but once he left, the heart seemed to go out of the side and it was they who finished 23rd, second to bottom in the League. City, ironically, finished 11th.

Twelve months later and the writing was on the wall for Avenue. Their best players were disappearing, some to City, others to more glamourous destinations. Bobby Ham, Pat Liney, Terry Dolan. Ten thousand had watched Avenue complete a famous double over City in the previous season. There was no segregation and supporters still changed ends at half-time, but by the end of 1967-68 they were bottom. City were almost promoted.

The following season, Avenue's fortune's slumped even lower. Twenty points from a possible ninety-two saw them bottom again. Home attendances were hovering around 2,000, and in spite of 11,000 turning up for what was to be the last professional fixture between the two Bradford rivals, it was an unmemorable goalless draw. In 1969-70, City, freshly promoted, finished 10th in Division Three. Avenue lost their place in the League. They played for a couple of seasons in the Northern Premier League, but attendances were cripplingly poor and the club was forced to sell their ground to a property company. To mark the end of professional football at Park Avenue, a challenge match was arranged between the two Bradford clubs which attracted a crowd of 3,154. Fittingly, it was a late John Hall goal that decided the match, and, until now, ended the series of games between the two clubs. The shouts echoed round the terraces. The tea-lady in tears. It was a night for farewells. Only 698 people turned up to watch Avenue's last game, against Great Harwood. During the close-season the club folded.

The old ground was eventually demolished in 1980. I went to pay my final respects. Cranes were pulling apart the roof of the old stand as workmen dismantled the seats. Everything was over-grown and rotten. I got a few souvenirs. Three seats from the old stand. A couple of metal half-time

scoreboard numbers and the old supporters club 'PASC Members Only' sign from the the club room. There was an old man standing on the terracing, leaning on his crutches, tears running down his cheeks. *"Ah nivver thowt it would 'appen,"* he said. *"Ah've been 'ere when there's been thirty thousand. Yer couldn't move. It's terrible."*

It is because of people like him that I am pleased that a new era in Avenue's history has dawned. In 1988-89 the newly reformed club played in the West Riding Amateur League Division Three. They finished second, applied for membership to the Central Midlands League Supreme Division and have been attracting well over 200 to home games in spite of having to play out of town at the ground of Bramley Rugby League Club. The atmosphere is excellent. Green and white scarves are very much in evidence. City seem to be taking them seriously enough, as they have protested at the amount of publicity Avenue have received and have banned the *City Gent* publication, *Avenue Fightback*, from their club shop.

To mark the start of the long road back, Avenue arranged a derby match with Bradford City. The game attracted 600, City fielded a team of reserves, and the result was a one-all draw. Even Kevin Hector made a second half appearance for the green and whites and almost scored. A while back I went for a meal in a West Bowling curry house. On the back of the toilet door someone had scrawled *"Bradford Park Avenue Are Back"*. Good luck to them.●

● Left: Kevin Hector, the idol of West Bowling. Above: Bradford PA, 1967-68. Bottom of the League, but with a kit like that who cares?

Avenue Update...

IN 1990-91 SEASON, BRADFORD PARK AVENUE finished a creditable third in the Bass North West Counties Division Two. Their support, particularly away from home, was the best in the league by far, and many home supporters looked askance at the green- and white-clad legions who descended on places such as Maghull and Castleton Gabriels.

The Avenueites, or Stans as we now call them after the *Bernard of the Bantams* cartoon character, hate with a passion anything to do with claret and amber. It was particularly ironic, therefore, that Avenue lifted their first 'major' trophy since re-formation, the West Riding County Cup, at Valley Parade last May. They beat Pontefract Collieries 5-1 after extra-time before a crowd of 935. City fans were there to taunt their neighbours whilst the Stans did their best to dismiss Valley Parade as *"not as good as Park Avenue."* Rumours had it that the crowd would have been greater but for the many Stans left waiting for the trolley bus specials that took them to games back in the Sixties! ●

THE MOST DAZZLING THING IN THE MATCH LAST SATURDAY WAS THE BRADFORD JERSEY.
THE COLOURS ALMOST PUT THE SPURS OFF THEIR GAME.
THIS SHOULD MAKE 'EM DIZZY!

Styles and tribulations

From sock tags to shadow stripes, RUPERT BASSETT *laments declining standards in football design.*

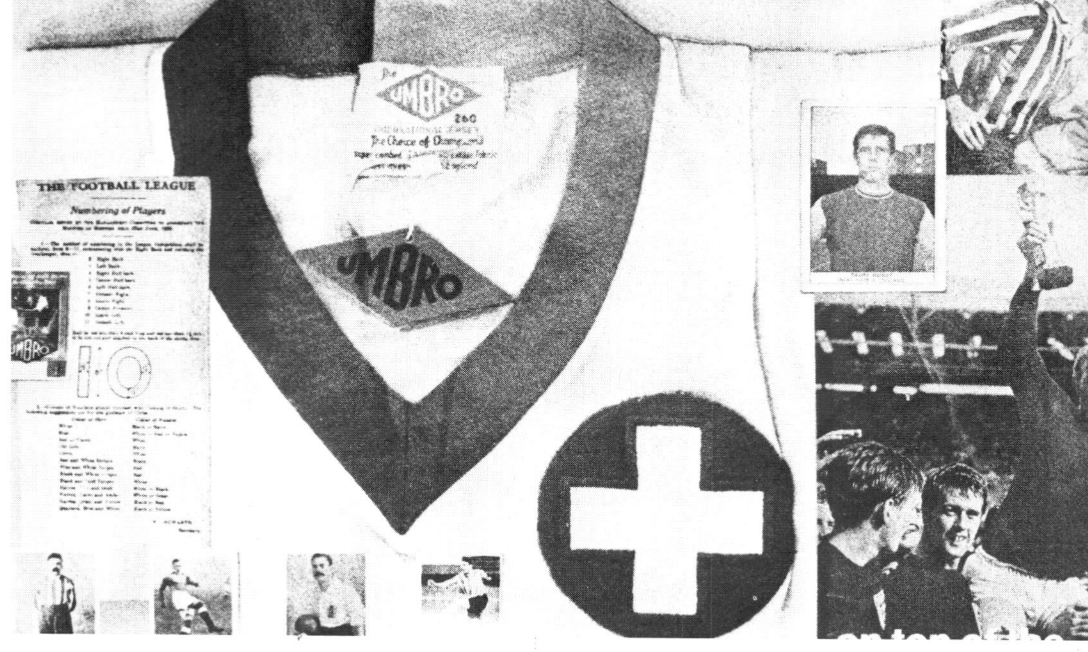

THE DESIGN OF FOOTBALL SHIRTS HAS BEEN appalling for far too long now, almost twenty years in fact. This really is a tragedy, because the visual appearance of footballers is symbolic of the many other outrageous abuses of the game which continue away from the public eye.

Ironically, the cause of the decline in the standards of football shirt design was England's 1966 World Cup triumph. Sir Alf Ramsey's world-beating squad were equipped with clothing and footwear that had been gradually developed by trial and error since the early 1800's, with the sole aim of enhancing the performance of the players. By 1966 this was at a peak, combining efficiency and economy of design with comfort and durability. The 1966 squad's kit was supplied by Umbro International Ltd, and featured a simple long-sleeved round-necked shirt of super combed 'Tangeru' cotton jersey, plain white or plain red, adorned only with the three lions of the English Football Association on the left breast and the player's squad numbers on the back. The Umbro logo was to be found only on the woven neck label. *"They were really beautiful shirts... simple, well-made, hard-wearing if you treated them right. Much more comfortable than these polyester things you can buy today."* - Arthur Toomer of Toomer's SportsHouse, Southampton, supplier of Umbro International kit to the Swiss national team for the 1966 World Cup.

The unfortunate side-effect of the 1966 victory was that it offered a clear demonstration of the enormous marketing potential of football. Since then, the inept performances of the England team have been matched only by the ridiculous designs of their strip, as sportswear manufacturers took advantage of the inadequacies of the laws governing player's equipment.

Until recently, the visual appearance of footballers was governed by Law IV (3), which stated: *"The goalkeeper shall wear colours which distinguish himself from the other players and the referee."* Fifteen words. That's all there was. As Dr Desmond Morris put it in 1981 in *The Soccer Tribe*: *"In theory, players could appear in evening dress or bathing suits without breaking the law."*

The existing seventeen Laws were drawn up in their 'modern' form in 1898 after many decades of trial and error. During the twentieth century, there has been little alteration to the laws governing the design of players' kit, only the 1990 rewriting of the Law IV (1) which states that *"The compulsory equipment of a player shall consist of jersey or shirt, shorts, stockings, shinguards and footwear."* Law IV (3), however, which governs the colouring of this equipment, remains full of loopholes, ready for exploitation.

The very first important change in the visual appearance of players was one small but significant addition to the team strip of just one Football League club. The intended function of this addition was remarkable only for its pointlessness, and was duly dropped after a couple of seasons, but its very existence had monumental repercussions for the game. The addition in question is the

infamous Leeds United sock tag number. On 18th March, 1972, Leeds dumped Tottenham Hotspur out of the FA Cup Sixth Round. Nothing remarkable about that, but while doing so they wore small rectangles of blue plastic canvas from their stocking ties, hanging down to display the players' numbers.

The sock tag number was a symbol of a team's uniquely flamboyant style of play, and marked the birth of the theory that an exceptional team deserves an exceptional visual appearance. Leeds' success continued while wearing their first Admiral strip (incorporating the infamous 'smiley' badge, kitsch enough to merit its place in '90s rave culture) and proved conclusively that a team's performance could be improved by wearing a unique strip.

I was sufficiently impressed by the sock tag numbers to demand a pair of number nine's for Christmas in 1972. I couldn't cope with the introduction of manufacturers' trademarks on the shirts and shorts, though. The rot set in at Freegrounds County Junior School in the Hedge End, Southampton, where the school team colours had traditionally followed those of the England

"The unfortunate side-effect of the 1966 victory was that it offered a clear demonstration of the enormous marketing potential of football."

team, and were consequently wrecked by the introduction of that first Admiral kit. The ensuing economic and ethical wranglings between adults and offspring resulted in those boys with parents who were dockers or Ford workers having the entire new kit, those with birthdays coming up having at least the shirt, those with parents on the PTA having nothing and, worst of all, those with zealous mothers simply having red and blue ribbons sewn down the arm of their old shirts. It was really sad.

Another significant event occurred during the 1976 FA Cup Final, when my father told me, *"A lot of money must have changed hands."* He was not explaining how come Bobby Stokes scored the winner, or why Her Majesty, the Queen, wore Southampton colours, but was referring to the reason why the ribbon down the sleeves of the new Saints' shirts contained repeated Admiral badges and not Southampton badges as I had naively assumed. I remember calculating at half-time that each player must have worn at least thirty-five Admiral logos, and wondering what the point of that might be.

In contrast to the intrusive Admiral designs, there has never been an aesthetic problem with the thousands of metres of Adidas' three stripes on football strips, even though they are a blatant piece of merchandising. This is because the stripes are a minimal and comparatively inoffensive graphic device which do not look out of place amongst the other graphic elements of the game which are essentially linear (pitch markings, goal posts, shirt stripes, ticket queues etc). It is also because they have been around for so long that they have become an integral feature of the game in the same manner as the theme to *Match of the Day*, jokes about Scottish goalkeepers, Wembley stadium and chants of 'Boring, boring Arsenal...'

The all-red kit supplied to Brian Clough's young Forest team in the late Seventies was one of the very first in the Football League to carry the three Adidas stripes, and was accompanied by a radical reduction of Forest's badge from traditional heraldic device to minimally linear graphic design. This unique strip was worn throughout their rise from the Second Division to European Champions, and rightly became the clothing of the first million-pound player.

A team's success on the field became associated with the uniqueness of their strip, and made individuality of design a must for every ambitious club, ie all of them. Supplying a Football League club with its outfit has become a highly lucrative business, manufacturers competing eagerly for design rights. The interest in football in this country produces extensive coverage in the press and broadcasting media. The televised football match has become a ninety-minute commercial for sportswear manufacturers. Their ranges of spin-off leisurewear are blatantly based upon patterns and fabrics of the strips of clubs they supply, and the manufacturer clearly expects the performance of their sales figures to match that of the team during a season of grasswalk shows.

Styles and tribulations

Tragically, with the ever-changing need to supply clubs with their individual look, a plethora of entirely non-functional and unnecessarily appalling 'fashion details' has been invented: stripes, piping, edging, cuff detailing, collar detailing, buttons, pockets, drawstrings... all liberally accompanied by the manufacturers' trademarks. Even the legibility of shirt numbers has been affected by this commercial exploitation. The shirt number has been devalued, replaced by the logo as the second most important symbol on the back of shirts. It is a tragic story. During the 1978 World Cup Finals, the Adidas shirts worn by over 30% of competing teams had numbers made up of the ubiquitous three stripes (ten out of ten for marketing, but minus several hundred for legibility), which caused such problems that commentators forced Adidas to change them between the first round group games and the second round play-offs.

During the Eighties, clothing became even more complicated with the introduction of fabrics with which more subtle and detailed changes could be made. Spurs' white became Le Coq Sportif's shadow stripe in 1982-83. On Merseyside during the 1983-84 season, Liverpool's red and Everton's blue became Umbro's pinstripe and shadow chequers respectively.

Adidas produced the next major fashionable effect in the form of a complex jacquard pattern for the Manchester United shirt, originally developed to hinder attempts at counterfeiting. The shirt fabric was finely knitted from a combination of matt and sheen polyesters, both dyed the same red, in a repeating pattern which covered the entire body of the shirt with MUFC graphic devices. One of the main problems with all this is that, as well as being nothing more than exercises in superficial styling, all those unnecessary fashion details are just badly designed.

"*It is a fact that no fashion/ textiles designer of any talent would work for a sportswear company.*"

It is a fact that no fashion/textiles designer of any talent would work for a sportswear company because the 'designwork' is so commercially led that no real creative work actually takes place. Manufacturers produce what is proven to sell, and their 'designers' spend all their time studying the opposition for ideas to rip off rather than creating anything truly original. It is the financial management of these companies, people with no visual training at all, who decide whether a design is good or bad: only a very weak 'designer' could tolerate such conditions, and this weakness is reflected in their work.

Sportswear manufacturers don't seem to realise that if fans are prepared to spend money on rubbish, then they would spend a lot more on a product of quality. Quality fabrics developed for sportswear are widely available in other disciplines, where natural cotton is properly appreciated and used with modern synthetic fibres (Lycra is an obvious example) and modern manufacturing processes to produce garments which really enhance athletic performance.

"I need quality jerseys when playing to feel confident in my game. The new Umbro range offers any keen soccer player style and comfort." - Ally McCoist, quoted from page one of the 1991 Umbro catalogue. Umbro must have paid Ally a lot of money to put his name to that, or else hidden the new Scotland away kit.

Decent football garments do exist, though: the Umbro drill cotton training suit is an absolutely splendid example of functional simplicity and sartorial elegance, worthy of inclusion in a Katharine Hamnett collection. Another classic is the Polisox football sock, with its all-cotton cushion foot with flat-linked toe seams and patented attached stocking tie...

Unfortunately, manufacturers want to keep costs low and profit margins high and they use rubbish designers for rubbish fabrics, but the real crime is when the garments are made up in the Far East in appalling working conditions, by people paid appalling wages.

Hands up everyone on the terrace who used to work in a textiles' mill...

Question Time

You were beginning to worry, we can tell. The book's nearly over and there has been no sign, not even a hint, that a ridiculously difficult quiz might be coming up. Honestly, as if we would forget. Get out your reference books. The answers are on page 96.

1. Identify the following ex-First Division players from their descriptions on 1970s' football cards:
a) *"Bulky, bustling spearhead who keeps defences on their toes."*
b) *"Lanky, long-striding winger with clever footwork."*
c) *"Speedy left flank operator with good shot."*
d) *"Plays in various positions but is at his best as a midfield shadower."*
2. Who are the only club to have won one of the major European trophies without ever having won either their domestic league or cup?
3. Name the Football League goalkeeper of the 1970s and '80s who appeared in a Persil advert?
4. Which club has played most seasons in the Scottish First Division since the re-organisation of the Scottish League in 1975?
5. Why do Notts County's floodlights points towards each other instead of onto the pitch?
6. Which Football League clubs played in the following colours during the 1890s: a) red shirts, grey shorts b) red and white quartered shirts, blue shorts c) red and blue striped shirts, black shorts?
7. Supporters of which Swedish club are known to rival fans as 'herring-stranglers'?
8. Who are the current holders of the Larchimage Windows Cup and what were the competition's previous names?
9. Identify the 'authors' of the following autobiographies: a) *Never Afraid To Miss*; b) *Attack From The Back*; c) *Striking For Soccer*; d) *Captain Fantastic*.
10. Which two current League teams are the only ones to have played solely in the Second and Third Divisions?
11. Who is the only member of the Royal Academy to have played professionally in the Spanish League and which club did he play for?
12. Which League footballer of the '60s and '70s had articles published in the humour magazine, *Punch*?
13. Name the only three French players to have played on the winning side in a major European club final?
14. Who were the first team to take a lap of honour around Wembley after the winning the FA Cup?
15. Which member of Celtic's 1970 European Cup Final team subsequently became co-owner of a snooker club in Dumfries? (Well, have a guess at least.)
16. To date, England have only once fielded a team containing six black players. Name the players and the opponents.
17. Which East European club has a kangaroo featured prominently on their official badge?
18. Manchester City's famous German goalkeeper, Bert Trautmann, was manager of which two African national teams in the 1970s?

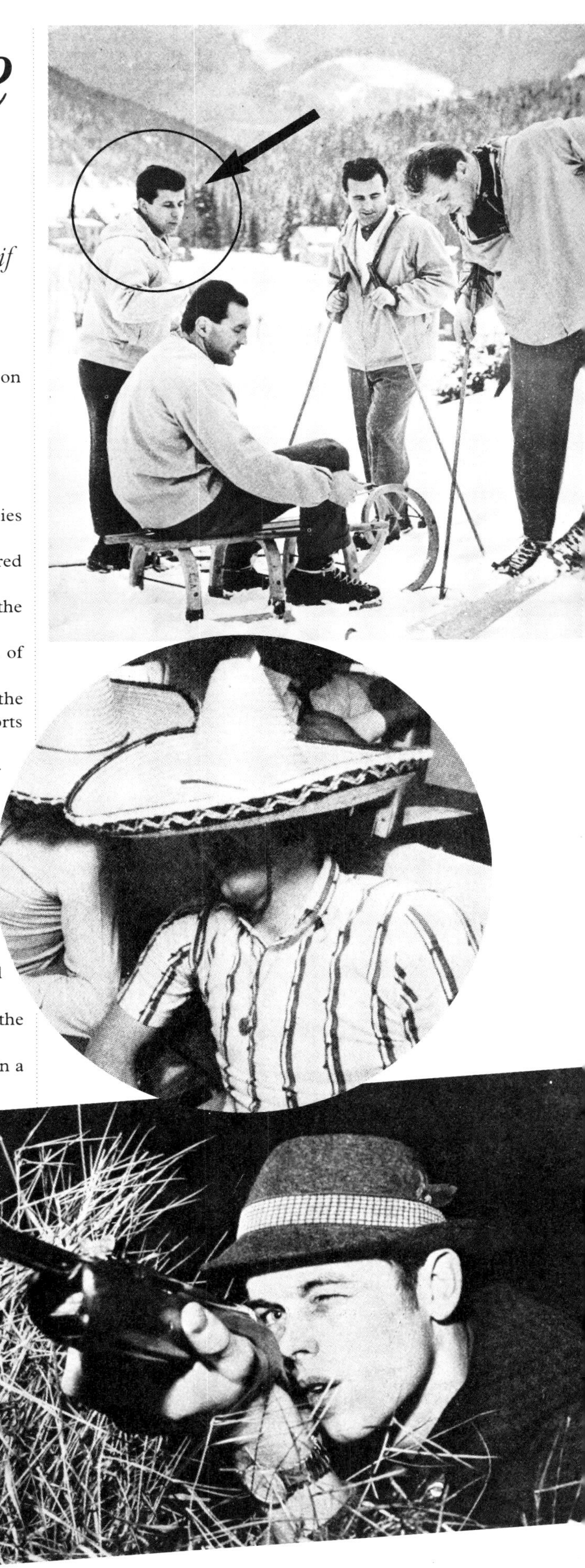

Picture Quiz
Name the three footballers on their hols.

Quiz Answers

1. a) Bobby Gould; b) Tommy Hutchison; c) Alan Hinton; d) John Boyle (ex-Chelsea and Orient - bet you didn't get him).
2. Bayer Leverkusen, UEFA Cup winners in 1988.
3. Phil Parkes (ex-Walsall, QPR, West Ham etc).
4. Hamilton.
5. We don't know. It's a rum do.
6. a) Port Vale; b) Newton Heath, later Manchester Utd; c) Stoke City.
7. IFK Gothenburg.
8. Chelmsford City; Bill Dellow/Westgate Insurance Cup.
9. a) Malcolm MacDonald; b) Phil Neal; c) Jimmy Hill; d) Mick McCarthy.
10. Plymouth Argyle and Bristol Rovers.
11. The sculptor, Eduardo Chillida; Real Sociedad.
12. Derek Dougan.
13. Michel Platini, Juventus - European Cup 1985 and Cup Winners' Cup 1984; Raymond Kopa, Real Madrid - European Cup 1957-59; Lucien Muller, Barcelona - Fairs Cup 1966.
14. Everton, 1966.
15. Jim Brogan.
16. The game was *v* New Zealand on 3rd June, 1991. The players were John Salako, Brian Deane, Des Walker, Paul Parker, Earl Barrett and Mark Walters.
17. Bohemians of Prague. It's a legacy of an Australian tour undertaken in the 1920s.
18. Tanzania and Liberia.

Picture Quiz: Josef Masopust (Czechoslovakia, European Footballer of the Year, 1962); John Toshack; John Galley (Bristol City and Rotherham among others).

TH
REVISION REVOLUTION

How to build a culture of effective study in your school

Helen Howell with Ross Morrison McGill

First published 2022

by John Catt Educational Ltd,
15 Riduna Park, Station Road,
Melton, Woodbridge IP12 1QT

Tel: +44 (0) 1394 389850
Fax: +44 (0) 1394 386893
Email: enquiries@johncatt.com
Website: www.johncatt.com

ISBN: 978 1 913622 93 0

Set and designed by John Catt Educational Limited

Reviews

Helen Howell debuts a fabulous book: the what, why and how to create an effective culture in schools. A must-read for any school leader or teacher. Helen is meticulous in her step-by-step approach to creating a positive revision culture, along with all the practical techniques to ensure children can thrive. We have needed this book for a long time. *The Revision Revolution* is evidence-informed and written by a practitioner who thoroughly understands the science of learning, the challenges many pupils face, curriculum design and, crucially, the difficulties of instigating effective change in schools. Highly recommended.

Allison Ash, headteacher, Brian Clarke Church of England Academy, Oldham

This powerful and important book sets out the compelling case for a revision revolution in our schools. Helen Howell argues for a new approach – embedded from Year 7 (or earlier) – that will address the often neglected, but crucial question of 'how' to revise. The step-by-step format provides a clear and achievable road map for the 'revolution': a cultural shift that involves all stakeholders and places revision – the process of making knowledge 'stick' – at the heart of learning. Part manifesto, part practical handbook and rooted firmly in the science, this engaging and accessible guide is packed full of strategies applicable across the curriculum. *The Revision Revolution* should be read by anyone who is serious about 'levelling up', not least because it is about establishing the independent study habits that will empower all students to achieve their goals, in the classroom and beyond!

Kath Monaghan, head of English, Oldham

If you are wondering how you can help your students revise with confidence then look no further. *The Revision Revolution* is packed with ideas and a clear step-by-step guide to building a revision culture in your school. It tackles all aspects of school life, from the classroom to the curriculum, the pastoral curriculum and supporting working at home. An excellent guide to supporting our students to revise using tried-and-tested strategies that they can take with them beyond schooling, enabling them to learn anything with a little hard work.

Darren Leslie, principal teacher, learning and teaching,
Bell Baxter High School, Cupar, Fife

This is an excellent and informative guide. *The Revision Revolution* is aimed at secondary school teachers but there are elements that primary schools should use, too. It is easy to read, well researched and includes key information on educational research and cognitive psychology, e.g. dual coding, cognitive load. This is a book that I wish my teachers had had access to when I was in school and it has plenty of ideas for me to take on board in my role as a primary school teacher. It will also help me with my own CPD!

Louise White, Year 4 teacher, Port Talbot

The Revision Revolution describes a strategy to embed revision into the school culture and everyday classroom practice. While examples from the English classroom are most prevalent, there are many ways given to use these elsewhere in the school. Concrete strategies are contained in every chapter. Emphasising the importance of student oracy and the role of student revision leads to practical suggestions for schools to develop a revision revolution for their students.

Zoë Watson, head of science, Nower Hill High School,
Pinner, Middlesex

The Revision Revolution is far more than a book about how to revise. It offers an approach to the curriculum that embeds revision at the heart of its practice, and through its delivery ensures an approach to adaptive teaching. Helen Howell offers a universal strategy for sequencing and scaffolding, while considering the challenges that so many pupils face (retrieval, cognitive overload) to ensure that young people with barriers to learning can access the same level of aspiration and challenge across the mainstream curriculum. This is a book for all staff, from trainee to ECT to SLT, and will be my 'go to' when explaining approaches to adaptive teaching.

Lauran Underwood, SENCO, Blue Coat School, Oldham

Since reviewing this wonderful book, I have been busy implementing some of the fantastic strategies and tweaking the ones I already use. Although I have helped my students to achieve exam success, I still want to help more achieve their true potential. This book, I believe, will help us (myself and my students) bring this dream to fruition.

Paulette Ennever, head of food technology,
Featherstone High School, West Yorkshire

I absolutely loved *The Revision Revolution*. It has totally changed my perception on revision, from being at the end of Year 11 to starting much earlier on. It was interesting to consider that sequence and scaffolding from KS3 is also part of the revision process. I can't wait to implement a revision website within our department.

Victoria Deavall, subject leader in computing,
Biddulph High School, Stoke-on-Trent

From start to finish, the book resonated with me. The format and suggestions are so clear that I wish they were around 20-plus years ago! Even though I'm primary school-based, there are several ideas I'm going to try to incorporate into my teaching. Rebuilding revision retrieval into whole-school practice, with a range of retrieval formats and regular modelled practice, allows all children to be much more independent. This is an ideal that now is achievable not just for some children, but for all those at school.

Christine Butterworth, Y4 teacher and PPA team leader,
Layton Primary School, Blackpool

The Revision Revolution offers a much-welcomed review of approaches to revision. Too often revision is thought of as something that comes at the end of a scheme of learning or in preparation for assessment. This book show that revision is more than that: it is about effective curriculum design and sequencing; careful and considerate use of assessment, while also skilfully selecting teaching and learning strategies that will develop metacognition and self-regulation within learners.

Rob Higgins, headteacher, Blue Coat School, Oldham

Contents

Foreword

'Learning' is a word we all use regularly – perhaps when discussing homework, reading a book or watching a video tutorial online. At some point each day, we all try to learn something. Sometimes this learning is subconscious. At other times it feels hard and we give up, try again (or not), and hope to establish a new way of thinking or doing with the information we have learned.

Even as a teacher, it has taken me decades to understand in finer detail how we learn, how our memory is shaped, and the things that can hinder or support this process. How far away are we from every teacher learning this information at the start of their careers, rather than in the autumn years, like me? How far away are we from every child succeeding at school and developing a love of learning? What will it take to bust myths about learning styles and how we learn, gender stereotypes, and misconceptions about reading, writing or how good we are at certain subjects?

If you think back to the time when you sat your public exams, what explicit study skills can you name off the top of your head? Were you taught 'how to learn' or was your schooling a hazardous journey? Were you taught how to support your brain through sleep, diet and hydration? I suspect you can remember certain techniques that you used as a student. How effective were those techniques when you studied for those exams? What would the experience have looked like for disadvantaged students or those with special educational needs?

Beyond the wider discussion about exam reform, vocational education and technical qualifications, what one thing could all teachers do to help students get off to a good start? I know I would have been a much more effective teacher had I known more about memory and how it's shaped, and about how to teach explicit study techniques to my students.

Summarisation, elaboration and retrieval practice are just some of the techniques that will be unpicked in *The Revision Revolution*. These study skills are commonly promoted in the later years of school before final exams, rather than embedded throughout the curriculum and taught explicitly within subject disciplines. However, this is beginning to change. Many schools are thinking much more carefully about curriculum decisions and how knowledge can be taught, assessed and embedded to develop further schema. Teacher professional development is being more carefully targeted to develop a collective approach that reaps rewards later on, particularly when these study skills are taught from a young age.

Whether we remember, retrieve, practise, rehearse or regurgitate facts (use whatever term you want) in order to strengthen the connections in our memory, the aim is to repeat to the point of automation so the information can be easily retrieved from long-term storage. This is how we learn, yet it is likely that the parents of today, who were the pupils of yesterday, have not been explicitly taught these study skills. Neither have some of the pupils in our classrooms. Many will dislike the words 'rote', 'repetition' or 'regurgitation', yet the terms 'rehearsal', 'revision', 'retrieval' and 'practice' elicit more favourable responses. Whatever term we use, to learn requires repetition.

We all admire those people who achieve great things. One thing they all have in common is that they have gone through countless hours of repetition, whether they are training to run a marathon, ace a memory test or perform a set of 30 songs to a crowd of 50,000 people. Being on top of your game requires practice.

This is no different to our work as classroom teachers. We refine our pedagogical decisions. We lead micro- and meso-assessment in class to determine what pupils do or don't know. We meet with colleagues to reflect on our teaching practice so we can become better at what we do. Just as we teach our pupils how to self-regulate their behaviour, we should also nurture their love of learning in and out of the classroom; this is not something to be left to chance.

Equipping all teachers and students with a better understanding of how we learn (not just for exams) is a social responsibility. When families learn these strategies and study skills, too, they can not only support their child, but also use this information to aid their own day-to-day living and working. Learning how to learn is a social justice issue that can unlock potential in everyone. The challenge is mastering each of the techniques and knowing how and when to apply them in and out of the classroom. The result? Critical thinking skills develop, communities are transformed and people are empowered.

In this book, Helen Howell brings together all the strategies, research and actions a teacher and school need to make this happen. *The Revision Revolution* is a call for schools to refine the way they teach and how they shape professional development. It is a call for a whole-school approach to improving the quality of teaching and learning.

One final point to make about resilience and learning to learn. This book has been almost three years in the making. When Helen and I pitched our idea to the publisher, John Catt Educational, in July 2020, the book was rejected. This was a first for me as an established author and for Helen as a new author. Naturally, having drafted almost 40,000 words, we were disappointed. John Catt provided us with the feedback we needed, and Helen and I had an in-depth discussion about a new approach.

We took the summer of 2020 off and revised our thoughts in the new academic year. We wanted the book to inspire a revolution of sorts in learning and study skills, so we set to work on redrafting. That redrafting process was very much an example of what this book aims to share with you: how refining, rereading, revision and many other approaches can help us become better teachers and help students become better learners.

Now, 18 months after that rejection, we have the book in our hands. I'm pleased to have supported Helen in the process of co-authoring this book, reading every word and contributing to the ideas, resources and references. *The Revision Revolution* builds upon the great ideas Helen has shared on www.TeacherToolkit.co.uk and our thoughts about how parents can support their children through school. It offers a range of techniques all in one place for teachers to use in their classrooms. Put simply, we hope this book will help you teach more effectively.

If we truly want to 'level up' post-pandemic, some of the key strategies we have outlined in this book can help you make a start in the classroom tomorrow. Helen and I agree strongly that our schools need a revolution from the ground up, and that this starts from the very first day of school. We hope *The Revision Revolution* will act as a conversation starter and help schools across the UK and further afield take steps towards social justice.

Ross Morrison McGill
www.TeacherToolkit.co.uk

Introduction
Igniting the Revolutionary Fires

When I was a student, there certainly wasn't a culture of revision at my school. But I still revised. In fact, I studied incredibly hard for my final exams and got really good grades. I defied all the science (not that there was much of that in education at the time!) and crammed in the weeks before my GCSEs, rather than spacing out my revision or making it any kind of habit.

So, why do we need a revision revolution in schools if success can be achieved in this way? Well, I was lucky. I was surrounded by positive influences: hard-working friends, supportive parents, even a private tutor. I was privileged. Not every student is afforded these advantages in life.

In addition, grades aren't everything. Yes, I performed well in my exams and got a clean sweep of A grades, but do I remember any of that learning? Very little. There's a big difference between performing well in a test and committing learning to long-term memory. If schools want to be more than exam factories, we need to ensure learning is meaningful, deep and transferable, and that comes from showing students not just *what* to revise but also *how* and *why*. We need to make revision accessible to all, enjoyable, even irresistible.

The aim of this book is to show you, step by step, how to start a revision revolution, creating a positive culture of revision in your school so students of all abilities and circumstances can thrive. They will leave school with more than great results. They will have the knowledge to challenge injustice; the knowledge to debate, communicate and question; and the knowledge to succeed in whatever future they choose to pursue.

Why don't students revise?

Too many students revise ineffectively or not at all, which is a source of huge frustration for teachers and parents. We might assume this is down to laziness, apathy or even defiance, but what if they simply lack the skills? It's a vicious cycle: if you lack the skills, you lack the confidence and consequently fail to prepare for exam success. You give up.

Consider the student who laughs when they receive their substandard test or exam results. Our go-to response as teachers is to chastise them for having such low aspirations, or perhaps to humiliate them in front of the class for seemingly taking pride in their underachievement (I have certainly been guilty of this). But all this does is cause extra embarrassment for the already ashamed student, who conceals their fear of failure with apathy because they don't know how to succeed. As educators, we have the power to change this and change it permanently.

No student enters school knowing how to revise. The more conscientious might attempt revision (as I did) by looking over their notes, answering exam questions and making revision timetables, but without really knowing how to make major gains. Rereading notes may seem an obvious and logical way to revise, but it is actually one of the least effective methods. How are students to know this if they aren't told what is and isn't effective?

Unlikely though it is, let's suppose a student types 'effective revision methods' into Google before creating their revision timetable. They will find a plethora of false and conflicting advice online, and their attempts to independently find effective revision methods will inevitably fall short. In fact, it's the modelling of effective study habits by their teacher that will help students the most. Even if students find some reliable videos online that model effective study habits, they will not be broken down using the expertise of the teacher who knows their students and their subject better than anyone else.

Teachers, parents, tutors and heads of year will tell students to revise – perhaps when, how often and how long for. They may even assist with creating revision timetables. Well-intentioned though this is, it doesn't address the all-important 'how' of revision and it won't create the long-lasting revision culture this book advocates. Even if techniques are covered in a lesson, this is probably a one-off and not a regular part of the curriculum, therefore it's unlikely to really help students establish effective study habits. There's a lack of knowledge among busy teachers about the best revision methods and how to explicitly teach them to students. Teachers may also worry that time spent teaching study skills will take away from their subject content, but in fact the opposite is true: teaching study skills will help ensure that content is remembered and knowledge can be built on.

Often, the resources given for revision include past papers and booklets of information that students are rarely shown how to use. At worst, the completion of exam papers leads to bad habits becoming entrenched. As Doug Lemov states, practice does not always make perfect, but it does make permanent (Lemov et al, 2012). Ideally, students should have a bank of well-practised revision and study methods that they can confidently select from. Only then will their fear and trepidation surrounding that loaded word 'exam' be reduced or even transformed into optimism. By using a step-by-step process to establish a revision culture in school, we can slowly develop these empowering life skills.

The traditional approach to revision – sessions laid on once or twice a week for Year 11 – simply won't cut it. I've never known these sessions to be beneficial for more than a handful of students (usually the ones who don't need it). They are a 'too little, too late' intervention: students are dragged to them, teachers are dragged into running them (sometimes during their holidays) and no one gains much.

Revision needs to be modelled in small, manageable chunks, allowing students time to practise and build gradually towards those daunting exam questions or full essay tasks. Equally, no scaffold should be provided without a plan to remove it. By teaching the revision process from the early years of secondary school, we can support students to mastery over time, slowly reducing the scaffolds and increasing their independence.

The achievement gap

By neglecting to teach the 'how' of revision, we risk widening the achievement gap. Low-attaining students lack the knowledge and skills to work out revision for themselves, whereas high-achievers may find relatively effective ways to revise without teacher intervention – or they may have private tutors to guide them in the right direction. The premise of this book is really very simple: show them how and tell them why, then let that 'how' and 'why' trickle through the school. If we immerse students in effective study habits, and arm them with the rationale behind what they are doing, we can raise their aspirations along the way.

Defining learning is notoriously difficult, but what most attempted definitions have in common is the idea of a 'change' – in memory, understanding or perceptions. For a change to become permanent, that learning needs to be stored in long-term memory. New learning enters the brain via working memory, but this is limited; forgetting occurs when it becomes overloaded or the knowledge is not successfully transferred to long-term storage. Those students who are already behind academically or have lower than chronological reading ages are further disadvantaged because of a lack of secure knowledge to draw from. In order to narrow the achievement gap, we need tangible and concrete ways to help students remember their learning. If we 'understand new things in the context of things we already know' (Willingham, 2009), it's crucial that students are given ways to remember important knowledge. Once learning enters long-term memory, it's much easier to recall either with or without a cue.

The achievement gap is sometimes compounded in schools by the misguided belief that 'less able' or lower-set students need easier activities or, even worse, an easier curriculum. This is what some educators believe to be effective differentiation but it actually widens the gap further, because while the most-behind students only ever complete basic work, their peers are sprinting ahead through exposure to complex texts, vocabulary and challenge. I prefer to think of differentiation in terms of levels of scaffolding: some students may need more support to complete a task than others, but the high expectations and intended destination are the same.

This book, therefore, offers suggestions for how you might add or remove scaffolding to meet the needs of your students: challenge remains high while threat is always low (Myatt, 2016). In my first years of teaching I had a bottom set for grammar and I remember feeling very proud of myself for not only finding a copy of Roald Dahl's *The Twits* (as opposed to Homer's *Odyssey*, which was being studied by the rest of the year group) but also finding a video of the worm-eating episode. While this may have been funny and memorable, the focus was on task completion over thinking (Myatt, 2020a) and on keeping students busy: one of Robert Coe's poor proxies for learning (Coe, 2015). By explicitly modelling effective study strategies, we can enable 'bottom set' students to access high levels of challenge by essentially developing their academic literacy.

However, this is not to say that some students shouldn't receive targeted interventions. Our weakest readers and writers may well need some phonics provision and will certainly benefit from a school-wide culture of reading for pleasure and progress. All these elements work in harmony to get the best out of every student.

Building a revision culture, then, is hugely important for our students' futures. It involves more than just a few tips on how to revise. It's a gradual process that will filter through the whole school: every year group, every key stage, every student. It should permeate lessons, assemblies, parents' evenings, staff meetings, form time, governor presentations. This is how we build a culture that empowers all stakeholders to become experts on revision – a culture where revision is irresistible. This culture is also about creating autonomous learners who are able to effect their own improvements. One of the key aims of *The Revision Revolution* is to create self-regulated learners who add to their knowledge, understanding and skills through their education and beyond.

Imagine a world in which every student knows not just what to revise but how. Where every student can match appropriate strategies to content and understand why they are doing it. Where every student can see what's in it for them and have ambitions far beyond leaving school with good grades. In this world, barriers are broken down and anything is possible. *The Revision Revolution* will help you build that culture of effective study one step at a time.

Mental health

Although this book isn't specifically about wellbeing, I strongly believe that students' mental health will benefit enormously from practising and developing confidence in effective study strategies early in their education.

I believe this for two reasons. First, a strong grounding in effective study methods removes an additional burden on students in the run-up to exams: it stops them wondering how on earth they should prepare for success. Second, spreading exam preparation out over time means no more unhealthy cramming, just useful and habitual study for optimum learning.

A word on the steps

This book offers a step-by-step approach to building a revision culture, but the order of those steps is not rigid and neither is each step necessarily designed to be done in isolation. Context is important here: where are you on your revision journey? What is your intake like? How supportive are parents? The timescale will be context-dependent, too, and is only a guide.

Start with the audit on the next page. Return to it a year into your journey in order to review and decide on next steps by evaluating your priorities. Nobody knows their school better than the teachers and leaders working in it!

Stakeholder		**RAG**
	Students	
Attitude	Students understand what revision is and its importance. They recognise the link between revising and future success.	
Understanding	Students across all year groups understand how to revise effectively.	
Skill	Students can revise independently, monitoring their strengths and areas for improvement.	
	Staff	
Attitude	Staff understand what revision is and its importance. They buy into building a revision culture.	
Understanding	Staff know what the most effective study methods are and the science behind each one.	
Skill	Staff have a bank of strategies they can use effectively to build students' revision skills towards mastery, fostering self-regulated learners.	
	Leaders	
Attitude	Leaders at department and whole-school level understand what revision is and its importance. They buy into creating a revision culture through staff training and other whole-school approaches.	
Understanding	Leaders know the science and research behind the most effective study methods in enough depth to run training and answer staff questions on rationale and implementation.	
Skill	Leaders are adept at using revision strategies in their own practice and happy to share their experiences with others, creating a dialogue around revision.	
	Governors	
Attitude	Governors are aware of the importance of revision and how it empowers students. They support the school's drive to create a revision culture.	
Understanding	Leaders regularly present to governors on whole-school revision strategies, explaining the rationale, aims and outcomes so that governors understand and invest in the process.	
	Parents	
Attitude	Parents support the school's drive to create a revision culture and understand the benefit of effective study strategies to their child's learning and future success.	

Understanding	Parents understand the important aspects of an effective study session, including creating the right environment, the optimum length of a study session and the types of strategy their child might use.	
Skill	Parents have enough understanding of effective revision to be able to support their child's home study (for example, quizzing them using the Leitner system with flashcards).	

Finally, here's a suggested timeline for the first year of your revolution:

Step 1
Revolutionary Curriculum

Designing a programme of study that enables all students to succeed in our subject areas

Summer term: June/July

In a nutshell
Curriculum is the programme of study we design for our students, whereas syllabus is the list of topics determined by governing bodies. In designing the curriculum, we decide how the syllabus is delivered. For a revision revolution to be successful, we first need to decide on the powerful knowledge to be revised and on important ways to communicate that knowledge, such as reading and oracy. This chapter looks at curriculum review and the features we might explore as we develop a rich curriculum.

There is little point in instilling effective revision habits in students if we lack a strong curriculum full of powerful knowledge that we want students to revise and remember. The summer term is a popular time for curriculum review – there's usually some release time owing to Year 11 leaving. But there's no requirement to start your revision revolution in June or July, and you may have reviewed your curriculum recently and feel it is strong. In this case, your revolution might start from Step 2.

To ensure all students achieve success, we need to construct a curriculum that not only includes the knowledge and skills we want students to master, but also involves the gradual removal of scaffolds so they gain independent mastery by the time they leave school. Thinking must stay effortful for students to continue to progress, therefore our curriculum needs to be challenging, but with the support in place to make it accessible to all.

Kat Howard poses some great questions to get subject teams thinking about curriculum review (Howard, 2020b), which I've paraphrased below.

1. What are the capsule pieces in your subject's curriculum?
2. What makes least sense? Is there a scheme that doesn't fit or interrupts the flow of your curriculum?
3. What is least connected? Are some schemes there because we enjoy teaching them rather than because they add value? For each scheme, can we say 'why this' and 'why now'?
4. What is most and least useful?
5. Does your subject's curriculum reflect the gold standard of your subject?
6. Does your subject's curriculum explore the big ideas?
7. Is there a level of depth that honours the knowledge?
8. Does your subject's curriculum reflect the students that make up your school's cohort?
9. Have you decided on the important core knowledge for your subject and ensured students repeatedly 'bump into' (Howard, 2020a) this knowledge along their curriculum journey?
10. Have you discussed the most useful hinterland knowledge to help explain and support the core knowledge? This might include concrete explanations, models, examples and strategies to support students in remembering and understanding the core knowledge of each subject's curriculum.
11. How are students supported to talk, read and write like subject experts?

The terms 'core' and 'hinterland' are used by Christine Counsell to facilitate thinking around the important (core) knowledge but also the extra knowledge (hinterland) that makes the core knowledge more memorable (Counsell, 2020). This might consist of analogies, anecdotes, stories, examples, models and explanations that illustrate and break down what we deem to be the powerful knowledge in our subject area. One example of delicious hinterland knowledge, which I decided to include in our Year 7 medieval scheme on *Beowulf*, is the idea that 'larger-than-life men … came into the poetic imagination due to medieval discoveries of fossilized mammoth bones, which, when incorrectly reassembled, look like nothing so much as tremendous human skeletons' (Headley, 2021). Although it's clearly not crucial that students retain this information about mammoth bones in order to become scholars in the subject of English, it's such a great and memorable anecdote about medieval characterisation, including the possible origin of the giant that continues to capture our modern imaginations.

Sequencing and stories

Curriculum is perhaps most helpfully thought of as a progression model and a narrative we weave around our subject. Therefore, sequencing and stories are arguably a good place to start.

Since the word 'sequencing' entered the Ofsted criteria for the curriculum, it has been subject to many different interpretations. Sequencing a curriculum means joining items of knowledge together into coherent schema or, in other words, finding ways to link different units of study together. We might give our curriculum flow through chronology, for example. By 'sequencing' a curriculum, we can weave the narrative of our subject through Year 7 to Year 11 and beyond.

For example, at my school, our key stage 3 curriculum is structured to tell the 'story of English' from Homer and the oral tradition, through Chaucer, Shakespeare, the Romantic poets and Victorian literature including the Gothic tradition, to 20th century war literature and 21st century dystopian fiction. Students do not study these as isolated units; rather they examine how one influenced and helped create the next, constantly looking back and forth across eras, adding to their developing schemata (our existing web of knowledge that we use to make sense of new information). This accumulation of knowledge from one scheme to the next makes revision crucial, in order to build upon and hang on to the learning accrued at each stage of the curriculum journey.

When my students study war literature in Year 8, they look back at Shakespearean descriptions of war, recognising and tracking common themes of propaganda, patriotism and trauma, as well as recognising conventions from the Gothic tradition in violent war imagery. They can begin to critique notions of bravery as a masculine trait, and how ideas of 'emasculation' and 'cowardice' have been used to manipulate soldiers throughout history. As David Didau says, 'You can't think about something you don't know' (Didau, 2020).

Students also look ahead to dystopian fiction, identifying the influence of the horrors of 20th century war on a new wave of dystopian writing, much of which (although fictional) is inspired by the real living nightmare of war, discrimination and tyrannical regimes in the 20th century.

Our brains privilege stories (Willingham, 2009). Therefore, by using the curriculum to tell the story of our subject, we can make it memorable and exciting for students. I remember a particular lesson with my 'low-ability' Year 8 class, when we had just begun our dystopian fiction scheme and study of George Orwell's *1984*. I asked them to draw parallels between war writing (the last scheme) and dystopian fiction using the vocabulary they had learned. Their responses were so impressive. The headteacher happened to be observing the lesson at the time (it wasn't a planned observation) and he watched previously struggling readers confidently use complex vocabulary to describe the similarities they were able to identify themselves using their developing schemata.

The results of making these links explicit in our daily teaching are potentially phenomenal, with students adding to their schemata each term. We are able to really challenge students at all levels and empower them to make incredible progress. The table opposite includes some of the parallels that my students commented on when moving between schemes.

Scheme	Vocabulary explicitly taught	Commonalities identified by students (themes: the 'what' and techniques; the 'how')
The Gothic tradition (*Frankenstein*)	Benevolent, malevolent, supercilious, malicious, xenophobia, inherent, fiend, callous, satiated, dehumanise, protagonist, anti-hero, omniscient, omnipotent, gruesome, grotesque, grim.	From Year 7 study (the *Iliad*, the *Odyssey*, Shakespearean rhetoric): • Abuse of power. • Violent imagery. • Hubris of protagonist.
20th century war literature	Envelop, consume, devour, withered, oppressive, decomposing, endure, contempt, malevolent, disembodied, bleak, callous, apparition, fatigue, foreboding.	• Abuse of power. • Grotesque imagery. • Loss of faith (theme of religion/God). • Fear of science/technology. • Appearance versus reality – who is the real monster? (e.g. government/war).
Dystopian fiction	Omnipresent, totalitarian, decay, manipulate, ominous.	• Abuse of power. • Real dystopia of early 20th century. • Themes of persecution and control. • Resistance and rebellion. • Bleak, decaying settings.

Knowledge and cultural capital

This is another hotly debated topic in education at the moment. At one end of the spectrum, educators believe that for too long knowledge of 'the best which has been thought and said' (Arnold, 1869) has been reserved for public schools and potential Oxbridge students, while the majority of comprehensive students study 'lighter' or 'engaging' curricula with lots of practical activities and 'popular' texts (remember my example of using *The Twits* to teach grammar to a bottom-set class?). These educators argue that all students deserve access to knowledge of Latin, ancient Greek, Dickens, the classics and higher-level concepts in order to give them 'cultural capital'. This phrase refers to the ability to debate, converse and communicate on an intellectual level, and to understand references used in conversation and writing – what Didau calls shared knowledge (Didau, 2020).

At the other end of the spectrum, educators are frustrated that a focus on memorising facts is 'drying up' creative subjects. Some also believe we are in danger of creating a 'hierarchy' in humanities and arts subjects that places importance on 'dead white males' and colonises the curriculum. The counter-argument here is that it's impossible for students to think about something they don't know – higher-order thinking and creativity can only come from a foundation of solid, secure and ideally transferable knowledge. Some students may come to us culturally poor, since they haven't had the same opportunities as their peers to explore the world, read (or be read to) or talk about their interests with adults. A potentially huge knowledge and word gap is in place before school even begins. Obviously, we want to avoid compounding this gap when constructing a curriculum.

Perhaps our response to this debate when designing and reviewing a curriculum should be balance. Knowledge is important but only as a starting point. For example, a core curriculum in English might focus on classics from the canon, but also weave a range of interesting linked modern and multicultural texts through the wider curriculum, thus ensuring students are exposed to high-quality texts from around the world and from different eras. Returning to my 'hinterland' example from our medieval scheme on *Beowulf*, we immediately consider characters such as Grendel's mother from the critical perspective of problematic representations of gender, exploring Maria Dahvana Headley's argument that 'Grendel's mother doesn't behave like a monster. She behaves like a bereaved mother who happens to have a warrior's skill' (Headley, 2021).

Another important part of this argument is challenge. All students deserve to be challenged, no matter their background or starting point, and exposing them to 'the best which has been thought and said' with careful teacher scaffolding ensures they are challenged throughout the curriculum. The argument here is that 'what works best for the most disadvantaged works best for all' (Didau, 2020); if we look after those students in our curriculum design, we will serve our entire cohort well. The 'best' is, of course, subjective and choices made in curriculum design inevitably involve eliminating as well as selecting great topics. But, arguably, it's the opening up of this continuous dialogue that is important.

I think it's necessary to ask, firstly, what the important or 'shared' knowledge is in your subject area, or what the big picture is in your subject. What do students need to know in order to speak, read and write like scholars or professionals? Ideally, we want to give students the tools to enter the academic world of university, whether they choose to or not. If creating a level playing field of 'student-scholars' is our aim then devising a curriculum with this crucial knowledge peppered throughout is perhaps the best way to achieve this (see the 'Mapping and fading' section on page 34). In this way, we prevent days of frustration with Year 11 students who struggle to identify basic concepts, and keep ourselves from repeating the same simple mistakes in our respective subject areas.

Extra support

In order to devise an ambitious and challenging curriculum that is 'unapologetically academic' (Webb, 2019), certain students will need to be supported with lots of scaffolding, in the form of modelling and breaking down processes and complex texts into manageable chunks. We will always come across the argument that 'my students cannot access this', but that perspective only widens the achievement gap. There are ideas throughout this book on how to make challenging work accessible for all.

Extra challenge

Hopefully, the inclusion of challenge in a curriculum will inspire some students to read more widely around topics. It's worth making wider reading lists available, as well as academic texts such as journal research articles that students can explore outside the classroom. The online lecture series Massolit,[1] although not currently available for every subject area, is a great example of wider scholarship. There are ideas to support students on accessing this kind of wider scholarship in Step 8.

Oracy

'Talk is the sea upon which all else floats' – James Britton, 1970

1 www.massolit.io

Oracy is the foundation of effective reading and writing. By getting students to talk in a structured way using academic vocabulary, sophisticated sentence structures and a formal register, we are giving them great rehearsals for writing, setting our expectations for the quality of language they use and raising their confidence with an academic metalanguage that can feel quite alien to them.

Sometimes, mathematicians and scientists argue that oracy and developmental writing – writing designed to teach students how to write and improve syntactic control (Lemov, 2017b) – are irrelevant to their subject areas. However, fantastic blog posts have been written by teachers on using both these approaches to develop scientific and mathematical scholars. See, for example, 'Writing in science: a symposium' (Raichura, 2018), a series of blog posts written by a range of science teachers and collated by Pritesh Raichura, head of science at Michaela Community School in North London.

Oracy can easily be neglected in the classroom. When exams and assessments typically involve writing in silence, it's easy to get into the habit of regularly setting tasks that involve silent reading and writing, especially as this makes it easy for teachers to check all students are on task and to circulate, reading and marking work. However, oracy is 'cognitively sticky' (Didau, 2018a). When we consider how toddlers acquire language, they instinctively pick up grammatical patterns and this is why they often form irregular past-tense verbs incorrectly: I eated/I goed, etc. My four-year-old son recently described the doors of the trams closing 'bangerly' – clearly this isn't a word, but his instinctive knowledge of how to form an adverb that reflects the noise he heard shows the naturalness of oral language acquisition. Oracy is a natural process that struggling readers and writers engage in daily, which makes it perfect for 'low floor, high ceiling' activities that are accessible for all but can be extended to high levels. Tom Sherrington warns that students may often sit through 'whole lessons without rehearsing using language, airing their thoughts, practising explaining concepts or sharing ideas with others' (Sherrington, 2021).

The oral activity I use most often in my classroom is timed discussion in pairs, but I also frequently use a listing activity.[2] I always allow thinking

2 In pairs, students take it in turns to list things they can remember about a topic – ways to describe something or the conventions of a genre, for example. This activity is low-threat and each student contributes equally while being supported by their peer.

time and often let students write notes or full sentences in preparation for their discussion. The following ideas get more students involved in whole-class discussion and ensure the quality is high.

1. **No opt out, choral response and cold-calling**. All these activities are from Doug Lemov's *Teach Like a Champion* (2015) and are wonderfully simple. 'No opt out' involves returning to a student who was previously unable to answer once the correct answer has been given. This serves several purposes: expectations are high, attentive listening is expected and giving the correct answer (even if parroting it at this stage) helps cement it in the student's memory. Choral response involves the whole class responding in unison to a question or stem. This can work well with definitions such as 'Photosynthesis is the process of…'. Finally, cold-calling is simply choosing students to call on, rather than allowing hands up, and is another way to keep students alert at all times!
2. **Pose, pause, pounce, bounce**. The teacher poses a question and pauses to allow students to rehearse their answers in their heads, on paper or orally with a partner. The teacher pounces on a student to answer, then bounces their response to another student for additional detail, clarification, analysis, etc. This process can be repeated many times, particularly the 'bounce' part, ensuring wider participation than constantly questioning the same student(s).
3. **Paraphrasing**. A number of students are asked to explain in their own words the learning, teacher explanation or answer of their peer. This ensures they have been listening and have understood.
4. **Probing**. Students are asked 3-5 follow-up questions to add detail, depth and improved quality to their answer.
5. **Say it again, better**. Students are given certain criteria, vocabulary or details to add to their answer in order to improve it.

Patrice Bain discusses the importance of oracy in *Powerful Teaching*. She states that 'if a student asks a question in class, I encourage other students to provide a response with elaborative feedback – beyond a simple explanation … Once a student jumps in with an explanation, I ask a second student to add on to the first student's explanation' (Agarwal & Bain, 2019). This is similar to 'pose, pause, pounce, bounce' and 'say it again, better', but it gradually removes reliance on the teacher while providing an assessment tool as teachers listen to the responses offered by the class.

Below are some 'rules for talk' that might be helpful in designing a memorable curriculum with a strong oracy thread. They will, of course, be more effective and habitual for students if used across the school.

1. **Full sentences**: always speak in full sentences.
2. **Vocabulary**: use key words and academic vocabulary when speaking.
3. **Eye contact**: look at the person or people you're addressing, listening to or responding to.
4. **Projection**: speak loudly and clearly, articulating each word.
5. **Listen**: always listen to your peers and teacher – you may be asked to paraphrase what they have said!

Extra support

At my school we have displays and resources to support all students to talk like scholars. One of the most effective presents key academic verbs and a list of synonyms, so teachers can simply point and say, 'What word might we use instead of [show]?' These are 'working displays' that can aid exploration of the subtle nuances between different synonyms, and words can be added as and when they are learned. Sentence stems are on display that students can practise using in oral activities, as well as a 'rules for talk' poster.

Extra challenge

Students could be encouraged to use certain grammatical structures in oral activities, such as a noun appositive, conjunction, participial phrase or subordinate clause, to increase the complexity of their speech and make it closer to written language.

Reading

For most subjects, reading will consist of non-fiction texts in the form of articles, research papers, letters, studies, eyewitness accounts or textbook explanations. This type of reading is often difficult for students for a multitude of reasons: most students will be unfamiliar with the conventions of non-fiction, the vocabulary can be highly academic, and the syntax is often far more complex than the spoken word or fiction texts. However, non-fiction texts are an important source of knowledge, challenge and wider perspectives. Subjecting students to a range of non-fiction throughout the curriculum broadens their knowledge, vocabulary and familiarity with complex sentence structures and the conventions of different non-fiction texts. It will also help prepare students for the type of independent reading they will need to complete in further and higher education. However, careful scaffolding is needed to make these texts accessible.

Here are some ideas for scaffolding the reading of non-fiction texts.

1. **Summarise the text**. By giving students a brief explanation of what the text is about, we reduce cognitive load, leaving them free to concentrate on the content of their reading rather than working out the key message. For example, 'This article is an opinion piece about behaviour in schools in which the writer explains why they do not agree with isolation as a punishment for poor behaviour.' Or, 'This text explains what is meant by "nutrition" and goes through the different nutrients needed for a balanced and healthy diet.' You could then model strategies for independent summarising, such as providing a heading and bullet points for each paragraph and using the topic sentence in a paragraph to work out what it's about.
2. **Make the conventions explicit**. For example, 'This is a newspaper article, therefore it has a headline, subheading, image and caption that give us clear indications about the content of the text. Because it is a feature article, the heading expresses an opinion and it is important to be aware of this biased perspective.' Or, 'This is an informative text, therefore it includes factual information and breaks down difficult, multisyllabic words so that we know how to pronounce them phonetically, such as "car-bo-hi-drayt".'
3. **Front-load the vocabulary**. With difficult texts, we cannot teach every word. Doug Lemov et al write about which words we might 'gloss over' (Lemov et al, 2016), asking students to write a synonym in the margin rather than giving them detailed definitions and practice using the word. With words that are necessary for

understanding or are part of word families, we might offer student-friendly definitions, example sentences, concrete examples of the word and questions to assess student understanding before reading the text. This reduces cognitive load: when students read the text, they have already encountered key words and feel a certain amount of familiarity and confidence with them.

4. **Break down difficult sentences**. If we are explicit about the sentence structures used by writers, students will become more familiar with them. We could say: *'A conditional sentence uses "If… then" or its equivalent (unless/provided that/supposing/except/as long as/in case) to show how something may happen or be true as a result of something else, such as, "If you take in more energy than you use up, then your body will store this as fat." This sentence is made up of an "if" clause that sets the condition and a main clause that explains the result of that condition. In a multi-clause sentence – for example, "Electrons, particles that are negatively charged and tiny, move around the nucleus in electron shells" – the main clause (which makes sense on its own) contains the most important information and the main idea, while the extra clauses offer additional, less important information. In this sentence, the main clause tells us what electrons do (move around the nucleus in electron shells) while the subordinate clause provides extra detail about their characteristics (negatively charged and tiny).'*

And here's a suggestion for whole-school literacy. Since becoming a parent, I've realised the difference it makes to a child's learning when you tap into their interests. For example, my four-year-old son is currently obsessed with dinosaurs. He costs me a fortune in dinosaur magazines, games and books; however, through engaging with these, he now knows complex words like 'herbivore' and 'volcanic'. He's constantly asking 'What's that?' and he loves learning the different dinosaur names and information about other prehistoric animals.

By asking students what they are interested in and ensuring the school library (or classroom library) is well stocked with non-fiction books on those topics, we can pique students' curiosity and build their knowledge in a way that is driven by them and their passions.

Vocabulary

Vocabulary is fundamental to understanding in every subject area. Studies show (not surprisingly) that vocabulary is one of the biggest reasons for the achievement gap, so it's crucial to make it an integral part of our curriculum. Here are some ways you might do this.

1. Decide on the key words for each scheme and allow students plenty of opportunities throughout the scheme to practise using these words, in oral discussions and in writing.
2. Pick out important words from texts and teach them explicitly.
3. Teach a range of tier 2 and tier 3 words.
4. Include cumulative low-stakes testing of key words and set vocabulary homework, using strategies such as the Leitner system (see page 68) to prevent forgetting.

If you're compiling word lists to enable students to write with sophistication in your subject area, consider whether you have included enough tier 2 words. In *Bringing Words to Life* (2013), Isabel Beck et al categorise vocabulary in three tiers: tier 1 words occur in speech, therefore they are simpler and also tend to be more familiar to students; tier 2 words occur mainly in texts and span different subject areas; and tier 3 are subject-specific terminology words. Tier 2 words are not often explicitly taught because teachers tend to focus on their subject's tier 3 vocabulary; however, they are high-utility words often unfamiliar to students, particularly those who are not 'readers'. Tier 2 words also aid reading comprehension because they are common in texts but not speech.

You can consider writing bespoke student-friendly definitions of tier 2 words that fulfil the following criteria:

1. They use **everyday language** that students can understand, i.e. words they already know.
2. They provide ideally **more than one example sentence** using the word in context.
3. They are written in **full sentences** (avoid synonyms) while being as concise as possible.

4. They **capture the essence**, i.e. show what makes the word different to its synonyms.
5. They use the correct **tense** and **part of speech**.

Bringing Words to Life offers an absolute plethora of suggested activities for vocabulary practice. Studies completed by Beck et al (2013) have identified the following as best practice for explicit vocabulary instruction in the classroom:

1. Introduce words through explanations in everyday language.
2. Provide several contexts in which the word could be used to avoid surface-level understanding.
3. Get learners to interact with word meanings straight away.
4. Use activities that require students to process the meanings of words in deep and thoughtful ways.
5. Provide examples, situations and questions that are interesting and therefore memorable.
6. Provide many encounters with target words.

Alex Quigley, in *Closing the Vocabulary Gap* (2018), writes about the power of etymology (word origins and how meanings have evolved over time) and morphology (the forms of words). He suggests breaking words down into their constituent parts to encourage pattern-seeking.

Mapping and fading

I wrote earlier about working backwards with curriculum: asking ourselves what we want students to know and be able to do by Year 11 (or Year 6 or Year 13) and mapping these items of knowledge and skills into our curriculum, ensuring they are repeatedly covered. Initial teaching should be 'massed', only moving on to the next scheme once a high success rate has been obtained. As Mary Myatt advocates, we should teach to mastery (Myatt, 2020a). Powerful revision in the form of retrieval quizzes, homework and other activities can be used to space the coverage of the same key knowledge and skills so they are not forgotten. This is what we will turn our attention to in Step 2 of this book.

As well as mapping important knowledge and skills into the curriculum and considering how best to sequence them, we need to think about the gradual removal of cues. We need to consider how to move from direct teacher-led instruction to student autonomy over the course of the curriculum. Deciding when, where and how to remove scaffolds is a mammoth task but a worthwhile one. In *The Writing Revolution* (2017), Judith Hochman and Natalie Wexler include level 1, 2 and 3 activities – a helpful way to think about difficulty levels within a skill. We need to reduce cues so that eventually students can complete the skill with no support whatsoever. This is teaching to mastery. Once a skill becomes automatic, it reduces cognitive load, freeing students up to concentrate on more advanced thinking.

Siegfried Engelmann's model of direct instruction uses 'backwards fading' (Needham, 2019) to teach important skills, advising that we begin with the easiest skill and obtain a high success rate from students before moving on. Backwards fading is a strategy where worked examples are gradually reduced and replaced with practice problems as learners gain expertise in the subject (Kirschner et al, 2006).

Here's an example of how I might gradually remove scaffolds across a series of lessons for the teaching of topic sentences.

Lesson	**Activity**
Lesson 1	• Define topic sentence. • Worked examples of topic sentences with clear criteria (subject, verb and object, expresses paragraph's main idea in one sentence). • Draw students' attention to use of topic sentences in pieces of writing. • Teacher writes modelled annotated topic sentences and students copy down. • Students distinguish topic sentences from supporting information. • Students work in pairs, orally rehearsing topic sentences for a given topic and ensuring they have included all the criteria from the start of the lesson.
Lesson 2	• Teacher provides topic sentence and asks for extra detail (e.g. Achilles is characterised as petulant. What else do we know about Achilles?). • Teacher models how to add this information as an appositive (e.g. Achilles, a demi-God warrior, is characterised as petulant). • Students orally rehearse adding appositives in pairs.

Lesson 3	• Teacher provides topic sentence and asks 'when', 'where', 'why' and 'how' questions, noting down student answers. Teacher then models expanding the topic sentence with these ideas (e.g. Achilles, a demi-God warrior, is characterised as petulant at the beginning of the *Iliad* because he abstains from war to punish Agamemnon). • Students rehearse using these questions to add detail to their topic sentences.
Lesson 4	• Teacher provides topic sentence and models beginning with a subordinate conjunction. • Students rehearse using conjunctions to improve basic topic sentences.
Lesson 5	• Retrieval quiz (1. What is a topic sentence? 2. What must be included in a topic sentence? 3. In what ways can you add detail to a topic sentence? 4. Identify the topic sentence and supporting information). • Teacher provides topic sentence and asks students how it could be improved. Teacher prompts students to choose more precise, academic and sophisticated vocabulary, as well as techniques such as appositives.

Hopefully, you can see how the lessons described above progress from highly didactic and teacher-led to more student-centred after the students have had multiple opportunities to practise and a high success rate has been achieved. Obviously, this is dependent on how the lessons progress. I'm not suggesting that students will have mastered topic sentences in five lessons, just that they may be able to work on them independently with some teacher prompting by lesson 6.

One skill I definitely want Year 11 students to have mastered is crafting effective analytical paragraphs. I teach this using the WHY method:

- **What** is the writer telling us about the character, theme or setting? This is your topic sentence and quote.
- **How** does the writer use language or structure to convey their message? This is where we analyse the writer's craft and zoom in on important words, phrases or techniques.
- **Why** does the writer employ this technique? This is where we explain the writer's intention and the effect of their writing on the reader or audience.

The easiest part of a WHY paragraph is the 'what' (topic sentence) so this is my starting point in Year 7. The aim is to teach topic sentences to mastery so that students can write them with fluency and flair, leaving them free to concentrate on the more challenging 'how' and 'why' parts of analytical paragraphs.

Here's an example of how I might map the teaching of analytical WHY paragraphs across the KS3 curriculum.

<table>
<tr><th>Year</th><th>Focus</th><th>Skills</th><th colspan="2">Academic vocabulary</th></tr>
<tr><td rowspan="3">7</td><td>Term 1
'What' sentences: what is the writer telling us?</td><td>Simple, compound and complex topic sentences, and embedding quotes using academic verbs.</td><td colspan="2" rowspan="3">• Depict
• Illustrate
• Evoke
• Characterise
• Present
• Elicit
• Provoke</td></tr>
<tr><td>Term 2
'What' sentences: what emotions are being conveyed?</td><td>Topic sentences including noun appositives and embedding quotes using academic verbs.</td></tr>
<tr><td>Term 3
'What' sentences: what does the writer want the reader/audience to feel?</td><td>Topic sentences using present and past participles, and embedding quotes using academic verbs.</td></tr>
<tr><td>8</td><td>Term 1
'How' sentences: how does the writer do [what is described in the topic sentence]?</td><td>Zooming in on words and phrases.</td><td rowspan="3">• Utilise
• Employ
• Implies
• Suggests
• Portrays
• Signifies
• Foreshadows
• Embodies
• Encapsulates</td><td rowspan="3">• Simile
• Metaphor
• Alliteration
• Sibilance
• Adjective
• Noun
• Verb
• Adverb
• Assonance
• Consonance
• Imagery
• Onomatopoeia
• Personification
• Animalistic
• Society</td></tr>
<tr><td></td><td>Term 2
'How' sentences: how does the writer use [words, phrases, techniques, structure] to do [what is described in the topic sentence]?</td><td>Identifying and analysing the effect of techniques.</td></tr>
<tr><td></td><td>Term 3
'How' sentences: how does [what is described in the topic sentence] link to context?</td><td>Linking writer's craft to context.</td></tr>
</table>

<table>
<tr><td>9</td><td>Term 1
'Why' sentences: why might the writer do [what is described in the topic sentence]?</td><td>Identifying writer's attitude using tentative language.</td><td rowspan="3">• Emphasise
• Highlight
• Accentuate
• Criticise
• Contradict
• Reinforce
• Celebrate
• Condemn
• Tone
• Mock
• Idolise
• Expose
• Theme</td></tr>
<tr><td></td><td>Term 2
'Why' sentences: why might the writer use [the technique analysed in the 'how' sentence(s)]?</td><td>Identifying writer's purpose/effect on reader using tentative language.</td></tr>
<tr><td></td><td>Term 3
'Why' sentences: why might there be multiple interpretations? Why does this idea/theme/motif permeate the text?</td><td>Multiple interpretations using tentative language; cross-references.</td></tr>
</table>

It's worth emphasising that this teaching is cumulative, so students will continue to write topic sentences while learning and writing about the author's craft (the 'how') and they will continue to write topic sentences and analyse quotes while learning about the author's intention (the 'why'). The knowledge is constantly practised and reinforced.

This approach of mapping and backwards fading is perhaps more obvious in subjects like maths where knowledge is mainly hierarchical: you can't add and subtract until you can count forwards and backwards; you can't multiply and divide until you can add and subtract; and you can't understand fractions until you can multiply and divide. Although knowledge in English is arguably more cumulative, there are certainly hierarchical elements. For example, a student can't understand a noun phrase without first having a secure knowledge of nouns and other word classes. It makes sense, then, to start with the easiest skill and teach this to mastery, before moving on and gradually reducing the level of teacher support.

We've reached the end of Step 1. At the end of each step in our revision revolution you'll find a short quiz about what we've covered, as well as some reflection questions and a summary. In Step 2, we'll explore how to make the revision revolution a reality in your school, by identifying key stakeholders to bring on board and training staff in the essential study skills that we want to equip our students with.

Quiz

1. What important questions might you explore as part of a curriculum review process?
2. What does the term 'curriculum' mean?
3. What are the key debates surrounding curriculum design?
4. Why are writing and oracy important?
5. What is backwards fading?

Reflection

1. Are all curricula across your school of a similar high quality?
2. Are there opportunities to make links across subjects so that learning is transferable?
3. Is the curriculum in each subject progressive?
4. Do all subjects offer opportunities to read relevant texts and scaffold writing?
5. Do all subjects offer opportunities for high-quality oracy, whether this is through teacher-led feedback or student-led discussions?

Summary

- Curriculum review is important so we know what powerful knowledge we want students to revise.
- A rich curriculum might include reading, oracy, writing and vocabulary instruction.
- A carefully structured curriculum might involve mapping and fading in order to build students to independence and mastery.

Step 2
Calling All Comrades

Getting stakeholder buy-in to your revision revolution

Autumn term: September onwards

> **In a nutshell**
> Once you're happy with your curricula, the next step in the revision revolution is engaging stakeholders. This chapter begins by looking at who the key stakeholders are and their importance in the revolution, and then focuses on school staff and how to rally their support.

Four years into teaching, I was promoted to English and literacy AST.[3] I was ecstatic. My mind was buzzing with ideas that I was desperate to share and implement. This abundance of ideas, I soon realised, is both a blessing and a curse. Yes, it's exciting to be constantly innovating, but my naive and inexperienced self knew very little about effective implementation. In other words, I was a great starter but not a great finisher. Lots of initiatives were introduced and, in time, we made fantastic gains in both English and whole-school literacy. However, I now realise that less is more:

3 AST stands for advanced skills teacher – it was a way to keep ambitious teachers in the classroom by giving them a promotion that was based on improving classroom practice. Sadly, it doesn't exist any more.

implementing one idea slowly and thoroughly, involving all stakeholders and including time to reflect are crucial to sustainable change management.

One of the key takeaways from John Kotter's eight-step change model is that if you're 'too impatient, and if you expect too many results too soon, your plans for change are more likely to fail' (Mind Tools, 2007). The high-stakes nature of education means we're not always good at being patient, but it's important to acknowledge that real, sustainable change takes time. That's why this book is structured in steps. How long you spend implementing each step will depend on you and your context, but slow and steady wins the race if we want our revision culture to be sustainable.

An important focus for your revision revolution is stakeholder buy-in. If everyone is invested in a collective vision for student revision, it's much more likely to be successful. Kotter's change model begins with creating urgency: 'For change to happen, it helps if the whole company really wants it. Develop a sense of urgency around the need for change. This may help you spark the initial motivation to get things moving.' The suggestion is that 'for change to be successful, 75% of a company's management needs to "buy into" the change' (Mind Tools, 2007). This involves a clear rationale but also an open and honest dialogue, both of which we will explore here in Step 2.

Stakeholders

Here are some of the stakeholders we need to call to arms.

1. **Staff**. First and foremost, we need the support, enthusiasm and expertise of staff. This includes the full support of the school's leadership team, effective and persuasive training for teaching staff, and a consistent approach that involves time to reflect and refine. One of my biggest mistakes when introducing new initiatives to staff was false assumptions: I assumed my colleagues shared my enthusiasm and workaholic tendencies, and that they would implement the initiative perfectly. In hindsight, this was very naive. It takes time to implement an initiative well and to get it right. Teachers are ridiculously busy – why should they invest in 'my' initiative, especially if I don't explicitly outline what's in it for them?

Students will easily sense if a member of staff is doing something because they have to, rather than because they believe in its value.

2. **Parents**. What do we do with our most difficult students? We ring their parents, because we know what a valuable resource they are when we work in partnership with them. This is not limited to behaviour. We should also share our vision for a revision revolution and the reasons behind it. Parents will be more inclined to support our initiatives and encourage their child to engage if they can see exactly how it will benefit them. Of course, parents also face competing pressures on their time, so the key is to convey a simple and concise message that is easy to digest and implement.
3. **Governors**. Governors don't need the same level of detail about each individual revision strategy, but it's worth sharing a long-term plan with them so they understand the intentions and how you plan to achieve your goals. This means they will be confident when speaking to parents, students or the dreaded Ofsted. We want every stakeholder to be able to talk with the same degree of eloquence about the revision revolution – its intent, implementation and impact. The revolution truly becomes a collective endeavour!
4. **Students**. We will focus on this all-important stakeholder in forthcoming chapters. Students can become demotivated or disengaged when the purpose of what they're doing isn't clear. We shouldn't underestimate the power of being explicit about the benefits of our approach to revision: students are intelligent, perceptive young people who will buy into learning if they can see the benefits. Nowhere has shown the potential of our young people better than the fantastic Michaela Community School, where a disadvantaged cohort are treated like future Oxbridge graduates. This is the power of high expectations and academic rigour. I truly believe students respond to our expectations – treat them as capable of greatness and they will emerge as such. The revision revolution involves trusting students to be part of the conversation around revision and learning, even allowing them some ownership and leadership of it.

Later chapters in this book will explore how we can immerse students, parents and governors in our revolution, but first we need to get staff excited and invested in this process.

Senior leadership

The second step in Kotter's change model is forming a 'powerful coalition'. This involves 'strong leadership and visible support from key people within your organization' – the coalition should be a team of 'influential people whose power comes from a variety of sources' (Mind Tools, 2007). Consider your context: who are the visible and well-respected leaders that will drive the revolution forward? They might be middle leaders, pastoral leaders or data managers, in addition to members of your senior leadership team, to reflect the variety of power sources.

No initiative can be truly successful without the support of senior leadership and particularly the headteacher. A former headteacher of mine had a favourite quote about how teachers 'make the weather', which he advised us to stick in our planners every year. It always occurred to me that this was true of leaders, too: the 'weather' in their departments or schools is created through their approach, be it warm or abrasive, proactive or lazy. When a headteacher and leadership team give an initiative their support and provide a dose of enthusiasm, it's contagious and staff will follow suit.

There's always a balance to be found between carrot and stick, therefore the backing of the senior leadership team (SLT) is essential. Depending on your context, it may be worth having a conversation with SLT about how you want their support to look. Any initiative is vulnerable to lethal mutations (we've all seen the dreaded tick list for observing and grading lessons) and your revision revolution is likely to be much more successful if SLT express their positivity and belief in it, rather than chastising people for not rigidly following the principles introduced in staff CPD. SLT may not necessarily lead staff training but they should certainly attend it with great levels of enthusiasm. They should be part of ongoing dialogues with staff about revision in their subject areas. This is important for students, too – they need to see that school leaders believe in revision and its importance.

Depending on your role in school, you may want to present a short- and long-term plan for building a revision culture to your SLT and gain their support from the beginning. If you're leading departmental or whole-school training, a word from a member of SLT is so helpful in ensuring that staff can see you have their backing. As far as students are concerned, having members of SLT lead assemblies on revision is a great way to reinforce the message of its importance (see Step 7).

Share the science

This book takes a research-based approach to revision using strategies proven to be the best bets for our students. Therefore, at different points in your revision revolution journey, you will need to share with staff the study methods that are shown to be the most effective. The table below is not an exhaustive list, but it includes the six strategies with the most evidence behind them, in order of what you might focus on first and why.

Study method	What is it?	When to share with staff and why
Retrieval practice	Retrieval is recalling previously studied information from memory. There is a very strong evidence base showing this approach to be effective.	This is a fairly simple and very effective revision strategy, therefore it makes sense to train staff on this first and ensure it's used across the school. There are lots of different retrieval practice activities, so it's worth spending quite a bit of time in staff training exploring these and how you might use them in different subject areas.
Spacing and interleaving	Research shows that it's beneficial to space revision out, so it's completed little and often, rather than 'crammed'. Not only this, but forgetting can actually be a good thing in terms of allowing important knowledge to enter long-term memory. Therefore, it's best to leave a gap after learning the key information and before revising it. This will inevitably make revision feel harder, but it will be more effective in the long term. While spacing means leaving gaps between study sessions, interleaving means inserting different topics into those gaps so you don't spend too long studying or revising one topic in isolation. Research shows that studying in this way helps to reveal connections between ideas, as well as aiding long-term retention.	Once retrieval is being consistently and effectively used across the school (or in Year 7 at least), you may want to introduce staff to the ideas of spacing and interleaving. When designing retrieval tasks, it's worth introducing challenge through some spacing of topics (e.g. including recall questions on topics from last week, term, year, etc). Spacing, interleaving and retrieval work best in tandem. It's also worth asking staff to think about the effects of spacing and interleaving when planning and setting homework. For example, homework set on a previously studied unit rather than the current one is likely to be more effective for long-term memory. Also, interleaving different topics in revision lessons and asking students to make links between those topics is likely to be more effective than revising in blocks.

Elaboration	Elaboration as a study method means developing detailed explanations of ideas by answering questions about how, when, why and what, as well as connecting the ideas to personal experiences, memories and daily life.	The reason this is a great study method to encourage staff to use is that, once students are trained in asking 'how', 'when', 'why' and 'what' questions, they can construct their own revision questions and work independently or in pairs to answer them. This takes time to achieve, but ensures students think deeply about their learning, questioning rather than simply rereading or memorising. Ultimately, we need students to become self-regulated learners able to structure their own effective revision sessions without teacher instruction. When introducing challenge and scaffolding retrieval, it's worth considering using elaborative interrogation as part of this process.
Dual coding	Very simply, dual coding is combining visuals and words. Our brain receives information through two channels, visual and auditory, therefore the brain remembers information better when there are two prompts: visual and verbal. This is also the reason why we shouldn't talk while asking students to read something, as it's very difficult – almost impossible – for them to listen and read simultaneously. The visual doesn't have to be a picture, neither do you need to be an artist. There are many different types of visuals, and some will suit certain information better than others, but combining words and visuals helps students understand and retain information.	Dual coding at its most simple is a very easy strategy to implement. It involves teachers using visuals to explain concepts and students doing the same in their revision. For example, it may be easier for a student to remember the quote 'Small circles glittering idly in the moon' from Wordsworth's *The Prelude* if they pair it with an image of spots of moonlight trailing the poet's boat in the water.
Metacognition	Metacognition involves students thinking explicitly about their learning, usually through evaluating their work, setting goals and monitoring their own academic progress. It involves a level of independence and autonomy that has to be achieved gradually.	Enabling students to become self-regulated learners is a key part of revision and there are many ways this can be modelled and practised in the classroom (see Step 4).

Concrete examples	Many of the ideas that students need to master in order to be successful in different subject areas are fairly abstract and therefore more difficult to understand than concrete ideas. This also makes them hard to explain, but creating real-world, concrete examples that students can relate to is one effective way to achieve this.	I've left this until last because, although it's important for teachers to have an arsenal of examples to make the abstract concrete for students, this is part of a much wider training focus on explanation that could include looking at anecdotes/stories, analogies, metaphor, explanation design and so on (Tharby, 2018). It would undoubtedly be beneficial for students to become proficient in developing these kind of examples themselves; however, it's arguably a separate area of training.

Although these research-based study methods have been found to be effective, they are susceptible to lethal mutations when not fully understood. This is why ongoing staff training is crucial to ensure the strategies are used in a way that enhances rather than inhibits student learning. This training might include learning walks that look at consistency and effectiveness of implementation. It's important, however, that this is about opening up a dialogue and doesn't become a checklist-type exercise where staff quickly shoehorn in the strategies they think you want to see.

The Revision Revolution Year 1: staff training on retrieval

Teachers lead incredibly hectic lives. Staff training sessions add to their already overflowing list of things to cover and can potentially breed resentment. At my first school, staff training was always on a Wednesday after school – I had usually been teaching all day and was exhausted. We need to acknowledge that the typical teacher has had a day of ringing parents, detaining students, marking, teaching, completing admin and trying to keep on top of emails. Therefore, they need this additional demand on their time to be purposeful (and it does help if it's accompanied by a cup of tea and some biscuits!). I have sat in staff training where we made wedding dresses and decorated T-shirts that we modelled on a hugely embarrassing catwalk. To this day, I have no idea what the point of that training was and it certainly did nothing to improve my teaching.

Most teachers I know are glad of the move towards a research-based approach to our profession. It certainly makes gimmicky staff training less likely – it's simply not excusable any more. Staff deserve to know the rationale and evidence behind any initiative. After all, why should they buy into it if you can't prove it will have a positive impact on students? Every teacher wants the best for their students, so if we can show how what we're asking teachers to do will add value, this will make our training session much more credible and compelling. To make your revision revolution seductive to all stakeholders, not just staff, talk with great passion and belief about the steps you're taking towards building a revision culture. Be the best salesperson with the most fantastic product!

To support this CPD, the rest of this chapter presents a suggested outline for your initial sessions with staff. You can use the QR code to access ready-made presentations with possible activities and research to include in the training.

www.teachertoolkit.co.uk/wp-content/uploads/2021/12/ The-Revision-Revolution-Resources-1.pdf

Teacher training session 1

Before you introduce retrieval, present the overriding aim of this training: to kickstart a revision revolution! Why is this revolution needed? What happens currently in your context and how could this be improved? An 'Imagine a world...' approach might help create the urgency needed for that all-important buy-in:

> *Imagine a world where revision is a habit. Where students revise for every exam in every subject area using a bank of strategies they have practised since Year 7. Where they are not only fully confident with these strategies but also know exactly which strategy to choose*

in different circumstances, what kind of environment to create for an effective study session, and how to evaluate each session in order to make gains in the next one. Gone are the days of 'Well, you can't really revise for [your subject], Miss/Sir'. Gone are the days of students blindly completing practice question after practice question without making meaningful improvements. Students know exactly how to revise effectively, as do their parents, and they are enthusiastic about their revision as empowered, independent learners heading for success. The stress levels of students and staff are massively reduced as anxiety is replaced with confidence. Revision has become irresistible!

Now you've set the scene, it may be worth spending some time debunking any myths. The audit you completed in the introduction to this book (see page 19) will help you ascertain whether this is necessary in your context, but in my experience there are always those delegates who need a bit more convincing.

First, reassure staff that you're not advocating that students revise for their GCSEs from Year 7. Rather, the revision revolution will involve creating 'self-regulated learners' (Quigley et al, 2018) who know how to use the most effective study methods to make gains in their learning. If the curriculum has been well designed and well sequenced from Year 7 onwards, it will be brimming with powerful knowledge; the aim of our revision revolution is to make this knowledge stick. We will model and practise these strategies thoroughly and repeatedly enough for students to be able to use them independently. What better way to prepare your students for Oxbridge, should this be their aspiration?

The revision revolution is about creating high expectations and future opportunities for all; it's about creating choice and removing barriers. Whatever students choose to do, they have the tools to achieve their ambitions. It may be worth asking how many staff ever received this kind of explicit instruction in study methods? Imagine how much better prepared it would have made us for the demands of further and higher education. As part of my research for this book, I spoke to my mum about how I explicitly teach note-taking. My mum has dyslexia; she was academically successful and graduated from university, but she was amazed by the concrete approaches to teaching academic skills that she never had access to. She was sure these would have helped her overcome some of the barriers she faced through her undiagnosed dyslexia.

It might be worth presenting to staff the differences between traditional revision and effective revision in a simple table like this one.

Traditional revision	**Effective revision**
• Completing past papers. • Rereading notes. • Highlighting. • Cramming. • Can't revise, won't revise. • Last-minute interventions and after-school 'free-for-alls'. • Little or no modelling of how to revise.	• Retrieval. • Spacing. • Dual coding. • Interleaving. • Concrete examples. • Desirable difficulties. • Lifelong study skills. • A regular habit as all strategies are explicitly modelled to students across the school.

Now you (hopefully!) have the staff convinced and onside, it's time to explore the first effective study habit.

Session aims

Present the aims of the session: 'To explore the science behind retrieval practice and what constitutes powerful knowledge in different subject areas.' Explain to staff that embedding retrieval into our curriculum will help us on the path towards a revision revolution. If you set some prereading, this is an opportunity to quiz staff on what they know. Possible quiz questions include:

1. What is retrieval practice?
2. List as many benefits of retrieval practice as you can remember.
3. Name one retrieval activity and how it works.
4. What should we bear in mind when setting retrieval tasks?

These questions will help you eliminate misconceptions from the outset and address any remaining scepticism about the value of retrieval.

Analogies

Analogies are very powerful in capturing the attention of staff or students and delivering effective explanations. One analogy I've heard to explain the usefulness of retrieval practice is learning to drive. Just as learning to drive involves gradually mastering each part of the process before reaching a point of automaticity, students need secure component knowledge before they are able to access the higher-order ideas in our subject areas. For many, learning to drive is a challenge that does not come naturally, so you may find that a lot of staff are able to relate to the journey from anxious novice to automaticity in the act of driving. I passed my driving test on the fourth attempt after years of lessons with several different teachers. This was partially due to the gaps I had between lessons, which meant I never really built on the knowledge and skills learned from one cluster of lessons to the next. After passing my test, I drove on the motorway every day and the process soon became automatic. It's the same with knowledge – essentially we use it or lose it.

Effective study patterns

I find David Didau's blog post exploring different study patterns very powerful (Didau, 2013a). Ask staff which of these study patterns is most likely to result in long-term learning:

1. 'Study study study study – test.
2. Study study study test – test.
3. Study study test test – test.
4. Study test test test – test.' (Didau, 2013a)

Our schemes and curricula are generally set up for study pattern 1, but research suggests this is the least effective and it's actually study pattern 4 that's most likely to aid students in retaining what they have learned. The implications of this are that we should be regularly quizzing students throughout our schemes. It's important, however, that this testing is 'low-risk, frequent, and designed to include variation and distracting difficulties' (Didau, 2013a). It's necessary, therefore, to explore what these kinds of tests (or quizzes, if you want to make them sound less threatening) might look like in different subject areas.

Schema

You will almost inevitably encounter concerns from some staff that retrieval equals rote learning. In order to unpick this, I suggest exploring Daniel Willingham's statement that 'understanding is remembering in disguise' (Willingham, 2009). This can be explained by looking at schema: we all make sense of new knowledge by connecting it to items of knowledge that already exist in our schema. In other words, knowledge recall is essential to learning and goes far beyond factual recall – it is how we form understanding. Retrieval should not only test factual knowledge, although this should almost definitely be the starting point, so that students can build on this foundation of facts to access more complex thinking.

I like to illustrate the idea of schema a bit further with an anecdote about my son:

> *For example, my toddler is slightly obsessed with trains. He has learned that they have carriages and wheels, but beyond that does not yet have a confident grasp of the different characteristics of a train. For this reason, he thinks his toy tractor, which pulls a trailer of animals, is also a train and gets quite cross when I suggest otherwise! His schema is not developed enough to recognise the difference in the wheel size, the shape and the purpose of these different vehicles. Experiences also play a part in schema development. Alfie has ridden on a train and a tram, therefore he knows the difference between these methods of transport, but, in our urban setting, he has never ridden on or even seen a real-life tractor.*

In *Powerful Teaching*, Agarwal and Bain list 10 benefits of retrieval practice. Some of these have been explored already, but it's still worth projecting this list at this point in the session:

1. 'Improves students' learning and retention of information over the long term.
2. Increases students' higher-order thinking and transfer of knowledge.
3. Identifies students' gaps in knowledge, which provides formative assessment for teachers and students.
4. Increases students' metacognition and awareness of their own learning.

5. Increases students' engagement and attention in class.
6. Increases students' use of effective study strategies outside of class.
7. Increases students' advance preparation for class.
8. Improves students' mental organisation of knowledge.
9. Increases students' learning of related information that isn't initially retrieved.
10. Increases students' learning in the future by blocking interfering information.' (Agarwal & Bain, 2019)

The forgetting curve

It may be helpful to refer to Hermann Ebbinghaus' forgetting curve, which illustrates the importance of revisiting knowledge to prevent forgetting, as well as spacing these recaps so that knowledge is revisited weeks, months, terms and years later.

Powerful knowledge

You've now introduced quite a lot of science for one session and, at this point, it may be worth asking departments to look at their curricula and decide on the powerful knowledge that students need to remember in order to gain understanding, achievement and opportunities. You might decide to give heads of department some prompt questions (see below) in advance of the session, so they have their curriculum to hand and understand the aims of the discussion.

- What knowledge do we want students to retain at KS4 and KS5?
- What knowledge will add to students' cultural capital?
- What knowledge will enable students to be part of 'the conversation'?
- What knowledge opens doors and enables choice and opportunities?
- You may want to consider vocabulary, your subject's 'canon', skills (knowing how) and so on.

Once staff have decided what constitutes powerful knowledge in their subject area, you can use this information to move on to strategies for retrieval practice in session 2.

It's extremely beneficial to spend time working across departments, looking at any powerful knowledge you have in common and therefore creating that disciplinary approach. For example, while the term 'crescendo', meaning increasing in volume, is key to students' understanding in music, we also use it in English when examining an increase (crescendo) in tension within a text. Making these links helps students add to their schema, aiding understanding and long-term memory, and encouraging the transference of knowledge across and between different contexts.

Teacher training session 2

Quiz

You might begin this session with a retrieval quiz on session 1, in order to unpick misconceptions and address misgivings. Questions could include:

1. What is the testing effect?
2. What does Ebbinghaus' forgetting curve tell us about newly learned information?
3. What is spacing and why is it important?
4. What is a schema and what does it show us about memory?

Implementing retrieval practice

Because this second session will focus on the 'how' of retrieval and successfully implementing it into the curriculum, it's worth offering guidance on how to set up retrieval successfully and the possible pitfalls to avoid. Robert Coe offers excellent advice on this:

1. 'Teachers might generate retrieval questions that focus solely on factual recall (these questions are easier to generate) rather than requiring any higher-order thinking.
2. Questions might be too easy and boost confidence without providing real challenge, which is likely to be a key ingredient for generating the kind of learning hoped for.
3. Teachers might allocate too much time to the quizzes, effectively losing the time they need to cover new material.' (Coe, 2019)

I would also emphasise the importance of feedback. There are certain conditions that make retrieval a waste of time:

1. **Students copying out the answers from their books**. This clearly involves no thinking whatsoever and negates the 'desirable difficulty' (Bjork & Bjork, 2011) element of retrieval practice, as well as preventing any type of assessment of learning by either student or teacher.
2. **Lack of feedback**. If students don't receive corrective feedback on their retrieval tasks – however this may look – the task will add no value to their understanding of the topic and errors may become embedded into memory.

It may be worth mentioning the hypercorrection effect at this point. This suggests that the more confident students are that their (incorrect) answer is correct, the less likely they are to repeat the error if corrected. In other words, errors made with high confidence are easier to correct than those made with low confidence. This is why it can be a good idea to get students to RAG (red, amber, green) their answers before feedback. This also helps avoid the illusion of knowing – the belief that we know more than we actually do.

At least some of students' feedback should involve self-correction, where they mark their own answers. This needs careful thought in terms of ensuring that errors and misconceptions do not go uncorrected. After all, teachers are the experts and students are the novices; they rely on our guidance in order to move along the novice-to-expert continuum. To encourage this culture of self-reflection, teachers will need high-quality resources such as knowledge organisers, flashcards and answer sheets. They will need to model the process of self-correction to students to enable them to complete this process effectively and confidently.

In *Powerful Teaching*, Agarwal and Bain suggest a simple way to make use of the hypercorrection effect: the 'four steps of metacognition', which I've paraphrased below. Metacognition, in the simplest terms, can be described as 'thinking about your own thinking'.

1. Students place a star next to the questions they can answer and a question mark next to the ones they can't.

2. Students answer all the questions they have marked with a star.
3. Students look up the answers to all the questions they have marked with a question mark.
4. Students verify all the starred answers are correct. (Agarwal & Bain, 2019)

You could, of course, add an extra layer of checking by feeding back as a class, with the teacher leading and quality-controlling answers. Bain writes that she circulates and lets students know when there is an error, but not where the error is (Agarwal & Bain, 2019). This forces students to be more independent in their problem-solving and makes learning more effortful – a desirable difficulty. Students become explicitly aware of what they know, and of what they don't know and need to revise in future study sessions.

The benefit of this kind of strategy is that students cannot fail: they simply look up answers they do not know. It's a simple, effective technique for students to use in home study sessions.

Varying the conditions

It's important to vary the conditions of retrieval practice. Tom Sherrington outlines the issues with solely using quizzes written by the teacher:

> *'Remembering takes many forms. When [retrieval tasks are] more complex, less easy to define and control, messier, harder to give precise feedback on, they're probably going to deepen learning more than a daily quiz produced by the teacher can for the very reason that they are more complex, linking more ideas together. For some students, an overemphasis on quizzing processes may continually misfire because their experiential platform for the knowledge just isn't adequate or they can't apply the knowledge in new contexts due to lack of practice.'* (Sherrington, 2020)

Adding challenge

Offer examples of how to vary the conditions of retrieval and make it more challenging for students:

- Practise explaining something verbally in pairs.

- Use their knowledge to demonstrate why a particular argument/thesis statement is true.
- Close books and engage in a discussion using the vocabulary they have learned.
- Produce a timeline or essay plan exploring how a character in a novel develops as the story progresses.
- Engage in a paired questioning exchange, devising and exchanging questions and answers.

Here are some other ways to add challenge:

- **Spacing**. The longer the gap between initial teaching and retrieving, the harder the information will be to retrieve – a desirable difficulty.
- **Extended questioning**. It's important that, in feedback, teachers ask 'why' and 'how' questions to extend students' thinking to higher-order ideas.
- **Mixed retrieval quizzes**. These are quizzes that build from factual recall to more challenging 'how' and 'why' questions that reflect the higher-order processing they will need to use in an essay/exam.
- **Linking**. Getting students to find similarities and differences with other schemes/texts/characters/themes will add challenge and aid memory through schema-building.

Embedding retrieval in Year 7

The rest of the training session can be spent looking at a range of retrieval activities in departments and planning these into a Year 7 scheme of work in a way that gradually reduces scaffold.

Teacher training session 3

By session 3, hopefully there will be lots of retrieval practice going on in lessons, particularly across Year 7. This is a great step forward but quality control is clearly necessary, so I would set aside time in this session to discuss what has been trialled, the benefits and the pitfalls. As a staff body, what have we learned about retrieval this year and how can we ensure this is effectively implemented across all year groups? Where possible, schedule some learning walks across and within departments. Sell this as a positive and supportive process that facilitates the sharing of great practice and opportunities to learn from one another.

You could start the session with another retrieval quiz, but this time bring in some spacing. The plan included below could work well, demonstrating how to incorporate desirable difficulties into your retrieval task.

Last session	Last month	Last term
Name one possible pitfall of retrieval in the classroom.	What is the testing effect?	What is retrieval practice?
How can we add challenge to retrieval tasks?	How might we vary the conditions of retrieval practice?	Why is retrieval practice beneficial?
What is the hypercorrection effect?	Why is it important to vary the conditions of retrieval practice?	Name at least one retrieval activity.

As previously mentioned, one of the main criticisms of retrieval (particularly from subjects that involve essay-writing, like English and history) is likely to be that factual recall questions do not mirror the final test. Even in Year 7, when students are still years away from final exams, students are required to apply their knowledge in the form of a piece of writing or product of some kind.

To mitigate this concern, spend some time in session 3 discussing the importance of developing a high success rate with factual knowledge before moving on to higher-order questions. Ideally, students' knowledge needs to move from inflexible to flexible, which means knowledge of the important facts (vocabulary, dates, equations) is fluent, accurate and retained. The key messages here are:

1. Firm up factual knowledge first.
2. Then include questions in your retrieval tasks that involve a deeper level of processing than mere factual recall.

To firm up factual knowledge, it's worth 'overlapping' questions. This means testing the same knowledge repeatedly, but phrasing it differently to check students are not learning by rote. Have they really understood this knowledge to a point of fluency? For example, I might ask, 'What is the Aristotelian triad?' and then, in a subsequent lesson, follow up with 'Ethos, logos and pathos are known as what term in classical rhetoric?'

You might consider looking at the pros and cons of different retrieval tasks. An interesting research paper by Pooja Agarwal explores the benefits of mixed retrieval quizzes (Agarwal, 2019) that are scaffolded to include both factual and higher-order questions (see example below). Agarwal found that the effect size of this kind of quizzing was greater than isolated factual recall quizzes.

1. **List** the characters that Iago manipulates in his plan to destroy Othello.
2. **Why** does Iago claim he wants revenge?
3. **How** does Iago bring Cassio down?
4. What is the **link** between Iago's conversation with Montano and Cassio's reputation?
5. For one of the characters you listed in question 1, **explain how** Iago manipulates them.
6. 'Rhetoric is the art of ruling the minds of men.' Explain this statement.

You can see how this quiz builds up to the challenging and provocative statement in question 6. In a blog post, David Goodwin presents an example of a mixed retrieval quiz from geography:

1. 'What is the average temperature and precipitation of the Arctic?
2. Why might the climate of the Arctic be considered "hostile"?
3. At which latitude can the Arctic ecosystem be found?
4. What is the link between the latitude and climate of the Arctic ecosystem?
5. Name one plant and one animal that live in the Arctic. For each briefly describe how they adapt to the conditions.
6. "Plants and animals adapt to survive in a hostile environment." Explain this statement.' (Goodwin, 2020)

Another great technique for scaffolded retrieval is Kate Jones' retrieval pyramids (Jones, 2021). They deliberately build from factual to higher-order thinking, with this build-up of knowledge reflected visually through the pyramid structure:

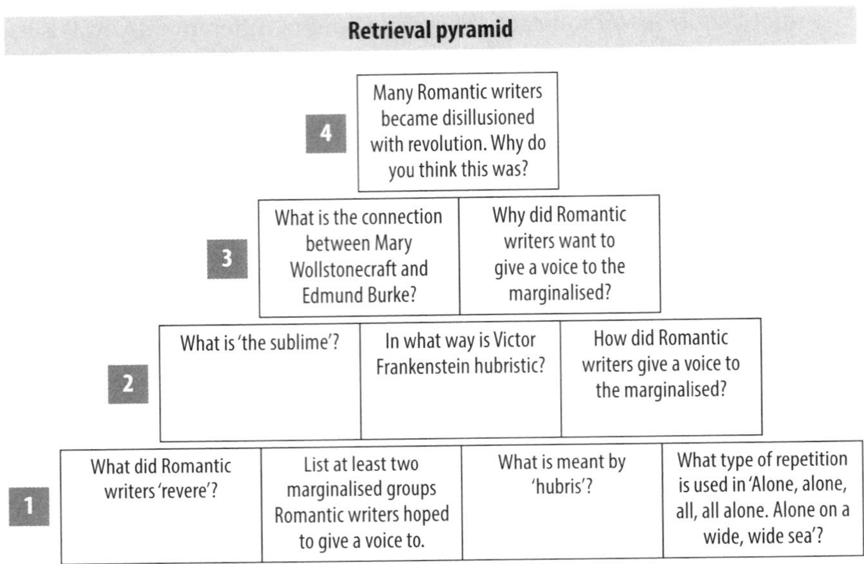

The diagram below shows how we might think of retrieval across a scheme of learning (Needham, 2020a).

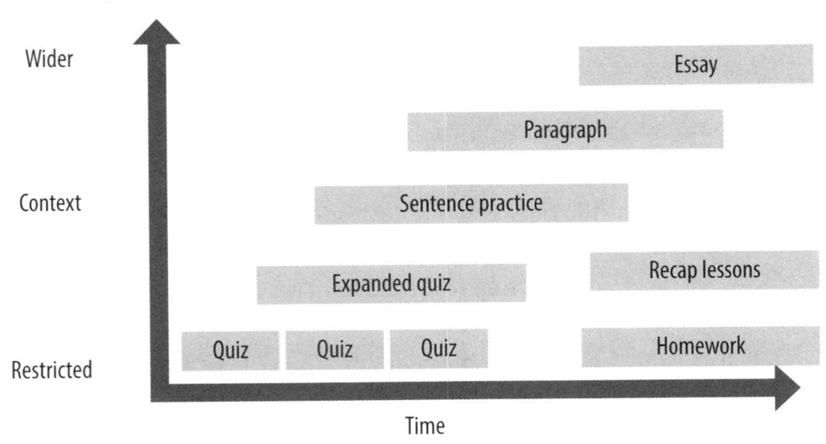

In terms of building to sentence level, I love the following idea from Assad Javed, KS3 coordinator at the Blue Coat School in Oldham, fusing grammar skills and factual knowledge:

Plenary: Edit the following paragraph by inserting embedded clauses with present and past participle phrases and by inserting missing words.	**Year 7 homework returned**
Ferdinand and Miranda's courtship, [influenced by ...], is an important part of the play, [allowing Prospero...]. Miranda, [representing...], is completely in ________ with Ferdinand since she has not met many other men on the island. Shakespeare, [critiquing...], shows how fathers utilised their daughters as property to further their power, through P________ and M________'s relationship. Manipulation, [reinforced through...], is the primary tool for Prospero's journey back to power.	Ferdinand and Miranda's courtship, influenced by Ariel's magic, is an important part of the play, allowing Prospero to gain control. Miranda, representing naivety, is completely infatuated with Ferdinand since she has not met many other men on the island. Shakespeare, critiquing patriarchy, shows how fathers utilised their daughters as property to further their power, through Prospero and Miranda's relationship. Manipulation, reinforced through magic, is the primary tool for Prospero's journey back to power.

In the introduction, I wrote briefly about mental health and how I believe the explicit teaching of study skills will ease stress and anxiety for students. Interestingly, a study shared by Edward Watson and Bradley Busch in *The Science of Learning* (2021) has shown that 'increased stress did not negatively affect the memory of those [students] who used retrieval practice'. Watson and Busch explain that retrieval practice was 'so effective at combating the negative effect of stress on memory that stressed retrieval practice students performed better than those who weren't stressed' but 'had used [the ineffective strategy of] rereading for their revision'.

Finally, 'nothing motivates more than success' (Mind Tools, 2007), so think about a short-term, achievable goal that you could implement. For SLT and governors, this might be all staff being able to articulate the benefits of retrieval. For teaching staff, it might be students confidently quizzing as part of lesson routines. Giving staff some ownership of these short-term goals will help achieve the aim of Step 2: staff buying in to the revision revolution.

Quiz

1. What are the six research-based study methods?
2. What is retrieval practice?
3. List some of the benefits of retrieval practice.
4. What is the hypercorrection effect?
5. How can retrieval be made more challenging?

Reflection

1. What kind of staff training calendar would be appropriate for your context and who will form your 'powerful coalition'?
2. How much do staff know already about the most effective study methods? How will you assess this and adapt your training plans appropriately?
3. How will you ensure you have the support of SLT?
4. How will you work alongside staff to support them with implementing effective study methods?
5. How will you monitor the implementation of retrieval as a starting point?

Summary

- It's important to engage key stakeholders – staff, parents and students – in the revision revolution.
- A good first study strategy to focus on is retrieval: the act of recalling learning from memory.
- To engage staff effectively in the revision revolution, ensure time is dedicated to thorough staff training, a dialogue around revision, and reflection in the form of learning walks and departmental discussions.

Step 3
Junior Revolutionaries
Training up Year 7 to use effective study skills

Autumn term: September/October

> **In a nutshell**
> The third step in our revolution is to begin creating our brave new world of revision by focusing on those perfectly malleable Year 7 students. The transition to secondary school is the ideal time to introduce them to a culture of effective study through simple strategies they can use immediately and independently, making revision accessible for all.

All staff on board? Tick! OK, this is optimistic and you may have experienced resistance, but the important thing to remember is that this is the beginning of a journey. Everyone will eventually get on the bus, particularly once the benefits begin to materialise.

Now let's turn our attention to our favourite stakeholder: our students, the generation of the future!

Picture those shiny new Year 7s entering secondary school on their first day in September, bright-eyed, bushy-tailed and eager to please. This new beginning is the perfect time to introduce effective revision habits. You may question introducing revision this early, but I would advocate going even further and making it part of primary education. Training students to use beneficial study skills is not the same as training them to pass an exam. It empowers them to become independent learners who are aware of their strengths and weaknesses and equipped to enter further education should they wish to. This message needs to be reinforced from every angle and at every opportunity, eliminating all the negative connotations that surround revision.

Before getting into the 'how' of revision with Year 7, unpick the word with them. Students are likely to have negative perceptions of revision as something hard, abstract and possibly unreachable. Perhaps they have witnessed an older sibling grappling with revision as they prepared for looming exams. Try asking students the following questions:

- What is revision?
- Why do students revise?
- How should you revise?

The answers you receive are likely to be along the lines of: 'Revision is something you do before an exam. Students revise so they can get good grades. You should revise by rereading your exercise book and practising exam questions.' Or they might simply have no idea how to revise.

When I sought student voice on revision at my school, lots of responses acknowledged the importance of revision, but there were many unsurprising misconceptions. Many students linked revision to assessments, tests or exams. Most students thought you should only revise in preparation for the aforementioned exams (there was no awareness of the science behind spacing revision out). A third of students were particularly negative about revision, using words like 'stressful', 'boring' or 'difficult'. The most heartbreaking response was, 'I don't know how to do it.' This is where the achievement gap comes back in: the students who suffer the most are those who lack home support with revision. It's completely unnecessary for students to be left in the dark about how to revise: the science is there in education, it's simply a case of sharing it to make the process transparent and explicit.

What actually is revision?

Here's a perfect opportunity to demystify revision. First, share the word's origins: the prefix re- means 'again' and 'vision' is to see, so revision is simply 'seeing again'. It's a revisiting of key knowledge, skills and topics. Revision can take many forms and helps secure understanding at all levels, not just for exam preparation but for lifelong learning and continually improving intelligence. It should be an exciting endeavour, not a means to an end (i.e. not purely focused on exam performance). Revision is also a polysemous word (a word with more than one meaning) and it's worth pointing out to students that every definition of revision has positive connotations: it can mean 'seeing again'; it can also mean improving something through making changes to it. This second definition is crucial in the revision process – if we study we can make gains and improvements as a result.

Why do students revise?

Revision should be seen as an integral part of the learning process. Changing mindsets, starting in Year 7, will enable students to redefine revision simply as returning to prior learning in order to make it secure. Additional reasons to revise might include improving confidence in independent study, feeling better prepared for higher education and being empowered to add value to your work. Excitingly, independent learning is when true creativity occurs. It was only when I reached university and had to study independently in order not to fail that I began discovering my own ideas, prompted through research. If students are equipped to study independently from a much younger age, we potentially open up a world of academia beyond the classroom where imaginative ideas can flourish.

How should you revise?

You may need to do a bit of debunking here before looking at how to revise effectively. First, look at some non-examples: how not to do it! Rereading, highlighting and watching revision videos may be popular revision techniques but studies show they are of minimal benefit. This is because they are broadly passive methods that don't require students to think hard. Having said that, with a few little adjustments, these methods can be adapted to have much more value. Rereading becomes quizzing. Highlighting becomes summarising or retrieving key points. Watching a revision video becomes 'retrieve-taking' (Agarwal & Bain, 2019) where students watch, pause and take notes on what they have seen so far, selecting the most important information. The passive methods are now active, or generative: they involve generating information rather than simply reading it. And if students are going to reread notes, studies show reading them aloud is more effective than silent reading, but this is still much less effective than retrieval (Watson & Busch, 2021).

Share with students that retrieval is the foundation of effective revision, therefore this will be our starting point. Not only is retrieval backed up by a strong evidence base, but it ensures learning is not lost and can be built on. Explain retrieval practice to students in simple terms: teachers tend to spend a lot of time trying to get information into students' heads but retrieval is the opposite – it's getting information out. What can students remember or what do they already know about topic X? In *Powerful Teaching*, Agarwal and Bain suggest a semantic change from 'information' to 'outformation'.

I'm a big believer in sharing the science of learning with student's. They don't need to understand it in minute detail but, just like adults, why should we expect them to do something if we haven't explained the rationale behind it? I would therefore show Ebbinghaus' forgetting curve to Year 7, explaining the typical pattern of forgetting newly learned information and thus revealing the importance of constantly revisiting knowledge through spaced retrieval.

I would also show an image illustrating schema and debunk the idea that retrieving information is simply memorising facts. Retrieving information is actually how we make sense of things: by connecting it to existing knowledge in an ever-growing schema. The analogy suggested for staff training on page 52 (my toddler's partially developed schema, as illustrated by his tractor/train confusion) would work well as a concrete example, especially as students love a peek into teachers' private lives!

Another great analogy for schema is suggested in a blog post by Blake Harvard. He likens it to a spider's web, with each piece of knowledge adding to the ever-growing web (Harvard, 2019). Not only does this offer a clear visual for students, but it also means you can explore questions with them such as 'What would happen if the web did not have enough connecting lines?', eliciting answers such as 'This would make it less secure and more susceptible to breaking'. It's the same with knowledge: the more pieces of knowledge we have to interconnect with new pieces of knowledge, the more structurally secure our understanding will be. The fragility of a spider web, however, also helps demonstrate the fragility of knowledge: if knowledge is not revisited, our schema may disintegrate. Just as spiders keep spinning their webs, we need to keep revisiting our knowledge, making it secure and adding to our schemata.

Of course, I would argue that this is an invaluable prelude to your subject-specific curricula, but if you're worried about spending too much lesson time exploring the whys and hows of revision, Step 6 suggests how you might include it in a pastoral curriculum to use in PSHE lessons or form time.

Explain to students that retrieval practice is even more effective when it's responsive. This means teachers and students identifying the common misconceptions and sticking points in their particular class, and writing retrieval activities based on this information. Retrieval practice is also most effective when it's used regularly and cues are gradually reduced. As Peps Mccrea explains, 'the less assistance we provide students during retrieval, the greater the strengthening effect' (Mccrea, 2017). Therefore, moving towards 'free recall' without cues or scaffolds is essential.

You've now laid the foundations for Year 7 to buy into retrieval as the first effective study habit they will learn to use, making it irresistible and hopefully generating some excitement about being empowered by learning how to learn at secondary school. Retrieval comes in many different forms and these can be built on over time to include dual coding, spacing and elaboration. But, as explained in Step 1, it's a good idea to start small, getting all staff and students using certain strategies well before adding additional tools to the toolkit.

So, what simple retrieval habits can we instil into our perfectly malleable Year 7s as we begin this journey towards becoming a revision-centric school? The rest of this chapter looks at three ideas. Ensure your staff training takes place before this point, so teachers are confident introducing students to these methods and modelling them in the classroom, explaining why and how they will help students learn. Remember, it's not enough for just a handful of teachers to adopt these methods. The success of the revision revolution depends on a whole-school approach!

1. Self-testing flashcards

Why?

Flashcards are a very simple and effective way to test recall and students love using them. They are low-threat (therefore accessible for all) but the content can be as challenging as you like. Once students are confident using them, flashcards can become a regular part of revision homework.

How?

A flashcard is a card that contains a small amount of information and is used as a learning aid. For revision, students can write questions on one side and answers on the other, testing themselves and reordering the cards according to which answers they were able to correctly recall. For flashcards to be effective they should contain just a small amount of information – for example, a key word and definition or, for foreign language learning, an image and a sentence in the target language related to that image.

One strategy suggested by the coaching company InnerDrive[4] is to have five boxes, initially putting all the flashcards into box 1. When a flashcard is recalled correctly, the student moves it into box 2; if not, it stays in box 1. Every time the flashcard is recalled correctly, it moves into the next box and by the time it reaches box 5, the information has hopefully entered long-term memory. Students test themselves on the flashcards in box 1 daily, box 2 on alternate days, box 3 every third day, box 4 every fourth day and box 5 every fifth day.

A simpler method, called the Leitner system, can be used with three boxes. It works like this:

4 https://blog.innerdrive.co.uk/flashcards-what-when-how-where

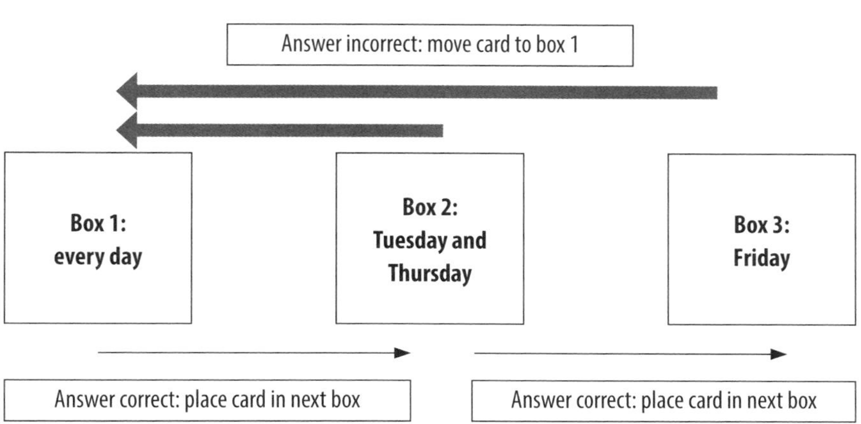

Let's say it's Monday. If the information from a flashcard is recalled correctly, the student places the card in box 2. If they cannot remember the answer or they answer incorrectly, the card is placed in box 1: tested daily. On Tuesday, students test themselves on all the cards in boxes 1 and 2. If a card from box 1 is answered correctly, it moves to box 2. If it's answered incorrectly, it stays in box 1. If a card from box 2 is answered correctly, it moves to box 3 (tested weekly). If it's answered incorrectly, it moves back to box 1. On Wednesday, students test themselves on box 1 cards, on Thursday boxes 1 and 2, and on Friday boxes 1 and 3. If a card from box 3 is answered correctly, it stays there, but if it's answered incorrectly, it moves back to box 1 to be tested daily.

This system means students gain the most practice on the flashcards they are weakest on. Daniel Willingham's research into cognitive psychology has found that 'memory is the residue of thought' (Willingham, 2009). The Leitner system works on the premise that we remember what we think about: students can achieve success by thinking about the knowledge that is least secure most regularly.

Increasing the spacing slightly each time the information is correctly recalled is the most effective way to ensure that information enters long-term memory. Students test themselves on information *just before* they forget it. The idea is that by making key knowledge secure in their memories, students build a foundation on which they can form excellent exam answers, add more knowledge and reduce cognitive load in their writing, thus enabling them to become 'experts'. As explored in Step 1, it's about building the factual recall to a point of automaticity so that students can more easily access higher-order thinking and ideas.

It makes sense to start small, so students might begin by testing themselves on one part of one topic (e.g. key vocabulary about the Tudors). As they travel further along the curriculum journey (from KS4, perhaps), they can interleave flashcards from different topics and even different subject areas.

Agarwal and Bain suggest using the 'retrieve, reorder, repeat' strategy with flashcards:

1. '**Retrieve**: students must retrieve the information before turning the flashcard over (even if they retrieve it incorrectly). They could write their answer down to provide evidence of this retrieval and hold them accountable.
2. **Reorder**: students should shuffle their deck. This will create desirable difficulties by changing the order, creating spacing and interleaving.
3. **Repeat**: students should keep their cards in their deck until they have retrieved the answer correctly three times.' (Agarwal & Bain, 2019)

Although these are simple and effective strategies, they will need to be modelled to students (possibly quite a few times) until they can use them independently. You might also consider sharing the strategies with parents. I've seen videos on Twitter that show teachers very clearly explaining the flashcard process with visuals, so parents can confidently support their child. Creating and sustaining a revision revolution depends on reinforcing key messages to all stakeholders.

Initially, model to students precisely how to create effective flashcards and support them to make these in class for a specific topic – for example, key words on the topic of 'environment'. On one side would be a single word and on the other a definition and example sentence. Any more information than this would render the flashcard ineffective. Homework is simply to use the flashcards to revise vocabulary on the environment. Ensure you model the process of moving the cards around according to whether they are answered correctly or incorrectly.

Extra support

As explained above, the flashcard process will need to be modelled in order for students to be able to complete it independently and correctly. However, once the process is part of students' revision routine, ideally from Year 7, it is incredibly powerful. Before setting this as homework for the first time, you could use 'I do, we do, you do' modelling in class: after watching you, students practise in pairs as you circulate, checking the process is being completed effectively. You could follow up with a questioning session: where does the card from box 1 go if it's answered correctly? How often do we quiz on the cards from box 3?

Extra challenge

Students can introduce more flashcards if they are regularly getting correct answers, even adding questions from other subjects. They can increase the difficulty of the questions with more complex vocabulary, higher-level questions or questions beyond the key information on the knowledge organiser. At my school, we introduced our lecture students to Marxist theory that they don't need to know, but it opens up original ideas and interpretations of their own. This could become part of their revision once the key knowledge is secure. If testing vocabulary, you could follow up with activities such as a writing task or a Frayer model using the key word.

A Frayer model is a type of graphic organiser that can be used to explain key vocabulary (see the example on the next page). The page is split into four boxes, with the key word written in the middle along with its category (e.g. 'adj' for adjective). The first box has the heading 'Definition' and this is where a student-friendly definition of the word should be written. The heading for the second box is 'Characteristics'; you can increase students' comprehension by listing the attributes of the word. The third and fourth headings are 'Examples' and 'Non-examples'; these help students differentiate the word from other similar words as well as ironing out any misconceptions.

Definition	**Characteristics**
A dictatorial style of government that regulates every aspect of life.	• Oppressive treatment. • Lack of freedom. • Everything is controlled (even thought). • Strict rules. • Harsh punishments. • Constant surveillance. • Citizens not trusted. • Culture of fear. • Dystopia. • Patriarchy. • Hierarchy. • Persecution and discrimination (e.g. of Jews, foreigners, etc.)

TOTALITARIAN
(ADJ)

Examples	**Non-examples**
Big Brother (Orwell's *1984*). Hitler. Dystopian regimes. *The Hunger Games.* Repression.	Democracies. Societies with freedom of speech. Welfare state (NHS). Equality. Socialism. Expression.

2. Self-quizzing

Why?

Self-quizzing may be done with a knowledge organiser or other knowledge-rich resource. Knowledge organisers can be used in different ways: for students to self-quiz (a very simple revision and self-assessment activity) and for teachers to facilitate retrieval by asking students to add all the information they can remember to a blank organiser.

Knowledge organisers have become very divisive recently and I would argue that this is because (like retrieval itself and most other educational strategies), they have been subject to lethal mutations. A well-designed knowledge organiser can be a powerful tool, but it's important to carefully model the self-quizzing process or the organiser may become a resource that is used badly or not at all. Subject specialists need to think carefully about what knowledge to include in their organiser. For example, in English there's little point in asking students to memorise the definitions of 'metaphor', 'simile' or 'adverbial', as they are all abstract concepts – parroting a definition does not equate to an understanding of these complex constructs. Instead, I would include key contextual information about an author, overriding themes, characters and perhaps some key vocabulary (that has been explored and practised in lessons). An example of how not to do it is the grammar knowledge organisers I produced to help students memorise the definitions of all word-level and some sentence-level grammar. As explained above, grammar definitions are abstract and complex, and students knowing their definitions by heart does not mean they can recognise and use them. Concrete examples of grammatical constructions and discussions about their effect are a much more effective way to build understanding of grammar.

How?

A knowledge organiser is a resource, typically put together by the subject teacher, that includes the key information needed to understand a scheme of work. It should contain the core knowledge that students need to know and commit to memory in order to access higher-level, more complex ideas about a topic. I always take care to emphasise to students that this is the minimum knowledge they need and not an exhaustive list. Because of the recent popularity of knowledge organisers, it would be relatively easy (and tempting for busy teachers!) to google 'knowledge organiser Othello' and lift a ready-made resource. However, this knowledge organiser will have been designed by someone else for a different department's scheme of work and a different cohort of students.

I've seen many flawed knowledge organisers: sometimes they are overwhelmingly (and unnecessarily) detailed, sometimes they include superfluous information and sometimes they lack key information. In the latest book from Michaela Community School, Katie Ashford writes about 'proceeding with caution' when it comes to knowledge organisers (Ashford, 2020): we need to use them as a starting point, not a means for students to 'perform' in lessons by reciting key information they have committed to memory. See Step 4 for how you might build on self-quizzing homework in a lesson, making it a meaningful platform for learning.

Here's an example of 'performing'. Just this morning, my four-year-old declared, 'A sea cow is a manatee.' I frantically messaged my husband to let him know we were the parents of a genius. Five minutes later my husband rang. I put my son on the phone to demonstrate his genius and here's how the conversation went.

Husband: What's a sea cow, Alfie?

Alfie: A sea cow is a… a sea cow is a… is a… walrus!

Me: No, Alfie, you just said it's a manatee.

Alfie: A sea cow is a manatee.

Husband: Where did you learn that, Alfie?

Alfie: It was on *Paw Patrol*.

Five minutes later, I asked Alfie the same question:

Me: What's a sea cow, Alfie?

Alfie: A sea cow is a… whale.

As you can see, Alfie didn't know what a sea cow was at all. He had simply repeated something he had heard on *Paw Patrol*, mimicking the information and 'performing' it, not actually learning it. This is where we need to be careful with self-quizzing. The important part is recalling the information, extending this recall (see Step 4 for expanded retrieval quizzes) and evaluating what has and hasn't been remembered, not simply memorising and repeating.

For mastery, it's about practising something not until students get it right, but until it's difficult to get it wrong. There's a reason why British motorists struggle to drive on the 'wrong side of the road' when abroad: their driving has become automatic and habitual and strong habits are difficult to break. This can, of course, work for and against us, as practice becoming permanent can involve the internalisation of misconceptions, which is why the corrective feedback element of retrieval is essential.

To offer another analogy, I'm part of an amateur operatic quartet. When preparing for a concert, I need to learn the words for several songs in a number of different languages. I learn them by writing them down, sticking them up on my wall and singing them repeatedly. This rote learning does not make me a better singer. However, knowing the words to a point of automaticity does two things to enhance my overall performance: it eases my nerves and it frees me up to think about technique. I learn the lyrics not until I remember them, but until I can't forget them! Similarly, when certain surface-level knowledge becomes part of students' long-term memory through techniques like repeated self-quizzing, this leaves them free to consider more complex ideas and thinking.

The knowledge organisers I've designed for schemes of work in English are typically divided into plot, key characters, context and vocabulary. Careful design is essential, ensuring the inclusion of the most important information that allows students to be successful in an individual topic. It's also worth considering wording, sentence structure and layout, so weaker readers can easily access the knowledge organiser and there's no danger of cognitive overload. Spending time designing the perfect knowledge organiser in subject teams is undoubtedly time very well spent.

Of course, knowledge organisers are not the only resource to support self-quizzing. Students might self-quiz with their flashcards, a relevant text or lesson notes. The process of retrieving valuable knowledge and understanding is what's important here.

Extra support

Model the self-quizzing process in stages while students watch and take notes.

- **Step 1**: read the section you're memorising.
- **Step 2**: cover the section up.
- **Step 3**: write down everything you can remember.
- **Step 4**: check your notes against the section you're studying.
- **Step 5**: with a different colour pen, write down any information you missed so you can visually see the gaps in your knowledge.

In my experience, you need to repeatedly emphasise and model the importance of step 5 to ensure it's completed. Otherwise, you may find students take the easy option by copying out information rather than 'retrieving' it. You could also demonstrate self-quizzing in the classroom using the 'I do, you do, we do' strategy.

Start by asking students to self-quiz on a relatively straightforward section of the knowledge organiser, such as key words and definitions, rather than the more complex sections. You might want to adapt the organiser to use less complex vocabulary or phrasing.

Extra challenge

Give students the option of memorising more than one section at a time. They could then apply this knowledge by creating their own carefully crafted sentences.

Self-quizzing revision homework

Subject	Self-quizzing homework
English	Self-quiz on the vocabulary section of your 'Myths and legends' knowledge organiser.
Science	Self-quiz on the 'Organs and their function' section of the body knowledge organiser.
Maths	Self-quiz on the meaning of BIDMAS.
Geography	Self-quiz on the erosion section of the 'Natural forces' knowledge organiser.
History	Self-quiz on the 'Key figures' section of the WW1 knowledge organiser.
Art	Self-quiz on the 'Important artists' section of the 'Surrealist art' knowledge organiser.
Drama	Self-quiz on the 'Globe theatre' section of the Shakespeare knowledge organiser.
Music	Self-quiz on the notation section of the 'Elements of music' knowledge organiser.
PE	Self-quiz on the 'Dribbling' section of the football knowledge organiser.

As noted earlier, a key part of the self-quizzing process for students is the final step, where they cross-reference their answers with the information on the knowledge organiser, filling in any missed information with a different colour pen. This is where they become aware of the gaps in their knowledge and can reflect on which parts they struggle to remember. The teacher can help with strategies to remember this information in future self-quizzing sessions. It may even be worth doing a reflection activity to discuss questions such as:

- Which parts of the information were hard to remember? Why?
- How could we ensure we remember these parts in future?

- Is there anything you didn't understand and would like to go over as a class?

By answering questions like these, students engage in metacognition by thinking about their learning – a crucial part of their journey towards becoming self-regulated learners and one that we'll discuss at many points in this book.

Alongside seeing evidence of their homework (I stipulate how many pages of self-quizzing I expect and emphasise that I want to see two different colours on there!), the above questions are a good way to ensure all students are engaging with the homework and reflecting on their progress. If students aren't quizzed on their self-quizzing homework in class, they are unlikely to see the purpose of it. A key part of developing our revision culture is quizzing students on the knowledge they should have learned, asking follow-up questions so they can see exactly how it fits with their learning in the subject area. This could take the form of a traditional retrieval quiz or an online quiz using Microsoft Forms or other software, which has the additional benefit of putting all the results together so you can see the sticking points and any examples of excellence in terms of students' explanations or understanding.

3. Brain dump/knowledge splat

Why?

This is another very simple activity, but this one can be cue-free, meaning it's the kind of free recall that Peps Mccrea advocates as particularly effective (Mccrea, 2017). It's a very easy strategy for students to use independently as homework.

How?

Arguably the simplest retrieval practice activity to deliver and complete, a brain dump or knowledge splat involves listing everything you can remember about a topic. As it's a free-recall activity, it removes the cues and strengthens memory of the information – but only if students are able to produce an answer. Therefore, it's important to consider *when* in the teaching of a scheme to use this activity. It's perhaps better suited to a time when students' knowledge is fairly secure (e.g. after a series of lessons on a particular topic or to revise last term's scheme).

A brain dump or knowledge splat involves dumping everything from your brain on to the page. It can be as specific or general as you like. For example:

- What do you know about the character/theme/topic/text/question?
- How should you approach passing a ball/painting a portrait/composing a harmony/solving an equation/dividing a fraction?
- How many things can you say about this quote/causes can you give for the Second World War/features can you list of baroque music?
- How many links can you make between X and Y?

Extra support

You could provide prompts in the form of questions or subheadings to direct students' thinking. For example, if the brain dump is on *Romeo and Juliet*, you might ask students to use these headings:

- Themes.
- Characters.
- Plot.
- Context.
- Key quotes.

Alternatively, you could provide sentence stems that help students practise academic phrasing, such as 'The play *Romeo and Juliet* explores themes of. . . .'

Extra challenge

You could get students to look for patterns, making links between themes, characters and context, for example, and considering how they fit with the writer's intentions. They could even make links to other schemes.

Brain dump revision homework

Subject	Brain-dump homework
English	List everything you can remember about the character of Achilles, including key quotes.
Science	Draw a diagram of the respiratory system in as much detail as you can.
Maths	Write down everything you can remember about fractions, including how to add, multiply, subtract and divide.
Geography	Write down as many differences as you can between urban and rural environments.
History	List as many reasons as you can for Hitler's rise to power.
Art	List the features of Surrealist art.
Drama	What is method acting? Give as many examples as you can.
Music	List as many features of Renaissance music as you can, including instruments, dynamics, structure and composition.
PE	List the characteristics of a perfect tennis serve.

Make it clear to students that they should use no notes or other resources when completing brain dump activities at home. They need to think hard, otherwise the process is meaningless.

Ideally, students should complete their homework and then check their answer against models completed in class, identifying what they did and didn't remember and noting this for further study. Even better, they could write down ways to ensure they remember certain details in future. For example, 'I know that pianos play chords, so it should help me to remember that a harpsichord was an early version of a piano.' This is a difficult skill, so it may be best to complete this process and reflect on homework in class several times before expecting students to identify strengths and targets themselves.

You could add certain scaffolds to your brain dump retrieval task by using visuals. For example, students recall everything they can about the Second World War supported by images of Hitler, Churchill and a concentration camp. You could also provide headings such as 'Causes', 'Consequences', 'Allies', etc.

One of the major benefits of introducing these strategies in Year 7 is that by the time students reach Year 11 they are so ingrained that revision is second nature. The process of revision is not this abstract thing that students have no idea how to approach; they have a bank of clear, tangible methods to revise effectively and with confidence. Hopefully, this will signal an end to tasks such as 'Revise *The Merchant of Venice* for next week's assessment'. These set students up for failure and non-compliance: the majority will not do any revision for the assessment because they don't know how to approach it. Instead, we can tell students specifically 'how' to revise and make it habitual, not assessment-focused. We can even explicitly model what their study session should include.

If you can make these three effective retrieval tasks part of lessons and homework in Year 7, it will be a great start to your revision revolution, building a revision culture from the ground up. Consistency and immersion are key. Consider how you'll make sure these methods are used correctly across the school, with student, parent and staff buy-in. Here are some ideas: present the strategies to governors; include a video explaining the strategies on the school website so parents can watch it; explore the strategies in assemblies; make them the focus of form-time for the first term of Year 7; make them part of induction or transition days; give all Year 7 students a revision exercise book and/or guide.

Imagine how proud Year 7 will feel to know they are the first cohort in the school to be explicitly taught how to revise: their knowledge, therefore, is superior to any other year group in school. They will be future revision leaders, able to guide others to succeed through effective study just like they have.

Quiz

1. When we break the word 'revision' down into its prefix and root, what does it mean?
2. Name one study strategy we could explicitly teach to Year 7.
3. Name one self-quizzing or brain dump homework you could set in your subject area.
4. How does the Leitner system make use of spacing?
5. How could you add support and challenge to any of the strategies in this chapter?

Reflection

1. How will you continue to train staff to teach these three revision methods: flashcards, self-quizzing and brain dumps?
2. How will you ensure you have staff buy-in and that staff use the strategies consistently and correctly across the school?
3. How will you ensure student buy-in?
4. How will you ensure parent buy-in?
5. How will you monitor and evaluate the effectiveness of these approaches to revision?

Summary

- Brand-new students starting in Year 7 provide a perfect opportunity to introduce effective study methods.
- Begin by debunking revision and opening up a dialogue. Students will have misconceptions that need addressing – let's change their mindset from negative to positive!
- The language used around revision is important. Consider how you might make reference to 'quizzes' rather than 'tests', and to 'assessments', 'memory' and 'learning' rather than 'grades' and 'exams'. This can help build positive attitudes towards revision.
- Introduce students to the idea of retrieval.
- Introduce three retrieval techniques: flashcards, self-quizzing and brain dumps. These will need careful and explicit modelling.

Step 4
Revolutionary Lessons

How to model effective study methods in the classroom

Autumn term: November/December

In a nutshell
This chapter explores how we can integrate study skills into lesson routines so that students encounter and practise them on a daily basis. Of course, not every lesson will look the same, but by explicitly modelling certain strategies we can develop students into confident learners who understand how revision fits into the bigger picture of learning.

I trained to teach at a time when we were encouraged to 'perform'. My trainee friends and I were constantly striving for that 'outstanding' observation by searching for ways to make lessons fun. I achieved my first 'outstanding' by using a big tree of knowledge that students added leaves to throughout the lesson. I might as well have held up a big neon sign every 10 minutes saying 'Look – they're learning!' but, in reality, I was stopping the learning for students to get up and stick leaves on a tree. To be fair to school leaders, it was the time when Ofsted was obsessed with the 'mini-plenary', so lesson observers were simply following suit.

However, on reflection, could this time have been better spent using careful questioning to assess student knowledge and check for understanding, building on gaps and misconceptions? Could my time blowing up tree posters and cutting out leaves have been better spent brushing up on my subject knowledge? Absolutely.

It was in this particular phase of education that I experienced my second Ofsted inspection. I remember being terrified about students getting things wrong during my lesson observation, because it might 'look bad' and scupper my chances of getting a good grade. This is a high-stakes environment and, ironically, it deters teachers from taking the kind of risks necessary to improve as professionals. There's such pressure attached to being an 'outstanding teacher' or one who 'requires improvement'. Just one observation below that particular teacher's 'normal' grade can affect their whole reputation within the school, particularly if it's from Ofsted. Just as we need to take risks to develop professionally, we need to build a low-stakes classroom culture where student mistakes are welcomed as learning opportunities. This is another key part of our revision revolution.

David Didau has written about one of his 'most memorable biology lessons'. His teacher 'knocked over the model skeleton (it's the law that there must be at least one lab per school to contain a full size model skeleton) and told us that we'd remember the lesson for the rest of our lives. I have. But I cannot for the life of me recall what the lesson was about' (Didau, 2013b). This illustrates the danger of creating experiences that serve no purpose beyond being memorable or fun. Remember my staff training where we made dresses and T-shirts? Zero professional learning took place. For many, 'engagement' has become a dirty word in education and this is a result of 'engagement' being associated with fun activities rather than deep learning. Can students be engaged through high challenge, academic rigour and rich learning opportunities? Of course they can, and any school that relies on games rather than powerful knowledge to engage is drastically underestimating its students.

It took me a good few years of teaching to realise that I don't need to make lessons 'fun' for them to be enjoyable. Neither do I need to be a 'funny' or popular teacher to be effective. Students are inspired by knowledge and they are enthused through sky-high expectations. What's more, the popularity of mini-plenaries (the leaves in my tree of knowledge) was misguided: students are simply 'performing' and there's no evidence that they will actually retain this knowledge over a week, month or year. If my students are busy thinking about the leaves they are sticking to a paper tree when I want them to remember the conventions of iambic pentameter, I am working very hard to prevent rather than enable learning.

The recent popularity of Barak Rosenshine's principles of instruction (2012) has been refreshing in the sense that it reassures us as professionals that no gimmicks are required. Rosenshine's first principle advocates beginning each lesson with a short review of previous learning, as well as engaging students in weekly and monthly reviews because 'prior knowledge is a major factor in our capacity to learn new information' (Sherrington, 2019). Focusing on effective retrieval, then, will surely narrow the achievement gap by allowing all students to gain and retain the powerful knowledge necessary to succeed in each subject area.

Many would argue that there's nothing revolutionary about Rosenshine's principles of instruction; they advocate a fairly traditional approach. But they are revolutionary in terms of countering the mindset I described at the beginning of this chapter, where we overcomplicate teaching or feel pressured to 'put on a show'. These principles have learning at their heart – pure and simple.

So, let's explore some ideas for immersing students in effective study habits within our lessons. Although we wouldn't necessarily include all these stages in one lesson, it's worth thinking of learning in terms of a cycle that starts with retrieval of prior learning, followed by the presentation of new material and teacher modelling, and then student practice and feedback.

1. Retrieval

Beginning each lesson with some form of retrieval practice is without doubt beneficial, but careful thought is necessary in terms of what form this retrieval practice takes. In my experience, it's too easy for students to look back through the pages for the answers when using exercise books. It might be a good idea, therefore, to give students retrieval or revision books. It's even better if they carry these around school and are in the habit of getting them out at the start of a lesson or whenever a task involves retrieval practice. If retrieval tasks have been well designed, this is also a way for students to see all the important knowledge and their strengths and targets in one place.

James Shea outlines the importance of 'warm' retrieval that is completely threat-free (Shea, 2021). A question like 'Complete the quote for Lady Macbeth' becomes 'Do you like Lady Macbeth?' so there's no right or wrong answer at this first reactivation stage. Shea, a lecturer in teacher education, also discusses the importance of 'priming' the memory with retrieval relevant to the lesson. Shea and his colleagues have launched a project 'to investigate the concept of priming and enhancing the formation of memory using these ideas'.

According to Tom Sherrington, 'It's not enough for teachers to own the knowledge checking process – always setting the quiz questions and framing the terms of how knowledge is encountered and tested. Ultimately students need to learn to do this themselves, generatively constructing and evaluating what they know and don't know and learning to explore a knowledge domain with purpose' (Sherrington, 2020). Clearly, this will take time, but Sherrington argues that 'richer retrieval practice experiences' can be created by varying the conditions of practice (see Step 1 and the staff CPD resources for some examples).

By giving students ownership over retrieval in this way, Sherrington says the retrieval is 'more complex, less easy to define and control, messier, harder to give precise feedback on' and is therefore 'probably going to deepen learning more than a daily quiz produced by the teacher can for the very reason that they are more complex, linking more ideas together. For some students, an overemphasis on quizzing processes may continually misfire because their experiential platform for the knowledge just isn't adequate or they can't apply the knowledge in new contexts due to lack of practice' (Sherrington, 2020).

Of course, in creating our revision revolution, we want to train students to retrieve independently in a variety of ways. Here are some key principles, informed by Sherrington's blog post, for effective retrieval practice design as part of the lesson-planning process.

1. **Involve everyone**. Your retrieval activity should be set up so that every single student is required to respond.
2. **Make checking accurate and easy**. There should be a way for students to mark their answers and identify gaps in their knowledge.
3. **Keep it generative**. It takes time to form a habit, but students need to become used to not using any cues so that retrieval is truly a test of their memory and understanding. I spend a lot of time telling students that copying down information from their books is a pointless process.
4. **Make it time-efficient**. Be clear on how long students have to complete their answers. If they finish before the time is up, offer prompts such as 'Rephrase this answer as a full sentence', 'Explain why nitrogen is an unreactive gas', 'How does syncopated rhythm add interest to a piece of music' and so on. These kinds of prompts are also a way of modelling elaborative interrogation – something we want students to do independently in their revision.

You may want your retrieval quiz to build on self-quizzing homework (as described in Step 3, see page 76). Here's an example script that uses retrieval to build on students' self-quizzing.

> **Teacher**: I asked you to self-quiz on the four types of allusions for homework. What are they? List all four please; you have 60 seconds. I will not be accepting hands up as it was your homework to memorise this information, so be ready! [Instead of allowing hands up, cold-call by selecting a student to answer. This way the whole class are kept on their toes.]
>
> Time's up! What are the four types of allusion, Hamza? [By asking the question and then naming the student to answer, all students are required to think in case you say their name.]
>
> **Hamza**: Literary, classical, historical and biblical. [If they don't know or can only partially remember, you could use 'no opt out' here; see page 29.]
>
> **Teacher**: Thanks, Hamza, and well done for getting all four. In front of you, there are examples of different types of allusions. Match each one to the correct type; you have three minutes…

> Now turn to your partner and explain your answers. If your answers are different, discuss why and try to reach a consensus ready to feed back. [Take feedback, addressing misconceptions.]
>
> The biblical allusion is from the next chapter of our text, which we will explore in today's lesson. Why does the writer use this biblical allusion here? What is the intended effect? Why this type of allusion rather than any of the others?

This lesson starter uses retrieval linking to the homework and then explicitly connects this to the content of the lesson, making it knowledge that students will apply and build on. The purpose of the revision homework is made clear to students, increasing the chance that they will buy into the revision process.

Agarwal and Bain point out that there are two types of feedback we can give after retrieval: elaborative feedback and correct-answer feedback (Agarwal & Bain, 2019). Elaborative feedback is where we explain why an answer is correct, whereas correct-answer feedback simply states whether the answer is correct or incorrect. As teachers, we probably use both of these naturally, knowing which questions are subject to misconception – and are therefore in need of explanation – and which questions require only a simple answer. We are sometimes reactive with these decisions: if it's clear that the majority of the class have struggled to remember or explain something then we need to elaborate and reteach. However, a high success rate suggests this particular item of knowledge has reached a level of automaticity and requires no further explanation at this point. This, of course, does not mean we won't return to it, utilising the spacing effect to test again when students have nearly forgotten.

One strategy I use regularly for spacing retrieval and connecting key knowledge is Andy Tharby's excellent 'memory platform', which works like this:

- **Question 1-3**: last lesson.
- **Question 4**: last week.
- **Question 5**: last term.
- **Question 6**: link last lesson to last term. (Tharby, 2014)

Here's an example of a memory platform and some follow-up questions we might ask to extend students' knowledge and thinking.

Memory platform

1. What is a counter-argument?
2. What do the words 'opponent' and 'refute' mean?
3. What are the coordinating and subordinating conjunctions? Can you give some examples?
4. What techniques might you use in a speech opener to establish ethos, logos or pathos?
5. Can you remember both of Achilles' opponents in the *Iliad*?
6. How are modal verbs and subordinating conjunctions used to characterise Agamemnon in this quote: 'you must prepare, however, a prize of honour for me'?

Memory platform

Answers and suggested follow-up questions for teachers. DO NOT PROJECT!

1. A counter-argument states the opposite argument in order to disprove it. Follow-up question: Why are counter-arguments important in rhetoric?
2. An opponent is a challenger or someone who is against something, and refute means to prove something is untrue. Follow-up questions: How are these words linked? How are they relevant to counter-arguments?
3. Coordinating and subordinating conjunctions signal contrasting ideas. See previous lesson for examples. Follow-up questions: What is the difference between subordinating and coordinating conjunctions? How might you use them for different effects?
4. A story, evoke an image, provocative questions, shocking statistics, anecdote... Follow-up questions: Why are these methods effective? What might be an ineffective way to open a speech?
5. Agamemnon, then Hector (Hector's crimes trivialise Achilles' feud with Agamemnon and completely negate it, though.) Follow-up questions: Why does Achilles have opponents on both sides? Can you link this to the idea of Homeric heroes?
6. The modal verb 'must' connotes necessity and sounds like a threat – establishing authority. 'However' emphasises Agamemnon's sacrifice and that it won't come without consequences. Follow-up questions: How does this characterisation explain the conflict between Agamemnon and Achilles? How does it foreshadow later events?

Extended retrieval quizzes

Studies show, and perhaps it's obvious, that retrieving facts on their own will not lead to exam success (but it's a good starting point). Students need to build on their foundational knowledge, working towards longer and more complex answers once this is secure. Tom Needham writes about bridging this gap by extending retrieval quizzes (Needham, 2020b). Students start with a factual quiz that includes important knowledge needed to answer the higher-order questions. For example, if teaching JB Priestley's *An Inspector Calls*:

1. What does the word 'supercilious' mean?
2. Write down the names of two characters who take no responsibility for Eva Smith's death.
3. What is the key difference between the characters who do and don't take responsibility?

This factual quiz includes three related questions, the answers to which can be built on to form a plan for an essay answer. For example:

1. 'Supercilious' means behaving as if you are better and more important.
2. Both Mr and Mrs Birling take no responsibility for Eva Smith's death.
3. The key difference between the characters who do and don't accept responsibility is age.

The teacher will build on the answers with follow-up questions, asking 'why' and 'how' – higher-order questions moving towards the kind asked in an exam, which are often analytical or evaluative rather than factual. The teacher will use these follow-up questions to make the links between the answers explicit. They may use a combination of questions for understanding (QU), questions for analysis (QA), questions for evaluation (QE) and probing questions (PQ):

1. **Which characters may be described as 'supercilious' (QU) and why (QA)?** Students should answer 'Mr and Mrs Birling' because they patronise others, threaten the Inspector and repeatedly reference their position, power and connections.

2. **Who might you describe as the most supercilious (QE)? Why (PQ)?** Students need to justify their answer here, but they could argue for Mr Birling because of his confident yet hugely incorrect predictions and constant references to his wealth and achievements, or Mrs Birling because of her distance from her children and attitude towards the Inspector.
3. **Why is age significant here (QA)?** Students should answer that the generational gap illustrates Priestley's perspective that the young represent hope and are capable of change, unlike the older generation who are too indoctrinated and set in their ways.

Needham (2020b) writes about giving students certain criteria to include in an answer in order to move towards this higher-level thinking. For example, if the exam question is 'How is the theme of age explored in the play?', students could be told to include the following:

- A subordinate clause including the word 'supercilious'.
- Dramatic irony, the quote 'unsinkable' and the context of a post-war audience.
- The quote 'girls of that class'.
- Symbolism of young versus old.

In this way, we move students from factual recall towards the completion of exam questions, putting together different pieces of knowledge into an analytical or evaluative higher-order answer. Here's how this might look in a history lesson, starting with a factual recall quiz.

1. What does the word 'rearmament' mean?
2. List three ways in which the Nazis reduced unemployment.
3. What is conscription?

Again, the teacher would build on students' answers with 'how' and 'why' questions and address any misconceptions arising from incorrect responses. They would then use follow-up questions to make the links between these answers explicit:

1. **How did rearmament reduce unemployment (QA)?** Students should answer that the increased manufacturing of military

equipment meant businesses needed to employ more people/many more jobs were created.

2. **What part of the German population was involved in conscription? How did conscription reduce unemployment (QA)?** Students should answer that men aged 18-25 were forced to undertake two years of military service, therefore all of this particular demographic was employed in the German military.
3. **Which of the Nazis' strategies to reduce unemployment was the most effective (QE)? Why (PQ)?** Students need to justify their answer here, but could argue that removing citizenship from Jews and unemployed women was the most effective because they were no longer included in the figures, or that the labour service was the most effective because young unemployed men were forced to work on public programmes and were therefore not permitted to be unemployed.
4. **How were unemployment figures skewed (QU) and what does this show us about the Nazi party (QA)?** Students should answer that unemployment figures were skewed because certain groups of people lost their citizenship in 1935 and therefore were not included in the figures, which shows the discriminatory, prejudiced, anti-Semitic and misogynist nature of the party.

After using the factual recall quiz as a basis for the higher-order questioning above, students should be fairly well equipped to answer the following exam question: 'How did the Nazis reduce unemployment?' Again, they can be given certain criteria to include in their answer:

- The words 'rearmament', 'conscription' and 'citizenship'.
- Reference to skewed statistics.
- Figures such as dates and ages (e.g. 1935, men aged 18-25).

Finally, here's a music lesson example, starting with the factual recall quiz.

1. List as many musical elements as you can.
2. What is syncopation?
3. What is meant by the word 'innovative'?

Again, the teacher would build on students' answers with 'how' and 'why' questions and address any misconceptions arising from incorrect responses. They would then use follow-up questions to make the links between these answers explicit:

1. **What is meant by rhythm, metre, harmony, tonality, texture, melody, timbre, dynamics and structure (QU)?**
2. **How might syncopation be used to add interest in a piece of music (QA)?** Students need to justify their answer, but could argue that by putting accents on weak beats, the normal or expected pattern is subverted and this challenges our expectations as listeners.
3. **What other rhythmic features might musicians use to make a piece unusual or innovative (QA)?** Students might answer dotted rhythms, varying tempo, accents, polyrhythms, pauses, etc.
4. **How else could a composer use musical elements to create an innovative piece of pop music (QE)?** Students need to justify their answer, but could list anything that breaks the traditional conventions of pop music or subverts/defeats the listener's expectations, such as use of unexpected or sudden changes in dynamics, contrasts between melody and harmony, unusual chord progressions, unexpected key changes, etc.

After using the factual recall quiz as a basis for the higher-order questioning above, students should be fairly well equipped to answer the following exam question: 'Explain how The Beatles used musical elements to transform the basically simple structure of *With a Little Help From My Friends* into an innovative song.'

Again, they can be given certain criteria to include in their answer:

- The words 'syncopation', 'transition' and 'chromatic'.
- Reference to contrasts.
- Bar lengths to analyse structure (e.g. a two-bar pause creates a ____ effect).

So, we start with factual recall but include follow-up questions, making the link between this factual knowledge and the exam question explicit through modelling. This is a sensible approach to retrieval practice. It's essential to work backwards to decide what knowledge students need in order to be successful in each part of our subject, and ensure this knowledge is included in regular retrieval quizzes. It's also essential to repeat questions that students seem to struggle with or where they might hold misconceptions. If the curriculum is well designed (see Step 1), the important knowledge for each subject should already be mapped for students to repeatedly 'bump into' (Howard, 2020a) through these kinds of retrieval quizzes. An example of bridging that gap between factual recall and higher-order thinking could be initially prompting students to correctly recall that Priestley uses dramatic irony to ridicule Mr Birling, then expanding on this knowledge with a but/because/so sentence:

- Priestley uses dramatic irony to ridicule Mr Birling because he wants to expose the flaws of the upper classes.
- Priestley uses dramatic irony to ridicule Mr Birling so that the audience immediately dislike him and sympathise with Eva Smith.
- Priestley uses dramatic irony to ridicule Mr Birling but the post-war audience would feel enraged by Birling's arrogant assertions.

The staff CPD chart from Step 2 (see page 60) is relevant here as it shows how we aim to move from factual recall to higher-order thinking, while also moving through sentence to paragraph to whole-text level. This will, of course, look different for subjects like PE or maths. In PE, students might move from discrete tennis skills such as serving the ball to full games and matches. In maths, students might move from simple numeracy to more complicated equations. In each case, the building blocks of knowledge are established before practising the more complex processes of essay-writing, equation-solving and match-playing, which means cognitive load is reduced and stamina built.

2. Presenting new material and modelling

Rosenshine's second principle of instruction advocates presenting new material in small steps, with student practice after each step (Rosenshine, 2012). He suggests asking a large number of questions and looking over all responses to check for student understanding. When presenting new material, it's worth considering how students will organise this in a way that connects to existing knowledge – for example, through a graphic organiser or note-taking system.

For this part of the lesson, students may be asked to read or listen to something that introduces new ideas. One effective way to make this part of the lesson active rather than passive, and to leave students with a revision resource, is the use of Cornell notes. In this approach, students take notes from a text or as teachers are delivering new content. They write a heading at the top, notes down the page, a summary at the bottom and questions/ cues down the margin. The idea is that students cover up or fold over their notes and use the questions to self-quiz and retrieve the answers from memory. This could be made more challenging by using 'how' and 'why' questions, because they tend to go beyond surface-level knowledge and require students to demonstrate or explain their understanding. Here's an example of Cornell notes from a lecture on Aristotelian tragedy.

Aristotelian tragedy	
Cue:	**Notes:**
How does Aristotelian tragedy work?	• Aristotle's principles of tragedy: a change of fortune, good-bad (peripeteia), linked to error in judgement. • Creates pathos-catharsis. • Hero has sudden realisation (anagnorisis).
How does the concept of a 'tragic hero' work?	• Tragic hero: morally good, excessive pride (hubris), fatal flaw (hamartia), tragic death because of irreversible mistake, accepts death with honour.
What is the result of Macbeth's hamartia? Where do peripeteia, catharsis and pathos happen?	• Macbeth's hamartia: ambition and hubris. • Peripeteia: regicide. • Macduff killing Macbeth: catharsis? Pathos: killing of Macduff's family.
Why is Macbeth controlled and never free?	• We all have 'dark desires' and can identify with Macbeth. • Visionary tragedy: preoccupied with future. • Macbeth as least free hero: controlled, never content.
Summary: Shakespeare both conforms to and subverts principles of Aristotelian tragedy through clear peripeteias but arguably no cathartic moments, although anagnorisis occurs both in Macbeth's nihilistic speech and the interaction with Macduff where he becomes aware of the witches' equivocation and trickery.	

Note-taking is a skill, so it needs to be modelled to students – they need to be shown how to pick out the most important information and write it down in their own words using appropriate abbreviations. It may take a lot of practice before students are confident and competent enough to take notes independently. In *The Writing Revolution*, Hochman and Wexler suggest particular shorthand for students to use, though this may vary from one subject to another depending on what your common words are. Below is an example of what your abbreviations might look like. Again, the more the use of shorthand is modelled across the school, the more likely students are to develop this essential skill.

Note-taking symbols

Abbreviation/symbol	**Meaning**
→	Result of/consequence
∴	Therefore
=	Equal to/the same as
:	Causes
↑ ↓	Increase/decrease
Cont'd	Continued
Dev'p	Develop/development
Sim/diff	Similar/different
W	Writer
R	Reader
Bc	Because
e.g.	For example
Ch	Chapter
i.e.	In other words
Gov't	Government
Max/min	Maximum/minimum
P	Page

Abbreviation/symbol	Meaning
Re:	Regarding
Vs	Versus
w/	With
*	Important
()	Less important/extra information
#	Number
@	At
£	Money/financial

In *The Science of Learning*, Watson and Busch report how students who took notes during a lesson 'performed 12% better … compared to those who took no notes at all'. However, the type of notes matters: 'students who took summary notes at the end of each lecture or topic did 10-15% better on problem-solving questions and 13-17% better recalling facts than those who just took notes during the lesson' (Watson & Busch, 2021). It may be worth following up note-taking in class with further notes, or with self-quizzing of the notes after a gap, in line with the spacing effect.

There are many clear benefits to modelling note-taking and it's arguably a gap in current teaching practice; taking effective notes is a lifelong study skill that students will certainly need in further and higher education. The Cornell approach means students have to listen very carefully to the content delivered by the teacher in order to process it into answers to specific questions, rather than just copying down chunks of information or noting what the teacher tells them to. Students have to decide what information to record and how, which encourages them to take responsibility and play an active role in their learning.

One thing to bear in mind when teaching students to master this challenging skill is explicitly modelling abbreviations such as e.g., i.e. and etc. Even if students are avid readers of fiction, they may not be familiar or confident with using these abbreviations as they are more common in non-fiction writing. Have a key of abbreviations for important words, phrases or concepts in your subject area, and a way of highlighting more and less important information, such as underlining, asterisks, brackets and margins. It's also important to model how to turn notes into full sentences, paragraphs and even essays. This could be included in a pastoral curriculum (see Step 6) as well as core lessons.

In terms of our revision revolution, techniques like Cornell notes are key, because students' exercise books become revision tools that help them test their knowledge. It becomes easy to show students how they should complete a study session (e.g. revise using Cornell notes on X topic, then apply this knowledge to your own practice sentence/paragraph/essay). Similarly to self-quizzing, students cover up the summary section of their Cornell notes, revealing just the cues. They use these cues to write answers from memory, before checking their answers and adding to them where necessary. Encourage use of a different colour pen to make gaps in knowledge visual to students. If they complete an activity like this before drafting an analytical paragraph or any piece of writing relevant to your subject area, the quality is likely to be higher because they have reviewed their knowledge of the topic first. It will also serve to reduce cognitive load as they write. Quizzing using Cornell notes is an ideal activity to do in pairs, either with another student, a parent or a sibling.

Agarwal and Bain recommend a process they called 'retrieve-taking': this involves students reading their book (or perhaps their Cornell notes), closing their book, writing down what they can remember and then opening their book back up to check their answers (Agarwal & Bain, 2019). This is a wonderfully simple process and the small tweak from rereading to 'retrieve-taking' makes the process active rather than passive, and therefore much more beneficial. It also offers students a way to check their retrieval and identify gaps in their knowledge independently; we build self-regulated learners with knowledge of their strengths and targets.

Bain strongly advocates the retrieve-taking process: 'By simply having a discussion, followed by time to ponder, followed by time to retrieve notes, students are able to pull information out of their heads to make sense of it as we go along. Because of this opportunity for Retrieve-Taking, students listen and participate during my teaching and discussions because they are confident they will be given time for writing and retrieving later on' (Agarwal & Bain, 2019). Bain also mentions 'retrieval guides', where the teacher models picking out important concepts in a text, article or lecture and noting them down. This, again, becomes a strategy students can use independently.

Small changes to our questioning can be made in this part of a lesson to encourage high levels of understanding, such as asking 'What have you understood?' rather than 'Have you understood?' and 'What questions have you got?' rather than 'Have you got any questions?' Once this process has been repeatedly modelled to them, students can use these questions to reflect on their own understanding in independent study.

Extra support

Note-taking is a skill that needs explicit and regular modelling, and Cornell is a very prescriptive type of note-taking, therefore students will need a lot of guidance to master it. Take them through the process step by step and gradually reduce the amount of teacher direction over time. Give students a printout of the shorthand they can use for their note-taking to help them get used to this type of writing and know when its use is appropriate.

Extra challenge

Cornell notes could be used in conjunction with any of the strategies listed above. For example, students could be encouraged to include certain vocabulary or sentence structures in their notes. They could also include different types of questions as cues to extend their understanding when they use their notes to revise.

3. Student practice

Rosenshine emphasises the need to guide student practice, providing scaffolds for difficult tasks and monitoring independent practice. Tom Sherrington suggests that many learning experiences move through the following sequence:

- 'Teacher explains.
- Teacher models.
- Teacher checks for understanding.
- Guided student practice with scaffolding.

- Scaffold and support gradually withdrawn.
- Independent practice.
- Fluency.' (Sherrington, 2019)

Fluency is, of course, our ultimate goal. This book is all about empowering students to be fluent in their study strategies, but with the acknowledgement that this is a gradual process.

Once students have completed their Cornell notes on Aristotelian tragedy, the student practice stage could involve them applying this knowledge in a paragraph on Macbeth. Equally, it could be a discussion with a partner about how principles of Aristotelian tragedy are relevant to the play, or any other activity where this knowledge is used as a springboard into higher-order thinking.

4. Feedback

Rosenshine's principles advocate 'checking the responses of all students' and 'monitoring students when they begin independent practice' (Rosenshine, 2012).

Studies cited in *The Science of Learning* show that the most effective feedback after checking and monitoring 'focused on how to do the task better' but, alarmingly, 'over one third (38%) of feedback interventions [did] more harm than good' (Watson & Busch, 2021). Ineffective or even detrimental feedback tended to focus on ability. A study by John Hattie and Helen Timperley found that effective feedback should focus on these key questions:

- **Where am I going?** This makes the goal crystal clear.
- **How am I going?** This gives an indication of progress.
- **Where to next?** Perhaps the most important question as it focuses on the strategies needed in order to improve. (Hattie & Timperley, 2007)

Hattie and Timperley looked at four types of feedback and found that 'feedback about the person', commenting on things like natural ability, was least effective. 'Feedback about the task' was found to be 'often effective if students had a faulty interpretation of what was needed'. However, the less common 'feedback about the process ... prompts [students] to search out more information and often leads to deeper learning than just feedback on the task'. Finally 'feedback about self-regulation ... how well students monitored their performance, regulated their actions and tweaked their strategies' is 'more effective for novice learners' (Watson & Busch, 2021). Essentially, when monitoring and checking, the feedback provided should result in the learner thinking deeply about how to make further improvements to their work.

Students should first proofread any written work, so your feedback isn't focused on basic errors that they could have corrected themselves. Here's a possible proofreading code that would ideally be used across the school.

Literacy marking key

Code		
NP	A new paragraph is needed here.	
Sp	I'm unsure of this spelling and have circled the part I'm struggling with.	
CL	I'm unsure if this word(s) needs a capital letter.	
KW	I've used a key vocabulary word here.	
COL	I'm unsure if this is phrased academically or I've used colloquial language.	
?	I'm unsure if this part makes sense.	
SS	I've used a sophisticated sentence structure here.	? I'm unsure of the sentence structure here.
P	I've used sophisticated punctuation here.	? I'm unsure of the punctuation here.

Becoming a self-regulated learner will not happen overnight and students may feel uncomfortable and unfamiliar with this way of working to begin with. Making it part of your classroom routine and modelling it regularly – as well as encouraging students to use these kinds of questions in talk, while working in pairs and in whole-class discussion – will eventually result in students feeling able to ask and answer questions that enable them to plan, monitor and evaluate their work effectively.

It can be helpful for students to zoom in on their work, explaining which part they are particularly proud of, where they have taken a risk and how they might make further improvements. By doing this, students reflect on their work and engage metacognitively with their learning, becoming more aware of their strengths and weaknesses. Ideally, they learn to quality-control *as they work*, rather than this being an additional task at the end of a piece of work. Consider the following example:

An omnipotent light, devoured by a thick, ominous, tenebrous fog, looking fearful, shines a lustrous beam of light only Heaven can provide. Beyond the light, a blinding fog prowled as though a predator was hunting its prey, slowly yet surely covering every inch of the vast blue sky, like a disease, slowly yet surely it will devour its victim in the worst way possible.

- *I am proud of the juxtaposition of light and dark images to evoke a foreboding atmosphere.*
- *I took a risk by including two similes within one sentence.*
- *I could improve by varying my vocabulary and avoiding repetition unless it is for deliberate effect. Do I need to state 'looking fearful' when I have implied this through the dark language used?*

This student knows exactly what they are aiming to do in their writing and is very successful at reflecting accurately on their work, independently identifying areas for improvements. This will be the result of lots of teacher modelling, paired coaching and redrafting work as a class.

Alex Quigley suggests that feedback should be thought of as a wedding cake: the biggest layer (where the most effort is exerted) is self-assessment, the next biggest is peer assessment and the smallest (icing on the cake) is teacher assessment. By the time the work reaches the teacher, several improvements and checks should already have taken place, leaving the teacher free to really push the student towards the next level of excellence (Quigley, 2014). Clearly, for this to work well, effective self- and peer assessment needs to be taught, modelled and repeatedly used and refined in the classroom.

In a blog post on metacognition, Elizabeth Mountstevens writes about a 'reflection-feedback sandwich' where students reflect on their performance, receive feedback and then reflect on their judgement accuracy (Mountstevens, 2021). As a final part of this metacognitive process, students could discuss which of the revision strategies might be most well suited to revising the content of today's lesson. Or perhaps a mixture of strategies could be used – for example, a brain dump followed by creating flashcards on the areas that appear to be sticking points. In this way, students are constantly thinking about how to revise, making it more likely that they will use these concrete strategies to remember their learning.

Extra support

With this kind of self-assessment, I have often found that students highlight with no explanation given, or highlight with the word 'proud' or the phrase 'I am proud of this sentence' even after I have modelled the process. This is a total waste of time (and I tell them this!). The important part of their self-assessment is the reasoning and explanation, as this is where they really think about their choices and evaluate their work.

Extra challenge

Asking 'Why?' even when students have given a reason can sometimes prompt them to develop their thinking even further. For example: why is including two similes a risk? Why might it work/not work? Why are you proud of the juxtaposition? How does it evoke a foreboding atmosphere more than just using light or dark images? How could you improve your vocabulary? What effect would removing 'looking fearful' have? These questions then become metacognitive, encouraging students to evaluate their work in detail.

Another way to make feedback actionable is using questions. Phrasing feedback as a question that students answer when redrafting ensures they add value to their work. Consider the following example feedback questions:

- Why does the writer use [insert technique/word/phrase] here? Can you include the phrases 'evokes an image of' or 'impacts the reader through connotations of'?
- What sum did you do to reach this number?
- Why is this word/phrase/technique powerful?
- How does this conclusion reinforce/contradict your prediction about the experiment?
- What might be a more precise/sophisticated/academic/formal word here?

- How could you phrase this more clearly?
- How might you combine these closely related sentences for better phrasing?
- What unnecessary/repeated information could you remove from this section?
- How could you order this paragraph/text more logically/chronologically by using some time-transition words and phrases?
- How could you explain this part more thoroughly/clearly/concisely by adding the word 'because'?

Another principle of effective feedback is that the more effort students put into improving their work, the more this learning will stick. You may be familiar with Ron Berger's famous 'Austin's Butterfly',[5] a lesson where student Austin makes improvements on a drawing of a butterfly based on comments from his peers (carefully scaffolded and guided by the teacher). By draft 6, his work is an accurate depiction of the butterfly, a huge improvement on draft 1 and a very impressive drawing from a six-year-old. The mantra 'If it's not perfect, it's not finished' seems to work here. The fact that the student redrafts five times before the finished product is accepted as a standard of excellence shows the importance of supportive feedback in enabling effective redrafting.

In *Making Every Lesson Count*, Shaun Allison and Andy Tharby suggest the STAR acronym to help students approach redrafting:

- '**Substitute**. What could you change in order to improve this work?
- **Take away**. What information is unnecessary and could be removed?
- **Add**. What could you add in order to improve this work?
- **Rearrange**. How might the order of ideas be improved?' (Allison & Tharby, 2015)

In order to encourage proofreading and editing, a marking key can be used to help students check their work. For example, if students are unsure of a spelling, they could use 'sp' to identify that they think this spelling is incorrect and then circle the part of the word they are unsure of. This

5 https://youtu.be/hqh1MRWZjms

ensures they are thinking about areas for improvement at word level, by identifying the specific part of the word they struggle with, rather than relying on the teacher to correct all their spellings.

In all these ideas for feedback, the initial targets come from the teacher but the effort in making those improvements crucially comes from the student. Through careful and repeated modelling of the feedback process, students should become better at evaluating their own work. Framing much of the feedback as questions makes students less reliant on teachers to correct things like basic punctuation. I always tell my classes that if I'm busy adding capital letters to their work, I'm unable to focus on pushing them towards the higher-order thinking necessary for success.

Quiz

1. How can Rosenshine's principles inform our teaching?
2. Why is modelling important?
3. What is metacognition and how does it help create self-regulated learners?
4. Why is feedback important?
5. Why is reaching fluency a gradual process?

Reflection

1. Do lessons in your context incorporate regular reviews of learning?
2. Is modelling used to move students along the novice-to-expert continuum?
3. Are there lots of opportunities for student practice in order to achieve a high success rate?
4. Is feedback regular and does it add value?
5. Are students explicitly taught metacognitive strategies so they can reflect on their own work effectively?

Summary

- It's beneficial for most, if not all, lessons to begin with some form of review.
- The review should incorporate spacing (weekly and monthly review).
- The student practice part of a learning sequence is essential to develop fluency.
- Scaffolds are often needed at first but should be gradually removed.
- The feedback part of a learning sequence is important in identifying where and how to improve. Through metacognitive questions, students can develop the skills to reflect and feed back on their own learning.
- You can empower students by teaching them explicit methods for note-taking, planning and sentence crafting.

Step 5
Revolutionary Coaching

Training students up to coach one another as effective revision buddies

Spring term: January

> **In a nutshell**
> Students are, of course, the most important part of our revision revolution. This chapter looks at how we can train students to become effective learners and to support others in their learning and revision, too.

In Step 4, I wrote about the mistakes I unwittingly made in my lesson planning that disadvantaged my students. While I was busy designing these 'fun' lessons with engagement and performance at their heart, I neglected one of the most important parts of effective teaching: modelling. David Didau explains the importance of modelling well when he writes about wanting to improve his tennis skills; he decided to take some lessons after realising he was never going to improve just by watching Wimbledon every year (Didau, 2015a). Watching fully formed experts perform does little to improve the skills of the novice. However, working with a coach who breaks down and carefully models each specific skill, and allows time to practise these skills in isolation before putting them together, will make a difference. Of course, this is much harder, but that's the point: learning needs to be effortful for students to progress.

Students are reliant on us, as subject experts, to model our thought processes and the steps we take in order to reach a level of excellence. By modelling these explicitly, we can encourage students to model to one another, explaining their own thought processes and making adjustments and edits as they go. This is an essential part of becoming a self-regulated learner. We must not underestimate the power of oral conversations in which students explain their writing, modelling their understanding to one another verbally. Research suggests that oracy is 'cognitively sticky' (Didau, 2018a): students are likely to remember the learning better when they have had opportunities to discuss and articulate it verbally.

Despite the obvious importance of immersing students and stakeholders in the world of revision, what lies at the heart of this culture is the classroom. We need to train our students up in a way of thinking that will empower them not only to succeed but also to support one another in succeeding. As a starting point, Agarwal and Bain recommend adding some peer checking after students complete a retrieval quiz. This could take the form of a paired discussion where students cross-reference their answers, asking questions such as:

- 'Is there anything in common that both of us wrote down?
- Is there anything new that neither of us wrote down?
- Did either of us write down any misinformation?
- Why do you think you remembered what you did?' (Agarwal & Bain, 2019)

I would also suggest asking students to look at any different answers and discuss which they think is correct and why. You could, of course, provide a resource to enable them to check the answers they are unsure of, such as a knowledge organiser or a worksheet in their exercise book.

Agarwal and Bain suggest further ways to extend feedback through student discussions, which I've paraphrased here:

- Students discuss similarities and differences in their responses following a brain dump (see prompt questions above).

- Students write down two things they remember about a topic. They swap answers with a partner, adding a further point to each other's responses.
- Two pairs of students make a Think-Pair-Square for a group discussion following retrieval.
- After feedback, students could be asked what surprised them, why they got X correct and Y incorrect, what is their next step, etc. (Agarwal & Bain, 2019)

Before we explore approaches to get students working in collaboration – not competition – to support each other to be great learners, it's important to ensure high-quality modelling takes place first so that students can act as effective peer coaches. The modelling part of a learning sequence is crucially important, since this is how we verbalise our expert thought processes to students. There are lots of options here: live modelling (one of my favourites), pre-prepared models, worked examples, silent modelling and 'I do, we do, you do'. The table below summarises each of these approaches, along with the benefits and when you might choose to use each one.

Type of modelling	What is it?	Benefits
Live modelling	Live modelling is completing a task while simultaneously explaining the thought process and steps being taken. Although this is usually used by teachers, it can also be a very effective independent revision activity, especially if students are able to pair up, answering an exam question while explaining to their partner what they are doing and why, using the language of an expert as much as possible. Even if revising on their own, students can annotate their work to show the steps and thought process.	I love live modelling because I think it breaks down the process that students need to go through and therefore is much less overwhelming than presenting a completed answer. It's a bit like watching someone on a cooking programme go through the steps of baking a cake, rather than just showing you the finished product and expecting you to be able to replicate it.

Pre-prepared models	Although live modelling can be very helpful, pre-prepared models have their uses, too. One benefit is having a range of answers of different qualities and being able to show the differences between a low-mark and a high-mark answer. When revising, it can be very effective to study completed answers and examine the ingredients of a full-mark answer, then use these to create your own answer to a similar question.	Not only can pre-prepared models help students see the difference between poor and high-quality answers, but they can also be used to explore common misconceptions. You can tailor pre-prepared models to the needs of your class, giving them your full attention free from the many distractions when modelling live in a classroom. Clearly, it's more work to create models in advance; however, once you have them they are permanent. Many teachers I know keep folders of model answers reflecting different grades, which can be used repeatedly with classes as and when needed.
Worked examples	Worked examples show each step involved in solving a problem or completing an exam question, essay paragraph, piece of artwork, etc. The idea is that teachers gradually reduce the number of steps they complete, moving from worked examples to partially completed examples until eventually students complete the answers themselves. When revising, students could look at a completed example, then attempt a partially completed one and finally complete their own answer while checking they have followed the steps shown in the models. This is another scaffold that students need to rely upon less as they move nearer to their final exam, once they are confident with the process.	I really struggled with maths at school but I had a fantastic teacher called Mrs Mann. We had a separate exercise book and notebook full of worked examples that we referred to when completing our own maths problems. I ended up with an A for GCSE maths, which I attribute to Mrs Mann's fantastic explanations and step-by-step worked examples. This is the power of worked examples. But this highly scaffolded approach does need to be removed at some point and certainly as students near the exam. It is, however, a great strategy for addressing misconceptions when providing feedback on mocks and practice papers.
Silent modelling	Silent modelling probably sounds quite strange. However, it has the benefit of focusing full attention on the process because it's not accompanied by a commentary explaining how the model is being put together.	Because students are being asked to watch and not listen, this type of modelling reduces cognitive load. You may want to give students an opportunity to ask questions after the silent model has been completed. Students could then complete their own similar question having watched the teacher at work.

I do, we do, you do	*Stage 1: I do* This is where you, as the expert, show students how to do something, breaking it into manageable steps. *Stage 2: We do* This is where you and the students work through a process together. The teacher leads with prompt questions to guide students towards proficiency. This is often the first stage in the classroom, with the 'I do' part left out completely. However, by first talking students through your expert thought process, without asking anything from them except their attention, you not only reduce cognitive load but also avoid incorrect answers from students, giving them an extra layer of scaffold before addressing misconceptions in the 'we do' and 'you do' stages. *Stage 3: You do* This is where control is handed over to the student(s) so they can practise the skill that has been modelled. That's not to say that this stage can't be scaffolded with prompts, paired work, templates or teacher/peer support while students complete the task. However, all this should eventually be removed to mirror the conditions that students would face in an exam.	This method can be a great way to teach a new skill, gradually reducing the level of support. Equally, when going over something that students are finding hard or haven't tackled for a while, it can make that process explicit and ensure students have the confidence to complete the task themselves after experiencing two examples with teacher support.

Pre-prepared models

On the next page is a pre-prepared model that includes two examples of essay introductions, based on *An Inspector Calls* by JB Priestley. Students typically struggle to write engaging introductions and often waste time by just telling the story, picking up no marks (see introduction A). The model also includes some common spelling errors (Priestly, inspecter, hypocriticly) and examples of less academic language ('show' used repeatedly). Students often tell me one introduction is better than another simply because it's longer, so I've made sure both are the same length. Introduction B concisely covers characterisation, the writer's intention and the effect on the audience in accurate, academic language, picking up marks immediately.

Introduction A:	Introduction B:
In this essay, I am going to write about the hypocrisies of the upper classes. In An Inspector Calls, characters behave hypocriticly and Inspector Goole shows how this is wrong. The behaviour of some of the Birling family does change, however, after the inspector's questioning. *Priestly shows us how this hypocrisy is wrong and presents the Birling family in a way that makes us hate them but have sympathy for Eva Smith.* *The upper classes are shown in a way that make us dislike them, preferring the down-and-out working class Eva Smith whose story is told through the inspecter as she is never present in the play.*	*Behaving hypocritically means claiming to have higher standards or more noble beliefs than is the case. At the beginning of the play, the Birling family behave as though they are a perfectly content family unit with the cracks only beginning to be exposed on the Inspector's entrance.* *Mr and Mrs Birling behave in a particularly superior way, claiming to be more knowledgeable, intelligent and moral than the lower classes.* *Priestley forces us to question this hypocritical behaviour and the terrible, irresponsible consequences for vulnerable, marginalised members of society in this capitalist world.*

The reason for these pre-planned models is that students often struggle to write an original and engaging introduction to a piece of transactional writing. In the example below, a pre-prepared model of an article introduction, introduction A is typical, reverting to 'I think', repeated basic vocabulary and run-on sentences. Introduction B gives students an alternative: it paints a picture with an anecdote that encourages the reader to invest in the story and to feel something. It also provides an opportunity to discuss the Aristotelian triad of ethos, logos and pathos, and how this works in persuasive writing and speeches. Finally, it models how to smoothly link the introductory anecdote to the purpose of the article through a powerful statistic that gets to the heart of the argument: fighting against animal cruelty.

Introduction A:	Introduction B:
I think we need to do more to help animals because it isn't their fault people treat them badly and we should show we care about them and will save them. *Many animals have suffered terrible treatment and abuse from their owner which is beyond their control. This can make them behave badly and become difficult pets but they are just scared and helpless. We should help them. It's not their fault.*	*Heavy breathing could be heard through the ground floor bathroom window. Pudsey shivered with cold and fear as he wondered when the next beating would be. Pudsey never chose to be here. He could have had a caring owner who fed him, cuddled him and loved him. Instead, he was suffering from multiple injuries: swollen eyes and head wounds that caused him terrible pain and suffering.* *According to the RSPCA, the Royal Society for the Prevention of Cruelty to Animals, Pudsey is just one of 102,900 animals who were rescued from neglect, cruelty and abuse last year.*

Worked examples

The worked example below looks at how a teacher might model fractions, gradually reducing levels of scaffold so that students eventually complete the fraction sum with no support. By looking at the steps modelled in the worked examples, students can see how to solve the fraction independently.

Completed example	**Partially completed example**	**Student-completed example**
1/3 + 1/6	1/2 + 2/5	1/4 + 3/5 = ?
1. Find the common denominator (smallest number that will divide by both 3 and 6): 6. Use this as the new denominator for each fraction in the sum.	1. Find the common denominator (smallest number that will divide by both 4 and 5): 20. Use this as the new denominator for each fraction in the sum.	Follow the steps and show your working.
1/3 + 1/6 = /6 + /6	1/2 + 2/5 = /10 + /10	
2. Work out what you need to multiply each denominator by to make 6.	2. Work out what you need to multiply each denominator by to make 10.	
1/3 + 1/6 = /6 + /6	1/2 + 2/5 = /10 + /10	
3. Multiply each numerator by this number.	3. Multiply each numerator by this number.	
1/3 + 1/6 = 2/6 + 1/6	1/2 + 2/5 = /10 + /10	
4. Add the new fractions together.	4. Add the new fractions together.	
1/3 + 1/6 = 3/6	/10 + /10 = /10	
5. Reduce if possible – will the numerator and denominator divide by a common number?	5. Reduce if possible – will the numerator and denominator divide by a common number?	
Yes, both divisible by 3 = 1/2		

Adding subordinate clauses to topic sentences

This second worked example looks at how we might model teaching subordinate clauses by gradually removing the steps to creating a sentence including a subordinate clause.

Worked example	Partially completed example	Student-completed example
Hermia elopes with Lysander. 1. Why does Hermia elope with Lysander? Use the word 'because' in your answer. Hermia elopes with Lysander because her father wants her to marry Demetrius. 2. Underline the subordinate clause (extra information that does not make sense on its own). Hermia elopes with Lysander because her father wants her to marry Demetrius. 3. Move the subordinate clause to the beginning of the sentence, separating it with a comma. Because her father wants her to marry Demetrius, Hermia elopes with Lysander. 4. Examine your word choices – can you replace any words with more sophisticated or precise alternatives? Because her father commands her to marry Demetrius, Hermia elopes with Lysander.	Egeus grows angry with his daughter. 1. Why does Egeus grow angry with his daughter? Use the word 'because' in your answer. Egeus grows angry with his daughter because she refuses to marry the suitor of his choice. 2. Underline the subordinate clause (extra information that does not make sense on its own). 3. Move the subordinate clause to the beginning of the sentence, separating it with a comma. 4. Examine your word choices – can you replace any words with more sophisticated or precise alternatives?	Theseus feels sympathy for the lovers. Follow the steps to complete your own complex sentence with a subordinate clause at the beginning.

A note on metacognition

The revision revolution is ultimately about empowering learners to take control of their learning. It would be remiss, therefore, not to mention the work of John Flavell on developing self-regulated learners. According to Flavell's research, self-regulated learners actively participate in their learning and are able to independently adjust their learning processes to respond to feedback. This requires motivation, but how do we build this in our students? It's worth delving into some of the Education Endowment Foundation's recent research in this area.

An EEF report, entitled *Metacognition and Self-Regulated Learning*, breaks down our metacognitive knowledge as:

- 'Our own abilities and attitudes (knowledge of ourselves as a learner).
- What strategies are effective and available (knowledge of strategies).
- This particular type of activity (knowledge of the task).' (Quigley et al, 2018)

The EEF has also put together an audit for schools (Quigley et al, 2021) that describes the knowledge and behaviour of students as they demonstrate exemplary metacognitive skills:

- **Pupil knowledge**. 'Pupils are self-regulating (aware of their own strengths and weaknesses) and can motivate themselves to engage in and improve their own learning. Pupils understand how they learn, exhibiting knowledge of themselves as learners, understanding how to deploy a range of available strategies for different tasks. Pupils show a deep understanding of how planning, monitoring and evaluating their learning is different across subject domains and tasks, as well as understanding commonalities in their learning.'
- **Pupil behaviour**. 'Pupils consistently plan for tasks with independence, reflecting upon the success of their plans. Pupils engage in metacognitive talk with their peers with relative independence. Most pupils effectively manage their learning outside of the classroom, utilising a range of strategies with increasing independence. Most pupils fully engage with feedback to monitor their learning with increasing independence.'

In the EEF report, the authors state that self-regulated learners plan, monitor and evaluate their work (Quigley et al, 2018). This means students ask questions of themselves as they complete a piece of writing or solve a problem. Students could approach the planning stage by asking questions like: how have we completed this question/solved this problem before? What is the best strategy? What key terminology should I include? How can I construct the best opening sentence? What is the most logical order for my points? Have I answered a question/solved a problem like this before and was it successful? Why/why not? What have I learned from in-class models and examples about this type of question?

The monitoring stage could include questions like: am I doing well so far? How do I know? What other strategies or techniques might I include to improve my work so far? Am I finding this easy or difficult? Why? Could I stop and change/add/take away anything to improve my work so far?

Finally, the evaluation stage might include questions like: how did I do? Did X strategy/technique work? Why/why not? How could I answer this question better/solve this problem more effectively next time? Are there any strategies or techniques that may be better? Did I include enough/the right terminology?

Obviously, if students are completing an exam question in timed conditions, they are not going to spend time answering all these questions, but they can be helpful at the first stages of revision. Once this is a habit, students can pick and choose between the questions appropriately in terms of which will help them make further improvements.

Clearly, for students to be as reflective as described by the EEF, this will need to be modelled to them and be part of regular classroom practice. Now let's consider some ways to get students studying collaboratively as effective 'revision buddies', contributing to the culture of study we're aiming to create.

1. Paired coaching

In this book we've explored the importance of metacognition for developing self-regulated learners. A powerful and potentially transformative strategy for developing that metacognition is paired coaching.

The Science of Learning sheds more light on why coaching is a powerful approach, reporting on a study that shows 'effort is contagious' (Watson & Busch, 2021). The study found that 'students were more likely to work harder on a task if the person next to them was working hard', suggesting this was due to 'the bandwagon effect … when people adopt the behaviour of those around them' and to 'our automatic need to imitate those around us'. Sport psychology has shown that 'people would cycle faster on a bike machine if they were being observed by others' (Watson & Busch, 2021). For improved effort, someone else must also be working hard and students must know their performance is being tracked. Strategic pairings are also important: 'pairing students with someone who will encourage them to work hard' (Watson & Busch, 2021). This study reinforces the idea that building a culture of effective study is incredibly powerful, as students will 'raise their game' as a result of the hard work and academic rigour happening around them.

Like everything, paired coaching needs to become part of the classroom culture – and ideally the school culture. The first time I do this with a class, I give very explicit instructions about how it works and we revisit these instructions in every successive coaching session. I usually use some form of checklist or success criteria that has been thoroughly modelled beforehand, with concrete examples, so the student coach knows exactly what they are looking for in their partner's work.

I also use a visual of two students engaged in paired coaching, pointing out that the student coach's eyes are constantly on their partner's work: watching, checking and asking probing questions. The student coach should clear their workspace and close their exercise book, so the student writer can move their book into the middle of the shared space. I tell the student coaches that they have two jobs. The first is to check for accuracy: are all words spelled correctly? Has punctuation been used correctly? Do all sentences make grammatical sense? Accuracy will, of course, look different in certain subjects. In maths, it might be checking the placement of decimal points; in music, it could be the formation of the clef and time signature. Their second job is to quality-control and push their partner: could they use a better or more precise word here? Could they structure this sentence in a more sophisticated way? Could they add variety? Have they hit this part of the criteria? What is missing or needs more detail?

The student writer, on the other hand, needs to vocalise their thought process: what are they writing and why? What will they write next and why? They should explain their choices and reasoning at every stage: this is the heart of metacognition. Of course, the students need to swap roles and should ideally spend the same amount of time in each role. With a process like this, there is no way students can revert to task completion over thinking (Myatt, 2020a) as they are forced to explain and justify their choices at every stage.

At this point, I want to emphasise that I would never set students off on a task like this before I had carefully modelled whatever skill it is I want them to practise. For paired coaching to be successful, students need a good understanding of what is being asked of them and what success looks like, which is why some criteria or a checklist can be helpful, as well as lots of explicit modelling and chunking. The teacher (the expert) is always available during paired coaching, but only if both students are unsure – the teacher becomes an extra layer of quality control when needed.

The reason the paired-coaching process is so powerful is that not only do students have to explain and justify their thinking, but they also push each other to take risks in a safe and supported environment. Success in their partner's work is success for them, and they are often very proud of the paired outcomes. Once this becomes a habit, students are able to internalise this way of thinking and it becomes a scaffold for writing or revising without peer support.

To encourage pride in the paired-coaching process, you could follow it up with one of Doug Lemov's strategies from *Teach Like a Champion*: show call. This involves showing the whole class one or a series of examples to evaluate. What makes this great? What further improvements could be made? This strategy ensures two things become part of classroom culture: mistakes and high expectations. Mistakes are valued as a learning opportunity and students support each other in a continual process of reviewing, redrafting and improving their work. High expectations are constantly modelled: no matter how great the show-call example, it can always be improved.

A perhaps unintended benefit of this approach to peer study is that it really improves class relationships. I usually pair up students who would never choose to work together, but end up rooting for each other and sharing their work with pride, seeing it as a team effort. Of course, it's also worth considering strategic ability pairings: the more able students coaching the less able and vice versa. And the process works equally well in practical subjects, where students can work together to talk and coach each other through the technique for serving a tennis ball; the method in a science experiment; the process of shading in art; the construction of a product in design technology.

Ideally, by the time students reach Year 11 (or maybe before), they will be revising in pairs or small groups, using coaching techniques to support each other in making gains in their learning. Imagine seeing this in action in the school library: no nagging, just spontaneous and enjoyable revision!

2. Paired quizzing

Paired quizzing is a very simple process: partners ask each other questions and assess whether the answers are correct or incorrect. There are several ways of doing this and you may want to vary the process depending on where students are up to in the topic.

You could provide answers in the form of a knowledge organiser or crib sheet, and get students to take turns asking questions. For example, what is important about the context of *Macbeth*? In this case, students will probably need some training in how to write questions and you may want to get them to prepare these in advance.

Alternatively, you could provide the questions and answers. This approach avoids any misconceptions about whether responses are right or wrong, but runs the risk of students 'parroting' answers without necessarily understanding them. You will probably want to listen in and do some whole-class follow-up.

A mixture of these approaches is probably the best option, depending on where students are up to in the learning. If you're near the beginning of the scheme, perhaps provide the answers; if you're at revision stage, students could write their own answers while you circulate and check for errors.

Whichever approach you choose to take, it's important to train students in how to quiz effectively. It will not be at all productive if they tell their partner that their answer is wrong and simply reel off the correct answer. I would suggest an approach such as 'tip, tip, teach, try again':

> **Student 1**: What does 'equivocation' mean?
>
> **Student 2**: I can't remember.
>
> **Student 1**: It relates to the witches [tip].
>
> **Student 2**: Something to do with lying.
>
> **Student 1**: Yes, but think more along the lines of trickery [tip].
>
> **Student 2**: When they trick Macbeth.
>
> **Student 1**: Think about what they say and how this tricks Macbeth [tip].
>
> **Student 2**: They tell him he will be king.
>
> **Student 1**: Equivocation is use of unclear language to tell half-truths. For example, the witches tell Macbeth he can't be killed by any man born of woman, which makes him feel invincible. But the witches know Macduff was born through caesarean section and will kill Macbeth – this is how they trick him into feeling invincible [teach]. Can you repeat back to me the definition of 'equivocation' with an example [try again]?

The 'teach' part is crucial, as teaching is shown to be an effective study strategy (Enser & Enser, 2020). Of course, this kind of coaching by students requires practice, but it's very powerful once they have mastered it, helping them explore and discuss important knowledge for each unit.

Although it's important that we, as subject experts, quality-control this process by providing answers for coaches and checking for misconceptions, the eventual aim is for students to teach each other without notes, retrieving the knowledge and understanding from memory. Remember, our aim is to gradually reduce scaffolds. It's perhaps best to think of a trajectory from high challenge/high scaffold to high challenge/low or no scaffold.

3. Questioning/elaborative interrogation

Research shows that elaborative interrogation (asking 'how' and 'why' questions about a topic) is an effective way of developing depth of knowledge and understanding (Smith & Weinstein, 2016).

If provoking students to think hard about a topic improves learning and memory, it makes sense that asking questions to explore how and why things work will not only develop a deeper understanding, but also result in better retention. Elaboration is most effective when there's some prior knowledge to connect the new information with. The questions you use will depend on the topic being revised, but the Learning Scientists suggest the following possible generic questions:

- 'How does X work?
- Why does X happen?
- When did X happen?
- What caused X?
- What is the result of X?' (Smith & Weinstein, 2016)

Studies also show that elaborative interrogation works best with factual information; there isn't enough evidence yet to suggest it's useful for exploring interpretations in English, for instance. On the next page is an example that uses questions to revise grammar.

What are adjectives?	An adjective describes a noun.
Why is an adjective not simply a 'describing' word?	Other parts of speech, such as adverbs, can add description, but adjectives specifically describe nouns.
How do adjectives work?	An adjective forms part of a noun phrase by adding description to the noun.
What is the result of using too many adjectives?	Too many adjectives in a phrase or sentence can be less effective than using carefully selected verbs and nouns. The description can become confusing, instead of clear and vivid.
Why is adding an adjective not always the best way to improve a sentence?	Carefully chosen adjectives can be very effective but there are many other options to improve writing, such as using different types of verbs, adding a subordinate clause or using an adverbial.

Research also shows that elaborative interrogation works better when used with an extract rather than a long text (Kingsbridge Research School, 2019). Consider the following example:

Respiration

The primary organs of the respiratory system are the lungs, which function to take in oxygen and expel carbon dioxide as we breathe.

The gas exchange process is performed by the lungs and respiratory system. Air, a mix of oxygen and other gases, is inhaled.

In the throat, the trachea, or windpipe, filters the air. The trachea branches into two bronchi, tubes that lead to the lungs.

Once in the lungs, oxygen is moved into the bloodstream. Blood carries the oxygen through the body to where it is needed.

Red blood cells collect carbon dioxide from the body's cells and transport it back to the lungs.

An exchange of oxygen and carbon dioxide takes place in the alveoli, small structures within the lungs. The carbon dioxide, a waste gas, is exhaled and the cycle begins again with the next breath.

The diaphragm is a dome-shaped muscle below the lungs that controls breathing. The diaphragm flattens out and pulls forward, drawing air into the lungs for inhalation. During exhalation the diaphragm expands to force air out of the lungs.

Adults normally take 12 to 20 breaths per minute. Strenuous exercise drives the breath rate up to an average of 45 breaths per minute.

(www.livescience.com/26825-human-body-system-respiration-infographic.html)

Read lines 1-4

How does respiration work?

Read lines 11-13

Why is oxygen inhaled and carbon dioxide exhaled?

Read lines 14-17

Why is the movement of the diaphragm important in this process?

Read lines 18-19

What is the result of strenuous exercise on respiration?

It's worth being explicit with students about question types. Sarah Cullen describes some questions as 'pulling' (supporting students with prompts that pull them to a certain answer) and others as 'pushing' (for stretch and challenge) (Cullen, 2019). Pulling questions could include: X is the most important idea – can you explain why? What technique is being used here? Can you remember what we said was the effect of this technique? These kinds of questions coax students towards a specific response. 'Pushing' questions prompt students to reach answers independently and tend to be more open; there's less scaffolding in these questions. For example, how does the writer want us to respond to this character? Why is chiasmus used here? As Cullen explains, 'pushing' questions are also a form of fading, because they 'prompt learners to reach new conclusions independently, a key step towards achieving automaticity' (Cullen, 2019).

Below is a useful template that guides students in how to craft questions for surface-level and deeper understanding. This one uses a visual, but it could be adapted to develop questions around a specific topic or skill.

Second / First	Is/does *Present*	Did/was *Past*	Can *Possibility*	Could/ would/ should *Probability*	Will *Prediction*	Might *Imagination*
What... *Event*						
Where... *Place*						
When... *Time*						
Who... *Person*						
Why... *Reason*						
How... *Meaning*						

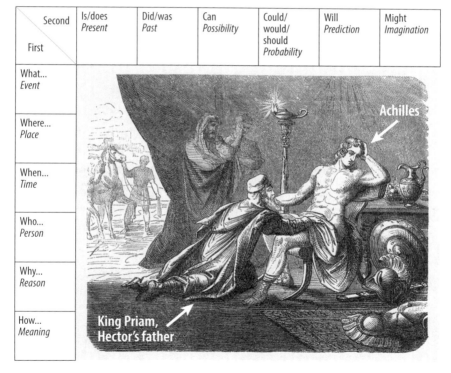

Image: iStock/ZU_09

As with everything we want students to master, two things are key: expert modelling and repetition. Repeated modelling of these strategies, where students listen to the thought process, language and methods of an expert, will lead them along the novice-to-expert continuum. They will gain in confidence and proficiency – and learn from their mistakes.

Quiz

1. What questions could students ask when coaching?
2. What is 'tip, tip, teach, try again' and why is it useful?
3. What is elaborative interrogation?
4. Name one elaboration stem.
5. Name one other type of questioning.

Reflection

1. How is questioning taught in your context?
2. Is CPD needed on questioning strategies?
3. Do students have opportunities to 'coach' each other in your context?
4. Do students have opportunities to explain their thinking aloud in your context?
5. Is there a supportive environment among students in your context?

Summary

- Training up students to support each other with the revision process is very powerful.
- Although it takes practice, and careful and repeated modelling, students acting as coaches is very effective and requires them to develop metacognition.
- Explicit teaching of question crafting and the answering of different types of questions are key to effective revision.

Step 6
Revolutionary Wellbeing

Using the pastoral curriculum to teach students the science of learning

Spring term: January/February

> **In a nutshell**
> For a sustainable revolution, effective revision needs to become part of the school culture. It needs to be seen everywhere! This chapter considers how we can make use of the pastoral curriculum to teach students about the science of learning, transforming revision from a mysterious task that students know they 'should' do, but have no idea how to approach, into something clear and transparent.

In my university days, there was a thing called 'pulling an all-nighter'. Not as glamorous as it sounds, this involved studying for the majority of the night before an assignment deadline or exam. This was a firm part of university culture and people would declare with pride, 'I had to pull an all-nighter to get this essay in!'

Where should I begin with the problems surrounding this? First, there are the health implications of forgoing sleep in order to hit a deadline, undoubtedly fuelled by sugary snacks and high-caffeine drinks. Second, the 'cramming' nature of this learning means it's likely to be forgotten quickly – certainly not what we want for our students as they enter the world of academia. Third, what terrible preparation for the real world, where this kind of behaviour would be seen as unprofessional.

This is why we need a culture shift. We know cramming is ineffective, but students gravitate towards this approach. It seems to be human nature to need a sense of urgency in order to actually practise or prepare for something. For example, I love singing. During lockdown – arguably the best opportunity to get lots of singing practice in – I didn't sing at all except for bedtime lullabies to my children. I need something high-stakes hurtling towards me – such as a concert, audition or show – in order to thoroughly practise. It seems I'm not alone. The rest of my quartet said the same and in our first rehearsal after lockdown we were all back to using our previously memorised music sheets. If this is such an ingrained part of our modern lifestyle, prioritising social media over study until something high-stakes is looming, it's going to take real effort to shift away from these habits to more effective, spaced practice.

Students need constant reminders not only of the drawbacks of cramming but of the better, more healthy alternatives. They need to know about spacing, why it's effective and how to implement it into a revision timetable. Also, as previously mentioned in this book, for our revolution to be successful and sustainable, revision needs to be a whole-school endeavour: something everyone believes in and values. This should be a consistent message received by both students and parents. Visitors to the school should feel a tangible culture of revision. Making effective study methods a part of the pastoral curriculum will not only place staff in a position where they are driving this culture shift, but will also serve as CPD by improving their knowledge of research-based study methods. After all, what's one of the best ways to learn something? Teach it!

I fully recognise and support the statutory inclusion of certain topics in a PSHE curriculum, such as drugs, child exploitation and sex education. However, I doubt that all schools always use their PSHE time effectively. When I was at school, I spent quite a lot of time making posters and colouring in during PSHE. Admittedly, this was a while ago, but more recently I covered a PSHE lesson where students were tasked with writing a letter to their future selves for 25 minutes. Although this will not have a hugely detrimental impact on the vast majority of students, activities such as this, which are arguably time-fillers, can further disadvantage those students who simply can't afford to not be learning.

In *Powerful Teaching*, Agarwal and Bain split students into three categories:

1. 'Group 1 tends to be students who learn easily and retain information through the use of feedback. They generally do well in all their lessons.
2. Group 2, the most common, includes the students who learn best when a topic is introduced, followed by review and reinforcement through feedback, and then additional review and reinforcement through feedback.
3. Group 3 includes the students who, despite the introduction, reinforcements, and feedback, still struggle with information. Their frustration often impacts their motivation.' (Agarwal & Bain, 2019)

We owe it to all students, but particularly this third group, to make the most of all the time we have with them. These students need to be explicitly taught how to learn. They need to know what they know and what they don't know. We need to take all opportunities to increase their motivation. As Bain says, 'once students see that they are able to pass, I see their pride and effort increase.'

In this chapter we'll discuss a pastoral curriculum model designed to advantage all students, especially that third group. It's intended for use in PSHE or wellbeing lessons and slides for all year group sessions can be accessed by following this QR code.

www.teachertoolkit.co.uk/wp-content/uploads/2021/12/ The-Revision-Revolution-Resources-1.pdf

A note on diversity

A lot has been written recently about the importance of diversifying the curriculum in order for students of all backgrounds to see themselves reflected in it. I've aimed to use a range of example role models in this pastoral curriculum, from inspirational working-class footballers, such as Marcus Rashford, to girls who defy the odds, such as Malala Yousafzai and Greta Thunberg. Hopefully, these sessions will demonstrate to students how success comes in all forms, backgrounds and ethnicities.

Building a pastoral revision curriculum

	Session 1	**Session 2**	**Session 3**
Year 7	Demystifying revision. What is revision? What is retrieval? Self-quizzing, brain dumps and flashcards.	How we learn. Desirable difficulties. How memory works: the Ebbinghaus forgetting curve and schema.	Automaticity and the benefits of overlearning.
Year 8	Creating the best environment for study. Effective study habits: metacognition.	How to take notes effectively: Cornell notes; abbreviations.	Retrieve-taking; developing notes into sentences/ paragraphs.
Year 9	Writing process: planning – drafting – editing – redrafting.	Effective study habits: interrogative elaboration	Effective study habits: dual coding (mapping/drawing and graphic organisers).
Year 10	Effective study habits: concrete examples, analogies and anecdotes. Examples and non-examples using the Frayer model.	Generative learning strategies: self-explaining and teaching.	How to design an effective revision timetable and remain healthy during exam season.
Year 11	Independent revision.	Independent revision.	Independent revision.

Year 7

I've suggested starting in Year 7 with a session that demystifies revision. The headteacher Sonia Thompson reminds us that students arrive with 'backpacks of knowledge' (Newmark, 2021); they also arrive with backpacks of preconceptions and misconceptions. They all have their own ideas about revision, informed either by older siblings, teachers or their own personal experience. Session 1, therefore, begins by debunking revision myths and establishing three simple strategies for effective study: brain dumps, self-quizzing and flashcards. These strategies will be used across the pastoral curriculum to help students remember and understand the learning.

The focus for session 2 is how we learn. We look at desirable difficulties, because effortful learning doesn't feel comfortable and this may lead to resistance from students. We need to explain the science behind learning, so students know that with challenge comes success – but not overnight. Difficulty can feel unpleasant, frustrating, even maddening and I think we need to be honest about that. Nevertheless, there are huge long-term benefits, so students should stick with it! This doesn't mean they should silently struggle – support will always be available. With knowledge, we either use it or lose it, but using it can feel hard, especially at first.

By explaining about schema, and about Ebbinghaus' forgetting curve, students can see how quickly we forget, but also how items of knowledge connect to enable us to understand. I often tell my classes that I know a lot of their set texts off by heart, particularly the important quotes. Why? Because I've taught them repeatedly, planned lessons on them, assessed them and thought deeply about them. For me, reeling off these quotes has become automatic – I rarely forget them and, if I do, a small cue recalls them to me.

Session 3 in Year 7 explores automaticity and how learning something to a point of mastery can be helpful in accessing more complex thinking. As an example, I struggled with maths at school, but my mum ran a programme of 'overlearning' simple maths. It was through this programme that basic addition, subtraction and multiplication became automatic for me. I remember finding fractions easy while the rest of my class found them hard (a first for me!) and this was without doubt because of my ability to quickly work out the steps involved in solving the fraction.

Year 8

The modern world is full of distractions and in Year 8 our pastoral curriculum begins by exploring with students how to create an environment conducive to learning. This means the removal of technology. Of course, they might be using technology to facilitate their revision – watching a video, for example. In this case, phones need to be in flight mode so that texts, social media updates and phone calls don't distract from learning. Barry Zimmerman states that effective learners restructure their 'physical and social context to make it compatible with [their] goals' (Zimmerman, 2002). Without a teacher present, students need to independently manage their motivation for study. As Alex Quigley says, they need to 'delay immediate gratification' to support their long-term learning goals (Quigley, 2018).

Session 1 also looks at metacognition and its relevance to an effective study session: students can round off their revision by making a note of their successes, as well as areas where they struggled and therefore need to focus their attention in future study sessions. We want students to be trained to use metacognition as soon as possible. As John Flavell explains, 'I am being metacognitive if I notice that I am having more trouble learning A than B; if it strikes me that I should double-check C before accepting it as fact' (Flavell, 1976). Metacognition is, however, only part of becoming a self-regulated learner who has the following characteristics: goal-setting, independent, team worker, knows when to ask for help, knows where to find support, conscientious, driven.[6]

Session 2 focuses on writing as a key study skill. Effective note-taking is a skill that many sixth-form students and even undergraduates don't have, simply because it's not something they have ever been explicitly taught. However, effective note-taking is incredibly important in all subject areas – there's no subject that does not require students to read. Learning hinges largely on reading, and more so as students move into higher education, where they are expected to do significant amounts of independent study and research.

This second session looks at a set of abbreviations, modelling how to use these when picking out and summarising important points. Another

6 https://metacognition.org.uk/speedy-cpd

useful approach to summarising is providing each paragraph of text with a heading and reducing it to three key words. As always, this will need clear and repeated modelling.

The final session considers how to develop notes into beautiful sentences and paragraphs. It's worth using some of the strategies from *The Writing Revolution* here, such as explicit modelling of noun appositives, discourse markers and paragraph plans (Hochman & Wexler, 2017).

Year 9

Year 9 begins by looking at the writing process. Students need to see writing – in all subject areas – as an ongoing process of planning, drafting, editing and redrafting. See page 158 for an assembly that presents some first drafts of writers' masterpieces, full of scribbles and messy notes; they are far from perfect because they are works in progress. A recent study on writing for pleasure stresses the importance of explicitly teaching the writing process, as well as teaching self-regulation strategies (Young, 2019). Elisabeth Bowling's fantastic CPD session on teaching 'beautiful writing across secondary subjects' contains lots of ideas (Norwich Research School, 2020).

In session 2 we explore elaboration. Introducing students to some question stems and modelling how to use them in revision is a good starting point. If students are unable to use elaboration correctly, it could be counterproductive. By modelling how to write elaborative questions, where to find the answers, how to compare and how to look for connections to real-life experiences and memories, you make this skill explicit to students and enable them to use it successfully. Consider the following sample script that guides students through the process.

> **Teacher**: Most elaborative questions use 'how' and 'why' because these question stems require deeper understanding to reach an answer. Therefore, if we want to write questions to test our understanding of the oral tradition, our initial questions might be 'How does the oral tradition work?' and 'Why did the first storytellers use stock phrases, rhyme and epithets?' We could also ask, 'Why did storytellers recite their work from memory instead of reading from a script?' The answers to these questions are on our knowledge organiser and in

your exercise books from our first lesson on the *Iliad*, but our aim is to be able to retrieve the information without looking it up. In order to answer these questions, we need a secure surface understanding that the oral tradition meant storytellers recited their tales from memory, using stock phrases, epithets and rhyme to make their stories more memorable because they were not able to write their story down.

[Pause here and allow students to create their own elaborative questions on a topic they are familiar with, perhaps working in pairs. They should also attempt to answer them.]

To take this understanding further, we could compare this to modern advertising, which is full of types of epithets: slogans and rhymes specifically designed to be memorable so the consumer will buy the product. Some of them are influenced by Greek mythology. We could ask, 'Why are the brand names Hermes and Ambrosia derived from Greek mythology?' Answering this question requires us to understand that Hermes was the messenger god, suggesting the effectiveness and 'godly' speed of the parcel company, while Ambrosia was the food of the gods, forbidden for mere mortals, implying the custard is irresistible, 'heavenly' food.

[Pause here and allow students to compare two closely related topics or concepts, or to look for examples of a topic's usage in the modern world.]

In Step 2, I included a table of the most effective study methods (see page 45), which I suggested that you try to incorporate into your revision revolution. One of these methods is dual coding: the combining of visuals and words. In the third Year 9 pastoral session, which explores dual coding, you could show an image of Icarus to illustrate the word 'hubris'. Hubris is such an important concept across the curriculum: the hubristic scientist who uses genetic modification to create a new species; the psychology behind hubristic murderers who play God with human life; the hubristic media that can make or break careers. By telling the ancient story of Icarus, who attempts to transcend the limitations of human capability with dire consequences, students will understand the origins of the word – a punishment from the gods for human arrogance – and connect that to different areas of the curriculum. Because our brains privilege stories (Willingham, 2009), this combination of dual coding and storytelling makes the target word and concept much more memorable – irresistible, even! Of course, there are countless examples of hubristic politicians in our modern world that students will be able to recognise.

Students can apply dual coding to their own revision, using images on flashcards to explain key concepts or vocabulary words, telling the story that goes with them where appropriate. This third session, however, is about more than just images. Graphic organisers can be used to organise knowledge, helping identify links and strengthening memory and understanding. The more visuals students create to represent one single idea, the clearer it should become. Look at the examples below: three graphic organisers to represent the chain of events leading to the deaths of Romeo and Juliet.

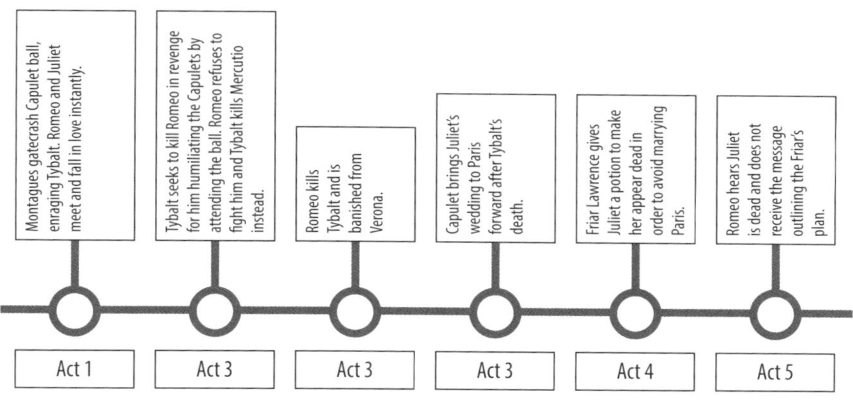

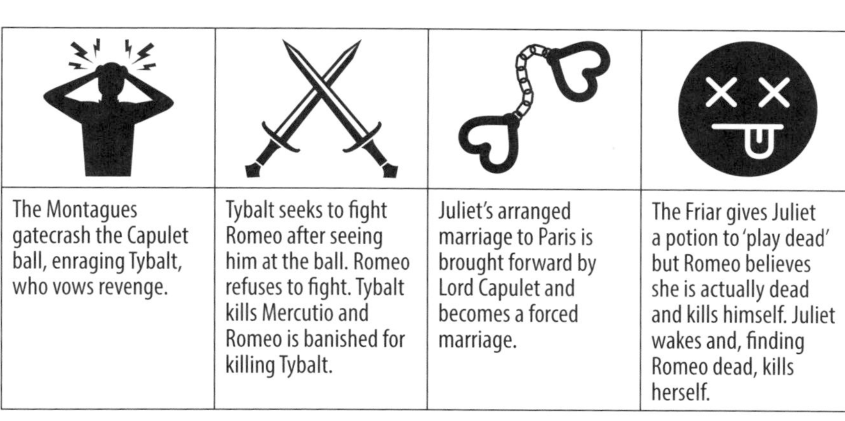

The Montagues gatecrash the Capulet ball, enraging Tybalt, who vows revenge.
Tybalt seeks to fight Romeo after seeing him at the ball. Romeo refuses to fight. Tybalt kills Mercutio and Romeo is banished for killing Tybalt.
Juliet's arranged marriage to Paris is brought forward by Lord Capulet and becomes a forced marriage.
The Friar gives Juliet a potion to 'play dead' but Romeo believes she is actually dead and kills himself. Juliet wakes and, finding Romeo dead, kills herself.

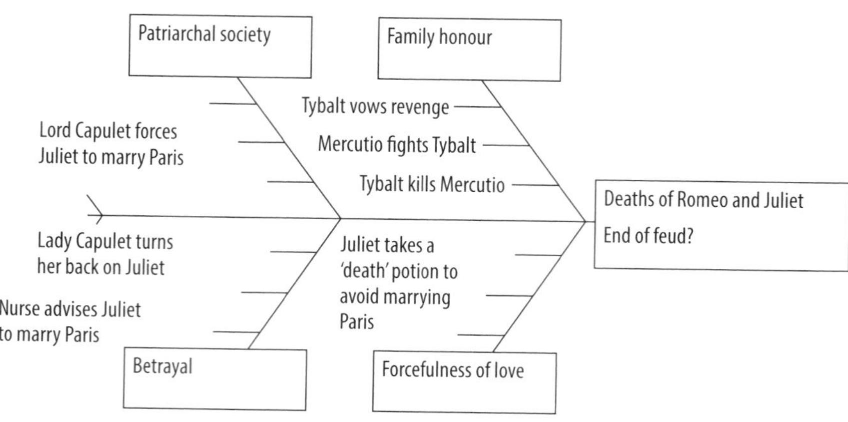

Each organiser presents the events in a different way, encouraging students to think deeply about the theme of blame in the play. The first is a timeline, putting the events in order. Students should see that many pivotal events happen in Act 3 and begin to think about the significance of this – or about possible exam questions focusing on this act. The second organiser is a cartoon strip, using simple pictures to represent important events in the chain. The third is a fishbone diagram that shows cause and effect; it's more complex as it categorises the events into themes, forcing students to consider Shakespeare's intentions in using this chain of events. These same diagrams could easily be used for history. Students could timeline the chain of events leading to Hitler's rise to power; they could use simple pictures to represent the most important events in cartoon strip form; and they could use a fishbone diagram to group the events into economic, social and political factors.

When I began my teacher training in 2009, we were taught to appeal to students' learning styles. We were led to believe each student had a natural preference: visual, auditory or kinaesthetic. Whether or not this is a myth, it has caused problems in education such as some students developing a fixed mindset: they might believe they 'can't do' certain subjects because they are a 'visual learner', or that they need to act out how particles move in science lessons because they are a 'kinaesthetic learner'. A better approach, as advocated by the Learning Scientists (Sumeracki, 2019), is to think about the most appropriate multimodal approach for the skill being taught, as well as how many different ways you can present, explain and teach that same skill. For example, a food technology teacher is unlikely to teach their students to bake a cake through reading instructions in a textbook alone; they are more likely to show them the process step by step, as you would see on a cooking programme. Similarly, a geography teacher is unlikely to rely solely on a verbal description of a map, as they know students need to see a visual representation of it.

My sister is a physiotherapist. As part of her training, she watched several procedures on patients (visual), performed procedures herself (kinaesthetic) while receiving auditory feedback, and completed set journal reading on important research linked to physiotherapy. No one tested her to ascertain her preferred learning style before her training, because this kind of multimodal approach is beneficial for all learners. It's about 'considering what representations … best match the topic being learned' (Sumeracki, 2019). None of us would get very far learning to drive by reading a book, or learning to play tennis by watching Wimbledon (Didau, 2015a)!

Graphic organisers can also be used to make connections between different items of knowledge, which helps to ensure learning enters long-term memory. Categorising information by comparing, contrasting or listing (according to importance, etc.) can therefore be a useful revision strategy. Students might explore pros and cons, advantages and disadvantages, reasons for and against, or similarities and differences. Consider the following examples:

Achilles is a valiant, benevolent hero	**Achilles is a bloodthirsty murderer**
'Why all the weeping? Speak out now, don't conceal it, let us share it' 'No other Achaean had the strength to wield it, only Achilles' 'As you wished sir the body of your son is set free'	'Achilles picked twelve young men to pay the price for dead Patroclus' 'Would god my passion drove me to slaughter you and eat you raw, you've caused such agony to me!' 'Achilles had in mind for Hector's body outrage and shame'

Nuclear power	
Pros	*Cons*
Cheap. High power output. Creates jobs for local community.	Non-renewable. Danger of nuclear explosion. Pollution.

Judaism and Christianity	
Similarities	*Differences*
Based on the Old Testament. Monotheistic religions. Belief in Jesus. Suffered persecution.	Place of worship: church versus synagogue. Traditions: Christmas versus Hanukkah. Religious figures: priests versus rabbis. Views on messiahs.

In the first example, I've modelled the categorisation of quotes into those that show a benevolent side of Achilles and those that show a malevolent side. I can then extend this into a paragraph, explaining the quotes and ideas. This encourages students to explore different interpretations and viewpoints, adding extra layers of analysis to their writing. The factual knowledge of the character Achilles, the plot of the *Iliad* and relevant quotes enable students to develop complex arguments and debates.

The second example categorises the advantages and disadvantages of nuclear power, which could then be compared to other power sources to evaluate and debate its use for electricity. The third example compares Christianity and Judaism to help students understand the important and sometimes subtle differences between these beliefs. Explicitly modelling for students how they might categorise different information will help them 'form sound schemata of their own' (Sherrington, 2019) by making links between items of knowledge and embedding these into long-term memory.

It's a good idea to model strategies that can be used for comparison, such as Venn diagrams. The following example explores some similarities and differences between classical and baroque music.

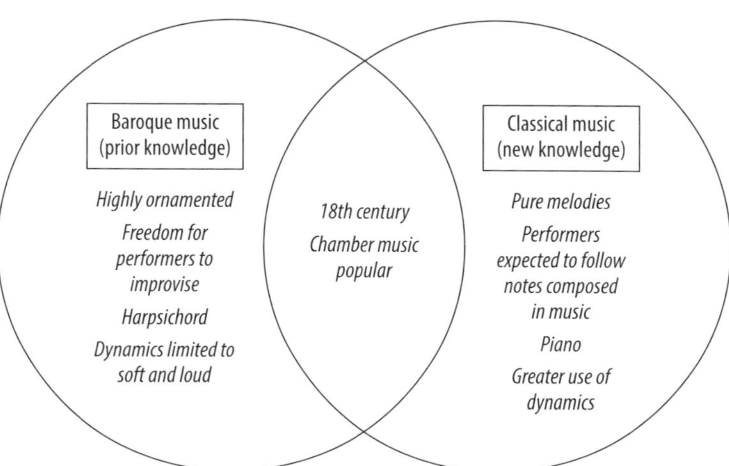

In this diagram, students' understanding of the classical era is framed by their existing knowledge of baroque music. They are able to understand pure melodies because they have already studied and listened to 'highly ornamented' music, therefore will notice the absence of these ornamentations and flourishes. They already understand the concept of improvisation, therefore will know what it means for musicians to be restricted to the notes written. They will be familiar with the harpsichord and recognise it as a predecessor to the piano with a different sound, and they will know what is meant by dynamics, though they will hear more layers of volume in classical music. They are adding to their schema of knowledge. This is how elaboration works: by making connections to a secure prior knowledge base.

As David Didau explains, 'the more items [of knowledge] and the greater the number of connections between items, the easier it becomes to draw the entire schema into working memory' (Didau, 2018b).

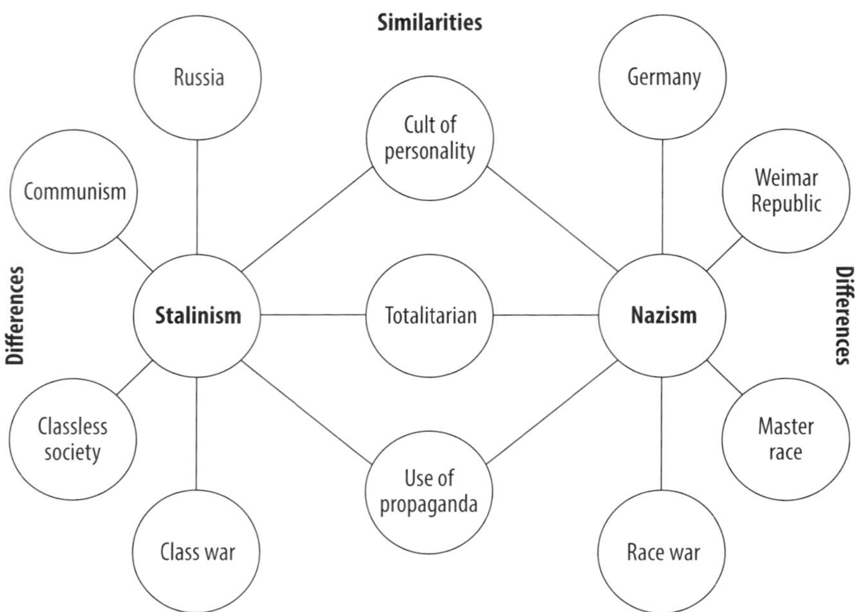

This graphic contrasts the ideologies of Nazism and Stalinism. It's a simple and visual starting point, but each point of similarity and difference can be elaborated on and developed into a sentence or full paragraph of revision. For example, students could take the 'totalitarian' point and develop it into: 'Both Stalinism and Nazism were totalitarian regimes with total control, restricting any opposition to their rule.'

When explaining dual coding to students, it may also be worth talking about cognitive load and how this can inform their use of diagrams. Essentially, the simpler the diagram, the more effective it will be in not overwhelming working memory. *The Science of Learning* cites the 'split-attention effect', where 'having to receive information from two or more sources can place a burden on working memory, as focus is being spread too thinly' (Watson & Busch, 2021). Watson and Busch report that 'integrated diagrams', where parts of the image and its explanation are combined, are more effective than 'conventional diagrams' that might include a key, requiring students to look at both the image and its explanation separately.

Year 10

Although concrete examples is one of the effective study strategies cited in Step 2 (see page 45), it is one of the more complex, which is why our pastoral curriculum introduces concrete examples in Year 10, once students have a secure understanding of retrieval, spacing, dual coding and elaboration.

In Andy Tharby's *How to Explain Absolutely Anything to Absolutely Anyone* (2018), he writes about the power of stories and metaphor in explanations. We know our brains are wired to create and remember stories – metaphors and analogies can be effective in making the abstract concrete.

One aspect of maths that students typically struggle with is fractions, but understanding fractions is key to understanding other areas of maths, and to being able to complete daily activities such as following recipes, working out discounts, comparing bank accounts and more. It can be very helpful to use concrete examples when teaching fractions, so students don't just see an abstract figure. On a very simple level, this may involve an image of a cake split into four pieces to represent quarters. Two of those pieces could be shaded to represent two-quarters or a half, which could lead into a concrete example of calculations such as ¼ + ¼ + ¼ = ¾ and an introduction to technical terms such as 'denominator' and 'numerator'.

With a toddler living in our house, I watch a lot of CBeebies. These programmes use concrete examples in order to explain abstract ideas and technical terms to young children. For example, *Go Jetters* (if you're not familiar with this programme, four characters 'jet' round the world visiting different landmarks) explains 'climate' and 'irrigation' by showing how different food crops are grown in different countries depending on their 'patterns of weather' (climate). The characters explain how some crops prefer a warm climate whereas others need wetter climates. Therefore, in dry climates some farmers store water and move it to the fields using special pipes; this is called 'irrigation'. Instead of beginning with an overly complex, technical definition, the programme presents accessible and tangible examples followed by simple child-friendly definitions, all using everyday language. What a fantastic, broken-down explanation of a potentially very complex concept, particularly for toddlers.

In his blog, science teacher Pritesh Raichura writes about how he used to start lessons with a definition ('a vacuous string of words devoid of meaning') but now begins with concrete examples – something 'pupils will have experienced so know exactly what they mean' (Raichura, 2019). He discusses how students can link those concrete examples to the definition, making it easier to comprehend. The example he gives is homeostasis. Instead of the incredibly complex and abstract definition, Raichura starts with several concrete examples (the more, the better):

- 'Imagine you are exercising. Your body temperature goes up. How does your body respond? You sweat, cooling your body down. On the other hand, on a cold winter day, as soon as your body temperature goes down, your muscles start shivering which warms you back up. So, when your body temperature goes up, your body does something to bring it back down. When it goes down, your body does something to bring it back up.'
- 'What happens if you drink too much water? You may need to visit the loo more often – you urinate more. What happens when your body loses too much water, say on a really hot day? Well, you feel thirsty to increase your water levels. So: when your water levels go down, your body does something to make it go up and vice versa.'
- 'We call things like "body temperature" and "water levels in the body" our *internal environment* because they are *conditions inside* the body that might change.' (Raichura, 2019)

Raichura talks about examples and non-examples as an important part of making the abstract concrete and unpicking misconceptions. He says 'non-examples highlight concept boundaries', meaning they help to show the core feature of a concept as supposed to the surface feature(s). He cites the example of condensation: students are given the concrete examples of breath on a cold window, water droplets on a saucepan and steam on a bathroom mirror. All these examples share the core feature of a gas turning into a liquid as it cools, but also the surface feature of water droplets on glass. For this reason, Raichura emphasises the importance of sharing raindrops on a window as a non-example: these are water droplets on glass, but this is *not* a gas turning into a liquid. The diagram opposite illustrates how to use non-examples.

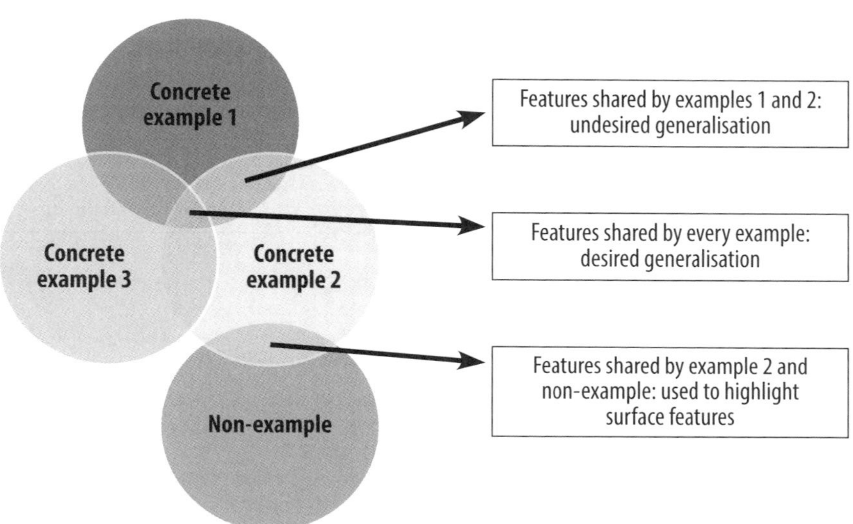

As part of their revision, students could use a Frayer model (see page 72) to outline examples and non-examples. Or they could be given a completed Frayer model and ask themselves why the non-examples do not share the core feature of the key term or concept. In the example overleaf, the non-examples of hubris all involve a form of arrogance or confidence but do not involve 'playing God' with lives or result in a fall.

Definition	Characteristics
Excessive pride before a fall. It was originally a punishment from the gods for too much arrogance.	• 'Playing God'. • Attempting to transcend boundaries of human limitation. • Arrogance. • Usually dire consequences.

HUBRIS
(N)

Examples	Non-examples
• Icarus flying too close to the sun and plummeting to his death. • Hitler attempting to take over the world and create a master race. • Victor Frankenstein's creation of a new species. • The corner-cutting making of the Titanic, which ultimately sank.	• Boxer Muhammed Ali saying 'I am the greatest'. • A rap battle where each rapper says they are better than the other. • Preparing well for an exam and believing you will get a high grade.

One of the best teachers I know uses analogies all the time and it's no coincidence that her students (of all abilities) do really well. I would advise pre-planning these analogies to make them really effective, unless you're very good at thinking on the spot (I am not!). Examples from the world around us can make abstract ideas more engaging and easier for students to understand, as well as adding to their cultural capital.

Here are two examples I use regularly in my teaching to make 'abstract' ideas concrete:

1. The idea of **desensitisation** is crucial when teaching literature, as many writers explore people's apathy towards suffering, death and destruction (for example, Carol Ann Duffy in the poem *War Photographer*). Many protagonists grow desensitised over time (Macbeth and Achilles both become less affected by the murders they commit). To explain this idea, I tell students about my sister, a physiotherapist, and how at the beginning of her training she would feel faint watching surgery. Over time it affected her less and less: she became desensitised and this was necessary for her to be effective in her job. Using a personal story makes it memorable to

students, as well as easy to understand. However, it's important to explain that this is a positive example of desensitisation, whereas the desensitisation we develop to horrors portrayed in the media is an element of human nature bemoaned by writers. I combine this with teaching the morphology of 'desensitisation', drawing students' attention to the prefix de- (meaning 'not'), the root 'sens' (meaning to feel) and the suffix -tion (which forms nouns = literally the act of no longer feeling).

2. To explain the idea of **hierarchy**, I often use the example of Premier League football (I know very little about football so have to check my facts beforehand!). At the top of the hierarchy, we have clubs like Manchester City that are successful in terms of matches won; this places them at or near the top of the Premier League. Manchester City is also one of the richest clubs, which means it can afford the best players, manager, training, etc. and is therefore at the top of the football hierarchy. Another example is the hierarchy at work in a school, with the headteacher at the top and students at the bottom (although this hierarchy could, of course, be contested!).

With these concrete examples, it's important to make the link explicit in order to avoid the 'curse of the expert', where we expect students to understand the connection between our example and the idea we're explaining. For my hierarchy explanation to be effective, I need to be explicit about how this relates to the topic being studied. I might say: 'Similar to the power held by the parents in the family home, the headteacher in school and the football club at the top of the Premier League, Macbeth – as King of Scotland – was finally at the top of the hierarchy, while female peasants were at the bottom, with no money or power and therefore very little status.' A table like the one overleaf could help make the link clear.

	Manchester City	**King Macbeth**
Status	Their position at or near the top of the Premier League.	His title of king.
Power	They are a rich club, therefore have the power to buy the best players, manager, coaches, etc. This directly influences their status.	As king, he makes all the decisions about Scotland: who to wage war against, who to honour, who to punish, etc.
Wealth	See above.	As king, Macbeth has the most luxurious castle, food, armour, etc.
Gender	Men's football has a higher status than women's, having been established for much longer, and the players are on much higher wages. I have two friends who are female football coaches and have to work very hard to be respected in a 'man's world'.	Being male in a patriarchal society meant Macbeth had more power/respect than a queen would have, especially with his military background where he proved his bravery and physical strength.

Equally, metaphors can be a very effective way of explaining abstract concepts. They are all around us, explaining everything from feelings ('I feel down/blue/a black cloud hanging over me') to attitudes ('she was put on a pedestal while I was talked down to') and descriptions ('silence is golden', 'the traffic flowed'). Tharby writes about how human beings think in metaphors (Tharby, 2018). He also cites Aristotle's belief that 'the soul never thinks without a picture'. Visual metaphors, therefore, can be helpful, especially when some students lack the shared cultural references the metaphor depends on.

Tharby gives the example of a geography teacher drawing a hard-boiled egg to represent the earth's layers – 'the crust is brittle and broken into pieces like the cracked shell of a hardboiled egg. The mantle is like the egg white, the core is like the yolk in the centre' (Tharby, 2018). The effectiveness of this metaphor lies in its simplicity, but also in the way it allows students to 'see what is not visible. In this case, the seemingly unknowable depths of the earth beneath our feet.' Tharby does warn, however, that 'simple sources … belie the complexity of the targets on which they aim to shed light'. This underlines the importance of non-examples to illustrate how the egg is like the earth but also unlike the earth.

Students may be able to link abstract concepts to analogies in their own lives, although metaphors are much harder. They could, however, collect analogies and metaphors used in class and practise retrieving them in a study session, explaining how they are relevant.

With concrete examples, it's important to provide multiple examples so that students don't associate desensitisation just with the sphere of medicine or hierarchy just with the Premier League. And a 2007 study highlights the idea of 'concreteness fading': it's important that, over time, key components of the concrete example are replaced by abstract representations. For example, 'Initial learning about the ecological concept of competitive specialisation used images of ants seeking food [concrete example] ... as students gain experience with the concept, the ants were replaced with black dots, and the food sources with green patches' (Pashler et al, 2007).

The second session in Year 10 looks at Fiorella and Mayer's generative learning strategies. Generative learning links back to the work done in Year 7 on schema, as it's a 'theory of learning that suggests pupils create understanding of what is to be learnt through a process of selecting information, organising it and then integrating it into what they already know' (Enser & Enser, 2020). It's based on an idea we've already explored: that 'learning depends on what students think about' (Enser & Enser, 2020), which depends on what they already know. You can't think about what you don't know! Eight generative learning strategies are listed in the table on the next page, along with their effect size (Enser & Enser, 2020). Some have more evidence behind them than others, and some (e.g. drawing, enacting) could be subject to lethal mutations if not explored in enough depth.

	Effect size	Why included/not included in pastoral curriculum
Summarisation	0.5	Summary skills are explored in Year 8 as part of the writing focus.
Mapping	0.62	Mapping and drawing can both be explored as part of the dual coding session in Year 9.
Drawing	0.4	As above.
Imagining	0.65	Difficult to pin down!
Self-testing	0.62	Explored as part of retrieval.
Self-explaining	0.61	High effect size and linked to metacognition.
Teaching	0.77	As above.
Enacting	0.51	Subject to lethal mutations unless explored in depth.

Self-explaining and teaching are two key strategies that link to metacognition. Self-explaining has similarities to elaboration, in that it involves elaborating on material covered in order to explain it to yourself. Students explain by asking themselves questions like 'Why is this the case?' and 'What would happen if…?' The key difference, however, is that they should reach a point where they are able to interrogate their own explanation. In their book *Fiorella & Mayer's Generative Learning in Action*, Zoe and Mark Enser suggest the following prompts:

- '**Classify their thinking**: "What do you already know about this topic?"
- **Probe assumptions**: "What additional evidence would lead to you reaching a different answer to this question?"
- **Demand evidence**: "What evidence have you got for the conclusion you have reached?"
- **Alternative viewpoints**: "Who would disagree with the conclusion you have reached?"
- **Explore implications**: "What are the implications for your conclusion? What would need to happen or change?"
- **Question the question**: "Why do you think this was an important question to ask?"' (Enser & Enser, 2020)

Enser and Enser also offer the following examples of how self-explaining might be used in different subject areas:

- 'In maths, before embarking on a set of questions, the learner might explain the process to themselves.
- In science, before completing a practical, the learner might explain the process they will be carrying out. This should enable them to then concentrate on what is to be learnt rather than the mechanism of carrying out the work.
- In religious education, the learner might explain to themselves the origin of the views of a particular faith on an issue being studied.' (Enser & Enser, 2020)

Whenever I teach something, my knowledge and understanding of the topic develop and I'm forced to be very reflective on the gaps in my own knowledge and about how I could have taught the topic better. Teaching has been found to be most effective as a generative strategy when students *know* they will be called upon later to teach the learning. This is for the same reason that closed-book quizzes are more effective than open-book ones – students know they will be held to account!

Enser and Enser outline some of the benefits of teaching as a generative learning strategy:

- 'Firstly, the preparation stage, in which students would select and begin to organise their understanding of the materials, thinking hard at this initial stage in order to make appropriate selections as they study.
- Secondly, the act of explaining encourages students to actively engage in the materials, again selecting, reorganising and drawing on prior knowledge in order to make the ideas as clear as possible.
- Finally, when interactions take place between tutor and tutee such as through deep questioning, metacognitive processes are employed as the teacher reflects on their own understanding of the material and restructures it as necessary.' (Enser & Enser, 2020)

This can be an incredibly simple and effective revision strategy: students just need a partner to teach their topic to, and they could even quiz them on it afterwards to see how effective their teaching was. Enser and Enser recommend providing access to teacher guidance and/or high-quality resources at the preparation stage to avoid students sharing misconceptions.

In *The Science of Learning*, Watson and Busch report that 'students who had been expecting to teach the material to someone else remembered more of the material and did so in a more efficient way than those who thought there was going to be a test' (Watson & Busch, 2021). 'Expecting to teach someone helps the learner categorise the most important information and encourages them to thoroughly go over what they do and don't know in preparation for tough questions', and it also 'encourages self-explanation and elaborative interrogation' (Enser & Enser, 2020).

One possible homework could be asking students to watch different Massolit lectures[7] and to teach the lecture to a partner. They could even write a retrieval quiz to test understanding.

Many schools use peer-tutoring programmes for reading and numeracy. The success of these programmes may depend in part on the quality of the training, but the act of students teaching each other can be empowering as well as impactful. At my old school, I ran a Literacy Leaders programme. Students had to apply and, if successful, they would listen to our weakest readers read aloud every week. Two particularly reluctant readers returned week after week and became regular library users, partly owing to the bond formed with these older 'role model' students.

The final Year 10 session explores wellbeing and the creation of an effective revision timetable. As we know, revision and wellbeing often do not go hand in hand and students are sometimes overwhelmed with stress during exam season. Hopefully, through the deliberate teaching of effective study habits, you will already have made great headway on reducing stress levels. It's always worth reminding students, however, that as much as they may feel the need to revise until 2am, the fact is that sleep, relaxation, nourishment and 'little and often' revision will much better prepare them for exam success.

Year 11

I've dedicated the whole of the Year 11 pastoral curriculum to developing a revision timetable and putting it into practice. At this point, students should be aware of the rationale behind spaced revision, retrieval practice, interleaving schemes, etc.

7 www.massolit.io

Below is a sample revision timetable that could form part of the pastoral curriculum for Year 11.

Monday	Tuesday	Wednesday	Thursday	Friday	Saturday	Sunday
One hour Revise theme of power in: *Macbeth* (20 mins) *Ozymandias* and *My Last Duchess* poems (20 mins) Make connections between presentation of power in above texts (20 mins)	Break day	One hour Revise theme of power in: *An Inspector Calls* (20 mins) *A Christmas Carol* (20 mins) Make connections between presentation of power in above texts (20 mins)	Break day	One hour Revise terminology for structure question (10 mins) Revise Dickens' structural choices in stave 1 of *A Christmas Carol* (20 mins) Revise Priestley's use of cliffhangers in *An Inspector Calls* (20 mins) Answer a structure question (10 mins)	One hour Revise theme of guilt in: *Macbeth* (20 mins) *Kamikaze* and *Remains* poems (20 mins) Make connections between presentation of guilt in above texts (20 mins)	Break day

Monday	**Tuesday**	**Wednesday**	**Thursday**	**Friday**	**Saturday**	**Sunday**
Break day	One hour Revise characterisation of witches in *Macbeth* (20 mins) Revise writers' attitudes by looking at two non-fiction texts on witches (40 mins)	Break day	One hour Revise theme of power in: *An Inspector Calls* (20 mins) *A Christmas Carol* (20 mins) Make connections between presentation of power in above texts (20 mins)	One hour Use opening of *A Christmas Carol* as mentor text for writing opening of a ghost story Reread opening, picking out effective techniques to create a frightening atmosphere (20 mins) Write descriptive piece using techniques identified above, aiming to evoke an eerie setting (30 mins) Proofread and edit (10 mins)	Break day	Break day

I'm not suggesting creating separate timetables for each subject area. This timetable is an example of how connections could be made across different topics in English, but you could spread this out further and interleave different subject areas into each study session. The timetable utilises *little and often* by scheduling an hour of revision most days, but it also takes into account research that shows leaving *small gaps* between study sessions (break days) is beneficial. The timetable also considers research that shows *making connections* between different topics and ideas strengthens memory; it's structured to revise by theme, writers' attitude and craft, rather than revising one topic in isolation. The topics are *mixed up*; however, it is important to return to each topic (the length of spacing will depend on the nearness of the exam).

For teachers going back over material, it's worth considering interleaving different topics and making explicit links between them, as well as including lots of retrieval quizzes as you go. Remember also to consider the forgetting curve and the optimum intervals to allow learning to enter long-term memory.

Quiz

1. How might automaticity contribute to effective learning?
2. What features are important in creating an effective study environment?
3. What is elaboration?
4. How can we develop effective concrete examples?
5. List some generative learning strategies.

Reflection

1. How could you include a pastoral revision curriculum within your context?
2. In what ways might you gradually increase the challenge and reduce the scaffold of your revision curriculum?
3. Which staff are best placed to lead on and develop a revision curriculum?
4. Could you align this curriculum with ongoing study skills CPD for staff?
5. How might you design a revision curriculum around statutory PSHE content?

Summary

- A pastoral curriculum can be a great opportunity to teach students effective study methods and continue staff CPD.
- Exploring the science of learning in the wider curriculum will support the strategies being used in core lessons.
- The pastoral curriculum should improve student wellbeing and create the culture of effective revision we are striving for.

Step 7
Senior Revolutionaries

Engaging adults and older students in the revision revolution

Spring term: March

In a nutshell
This chapter focuses on how we might engage SLT, pastoral leads, parents, governors and older students in supporting and driving forward our revision revolution. In order to build a tangible culture of effective study, all stakeholders need to have a shared vision and collaborate to create and sustain this culture.

I can't remember many assemblies from secondary school but I do have fond memories of primary school assemblies: singing hymns and listening to bible stories. I'm not religious, but there's something about the storytelling that is both seductive and memorable. The first part of this chapter will explore how assemblies can be used to tell powerful stories about success gained through studying, embracing desirable difficulties and critiquing the world in which we live. Assemblies are typically delivered by SLT or heads of year, so they are a great way to involve these key leaders in driving the revision revolution forward.

The second part of the chapter will explore how we can engage 'senior revolutionaries' in our revision revolution, by getting senior leaders to deliver study skills assemblies, recruiting senior students as revision role models and bringing parents on board with the revision process.

Using assemblies to reinforce effective study habits

Assemblies are brilliant for getting important messages across to entire year groups and for instilling healthy habits. For this reason, they can be a fantastic resource when it comes to reinforcing messages about revision.

Before explaining the assembly ideas included in this chapter, I want to emphasise that these are suggestions; choosing appropriate role models for an assembly, as well as inspirational stories, will be context-dependent. Your intake may include lots of students from a particular ethnic minority or who have different types of disadvantage. There may be issues within the community that you can tap into by citing a carefully chosen historical figure or anecdote. The assembly sessions explored in this chapter are aligned with the pastoral curriculum (Step 6) where it's possible and logical to do so.

Opposite is a suggested assembly timetable, accompanied by a QR code that will take you to a fully resourced set of slides to use for this chapter's assemblies or adapt as appropriate for your context. Assemblies are a great way to reward students for hard work and effort. Consider implementing a revision rewards system in your school. Form tutors could lead on this, as they know the students in their form incredibly well and are aware of their strengths, their struggles and their levels of confidence, as well as having regular interactions with parents. Which students have form tutors noticed putting effective study strategies into action regularly and successfully? What have they achieved or what gains have they made as a result? Is there a student who struggles in maths but has used the Leitner system to practise their times tables to mastery, so they now find fractions much easier? At the end of each assembly, I've included a slide to reward exceptional study should you wish to.

Year	Assembly 1	Assembly 2
7	Embracing desirable difficulties. Concrete example: endless possibilities – Newton, Einstein, Hawking, etc.	Sweating the small stuff: how to make marginal gains. Concrete example: British Cycling team.
8	Developing automaticity: the power of repetition. Concrete example: professional musicians/ learning to drive.	The making of a masterpiece. Concrete example: famous writers' first drafts.
9	Metacognition and challenging the world! Concrete example: Greta Thunberg and Malala.	Metacognition and the danger of fake news. Concrete example: the internet.
10	The power of pictures and stories. Concrete example: Picasso's *Guernica* and Klimt's *The Kiss*.	Teaching as revision. Concrete example: Einstein.

www.teachertoolkit.co.uk/wp-content/uploads/2021/12/The-Revision-Revolution-Resources-1.pdf

Year 7

In the first of our assemblies for Year 7, we can let students know they are all capable of brilliance if they embrace desirable difficulties. There are so many examples we could use here. Perhaps start with a picture of some 'greats' – Newton, Einstein, Shakespeare, Martin Luther King Jr, Bill Gates, Marie Curie, Picasso, Stephen Hawking, Leonardo da Vinci, Marcus Rashford – and ask what they all have in common. Did their achievements come easy? Of course not. Newton's *Principia* was the culmination of more than 20 years of thinking. Einstein, although his name is now an eponym for genius, did not consider himself one; he recognised the importance of continually asking questions and described himself as 'passionately curious'.

In *The Science of Learning*, Watson and Busch report on a study that found 'hearing about successful scientists who struggled either in their personal or professional lives ... led to these students going on to achieve better grades than those who had just heard about their greatest achievement' (Watson & Busch, 2021). Interestingly, 'this effect was most pronounced in students who were currently struggling academically in their science lessons', which emphasises the importance of building a culture of effective study for all in order to narrow the achievement gap and address educational disadvantage.

The research concluded that 'teaching students about how others have had to overcome struggles on their way to success can be implemented in classrooms to improve motivation and learning in science, and likely other subjects too' (Watson & Busch, 2021). The important mindset shift is away from believing that success in a subject is down to natural talent and towards recognising that hard work and determination can overcome barriers. Watson and Busch write of a 'self-fulfilling prophecy' where students link failures to lack of intelligence and therefore reduce effort, 'as they believe they can do little to affect their outcome'. This is called 'learned helplessness'.

Taking risks and learning through failure are important desirable difficulties. You might, of course, have your own stories of overcoming difficulties to share in an assembly. Perhaps this is a slightly dated example, but I always return to Alex Ferguson's description of David Beckham as 'Britain's finest striker of a football not because of God-given talent but because he practises with a relentless application that the vast majority of less gifted players wouldn't contemplate'. Marcus Rashford is a more contemporary example of someone with humble beginnings who has gone on to play football for a Premier League club through sheer hard work and self-belief.

In the second Year 7 assembly, we can debunk the famous phrase 'practice makes perfect'. In fact, only perfect practice makes perfect (Lemov et al, 2012). As any successful professional will tell you, in order to improve we need to fine-tune small areas; it's this ability to focus on the detail that separates a good amateur from a professional. I remember watching a professional singer perform one of the songs from my repertoire: she could sing even high notes quietly, but with power and expression. Singing softly in the upper range is incredibly difficult, but she had clearly spent hours perfectly practising this skill. This is one of the ways to differentiate an amateur from a professional: their absolute mastery of their craft.

There's a theory that if you practise any skill for 10,000 hours, you can master it. This can be traced back to a study showing that, by the age of 20, elite violinists had practised for an average of 10,000 hours, compared with the 4,000 hours completed by their less proficient counterparts (Ericsson et al, 1993). However, it can be argued that the *quality* of practice is more important.

Students love learning about their teachers' private lives, so a personal example might work well here. For instance, when I'm preparing for a concert with my operatic quartet, I don't make any progress by just singing the songs again and again. I isolate tricky phrases, rhythms or harmonies and practise them repeatedly, sometimes taking the words out and singing on a vowel before slowly adding the words back in. I might practise a phrase slowly and then speed it up. Mastering singing the phrase too fast ensures I can sing it easily at the correct speed. In other words, I 'overlearn' it. It's the same with revision. Repeatedly completing exam questions won't improve students' exam grades. Students need to practise the tricky parts, refine them and put their answers together piece by piece.

Stories are powerful, as are quotes and ambitions, so there's lots of scope here for impactful assemblies. You could begin with an inspirational quote showing the equation between hard work and success, then lead into a story of someone who has developed effective habits to reach a goal. One example is the British Cycling team and their success in the Olympics. Dave Brailsford was hired as performance director in 2003 and focused on a strategy of marginal gains, 'the philosophy of searching for a tiny margin of improvement in everything you do' (Clear, 2018). Five years later, this previously mediocre team 'dominated the road and track cycling events at the 2008 Olympic Games in Beijing, where they won an astounding 60 percent of the gold medals available' (Clear, 2018). Brailsford had achieved hundreds of small improvements through changes such as redesigning the bike seats, giving the riders more comfortable pillows and mattresses, and making sure they washed their hands thoroughly to prevent illness.

Our brains privilege stories (Willingham, 2009) and these are the kinds of assemblies that will stick with students as long as the message is made explicit: how can they make small changes for big gains? The tweaks might include a bedtime routine, some dedicated time away from their phone or showing kindness to a friend.

This book has made several references to the importance of risk-taking. What better way to illustrate the necessity of risk than telling the story of a toddler learning to walk? Fear is a learned response. When my son first began to walk, I was constantly chasing after him; I was worried he might fall down the stairs or bang his head, but he was fearless. Over time, I realised that he knew how to turn his body around on the stairs and avoid trapping his fingers in the door. What's more, he *needed* a few minor falls to become secure in walking and climbing – no learning happens without risk and no learning happens without mistakes. A fall might result in some tears, but it didn't mean he gave up. He tried again and continued to get better until walking became automatic. It's how we respond to our mistakes, learning from them and building on them, that's important.

Year 8

I recently watched a lovely video[8] in which the singer-songwriter Paul Simon shares the inspiration behind the classic song *Bridge Over Troubled Water*. He starts by explaining that the beginning of the melody came from a Bach chorale, but he quickly became stuck. His next inspiration was a gospel group and the central lyric comes from a scat singer. This fusion of influences reminds us not only of the importance of knowledge in the creation of a masterpiece, but also how that knowledge becomes automatic. At one point Simon talks about how his knowledge 'subconsciously influenced' him to use 'gospel changes'. This is the power of repeatedly practising to the point of automaticity: it can get us 'unstuck'. This particular video is only four minutes long and, although dated, it conveys a powerful message for the first assembly in Year 8. If offers a rare opportunity to hear from a creator about their choices and influences and how they fit together to create something original. It should also be refreshing for students to hear about a master becoming stuck.

The second assembly includes pictures of writers' first drafts, and artists' tales of false starts and dead ends that resulted in a masterpiece. The

8 https://youtu.be/qFt0cP-klQI

common theme running through these assemblies is summed up succinctly in the following quote, which has been attributed to the basketball coach Tim Notke: 'Hard work beats talent if talent doesn't work hard.' Students should see their work as a draft, not a finished product. Perfection doesn't come easily and nor should we expect it to.

Year 9

By Year 9, hopefully students are getting used to the concept of metacognition. Thinking about thinking allows us to challenge the world, just as Malala Yousafzai and Greta Thunberg saw injustice and decided to act. Both these young people have faced barriers – such as Donald Trump's attempts to publicly humiliate Thunberg via Twitter and the attempted murder of Malala by the Taliban in Pakistan – but they have overcome adversity and built awareness of important current issues. This is what we explore in the first Year 9 assembly.

The second assembly looks at 'fake news'. A quick Google search will bring up lots of articles full of false information that young people need to be able to interrogate. This skill is particularly important in the age of social media. Metacognition is closely linked to critical thinking, as both involve students evaluating their own thinking: 'Critical thinking is a metacognitive process that, through purposeful, reflective judgement, increases the chances of producing a logical conclusion to an argument or solution to a problem' (Dwyer et al, 2014).

The self-regulation cycle of planning, monitoring and evaluating is relevant and helpful for critical thinking, as it involves asking questions such as 'What are reliable sources of information I can learn from?' (planning), 'Does this information seem reliable and trustworthy?', 'How are my feelings impacting my thoughts?' (monitoring) and 'Why might some of the sources I've used/seen/read not be trustworthy and reliable?' (evaluating).

Critical thinking and metacognition share the goal of accurate learning and therefore lend themselves to weeding out misinformation. According to the International Association for Media and Communication Research, 'instances of metacognitive awareness enable individuals to discern a biasing influence and make corrections to adjust their perceptions, which may result in a more realistic assessment of the news they receive'.[9] This is essential in the modern world, where 'fake news' abounds.

We have a moral responsibility to help prevent students from internalising delusions and misinformation that serve the interest of others at the cost of their own, making them vulnerable to exploitation. We need to get students looking at examples of fake news, questioning them, identifying a self-serving purpose and noticing the warning signs of unreliability. We also need to help students recognise their own biases that may affect their vulnerability to misinformation. This is a great starting point for protecting young people from the growing threat of online misinformation.

Year 10

In the pastoral curriculum model presented in Step 6, dual coding is explored at the end of Year 9. An interesting assembly for Year 10 would consider the ability of pictures to tell a story and therefore help us remember our learning. I like the idea of showing Picasso's *Guernica*, which depicts the horrors of the Spanish Civil War, and telling the story of Picasso choosing to remove this painting from Spain as an act of protest until democracy was restored. Klimt's *The Kiss*, on the other hand, depicts lovers embracing – from a study in hate to a study in love. This is the power of images to help us understand and make sense of the world. To link back to the 'fake news' assembly in Year 9, propaganda images could be shown for students to interrogate.

The second assembly explores teaching as revision. There's a great quote, which some people attribute to Einstein: 'If you can't explain it to a six-year-old, you don't understand it well enough.' This quote speaks to the importance of teaching something to demonstrate our understanding. I'm not necessarily advocating that we seek out six-year-olds for our students to teach in study sessions (although there may be an opportunity for a transition project here!) but the link between teaching and understanding is clear.

There are no assemblies included in this chapter for Year 11. This is not because I don't think they are needed. Rather, as students navigate this time of high-stakes exams and thoughts about the future, you may want

9 https://iamcr.org/node/13101

to return to certain topics, focus on the issue of exam stress, or invite guest speakers.

Using form time to reinforce effective study habits

It's important that all staff are trained in what effective study habits look like and strategies to implement them, so they can have discussions with students in their form about how they are revising, ensuring those students are putting theory into practice and have the support they need.

Form tutors are asked to deliver a lot in a short space of time, so their input can be as simple as checking planners or equipment, or asking students to identify a homework where they have used an effective study habit such as a brain dump or the Leitner system. These kinds of conversations mean students are surrounded by rhetoric about learning. Equally, the tutor could facilitate paired discussions, listening in and repeating back to the class any interesting snippets they hear. Alternatively, they could spotlight a pair to feed back, or use cold-calling. It's worth telling students in advance if you're going to do this, in order to keep them on their toes.

Many schools have tutor reading programmes, which are a great chance to use and model some of these study habits within the reading. You could try a quick retrieval quiz or brain dump on the previous chapter, a paired conversation about what's happened so far, some Cornell notes on an important character or some flashcard quizzing on key vocabulary – the opportunities are endless!

If form tutors do nothing more than speak to students about the reasons why study strategies such as rereading and highlighting are ineffective (i.e. they are passive rather than active), this is a great starting point and helps keep the revision dialogue going. These discussions could be part of their pastoral curriculum lessons if time permits.

You can reinforce all this by having a page in students' planners that lists the most effective study strategies, with reasons and concrete examples (see the table overleaf). You could even include an extra column in the traditional planner pages where students list a strategy they have tried, signed off by parents.

Study skill	What is it?	Why use it?	Examples
Retrieval	Retrieving information from memory without any cues.	Retrieval is proven to develop long-term learning.	• Brain dump: write down everything you know about... • Self-quizzing: ask yourself specific questions about a topic, perhaps using a knowledge organiser or Cornell notes. • Flashcards: write questions or vocabulary words on one side and answers or definitions on the other.
Spacing	Retrieving information after a gap.	Spacing makes retrieval more difficult (in a desirable way!) by retrieving information just before we forget it.	• Complete a brain dump on a previous topic. • Include questions from previous topics in your self-quizzing. • Include questions from previous topics on flashcards.
Interleaving	Retrieving information from different topics or subject areas.	Again, by mixing different topics and/or subjects, retrieval is harder but more effective in the long-term.	• Complete a brain dump on two different topics or in two different subject areas. • Include questions from different topics and/or subjects in self-quizzing. • Include questions from different topics/subjects on flashcards.

Metacognition	Understanding how you learn as well as what your strengths and gaps are.	This means you are not reliant on the teacher when they are unavailable and can evaluate your own learning.	• Before you complete a task, ask yourself when you have completed something similar and what strategy you used. • After you have completed a task, label or explain the steps you took to complete it. • After you have completed a task, check it against class resources or a modelled example, and make a note of your successes and areas to revise and develop next time.
Dual coding	Combining visuals with words to help remember learning.	Using images is a proven way to strengthen memory.	• Draw a picture to go with a vocabulary word (you do not need to be an artist!). • Create flashcards with pictures and words on one side, definitions on the other. • Use graphic organisers, such as Venn diagrams, to organise your ideas.
Elaboration	Using questions to expand on answers and explanations.	This helps improve your understanding by adding detail to explanations with reasons.	• Create 'how' and 'why' questions about a topic. • Use questions to make links between topics, e.g. How is X similar to Y? • Answer the questions!

Department/year group meetings

Time, of course, is precious in department meetings. However, having a short slot when study skills can be discussed will keep them on the agenda. One teacher could share a retrieval strategy and the misconceptions that arose or the knowledge gaps that were revealed. A form tutor could share how their students used a revision timetable to space and chunk their revision in a manageable way. This is about maintaining the professional dialogue around effective study and keeping staff excited about moving forward with the revision revolution.

Student role models/peer tutors

Let's not underestimate the power of older students to influence the younger ones. If you're lucky enough to have a sixth form in your school, think about training up some Year 12 and 13 students in retrieval strategies and the science of learning. It's even more effective if these students started out in the Year 7 cohort that you trained up in Step 3.

If you don't have a sixth form, why not involve Years 10 and 11? Once students are in-role, there are copious opportunities to utilise them: as speakers at parents' evenings, speakers in assemblies, tutors for students, and they could even teach a lesson from the pastoral curriculum! As you reach the third year of your revision revolution, you could involve students in Year 9, who have benefited from the first two years of the pastoral curriculum and have a good understanding of effective study methods. These 'revision leads' could also be tasked with noticing students who are 'revision stars' to nominate for rewards in assembly. Perhaps these are the students who repeatedly attend study sessions with the revision leads or make a significant effort in those sessions. Perhaps these are the students who arrive at the sessions knowing exactly what their strengths and areas for development are.

In my previous role as AST for literacy, I recruited a group of student literacy leaders. They promoted literacy across the school by running events like World Book Day and Readathon, reading in assemblies, and tutoring Year 7 students with low reading ages. I formalised this process with application forms and a selection process, then gave the successful applicants 'Literacy Leader' badges that they could wear with pride. Years 10 and 12 may be the perfect year groups to target, as they are thinking about their college applications. Being able to talk about their role as 'revision lead', 'leader of learning' or 'study lead' could make their application stand out.

Extra-curricular

Lots of subjects run revision sessions but, as explored in the introduction, these are often a last-minute affair in Year 11 that involves reteaching – or groups of students chatting and googling! Instead, could you open up the library once a week for study sessions, perhaps run by your student revision leads? Alongside this could be specific sessions for note-taking, dual coding, elaboration, etc.

A supportive, productive and lively environment is key to making revision irresistible. I recommend training up revision leads beforehand and perhaps stipulating what the study sessions will look like, then deciding whether you want them to be drop-in or to target a specific cohort of students – or even a mixture of both. Depending what the rules are in your school library, create a welcoming environment with drinks and biscuits.

Here's an example of what a study session might look like.

Activity and timing	Purpose
Introduction: Revision lead greets student and asks them what they would like to work on and why (5 minutes). Students attending will need to bring revision materials (e.g. exercise books or lesson resources) but materials for flashcards, Cornell notes, templates, etc. can be provided.	• Greeting the student by name is important in developing a positive relationship between mentor and mentee, creating a warm environment and making the mentee more likely to turn up to future sessions. • Asking the student what they want to work on and why gives them ownership of their revision but also forces them to think about their choice: are they choosing the easy option by selecting a topic they enjoy, or is it something they are struggling with? It's even better if revision leads are trained beforehand to look out for answers such as 'Because I have a test'. It's not that the student can't use the session to study for a test, but this is the perception of revision we ideally want to move away from.
Select strategies for revision: Revision lead suggests appropriate strategies to develop the student's learning (5 minutes).	• By opening up a dialogue about what the most appropriate strategies might be, revision leads force students to use metacognition to explain their choices. For example, 'I think we should start with a brain dump to see what I can remember about X and then make flashcards out of the information I forgot.'
Complete revision: Revision lead allows the student time to complete any activities, supporting as and when necessary (15 minutes).	• Although the responsibility is still with the student revising (we can't expect our revision leads to be expert in every topic!), this is a supportive process where the revision lead is a 'buddy', guiding the student to reflect and review where necessary. It's a good idea to train the revision leads up in 'Tip, tip, teach, try again' (see page 120) to help with this.
Evaluation: Revision lead guides the student to reflect on the strengths and weaknesses arising from the session, praises them for their effort and attendance, and says goodbye.	• This is a crucial part of the session. We must avoid the 'illusion of knowing' by encouraging students to note down their strengths and their targets. This also helps them know what to focus on next time. If they got all or most of the content correct with little effort, it's worth having a discussion about whether they should be focusing on something else. The revision lead might also set an aim for the next session, e.g. keep quizzing on X using the Leitner system or bring your notes on Y next time. • By praising the student (and potentially nominating them for an award in assembly) again we are creating positive relationships and experiences of revision. • You might also have an attendance card for the revision lead to sign linked to rewards for attending X number of sessions.

Revision lessons

Is there space in your curriculum to include revision lessons in each subject area? These could be incredibly beneficial, particularly if you use spacing to test students on information learned several weeks ago in order to prevent forgetting. In a study, Pashler et al suggest creating 10 questions that cover the key knowledge for a topic and using these questions to get students to rate their likelihood of getting the answer right, from 0-100. For a question they have answered correctly without hesitation in a study session, they might choose 100; for a question they hesitated on but eventually remembered, they might choose 60; and for a question they could not remember at all, they might choose 0 (Pashler et al, 2007). Students should then find the answers by looking through class materials (and checking with the teacher if necessary). This process means students know where the gaps are in their knowledge, and therefore know what to focus on in their home study sessions.

As always, think about your context: where are the opportunities for revision immersion?

Using parents' evenings to reinforce effective study habits

Although we all recognise the importance of this communication, parents' evenings can be fairly fruitless occasions. At my worst, I've repeated the same information to every parent, thinking it's what they want to hear. Here are your child's current grades. Here's their target. They are/are not on track to reach that target. Do they read regularly, ideally for at least 20 minutes a day? This dialogue isn't completely unhelpful and, of course, discussions about behaviour can be useful too, but it's of limited benefit to share little more than cold, hard numbers. We're missing an opportunity to empower parents with strategies to support their child's learning. Just as I've never taught a student who doesn't want to succeed (even if this desire is buried deep inside), I've never met a parent who doesn't want to help their child. The recurring question at parents' evenings is always: 'Is there anything we can do to support at home?'

Powerful Teaching describes 'a triangle of learning' where parent, child and teacher have shared strategies and language (Agarwal & Bain, 2019). Any chance to speak to parents about effective study habits should be grabbed with both hands. But this doesn't need to dominate discussions with parents. By simply having a handout that covers effective study skills in a parent-friendly way, you can encourage this key stakeholder to support their child in revising effectively. I've put together a parent guide that you can use or adapt to aid this ongoing dialogue; follow the QR code to download the guide.

www.teachertoolkit.co.uk/wp-content/uploads/2021/12/The-Revision-Revolution-Resources-1.pdf

Many schools have Year 6 induction meetings, options evenings for KS3 and KS4, and parent information evenings. And every school, of course, holds open days and evenings. These are all great opportunities to explain and reinforce how to study effectively. You can ask your revision leads to speak at these events – there's nothing more powerful than a student eloquently explaining how knowledge of effective study skills has benefited them.

Developing a revision website

In this digital age – and as we navigate a global pandemic, more dependent than ever on technology in our teaching – the internet is a tool we can't afford to ignore. By developing a revision website, we can make the abstract idea of revision concrete through videos that model the process explicitly and debunk the idea that revision is nothing more than completing exam questions and papers. This is helpful to students and parents.

The videos can be made in a way that breaks down revision, explaining why a technique is effective, how to do it and how to evaluate it – a crucial part of the process. Why not get some of your student revision leads to make and promote videos on the website? In my experience, most students are much more technologically literate than their teachers.

I would suggest including the following videos on a school revision website:

- Creating the right environment for revision.
- Deciding what to include in a revision session.
- The Leitner system.
- Brain dumps and self-quizzing.
- Reading and making notes.
- Writing for revision (sentence expansion and planning exercises).
- Using your exercise book/course materials to revise.
- Evaluating your revision session.

Presenting to governors

For any big whole-school initiative, it's important that governors know the purpose behind it, the short and long-term plans, the impact and how this is being monitored. All this will not be covered in one presentation, but regular updates to key stakeholders will mean everyone is on the same page and the language of revision is being spoken by all.

Another benefit of getting governors onside might be the securing of funds to develop your revision revolution further. There should be a process whereby you are able to report on impact – remember, this should be something to celebrate! Ideally, you'll have decided your measures beforehand. You might use the audit from the introduction (see page 19) to source some staff, student and/or parent voice, quote an Ofsted report, or cite data on improved results or entries into further education. It's important, however, that all stakeholders recognise this is a long-term endeavour. Results will not materialise overnight and perhaps not even within the first few years. Revolutions take time.

Your presentation to governors might take the form of an improvement plan, like this one:

Priority	**How and who**	**By when?**	**Success indicator**
Train staff in research-based study methods.	CPD sessions (three initially) on retrieval practice.	End of autumn term.	On learning walks, staff are confidently using retrieval activities that help students' learning in their subject area.
All Year 7 students taught about effective study methods.	All teaching staff.	End of summer term.	Student voice with Year 7 reveals students studying regularly using strategies taught and that their perception of revision is positive.
Pastoral curriculum that teaches all year groups about research-based study methods.	All pastoral teaching staff.	End of summer term and ongoing.	Student voice reveals whole cohort are more confident with revision. Improved results in tests. Increase in internal sixth-form applications.
Assemblies on importance of effective study.	SLT and year managers.	Implemented from autumn term.	Wellbeing survey shows reduction in anxiety levels of students.
Parent booklet on effective study.		End of autumn term	Parent voice on home study and school support reveals positive impact.
Year 2 of revision revolution: recruitment of revision leads, CPD on MCQs to continue to improve retrieval in the classroom, development of revision website.			

Of course, this document will be designed for your context: you may not have a sixth form and your 'powerful coalition' of staff (Mind Tools, 2007) will need to feature on the improvement plan to show their continued impact across the school. The example above is just to get you thinking about how to present ideas and their rationale to governors (and to other stakeholders if you're part of a trust).

Newsletters

Newsletters can be a great form of regular communication with parents. They are a useful way to direct parents towards important information and resources to help their child. I find it particularly helpful at parents' evenings to be able to refer parents to vocabulary, reading lists and assessment dates in the newsletter, for example.

The nursery that my sons attend uses the online system Tapestry to keep us updated on their progress, but I do remember being completely overwhelmed by two separate messages about Comic Relief Week, when they were both due to be involved in different themed days every day of the week. My husband and I both work full-time and mornings are chaotic – I had no idea how we would remember all these daily events. I mention this because busy parents need simple, easy-to-implement instructions or they are unlikely to be able to support the school's aims.

You might design a whole-school newsletter that includes a revision section in each edition, or faculty newsletters with revision strategies specific to English, maths, science, art, etc. Some schools also have year group newsletters that are tailored to the specific stage of the students. A transition newsletter could be a great way to inform parents of Year 6 students about simple study strategies that they could start practising, perhaps as part of a summer project. Whatever you prepare needs to be concise and relatively jargon-free, designed for busy parents who want to support their child in a simple, straightforward way.

Here are some possible topics for whole-school newsletters.

- **Demystifying revision**. A short explanation of what revision is and what it isn't (see Step 3). Creating a five-year revision programme does not mean preparing for GCSE exams from Year 7!
- **Creating the conditions for an effective study session**. A short guide on the importance of a distraction-free, quiet environment and how to motivate your child to work in these conditions (e.g. the reward of using their phone or watching a specific TV programme afterwards).
- **Structuring a study session**. An example study session (this will probably need to be subject-specific). For example, if a Year 7

student is studying myths and legends, they might start with a five-minute brain dump in which they write down everything they remember about the myths and then check this against their exercise book, adding to or amending their brain dump notes with a different colour pen. They could then spend five minutes using the Leitner system to quiz themselves on key vocabulary and quotes. Finally, they can apply this knowledge in a carefully crafted topic sentence with an embedded quotation.

- **Reflecting on a study session**. A short explanation of how and why students should make a note of the successes and targets that arise from the study session: to inform future sessions and even questions they might ask their teacher to address gaps in knowledge or areas of confusion.

The examples above continue the granular approach to revision advocated in this book. The Year 7 study session is focused on creating one beautiful topic sentence: in this way, students concentrate on mastering each skill in isolation, before accumulating more skills and building towards the kind of complex essay-writing or mathematical equations they will need to do by the end of school.

On the topic of keeping newsletters simple, I write a half-termly newsletter from the English department at my school, which I find a great way of communicating key information to parents. I talk about small changes that parents can make to support their child's learning and one of my favourites of these comes from *Powerful Teaching*: 'tell me three' (Agarwal & Bain, 2019). Here's the excerpt from our April newsletter:

> *One small change you can make to support your child is, rather than asking 'How was your day?', asking '**What are three things you learned today?**' You can also ask '**Remind me of three things you learned yesterday**' to help your child remember prior learning. If you have paper handy, you could get them to **write down three facts about a specific topic** (see current topics below). Finally, why not use the flashcards shared in last month's newsletter and encourage your child to **answer a card correctly three times** before it is removed from the deck!*
>
> *Studies show that encouraging children to retrieve information has a huge positive impact on long-term learning.*

Newsletters are not, of course, reserved exclusively for parents. Many schools have a 'learning and teaching' newsletter, which is a perfect opportunity to raise the status of revision by including a 'revision tip of the month' or something similar. To encourage buy-in, invite teachers to write about their experiences of trialling a retrieval task or revision strategy, thereby sharing their good practice with the school and offering a CPD opportunity to staff. You could, of course, have guest writers from different subject areas for your parent newsletter, too.

Quiz

1. How many hours of practice does it allegedly take to develop mastery?
2. What does evidence show about telling the stories of struggling scientists?
3. What is 'tell me three'?
4. How is metacognition linked to critical thinking?
5. What do we mean by automaticity?

Reflection

1. What assemblies might you include to promote revision in your context?
2. What is the best method for contacting parents in your context? If parents' evening attendance isn't high, what other means of communication might work? Do many families in your context have access to technology in order to engage with newsletters and websites? If not, what other methods could you use?
3. How hands-on are governors in your context? Are there opportunities to present to them on the progress of the revision revolution?
4. How does form time work in your context? Is there time to reinforce revision strategies?
5. Who presents assemblies in your context? Is this an opportunity to involve senior leadership and heads of year?

Summary

- Parents and governors should feel part of the revision revolution.
- There are simple ways to keep parents informed, such as newsletters and a handout at parents' evening.
- Presentations to governors summarising the aims of the revision revolution and its success so far will ensure everyone understands the rationale behind creating a culture of effective study.

Step 8
Revolutionary Home Study

Using homework to build effective independent study

Summer term: April/May

In a nutshell
In this chapter we'll explore effective homework as a way to build self-regulated learners. Homework is a key part of creating a strong culture of study, as a lot of student revision takes place at home. This is a crucial time, when students aim to add value to their learning without the support of their teacher, and we need to put scaffolding and resources in place to enable all students to complete their homework independently, regardless of ability.

In my first few years of teaching, I set homework out of expectation rather than need. Homework has become quite a contentious issue in recent times, with many teachers, parents and students questioning its effectiveness. There are several possible issues with homework, not least how to make it accessible enough for students to complete independently but challenging enough to be worthwhile. Homework can also add tremendously to teachers' workload, as not only do we need to mark and check the work, but we may also spend a lot of time chasing up incomplete homework, setting detentions or contacting parents. But there is another way.

The Science of Learning reports on a study that shows 'students who were set regular homework … performed significantly better than those who were only set it occasionally'. The researchers did find, however, that the frequency and quality of homework were more important than the amount of time students spent on it (Watson & Busch, 2021). This supports the 'little and often' premise of effective study. According to the researchers, 'extra time spent after one hour led to minimal gains that did not justify the extra time'. They also found that 'students who did their homework by themselves ended up doing around 10% better in their exams than those who did their homework with parents helping them'.

This relates back to the idea of desirable difficulties. I was certainly reliant on my dad when tackling my own maths homework and I would give up very easily when I 'just didn't get it'. If I didn't understand my dad's explanation immediately, this led to sulking rather than learning. Although my dad was trying to help me, I would have been better off working through the struggle of maths by myself. Doing homework independently 'encourages autonomy, which has been linked with developing self-regulation' (Watson & Busch, 2021).

Homework is an important part of creating self-regulated learners and testing students' ability to complete work independently. The EEF's planning framework for home learning states the importance of metacognition for successful homework:

> *'The most effective learners can self-regulate and organise their approach to learning. They are aware of their strengths and weaknesses and have well-developed metacognitive strategies that help them to learn. Metacognitive strategies can be taught, and are particularly powerful when they are subject-specific. These metacognitive strategies will be particularly important for your pupils if you can't be with them in the classroom, along with a consideration of how we learn and how we remember what we have learnt.'*[10]

10 https://educationendowmentfoundation.org.uk/public/files/Publications/Covid-19_Resources/Resources_for_schools/Home_learning_approaches_-_Planning_framework.pdf

Below, I've reproduced the EEF's framework for home learning, adapting and/or expanding the 'Examples' section.

Approach	**What is it?**	**Why include it?**	**Examples**
Activate	Prompting students to think about what they have learned previously to help with next steps.	An important aspect of metacognition is planning how you'll approach a task, using what you already know.	• Watch a video and complete Cornell notes and/or summarise from memory. • Complete a quiz. • Read a text and complete Cornell notes and/or summarise from memory. • Add to a partially completed concept map or worked example. • Revise key vocabulary related to a topic using Leitner flashcards or another retrieval strategy.
Explain	Explicitly teaching strategies to students and helping them choose when to use them.	Metacognitive strategies are most effective when they are context-specific, especially if students understand when and why to use them.	• Model thinking under a visualiser as you complete worked examples. • Use videos that explain a thought process and demonstrate a strategy. These videos could be uploaded to a school platform (we use Bloodle) for students to draw on at their convenience. • Explain each step in a worked example. • Model use of Cornell notes and note-taking, as well as how to turn notes into sentences and paragraphs. • Limit the amount of new information within one session and break explanations into chunks, where possible.

Practise	Students practise strategies and skills repeatedly to build independence.	Students need to practise strategies to develop independence. Scaffolds and support are needed at first but should decrease over time.	• A video leading students through practice questions, reducing the guidance with each example (again, an online platform could work well here). • A series of questions with partial prompts and links to further help where necessary. • Scaffolding: knowledge organisers, essay prompts, annotated examples. Prompts for students to label and/or explain each step with reasons why they were carried out. • Split tasks into components and allow students to practise these to a high level of success before combining them into larger tasks.
Reflect	Students reflect on what they have learned after completing a piece of work.	Self-regulated learners use tasks they have completed to evaluate what went well and what they will do differently next time.	• Key learning points for the group as a whole (e.g. whole-class feedback). • Prompts to help students with self-evaluation. • Quizzes after activities, supporting students to think about what they have learned, what they had trouble with and further help needed.
Review	Revisiting previous learning after a gap.	Retrieving things from memory, particularly when you have started to forget them, aids long-term retention.	• Quizzes that include questions from previous topics as well as current ones. • Brain dumps, etc.

In his book *What If Everything You Knew About Education Was Wrong?* (2015b), David Didau shares the findings of Cepeda et al (2008) on the optimal intervals for retaining information:

Time to test	Optimum interval between study sessions
One week	One to two days
One month	One week
Two months	Two weeks
Six months	Three weeks
One year	Four weeks

When designing a curriculum and setting homework, it's worth considering these intervals. Towards the end of Year 10, a teacher might cover a set text for the GCSE exam and set revision homework on it four weeks after they have finished teaching that particular text. Or the teacher could be even more specific and space the revision in terms of chapters, characters or themes (for example, revise chapter 1 when teaching chapter 4).

Amy Forrester has written a great blog post about how she used the intervals above to set quotation memorisation homework, with positive effects. Forrester used research on optimal spacing to create 'a programme of study for my year 11s, all of which would be undertaken as homework. They would have 5 tasks a week for learning quotations for each of their literature texts, and, after 3 weeks, these would be gradually replaced with recap tasks each week' (Forrester, 2017). She explains the positive impact of this on student memory and exam performance. Timing was crucial in order to avoid that undesirable cramming that students tend to revert to if we don't actively discourage them with concrete alternatives. If you've been following the revision revolution's steps so far, it won't be difficult to set homework that is meaningful and requires minimal teacher feedback. Here are some examples.

- Quiz yourself on your Cornell notes on the Gunpowder Plot. I would like to see one full page of answers, and corrections or additions in a different colour. You should also summarise at the bottom any areas of strength or struggle.

- Use the Leitner system to quiz on important vocabulary for understanding and explaining the nervous system. Follow this up with 3-5 sentences that include the key vocabulary explaining how the nervous system works.
- Explain to a friend or family member how the water cycle works. Ensure they have a copy of your knowledge organiser so they can give feedback on what you remembered and any areas of misconception or omission.
- Use the notes you made in lessons on Beethoven's symphony to write a paragraph explaining its structure. Label your topic sentence, supporting statements and concluding sentence. For extra challenge, include a noun appositive, the term 'ternary' and a colon followed by further explanation.

As the teacher, all you should need to do is see evidence of the homework and check it's set out in the way you instructed. Key questions might include:

- Where is evidence of corrective feedback? For example, have students used a different colour pen to correct their response or add missing information?
- Where is evidence of self-reflection? For example, have students used their metacognitive skills to summarise their areas of strength and weakness in this revision homework?
- Where is evidence of metacognition? For example, have students labelled the steps they followed to complete the homework?

The beauty of these homework tasks is that parents can get involved in a way that makes no demands on their subject knowledge, because the answers are available for them. This removes any anxiety parents may have around their working knowledge of complex grammatical structures, quadratic equations or the periodic table. Therefore, parents and students can enjoy learning together, both playing an active part in the learning process.

Many schools have recently subscribed to the online lecture series Massolit.[11] Retrieval homework works in perfect harmony with

11 www.massolit.io

programmes like this. Give students a link or QR code for the lecture you want them to watch and ask them to take Cornell notes: a lovely, marking-free homework! Once they have taken notes (therefore actively engaging with the lecture, rather than passively watching), you can design a retrieval quiz based on the lecture. There are lots of possibilities here: it could be a multiple-choice quiz, a brain dump on everything they can remember or a mixed-retrieval quiz building up to more complex higher-order thinking. Here's an example of a mixed-retrieval quiz based on a Massolit lecture about Dickens' *A Christmas Carol.*

1. What was life like in the time when Dickens was writing?
2. How had London changed as a result of the Industrial Revolution?
3. Why was Dickens particularly interested in poverty?
4. Name one character Dickens created to evoke sympathy for the poor. Briefly explain how he does this.
5. 'The rich and poor had a symbiotic relationship in capitalist London.' Explain this statement.

Powerful Teaching warns that, although open-book retrieval quizzes will increase learning, they may decrease home study (Agarwal & Bain, 2019). If you're setting revision homework, therefore, it's beneficial to tell students that they will complete a closed-book retrieval quiz. Closed-book retrieval quizzes in the classroom will help ensure students are studying at home. This is about motivation: if students can 'cheat' by looking up the correct answers, they are unlikely to prepare as thoroughly. With open-book quizzes, we can create the illusion of fluency and confidence in students. But by making things difficult in a way that is desirable, students are made to think about their strengths and areas of development.

In Step 2 we discussed Agarwal and Bain's four steps of metacognition (see page 55). This is an effective revision strategy for students to use at home; here's a reminder of how it works.

1. Students place a star next to the questions they can answer and a question mark next to the ones they can't.
2. Students answer all the questions they have marked with a star.

3. Students look up the answers to all the questions they have marked with a question mark.
4. Students verify all the starred answers are correct. (Agarwal & Bain, 2019)

*	?	Items to know	Answer
		Definition of 'hubris'.	
		How did Macbeth's hamartia create his downfall?	
		Divine right of kings.	
		Why does Macbeth descend into tyranny?	

Whether students have written their answer from memory or looked it up, there is guaranteed success in this activity, which helps build positive associations with study, rather than the traditional sense of dread that accompanies revision for many students.

Another really simple revision task for home study is what Agarwal and Bain call 'power tickets', which combine spacing, interleaving and retrieval:

	Today	Yesterday	Last week	Last month	Last term	Last year
	Suffragettes	Suffragists	Edwardian era	Gothic tradition	Victorian era	Romantics
Write one fact						
Write a second fact						
Write a third fact						

This could easily be made more complex by getting students to develop sentences using their retrieved knowledge:

	Today	**Yesterday**	**Last week**	**Last month**	**Last term**	**Last year**
	Suffragettes	Suffragists	Edwardian era	Gothic tradition	Victorian era	Romantics
Write one fact	The suffragettes used violence.					
Write a second fact	They gained global media attention.					
Write a third fact	Emmeline Pankhurst made a famous speech called 'Freedom or death'.					
Develop your facts into one beautiful sentence. Include a noun appositive, relative clause or present participle	Emmeline Pankhurst, a suffragette who believed their violent methods justified the cause, wrote a powerful speech called 'Freedom or death'.					

You could even ask for the inclusion of certain criteria – for example, a vocabulary word, type of punctuation or grammatical construct. And it would be great if students' planners included some of these templates, as quick and easy reminders of how to revise.

Agarwal and Bain point out that a lot of these study strategies are much quicker than traditional and less effective revision tasks such as rereading and highlighting – and they are also much more effective. Essentially, we're asking students to 'spend less time studying and more time learning' (Agarwal & Bain, 2019).

You can help students gain ownership of their home study by considering the following questions from *Powerful Teaching*:

- 'What strategy are you most interested in or most likely to try on your own?
- When and where would it be possible for you to use this strategy? Choose one particular situation and write that down.
- What can you do to remember to use this strategy? Write it down and set up a reminder.
- How will you keep track of whether you are using the strategy as you planned? Write down a tracking method and set it up right now.' (Agarwal & Bain, 2019)

These are perfect questions to be used by form tutors and in form-time discussions. They shouldn't take long to answer, but will ensure home study is happening in a way that is purposeful and well organised.

Revolutionary writing

For the rest of this chapter I want to explore the importance of revolutionary writing: a whole-school approach to the teaching of writing that involves explicit writing instruction. Our revision revolution aims to create self-regulated learners and this includes students who can take notes effectively, turn notes into full sentences, craft sentences in a range of sophisticated and academic ways, and plan paragraphs and whole pieces of writing.

To read more about revolutionary writing, see Judith Hochman and Natalie Wexler's excellent *The Writing Revolution* (2017). Many of the ideas presented in *The Writing Revolution* work hand in hand with our revision strategies, as I'll explain in the following sections.

Note-taking

In Step 4 we discussed effective note-taking (see page 95), including suggested abbreviations and different ways to teach note-taking to students. If note-taking is being taught across the school, students' exercise books become revision books that they can use to self-quiz and practise turning notes into full sentences and paragraphs.

Sentence-crafting

Writing is so automatic for many teachers and parents that we underestimate its complexity, often asking students to write paragraphs or whole texts when they desperately need to gradually build up to these tasks, starting with sentence-level work. Writing successful whole texts involves paying attention to spelling, handwriting, sentence construction, grammar, purpose, audience, punctuation, genre, vocabulary and paragraphs – it is incredibly demanding! Setting small writing exercises as homework can help students improve their knowledge and writing simultaneously.

The Writing Revolution warns that although students are typically assigned a great deal of writing in school, not much *learning to write* takes place, potentially resulting in lots of low-quality writing (Hochman & Wexler, 2017). Doug Lemov splits writing into three categories: developmental, summative and formative (Lemov, 2017a). Here I've paraphrased Lemov's definitions of each:

1. **Summative writing**: using a specific (taught) structure to 'explain and justify' an idea.
2. **Formative writing**: developing thoughts about an idea.
3. **Developmental writing**: teaches students how to write using deliberate practice.

Lemov argues that although developmental writing is the foundation of formative and summative writing, it is 'sorely overlooked' (Lemov, 2017b). Developmental writing teaches sentence construction and crafting, making the steps to improvement explicit through modelling. Sentences are the building blocks of writing and are therefore very worthy of our attention.

Sentence-crafting is an activity that I use a lot in the classroom and often set as homework. It relies on a good knowledge of grammar, so it needs to be modelled. Students are provided with a simple sentence and are given a variety of ways to improve the sentence, applying them step by step (see the table overleaf).

Seeds need light to grow.	
Can you use a more precise verb?	Seeds **require** light to grow.
Can you use more technical vocabulary?	Seeds require light to **germinate**.
Can you add a subordinate or relative clause?	**Because most seeds are light-sensitive**, they require light to germinate.
Can you change the position of the clause? Tip: you can replace the commas that separate a relative clause with dashes or brackets.	Seeds, **which are mostly light-sensitive**, require light to germinate.
Can you add a prepositional phrase?	**Before they can germinate**, seeds (which are mostly light-sensitive) require light.
Can you add a noun appositive? Tip: you can replace the commas that separate a noun appositive with dashes or brackets.	Seeds, **embryonic plants enclosed in a protective outer coating**, require light since they are mostly light-sensitive.
Can you add a present or past participle phrase?	**Being mostly light-sensitive**, seeds require light to germinate. **Found in plants and flowers**, seeds require light to germinate since they are mostly light-sensitive.

When you first model the steps, you can show the improved sentences and ask students what you have changed, testing that they can identify the verb, noun, subordinate clause, etc. When using this process, students should be encouraged to remove as well as add. A good sentence won't include all these criteria: it's about finding and evaluating what makes the best sentence, another skill that needs explicit modelling and repeated practice. Sentence-crafting also works really well as a paired coaching activity (see page 117).

The 'but/because/so' sentence-expansion activity from *The Writing Revolution* simply involves providing students with a sentence and asking them to expand it using these three conjunctions (Hochman & Wexler, 2017). The idea is that students will have to extend their understanding by adding an extra level of detail to their sentences. For example:

> *The body needs air to breathe but [contrast/change of direction].*
>
> *The body needs air to breathe because [reason].*
>
> *The body needs air to breathe so [cause and effect].*

The body needs air to breathe but this air is filtered by the trachea before it reaches the lungs.

The body needs air to breathe because air contains oxygen.

The body needs air to breathe so oxygen can be inhaled into the lungs and transported around the body through the bloodstream.

A second way to add detail to sentences is questioning. This is particularly good for revision: students can revise key knowledge by asking who, what, when, where, why and how. For example:

The British army prepared to fight.

We know who (the British army) so can eliminate 'who' as a question stem.

When? In 1914.

Where? Deployed to France.

Why? War declared on Germany.

How? Equipped with weapons from the Industrial Revolution.

In 1914, as Britain declared war on Germany, the British Army was deployed to France, equipped with weapons from the Industrial Revolution.

Students can also be given separate sentences to combine into one for homework. For example:

Kolkata is the capital of India's West Bengal state.

Kolkata was formerly called Calcutta.

Kolkata is known for its architecture, art galleries and festivals.

Kolkata has been home to many prominent people including Mother Teresa.

Students might write:

Kolkata (formerly Calcutta), the capital of India's West Bengal state, is known for its architecture, art galleries and festivals and has been home to many prominent people including Mother Teresa.

As with the sentence-crafting activity, modelling is essential before setting these kinds of activities for homework. In *The Writing Revolution*, the authors suggest following this process when introducing writing activities:

1. 'Model the activity.
2. Students practise orally in a pair.
3. Students try the activity on their own.
4. Teachers offer prompt feedback.' (Hochman & Wexler, 2017)

Texts tend to include much more complex sentence structures than speech, which is why giving students practice with conjunctions (words that connect phrases and clauses) and clauses (a group of words containing a subject and a verb) improves reading comprehension as well as writing skills. Consider the following examples:

- Revising is important so you can achieve good grades.
- Revising [subject] is [verb] important = independent clause [complete thought that makes sense on its own].
- so [conjunction] you [subject] can achieve [verb] good grades = dependent clause [incomplete thought that does not make sense on its own].

Here's how conjunctions could be explored in revision homework in order to improve writing. Start with a question:

> Did unemployment and poverty contribute to the rise of Hitler?
>
> *Although unemployment and poverty contributed to the rise of Hitler,* [contrasting information]…

Students might write:

> *Although unemployment and poverty contributed to the rise of Hitler, it was his powerful speeches that won over many of his supporters.*

This sentence demonstrates quite complex understanding by examining different reasons for Hitler's rise to power and evaluating the strength of each. This could, of course, be developed into a paragraph with evidence to support the statement.

> *Before the rise of Hitler* [understanding of chronology]…

Students might write:

> *Before the rise of Hitler, the Wall Street Crash of 1929 caused worldwide economic disaster.*

This sentence demonstrates understanding of the order of events. Students could add additional events to the sentence and develop it into a paragraph showing the relevance of those events to Hitler's rise to power.

> *Since* [cause and effect] ________________ ,

Students might write:

> *Since a triangle has three sides, there are three angles that always add up to 180 degrees.*

This sentence demonstrates understanding of the relationship between the number of sides in a shape and the number of angles.

> *Unless* [introduces a case in which a statement is not true] ______________ ,

Students might write:

> *Unless we are inhaling oxygen and exhaling carbon dioxide, our respiratory system is not functioning correctly.*

There is an opportunity here to develop students' understanding using morphology: the dependent or *subordinate* clause relies on the main clauses to make sense, therefore it's of less importance than the main clause. The prefix 'sub' means below, as in a 'submarine', which travels below water, and 'substandard', which means below the expected standard. By encouraging students to notice these vocabulary links, we develop their word consciousness as well as their subject-specific understanding.

Another way to teach clauses is to use noun appositives, which not only make sentences more sophisticated, but also add layers of detail and understanding to students' writing. They rarely occur in speech and are found mainly in text, therefore they need explicit teaching, especially for our 'non-readers'.

Very simply, a noun appositive renames the noun, explaining that noun more fully. For example:

The British army prepared to fight.

The British army, **a group of patriotic men**, prepared to fight.

The British army, **a group of patriotic men with expectations of glory**, prepared to fight.

The noun appositive can be moved to the beginning, as long as it remains next to the noun it renames:

A group of patriotic men with expectations of glory, the British army prepared to fight.

Planning

Giving students a way to plan their paragraphs and full texts supports the EEF report on metacognition (Quigley et al, 2018), which says students should plan, write, check and redraft, but also that it's important to model each of these steps.

The Writing Revolution suggests that before planning, students need to know what a topic sentence is and how to create one effectively (Hochman & Wexler, 2017). Students then need to practise generating relevant ideas about a topic and putting them into a logical order. Once the teacher has modelled and allowed time for students to practise creating full topic and concluding sentences, they can then have a go at creating single-paragraph outlines like the one below:

Topic sentence: The Taj Mahal, an iconic structure, is situated in the Indian city of Agra.

1. Commissioned = 1632.
2. Emperor Shah Jahan wished to house the tomb of his favourite wife.
3. Includes a mosque, guesthouse and formal gardens.

Concluding sentence: A piece of incredible architecture, the Taj Mahal is a sight to behold.

There are, of course, so many more approaches to setting homework that will help students remember the important learning from your subject area. You will want to consider the optimum remembering intervals, levels of scaffold and increased complexity depending on where students are on their curriculum journey. Homework, too, can become an irresistible part of the revision process once home-study strategies are explicitly modelled and made accessible to all.

Quiz

1. Why is homework often difficult for students?
2. What are the optimum intervals for remembering?
3. Name one retrieval task you could set as homework.
4. What is sentence-crafting?
5. How might students plan their writing?

Reflection

1. What is the homework policy at your school?
2. What type of homework do you set in your subject area? Does it add value?
3. What is the uptake like for homework? Could this be improved by using some of the ideas in this chapter?
4. How might you use remembering intervals to stagger homework topics?
5. How might you introduce note-taking and other explicit writing strategies?

Summary

- Homework can be made more meaningful for students and less labour-intensive for teachers.
- There are lots of simple retrieval tasks that can be used for homework.
- Sentence-level work can be a great homework activity to practise writing.
- Fusing knowledge retrieval and writing can help bridge the gap between factual recall and higher-order responses.

Step 9
Vive la Révolution

Next steps and how to sustain a culture of revision in your school

Summer term: June onwards to infinity!

In a nutshell
At the start of this book we looked at the tendency in education to introduce too many initiatives, which then become unsustainable. I've learned over time that less is more. Doing one thing well is better than paying lip service to lots of different projects, and it also keeps your workload in check. This chapter considers possible next steps after the first year of the revision revolution, and how to make it a sustainable, long-lasting endeavour that reaps rewards years into the future.

How do you make a revolution last? We've all experienced frustration when an initiative is introduced quickly and then dropped in favour of the next big thing, without actually being given a chance to have impact. Our education system is not good at patience. And it's no wonder, what with the pressures of Ofsted and the fact that moving from special measures or 'requires improvement' to 'good' or 'outstanding' would, until recently, only happen through a rapid rise in results. Of course, I'm not suggesting that changes and tweaks won't be needed along the way, but a process of continual reflection is very different from giving up on an initiative because it hasn't produced instantaneous results. It's about finding the best bets for the students in our care: those approaches to learning that have a strong evidence base behind them.

The revision revolution will not happen overnight and neither will results suddenly improve. As an education system, we have to get better at waiting. In *Slow Teaching*, Jamie Thom writes about how 'slowing down in all aspects of education can lead to improved student outcomes' (Thom, 2018) and although this may feel counterintuitive, it is so important. We all know that, given time and thoughtful implementation, doing one or two things well is far preferable to doing several things badly or superficially.

Mary Myatt writes about 'fewer things, greater depth' (Myatt, 2020b) and that is exactly what this book advocates: starting small with retrieval, allowing staff and students to develop an in-depth understanding of how it works, why it works and what strategies to use when.

We're constantly held to account in education and this is understandable. It's a hugely important job. But often we prove our worth through data, and data can be problematic and misleading: an immediate set of improved data may show students performing rather than learning. This is where we have to really 'sell' the revision revolution to our stakeholders (see Step 2), being clear that this is an exciting endeavour that will deliver long-term rewards.

In John Kotter's eight-step change model, the first part of the model focuses on the vision and the strategies needed to get there, while the final two stages are about *sustaining* change. For example, using desirable difficulties in the classroom will feel uncomfortable at first, but staff mustn't feel they are expected to get it right immediately. In this way, they are more likely to persevere. Departments may need time, therefore, to discuss the pitfalls of their revision revolution and how to overcome these. This time is necessary to allow true culture change.

One of the biggest challenges can be maintaining the momentum. The initial buzz is very exciting, but with so many things competing for our attention in the busy and chaotic world of education, this can be difficult to sustain. What is needed with any type of change management is a cycle of ongoing improvement, such as the model opposite.

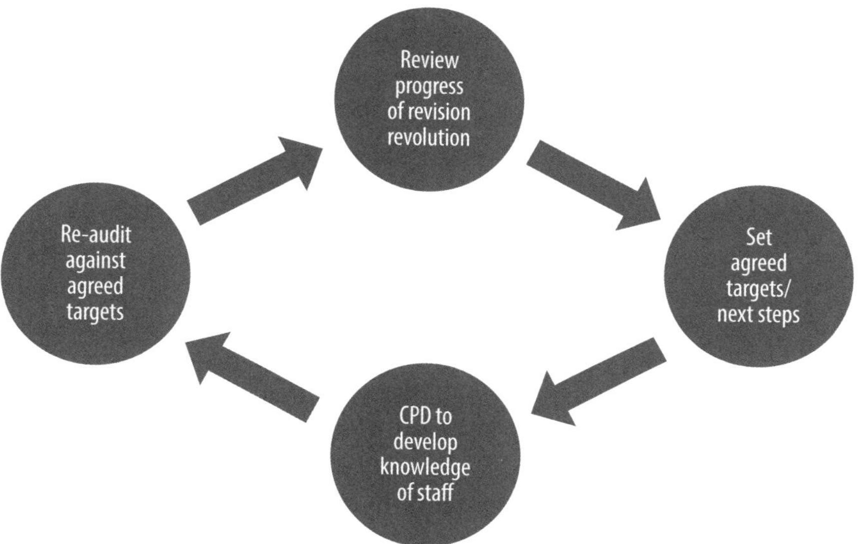

Just as the curriculum is never 'finished', neither is any meaningful revolution.

Review progress

After year 1, you'll probably notice a tangible culture shift and some great successes. In addition to reviewing your audit from the introduction to this book (see page 19), it may be worth conducting some student, staff and parent voice surveys to evaluate how attitudes to revision have changed. Despite all its successes, your revolution is still in its infancy. You may want to refer back to the short and long-term targets set in the document used with governors (see page 170) in order to check where you are against the success indicators.

Just like curriculum review, it's important to be as precise as possible with the diagnosis of strengths and areas of weakness, in order to make the next steps successful. Part of accurate diagnosis is asking pertinent questions. This also makes the review process a collaborative one, ensuring stakeholders remain on board with the revolution's rationale and next steps. You could make these questions part of department meetings or middle-leader meetings with SLT – ideally both. Another benefit of this approach is that you're acknowledging that the targets for each department might need to look different: not only are all subjects unique, but they may also be at different points of the revolution journey at the end of this first year.

Here are some examples of pertinent questions:

- What retrieval or other study strategies are you using in lessons to ensure students repeatedly bump into the powerful knowledge they need to store in long-term memory in your subject area?
- What retrieval or other study strategies are you using in students' homework?
- How are you reducing the scaffolding of retrieval (e.g. reducing cues) so that students work towards independence?
- How are you building students' metacognition through, for example, use of peer coaches or self-assessment of homework?
- What have you noticed about students' learning since beginning this revision journey? What are the strengths and the areas to develop? How do you know? Are there particular items of knowledge that students are able to recall easily, for example, and how are you assessing this?
- Are there particular cohorts of students who are excelling or struggling? Why might this be? Is there a need for more scaffolding or modelling for disadvantaged students?
- What are students' and/or parents' perceptions of revision in X subject? How do you know?
- What could I expect to see in students' exercise books? How does this help their book become a useful revision resource?
- What departmental CPD is needed to move to the next stage of the revision revolution in X subject?

You're not necessarily looking for 'perfect' answers here – it's not a test of who is the best head of department. What you are doing, however, is ensuring ongoing and purposeful dialogue around revision that moves the school forward on the revolution journey.

Set agreed targets/next steps

To keep the excitement going, it's important to reflect and decide on next steps. Where are you up to now? What's gone well and what needs further attention? If something hasn't worked or had the desired impact, why? What needs to be changed to improve this for next year? If retrieval is now a tangible part of school culture, is it time to look more closely at spacing and interleaving? Is one department doing a fantastic job of elaboration or dual coding, and could this be shared across the school? Is one department not really on board with the revision revolution?

Identifying these strengths and areas for development will enable you to come up with tangible solutions, such as pairing up departments or getting staff to lead CPD. You should now be in a position to show any resistant colleagues some explicit examples of the benefits behind sharing and using the science of learning (they are likely to be in the minority if all the revision revolution steps have been followed).

In my first English department, we would pride ourselves on 'never standing still' and being the most innovative department in the school. This didn't mean we ran ourselves into the ground. Rather, it meant we constantly reviewed and improved our provision based on the latest research and our own findings, as well as changing needs and cohorts. This reaped rewards in terms of student success and our reputation as a research-driven department that cared deeply about students.

Just as we start teachers off on that novice-to-expert continuum, with a high level of scaffolding that's gradually reduced until it's removed completely, we need to take the same approach with our revision revolution. We will necessarily start with lots of direct and explicit instruction for all stakeholders, but eventually revision will be such an embedded part of school culture that we will be able to metaphorically throw away the ladder. Students will be able to reach those academic heights independently, with a whole toolkit of study skills at their fingertips. Planning how and when to remove this scaffolding will depend upon the successful implementation of each step in this book and the timeframe in which you do this. Reflecting, evaluating and deciding on the next meaningful steps will be key.

CPD

CPD for year 2 of the revolution may include training staff in how to design effective multiple-choice quizzes. If retrieval is now being used across the school, introducing multiple-choice quizzing as part of that retrieval will require students to have very precise knowledge in order to identify the correct answer. MCQs can be time-consuming to create, owing to the level of thought required to design useful questions and 'distractors', and this is why I wouldn't start retrieval training with MCQs. But they are a great assessment tool.

To take this idea of assessment further, it may also be worth exploring in year 2 of your revolution an assessment system aligned with the study methods that are now fairly well established within school. According to Barak Rosenshine (2012) and Siegfried Engelmann (1980), it's important to obtain a high success rate in each skill before moving on. This makes absolute sense in subjects like maths, where you can't begin to understand fractions if you don't know your times tables. Equally, if a musician doesn't know their scales, they are unable to improvise. Those basic skills that are often demonised as less creative are fundamental to accessing the higher-level cognitive processes, opening doors to creativity and originality.

Although this is more complex in subjects like English and history, it's still crucial to find a way to make assessment granular so that students are not held back. If they can't write a thesis statement in English, presenting a clear and well-crafted argument with relevant evidence to support it, there's no way they can write successful analytical paragraphs and essays. A granular approach also allows us to diagnose where the issues are. By breaking down the assessment, we can more easily identify what students are struggling with.

In English, an assessment might include some sentence-level practice on constructing topic sentences, a quotes match-up and the listing of effects, before piecing all this together into a paragraph. In art, students might practise some shading or a section of a picture before drawing the complete image. In maths, questions on multiplication and division might be interleaved with fractions that build up to more complex equations. It's important, however, to consider fading. While it may be beneficial to construct highly scaffolded assessments in Year 7, by

Year 9 they will need to be less scaffolded and by Year 11 perhaps completely scaffold-free.

Multiple-choice quizzes

Staff will now be well versed in the benefits of low-stakes quizzing. MCQs are an effective and simple way to do this. They are great for identifying and addressing misconceptions, but there are certain criteria to bear in mind when designing MCQs.

An MCQ is a quiz with questions that have several pre-written answers to choose from. As mentioned earlier, the idea is that, by writing the answers strategically, teachers can use the quizzes as an assessment tool. Well-designed MCQs have several benefits: they reveal misconceptions, require precise understanding, and test ideas and deeper meanings as well as factual recall. Below are some guidelines for designing MCQs, paraphrased from a checklist sent to me by Stuart Kime.

1. They should be set out vertically.
2. All alternatives (incorrect answers) must be plausible but unambiguously wrong.
3. All alternatives should be similar in length and content.
4. The correct answer should vary in placement so there's no pattern (e.g. not always option A).
5. Three options to choose from is ideal (with no 'all of' or 'none of' options) as it reduces the difficulty of coming up with plausible distractors.
6. The question should not use a negative (e.g. Nazism was not a cause of WW1 because…)
7. Include a range of 'what', 'how' and 'why' questions.
8. The stem should be a question or partial statement.
9. Answers should begin easy, giving all students an experience of success, before increasing in difficulty or complexity.
10. Finally, incorrect answers must help test whether students have learned what was intended.

A video is available on YouTube in which Kime offers further advice on designing MCQs (ResearchED, 2020).

Example multiple-choice quizzes

	Poorly designed MCQ	**Well-designed MCQ**
Factual recall	Name the protagonist in *The Hunger Games*. A. Katniss Everdeen B. Winston Smith C. Victor Frankenstein The incorrect options are implausible as they are from other novels, therefore it's too easy to guess the correct answer.	Name the protagonist in *The Hunger Games*. A. Katniss Everdeen B. Peeta Mellark C. Prim Everdeen All incorrect options are plausible and this helps reveal misconceptions around the term 'protagonist'.
Inference	What does this line from *An Inspector Calls* show: 'girls of that class'? A. Mrs Birling is prejudiced against working-class women. B. Mr Birling is prejudiced against working-class women. C. Sheila is prejudiced against working-class women. The way this question is designed means it only tests who said the quote rather than the meaning behind it.	What does this line from *An Inspector Calls* show: 'girls of that class'? A. Mrs Birling is prejudiced against working-class women. B. Mrs Birling is sympathetic towards Eva Smith. C. Mrs Birling has realised the errors of her ways. The incorrect answers all ensure it's the meaning of the quote that's being tested, as well as anticipating possible misconceptions.
Deeper meanings	How does Juliet respond when she learns Romeo is a Montague? A. She asks why he must belong to the enemy family. B. She questions the significance of a name. C. She wants Romeo to forget his family loyalty. All answers are plausible. The incorrect answers need to be unambiguously wrong to be able to assess students' understanding.	How does Juliet respond when she learns Romeo is a Montague? A. She asks why he must belong to the enemy family. B. She decides family loyalty is more important than her love for Romeo. C. She rejects Romeo's love. All incorrect answers are unambiguously wrong, giving a more precise indication of what students have learned and any misconceptions that need addressing.

As with all retrieval quizzes, it's a good idea for students to mark and correct their own answers, making this another low-stakes retrieval test. Correcting their own work should help them recognise misconceptions, as well as giving teachers the opportunity to address misconceptions. If teachers ask follow-up questions during feedback, students can also be encouraged to explore deeper meanings.

Extra challenge

For extra challenge, you can include 'how' and 'why' questions as well as 'what' questions. This ensures students are tested on higher-order thinking that goes beyond simple factual recall. For example:

Why is pathetic fallacy used in Act 1, Scene 1 of *Macbeth*?

A. To portray the witches as sinister and frightening through their association with turbulent weather.

B. To portray the witches as outsiders who do not interact with human beings.

C. To portray the witches as prophets through the creation of an eerie atmosphere.

Extra support

For less literate students, lower reading ages and the demands placed on working memory can cause an extra level of misunderstanding. This needs to be taken into account when designing MCQs for these students. If the wording is too complex, students may answer incorrectly because the question is inaccessible for them, not necessarily because they don't have the knowledge to answer correctly.

	Poorly designed MCQ	Well-designed MCQ
Considering reading ages	How does Watson respond to the news that Mary will not inherit any treasure? A. He ecstatically proclaims his love for her, liberated from the threat of being perceived as having materialistic motivations. B. Although shocked, he vows to repress any remaining feelings for Mary and live his life a single man. C. He is heartbroken and perplexed by the news, attempting to comfort Mary who is also upset.	How does Watson respond to the news that Mary will not inherit any treasure? A. He is happy because he can now reveal his love for her. B. He decides not to reveal his true feelings for Mary. C. He attempts to comfort the upset Mary.

In the table above, the poorly designed MCQ includes unnecessarily complex vocabulary, while the long sentences contain multiple clauses. Some answers involve several concepts, placing an unnecessary strain on students' working memory. For example, option C includes: Watson is heartbroken; Watson is perplexed; Watson attempts to comfort Mary; Mary is upset.

How do we measure success?

As I write this, students across the country are receiving their A-level results after two years of disrupted education. Jeremy Clarkson has posted his annual tweet about how he failed his A-levels yet he has a personal chef, villa in St Tropez, etc.[12] This book has attempted to look beyond exam results when rethinking revision, making it instead about meaningful learning and opportunities for all.

Perhaps we need to spend time with students debating definitions of success. Is success defined by wealth, status and fame, as suggested by Clarkson? Or should we be looking to those scientists who have made breakthroughs in medicine and physics that have saved lives, or changed the way we see and think about the world? We're all aware of rich and famous people who are terrible role models, just as there are little-known artists who inspire others through the powerful messages they convey.

12 https://twitter.com/JeremyClarkson/status/1424988174502277135

What do we want for our students? I agree with Clarkson that exam results shouldn't be the sole determiner of success, but I disagree with the flippant disregard for the importance of study in achieving success. The revision revolution is about creating opportunities for students to be aspirational and get excited about their futures – they have access to tangible ways to succeed. But these tangible study methods require effort, therefore the key message is: work hard and anything is possible. The revision revolution is about creating choice and chances for students. Whatever avenue they choose to pursue, whatever their hopes and dreams, whatever and whoever they are inspired by, they have the knowledge and skills to get there. No doors are closed to them owing to background or ability.

It may be tempting to judge the success of our revolution on data alone, but even the most rigorous assessments can be poor proxies for learning. And it's learning we are interested in: learning that empowers students to see beyond superficial definitions of success. Learning that enables all students to achieve greatness in a world where the future is theirs to shape.

Quiz

1. What does Mary Myatt mean by 'fewer things, greater depth'?
2. Name some criteria of effective multiple-choice quizzes.
3. Name some benefits of multiple-choice quizzes.
4. What evidence-based strategies might staff CPD focus on in year 2 of the revision revolution?

Reflection

1. Reflecting on the first year of your revolution, what are the successes and the areas to develop further?
2. What does staff training need to be focused on in year 2?
3. Is retrieval now an established part of school culture?
4. Have student attitudes to revision changed?
5. Are parents on board with the revision revolution?

Summary

- Revolutions take time and year 1 is just the start of the journey.
- Staff need to feel empowered and supported to take risks in order for the revolution to be successful.
- Begin to think about how to gradually remove scaffolds so students and staff can move along the novice-to-expert continuum.
- CPD should build on the work done in year 1, rather than moving on to something new and unconnected.

Conclusion

If you take just one thing from this book, I hope it's this: the power of expectations. I really believe that all students are capable of brilliance. If we immerse everybody – from students to parents, teachers to governors, pastoral leads to SLT – in the world of revision, that culture of effective study will stick. And the exciting part is that it will raise standards for all, including the most disadvantaged students.

Revision is without a doubt a major contributor to the achievement gap. Too often it's done in a substandard, haphazard way – or not at all. It doesn't have to be this way. There are opportunities all around us to shift the culture: assemblies, a pastoral curriculum, enrichment, parental engagement, student advocates, staff CPD, homework and possibly many more that are unique to your context. If we grasp these opportunities, we can empower every student to see their limitless potential open up in front of them.

We are lucky, I think, to be in education at a time when research has become central to our profession. We would be foolish not to make the most of this advantage and use it to give our students opportunities we never had.

Admittedly, things happen on exam day or even the night before that we simply can't control (anxiety, a bad night's sleep, family issues, a break-up). But there are ways that we can create the conditions to allow success to happen:

1. Give students a secure knowledge of the subject, ensuring the learning has entered long-term memory so higher-level thinking can happen during the exam.

2. Develop a vocabulary that allows students to speak, read and write like academics.
3. Teach effective revision strategies and how to make regular use of them.

It's as simple as that. If we can make these three strategies part of our school culture and use them in a consistent way across the school, we will place students in a much better position than if we simply tell them to revise and chastise them when they fail to do so.

The revision revolution makes exam success possible for everyone. It makes the revision process accessible, even irresistible. Enjoy your journey – and vive la révolution!

Acknowledgements

This book has been a labour of love that began more than two years ago, around the same time as the birth of my second son. It would not have been possible without the support of my husband and parents, who kept me sane, entertained the boys and accepted all my distracted hours of writing and editing.

Thank you to my dad, a perfectionist who (like my mum) would do anything for his children and has proofread almost every word. Special thanks to Kath Monaghan, my inspirational ex-head of department, who is endlessly generous with her time and read all of my quite rubbish first draft, always responding with kind yet constructive feedback.

Finally, thanks to Ross Morrison McGill and John Catt Educational, for giving me the opportunity of a lifetime and enabling me to share my belief in what is possible for every child.

Bibliography

Agarwal, PK. (2019) 'Retrieval practice and Bloom's taxonomy: do students need fact knowledge before higher order learning?', *Journal of Educational Psychology*, 111:2, 189-209

Agarwal, PK, & Bain, PM. (2019) *Powerful Teaching: unleash the science of learning*, Jossey-Bass

Allison, S, & Tharby, A. (2015) *Making Every Lesson Count*, Crown House

Arnold, M. (1869) *Culture and Anarchy*

Ashford, K. (2020) 'Knowledge organisers: proceed with caution' in K Birbalsingh (ed), *Michaela: the power of culture*, John Catt

Beck, IL, McKeown, MG, & Kucan, L. (2013) *Bringing Words to Life: robust vocabulary instruction* (second edition), Guilford Press

Bjork, EL, & Bjork, RA. (2011) 'Making things hard on yourself, but in a good way: creating desirable difficulties to enhance learning' in MA Gernsbacher, RW Pew, LM Hough & JR Pomerantz (eds), *Psychology and the Real World: essays illustrating fundamental contributions to society*, Worth Publishers

Britton, J. (1970) *Language and Learning*

Cepeda, NJ, Vul, E, Rohrer, D, Wixted, JT, & Pashler, H. (2008) 'Spacing effects in learning: a temporary ridgeline of optimal retention', *Psychological Science*, 19:11, 1095-1102

Clear, J. (2018) 'This coach improved every tiny thing by 1 percent and here's what happened' (blog post), an excerpt from J Clear, *Atomic Habits*, Avery. Retrieved from: https://jamesclear.com/marginal-gains

Coe, R. (2015) 'What makes great teaching?' (presentation at the IB World Regional Conference), Centre for Evaluation and Monitoring/Durham University, www.ibo.org/globalassets/events/aem/conferences/2015/robert-coe.pdf

Coe, R. (2019) 'Does research on "retrieval practice" translate into classroom practice?', *Education Endowment Foundation Blog*, https://educationendowmentfoundation.org.uk/news/does-research-on-retrieval-practice-translate-into-classroom-practice

Counsell, C. (2020) 'Better conversations with subject leaders' in C Sealy & T Bennett (eds), *The researchED Guide to the Curriculum: an evidence-informed guide for teachers*, John Catt

Cullen, S. (2019) 'Fading: removing teacher presence in directed teaching' in A Boxer & T Bennett (eds), *The researchED Guide to Explicit & Direct Instruction: an evidence-informed guide for teachers*, John Catt

Didau, D. (2013a) 'Deliberately difficult – why it's better to make learning harder', *David Didau* (blog), https://learningspy.co.uk/featured/deliberately-difficult-focussing-on-learning-rather-than-progress-2

Didau, D. (2013b) 'Teaching sequence for developing independence stage 1: explain', *David Didau* (blog), https://learningspy.co.uk/featured/teaching-cycle-stage-1-explaining

Didau, D. (2015a) 'Cargo cult teaching, cargo cult learning', *David Didau* (blog), https://learningspy.co.uk/english-gcse/cargo-cult-teaching-cargo-cult-learning

Didau, D. (2015b) *What If Everything You Knew About Education Was Wrong?*, Crown House

Didau, D. (2018a) 'A broad and balanced approach to English teaching and the curriculum', *David Didau* (blog), https://learningspy.co.uk/english-gcse/a-broad-and-balanced-approach-to-english-teaching-and-the-curriculum

Didau, D. (2018b) 'How to explain… schema', *David Didau* (blog), https://learningspy.co.uk/featured/how-to-explain-schema

Didau, D. (2020) 'How should we decide what knowledge to teach?', *David Didau* (blog), https://learningspy.co.uk/featured/how-should-to-decide-what-knowledge-to-teach

Dwyer, C, Hogan, M, & Stewart, I. (2014) 'An integrated critical thinking framework for the 21st century', *Thinking Skills and Creativity*, 12, 43-52

Engelmann, S. (1980) *Direct Instruction*, Educational Technology Publications

Enser, Z, & Enser, M. (2020) *Fiorella & Mayer's Generative Learning in Action*, John Catt

Ericsson, KA, Krampe, RT, & Tesch-Römer, C. (1993) 'The role of deliberate practice in the acquisition of expert performance', *Psychological Review*, 100:3, 363-406

Flavell, J. (1976) 'Metacognitive aspects of problem-solving' in LB Resnick (ed), *The Nature of Intelligence*, Erlbaum

Forrester, A. (2017) 'Something that helped with learning quotations for the new GCSEs', *Defying Stars Teaching* (blog), https://defyingstarsteaching.wordpress.com/2017/05/27/first-blog-post

Goodwin, D. (2020) 'Retrieval practice for higher order thinking: making inflexible knowledge flexible', *Assembling Schema, Whilst Traversing Education's Age of Ultron* (blog), https://mrgoodwin23.wordpress.com/2020/05/25/retrieval-practice-for-higher-order-thinking-making-inflexible-knowledge-flexible-2

Harvard, B. (2019) 'Building a web of knowledge', *The Effortful Educator* (blog), https://theeffortfuleducator.com/2019/09/18/building-a-web-of-knowledge

Hattie, J, and Timperley, H. (2007) 'The power of feedback', *Review of Educational Research*, 77:1, 81-112

Headley, MD. (2021) *Beowulf: a new translation*, Scribe

Hochman, JC, & Wexler, N. (2017) *The Writing Revolution*, Jossey-Bass

Howard, K. (2020a) 'Litdrive CPD: designing an English curriculum' (presentation), Litdrive, https://litdrive.org.uk/remotecpd/kat-howard-designing-an-english-curriculum

Howard, K. (2020b) 'Curriculum is the heart: part two', *Kat Howard* (blog), https://saysmiss.wordpress.com/2020/04/30/curriculum-is-the-heart-part-two

Jones, K. (2021) *Retrieval Practice: Resource Guide – ideas and activities for every classroom*, John Catt

Kingsbridge Research School. (2019) 'Elaborative interrogation' (blog post), https://researchschool.org.uk/kingsbridge/news/elaborative-interrogation

Kirschner, PA, Sweller, J, & Clark, RE. (2006) 'Why minimal guidance during instruction does not work: an analysis of the failure of constructivist, discovery, problem-based, experiential, and inquiry-based teaching', *Educational Psychologist*, 41:2, 75-86

Lemov, D. (2015) *Teach Like a Champion 2.0: 62 techniques that put students on the path to college*, Jossey-Bass

Lemov, D. (2017a) 'Three types of writing in the classroom', *Teach Like a Champion* (blog), https://teachlikeachampion.com/blog/three-types-writing-classroom

Lemov, D. (2017b) 'Developmental writing: especially useful with short assignments and fast revision', *Teach Like a Champion* (blog), https://teachlikeachampion.com/blog/developmental-writing-especially-useful-w-short-assignments-fast-revision

Lemov, D, Woolway, E, & Yezzi, K. (2012) *Practice Perfect: 42 rules for getting better at getting better*, Jossey-Bass

Lemov, D, Driggs, C, & Woolway, E. (2016) *Reading Reconsidered: a practical guide to rigorous literacy instruction*, Jossey-Bass

Mccrea, P. (2017) *Memorable Teaching*, CreateSpace

Mind Tools content team. (2007) 'Kotter's 8-step change model', Mind Tools, www.mindtools.com/pages/article/newPPM_82.htm

Mountstevens, E. (2021) 'Metacognition: what lies beneath?' *Catalysing Learning* (blog), https://catalysinglearning.wordpress.com/2021/06/02/metacognition-what-lies-beneath

Myatt, M. (2016) *High Challenge, Low Threat: finding the balance*, John Catt

Myatt, M. (2020a) 'Are our resources useful and beautiful?', *Mary Myatt* (blog), www.marymyatt.com/blog/are-our-resources-useful-and-beautiful

Myatt, M. (2020b) *Back on Track: fewer things, greater depth*, John Catt

Needham, T. (2019) 'The 6 skills: an overview and skill 1: tentative language', *TomNeedham* (blog), https://tomneedhamteach.wordpress.com/2019/03/18/the-6-skills-an-overview-and-skill-1-tentative-language

Needham, T. (2020a) 'Low stakes quizzing and retrieval practice 4', *TomNeedham* (blog), https://tomneedhamteach.wordpress.com/2020/01/13/low-stakes-quizzing-and-retrieval-practice-4

Needham, T. (2020b) 'Low stakes quizzing and retrieval practice 5: extended quizzing', *TomNeedham* (blog), https://tomneedhamteach.wordpress.com/2020/02/03/low-stakes-quizzing-and-retrieval-practice-5-extended-quizzing

Newmark, B. (2021) 'How much curriculum should be insisted upon?', *Ben Newmark* (blog), https://bennewmark.wordpress.com/2021/07/05/how-much-of-curriculum-should-be-insisted-upon

Norwich Research School. (2020) 'Elisabeth Bowling: beautiful writing across secondary subjects' (video), YouTube, https://youtu.be/uscCuiiw5pE

Pashler, H, Bain, P, Bottge, B, Graesser, A, Koedinger, K, McDaniel, M, & Metcalfe, J. (2007) *Organizing Instruction and Study to Improve Student Learning: IES practice guide*, National Center for Education Research, Institute of Education Sciences, US Department of Education, https://files.eric.ed.gov/fulltext/ED498555.pdf

Quigley, A. (2014) 'Questioning and feedback: top ten strategies', *The Confident Teacher* (blog), www.theconfidentteacher.com/2014/11/questioning-feedback-top-ten-strategies

Quigley, A. (2018) *Closing the Vocabulary Gap*, Routledge

Quigley, A, Muijs, D, & Stringer, E. (2018) *Metacognition and Self-Regulated Learning: guidance report*, Education Endowment Foundation, https://educationendowmentfoundation.org.uk/public/files/Publications/Metacognition/EEF_Metacognition_and_self-regulated_learning.pdf

Quigley, A, Runeckles, C, Pearson, J, & Watson, J. (2021) *Metacognition and Self-Regulated Learning: school audit tool*, Education Endowment Foundation, https://educationendowmentfoundation.org.uk/public/files/Publications/Metacognition/7-SchoolAuditTool.pdf

Raichura, P. (2018) 'Writing in science: a symposium', *Bunsen Blue* (blog), https://bunsenblue.wordpress.com/2018/10/03/writing-in-science-a-symposium

Raichura, P. (2019) 'Class teacher explanations I: examples and non-examples', *Bunsen Blue* (blog), https://bunsenblue.wordpress.com/2019/10/20/clear-teacher-explanations-i-examples-non-examples

ResearchED. (2020) 'Stuart Kime: guidelines for using MCQs in distance learning' (video), YouTube, https://youtu.be/iFqxgg6b-lI

Rosenshine, B. (2012) 'Principles of instruction: research-based strategies that all teachers should know', *American Educator*, 36:1, 12-39

Shea, J. (2021) 'Cognitive science v neuroscience: "priming" – could it change the way we teach?', *Peer Reviewed Education Blog*, https://peerreviewededucationblog.com/2021/02/17/cognitive-science-v-neuroscience-priming-could-it-change-how-we-teach

Sherrington, T. (2019) *Rosenshine's Principles in Action*, John Catt

Sherrington, T. (2020) 'Schema-building: a blend of experiences and retrieval modes make for deep learning', *Teacherhead* (blog), https://teacherhead.com/2020/01/05/schema-building-a-blend-of-experiences-and-retrieval-modes-make-for-deep-learning

Sherrington, T. (2021) 'Everyday routines 2: everyone talking productively', *Teacherhead* (blog), https://teacherhead.com/2021/04/26/everyday-routines-2-everyone-talking-productively

Smith, M, & Weinstein, Y. (2016) 'Learn how to study using… elaboration', *The Learning Scientists* (blog), www.learningscientists.org/blog/2016/7/7-1

Sumeracki, M. (2019) 'Dual coding and learning styles', *The Learning Scientists* (blog), www.learningscientists.org/blog/2019/6/6-1

Tharby, A. (2014) 'Memory platforms', *Reflecting English* (blog), https://reflectingenglish.wordpress.com/2014/06/12/memory-platforms

Tharby, A. (2018) *How to Explain Absolutely Anything to Absolutely Anyone: the art and science of teacher explanation*, Crown House

Thom, J. (2018) *Slow Teaching: on finding calm, clarity and impact in the classroom*, John Catt

Watson, E, & Busch, B. (2021) *The Science of Learning: 99 studies that every teacher needs to know*, Routledge

Webb, J. (2019) *How to Teach English Literature: overcoming cultural poverty*, John Catt

Willingham, DT. (2009) *Why Don't Students Like School?*, Wiley

Young, R. (2019) *What is it Writing For Pleasure teachers do that makes the difference?* The Goldsmiths' Company and the University Of Sussex, https://writing4pleasuredotcom.files.wordpress.com/2019/09/what-is-it-writing-for-pleasure-teachers-do-that-makes-the-difference-report.pdf

Zimmerman, BJ. (2002) 'Becoming a self-regulated learner: an overview', *Theory Into Practice*, 41:2, 64-70

Index

M

N

O

P

Q

R

S

T

V

W

Z

OXFORD *Playscripts*

·low

Terry Pratchett

adapted by Stephen Briggs

Johnny *and the* Dead

Oxford University Press

Oxford University Press, Great Clarendon Street, Oxford OX2 6DP

Oxford New York
Athens Auckland Bangkok Bogota Buenos Aires
Calcutta Cape Town Chennai Dar es Salaam
Delhi Florence Hong Kong Istanbul Karachi
Kuala Lumpur Madrid Melbourne Mexico City
Mumbai Nairobi Paris São Paulo Singapore
Taipei Tokyo Toronto Warsaw

and associated companies in
Berlin Ibadan

Oxford is a trade mark of Oxford University Press

First published 1996
Reprinted 1997, 1998

ISBN 0 19 831294 6

Printed and bound in Great Britain at Cambridge University Press

Illustrations are by Neil Chapman

Contents

Characters

In order of their appearance on stage:

Johnny Maxwell	*a twelve-year-old boy who discovers he can talk to the Dead in the local cemetery*
Wobbler Johnson	*Johnny's school friend*
Alderman Thomas Bowler	*one of the Dead; a member of Blackbury Council when alive; he wears civic robes*
Grandad	*Johnny's grandad*
William Stickers	*one of the Dead; a communist when alive; he has a huge black beard and wears gold-rimmed spectacles*
Yo-less	*Johnny's school friend*
Bigmac	*Johnny's school friend*
Antonio Vicenti	*one of the Dead; ran a joke shop and worked as an escapologist and children's entertainer when alive; wears a red carnation in his button hole*
Mrs Sylvia Liberty	*one of the Dead; a suffragette who campaigned for votes for women when alive*
Solomon Einstein	*one of the Dead; a famous taxidermist when alive; a keen thinker*
Addison Vincent Fletcher	*one of the Dead; invented a form of telephone when alive*
Stanley 'Wrong Way' Roundaway	*one of the Dead (non-speaking); played for Blackbury Wanderers when alive; famous for scoring own goals; wears a 1930's football kit*
Eric Grimm	*one of the Dead; disapproves of the behaviour of the other Dead; has a mysterious past*
Radio Announcer	*(voice only) on BBC Radio Blackbury*
Disc Jockey	*(voice only) on BBC Radio Blackbury*
Johnny's Mum	*(non-speaking)*
Johnny's Gran	*(non-speaking)*
Nurse	*works at Sunshine Acres Old People's Home*
Mad Jim	*(voice only) DJ for BBC Radio Blackbury; hosts 'Mad Jim's Late-Night Explosion'*
Mr Ronald Atterbury	*from the British Legion*
Private Tommy Atkins	*a young soldier from the First World War (non-speaking)*

Ms Ethel Liberty	*a representative of Blackbury Council*
Mr Bowler	*a representative of United Amalgamated Consolidated Holdings*
Woman in the Audience	*at the meeting at the civic centre*
Radio Interviewer	*(voice only) for BBC Radio Blackbury*
First Man **Second Man**	*thugs hired to wreck the cemetery*
Police Officer	*(non-speaking)*
Police Officer	*who arrests the second man*
Other Non-speaking Roles	*other dead people (if required)* *old people at Sunshine Acres* *soldiers from the First World War* *people at the meeting at the civic centre*

Scene 1

The cemetery. ***Johnny*** *walks onto the stage, carrying his schoolbag. He sits on a tombstone and addresses the audience.*

Johnny I really discovered the cemetery after I started living at Grandad's, after my parents split up. I started taking a short-cut through here instead of going home on the bus. My pal Wobbler thinks it's spooky…

Wobbler *enters, carrying a schoolbag.*

Wobbler Why do we have to go home this way? I think it's spooky.

Johnny *(Still talking to the audience)*… but I think it's quite – friendly. Peaceful. Once you forget about all the skeletons underground, of course.

Wobbler *sits next to Johnny.*

Wobbler It's Hallowe'en next week. I'm having a disco; you have to come as something horrible. So don't bother to find a disguise.

Johnny Thanks.

Wobbler You notice how there's a lot more Hallowe'en stuff in the shops these days?

Johnny It's because of Bonfire Night. Too many people were blowing themselves up with fireworks, so they invented Hallowe'en, where you just wear masks and stuff.

Wobbler My mum's friend, Mrs Nugent, says all that sort of thing is tampering with the occult.

Johnny Probably is.

Wobbler She says witches are abroad on Hallowe'en.

Johnny What…? Like… Majorca, and places?

Wobbler *(Not very certain on this point)* 'Spose so.

Johnny Makes sense, I suppose. They probably get out-of-season bargains, being old ladies. My aunt can go anywhere on the buses for almost nothing and she's not even a witch.

Wobbler Don't see what Mrs Nugent is worried about then. It ought to be a lot safer round here, with all the witches on holiday.

Johnny I saw a thing in a book once, about these people in Mexico or somewhere, where they all go down to the cemetery for a big fiesta at Hallowe'en every year. Like, they don't see why people should be left out of things just because they're dead.

Wobbler Yuk. A picnic? In the actual cemetery? You'd get glowing green hands pushing up through the earth and nicking the sarnies.

Johnny Don't think so. Anyway… they don't eat sarnies in Mexico. They eat tort… um, tort… something.

Wobbler *(Confidently)* Tortoises.

Johnny Yeah?

A new thought occurs to ***Wobbler****.*

Wobbler I bet. I bet… I bet you wouldn't dare knock on one of those doors. You know, one of them doors on those big gravestones. I bet something really horrible would come lurchin' out!

Wobbler *stands and lurches about a bit, arms stretched out in front of him. Then another new thought occurs to him.*

Wobbler 'Ere, my dad says all this is going to be built on. He says the council sold it to some big company for five pence, 'cos it was costing too much to keep it going. It's going to be offices and things.

Johnny I'd have given them a pound just to leave it as it is. I bet the people here wouldn't be very happy about it. If they knew.

***Johnny** points at Alderman Bowler's tomb, which has an impressive door, over which is carved… 'Pro Bono Publico'.*

Johnny I bet he'd be really angry.

He crosses to the door and knocks.

Wobbler *(Looking worried)* Hey! You mustn't do that!

***Johnny** knocks again. The door opens and **Alderman Thomas Bowler** steps out. Although his face is a bit on the pale side, he looks comparatively normal, and is dressed in his civic robes.*

Alderman Bowler Yes?

***Johnny** cries out in surprise and takes a couple of steps back, bumping into **Wobbler**.*

Wobbler *(Startled)* What?

Johnny The door's opened! Can't you see it?

Wobbler No! No I can't! There's no point in your trying to frighten me, you know. Er… look, anyway, I'm late. Um. Bye!

***Wobbler** starts to walk off, but quickly breaks into a run. **Johnny** walks over to Alderman Bowler.*

Alderman Bowler What is it you want?

Johnny Are you dead?

Alderman Bowler *points to the sign over his doorway.*

Alderman Bowler See what it says there?

Johnny Er…

Alderman Bowler It says nineteen hundred and six. It was a very good funeral, I gather. I didn't attend myself… er… rather, I *did*, but not so's I could actually observe events, if you get my meaning. What was it you were wanting?

Johnny *(Not quite sure what he does want)* Er… what… er… what does 'Pro Bono Publico' mean?

Alderman Bowler It means 'for the public good'.

Johnny Oh. Well, thank you. Thanks very much.

Alderman Bowler Was that all?

Johnny Yes.

Alderman Bowler I didn't think it could be anything important. I haven't had a visitor since nineteen twenty-three. And even then they'd got the name wrong. And – they were Americans! Oh well, goodbye then.

Alderman Bowler *freezes.* ***Johnny*** *takes a few steps away from him and speaks directly to the audience.*

Johnny I was about to go home, and I thought: if I go I'll never know what happens next.

He turns and walks back to Alderman Bowler.

Johnny You're dead, right?

Alderman Bowler Oh yes. It's one of those things one is pretty certain about.

Johnny Are you a ghost?

Alderman Bowler Good heavens, no! I'm just dead.

Johnny You're no good at dancing, are you?

Alderman Bowler I used to be able to waltz quite well.

Johnny No, I meant… sort of… like this *(He does a passable impression of Michael Jackson dancing)* you know, with your feet.

Alderman Bowler That looks very energetic.

Johnny And you have to go 'Ow!'.

Alderman Bowler I should think anyone would, dancing like that.

Johnny No, no, I mean… no, never mind. But look, I don't see how you can be dead and walking and talking at the same time.

Alderman Bowler That's probably because of relativity. *(He moonwalks stiffly across the path)* Like this, was it? Ouch!

Johnny Yeah, a bit. How do you mean… relativity?

Alderman Bowler I'm not too sure. Einstein explains it better.

Johnny What, *Albert* Einstein?

Alderman Bowler *(Still doing a rather inexpert moonwalk)* Who?

Johnny He was a famous scientist.

Alderman Bowler No, I meant Solomon Einstein. He was a famous taxidermist in Cable Street. Very keen thinker. Got knocked down by a car in nineteen thirty-two.

It has been getting darker.

Johnny I think I'd better be getting home. It's getting late, anyway.

Alderman Bowler *(Still moonwalking)* I think I'm getting the hang of this. Call any time you like. I'm always in. That's something you learn to be good at, when you're dead. Er. 'Ow!' was it?

Alderman Bowler *moonwalks off stage as* ***Johnny*** *comes downstage to address the audience.*

Johnny And that was the first time I'd seen one of the Dead from the cemetery. It wasn't the last, though. The next day, I was walking through the cemetery with my grandad.

Grandad *enters.*

Johnny That was when I met William Stickers.

Grandad It's disgusting, what the council are doing. Selling off this cemetery, and for what? Another flippin' office block! There's history in here.

Johnny Alderman Thomas Bowler.

Grandad Never heard of 'im. I was referring to him. *(He points to a headstone)* – William Stickers.

Johnny Was he famous?

Grandad Nearly famous. Nearly famous. You've heard of Karl Marx?

Johnny He invented communism, didn't he?

Grandad Right. Well, William Stickers didn't. But he'd have been Karl Marx if Karl Marx hadn't beaten him to it.

Grandad *looks at the headstone, which is visible to the audience. It reads: 'William Stickers. 1897–1949. Workers of the world unit'.*

Grandad A great man.

Johnny *(Reading the writing on the headstone)* 'Workers of the world unit' ? What was the 'world unit'?

William Stickers *enters.* ***Johnny*** *sees him but does not react yet.*

Grandad It should have been 'unite'. 'Workers of the world unite.' They ran out of money before they did the 'e'. It was a scandal. He was a hero of the working class. He would have fought in the Spanish Civil War except he got on the wrong boat.

Johnny What was he like? Was he a big man with a huge black beard and gold-rimmed spectacles?

Grandad That's right. Seen pictures, have you?

Johnny No. Not exactly.

Grandad I'm going down the shops. Want to come?

Johnny No, thanks. Er… I'm going round to Wobbler's.

Grandad OK. See you.

Grandad *exits.*

Johnny *(To William Stickers)* Hello.

William Stickers It *was* a scandal, them not giving me the 'e'. You'd think somebody would have stumped up the extra couple of bob. What's your name, comrade?

Johnny Johnny Maxwell.

William Stickers What year is this, Johnny Maxwell?

Johnny Nineteen ninety-five.

William Stickers Ah! And have the downtrodden masses risen up to overthrow the capitalist oppressors in the glorious name of communism?

Johnny Um? You mean like Russia and stuff? When they shot the Tsar?

William Stickers Oh, I know *that.* I mean, what's been happening since nineteen forty-nine? No one tells us anything in here.

Johnny Er, well… tell you what… can you read a newspaper if I bring one in?

William Stickers Of course, but it's hard to turn the pages.

Johnny Um. Are there a lot of you in here?

William Stickers Hah! Most of them don't bother. They just aren't prepared to make the effort.

Johnny Can you… you know… walk around? 'Cos you could get into things for free and so on.

William Stickers It's hard to go far. It's not really allowed.

Johnny Oh yes. I read in a book once that ghosts can't move around much.

William Stickers Ghost!? Ghost!? I'm not a ghost! *(He starts to exit)* And don't you forget that paper, comrade!

***William Stickers** exits. Blackout.*

Scene 2

*A school classroom. **Yo-less, Wobbler** and **Bigmac** enter and sit at some desks. **Johnny** enters and joins them.*

Yo-less Hello, Johnny. We were just talking about you. You been in that cemetery again?

Johnny *(Defensively)* Yes.

Wobbler Why do you go there? It's a dump. Well, the canal bank behind it is, anyway: old prams, burst settees, busted TVs…

Bigmac Yeah, and on the other side is that waste ground that used to be the boot factory.

Yo-less They're going to build an office building on that site. It was in the papers. *(He pulls out a copy of the local paper)* Look.

Johnny *(Taking the paper)* It's huge. That'll take up more land than that factory site! *(Reading)* 'An Exciting Development for United Amalgamated Consolidated Holdings: Forward to the Future!'

Wobbler What do United Amalgamated Consolidated Holdings actually *do*?

Johnny It says here they're a multi-national information-retrieval and enhancement facility. It says they'll provide three hundred new jobs.

Yo-less For all the people who used to work at the Blackbury rubber boot factory. It all seems a bit pointless.

Wobbler Hey! How are your ghosts getting on?

Johnny No, not ghosts. They don't like being called ghosts. They're just… dead. I suppose it's like not calling people handicapped or backward.

Yo-less Politically incorrect.

Wobbler You mean they want to be called… post-senior citizens.

Yo-less Breathily challenged.

Bigmac Vertically disadvantaged.

Yo-less What? You mean they're short?

Bigmac Buried.

Wobbler How about zombies?

***Wobbler** staggers around, doing a 'zombie' walk, and grabs **Yo-less** by the throat.*

Yo-less *(Pushing him away)* No, you've got to have a body to be a zombie. You're not really dead, you just get fed this secret voodoo mixture of fish and roots.

Wobbler Fish n' roots? I bet it's a real adventure going down the chippie in voodoo country.

Bigmac *(To Yo-less)* You ought to know about voodoo.

Yo-less Why?

Bigmac Well, 'cos you're West Indian, right?

Yo-less What? You know all about druids, do you?

Bigmac No.

Yo-less Well, there you are then.

Johnny No, look, you're not taking it seriously. I really saw them!

Wobbler Yeah, but you once said you'd seen the Loch Ness monster in your goldfish pond.

Johnny All right, but…

Bigmac And then there was the lost city of the Incas.

Johnny Well, I found it, didn't I?

Yo-less Yes, but it wasn't that lost, was it? Behind Tesco's isn't exactly lost.

Johnny Yes. Yes. All right. But, you'll come down after school, won't you?

Wobbler Well…

Johnny Not scared are you? You ran away before. When the Alderman came out.

Wobbler I never saw no Alderman. Anyway, I just ran away to wind you up.

Johnny You certainly had me fooled. All right then. All three of you. After school.

Bigmac After 'Cobbers'.

Johnny This is more important than some Aussie soap opera.

Bigmac Yes, but tonight Janine is going to tell Mick that Doraleen took Ron's surfboard…

Johnny All right then. After 'Cobbers'.

Yo-less I've got some geography homework.

Johnny We haven't got any.

Yo-less No, but I thought if I did an extra essay on rainforests I could pull up my marks average.

Johnny You're weird. All right. Let's meet up later. Six o'clock. At Bigmac's place, 'cos that's near the cemetery. Weird, really.

Yo-less What is?

Johnny Well, there's a huge cemetery for dead people and all the living people are crammed up in that multi-storey block of flats where Bigmac lives. I mean, it sounds like someone got something wrong…

Bigmac Six o'clock, then.

Wobbler But it'll be getting dark by then.

Johnny Not scared, are you?

Wobbler Me? Scared? Huh! *Me*? Scared? Me? *Scared*?

Blackout.

• •

Scene 3

***Johnny**, **Wobbler**, **Bigmac** and **Yo-less** are now in the cemetery. **Bigmac** is hiding something behind his back. It is getting dark. Throughout the scene, **Johnny** is the only one of the living who can see the Dead. **Wobbler**, **Bigmac** and **Yo-less** must react as though Johnny is the only other person on stage.*

Wobbler *(Looking nervously around him)* Scared? Me?

***Yo-less** puts a hand on **Wobbler's** shoulder. **Wobbler** yells.*

Wobbler Aaah!

Yo-less Hey, don't panic. Look, there's crosses all over the place. See, it's sort of like a church, really.

Wobbler Yes, but I'm an atheist.

Yo-less Then you shouldn't believe in ghosts…

Bigmac Post-senior citizens.

Johnny Bigmac?

Bigmac Yeah?

Johnny What are you holding behind your back?

***Bigmac** produces a sharpened stake and a hammer.*

Johnny Bigmac!

Bigmac Well, you never know…

Johnny Leave them here!

Bigmac Oh, all right.

Bigmac *puts down the hammer and the stake.*

Yo-less Anyway, it's not stakes for ghosts. That's for vampires.

Wobbler *(Not much reassured by this)* Oh, thank you!

Johnny Look, this is just the cemetery. It's not Transylvania! There's just dead people here! Dead people are just people who were living once! A few years ago they were just mowing lawns and putting up Christmas decorations and being people's grandparents. They're nothing to be frightened of!

Yo-less Yes… It's peaceful, isn't it?

Bigmac Quiet as the grave. *(He laughs)*

Johnny A lot of people come for walks here. I mean, the park's miles away, and all it's got is grass. This place has got bushes and plants and trees, and…

Yo-less Environment. And probably some ecology as well.

Wobbler *crosses to Antonio Vicenti's grave.*

Wobbler Hey, look at this grave. Dead impressive. But why has it got such a big arch on it?

Yo-less That's just showing off. There's probably a sticker on the back saying, 'My Other Grave is a Porch'.

Johnny *(He thinks this is a bit irreverent)* Yo-less!

Antonio Vicenti *enters.*

Antonio Vicenti Actually, I think that was very funny. He is a very funny boy.

Johnny Oh. Hello.

Wobbler, ***Bigmac*** *and* ***Yo-less*** *watch* ***Johnny*** *talking 'to himself' in amazement.*

Antonio Vicenti And what was the joke exactly?

Johnny Well, you can get these stickers for cars, you see, and they say 'My Other Car is a Porsche'. It's a sort of sports car.

Antonio Vicenti *(Laughing)* Oh yes. Back in the old country I used to do entertainment for kiddies. On Saturdays. At parties. The Great Vicenti and Ethel. I like to laugh.

Johnny The old country?

Antonio Vicenti The alive country.

Wobbler You don't fool us. There's no one there.

Antonio Vicenti And I did escapology, too.

Yo-less You're just talking to the air.

Johnny Escapology?

Antonio Vicenti Escaping from things. Sacks and chains and handcuffs and so on. Like the Great Houdini? My greatest trick involved getting out of a locked sack underwater while wearing twenty feet of chain and three pairs of handcuffs.

Johnny Gosh. How often did you do that?

Antonio Vicenti Nearly once.

Wobbler Come on, joke over.

Johnny Shut up, this is interesting.

Antonio Vicenti And you're John Maxwell. The Alderman told us about you.

Johnny Us?

__Antonio Vicenti__ nods in the direction over Johnny's shoulder. __Johnny__ turns and sees the Dead – __Alderman Bowler, Mrs Sylvia Liberty, Solomon Einstein, William Stickers, Addison Vincent Fletcher__ and __Stanley 'Wrong Way' Roundaway__ – moving on to the stage. They are surrounded by mist (created by dry ice or smoke pellets).

Yo-less He's not joking. Look at his face.

Wobbler Johnny? Are you all right?

Bigmac It's gone cold.

Wobbler *(His voice shaking)* We ought to be getting back. I ought to be doing my homework.

Bigmac Blimey! You *must* be frightened!

Wobbler Shut up!

Johnny *(To his friends)* You can't see them, can you? They're all around you but you can't see them!

Antonio Vicenti The living generally can't see the dead. It's for their own good, I expect.

Bigmac Come on. Stop mucking about.

Yo-less Hang on. There's something odd…

Alderman Bowler John Maxwell! We must talk to you!

Johnny What about?

William Stickers *(Brandishing a paper)* This!

__Wobbler__, __Bigmac__ and __Yo-less__ gape open-mouthed at what, to them, seems to be a paper floating in mid-air!

Wobbler Poltergeist! I saw the film! Saucepans flying through the air!

Alderman Bowler What is the fat boy talking about?

Yo-less It's just a freak wind!

Bigmac I can't feel a wind!

Alderman Bowler What is a poltergeist?

Johnny Look, will everyone just be quiet! *(To his friends)* Um, look. These, er, people want to talk to us, er, me.

Wobbler Are they… breath-impaired?

The lights dim further as night draws in.

Yo-less Don't be so wet. That sounds like asthma. Come on. If you mean it, say it. Come right out with it. Are they… er *(He looks around at the darkening sky)* post-senior citizens?

Wobbler Are they lurching?

Alderman Bowler You didn't tell us about this. In the paper. Well, it is *called* a newspaper, but it has pictures of women in the altogether – which might well be seen by respectable married women and young children!

William Stickers They're wearing swimming suits.

Alderman Bowler Swimming suits? But I can see almost all of their legs!

Sylvia Liberty Nothing wrong with that. Healthy bodies enjoying callisthenics in the God-given sunlight. And very practical clothing, I may say.

Antonio Vicenti *(Aside, to Johnny)* That's Mrs Sylvia Liberty. Died nineteen fourteen. Tireless suffragette.

Johnny Suffragette?

Antonio Vicenti Don't they teach you about these things at school? Suffragettes campaigned for votes for women. They used to chain themselves to railings and chuck eggs at policemen and throw themselves under the Prince of Wales's horse on Derby Days.

Johnny Wow!

Antonio Vicenti But Mrs Liberty got the instructions wrong and threw herself under the Prince of Wales. Killed outright. He was a very heavy man, I believe.

Johnny Who's the man next to her? In the rather old-fashioned football kit.

Antonio Vicenti Old fashioned? Oh… yes. That's Stanley 'Wrong Way' Roundaway. Used to play for Blackbury Wanderers.

Johnny Right.

William Stickers *(Butting in)* It says in this newspaper that the cemetery is going to be closed. Sold. By the council. It's going to be built on.

Johnny Er, yes. Didn't you know?

William Stickers Was anyone supposed to tell us?

Bigmac What're they saying?

Johnny They're annoyed about the cemetery being sold.

Alderman Bowler This is our home. What will happen to us, young man?

Johnny *(To Alderman Bowler)* Just a minute. Yo-less?

Yo-less Yes?

Johnny They want to know what will happen to them if the cemetery's sold off.

Yo-less I think… that the, er, coffins and that get dug up and put somewhere else. I think there's special places.

Sylvia Liberty I'm not standing for that! I paid five pounds, seven shillings and sixpence for my plot! I remember the document distinctly. 'Last resting place', it said. It didn't say 'after eighty years you'll be dug up and moved so the living can build a…' what does it say… ?

William Stickers Modern purpose-designed offices. Whatever that means.

Johnny I think it means they were designed on purpose.

William Stickers That's the living for you. No thought for the downtrodden masses.

Johnny Well, according to the paper the council says it costs too much to keep up, and the land's worth more for building on… Look, it's not my fault. I like this place, too.

Alderman Bowler So what are you going to do about it?

Johnny Me? Why me?

Sylvia Liberty You can see and hear us.

William Stickers So you must go and tell the council that we… aren't… going… to… move!

Johnny They won't listen to me! I'm only twelve! I can't even vote!

William Stickers Yes, but *we're* over twenty-one. Technically, I mean.

Antonio Vicenti Yes, but we're dead.

Alderman Bowler I served this city faithfully for over fifty years. I do not see why I should lose my vote just because I'm dead.

Johnny Well… I'll see what I can do.

Alderman Bowler Good man. And we'd like a paper delivered every day.

Antonio Vicenti No, no. It's hard to turn the pages.

Johnny I'll think of something. Something better than newspapers.

William Stickers Right. And you'll tell these council people that we're not going to take this lying down!

*The **Dead** drift off stage. **Stanley 'Wrong Way' Roundaway** initially drifts off the wrong way, but is rounded up by a couple of the other **Dead** and goes off with the others. There is a pause.*

Wobbler Have they gone?

Yo-less Not that they were here.

Johnny They were here. And now they've gone. Let's go. I need to think. They want me to stop this place being built on.

Yo-less We'll help.

Wobbler Will we? It's meddlin' with the occult. Your mum'll go spare.

Yo-less No. It's a Christian cemetery. So it's helping Christian souls. That's OK.

Johnny I think there's a Jewish part of the cemetery.

Bigmac That's all right. Jewish is the same as Christian.

Yo-less Er… not quite, but near enough. We've got to stick up for Johnny. We stuck up for Bigmac when he was in juvenile court.

Bigmac It was a political crime.

Yo-less You stole the Minister of Education's car when she was opening the school!

Bigmac It wasn't stealing. I meant to give it back.

Yo-less You drove it into a wall. You couldn't even give it back on a shovel.

Bigmac Oh, so it's my fault the brakes were faulty. I could've been badly hurt, right?

Yo-less Anyway. We were behind you, right?

Wobbler Wouldn't like to be in front of him!

Yo-less The point I'm making, is you've got to help your friends, right?

Wobbler/Bigmac Yeah.

Johnny I'm touched.

Wobbler Probably. But we'll still help you.

__Yo-less__, __Wobbler__ and __Bigmac__ exit. Blackout.

Scene 4

Grandad's house. __Grandad__ is sitting in an armchair, reading the local paper. __Johnny__ walks in and sits on a stool by the chair.

Johnny Grandad?

Grandad Yes?

Johnny How famous was William Stickers?

Grandad Very famous. Very famous man.

Johnny I couldn't find him in the encyclopaedia. How about Mrs Sylvia Liberty?

Grandad Who?

Johnny She was a suffragette.

Grandad Never heard of her.

Johnny All right... how about Mr Antonio Vicenti?

Grandad What? Old Tony Vicenti? What's he up to now?

Johnny Was he famous for anything?

Grandad He ran a joke shop in Alma Street where the multi-storey car park is now. You could buy stink bombs and itching powder. He used to do conjuring tricks at kids' parties.

Johnny Was he a famous man?

Grandad All the kids knew him. Prisoner of war in Germany he was. But he escaped. Always escaping from things, he was.

Johnny He wore a carnation pinned to his coat.

Grandad That's right! Every day. Never saw him without one. Haven't seen him around for years.

Johnny Grandad? You know that little transistor radio? The one you said was too fiddly and not loud enough?

Grandad What about it?

Johnny Can I have it? It's… for some friends. They're quite old. And a bit shut in.

Grandad Yeah. All right.

***Grandad** freezes as **Johnny** steps forward to address the audience. As **Johnny** speaks, the lights fade out on Grandad.*

Johnny I took the radio down to the cemetery and left it for them. I also made some notes about the people who were in there: Alderman Bowler, Mrs Liberty, Mr Stickers – and a quiet, overgrown little grave in one corner; just a flat stone on the ground – just saying *(He takes a notebook from his pocket and consults it)* 'Eric Grimm 1885–1927'. No 'Just Resting', no 'Deeply Missed', not even 'Died', although probably he had. The next day, we all went down to the library…

Blackout.

Scene 5

The library. ***Yo-less*****,** ***Bigmac*** *and* ***Wobbler*** *are on stage, looking at copies of old papers.* ***Johnny*** *enters.*

Johnny Found anyone famous yet? Nearly everyone who's died around here is buried in that cemetery. If we can find someone famous, that'll make it a famous place. There's a cemetery in London that's only famous 'cos Karl Marx is buried there.

Bigmac Karl Marx? What's he famous for?

Wobbler You're really ignorant, you are. Karl Marx. He was the one with the curly blond hair and the carhorn. You know, the one that never spoke.

Yo-less No, he was the one that used to *(He adopts an awful Italian accent)* talk-a like-a that-a.

Johnny Oh, ha-ha-ha! Very funny. He was *not* one of the Marx Brothers.

Yo-less Yeah. We know.

Bigmac So what films was he in, then?

Wobbler What did you say the Alderman was called?

Johnny Thomas Bowler. Why?

Wobbler It says here that he got the council to build a memorial horse-trough in the square in nineteen hundred and five. It came in useful very quickly too, it says here.

Johnny Why?

Wobbler Well… it says here, the next day the first motor car ever to drive into Blackbury crashed into it and caught fire. They used the water to put the fire out. The council praised Alderman Bowler for his forward thinking.

Yo-less Forward thinking? Building a horse-trough when motor cars had just been invented?

Wobbler Let's face it, this is a town where famous people don't come from.

Yo-less *(Looking at another paper)* It says here, that Addison Vincent Fletcher of Alamo Terrace invented a form of telephone in nineteen twenty-two.

Wobbler Oh great. But phones had been invented years before that.

Yo-less It says, he said his one was better.

Wobbler Oh yes. *(He dials on an imaginary phone)* Hello? Is that… *(He pauses to ask the others)* who invented the telephone?

Yo-less Thomas Edison?

Bigmac Sir Humphrey Telephone.

Johnny Alexander Graham Bell. *(To Bigmac)* Sir Humphrey *Telephone?*

Wobbler Hello, Mr Bell. You know that telephone you invented years ago? Well mine's better. And I'm just off to discover America – but I'm discovering it better.

Bigmac That makes sense, actually. No point in discovering a place until there's proper hotels and stuff.

Wobbler It's impossible for anyone famous to come from round here, because everyone round here is mental!

Yo-less Got one.

Bigmac Who? Which one?

Yo-less The footballer. Stanley 'Wrong Way' Roundaway. He played for Blackbury Wanderers.

Johnny I saw him. At the cemetery.

Bigmac Any good?

Wobbler *(Looking over Yo-less's shoulder)* Says he scored a record number of goals.

Bigmac Sounds good.

Wobbler Own goals.

Yo-less Greatest number of own goals in the history of any sport, it says. He kept getting over-excited and losing his sense of direction. But he was a good footballer, apart from that, it says. *(He picks up another paper)* Now – look at this.

Wobbler What?

Yo-less This is from nineteen sixteen. They're all going off to war. The First World War. Says here, it was the Blackbury Old Pals Battalion. There's a photo of them all in the paper. They all joined up at the same time…

The lights dim on everyone but ***Johnny****, who looks thoughtful. There is a sound of orders being shouted, of machine-gun fire. The lights go up again.*

Yo-less … and look, here's a paper from a month or so later. It lists all the local men killed at… the Somme. Let's check them against the photo in that paper.

Yo-less*,* ***Johnny****,* ***Bigmac*** *and* ***Wobbler*** *pore over the two newspapers. There is a moment's silence as their eyes move from one paper to the other. The horror of the losses slowly dawns on them.*

Johnny *(Shocked)* They all died. Four weeks after this photo was taken. All of them.

Yo-less *scans the list of dead soldiers and then looks at the photograph again.*

Yo-less Wait a minute… except for Atkins, T. He didn't die. It also says here that a Pals Battalion was when people all from one town or even one street could all join the army together if they wanted, and all get sent to… the same place.

Bigmac But… four weeks?

Wobbler Yes, but you're always going on about joining the army.

Bigmac Well... yeah... war, yeah. Proper fighting, with M16s and stuff. Not just all going off grinning and getting shot.

Yo-less They all marched off together because they were friends, and got killed.

Johnny Except for Atkins, T. I wonder what happened to him?

Yo-less It was nineteen sixteen. If he's still alive, he'll be dead. Perhaps he came back from the war and moved somewhere else.

Bigmac It would've been a bit lonely round here, after all... *(They all look at him)* Sorry.

The lights fade down on them.

Scene 6

The lights come up on the cemetery where ***Alderman Bowler, Sylvia Liberty, Antonio Vicenti, William Stickers, Solomon Einstein, Stanley 'Wrong Way' Roundaway, Addison Vincent Fletcher*** *and* ***Eric Grimm*** *are listening to the radio.*

Radio announcer *(Voice only)*... and that brings to an end our programmes for this evening on BBC Radio Blackbury. We'll now hand you back to Radio 2. Goodnight, everyone.

Solomon Einstein *leans forward and switches off the radio.*

Addison Vincent Fletcher So that's wireless telegraphy, is it? Hah! So much for Count Alice Radioni!

Antonio Vicenti Radioni? It was Marconi who invented the radio.

Addison Vincent Fletcher Yes, but who do you think he stole the idea from?

Antonio Vicenti Good grief! Who cares who invented it? Did you hear what the living are planning? They're going to steal our cemetery!

Alderman Bowler Yes, but I didn't know all this was going on, did you? All this music and… the things they were talking about! Who *is* Shakespeare's Sister and why is she singing on the wireless? What is a Batman? And they said the last prime minister was a woman! That can't be right! Women can't even vote.

Antonio Vicenti Yes, they can.

Sylvia Liberty Hurrah!

Alderman Bowler Well, they couldn't in *my* time!

William Stickers There's so much we don't know.

Antonio Vicenti So – why don't we find out?

William Stickers How?

Antonio Vicenti A man on the wireless said that you can ring the wireless station on the telephone to 'discuss problems that affect us all today'. A 'phone-in' programme, he said.

William Stickers Well?

Antonio Vicenti There's a phone box out in the street.

Alderman Bowler But how would we work the machinery?

Addison Vincent Fletcher Oh, I'm sure Mr Einstein and I will be able to sort it out. After all, it's just a less refined version of my own invention, mm?

Sylvia Liberty Well, come on then!

***Eric Grimm** clears his throat. The **Dead** all turn and look at him.*

Eric Grimm You can't go outside. You know that's wrong.

Alderman Bowler Only a little way, Eric. That can't do any harm. It's for the good of the…

Eric Grimm It's wrong!

Antonio Vicenti We don't have to listen to him.

Eric Grimm You'll get into terrible trouble.

Antonio Vicenti No, we won't.

Eric Grimm It's dabbling with the 'known'. You'll all get into terrible trouble and it won't be my fault. You are bad people.

***Eric Grimm** turns and walks back to his grave.*

Sylvia Liberty Come on!

William Stickers Yes, but… that's… outside…

Antonio Vicenti Not far outside.

Alderman Bowler Yes, but…

Antonio Vicenti The little boy stood in front of us and talked to us. And he was so frightened. And we can't walk six feet?

William Stickers It's all right for you, Vicenti, you spent most of your life escaping from things! But this is our place! This is where we belong!

Antonio Vicenti It's only a few steps…

*The **Dead** start to make their way out of the cemetery (as before, **Stanley 'Wrong Way' Roundaway** starts to exit the wrong way to all the rest, but is brought back by one of the others).*

• •

Scene 7

The shopping mall. BBC Radio Blackbury is blaring out of the mall's sound system. ***Wobbler, Bigmac, Johnny*** *and* ***Yo-less*** *are sitting on a bench, eating burgers out of CFC-free styrofoam boxes.*

Wobbler Hey, d'you think I could get a job at the burger bar?

Bigmac No chance. The manager'd take one look at you and see where the profits would go.

Wobbler Are you saying I'm fat?

Yo-less Gravitationally enhanced. Anyway, there's loads of people want jobs there. You have to have three A-levels.

Wobbler What? Just to sell burgers?

Bigmac No other jobs around. They're shutting all the factories round here. No one's making anything any more.

Wobbler Well, how does all the stuff get in the shops, then?

Bigmac That's all made in Taiwanaland or somewhere. That's right, eh? Johnny?

Johnny What?

Bigmac You've just been staring at nothing, you know that? You OK?

Johnny What? Oh, yeah, I'm OK.

Wobbler He's upset about them dead soldiers.

Yo-less Look… that's all in the past, right? It's a shame they died, but… well, they'd be dead by now anyway, wouldn't they? It's just history. It's got nothing to do with now.

Johnny *(Unconvinced)* Right. Maybe. *(Snapping out of it)* What CD did you get, Yo-less?

Yo-less *(Pulling his CD out of the store bag)* 'Famous British Brass Bands'. Excellent.

Wobbler 'Famous British Brass Bands'!?

Yo-less It's a good one. It's got the old Blackbury Rubber Boot Factory Band playing the 'Floral Dance'. Very famous piece.

Wobbler You're just basically not black, are you? I'm going to report you to the Rastafarians.

Yo-less *You* like reggae and blues.

Wobbler That's different…

Over the speakers we now hear the Dead's phone conversation with Radio Blackbury. All the boys can hear the radio programme, and react to it.

Sylvia Liberty *(Voice only)* Hello? Hello? This is Mrs Sylvia Liberty talking on the electric telephone! Hello? I demand to be heard this instant!

Disc jockey *(Voice only)* Er, hi. The caller on line… well, er, on *all* the lines, actually…

Sylvia Liberty *(Voice only)* You listen to me young man! And don't cut me off to start playing any more phonograph cylinders! Innocent citizens are being evicted from their homes! No account is being taken of their many years of valued service to the community, merely because of an accident of birth…

William Stickers *(Voice only, singing to the tune of 'The Red Flag')* The people's shroud is deepest black...

Sylvia Liberty *(Voice only) Will* you get off the line, you dreadful Bolshevik! You're nothing but a…

The voices are cut off and, seconds later, music plays over the radio.

Wobbler You get some real loonies on those phone-ins. You ever listen to 'Mad Jim's Late-Night Explosion'?

Yo-less He's not mad, he just says he is. All he does is play old records and go 'yeah!' and 'yowsahyowsah!' a lot. That's not mad. That's pathetic.

Wobbler Yes.

Bigmac Yes.

Yo-less Yes.

They look at Johnny. They all know the voices were not the usual radio loonies.

Yo-less Er… that was *them*, wasn't it?

Johnny Yes. It was them.

Yo-less How can they use the phone?

Johnny I don't know. I suppose some of them knew how to use it when they were alive. And maybe being dead's like… electricity or something.

Wobbler Who was the one singing?

Johnny That was William Stickers. He's a bit of a communist.

Yo-less I didn't think there were any communists left these days.

Johnny There aren't. And he's one of them.

Yo-less I think you've started something. Giving them that radio.

Johnny That's what I think too. Look, I've got to go. I'm supposed to be going with my mum to visit my grandmother.

***Johnny** exits. Lights down.*

• •

Scene 8

An old people's home. ***Johnny****, his* ***mum****, his* ***gran*** *and* ***Grandad*** *sit in a semicircle. There are a few seconds of silence, before* ***Johnny*** *turns to the audience and speaks. A couple of old people shuffle past at random during Johnny's speech.*

Johnny It's not that Sunshine Acres is a bad place. It's clean enough and the staff seem OK. But somehow it's more gloomy than the cemetery. It's the way everyone shuffles around quietly, or sits around waiting for their next meal, just because there's nothing else to do. It's like… life hasn't stopped yet and being dead hasn't started, so all you have to do is hang around. Every week we come here, have the same conversation, and go again. Except that this week, I noticed that on one of the rooms the name was Mr T. Atkins.

A ***nurse*** *enters carrying a cardboard box.* ***Johnny*** *stands up and intercepts her.*

Johnny Excuse me.

Nurse Yes?

Johnny I thought, you know, I might drop in and have a chat with Mr Atkins. Er… I'm doing a project at school – about the Blackbury Pals.

Nurse A project? Oh, well that's different then. The Blackbury Pals?

Johnny They were… some soldiers. Mr Atkins was one of them, I think. Uh… where… ?

Nurse I'm really sorry, but I'm afraid he passed away yesterday, dear. Nearly ninety-seven, I think he was. Did you know him?

Johnny Not…really.

Nurse He was here for years. He was a nice old man. He used to say that when he died, the war would be over. It was his joke. He used to show us his old army pay book *(She draws it from the box)* Look. 'Tommy Atkins', he'd say. 'I'm the one, I'm the boy, when I'm gone it's all over.'

Johnny What did he mean?

Nurse I don't know. This was his stuff. I expect it's all right for you to see, as it's a project. No one ever visited him, except Mr Atterbury from the British Legion. They've asked for his medals, you know.

She gives ***Johnny*** *the box. He peers into it.*

Johnny A pipe, a tobacco tin, and a huge penknife. Scrap book. A box… *(He sits down, takes out the box and opens it)*… with some medals in it. *(He puts it back)* A photograph… *(He takes out a photo. It is a print of the photo that had been in the paper, a group photograph of all the Pals. He turns it over and reads the back)*… 'Old comrades! We're the boys, Kaiser Bill! If you know a better 'ole, go to it!' They've all signed it. All of them. And under every name – except Mr Atkins's – there's a pencilled cross.

Nurse What's that, dear?

Johnny This photograph. They all signed it.

Nurse Yes. That was him, in the Great War. He used to talk about them a lot.

Johnny Yes.

Nurse His funeral's on Monday. At the crem. One of us will be there. Well, he was a nice old man.

Johnny Yes.

Johnny *stands, looking at the photo, as the lights go down.*

• •

Scene 9

***William Stickers** is in a phone box just outside the cemetery fence. He is lit by a spotlight.*

Mad Jim *(Voice only)* … yowsahyowsahyowsah! And the next caller on Uncle Mad Jim's bodaaacious problem corner iiis…

William Stickers William Stickers, Mad Jim.

Mad Jim *(Voice only)* Hi, Bill. You sound a bit depressed, to me.

William Stickers It's worse than that. I'm dead, Jim.

Mad Jim *(Voice only)* Wow! I can see that could be a real downer, Bill. Care to tell us about it?

William Stickers You sound very understanding, comrade. Well… events seem to have passed me by. I mean, how is Stalin managing in the glorious Soviet Union?

Mad Jim *(Voice only)* Seems to me you haven't been keeping up with current events, Bill.

William Stickers I thought I'd explained about that.

Mad Jim *(Voice only)* Oh, right. You've been dead, right? You better now?

William Stickers It's not something you get better from, Jim.

Mad Jim *(Voice only)* So, tell us, Bill, what's it like… being dead?

William Stickers Like? *Like*? It is extremely *dull*.

Mad Jim *(Voice only)* Oh dear, oh dear. Well, look, for Bill and all the other dead people out there, here's one from the vaults by Michael Jackson… 'Thriller' –

*As the music starts, the **Dead** – including **Alderman Bowler**, **Sylvia Liberty**, **Antonio Vicenti**, **Solomon Einstein** and **Addison Vincent Fletcher** drift onto the stage and join in with the dance.*

***Stanley 'Wrong Way' Roundaway**, of course, faces upstage – the opposite of all the others! **William Stickers** joins them.*

Alderman Bowler *(Moonwalking backwards across the stage)* This is how you do it, apparently. Johnny showed me.

Sylvia Liberty It certainly is a syncopated rhythm. Like this, you say? *(She joins in)*

Alderman Bowler That's right. And apparently you spin around with your arms out and shout 'Ow!'. Get down and – what was it the man on the wireless said?

Sylvia Liberty Bogey, I believe.

*For a while, the **Dead** dance around, vaguely in the manner of Michael Jackson's 'Thriller'. After a moment or two, **Johnny** rushes on.*

Johnny You shouldn't be doing this!

Antonio Vicenti Why not?

Johnny It's the middle of the night!

Antonio Vicenti Well? We don't sleep!

Johnny I mean… what would your descendants think?

Sylvia Liberty Serve them right for not visiting us! We're making carpets!

William Stickers Cutting a rung!

Alderman Bowler A rug. Cutting a rug. That's what Mr Benbow, who died in nineteen forty-one, says it is called. Getting down and bogeying.

The music stops.

Sylvia Liberty That was extremely enjoyable. Mr Fletcher! Mr Einstein! Be so good as to instruct the wireless man to play something more!

***Addison Vincent Fletcher** and **Solomon Einstein** cross to the phone box and start to tinker. **Johnny** goes across to see what they are doing.*

Solomon Einstein Hello, Johnny. I don't think ve've met before. Solomon Einstein: eighteen sixty-nine to nineteen thirty-two.

Johnny Like Albert Einstein?

Solomon Einstein He vas my distant cousin. Relatively speaking.

***Solomon Einstein** and **Addison Vincent Fletcher** laugh.*

Johnny Who're you ringing up?

Addison Vincent Fletcher Well, we were going to call back the radio station, but I was just having a look at the world.

Johnny What's going on? You said you couldn't leave the cemetery!

Antonio Vicenti No one has explained this to you? They do not teach you in schools?

Johnny Well, we don't get lessons in dealing with gho… with dead people, I mean. Sorry.

Antonio Vicenti We're not ghosts, Johnny. We're something else. But now you see us and hear us, we're free. You're giving us what we don't have.

Johnny What's that?

Antonio Vicenti I can't explain. But while you're thinking of us, we're free.

***Eric Grimm** appears at the other side of the cemetery fence.*

Eric Grimm Send him away.

Johnny Who's that?

Antonio Vicenti Mr Grimm.

Johnny Oh yes. I couldn't find anything about him in the paper.

Antonio Vicenti I'm not surprised. In those days, there were things they didn't put in.

Eric Grimm You go away, boy. You're meddling with things you don't understand. You're imperilling your immortal soul. And theirs. You go away, you bad boy.

He walks off.

Antonio Vicenti Anyway, how are you? Are you doing anything tomorrow? We're all going to a funeral.

Johnny Mr Atkins?

Antonio Vicenti *(Surprised)* Yes.

Johnny I'll be there.

The lights go down.

• •

Scene 10

The cemetery chapel. ***Johnny*** *and the* ***Dead*** *are at Mr Atkins's funeral. Also there are the* ***nurse*** *and* ***Mr Atterbury*** *of the British Legion. The living are at the front of the chapel, with the* ***Dead*** *in the pews behind them. We can hear a bit of organ music, as the service comes to an end.* ***Johnny*** *turns around and whispers to* ***Addison Vincent Fletcher****, behind him.*

Johnny Why are you here?

Addison Vincent Fletcher It's allowed. We used to go to all the funerals in the cemetery. Help them settle in. It's always a bit of a shock.

Johnny Oh.

Addison Vincent Fletcher And seeing as we knew you were going to be here, we thought we should make the effort. Mr Vicenti said it was worth a try. We're getting better at it!

*The service ends. All rise. The **Dead** leave smartly, followed by the **nurse** (as usual, **Stanley 'Wrong Way' Roundaway** has to be helped out the correct way!). **Mr Atterbury**, carrying Tommy Atkins's medal box, starts to leave, but is stopped by **Johnny**.*

Johnny Excuse me? Are you Mr... Atterbury? From the British Legion?

Mr Atterbury Yes, lad.

Johnny My name's Johnny Maxwell.

Mr Atterbury And I'm Ronald Atterbury. How do you do?

Johnny Are those Mr Atkins's medals?

Mr Atterbury Yes, son. The lady from the home said you're doing a project?

Johnny Um. Yes. Can I ask you some stuff?

Mr Atterbury Of course, yes.

***Johnny** and **Mr Atterbury** sit down on a bench.*

Johnny Well, when Mr Atkins said that he was 'the one'... um. Well, I know about the Blackbury Pals, how they all got killed apart from him. But I don't think that's what he meant.

Mr Atterbury You know about the Pals, do you?

Johnny Yes. From the local paper.

Mr Atterbury But you don't know about Tommy Atkins? Why he was so proud of the name?

Johnny No. No, I don't.

Mr Atterbury You see... in the Great War, the First World War... when a new recruit joined the army he had to fill in his pay book, yes? Name and address and that sort of thing? And to help them do it, the army did a kind of guide to how to fill it in. And on the guide, where it said 'name', they put: 'Tommy Atkins'. It was just a name. Just to show them that that's where their name should be, but it became a sort of joke. Tommy Atkins came to mean the average soldier…

Johnny Like the 'man in the street'?

A sound of marching feet can be heard in the distance, and a military band playing 'Tipperary'. The lights start to dim. ***Private Atkins, T.*** *enters and stands to attention.*

Mr Atterbury Yes. Very much like that. Tommy Atkins, the British Tommy.

Johnny So… in a way… *all* soldiers were Tommy Atkins?

Mr Atterbury Yes, I suppose you could put it like that. Rather fanciful, of course. The army used it because it was a common sort of name. I know our Mr Atkins was very proud of it. He was a strange old boy. I used to see him regularly at…

The ***Blackbury Pals*** *march on (through the audience?). They look straight ahead, marching in slow motion, almost. As they pass* ***Tommy Atkins****, he joins them. They turn and march off the way they came.* ***Johnny*** *sees all this, but no one else does.*

Johnny He's going back to France.

Mr Atterbury What?

Johnny Tommy Atkins. He's going back.

Mr Atterbury How did you know that?

Johnny Uh…

Mr Atterbury I expect the lady from the home told you, mm? Yes, we're taking him back this week. He gave us a map reference. Very precise, too. We'll scatter his ashes there.

Johnny Where… the Pals died?

Mr Atterbury That's right. He was always talking about them.

Johnny Sir?

Mr Atterbury Yes?

Johnny There was a Sergeant Atterbury in the Pals. Are you related to him?

Mr Atterbury *(Surprised)* Yes. He was my father. I never knew him. He married my mother before he went off to war.

Johnny Can I ask you one more question?

Mr Atterbury Yes.

Johnny Mr Atkins's medals. Were they, you know, for anything special?

Mr Atterbury They were campaign medals. Soldiers got them, really, just for being there.

Johnny Yes. Sometimes being there is all you can do.

***Johnny** starts to leave. **Mr Atterbury** stays on the bench, staring ahead. **Johnny** pauses, looks at Mr Atterbury, and seems about to go back to him, when **Antonio Vicenti** enters.*

Antonio Vicenti No.

Johnny I was only going to…

Antonio Vicenti What… ? To tell him you'd seen them? What good would that do? Perhaps he's seeing them, too. Inside his head.

Johnny Well…

Antonio Vicenti It wouldn't work. *(A short pause)* They'll start taking us out of the cemetery the day after tomorrow, you know.

Johnny I'm sorry. I wish there was something I could do.

Antonio Vicenti There still might be.

***Johnny** and **Antonio Vicenti** exit. Lights out.*

Scene 11

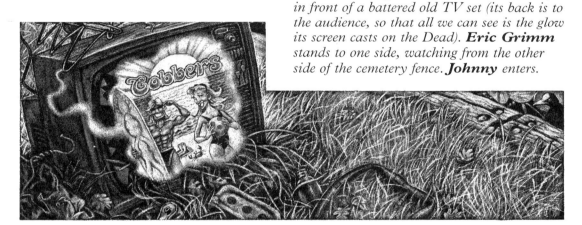

*The **Dead** are gathered, on the canal bank, in front of a battered old TV set (its back is to the audience, so that all we can see is the glow its screen casts on the Dead). **Eric Grimm** stands to one side, watching from the other side of the cemetery fence. **Johnny** enters.*

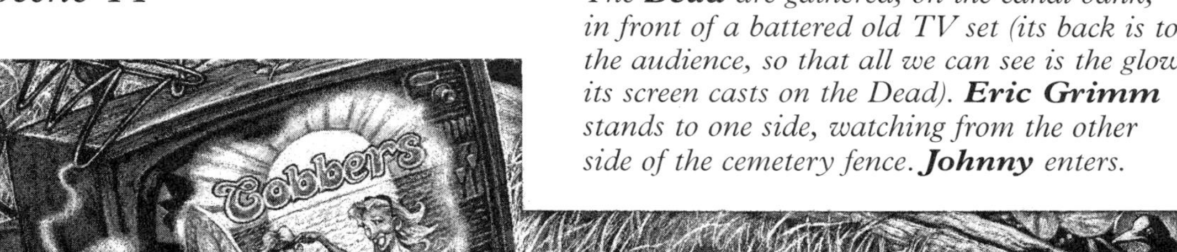

Johnny What's happened? Why are you all here on the canal bank?

Antonio Vicenti You know that old television set that had been dumped here? They made it work.

Johnny But how… ? I mean, the screen was smashed…

Addison Vincent Fletcher Another successful marriage of advanced theoretics and practical know-how, eh, Mr Einstein?

Solomon Einstein A shtep in ze right direction, Mr Fletcher.

Johnny Oh. I see. It's the ghost of the television!

Solomon Einstein Vot a clever boy!

Addison Vincent Fletcher But with improvements.

Johnny There's an old motor car, a Ford Capri, in the canal somewhere along there. Wobbler saw some men dumping it. D'you think you could make that work, too?

Addison Vincent Fletcher I shall see to it directly. The internal combustion engine could certainly do with some improvements.

Johnny But, look. Machines aren't alive, so how can they have ghosts?

Solomon Einstein But zey haf existence. From moment to moment. Zo, ve find ze right moment, yes?

Johnny Sounds a bit occult.

Solomon Einstein No! It is physics! It is *beyond* physics. It is – *meta*physics. From the Greek *meta*, meaning 'beyond' and *physika*, meaning… er…

Antonio Vicenti Physics.

Solomon Einstein Exactly!

Johnny Nothing finishes. Nothing's ever really over.

Addison Vincent Fletcher Correct! Are you a physicist?

Johnny Me? I don't know anything about science!

Solomon Einstein Marvellous! Ideal qualification!

Addison Vincent Fletcher Ignorance is important. It is an absolutely vital part of the learning process!

Eric Grimm There will be trouble because of this. This is disobedience. Meddling with the physical.

***Johnny** crosses to him.*

Eric Grimm There'll be trouble. And it will be *your* fault, John Maxwell. You're getting them excited. Is this any way for the dead to behave?

Johnny Mr Grimm?

Eric Grimm	Yes?
Johnny	Who are you?
Eric Grimm	That's none of your business.
Johnny	I didn't mean to…
Eric Grimm	No good will come of it.
Johnny	Look, I'd better be getting home for my tea.

__Johnny__ and the __Dead__ exchange waves, and he leaves.

Addison Vincent Fletcher	The principle is astonishingly simple. A tiny point of light, that's all it is. Whizzing backwards and forwards inside a glass bottle. Much easier to control than sound waves…
Sylvia Liberty	Excuse me. When you stand in front of the screen you make the picture go blurred.
Addison Vincent Fletcher	Sorry. What's happening now?
William Stickers	Mr McKenzie has told Dawn that Janine can't go to Doraleen's party.
Alderman Bowler	I must say, I thought Australia was a bit different. More kangaroos and fewer young women in unsuitable clothing.
William Stickers	I'm quite happy with the young women!
Sylvia Liberty	Mr Stickers! For shame! You're dead!
William Stickers	But I have a very good memory, Mrs Liberty.

The 'Cobbers' theme tune can be heard. The lights dim. It is starting to get dark.

Solomon Einstein	Oh, is it over? But zere iss ze mystery of who took ze money from Mick's coat!

Sylvia Liberty The man in the television said there would be another performance tomorrow night.

Antonio Vicenti It is getting dark. Time we were getting back. *(Pause)* If we want to go, that is.

Alderman Bowler Well, I'm blowed if I'm going back in there!

Sylvia Liberty Thomas Bowler!

Alderman Bowler Well, if a man can't swear when he's dead, it's a poor look-out. Blowed, blowed, blowed. And damn. I mean, there's all sorts of things going on. I don't see why we should go back in there. It's dull. No way.

Sylvia Liberty No way?

William Stickers That's Australian for 'certainly not'.

Sylvia Liberty But staying where we're put is proper.

Eric Grimm Ahem.

*The **Dead** look embarrassed, as if they have been caught doing something naughty.*

Eric Grimm I entirely agree.

Alderman Bowler Oh. Hello, Eric.

Eric Grimm Will you listen to what you're saying? You're dead. Act your age. It's over. You know what will happen if you leave. You know what will happen if you're too long away. What happens if the day comes and you're not here? The Day of Judgement. We must be ready. Not gallivanting off apeing your juniors. Not dabbling with the 'ordinary'.

Alderman Bowler Well, I've waited eighty years. If it happens tonight, it happens. I'm going to go and have a look around. Anyone else coming?

William Stickers Yes. Me.

Alderman Bowler Anyone else?

***Antonio Vicenti** and **Stanley 'Wrong Way' Roundaway** put up their hands.*

Eric Grimm You will get lost! Something will go wrong! And then you'll be wandering forever, and you'll… forget.

Alderman Bowler There's a world out there, and we helped to make it, and now I want to find out what it's like.

Antonio Vicenti Besides, if we stick together no one will forget who they are, and we'll all go further.

Sylvia Liberty Well, if you insist on going, I suppose someone with some sense should accompany you.

***Alderman Bowler**, **William Stickers**, **Antonio Vicenti** and **Sylvia Liberty** exit (again, one of them has to rescue **Stanley 'Wrong Way' Roundaway** and point him in the right direction). This leaves **Addison Vincent Fletcher** and **Solomon Einstein** watching the TV, and **Eric Grimm** observing from over the fence.*

Addison Vincent Fletcher What's got into them? They're acting almost alive.

Eric Grimm It is disgusting.

Solomon Einstein On ze other hand... zere voz a nice little pub in Cable Street.

Addison Vincent Fletcher You wouldn't get a drink, Solly. They don't serve spirits.

They both laugh.

Solomon Einstein I used to like it in there. After a hard day stuffing foxes. It voz nice to relax of an evenink.

*They look at each other, nod, and exit for the pub. **Eric Grimm** is left alone as the lights fade to blackout.*

Scene 12

The civic centre. ***Johnny*** *enters and addresses the audience. As he speaks, behind him, people are filing into rows of chairs in front of a table on a raised platform. The audience includes* ***Yo-less, Wobbler, Bigmac, Grandad****, the* ***nurse, Mr Atterbury*** *and others. Everyone has a sheet of paper – a handout from the council. Then* ***Ms Liberty, Mr Bowler*** *(from United Amalgamated Consolidated Holdings) and a couple of other people take their places at the top table.* ***Ms Liberty****, in mime, makes her introductory address to the meeting.*

Johnny The following night there was a public meeting at the civic centre to discuss United Amalgamated Consolidated Holdings' plans for the canal bank, boot factory site and cemetery. Quite a few people went. Even some of our teachers. Which is funny, 'cos you don't really think of them having a real life outside school. The lady from the council was called Ms Liberty; I s'pose she's a descendant of 'our' Mrs Liberty, but it's not really the sort of thing you could ask. There was also a man from United Amalgamated Consolidated Holdings.

Johnny *makes his way to the rows of seats and sits down.*

Johnny The meeting started off with Ms Liberty speaking to us, at great length, about nothing in particular…

Ms Liberty's *voice now becomes audible as we catch the end of her speech.*

Ms Liberty … providing a better future for the young people of Blackbury. And in the final analysis, it is not even a particularly fine example of Edwardian funeral architecture. And of course, full account of residents' views has been taken at every stage of the planning process. Now then, I would like to invite Mr Bowler from United Amal…

Johnny *stands.*

Johnny Excuse me, please?

Ms Liberty *(Dismissively)* Questions at the end, please.

Johnny When is the end, please? Only I have to be in bed by ten.

Mr Atterbury Let the lad ask his question. He's doing a project.

Grandad Here, here.

Ms Liberty *(A little ungraciously)* Oh… very well. What was it, young man?

Johnny Um, well, the thing is… the things I want to know is… is there anything that anyone can say here, tonight, that's going to make any difference?

Ms Liberty *(Severely)* That hardly seems an appropriate sort of question.

Mr Atterbury Seems damned good to me. Why doesn't Mr Bowler from United Amalgamated Consolidated Holdings answer the boy? Just a simple answer will do.

Mr Bowler We shall, of course, take all views very deeply into consideration. And furthermore…

Johnny But there's a sign up on the site that says you're going to build anyway. Only I don't think many people want the old cemetery built on. So you'll take the sign down, will you?

Mr Bowler We have in fact bought the…

Johnny You paid five pence. I'll give you a pound.

The audience laughs.

Yo-less I've got a question, too.

Ms Liberty Ah. Yes. Um. We'll, er, take the question from that other young man. *(**Wobbler** rises)* No, not you, the other one. The one with the shirt, er…

Yo-less *(Helpfully)* The black one. Why did the council sell the cemetery in the first place?

Ms Liberty I think we have covered that very fully. The cost of upkeep…

Yo-less But I don't see how there's much upkeep in a cemetery. Sending someone once or twice a year to cut the brambles down doesn't sound like much of a cost to me.

Johnny We'd do it for nothing.

Wobbler Would we?

Ms Liberty The fact, young man, as I have explained time and again, is that it is simply too expensive to maintain a cemetery that is…

Johnny No. It isn't simply too expensive.

Ms Liberty How dare you interrupt me!

Johnny It says in your papers that the cemetery makes a loss. But a cemetery can't make a loss. It's not like a business or something. It just *is*. My friend Bigmac says what you're calling a loss is just the value of the land for building offices. It's the council tax you'd get from United Amalgamated Consolidated Holdings. The dead don't pay council tax so they're not worth anything.

Ms Liberty We are a democratically elected council...

Mr Atterbury I'd like to raise a few points on that. There are certain things about this sale that I should like to see explained in a more democratic way.

Johnny I've had a good look round the cemetery. I've been… doing a project. It's full of stuff. It doesn't matter that no one in there is really famous. They were famous *here*. They lived and got on with things and died. They were *people*. It's wrong to think that the past is something that's just gone. It's still there. It's just that *you've* gone past. If you drive through a town, it's still there in the rear-view mirror. Time is a road, but it doesn't roll up behind you. Things aren't over just because they're *past*. Do you see that? *(Pause)* And… and, if we forget about them, we're just a lot of people living in… in buildings. It's wrong to throw all that away.

Ms Liberty Nevertheless, we have to deal with the present day. The dead are no longer here and I am afraid they do not vote.

Johnny You're wrong. They are here and they have got a vote. I've been working it out. In my head. It's called tradition. And they outvote us twenty to one.

Mr Atterbury *starts to clap. He is soon joined by the rest of the audience. Then he stands, and the applause dies down for him.*

Ms Liberty Mr Atterbury, sit down. I am running this meeting, you know.

Mr Atterbury I am afraid this does not appear to be the case. The boy is right. Too much has been taken away, I know that. You dug up the high street. It had a lot of small shops. People lived there. Now it's all walkways and plastic signs and people are afraid of it at night. Afraid of the town where they live! I'd be ashamed of that, if I was you. And we had a coat of arms up on the town hall. Now all we've got is some plastic logo thing. And you took the allotments and built that shopping mall and all the little shops went out of business. And then you knocked down a lot of houses and built that big tower block where no one wants to live.

Ms Liberty Now look, I was not on the council then. In any case, it is generally recognized that the Joshua N'Clement tower block was a… misplaced idea.

Mr Atterbury A bad idea, you mean?

Ms Liberty Yes, if you must put it like that.

Mr Atterbury So mistakes can be made, can they?

Ms Liberty Nevertheless, the plain fact is, that we must build for the future…

Mr Atterbury I'm very glad to hear you say that, madam chairman, because I'm sure you'll agree that the most successful buildings have got very deep foundations.

There is another round of applause.

Ms Liberty I feel I have no alternative but to close this meeting. Things are getting out of hand. This was supposed to be an informative occasion.

Mr Atterbury I think it has been.

Johnny But you can't close the meeting!

Ms Liberty Indeed, I can!

Johnny You can't. Because this is a public hall, and no one's done anything wrong.

Ms Liberty Then *we* shall leave, and there really will be no point to the meeting!

__Ms Liberty__, __Mr Bowler__ and the others at the table, sweep up their papers and storm out, to the accompaniment of a slow handclap and jeers from the audience. When they have gone, there is a silence.

Woman in the audience Can we actually stop it from happening? It all sounded very official.

Mr Atterbury Officially, I don't think we can. There was a proper sale.

Grandad There's plenty of other sites. The old jam works in Slate Road, and all that area where the goods yards used to be.

Woman in the audience And we could give them their money back.

Johnny We could give them *double* their money back.

There is laughter. __Mr Atterbury__ moves to the raised table and addresses the meeting.

Mr Atterbury It seems to me, that a company like United Amalgamated Consolidated Holdings has to take notice of people. Big companies like that don't like fuss. And they don't like being laughed at. And if they thought we were serious… and if we threaten to offer them, yes, double their money back… *(He chuckles)*

Woman in the audience And then we ought to do something about the high street.

Grandad And get some decent playgrounds and things, instead of all those 'amenities' all over the place.

Wobbler And blow up the Joshua N'Clement block and get some proper houses built.

Bigmac Yo!

Yo-less Here, here.

Mr Atterbury One thing at a time. Let's rebuild Blackbury first. We can see about Jerusalem tomorrow. But we ought to find a name for ourselves.

Grandad The Blackbury Preservation Society?

Mr Atterbury Sounds like something you put in a jar.

Grandad The Blackbury Conservation Society.

Mr Atterbury Still sounds like jam to me.

Johnny The Blackbury Pals.

Mr Atterbury It's a good name but… no. Not now. They were officially the Blackbury Volunteers. That's a good name.

Woman in the audience But it doesn't say what we're going to do, does it?

Johnny If we start off not knowing what we're going to do, we could do anything.

Mr Atterbury The Blackbury Volunteers it is, then!

The lights fade. They all exit.

• •

Scene 13

A street in Blackbury. ***Alderman Bowler, William Stickers, Sylvia Liberty, Antonio Vicenti*** *and* ***Stanley 'Wrong Way' Roundaway*** *enter.*

Sylvia Liberty Moving pictures have certainly come a long way since my day. That was a fascinating film.

Alderman Bowler Well, I think some of those tricks were done with mirrors. They can't really have bred a Tyrannosaurus Rex just for a moving picture.

William Stickers What should we do now?

Sylvia Liberty We should be getting back. To the cemetery.

Alderman Bowler Madam, the night is young!

Solomon Einstein *and* ***Addison Vincent Fletcher*** *enter.*

Alderman Bowler Hello, you two. Where did you get to?

Addison Vincent Fletcher The moon.

William Stickers What? The moon? What – *(He points up at the sky) that* moon?

Addison Vincent Fletcher Yes.

William Stickers But how?

Solomon Einstein Ve used a radio telescope. Travelled along ze radio waves.

Addison Vincent Fletcher Of all the forces in the universe, the hardest to overcome is the force of habit. Gravity was easy-peasy by comparison.

Alderman Bowler What was it like?

Solomon Einstein Ve didn't have time to see much, but I don't think I'd like to live zere.

Alderman Bowler *(Looking up at the shop names)* You know, I certainly don't remember all these shopkeepers from my time. They must have moved in recently. Mr Boots and Mr Mothercare and Mr Spudjulicay.

Sylvia Liberty Whom?

Antonio Vicenti Spud-u-like.

Alderman Bowler Is that how you pronounce it? I thought perhaps he was French. And electric lights all over the place and no horse… manure in the streets at all.

Sylvia Liberty Really! Please remember you are in the presence of a lady!

William Stickers That's why he said manure.

Alderman Bowler Shops full of cinematography televisions! Bright colours everywhere! The people seem taller, and they all seem to have their own teeth! An age of miracles and wonders!

Antonio Vicenti The people don't look very happy.

Alderman Bowler That's just a trick of the light.

Sylvia Liberty It's been fun. It's a shame we have to go back.

Alderman Bowler Go back?

Sylvia Liberty Now then Thomas. I don't want to sound like Eric Grimm, but you know the rules. We have to return. A day will come.

Alderman Bowler I'm not going back. I've really enjoyed myself. I'm not going back!

William Stickers Me neither! Down with tyranny!

Sylvia Liberty We must be ready for the Judgement Day. Supposing it was tomorrow, and we missed it?

Alderman Bowler Hah! Being dead's not what I expected. I just thought everything would go dark for a moment and then there'd be a man handing out harps. Isn't that what *you* expected?

William Stickers Not me. Belief in the survival of the spirit after death is a primitive superstition which has no place in a socialist society!

Solomon Einstein You don't zink that it might be worth reconsidering your opinions in the light of recent events?

William Stickers Just because I'm still here does not invalidate the general theory.

Alderman Bowler Anyway, I don't want to go back. I just wish that this night didn't have to end.

Solomon Einstein *(To Addison Vincent Fletcher)* Shall ve tell zem?

Addison Vincent Fletcher Times have changed. All that stuff about being home by dawn and not hearing the cock crow. That was all very well when people thought the earth was flat, but now we know different. Dawn is a place as well as a time. It's all relative. It's always night somewhere in the world. As long as we keep moving, we need never see another dawn!

Sylvia Liberty What on earth do you mean?

Solomon Einstein On earth, and around earth. One night and one day, forever chasing one another… We just follow the night around the world…

Addison Vincent Fletcher A night that never comes to an end. All you need is speed.

The ***Dead*** *exit. (****Stanley 'Wrong Way' Roundaway*** *needs showing the way again). Blackout.*

• •

Scene 14

The cemetery. ***Johnny*** *walks on, carrying a ghetto blaster. He addresses the audience.*

Johnny The campaign's going really well. Listen…

He switches on the radio in the blaster, and we hear the voices.

Mr Bowler's voice *(Voice only)* … at every stage, fully sensitive to public opinion in this matter, I can assure you. But there is no doubt that we entered into a proper and legal contract with the local authority.

Radio interviewer *(Voice only)* But the Blackbury Volunteers say too much was decided behind closed doors. They say things were never discussed and that no one listened to the local people.

Mr Atterbury *(Voice only)* Of course, this is not the fault of United Amalgamated Consolidated Holdings. They have an enviable record of civic service and co-operation with the public. I think what we have here is a genuine mistake rather than any *near-criminal activity*, and we in the Volunteers would be happy to help them in any constructive way and, indeed, possibly even to *compensate* them.

Mr Bowler *(Voice only)* Er, I don't think that will be necessary!

Radio interviewer *(Voice only)* Tell me, what exactly is it that United Amalgamated Consolidated Holdings *does*?

Johnny *switches off the radio.* ***Eric Grimm*** *enters.*

Johnny Where's everyone else?

Eric Grimm Haven't come back. Their graves haven't been slept in. That's what happens when people don't listen. Now they're going to fade away. If they don't get back here before dawn, they'll get more and more insubstantial until they forget who they are and fade away completely. It could be Judgement Day tomorrow, and they won't be here. Hah! Serves them right.

Johnny *(With a sigh)* I don't know where they've gone, but I don't think anything bad's happened to them.

Eric Grimm Think what you like.

He starts to exit.

Johnny Did you know it's Hallowe'en?

Eric Grimm *(As he exits)* Is it? I shall have to be careful tonight, then.

***Eric Grimm** exits. **Yo-less** and **Bigmac** run on.*

Bigmac Hey, Johnny! Look, in the paper! You're a real hero! Look! 'Council Slammed in Cemetery Sale Rumpus'!

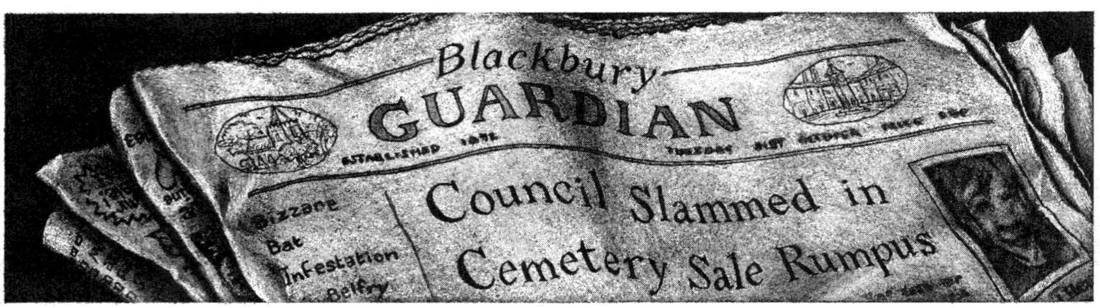

Johnny *(Reading from the paper)* 'War hero Ronald Atterbury told the *Guardian*: "There are young people in this town with more sense of history in their little fingers than some adults have in their entire committee-bound bodies".'

Yo-less And did you see over by the main gate? There's a local TV crew and everything. And there's ecologists who think they've found a rare breed of thrush.

Johnny They've gone.

Bigmac Gone where?

Johnny I don't know. Mr Grimm says that if they're away too long, they… they forget who they were… They're just not here.

Bigmac Then where are they?

Johnny I don't know!

Bigmac And it's Hallowe'en, too.

Johnny I wanted to tell them. I mean, we might win. Now people are here, TV and everything. I wanted to tell them and now they've gone!

Yo-less We ought to get back. I've got a project to do on projects.

Johnny I'm going to look for them.

Bigmac You'll get into trouble when they do the register.

Johnny *(Vaguely)* I'll say I've been doing something… social.

Yo-less Johnny? You OK?

Johnny Yes, I'm OK. You go on back. I'll see you at Wobbler's party tonight.

***Bigmac** and **Yo-less** exit, as **Mr Atterbury** comes on. He is carrying the old radio.*

Mr Atterbury Hello Johnny, exciting day, isn't it? You really started something, you know.

Johnny I heard you on the radio. You called United Amalgamated Consolidated Holdings public-spirited and co-operative.

Mr Atterbury Well, they might be. If they've got no choice. They're a bit shifty, but we might just win through. It's amazing what you can do with a kind word. *(He holds up the radio)* Look at this! Just dumped in the cemetery. People have no respect.

Johnny What are you going to do with it?

Mr Atterbury I was going to give it to those council men who are clearing the rubbish off the canal bank and dumping it into a skip.

Johnny Oh. Right.

Mr Atterbury Well, see you later, then.

Johnny Yes. Bye.

***Mr Atterbury** exits. **Johnny** looks around him.*

Johnny Mr Grimm? Mr Grimm? *(Pause)* I know you're here. You can't leave like the others. You have to stay. Because you're a ghost. A real ghost. You're not just hanging around like the rest of them. You're haunting. *(Pause)* What did you do? Were you a murderer or something? *(Pause)* I'm afraid they're clearing the canal bank. Sorry about the television.

***Johnny** pauses again. There is still no response. He turns and exits.*
*On the stage there is a pattern of moving lights as, over the speakers, we hear the voices of the **Dead**.*

Alderman Bowler *(Voice only)* How far to morning?

Antonio Vicenti *(Voice only)* Nearly there. We must go back.

Alderman Bowler *(Voice only)* What?

Antonio Vicenti *(Voice only)* We owe the boy something. He took an interest. He remembered us.

Solomon Einstein *(Voice only)* Zat's absolutely correct. Conservation of energy. Besides, he'll be worrying.

Sylvia Liberty *(Voice only)* Yes, but, if we go now… we'll become like we were, won't we? I can feel the weight of that gravestone now.

Antonio Vicenti *(Voice only)* We don't have to be frightened of the morning. We don't have to be frightened of anything. Come on.

Blackout.

. . . .

Scene 15

The cemetery. It is night. ***Yo-less*** *(dressed a bit like Baron Samedi),* ***Bigmac*** *(dressed as a skeleton),* ***Wobbler*** *(dressed as Dracula) and* ***Johnny*** *(dressed in a pink sheet) enter, warily.*

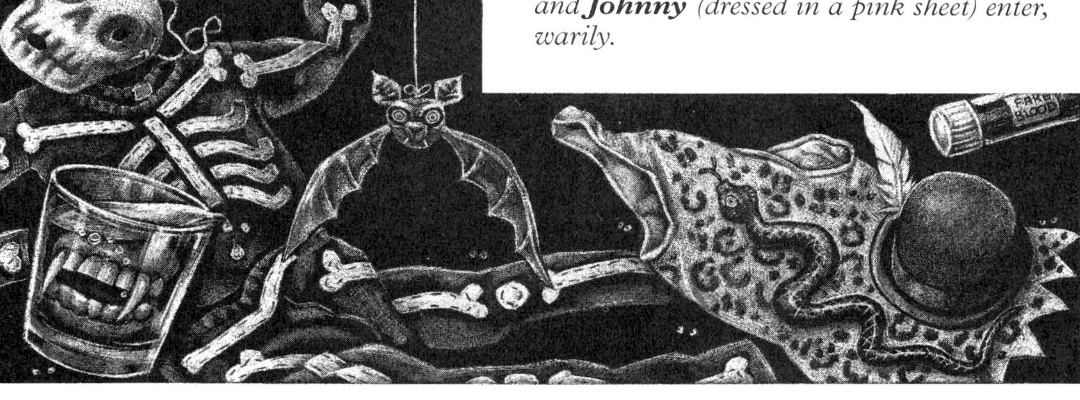

Wobbler D-did we have to come here on Hallowe'en?

Bigmac Well, let's face it, your party ran out of steam a bit when everyone decided to go trick or treating round the estate. Now that *would* be scary. Anyway, Johnny said he wanted to come.

Wobbler Yeah, what are you, Johnny, a gay ghost?

Johnny Look – Mum washed it with one of Grandad's red vests. It's the only one she'd let me cut a hole in. Anyway, there's nothing wrong with pink. Lots of people wear pink.

Wobbler Not very spooky, though, is it? Pink?

Johnny It's not that pink. But what's Yo-less supposed to be?

Yo-less Baron Samedi, the voodoo god. I got the idea from that James Bond film.

Bigmac That's racial stereotyping.

Yo-less No it's not. Not if *I* do it.

Johnny I'm pretty sure Baron Samedi didn't wear a bowler hat. I'm pretty sure it was a top hat. A bowler hat makes you look like you were off to an office somewhere.

Yo-less I can't help it. It was all I could get.

Wobbler Maybe he's Baron Samedi, the voodoo god of chartered accountancy. Anyway, why are we here, Johnny?

Johnny I wanted to try and get in touch with them again.

Bigmac Perhaps old Baron Samedi here could use his tarot cards, like in the film.

Yo-less No. Tarot is European occult. Voodoo is African occult.

Wobbler How're we supposed to contact the dead, then?

Bigmac What about the thing with the letters and glasses?

Wobbler The postman?

Bigmac You know what I mean.

Yo-less No. That could lead to dark forces taking over.

Someone coughs off stage.

Yo-less Listen!

Wobbler *(Whispering)* What?

There is a clank off stage.

Yo-less There's someone in the cemetery!

Wobbler It'll be Johnny's dead pals.

Johnny No. Wobbler, run back to Mr Atterbury's house over the road and tell him what's happening!

Wobbler Me? What? By myself?

Johnny You'll run faster if you're by yourself!

Wobbler Right!

__Wobbler__ exits. __Johnny__, __Bigmac__ and __Yo-less__ peer out towards the audience.

Yo-less What, exactly, are we doing?

There is the sound of a diesel engine being started up off stage.

Bigmac Someone's nicking a JCB!

Johnny I wish that's what they *were* doing. I reckon someone from United Amalgamated Consolidated Holdings is trying to wreck the cemetery!

Yo-less Listen, if someone's driving a JCB without lights at this time of night, I'm not hanging around!

Two lights come on. __Johnny__, __Bigmac__ and __Yo-less__ are illuminated in the headlights of the off stage JCB.

Johnny Is that better?

Yo-less No.

There is the noise of the machine driving forwards, getting closer.

Johnny *(Waving his arms in the direction of the machine)* Oi! Stop!

The engine stops. __Johnny__ whispers to __Bigmac__.

Johnny Run away! Quick! Tell someone what's happening!

__Bigmac__ runs off. Two __men__ enter, from the audience, and grab __Johnny__ and __Yo-less__.

First man You – are in real trouble, kid.

Second man Yeah. All this damage to the cemetery…

First man …which they'll find tomorrow morning…

Second man ... yeah. That's all your fault, that is.

First man Know what I think? I think it's lucky we happened to be passing and found them messin' around with that JCB, eh? Shame they'd already driven it through the place and wrecked everything. Kids today, eh?

Second man Yeah, and you'd just better go along with it, 'cos we know where you live, see?

Suddenly, as if from nowhere, ***Bigmac*** *charges on, wielding a length of lead piping. He strikes the* ***first man*** *across the shoulders. In the background, we hear the approaching siren of a police car.*

First man Hey! What the... ow!

The ***first man*** *runs off stage. The* ***second man*** *releases Yo-less in order to try and grab Bigmac.* ***Bigmac*** *hits him hard across the shins with the pipe. He yells and falls to the floor, holding his damaged shins.* ***Bigmac*** *dives onto him and starts to punch him.*

Second man Ow! gettim off me!

Johnny*,* ***Bigmac*** *and* ***Yo-less*** *help to subdue the* ***second man****. A* ***police officer*** *enters holding the* ***first man****. Another* ***police officer*** *enters, with* ***Wobbler*** *and* ***Mr Atterbury****.*

Police officer *(Lifting the* ***second man*** *to his feet)* Right, you. I think you and your friend had better come with us for a nice little ride down to Blackbury nick.

The ***police officers*** *and the* ***men*** *exit.*

Mr Atterbury Well done, you boys! Well done! I must say, though, I expected a bit more than this from United Amalgamated Consolidated Holdings. I suppose they thought everything would be a lot simpler if the cemetery wasn't worth saving. So they slipped a couple of likely lads a few quid to do... er... a Hallowe'en prank. Come on, I'll give you all a lift home. And then I shall take considerable pleasure in ringing up the chairman of United Amalgamated Consolidated Holdings. *Considerable* pleasure.

Mr Atterbury *exits, followed by* ***Yo-less*** *and* ***Bigmac****.*

Wobbler Well, that's it. Game over. Let's go home.

Johnny *does not move.*

Wobbler Come on.

Johnny It's not right. It can't end like this.

Wobbler Best ending. Nasty men foiled. Kids save the day. Everyone gets a sticky bun.

Johnny No. Something else is going to happen. I've got to go and see. You go with the others.

Wobbler No argument from me! You sure you'll be OK?

Johnny Me? Yes, yes, sure. See you tomorrow.

Wobbler *runs off after the others.*

Johnny Something's going to happen.

Alderman Bowler*,* ***Solomon Einstein****,* ***Antonio Vicenti****,* ***Sylvia Liberty****,* ***William Stickers*** *and* ***Stanley 'Wrong Way' Roundaway*** *enter .*

Johnny You're back!

Antonio Vicenti Yes. Hello, Johnny.

We hear the JCB start up again.

Johnny The JCB? What's happening?

Antonio Vicenti That's Mr Fletcher.

Johnny What are you doing?

Alderman Bowler Isn't this what people wanted? We don't need this place anymore. So if anyone's going to do it, it should be us. That's only right!

The JCB lights come on again, and the engine noise starts to get louder.

Johnny But you said this was your place!

Sylvia Liberty We have left nothing here of any importance.

William Stickers Force of habit is what has subjugated the working man for too long.

Sylvia Liberty He's right. We spent far too much time moping around because of what we're not, without any consideration of what we might be. We were trapped in the cemetery because we believed we were trapped. Instead of which, since we aren't encumbered by our bodies, we're even freer to move where we like.

Solomon Einstein That's right. We're… chronologically gifted.

Alderman Bowler Dimensionally advantaged.

William Stickers Bodily unencumbered.

Antonio Vicenti Enhanced.

Alderman Bowler So we're off.

Johnny Where to?

Solomon Einstein We don't know. But it iss goink to be very interestink to find out.

Johnny But… we've saved the cemetery! We had a big meeting! No one's going to build anything on it! Turn the machine off! We've saved the cemetery!

Alderman Bowler But we don't need it any more. We're dead. We can go where we like!

Johnny *We* do! We do. We… need it to be there.

The engine noise stops.

Solomon Einstein This iss of course very true. It all balances, you see. The living have to remember. The dead have to forget.

Addison Vincent Fletcher *walks on.*

Addison Vincent Fletcher Ah yes, conservation of energy, eh?

Solomon Einstein Indeed.

Antonio Vicenti We came to say goodbye. And thank you.

Johnny I hardly did anything.

Antonio Vicenti You listened. You tried. You were there. You can get medals just for being there. But now… we must be somewhere else.

The ***Dead*** *start to drift off.* ***Antonio Vicenti, Alderman Bowler*** *and* ***Sylvia Liberty*** *remain.*

William Stickers *(As he goes)* Goodbye, Johnny. Power to the people, eh?

William Stickers *takes* ***Stanley 'Wrong Way' Roundaway*** *off with him.*

Solomon Einstein *(As he goes)* Take good care of yourself, Johnny.

Addison Vincent Fletcher *(As he goes)* Goodbye, Johnny. Thanks for everything.

Johnny *(To Antonio Vicenti)* No… don't go yet. I have to ask you…

Antonio Vicenti Yes?

Johnny Um…

Antonio Vicenti Yes?

Johnny Are there… angels involved? You know? Or… devils and things? A lot of people would like to know.

Antonio Vicenti Oh no. I don't think so. That sort of thing… no. That's for the living.

Alderman Bowler I rather think it's going to be a lot more interesting than that. Mrs Liberty thinks we ought to tell you something. But… it's hard to explain, you know?

Johnny What is?

Alderman Bowler By the way, why are you wearing a pink sheet?

Johnny Um…

Alderman Bowler I expect it's not important.

Johnny Yes.

Alderman Bowler Well. You know those games where this ball runs up and bounces around and ends up in a slot at the bottom?

Johnny Pinball machines?

Alderman Bowler Is that what they're called? Right. Well… when you're bouncing around from pin to pin, it is probably very difficult to know that outside the game there's a room and outside the room there's a town and outside the town there's a country and outside the country there's a world, and so on… but it's there, do you see? Once you know about it, you can stop worrying about the slot at the bottom. And you might bounce around a good deal longer.

Johnny I'll… try to remember it.

Alderman Bowler Good man. Well, we'd better be going. Goodbye, Johnny.

Sylvia Liberty Goodbye, Johnny.

***Alderman Bowler** and **Sylvia Liberty** exit.*

Johnny Goodbye.

Antonio Vicenti Well, I think I might as well be off, too.

Johnny Why, are you all leaving?

Antonio Vicenti Oh, yes. It's Judgement Day. We decided. It's different for everyone, you see. Enjoy looking after the cemetery. They're places for the living, after all.

He exits. The lights go down on the cemetery. ***Johnny*** *turns to the audience. He is lit by a spotlight.*

Johnny So that's how we saved the cemetery. There was a *very* generous donation to the Blackbury Volunteers from United Amalgamated Consolidated Holdings. As Mr Atterbury said, it's amazing what you can do with a kind word – providing you've also got a big stick. After a few days, I went back to the cemetery.

The lights come up again on the cemetery. It is daytime.

Johnny Mr Grimm? Mr Grimm?

Eric Grimm *enters and sits.*

Eric Grimm Go away. You're dangerous.

Johnny I thought you'd be a bit… lonely. So I brought you this. *(He pulls out a pocket TV)* It'll work until the batteries die, and then I thought maybe it'd work on ghost batteries.

Eric Grimm What is it?

Johnny It's a pocket-sized television. I thought I could hide it right in a bush or somewhere where no one will know except you.

Eric Grimm What are you doing this for?

Johnny Because I looked you up in the newspaper. May the twenty-first, nineteen twenty-seven. There wasn't very much. Just the bit about them finding… you… in the canal.

Eric Grimm Oh? Poking around, eh? And what do you think you know about *anything*?

Johnny Nothing.

Eric Grimm I don't have to explain.

Johnny Is that why you couldn't leave with the others?

Eric Grimm What? I can leave whenever I like. If I'm staying here, it's because I want to.

***Johnny** moves downstage to address the audience.*

Johnny It wasn't a very long report. It said you were a respectable citizen, then your business failed and there'd been some trouble involving money and then… there'd been the canal. Seems daft to me, because suicide was against the law in those days. So if you failed, you could get locked up in prison to show you that life was really very jolly and thoroughly worth living.

He moves back up to Eric Grimm.

Johnny You'll be able to turn it on with your mind, I think.

Eric Grimm Who says I shall want to?

The TV picture comes on and we hear the 'Cobbers' theme.

Johnny Let's see… you've missed a week… Mrs Swede has just found out that Janine didn't go to the party… Mr Hatt has sacked Jason from the shop because he thinks he took the money…

Eric Grimm I see.

Johnny So… I'll be off then, shall I?

Eric Grimm Right.

__Johnny__ leaves __Eric Grimm__ looking at the TV. __Yo-less__, __Wobbler__ and __Bigmac__ enter and stand on the side of the stage. __Johnny__ crosses to them.

Yo-less Was he there?

Johnny Yes.

Yo-less What's he doing now?

Johnny Watching television.

Wobbler You all right?

Johnny I was just thinking about the difference between heaven and hell.

Wobbler That doesn't sound like 'all right' to me.

Johnny I was thinking about the world. It's… wonderful, really. Not the same as nice, or even good, but it's full of… stuff. We need never get to the end of it. There's always new stuff. *(Snapping out of it)* Yeah. All right. What shall we do now?

__Johnny__, __Wobbler__, __Bigmac__ and __Yo-less__ exit.

Activities

What the Author Says

It's not a good idea to ask a tightrope walker how they keep their balance, and it's not a good idea to ask an author why they wrote something in a certain way. But here goes...

I wrote a lot of **Johnny and the Dead** because I was angry. The little town I grew up in was something like Blackbury, and it has changed in the same way. Little shops have been killed off by a big supermarket. There are now about a million building society offices in the high street and hardly anywhere to buy food. It used to have its own council, even its own coat of arms. Now it's run from some other town ten miles away. It's not a place where people live anymore, it's just a place they park their cars.

Other things pointed the way towards the book. I actually met a man called Tommy Atkins, who *had* fought all the way through the First World War and was immensely proud of his name. And I was puzzled by the way in which the dead, in our society, always seem to be represented as evil. After all, they were our *ancestors*. Other societies don't think in the same way – some would gently dry grandad out when he passed away and then prop him high on the mountain somewhere to watch over his descendants (don't try this at home).

I wanted to write a book which said: the past might not have been better, but it is important and it was real. Real people lived and died. They weren't just jerky figures in old newsreels. Everything around us is the result of things they did, good *and* bad. We might learn something if we try to work out the difference. Some people feel that a concern for the past is 'against progress', but progress just means travel and is not automatically in a good direction – sometimes it makes the world a better place, and other times it means bad things happen fast.

I brought the Pals in because most of the Dead that Johnny meets are, well, funny, and I wanted to balance this up a little. I wanted him to understand that white-haired old Tommy Atkins was *also* a young man on a terrible battlefield. Tommy Atkins was not a lot older than Johnny when the Pals went off to war (some boys even lied about their age to get into the army) and I wanted Johnny and his friends to realize that if they'd been born earlier, it might have been *them*. And I wanted to say that the past is all around us, and sometimes we owe it something.

But if I was honest, I'd say that I also brought the Pals in because the image of the young ghosts of his friends marching back to greet Thomas Atkins when he died was *right*. I wasn't sure why, but I knew it was. Sometimes things just happen that way. Some things you don't work out in your head.

Terry Pratchett

What the Adapter Says

I first encountered Terry Pratchett and his writings when I wrote to him to ask if I could adapt one of his books, *Wyrd Sisters*, for the amateur stage. That was in 1990 and since then we have gone on to work together on various projects, mostly connected with his Discworld series of novels.

Like much of Terry Pratchett's writing, **Johnny and the Dead** appears on the surface to be a fantasy story, but closer examination shows that it is firmly rooted in reality. In **Johnny and the Dead** it is easy to see that the living's attitude to the dead neatly reflects the young and healthy's attitude to the elderly or disabled. Indeed, we can also see how adults react to children and the way that those at either end of the scale (the very young and the very old – or the dead) often get along better than the generations in between.

The methods used to adapt a novel for the stage are as varied as the authors you try to adapt. Some authors make heavy use of narrative and the adapter has then to weave that into the play as well, if they are to keep to the spirit of the original work. Some authors, like Charles Dickens and Terry Pratchett, write very good dialogue which helps the action to leap from the page. This makes the adapter's job easier – whole chunks of text can be lifted straight from the book into the play.

It is difficult to be hard and fast about 'rules' for adapting books, but here are a few useful guidelines that I do try to stick to.

- Do not change the principal plot. There is no point in calling a play Bram Stoker's *Dracula* if you are then going to have Dracula surviving at the end and starting up a flourishing law firm in Whitby.
- Never sacrifice 'real' scenes in order to add in some your own. After all, you have chosen to adapt the author's work because, presumably, you admire their writing. If you think you can improve on their humour/drama/characterization you should really be writing your own plots and not torturing theirs.
- Use the author's dialogue whenever possible. Same as above, really. Also try to have the same character saying the same lines as they do in the book – rather than giving them to another character.
- Don't add characters. Stick to the ones the author has given you.
- Don't be afraid to cut material. After all, you are trying to squeeze a three-hundred-page novel into a two-hour play; you just can't fit everything in, so don't try. Anything which does not help the main plot move forward should be on your list for potential dumping if your play over-runs.

Because this play is as likely to be used for reading in a classroom as for a stage production, I've also tried to keep the amount of stage directions to a minimum. Reading lots of instructions is *very* boring. However, if the characters just stand there and talk at each other in a performance of the script, the audience will find this very boring, too. The trick is to find things for the characters to do that make the things they say more effective. (See the Background Acting activity on page 93.)

I have tried to ensure that the special effects I have mentioned should be either easily achievable or not essential. I have also tried to arrange it so that the play can be performed with the minimum amount of scenery; in Terry's books the plot and the characters are the important things. Any scenic or other effects you can afford to conjure up on top of that are a bonus.

Stephen Briggs

Now Read On

Compare this play with the novel, **Johnny and the Dead**, on which it is based.

If you enjoy the novel, you can read more about Johnny and his friends in *Only You Can Save Mankind* and *Johnny and the Bomb.*

The LWT production of **Johnny and the Dead** has been released on video. There is also a soundtrack album available.

Terry Pratchett has more to say on the subjects of living, death and choice in his fantasy Discworld series; especially in *Small Gods* and *Interesting Times.*

A Dead Loss?

Incredibly the idea of selling a cemetery for five pence is not just an invention of Terry Pratchett's creative mind! In the late nineteen eighties Westminster Council sold three cemeteries in North London for fifteen pence in order to save the cost of maintaining the grounds. Within weeks, the company that bought the cemeteries sold a cemetery gatehouse for £170,000 and then sold the rest of the cemeteries to a Panamanian-registered, Swiss-based investment company. This company put the cemeteries up for sale at a price of £2.5 million.
Because of this, there was a public outcry over the sale. Legal and moral issues and questions were asked: Was it right to sell the land? Should the dead be left in peace? Should the land have been sold so cheaply? These questions were explored in a series of inquiries and reports that took several years to complete. These legal proceedings have cost an estimated £4.5 million. This money had to be paid by Westminster Council and the government. They got the money from people who pay taxes. And the result of all this? There hasn't really been one – the controversy still continues!

Read

'The district auditor said in his report...that they (the cemeteries) have no value.'

Lady Porter, Leader of Westminster Council

'In law, the city council were free to sell the cemeteries without safeguards for their future...but they clearly owed a moral obligation over and above their strict legal duties in relation to those whose relatives and loved ones were buried in the cemeteries.'

Dr David Yardley, local ombudsman for London and the South-East

Discuss

1. Are the dead worth anything?
2. Is it right that cemeteries should be used for building land?
3. Who should decide whether a cemetery is sold?
4. Should everything be given a price in terms of money, or are there some things that you cannot put a price on? In small groups make a list of things (e.g. people, places, objects) that cannot (or should not) be given such a price.

List

We Shall Remember Them
In our society, we remember people who have died in many ways. Make a list of the ways in which people who have died are remembered by the living. Below are some examples to start you off:

- memories
- war memorials
- park benches
- plaques

Changes for the Good?

Talk and Write

1 How much has your city, town, village or estate changed during the past few years?

2 Make a list of all the changes (no matter how small) that have occurred during the past five years.

3 Discuss whether these changes have been for the better or for the worse. Who do you think decided these changes could take place? Who *should* decide what changes should take place? What further changes would you like to see in your area?

Research

Try to find out how much your area has changed during the past:

- twenty years
- fifty years
- hundred years

Local libraries and history societies should be a useful source of old photographs and maps of your area. You could also talk to older residents of the area in order to find out what changes they can remember. Record their answers or write them up as an interview.

Exhibition

You could organize an exhibition of the changes. You could include photographs, recorded interviews, written accounts, maps. If you do organize an exhibition, you may like to ask people who see it to answer the following questions:

- What has changed for the better?
- What has changed for the worse?

Write

Points of View

In **Johnny and the Dead** (Scene 12), a public meeting is organized at Blackbury Civic Centre to discuss future plans for the canal, boot factory and cemetery. The local council and United Amalgamated Consolidated Holdings support the plans for the development of these sites; the local residents at the meeting are against them.

1 Imagine that you are a reporter covering the meeting for the local Blackbury paper. Write a front page article for the paper, describing the events of the meeting. Look back at Scene 12 and include quotations from the characters in your report.

2 Now assume that the local paper is owned by United Amalgamated Consolidated Holdings. They would obviously want the meeting reported in a way that reflected their views and helped put across their belief that the cemetery should be built on.

THUGS STOP MEETING

A group of local thugs disrupted last night's public meeting concerning the exciting future developments in Blackbury. Councillor Ms Ethel Liberty was forced to close the open meeting after being booed down by a group of bully boys.

United Amalgamated Consolidated Holdings spokesman, Mr Bowler, said afterwards: 'I don't understand all the fuss, all we are trying to do is...'

Continue this article or, if you prefer, write your own opening paragraph and continue the article.

3 Imagine that you are a member of the Blackbury Volunteers. Your task is to design and produce a one-page leaflet. This will be delivered to every household in Blackbury. The aim of the leaflet is to persuade local people to join the Volunteers in opposing the plans of United Amalgamated Consolidated Holdings. Before you start, you will need to consider the following things:

- Why do you oppose the plans?
- What alternative plans do you want to put forward?
- What sort of support do you need?
- What will be the next step in your campaign?

Look back at Scenes 2, 3 and 12 in order to gather evidence for your leaflet.

4 An alternative to writing a report for a newspaper would be to make an audio or video presentation for local TV or radio. Your report should contain a selection of the following:

- a summary, by the reporter, of the events of the public meeting
- local reactions both for and against
- brief statements by a spokesperson from both sides.

The Pals Regiments

Read

'...a Pals Battalion was when people all from one town or even one street could all join the army together if they wanted, and all get sent to...the same place.'

Yo-less

The Accrington Pals

Perhaps the most famous of all the Pals Battalions is the Accrington Pals. The battalion was made up of young men from Accrington, Blackburn, Chorley and smaller towns and villages of East Lancashire. Its official name was the 11th Battalion of the East Lancashire Regiment. Recruiting began in 1914 and within weeks the battalion had formed. Most of the young men in the area volunteered. They came from all social classes and all places of work.

After their initial training, the Accrington Pals were sent to Egypt to guard the Suez canal. However, two months later they were ordered to the trenches of Northern France. They arrived in March 1916 and began to prepare for a huge attack on the German trenches near the River Somme. The Accrington Pals were given the job of attacking Serre, a ruined village of thirty houses. They were told by their commanders that following a huge pounding by British guns, the German soldiers in the trenches guarding the village would be dead and they would be able to walk into the village without fear of attack.

The Battle of the Somme began on July 1st 1916. At 7.30 am, the Accrington Pals set off across No-Man's Land towards the German trenches. The German soldiers, hiding in deep cellars, had survived the British attack and were waiting for them. As the Pals poured over the top of their trenches, they were cut down dead by German artillery and machine gun fire. Those waiting in the trenches were killed or injured by German shelling. Some made it to the German trenches where hand-to-hand fighting took place, but the German artillery then shelled their own trenches and the Pals that made it that far were never seen again.

News of the attack filtered back to Accrington. The newspapers with their censored, optimistic reports told one story, but the letters sent back by the wounded told another. The people of Accrington surrounded the Mayor's house and demanded to be told the truth. The *Accrington Times and Observer* published accounts and photographs of the boys who had been wounded. By August 1916, the full horror of the losses was revealed and the newspaper began to print photographs of the young men who would not be returning to East Lancashire.

Research

Try to find out more information about Pals Battalions. You may find the following people and places helpful:

- There may be a local Pals regiment society in your area whom you could contact for more information.
- Your local branch of the British Legion might be able to help you.
- Older relatives might also be able to provide you with facts.
- Libraries will have relevant books and newspapers.
- War memorials will provide the names of those local people who were killed in World War I.

WORLD WAR I

* The First World War began in 1914 and ended in 1918.
* It was fought between two groups: the Allies and the Central Powers.
* The Allies were Britain, France, Italy, Russia, and the USA.
* The Central Powers were Germany, Austria-Hungary and Turkey.
* Lord Kitchener, the British Secretary of State for War, started a huge recruitment drive. In the first week of September 1914, 175,000 men volunteered.
* The German army began by invading Belgium.
* The French and British soldiers drove the Germans back.
* They soon reached a point where neither side could move so they both dug trenches and planned attacks on the enemy that might gain them a few metres of ground.
* The trenches stretched in a line, 700 kilometres long, from the Belgium coastline to Switzerland. This line was called the Western Front.
* The area between the two lines of trenches was called No-Man's Land. Here the ground was muddy, full of deep holes made by shells and scattered with barbed wire.
* Troops had to run across No-Man's Land to attack the enemy. They became easy targets for the machine guns of the enemy troops.
* The Battle of the Somme began in July 1916. It lasted for five months and resulted in enormous losses and huge numbers of casualties.
* The United States entered the war in 1917.
* Soon after, General Haig planned a huge offensive called the 'big push' to break through the German lines; thousands of soldiers died.
* Germany responded with a final big attack at Marne in 1918. This was unsuccessful.
* Germany surrendered in November of 1918 and the war ended.
* Ten million soldiers and civilians had died.

The Battle of the Somme

* The Battle of the Somme began on July 1st 1916.
* The plan was for British artillery guns to pound the German positions, which would kill their soldiers and destroy the barbed wire which defended their trenches.
* The barrage did not cut the barbed wire.
* The German soldiers took cover in deep trenches and were unharmed.
* By nightfall on the first day of the battle there were 57,470 allied casualties.
* In the first thirty minutes of the attack, 21,000 soldiers were killed.
* The Battle of the Somme lasted for five months and failed miserably.
* The Allies only gained seven kilometres of ground.
* Of the 700 men of the Accrington Pals Battalion who fought in the Somme campaign at Serre, 242 were killed and 350 wounded.
* In another area of the battlefield, the 10th West Yorkshire Division were annihilated in less than a minute.
* The British lost 420,000 men.
* The French lost 194,000 men.
* The Germans lost approximately 600,000 men.

Research

1 Try to find out more about conditions in the trenches during the First World War.

2 The following areas of research may also help you in your understanding of the war:
- photographs
- maps of the Western Front
- uniforms of the time
- medals awarded to soldiers

3 In Scene 10 of the playscript, Johnny sees the young soldiers from the First World War march past to the tune of 'Tipperary'. Try to find out which songs were popular during the First World War.

Further Reading

Poetry
World War I poets will provide a graphic description of life in the trenches. Look at some poems by:
- Siegfried Sassoon
- Wilfred Owen
- Robert Graves
- Rupert Brook
- Edmund Blunden

There are several books of collections of World War I poets, including: *Men Who March Away: Poems of the First World War* edited by I M Parsons, published by Heinemann Educational Books.

Novels
All Quiet on the Western Front is a novel by Erich Remarque, which gives a German perspective of life in the trenches.

Plays
The Accrington Pals is a play by Peter Whelan, published by Methuen.

Oh, What a Lovely War! This play, by Joan Littlewood and the Theatre Workshop, includes many songs popular during the First World War. It is published by Methuen. There is also a film version available.

Character Studies

Talk and Write

1 What words would you use to describe the following characters?

- Johnny Maxwell
- Yo-less
- Bigmac
- Alderman Thomas Bowler
- Ms Ethel Liberty
- Eric Grimm
- Addison Vincent Fletcher

Look for examples in the playscript to back up your description. If, for example, you think that Johnny is brave, find an incident in the play that supports this viewpoint. You might find it helpful to record the information on a chart like the one below.

CHARACTER	DESCRIPTION	EVIDENCE
Johnny	Brave	Scene 1 – He doesn't run away from the Dead
	Clever	

Continue this chart.

Discuss

Nicknames

1 What do the names Bigmac, Yo-less and Wobbler Johnson suggest about the characters?

2 Are these kind names?

3 Why do you think that Terry Pratchett uses the characters' nicknames rather than their 'proper' names?

Survey

1 What nicknames do people have in your class?

2 How did these nicknames begin?

3 Do all the people who have nicknames like them? If not, why do other people use that nickname?

4 What is the strangest, funniest or most weird nickname you have ever heard?

5 Do your teachers have any nicknames? Do they know they have them?

Read

Stereotypes

A **stereotype** is a standardized conventional idea or character. For example: the stereotype of a hero is one who is tall, strong, brave and good-looking.

In **Johnny and the Dead**, Terry Pratchett challenges character stereotypes. For instance Yo-less is a West Indian who likes brass bands rather than Reggae and Blues.

Talk and Write

1 Why do you think that Terry Pratchett does this? Just for humour?
2 Look through the playscript (especially Scene 15) to find other examples of stereotypes being challenged.
3 Make a list of these and discuss them in the class.

Talk and Write

1 You may have heard adults use the phrase 'typical teenager'. What do you think they mean by this?
2 Make a list of the qualities that adults might think a stereotypical teenager is like. We've started it off for you.

TEENAGE STEREOTYPE

Likes loud music
No respect for their elders

3 Now make a list of what the teenagers you know are really like. Compare the two lists. How do they differ?
There is further work on stereotypes in the section Attitudes to the Elderly on page 88.

Read

Political Correctness

'... They don't like being called ghosts. They're just... dead. I suppose it's like not calling people handicapped or backwards.'

Johnny Maxwell

Johnny and his friends have a lot of fun making up 'politically correct' terms to describe the dead in an 'inoffensive' way. For example:
- post-senior citizens
- breathily challenged
- vertically disadvantaged

The following are our 'politically correct' terms for certain groups of people:

• children:	pre-teen citizens
• teachers:	vacationally advantaged
• scaffolders:	tubular engineers
• sewage worker:	recycled food technician

Talk and Write

In a group, try to make up your own 'politically correct' terms. Discuss your own suggestions and write them down. Start with the list below:
- caretakers
- TV presenters
- school dinner servers
- police officers
- school secretaries

Can you think of any more terms for any other groups of people?

Attitudes to the Elderly

Talk and Write

1 What words do you commonly use to describe the elderly?
2 Make a list of words and phrases to describe a stereotypical old age pensioner as seen through the eyes of a young person. We've started it off for you:

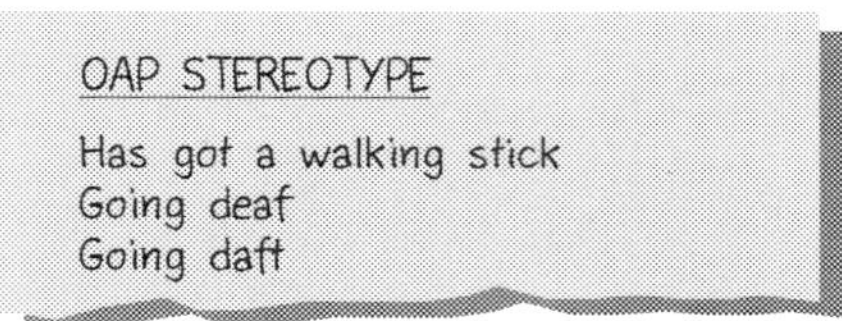

OAP STEREOTYPE
Has got a walking stick
Going deaf
Going daft

Is this a realistic view of elderly people?

Write

Make a list of the elderly characters in the play, with the most active and alert at the top and the least active and alert at the bottom.

Discuss

1 In the play, how are young people like Johnny expected to behave towards the elderly? (For example, why does Johnny feel he has to make 'doing a project at school' an excuse to talk to Mr Atkins?)
2 Do you think the attitudes in the play are realistic? Discuss in your group how you behave towards elderly people. If any members of the group have elderly relatives, how do they get on with them?

Rôle Play

1 Using the ideas and issues raised in your discussions, create a scene in the lounge of an old people's home like Sunshine Acres. Work in small groups, with one group member as the old person and the others as visitors.
2 As you play the scene, the teacher will freeze the action, and then move around and tap the 'old people' on the shoulder one by one, at which each character will say what thoughts are in his or her head at that moment.
3 Talk about the experience of the rôle play, concentrating particularly on the reactions of the 'old people'.

Write

Into the Future
Imagine that it is sixty years into the future and you are an elderly person. Write a description of a day in your life. Some of the following questions might help you:

- What kind of house do you live in?
- Are you able to get out and about?
- What activities do you do?
- Do you have family and friends?

Write

Growing Old
1 What do you fear most about growing old?
2 What sort of day-to-day life would you hate to have when you grow old?

Public Inquiry

In **Johnny and the Dead**, the cemetery is under threat of demolition from United Amalgamated Consolidated Holdings. The company wishes to build office blocks on the site of the cemetery and the old Blackbury boot works. In the play, UACH backs down (or appears to) when local people object and threaten to make the company look foolish.

A public inquiry is a way of reaching a decision in such cases if neither developers nor objectors are prepared to withdraw.

Rôle Play

Step One
Select an issue which your class identifies as a source of concern: this could be a local or a national issue. For example, you might decide to hold an inquiry over proposals for:

- a road development
- a shopping centre
- an opencast mine
- an airport
- a theme park
- a prison
- a laboratory (conducting experiments on animals)

You will find it easier if your inquiry concerns a development in your own area as you will be able to use your local knowledge. This development could be a real proposal, or you could decide to use an imaginary proposal and 'simulate' the inquiry. (Many top business people take part in 'simulations' to sharpen up their negotiating skills!)

Step Two
1 Divide the class into three groups.

Group one: those in favour of the development, for example:

- the developers
- their scientific advisers (who will argue that the development is harmless)
- local businesses (who stand to gain from increased trade)
- local workforce (especially those currently unemployed)

Group two: those against the development, for example:

- local residents
- their scientific advisers (who will argue that the development is harmful)
- environmental pressure groups: national (Greenpeace, Friends of the Earth) and local (Conservation Society, Wildlife Trust)
- national and local historical groups

Group three: those in two minds, for example:
- local landowners
- local councillors

2 Each group will plan its strategy for the inquiry. The following typical arguments may be helpful.

The developers' side may argue that:
- The development will bring prosperity to the area.
- New amenities will be created.
- Improved access will lead to better communications for the area.
- This facility is needed for the benefit of the locality or the nation.
- The objectors are showing a NIMBY ('Not In My Backyard') attitude.
- There is no proven threat to public health in their plans.
- They have taken steps to preserve the history of the site and minimize environmental damage.
- Their plans will bring new jobs for the local workforce.

The objectors' side may attempt to counter these arguments by saying:
- The destructive effects of the development will outweigh the benefits.
- There will be a high cost to residents in terms of noise and pollution.
- Access to the site (for heavy lorries etc.) will make the roads more dangerous.
- The facility will or may be dangerous to the health of residents.
- The facility is not to the benefit of anyone except the people who stand to make money from it.
- The objectors are not being NIMBYs, they object to all such developments: they don't want this development to be built elsewhere, they don't think it should be built at all.
- Irreplacable historical objects / buildings / landscapes / traditions will be lost.
- Irreparable environmental damage will be done.
- There is no guarantee that the jobs created by the development will go to local people.

Those caught in two minds may find themselves in this position:
- Local landowners will stand to gain from an increase in the value of their land and property; but they may be worried about the long-term effects of development on the quality of life both for themselves and the area.
- Local councillors will generally wish to improve the prosperity of the area, but not at the cost of serious damage to it.

Step Three

1 Each member of the group needs to adopt a rôle. Here are a couple of examples:

- A long-term unemployed man who supports the development because it might provide him with a job.
- A university professor who wants to organize a dig for Roman remains on the site of the proposed development.

2 The inquiry will be conducted with everyone taking part in rôle at all times. Each person must be sure of the following:

- his or her character's name and occupation
- basic facts about the character
- his or her views on the subject of the inquiry.

Step Four

Each group must then select a spokesperson. When the inquiry begins, it is the task of this person:

- to call on different members of the group to explain different parts of their case
- to sum up the group's arguments at the end of its presentation.

Step Five

1 Appoint a chairperson. This might be your teacher, or a visitor who does not know you and can therefore give all sides an equal hearing. You might also invite a group of impartial observers to listen to the inquiry and decide who has made the best case.

2 Begin the inquiry following the procedure set out below.

- The chairperson of the inquiry will invite each group to state its case without interruption.
- The chairperson may ask questions to make things clearer.
- At the end of each group's presentation, the spokespersons from other groups are allowed to ask questions.
- Only one person is to speak at a time.

Step Six

1 At the end of the inquiry, the chairperson will sum up the arguments from both sides.

2 The chairperson (or the invited observers) will then decide which side has made the best case.

Remember

- You must stay in rôle throughout the inquiry.
- All the arguments must be heard fairly.

Staging

Read

Johnny and the Dead is a fast moving play: one scene flows into the next. Therefore there is no need for a big set as complicated scene changes would interrupt the flow of the action. The position of the audience is also important to the staging of the play. There are five main ways of presenting the action.

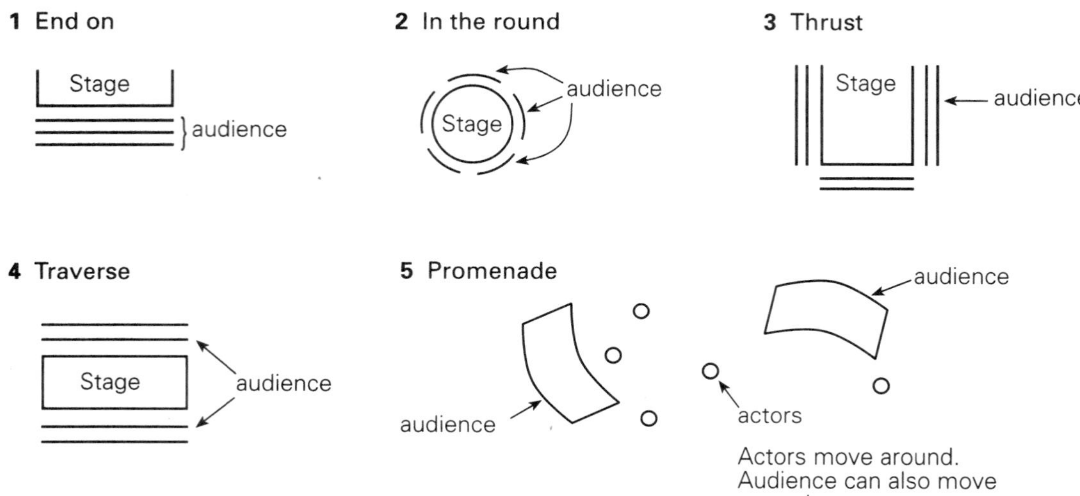

Talk and Write

Each type of staging has advantages and disadvantages.
Answer the following questions:

1. Do you want the audience to feel involved?
   If so you might not want to choose end on staging. Why not?
   Which type of staging would best help get the audience feeling close to the action?
2. Do you want the audience to see the actors' faces all the time?
   If so, you should not choose in the round or traverse staging. Why not?
   Which type of staging would help the audience see the actors' faces all the time?
3. Do you want the audience to move about during the performance?
   If so, you should not use end on staging. Why not?
   Which type of staging would allow the audience to move about during a performance?

Group Work

Preparing a Scene
Which type of staging would you wish to use for your production of **Johnny and the Dead**?

1 Divide into small groups and look at Scene 2.
2 Each group should choose a different way of staging this scene from the five main ways of presenting the action outlined on page 92.
3 Practise the scene and think carefully about:
- where your audience is going to be
- where the actors will move.

4 Each group should then perform the scene, positioning the audience according to their chosen way of staging.
5 When all the groups have shown their version of the scene, discuss which way of staging worked best and which was the least successful.

Read

Background Acting
As Stephen Briggs says in his introduction, '…if the characters just stand there and talk at each other in a performance of the script, the audience will find this very boring…The trick is to find things for the characters to do that make the things they say more effective.'

Improvise

Try the following activity.
In Scene 3, the Dead find out about the sale of the cemetery by reading a newspaper. Look at Scene 3 and improvise all the ways the Dead can find to pinch the paper from each other. You must bear in mind that the Dead find it difficult to grasp material things. You could start this 'business' with Alderman Bowler's speech on page 21, 'You didn't tell us about this. In the paper…'.

Draw

Costume
Design costumes for the Dead. You will need to find out the types of clothes the characters would have worn in the period they lived. There are clues in the list of Characters on page 4.

Design

Poster
Design a poster for a production of **Johnny and the Dead**. You will need to think about the following things:
- what images you want to use
- what information you have to convey
- how to make the poster eye-catching.

Afterthoughts

Who Makes the Rules?

The Dead have been told that they must not leave the graveyard because 'a day will come' though at first they seem pretty unclear about what will happen on the 'day' in question.

Read

In the Christian tradition, when the world ends, God will sit in judgement upon every soul that has ever lived. The good and innocent souls will go to heaven, but the bad and wicked souls will go to hell to be punished for all eternity.

Discuss

1 If your group contains followers of other faiths, discuss with them the concept of Judgement. Do other faiths have a similar belief?
2 As the Dead are about to leave, Antonio Vicenti says, 'Oh, yes. It's Judgement Day. We decided. It's different for everyone, you see.' (Scene 15, page 71). What does he mean by this?
3 How is Antonio Vicenti's new understanding of Judgement Day different from the traditional Christian version?

Discuss

1 Gradually, the Dead rebel against the rule that they cannot leave the cemetery. Where do you think the rule came from?
2 Only Eric Grimm eventually stands by the rule and refuses to leave the cemetery. Can you explain how this ties in with what we learn of him later in Scene 15?
3 After Johnny leaves Eric Grimm for the last time, he tells his friends he is '...just thinking about the difference between heaven and hell.' (Scene 15, page 73.). What does he mean?
4 Has Eric Grimm been judged? If he has, who has judged him?

Discuss

Addison Vincent Fletcher says, 'Of all the forces in the universe, the hardest to overcome is the force of habit.' (Scene 13, page 56.)

1 What does he mean by this?
2 How does this tie in with the Dead learning to break the rule?

Talk and Write

1 On your own, make a list, in two columns, of the rules that affect you most. In the first column write down all the rules that you think are reasonable and necessary and in the second column list all the rules that you find restrictive and pointless.
2 How do you decide which rules are necessary and which are not? Write down your method of deciding which is which.
3 Form a group and discuss each other's lists. Write down a list of ways in which you can test whether a rule is reasonable or not.
4 Make a group list of necessary and unnecessary rules that you can all agree on.

Discuss

The Abuse of Power

1 Why does United Amalgamated Consolidated Holdings hire thugs to rip up the cemetery late at night (Scene 15). What do they hope to achieve?
2 Are UACH wrong to do this? If so, why?
3 How does Ms Liberty abuse her power in Scene 12 of the play?
4 Is her abuse of power more or less serious than UACH's? Why?
5 Can you think of any similar instances in real life of companies or individuals abusing their power?

The Afterlife

Johnny and the Dead is a play concerned with the discoveries made by the Dead when Johnny starts to take an interest in them; but it is mostly a play about how to live.

Discuss

Johnny asks Antonio Vicenti about being dead: 'Are there…angels involved? You know? Or…devils and things? A lot of people would like to know.' Antonio Vicenti replies: 'Oh, no. I don't think so. That sort of thing…no. That's for the living.' (Scene 15 page 70)
What does he mean by this?

Brainstorming

In brainstorming, the whole group is invited to contribute ideas on a particular subject. These ideas are not discussed or edited; everything that anyone has to say is written down. Following a brainstorm, a discussion is usually held to sort out the most useful ideas and suggestions.

We don't actually know what happens when we die, but there are a lot of theories.

1 Have a brainstorming session of ideas about what happens when we die.
2 Write these ideas down on a board or flipchart, without discussing them. (It would be interesting to have ideas from as wide a range of beliefs as possible and it may be a good idea to use colour coding to keep track of which faith holds which belief.)
3 Once you have the ideas written down, discuss the ways in which these ideas about what happens when we die affect the way we live. You can set these out in two columns headed 'Belief' and 'Consequences'. Here is an example to set you off:

BELIEF	CONSEQUENCES
(Christian) If you live a wicked life, you will go to hell when you die	You either: - lead a good life, or - do bad things and get very frightened

Finding the 'consequences' is the hardest bit, but don't worry. There aren't any right or wrong answers, just say and write what you think!

Plays in this series include:

Across the Barricades — ISBN 0 19 831272 5
Joan Lingard *adapted by David Ian Neville*

The Bonny Pit Laddie — ISBN 0 19 831278 4
Frederick Grice *adapted by David Spraggon Williams with Frank Green*

The Burston School Strike — ISBN 0 19 831274 1
Roy Nevitt

The Canterbury Tales — ISBN 0 19 831293 8
Geoffrey Chaucer *adapted by Martin Riley*

Carrie's War — ISBN 0 19 831295 4
Nina Bawden *adapted by Robert Staunton*

The Demon Headmaster — ISBN 0 19 831270 9
Gillian Cross *adapted by Adrian Flynn*

Frankenstein — ISBN 0 19 831267 9
Mary Shelley *adapted by Philip Pullman*

Hot Cakes — ISBN 0 19 831273 3
Adrian Flynn

Jane Eyre — ISBN 0 19 831296 2
Charlotte Brontë *adapted by Steve Barlow and Steve Skidmore*

Johnny and the Dead — ISBN 0 19 831294 6
Terry Pratchett *adapted by Stephen Briggs*

Paper Tigers — ISBN 0 19 831268 7
Steve Barlow and Steve Skidmore

A Question of Courage — ISBN 0 19 831271 7
Marjorie Darke *adapted by Bill Lucas and Brian Keaney*

Smith — ISBN 0 19 831297 0
Leon Garfield *adapted by Robert Staunton*

A Tale of Two Cities — ISBN 0 19 831292 X
Charles Dickens *adapted by Steve Barlow and Steve Skidmore*

The Turbulent Term of Tyke Tiler — ISBN 0 19 831269 5
adapted from her own novel by Gene Kemp